| Due   Return | Due Return |
Date Date	Date Date

CONFIGURATIONS OF
CULTURE GROWTH

CONFIGURATIONS OF CULTURE GROWTH

By

A. L. KROEBER

University of California Press

BERKELEY AND LOS ANGELES

1963

UNIVERSITY OF CALIFORNIA PRESS
BERKELEY AND LOS ANGELES
CALIFORNIA

❖

CAMBRIDGE UNIVERSITY PRESS
LONDON, ENGLAND

CB
53
K7

SECOND PRINTING, 1963
MANUFACTURED IN THE UNITED STATES OF AMERICA

PREFACE

ONE OF *the recognized characteristics of human culture is the tendency of its successes or highest values to occur close together in relatively brief periods within nations or limited areas. While reasons have been adduced for the phenomenon, no systematic examination of the facts seems ever to have been made. I present here the more readily datable facts—for time lapse seems an essential factor of the phenomenon—in an orderly arrangement, as ᴜasis for an inductive comparison. The purpose is not so much to offer a final explanation as to make the most pertinent data readily available for those who wish to search farther for a causality. I am convinced that, the phenomenon being cultural, the explanation must first of all be made in cultural terms, even if it be essentially only a descriptive interpretation. The underlying psychology may ultimately be discoverable; but that will necessarily be later. I have offered an adumbration of an explanation in terms of cultural patterns. This will perhaps be considered insufficient. It does not wholly satisfy me. While we know a good deal in detail about some specific culture patterns, we are only in the beginning of understanding of the nature of such patterns; even their theoretical recognition is recent. How some sharply marked patterns in civilization have actually behaved, historically, seems worth knowing as a first empirical step toward understanding; and my main endeavor has been to present organized materials on this behavior.*

That this book dealing with data from history should have been written by an anthropologist will perhaps seem fitting to those interested in the development of the two studies. The aim of the work is obviously more or less sociological. The principal current of anthropology, and its soundest findings until now, I believe to be culture-historical. Nevertheless, if we can also generalize validly, it will be most important.

[vii]

I worked on this book, as time was available, from 1931 to 1938. It is a pleasure to remember that the Rockefeller Foundation and the University of California combined to free two half-years of my time for the work. In view of the Foundation's interest in furthering interdisciplinary researches, I trust that they too are satisfied. The plan formed itself some years before 1931; its theme I have been exercised over as far back as I can remember. Many years of specifically anthropological preoccupation seemed for a time to have led me away, but eventually they brought me back to it.

A. L. K.

Kishamish, Napa Valley, California
August 1, 1938
Final reading in type, August, 1944

CONTENTS

Chapter I

PROBLEM AND PROCEDURE

Chapter I

PROBLEM AND PROCEDURE

§1. The Undertaking

EDUARD MEYER, by some considered the greatest historian of our time, assigns to anthropology the task of determining the generic or universal features in human history. He accepts, of course, like all historians, what have been called the principles of the continuity or unity and of the uniqueness of history. That is to say, he holds as primary assumptions that every historical phenomenon has antecedents which in turn have antecedents; that it never originates out of nothing; that every effect also becomes a cause or influence; that exact repetition of phenomena is therefore impossible; in short, that all historic events possess individuality or uniqueness while occurring in an interconnected continuum. Beyond this there seem to lie certain forms of happenings which are more or less recurrent or generic, perhaps necessary and universal. These are no longer the province of the historian as such. Formerly, concern with them was left to what was called the philosophy of history—a field of inquiry on the margin of philosophy proper, somewhat sociological in intent but readier than sociology to deal primarily with historical data as such. The significance of Meyer's allocation of the study of the generic or repetitive forms in history to anthropology rather than to "Geschichtsphilosophie" lies in the facts that anthropology is not a philosophical science, but an empirical one; that it has been rather freely admitted by scientists to fall within the domain of natural science; and that its bent, as compared with that of sociology, has been overwhelmingly investigatory and not practical or ameliorative.

On the other side, anthropologists have prevailingly been inclined to construe their discipline as a historical science; at any rate, since about 1890, the majority have come to avow explicitly that the cultural phenomena with which they deal are properly intelligible only in a historic context.

These remarks are made in justification, if such be needed, of an anthropologist's dealing with wholly historical data. The two approaches are closely related. However, they are also indubitably distinct; and the differentiation is of moment—precisely because it is historically founded.

The immediately available data of history normally are records of events, acts performed by persons. From these, plus surviving monuments, works of literature, and the like, the "institutions and manners" or cultures of the past are inferred and reconstructed; and these reconstructions are again used in helping to explain why particular events happened. The historian may make pauses in which he depicts the culture of an area in a period. On the whole, however, these static sections tend to be incidents or interludes. Ordinarily the business of history is the narration of a sequential series of events in their connections or coherences, with culture as a context.

The anthropologist's situation is essentially the reverse: he deals with culture as such, in a context of history. Concerned, not in principle but usually *de facto,* with recordless peoples, the "primitives," he can learn relatively little of particular events among them, and concentrates on the facts and forms of their culture. Are the Dayaks archers, headhunters, weavers, matrilineal, totemic; were the Magdalenians archers, potters, weavers, fishermen? These are the kinds of data which he has developed methods for collecting more or less competently. In what spot or year, and by what individual, pots were first made among a certain tribe, is usually beyond his power of ascertaining; or even the name of the chief who led in a victory over a neighboring tribe, or the date of the fight, unless it occurred within the memory of the living.

True, these differences intergrade. Even the avowedly biographic historian brings in much culture by implication; and an anthropologist who disregarded such historical events as he might learn of would be considered a deficient workman. There is archaeology, of Egypt for instance, from which history with names, acts, dates, and places is reconstructed. There are historians who debate each other's "interpretations" or reconstructions of the socioeconomic pattern of the typical early mediaeval town very much as anthropologists debate whether pyramids and kingship and calendar were or were not imported from Asia into Central America, or whether matrilineal or patrilineal institutions, or totems or moieties, were the earlier in Australia. Nevertheless, using culture as an instrument to infer or understand the sequence of events, or using events to understand culture, are diverse processes of intelligence. Events are specific facts; culture by comparison is a generalized abstraction. History is therefore particular, and scarcely ever has detached itself wholly from individual persons. Anthropology often becomes technically detailed, but it can operate successfully without any knowledge of particular persons. The cultures which it depicts or analyzes are summaries or averages of a large number of individual acts.

It will accordingly be clear why Meyer leaves to anthropology the task of investigating the general or universal forms of human history: such forms are cultural.

The problem I have set myself in this book is an investigation of one of the forms which culture takes. This form is the frequent habit of societies to develop their cultures to their highest levels spasmodically: especially in their intellectual and aesthetic aspects, but also in more material and practical respects. The cultures grow, prosper, and decline, in the opinion of the world. How far they tend to be successful in their several activities simultaneously, or close together, or far apart in time, and how much variation in this regard is of record, is part of the problem. The type of phenomenon has been frequently noted, or has been widely taken for granted; it has not been systematically investigated, so far as I know, by a comparison of all available facts; that is to say, investigated empirically instead of intuitively or *a priori*.

The first question is whether such clusterings or spurts of higher cultural productivity are real or are perhaps only illusions of our minds. Then arises a series of more specific questions. Is there a tendency toward a norm of duration for such successful growths, or anything to show of what the duration is a function? Must the florescence extend over the whole of the culture, or may it be partial? Is there an order, or tendency toward order, for the several activities to come successively to their zeniths? Can a culture pass through a cycle to full decline and then enjoy another cycle of prosperity, or are we in that case dealing with two cultures? Can the cycles or bursts be induced from without, or must they develop from within? Do the peaks tend to come early within growths, toward the end, or is the growth curve most often symmetrical? We have here a whole set of problems, or possible problems, on which there exist abundant data, but of which there has been little systematic comparative research.

It is also evident that this set of problems is only one of a number that confront us in regard to the nature of culture. It confines itself to those cultural productions which seem qualitatively successful to other times and places—which have impressed and commanded a certain respect for their values from other cultures. Besides dealing with cultural quality, the problem deals with its distributions in chronological time and geographical space. But I have deliberately refrained, except incidentally or when necessary, from examining the content of the cultural growths. I have not tried to write a summary or comparative history of philosophy or science or painting with reference to what each civilization achieved in these activities. I have tried to see how far the several civilizations have behaved alike or unlike in the course of producing their highest manifestations in these activities. Nor again, except so far as it seemed necessary, have I dwelt on the sources of the culture material worked into florescences, nor on the influences and stimuli which disparate civilizations received from one another. In short, the characteristic content and specific quality of high cultural developments have been disregarded here, and with them their possible "causes," in favor of their growth configurations—configurations in time, in space, and in degree of achievement. Such a limitation has the merit of focusing attention on certain aspects of the phenomena, and of dealing with comparables, or near-comparables, instead of with everything at once. Obviously, an examination thus limited will not reveal causes. But I cheerfully renounce present search for these, because a clearer and surer understanding of how cultures behave historically seems antecedent to why they behave as they do. The treatment, in short, is behavioristically factual rather than explanatory.

§ 2. Genius

In tracing the historic configuration of the growth of patterns of higher culture, I have used as chief evidence the productions of individuals recognized as superior. This is because there is a strong tendency, ever since there has been history and even before it was written, to associate great cultural products and great men. Whether or not there was a Homer, we invent one. Little as we know of the life and personality of Shakespeare, we use his name to typify a flowering of culture. There is more written about him, probably, than about Elizabethan literature. Most of the readily accessible data of history are attached to personalities.

If the reverse were the case, and history came without names of people, with record only of events and achievements plus their dates and places, the evidential material listed in this book would have had a thoroughly different appearance. And yet it would have shown the same growth configurations, and the culture patterns discussed would have revealed themselves, if anything, more sharply. It is thus clear that while personalities are the medium through which an approach like the present one must largely operate to express itself, they are not of its essence or its goal.

It might be said that what is ordinarily called history deals primarily and cheerfully with persons, though giving their lives the wider illumination of institution and of social or cultural setting; whereas culture history aims consciously to analyze and reëxpress cultural movements, freed so far as possible from the entanglement of individualities. However, culture history has hardly as yet come to be regarded as more than one phase or subdivision of history. The natural or spontaneous procedure is to think of people and events rather than of intangibles like social currents or cultural developments. Behind the conventional historian's habits, and reinforcing them, lies the popular assumption that because persons have done whatever is recounted in history, therefore the springs of their actions, and consequently of all historical happenings, must lie in their individualities. That personalities are exceedingly plastic, as all observational psychologists tell us, is partly overlooked in this assumption. So is the fact, most consistently emphasized perhaps by anthropologists, of the tremendous molding power of the cultural environment or social milieu. The more naïve attitude—which the abler historians have pretty well transcended without formally repudiating it—is obviously akin to the view that the human will is free. One can write history without holding this belief, but much history is written as if the will were free. The culture-historical approach, which eliminates individual personalities as much as possible, therewith also eliminates this assumption, and so remains at liberty to consider social or cultural happenings and relations as such and in their own plane. The involved causality therefore tends to become different. Analysis and interpretation proceed without reference to individual human wills.

However, this curious situation results. In analyzing out as many as possible of the principal culture growths of admittedly higher value, I have perforce had to express myself in terms of superior personalities or genius; and I foresee that the main point of my work may be lost, in some quarters, because my recitals of data will be construed all over again as confirmation of the presupposition that personalities are primary and that therefore genius produces or "causes" higher cultural values and forms.

I can meet this view only by saying that culture patterns and their values are indeed most fully expressed by genius, but that the subject of this inquiry is not *who* expresses, but *what* is expressed, and *how:* that is, the relations in time, space, and substance of each expression to other expressions of higher culture. Every sophisticated person today will admit that Newton's Principia could not have been formulated either in Hottentot culture or even among Newton's Anglo-Saxon ancestors a thousand years earlier. In short, though the Principia could have been produced only by a genius like Newton and are the true expression of his personality, it is nevertheless clear that the existence of a certain body of science was needed before his genius could be touched off to realize itself in the Principia.

Now if we turn the situation around, so that it can be examined from its other side, it becomes clear that we can just as well focus interest on the growth of science, investigate its development, and look upon Newton as nothing more than the genius that was needed to touch off to its fullest realization the condition to which science had arrived in 1687. This second viewpoint is the one I am occupying; and it will perhaps be conceded to be as legitimate as the first and more spontaneous one.

It has, in fact, this advantage: while understanding of the pattern of seventeenth-century science and knowledge of its growth will never explain the psychology of Newton as a man, it will help understanding of the Principia as a cultural product, that is, as a historical phenomenon. On the contrary, the fullest possible understanding of Newton as a personality relates essentially only to the understanding of other personalities, or of genius as a type of personality. It will not explain the Principia, which are explainable only in terms of the growth of science. Historically, the work of Newton is a phenomenon inherently related to the phenomena represented by the works of other scientists, in time, place, and cultural substance. But Copernicus, Napier, Galileo, Kepler, *as personalities* or individual aggregations of psychic activity, have of course as good as no specific historical relation to the personality of Newton. And as for the psychological relation which almost certainly exists between them, not alone in type but also in degree or potence of personality, this sort of problem can probably be better studied on living, reëxaminable, or more or less controllable individuals than on long-dead ones. At any rate, such seems to be the opinion of psychologists, who as a group are notoriously not historical-minded and presumably see little relation between history and psychology.[1]

At bottom, then, the difference between the two attitudes is one of interest. Each is as legitimate as the other. If we are interested primarily in personalities, we are dealing with psychology, and bring in the culture only as a setting which cannot wholly be left out of the picture. If we are interested primarily in culture and how it behaves, we can disregard personalities except as inevitable mechanisms or measures of cultural expression.

It seems that this disregard of personalities, except as symptoms, is justified precisely by the fact that apparently greater, culturally productive individuals appear in history, on the whole, prevailingly in clusters. This makes their appearance a function of sociocultural events. If it were not so, they should appear much more evenly spaced or scattered, except for such minor or mild clusterings as will be produced in a continuous distribution by random accident and can be accounted for by the laws of probability.

It is universally accepted that every human being is the product of two sets of forces: his innate heredity or genetic constitution, and his environment. To attribute the appearance of genius primarily to biological heredity leaves the clusterings or constellations wholly unexplained. The moment we admit these as real, we must admit an important other factor, and it then becomes idle opinion to hold to the primacy of heredity. In fact, the finding of the whole science of genetics is that heredity is normally transmitted according to the laws of chance. Genetics leaves only an infinitesimal possibility for the racial stock occupying England to have given birth to no geniuses at all between 1450 and 1550 and a whole series of geniuses in literature, music, science, philosophy, and politics

---

[1] Wundt is the outstanding apparent exception, in his *Völkerpsychologie,* but this deals professedly with sociocultural phenomena and not at all with personalities. The psychoanalysts have shown some inclination to interpret historic figures, but in this they are only applying to interesting and widely but imperfectly known dead persons tne processes which they have learned by clinical dissection of living ones.

between 1550 and 1650. Similarly with the Germany of 1550–1650 and 1700–1800, respectively; and innumerable other instances in history.

It was a situation like this which Galton clearly recognized in the difference of genius production between fifth-century Athens and nineteenth-century England. He misinterpreted it by giving the Athenians a hereditary rating as many degrees superior to that of the modern English as these are superior to the African negro. His mathematics is sound—in fact, the greatest tribute is due his insight in applying the laws of probability to problems of this sort. His measurement of genius is probably also reasonably sound; at least, the results of his measurements do not appear to have been seriously challenged. But his explanation in terms of hereditary racial change is simply contrary to all we have learned about heredity since his day. His problem, his method, and his facts stand; it is his conclusions that have collapsed. Why? Evidently because there is a powerful factor of "environment" at work which he ignored in his search for a biological cause. The presence of this environmental factor could be, and was, suspected or taken for granted in some quarters. But cultural evidence and explanation as such could hardly have disproved positively the primacy of hereditary causality. It remained for the geneticists themselves—fellow biologists—to bring the disproof. And therewith the situation to which Galton pointed, which is a situation of the very type that I am examining, was reopened to explanation by the factor—or, better, factors—of environment.

Environment is, in its mechanism, of two kinds: biological, and sociocultural. Biologically operative environment would include selection, as effective ultimately on heredity; and physiological factors, such as malaria, syphilis, hookworm, iodine deficiency, inhibiting or retarding climate, and the like. Ordinary diseases, which either kill or leave the organism essentially unimpaired, hardly come into question, because there is no indication that either their incidence or their mortality is different for genius and the average. There are left, then, diseases which are "hereditary" or which by their prevalence can sap whole populations and bring them down below their normal potentiality of performance. In regard to these, or to genuinely selective factors in the Darwinian sense, no more need be said than that no real evidence has been offered with respect to their being a material influence on cultural productivity, and that in general the efforts in this direction have been naïve. It is legitimate enough for a biologist accustomed to biological thinking to suggest that the decline of Roman civilization was brought about by the introduction of malaria. Almost invariably, however, biologists have thrown off such ideas only in passing, as a possibly fruitful hint. They know their inability to handle historical phenomena with professional competence, and in general they refrain from attempted demonstrations, however strong their convictions may sometimes be. It is half-scientists, scientists who have become propagandists, and above all it is educated layman, that have pushed such theories; which therefore it is needless to refute. Historians have never taken them seriously. Such theories represent the taking of an opinion, or side, and propping it up with such evidence as can be assembled with convenience or industry, without control of contrary possibilities. It would be dogmatic to say that explanations of this type are wholly unfounded; but it would be a waste of intellectual energy to refute or analyze them until some positive and critical showing shall have been made for them.

This leaves culture as the part of environment giving rise to the uneven distribution or clusterings of the appearance of genius. The type of phenomenon included under the term "culture" in this connection is illustrated by the frequency of simultaneous but independent discoveries and inventions. This simultaneity may now be considered as well established.[2]

---

[2] So far as I am aware, the significance of co-inventions and discoveries was first formally pointed out by me in 1917. Within five years, Ogburn and Thomas ("Are Inventions Inevitable?" *Political Science Quarterly*, 37:83–98, 1922) cited a list of instances about ten times as numerous. I suspect that we had not only contemporaries but predecessors, and that if their and my recognition of the phenomenon as a recurrent one had been considered sufficiently important to be worth fighting over, our priority would have been contested and quite likely taken away from us by proofs. In short, the principle applies, as it ought if true, to the origin of its own recognition.

Familiar examples are the devising of calculus by Newton and Leibnitz, the discovery of oxygen by Scheele and Priestley, the formulation of the principle of natural selection by Darwin and Wallace in 1858, the discovery of anaesthetics by four separate American physicians, the invention of the telephone in the same year by Bell and Gray, and innumerable others. Probably a large proportion of the many contested priorities of discovery are due precisely to this fact: the discoveries were made in genuine independence, so far as relations of the personalities are concerned; the independence was then stretched into priority by their partisans, national or other. The same sort of simultaneity obviously occurs in aesthetic innovations: the first use of blank verse, of a metrical form, of a chord, of an architectural proportion, of a theme in painting such as shadow or atmosphere or a manner of brush handling.

In a world only partly conscious of culture, these contemporary and near-identical phenomena are apparently attributed to chance, and are noted as dramatic coincidences. They are, however, far too numerous for that. The explanation now generally given is that "the times were ripe"—the development of a science or art was sufficiently advanced for a certain next step to be in order. I have used in this book the concept of pattern growth, saturation, and exhaustion. These are all ways of saying substantially the same thing, however vaguely we can yet express it: the causal participation of a cultural factor, the intervention of a superpersonal element in the personal activity of genius. In proportion as a greater number of sociocultural innovations can be shown to have begun independently with several persons at or near the same time, the influence of superpersonal or cultural factors, in distinction from personal ones, will be construable as greater.

The contemporaneity of inventions is of course only one special aspect of cultural "environment" or influence. Any approach that primarily considers patterns of culture as such, that abstracts them so far as possible from the individual personalities associated with them, involves the recognition of cultural phenomena or factors as cultural. It is such factors, whatever their specific shape, that we must look for as the principal determinants, not indeed of the birth or existence of genius, but of its historic appearance, functioning, and productivity.

This view of course does not deny the superiority of certain individuals over others. It assumes such superiority. It also assumes that the finest flowerings of culture growths are expressed through such superior personalities. In fact, it assumes that, in general, genius will be at hand to express the highest manifestations of culture developments. This belief in turn almost necessarily involves the assumption that geniuses are presumably being born at nearly the same rate per thousand or million, century after century—at any rate, within a given race. Of course in this connection genius means potential, not realized genius: innate, hereditary, psychological superiority as distinct from manifest, historically expressed superiority. This hypothesis is certainly in agreement with what we know of psychobiological inheritance: high capacity ought to be born with but little fluctuation from an average rate, standard for each larger hereditary stock. But inasmuch as historically recognized geniuses do not ordinarily appear in an even flow, but in clusters separated by intervals, it is evident that cultural situations or influences must at times allow and at others inhibit the realization of genius. In short, it would seem that a large proportion, probably a majority, of eminently superior individuals never get into the reckoning of history. There are long stretches in which first prizes are not awarded, or at least are not recognized by posterity.

In Occidental sculpture, Italy holds preëminence; and in five centuries of Italian preëminence, Michelangelo, born in 1475, is considered as marking the culmination. But can we be certain that he was inherently, by his innate gifts, a greater sculptor than Ghiberti, born in 1378, Donatello, 1385, Bernini, 1598, or Canova, 1757? Ghiberti had nothing to build on, but he "initiated the Renaissance." Donatello reached higher, but he stood on Ghiberti's shoulders; and Michelangelo on Donatello's. Here the pattern began to strain and wilt; and we rate Bernini much lower. But can we be at all sure that in imagination, sense of form, technical skill, he was inferior to Michelangelo? His themes, his invoking of emotions, and perhaps his taste were on a lower level; but they were the emotions and taste of his age. The same holds for Canova. For sculptural ability we cannot really with certainty rate him one notch below the highest; it is the tepid neoclassicism of his period which we rate below Renaissance intensity. It is true that Michelangelo almost surely remains the greatest personality of the five; but on the extrinsic ground that he was painter, architect, and poet also, the other four are chiefly sculptors only.

What this example shows is that in ranking geniuses we evidently do not rank them according to intrinsic ability, which we have little means of estimating as such; rather, they appear to us as the composite product of personal superiority and cultural influence. If the cultural pattern which they express is still unformed, or is manifestly declining, we tend to evaluate them as lesser individualities than the geniuses at the pattern peak; but it is uncertain that they really are lesser. It does seem somewhat naïve to assume, because Donatello's and Michelangelo's presumptive native endowments plus the known state of art in Florence in 1430 and 1510 come to a higher total than Bernini's and Canova's presumptive native endowments plus the obviously decadent state of Italian art in 1650 and 1800, that Donatello and Michelangelo were therefore the greater men. Yet in our general thinking that is what we do. We veil the imperfect logic of the procedure by assuming that Florentine sculpture of 1450–1500 was made great by some miracle of Donatello's and Michelangelo's ancestral germ plasm.

To this assumption the simplest objection remains that historically such miracles mostly come in clusters, whereas if they were really accidents of the germ plasm they should come scattered.

On the contrary, culture florescences, viewed as such, reveal themselves as tending strongly to come in pattern waves. Hence the inference is justified that it is something in the wavelike character of culture growths which is at the bottom of the otherwise unexplainable clusterings of genius.

It will be clear that I am not denying or minimizing the existence of individual superiority. I am denying it as the cause of cultural superiority. The cause or causes of this latter remain unknown, and constitute a great problem of inquiry: this volume is an attempt to organize data so as to define the problem. Cultural superiority obviously avails itself of individual superiority as an important channel of expression. It therefore helps personally superior individuals to realize themselves as significant historical figures. On the other hand, absence of cultural superiority tends strongly to prevent inherently superior personalities from being realized as such, historically.

Evidently, a majority of born geniuses never come to fruition for the world. If we could keep culture permanently at its best level, the number of productive geniuses would be perhaps three or ten times as great as it actually is on the average in human history. This proposition is aside from the main line of the inquiry into how culture behaves; but it has a deserving interest of its own.

§3. The Problem

Recognition of the prevalence of clustering of genius and of the constellating of production of high cultural values is widespread and old. Probably most historians and most nonhistorians would accept it as a fact. On the contrary, there has been curiously little serious endeavor to see implications of general significance in it. The first step in such an endeavor obviously is the systematic collocation of the more available pertinent data, accompanied by analysis to insure their empirical comparability. Such an attempt cannot be said to have been made. The problem has been left to the historians of the arts, who deal with no more than single aspects of cultures, and to the philosophers, who are not empiricists. Spengler both saw the problem and felt passionately its profound importance; but he also felt that he knew the solution, and he was neither analytical, critical, nor orderly. So far as I am aware, no able orthodox historian, or scientist other than Galton, has dealt systematically with the problem.

The essential phenomena were recognized nearly two thousand years ago by Velleius Paterculus. Velleius was not a profound thinker, and obviously did no more than reflect, with his characteristic spontaneity, the opinion of his time. He is worth quoting in full.

Although this portion of my work has already, as it were, outgrown my plan, and although I am aware that in my headlong haste—which, just like a revolving wheel or a down-rushing and eddying stream, never suffers me to stop—I am almost obliged to omit matters of essential importance rather than to include unessential details, yet I cannot refrain from noting a subject which has often occupied my thoughts but has never been clearly reasoned out. For who can marvel sufficiently that the most distinguished minds in each branch of human achievement have happened to adopt the same form of effort, and to have fallen within the same narrow space of time. Just as animals of different species when shut in the same pen or other enclosure still segregate themselves from those which are not of their kind, and gather together each in its own group, so the minds that have had the capacity for distinguished achievement of each kind have set themselves apart from the rest by doing like things in the same period of time. A single epoch, and that only of a few years' duration, gave lustre to tragedy through three men of divine inspiration, Aeschylus, Sophocles, and Euripides. So, with Comedy, a single age brought to perfection that early form, the Old Comedy, through the agency of Cratinus, Aristophanes, and Eupolis; while Menander, and Philemon and Diphilus, his equals in age rather than in performance, within the space of a very few years invented the New Comedy and left it to defy imitation. The great philosophers, too, received their inspiration from the lips of Socrates—their names we gave a moment ago—how long did they flourish after the death of Plato and of Aristotle? What distinction was there in oratory before Isocrates, or after the time of his disciples and in turn of their pupils? So crowded were they into a brief epoch that there were no two worthy of mention who could not have seen each other.

This phenomenon occurred among the Romans as well as among the Greeks. For, unless one goes back to the rough and crude beginnings, and to men whose sole claim to praise is that they were the pioneers, Roman tragedy centres in and about Accius; and the sweet pleasantry of Latin humor reached its zenith in practically the same age under Caecilius, Terentius, and Afranius. In the case of the historians also, if one adds Livy to the period of the older writers, a single epoch, comprised within the limits of eighty years, produced them all, with the exception of Cato and some of the old and obscure authors. Likewise the period which was productive of poets does not go back to an earlier date or continue to a later. Take oratory and the forensic art at its best, the perfected splendor of eloquence in prose, if we again except Cato—and this I say with due respect to Publius Crassus, Scipio, Laelius, the Gracchi, Fannius, and Servius Galba—eloquence, I say, in all its branches burst into flower under Cicero, its chief exponent, so that there are few before his day whom one can read with pleasure, and none whom one can admire, except men who had either seen Cicero or had been seen by him. One will also find, if he follows up the dates closely, that the same thing holds true of the grammarians, the workers in clay, the painters, the sculptors, and that pre-eminence in each phase of art is confined within the narrowest limits of time.

Though I frequently search for the reasons why men of similar talents occur exclusively in certain epochs and not only flock to one pursuit but also attain like success, I can never find any of whose truth I am certain, though I do find some which perhaps seem likely, and particularly the following. Genius is fostered by emulation, and it is now envy, now admiration, which enkindles imitation, and, in the nature of things, that which is cultivated with the highest zeal advances to the highest perfection; but it is difficult to continue at the point of perfection, and naturally that which cannot advance must recede. And as in the beginning we are fired with the ambition to overtake those whom we regard as leaders, so when we have despaired of being able either to surpass or even to equal them, our zeal wanes with our hope; it ceases to follow what it cannot overtake, and abandoning the old field as though pre-empted, it seeks a new one. Passing over that in which we cannot be pre-eminent, we seek for some new object of our effort. It follows that the greatest obstacle in the way of perfection in any work is our fickle way of passing on at frequent intervals to something else.

From the part played by epochs our wonder and admiration next passes to that played by individual cities. A single city of Attica blossomed with more masterpieces of every kind of eloquence than all the rest of Greece together—to such a degree, in fact, that one would think that although the bodies of the Greek race were distributed among the other states, their intellects were confined within the walls of Athens alone. Nor have I more reason for wonder at this than that not a single Argive or Theban or Lacedaemonian was esteemed worthy, as an orator, of commanding influence while he lived, or of being remembered after his death.

These cities, otherwise distinguished, were barren of such literary pursuits with the single exception of the lustre which the voice of Pindar gave to Thebes; for, in the case of Alcman, the claim which the Laconians lay to him is spurious.[3]

That a problem is old may mean that it is insoluble, but it does not mean that it is vain or unworthy. Velleius has stated its essentials. To them we can add the facts of the history of Islamic and European civilization, of Egyptian, Indian, Chinese, Japanese, even some beginnings of understanding of Mesopotamian and native American. Instead of two cultures, one largely derived from the other, we can compare half a dozen major ones. This is the scope of the examination.

On the other hand, I deliberately refrain from any ultimate explanation. If we can do no better than to find the causality of the phenomena in "emulation," like Velleius, or in any other commonplace factor of individual psychology, we had better leave the problem alone. The phenomena are cultural, and their first understanding must be in cultural terms: how they actually behave culturally; how far they are historically alike or unlike; whether there is a type of events underlying the several cultural physiognomies. At present, any explanation can hardly be more than descriptive. The nearest I have ventured to an interpretation is in terms of realization of culture patterns. But I recognize that as an explanation this is only perceptive or descriptive. We are becoming increasingly aware of culture patterns. But we know extremely little, in any systematic or coherent way, about how they function and operate; and beyond that lies the problem of the why of their behavior, which may ultimately lead us back into psychology, or into the complex and obscure field in which psychobiological and sociocultural factors are enlaced. Short-circuiting by means of a spurious answer in terms of such causalities, which at present can be only verbal, I am specifically conscious of trying to avoid.

Another type of interpretation I mention only to dismiss as trivial: the specific historic explanation, such as that Elizabethan drama arose to its heights because of the victory over the

[3] *Roman History*, Bk. I, pp. 16–18. Translation by F. W. Shipley, 1924.

Armada, or that the Thirty Years' War made Germans write poor poetry and do feeble science for a century after. Historians have long and increasingly been sheering away from such immaturities, but they persist in textbooks and amateur pronouncements. Some explanations of this type may contain some truth, though even then it is likely to be of the kind which makes the trigger responsible for the shot. Invariably, however, they are more wrong than right, because any single specific cause is always only one of many: the realest "reason," the best understanding we can arrive at, in regard to any cultural phenomenon, is always the complex nexus of the largest historical totality with which the phenomenon can be brought into relation. The whole understanding of history is a matter of depth or perspective, as against which the singling out of obviousnesses in the immediate foreground is intellectually infantile. A cultural or historical pattern is a larger nexus which we perceive as possessing a certain objective validity.

If in the course of this study I allude to such shortsightednesses, it is to correct those which still have some currency: such as the concept of an Augustan age, whereas Roman literature came into flower during the dissolution of the Republic and died under Augustus. Or again, it is significant that mediaeval French architecture, sculpture, literature, and royal power had all declined before the Hundred Years' War; presumably, therefore, this war is more properly to be construed as the effect of a general decline in French national fortunes, perhaps as the product of a sag or interval between the working out of two successful sets of French patterns. Similarly with the four centuries following the Han breakup in China: the arts, instead of being destroyed by barbarian conquest and civil war, were actually progressing through a formative stage, of which the earlier T'angs reaped the fruits; it was the alleged political prosperity of the Hans under which the older Chinese culture reached its terminal stage. The inspection of cultural phenomena with an eye to their constellations, to the growth curve of their patterns, leads to a number of such corrections of particular perspective.

§4. Procedure

The most feasible plan for the study seemed to be to examine separately each separable course of a recognized intellectual or aesthetic activity and to determine as nearly as possible the growth of its quality or value curve in terms primarily of time, but of geographic localization also. This means that the quality-time configurations of Chinese philosophy, Indian philosophy, Greek philosophy, Arabic philosophy, and so on, were separately expressed. These in turn were then compared with one another. Thereupon science was treated in the same way; then sculpture; and so forth. This more or less sociological procedure has the disadvantage of lifting each growth out of its context of actual historical association. It seemed necessary, however, to begin an empirical operation analytically, with minimal groups of phenomena, and to compare and synthesize later. Theoretically, objection might also be made to this method because it assumes without proof the equivalence of each pattern growth, whereas science functioned differently in the total cultures of ancient China and modern Europe, philosophy was interwoven with religion in India and the Middle Ages but much more dissociated from it in Greece, and so on. In short, the supposedly comparable activities are not strictly comparable. I concede the point; but know of no other procedure. Roughly, at least, everyone is in agreement upon what constitutes philosophy or sculpture or poetry, especially when attention is focused upon activities which attained recognized achievement value and not with fumbling endeavors, undifferentiated gropings, half-articulate attempts. I have tried to do justice to major departures of direction by mentioning them, without allowing them to prevent comparative investigation altogether. After all, there are great similarities, and these must have significance, underneath the endless variability of particular historic expression.

A second treatment of the data crosscuts the first: the several activities within one area or nationality are considered together, in conjunction with political fortunes. This yields a profile of national- or integral-culture developments. This review (in Chapter Ten) is briefer, since most of the data have already been given in the preceding chapters.

The third part of the work (Chapter Eleven) consists of review and discussion.

As for the activities considered, they are, apart from the military-political data introduced in Chapter Ten, taken from the fields of aesthetic and intellectual exercise. These are, of course, not the most fundamental cultural activities; but they lend themselves best to the kind of examination proposed—perhaps because they are like flowers and fruits, from which the classifying botanist can in general extract more classification and history, or at least a readier classification, than from roots, stems, and leaves. They cycle more definitely, whereas technical arts and economies tend to go on with less evident fluctuation. Sociopolitical structure, population size, and wealth are factors which vary and which should be studied in this connection. But it is very difficult to obtain precise data on the last two over any lapse of time.

Of the several activities, philosophy and science speak for themselves. Of the arts, sculpture, painting, architecture, music, and literature obviously come into question. Of these I have reluctantly omitted architecture, except for some superficial cognizances in the combined national treatments in Chapter Ten. Almost alone among the arts, I found myself unable to follow the histories of architecture with sufficient empathy to induce a conviction of understanding their judgments. Structural features, which I evidently have not mastered sufficiently, interplay with aesthetic ones. Apparently, almost any building of sufficient mass or engineering difficulty will produce a strong psychological impression, to which the historians of architecture, like the mass of mankind, have yielded. A huge pyramid of masonry, even a stupa of heaped-up earth, an aqueduct, or a modern office building, are indubitably powerful symbols in emotional effect; but they may express but little direct aesthetic impulse. Then, too, the conventional classification—as into Doric and Ionic, Romanesque and Gothic, Renaissance and Baroque—proved confusing with respect to many particular structures. These terms are labels which at times refer to essential design and at times to externals; the initiate is supposed to know when and which. In my bafflement, I retain the suspicion that a culture-historically intelligible history of architecture is yet to be written.

Music I have had to restrict to that of the later Occident. The histories of other musics are mainly histories of their theories or instruments. The compositions are lost, or we do not know how the occasionally preserved records really sounded.

As for drama, there seemed reason both for separate discussion and for inclusion in literature. At the risk of some repetition, I met the dilemma by treating drama both ways. Prose proved difficult to separate consistently from poetry, and history from other prose writing. Rather against my preconceptions, historiography often failed to yield clear-cut constellations of its own; I have therefore reluctantly left it as a strain of literature. On the other hand, at the risk of some disproportion, I have allowed a chapter to philology: though it is the least important of the activities dealt with, its configurations are neat.

Another disproportion is of size. The chapter on Philosophy is briefer than that on Science, and that on Music than those treating of the other arts: they were the first written. If this is an injustice, I hope it will be compensated for by compactness, to which I could not always attain in later chapters.

My rating of genius and values, at any rate relatively within any one culture, is in the main the currently conventional one: I have followed the books, and their consensus is fairly close. Textbooks especially have been convenient in this regard, on account of their timidity about departing from the accepted norm. Encyclopaedias likewise, in the space they assign; and they give the facts which I principally needed—achievement, degree of eminence, dates, and place—concisely and with freedom from argument or novel opinion. The space measurements within books are not valid internationally: of Chinese, Hindus, and Arabs only the more outstanding penetrate to our encyclopaedias, as against many second-talent Europeans; and of course every French, German, English, or American encyclopaedia favors its nationals. But within the frame of one culture or nationality both the dicta and the space allotments of the secondary works are equitably significant. Where I have followed my personal judgment in place of the usual rating, I have tried to remember to designate it as such.

Certain disproportions are deliberate. Japan, for instance, developed a highly specialized mathematics which is of the greatest intrinsic interest culture-historically, but it remains unknown to most scientists and most historians; I have therefore given more space to this than to the configuration history of the familiar European mathematics.

In the choice of cultures I have also been guided largely by practical considerations appearing in the course of the work. Obviously I have had to work largely at second hand, from extant histories. These vary in their utility according as knowledge has been made available in European languages. For China and Japan the histories are excellently dated, but the currents are traced and evaluations are made according to plans, presumably native in origin, rather different from those followed in most other histories. For India, the value judgments are rather like our own, but the dating is of the haziest. For Egypt, the currently accepted picture of constellations, though unique in its repetitiveness, is remarkably clear; so sharp, in fact, as to arouse a suspicion of overschematization. Mesopotamia, on the contrary, is a chaos of discontinuities and uncertain dating; little that would make a picture emerges, and I have had to omit the culture from most chapters. The native American civilizations I would have liked to include, on account of their presumably complete historical disparateness; but the facts are insufficiently clarified. We have an inscriptional chronology from the earlier Maya which is internally certain but unplaced in universal time. We have a documentary history for the later Maya and Toltec-Aztec, but it is more or less legendary both in dates and content; it seemed wise not to build on materials so much less certain than most of the others. Ancient Peru I know something of at first hand; but we possess no dates whatever, and some of the culture sequences are not yet out of controversy, so it seemed wise to forego any interpretations based on personal certitude.

European or Occidental civilization I treat differently from any other: first, nation by nation, in each activity; and then as a composite whole. This procedure, together with the fullness of readily available data, has produced the result that the European section of several chapters has become as bulky as all the other sections combined. This I regret, because it will inevitably tend to produce an impression which I do not hold, namely, that European culture is more important than any other. In any genuinely sociological or comparative investigation the reverse is of course true: each essentially independent growth should count equally; if anything, the culture we participate in ought to weigh less heavily than the others, because our knowing it subjectively tends to impede our objective understanding of it. However, Occidental culture is extremely interesting as multinationally symphonic to a greater degree than any other. Each nation, as it were, contributes its own timbre and its own part to the unity of the larger composition. The way in which the national configurations proved to build up into the pan-European one has been, to me, one of the most fascinating results of the study.

Obviously, I have not read every writer, philosopher, or scientist whose name is cited as material, nor can I identify the product of each sculptor or painter named. I have tried to acquire at least a little firsthand acquaintance with some sample of each culture growth dealt with; not so much because this would suffice for a control, but for my own satisfaction and assurance. I am not a polyhistor nor writing a work of polyhistory, but have selected facts, from among those on common record, as they are pertinent to the problem set.

I have tried to exercise due care for exactness, but the range of history referred to is wide and some errors have no doubt crept in, especially in dates. Not all of these are due to my own carelessness of transcription: the sources I have used have a way of differing. Encyclopaedists evidently have a habit of borrowing from one another more frequently than is avowed, and in this way birth dates come to be perpetuated in two traditions. Deaths are more frequently given uniformly, but they are less important for my purposes. Names and birthplaces are also subject to error. "A of X" is a frequent Greek and mediaeval designation, in which "X" most frequently is the birthplace, but not always; sometimes fairly intensive biographical research would have to be conducted to insure accuracy, and then not always with certain result. Since my theme is constellations, and not biography, individuals become as it were only stones in a wall, and smallish inaccuracies are of less consequence than they would be in personal history. Errors would have to be gross to affect the argument.

I do not read Arabic, Persian, Sanskrit, Chinese, or Russian, and so cannot control the orthography of names from these languages, for most of which two or more systems of transcription are in use. According as my authorities employed one or the other, I followed. In a work of primary scholarship or permanent reference for factual detail, it would generally be considered necessary to transcribe into a consistent system, and this would require knowledge of the language. In this book, where names primarily serve identification, such correctness would have added a grace of workmanship which nobody would have appreciated more than I; but it might have added another seven years to the writing.

Certain recurring metaphors, I am certain, will provoke irritation and criticism: growth, patterns, saturation, realization, pulse, dissolution, and the like. If I could have found more precisely denotive terms, I should certainly have used them, and I shall welcome any substitutions that are either more definable or more aptly connotive. It must be remembered that history has the least technical vocabulary of any learned study, and that in all of what it has become customary to call social science the choice is largely between using figurative terms for fairly well understood groups of phenomena, or quarreling over definitions of concepts which tend to lead an existence of their own because their relation to phenomena is loose. "Diffusion," for instance, began as a hesitant figurative extension of meaning, but has become a standard term in anthropology and culture history. It includes a variety of processes, such as diffusion by war, trade, long contact-residence, missionization, or force. Where the mechanism is less of an issue than is the result, or where the result is clear but the specific mechanism is unknown or dubious, "diffusion" without further qualification may be a perfectly adequate description of the phenomena dealt with. Similarly in the present work, the concern of which is with the inherent grouping of certain phenomena of history and which largely begs the question of the basic causal mechanism involved, "growth" soon takes on a reasonably definite descriptive meaning. I could perhaps have found a more vividly expressive and sonorously impressive term, at the risk of overemphasizing some one aspect of its meaning. "Cycle" I have tended to avoid because of the implications that have become attached to it; and "return" and "progress" are not salient qualities of the phenomena I am concerned with.

When I have used the old Greek term "generation," it is usually with the implication of a third of a century, which is sometimes a more convenient approximative measure than century halves and quarters. For the peak of productivity of individuals, my experience is that the Greek *acme* or Latin *floruit* at age 40 is an unusually sound average estimate. Reputation and influence of course tend to arrive later and to persist after important productivity has ceased.

Chapter II

PHILOSOPHY

Chapter II

PHILOSOPHY

§5. The History of Philosophy

THE HISTORY of Ancient and Western philosophy offers an excellent opportunity for the study of concentrations because of the very continuity. For the last two and a half millennia, this story, as customarily told, constitutes a long strand, or at least a continuous roving of many fibers of thought, joining and disjoining, but stretching on. The interest of the recounters normally is in the relations of the interwoven elements of which the continuum consists. As long as attention is given to the content of thought, continuity is certainly to be recognized. God and the world, origin and end, motion and stability, the permanent and transient, body and mind, form and substance—most of these topics are dealt with by all men who philosophize; and in cultures that transmit themselves in writing it is to be expected that there will be dealing, avowed or indirect, with the conclusions of predecessors. If, however, we temporarily ignore the content of philosophy so far as possible, in order to direct attention to its productivity of new cultural values with reference to the occurrence of these values in period and region, it becomes plain that concentration is the salient feature, instead of continuity; that segregation is as outstanding as relationship. It is a matter of two points of view. Like science, philosophy in its nature tends to incorporate in each generation what its past has produced, to a degree that does not hold in the fine arts. In spite of this, the concentration in time and space of value productivity is about as marked in the intellectual as in the aesthetic fields.

I shall review what is customarily called "the" history of philosophy, from Thales to ourselves, in its usual frame, merely emphasizing its space, time, and value segregations instead of the relations of its content. The two other great philosophic growths of which we have record, those of China and India, I shall afterward consider separately.

Where dates are uncertain, the old assumption seems a good enough rule—that a man's "floruit" falls around his fortieth year. For a reflective activity like philosophy, fifty might seem a more appropriate age, though I doubt it; but the change would make little material difference.

The grand units generally recognized are Ancient, Arab, Mediaeval, and Modern philosophy. The last two of course are the products of the same people of western Europe, and therefore merely successive phases of the same greater culture growth, the Occidental. Ancient or Mediterranean philosophy, on the other hand, I divide into two, the earlier and purely Greek phase, and the later and religiously tinctured international one. The Arab development comes in two pulses, more distinct in region than in time; and in India probably, and in China certainly, two well-separated periods of growth must be recognized.

§6. Greek Philosophy

In Greek philosophy, two grand divisions must be distinguished: a productive period, little more than three centuries long; and a period of essentially nonproductive continuation, which is of indefinite duration.

The productive period, if we begin with the conventional date for the conventional initiator, Thales, runs from 585 to about 270, when the Stoic, Epicurean, and Skeptic doctrines had taken shape. The culmination is universally set with Plato and Aristotle, and may for convenience be put at 350, when both were alive and adult. Within fifty years of Aristotle's death, nothing new was any longer being produced in Greek philosophy, even by able men. The patterns which it had developed were evidently exhausted. They merely continued to be refilled, in more or less new combinations, thereafter.

The following constructive stages or phases, each of about fifty or sixty years, can be recognized within the productive period of Greek philosophy.

1. 585–535	Ionian Miletus	Thales, Anaximander, Anaximenes
2. 540–490	Ionia	Pythagoras, Xenophanes
3. 490–430	Asia Minor, Italy, Thrace?	Parmenides to Leucippus
4. 430–385	Athens and Greeks generally	Socrates, Democritus; Sophists; Cynics, Cyrenaics, Megarics
5. 385–320	Athens and Greeks generally	Plato, Aristotle
6. 320–270	Greeks generally	Stoic, Epicurean, Skeptic schools

1. Milesians: to Anaximenes' fiftieth year about 535, or death about 525.

2. Other Ionians, 540–490. Less preoccupation with nature and more with the divine than in the preceding.

Pythagoras of Samos, fl. 532.
Xenophanes of Colophon, born in the Olympiad of 580, lived to age 92.

3. Ionians, Aeolians of Italy, Dorian of Sicily, perhaps Ionian of Thrace, 490–430. The Pythagorean movement continued, but it had fallen into political troubles in southern Italy and almost no names are known from it. So far as its effects are concerned, it was now definitely a cult or order rather than a philosophy. Xenophanes is reckoned as the founder of the Eleatics, but the most important member of the "school" was Parmenides of this period. Ionia, which alone had so far produced philosophers, now shared this function with lower Italy, Sicily, perhaps Thrace; and the first Aeolians and a Dorian join the Ionians. The schools were markedly diverse in their teachings. The leading figures are:

Parmenides of Elea, b. ca. 540 or 515, in Athens 460.
Zeno of Elea, ca. 490–430.
Melissos of Samos, ca. 440.
Heraclitus of Ephesus, 540–480.
Empedocles of Agrigentum, ca. 490–430 (496–432).
Anaxagoras of Clazomenae, ca. 500–428.
Leucippos of Abdera or Miletus or Elea, ca. 450.

4, 5. Greeks generally, including Athenians, 430–320. The fourth and fifth phases are those of culmination and are marked by the four great names, Socrates, Democritus, Plato, Aristotle, though not exhausted by them. Taking the respective dates of these four as 469–399, ca. 460–360, 428–347, 384–322, the age-50 gauge yields approximately 419, 410, 377, 334 as their crystallizing moments. On the basis of age 40 to 60, 430 to 320 covers the great period. Obviously a subdivision is indicated between the two first and somewhat lesser figures and their two greater successors, the demarcation falling around 385 or 380.

Socrates and Plato were born Athenians; Democritos and Aristotle, Ionians from Abdera and Stagira on the coast of Thrace.

The sophists, Protagoras of Abdera, Hippias of Elis, Prodicus of Ceos, Antiphon of Athens, can mostly not be dated exactly, but fall generally into the generation around 430. Protagoras's time was about 480–410 (485–411?). Hippias, Antiphon, and Socrates were the first important thinkers to be born in Greece proper.

Three minor schools, the Cynic, Cyrenaic, and Megaric, were initiated respectively by Antisthenes of Athens, Aristippos of Cyrene, and Euclid of Megara, whose dates of birth are given as a little earlier than Plato's, namely, 444, ca. 435, ca. 444 (or d. 360). This would put their time of creative impetus at about 400 and in the decade or two just after. These schools, like the Sophists, indicate the experimenting vigor of Greek philosophy of the period, and that it was by no means confined to the current of Socrates-Plato-Aristotle.

6. Greece generally, 320–270. Another triad of schools—the Stoic, Epicurean, and Skeptic—typifies the sixth or post-Aristotelian phase, when constructive system building was beginning to terminate and interest was shifting from understanding for its own sake to ethics, understanding for the sake of conduct. The founders are Zeno of Kition in Cyprus, Epicurus of an Athenian family in Samos, and Pyrrho of Elis, whose dates are ca. 336–264, 341–270, ca. 360–ca. 270. Stoic doctrine

is said to have taken shape in the decade 310–300; the other formulations must have been about contemporary. The period is now Hellenistic instead of Hellenic. So is the geography. Thus Zeno was followed by Kleanthes of Assos in the Troad, born ca. 330, and Chrysippos of Soli in Cilicia, ca. 282–209. Zeno himself is said to have been a Phoenician; at any rate, Kition was a Phoenician city. It is evident that Stoicism was highly peripheral to Greece in its formative period. Each of these three men came from a region hitherto unrepresented by philosophers.

For Stoicism, the creative period may be somewhat longer than I have allowed. There is an old saying, "Without Chrysippos, no Stoa." I incline to assume that Zeno, as the founder of an organized and localized school, produced its fundamental viewpoint and ideas; and that Chrysippos elaborated and enriched these, perhaps also was the more successful expositor. If on the contrary the really new ideas are mainly the contribution of Chrysippos, the productive period of Greek philosophy would have to be stretched some forty years, to close about 230 instead of 270. The "Middle Stoa" under Panaetios of Rhodes, ca. 180–110, is already somewhat eclectic, and is significant historically rather than philosophically: it spread Stoic views to Rome. Still more is this true of the "New Stoa" in Roman imperial times, with Seneca, Epictetus, and Marcus Aurelius. Their writings were influential on posterity, but are only new expressions or shadings of ideas three to five centuries old.

With the development of a common Greek speech and civilization, the older Greek tribal grouping into Dorians, Ionians, Aeolians-Achaeans had become meaningless. Up to the time of Plato and Aristotle it retained some force, at least as a traditional influence. It is clear that Greek philosophy as a whole was an Ionian product, not only in its beginnings but in the majority of participants and in its peak. The exceptions are the following few:

Aeolian-Achaean: Parmenides, Zeno, Hippias.
Dorian: Empedocles, Aristippos, Euclid.

Even more striking is the nonparticipation of most of the Greek cities of the homeland. Thebes, Sparta, Argos, Corinth, nearly all the Peloponnesus and all the mainland north and west of Boeotia, produced not even one philosopher of the second rank. Megara and Elis are about the only birthplaces in Greece proper, besides Athens. Greek philosophy was the product of Ionia, Thrace, the Aegean islands, Italy, and Sicily—the Greek colonial world—plus Athens. It began peripherally and it remained peripheral plus Athenian to the end. Even though, around the peak, Athens drew most talent to her, she never produced more than part of it, and the rest of Greece proper almost none. In the arts the balance is much more even.

With the Stoic and Epicurean formations, Greek philosophical creativeness was exhausted. Men of ability continued to be born, but there was nothing left for them to do except to rephrase, to recombine, or translate. A philosophy on thoroughly new lines was evidently impossible for them: the old great forms were established too firmly to be broken, for centuries to come. Hence the Middle and New Stoa, and the Academy and Lyceum, went on, through Hellenistic and Roman times, even after Christianity was established, until the closing of the last school of philosophy at Athens by Justinian in 529. This means that the final spark from the past was then trod out; but the significance of the act is in marking the completeness of the triumph of another order of thought. Or, equally, the significance is the strength of the old channels, which were not obliterated until eight centuries after they last contained a current flowing strongly enough to deepen them: from 270 B.C. to 529 A.D. is just 800 years.

Here we have one of the skew curves that we shall encounter again and again: three centuries of rising development, eight of decline to extinction. Ancient and modern drama show the same phenomenon, except that the rise is more rapid. An activity begins, develops, reaches a peak, begins to decline, and there freezes. Thereafter it may continue indefinitely with imitation, repetition, or reduction. What we have is evidently phenomena of two orders. First comes a genuine growth, an increasing development of patterns or ways; but, this accomplished, there follows, instead of equally increasing disintegration, an institutionalization to perpetuate the patterns.

Apparently the perpetuation is one of inertia. Provided the forms achieved are reasonably rich and have been worked out to their limits, they seem to possess almost indefinite capacity of remaining in use if the civilization of which they are part survives. Egypt and China are the stock examples. Greek civilization did not break up, but dissipated into Graeco-Roman, which in turn assimilated the new Christian trends. There was therefore no overthrow from without; and the old philosophy could go on, weaker and weaker as a force, until it was crowded out of existence almost painlessly, and partly absorbed, by the incompatible Christian growth.

These are the epigones:

Middle Stoa
   Panaitios of Rhodes, 185/80–110.
   Poseidonios of Apamea in Syria, 135–50.
New Stoa
   Seneca, Spaniard, 3–65.
   Epictetus, Phrygian, 50–120/30.
   Marcus Aurelius, 121–180.
Epicureans
   Lucretius, 97/6–55 (95–52).
Skeptics
   Timon of Phlius, ca. 320–230.
   Arkesilaos of Pitane in Aeolia, ca. 315–241.
   Carneades of Cyrene, ca. 214–129, also head of Middle Academy.
   Aenesidemos, 1st cent. after Christ.
   Sextus Empiricus, fl. ca. 200.
Eclectics
   Antiochos of Ascalon, d. 68 B.C.
   Cicero, 106–43.

Latin writers like Cicero, Lucretius, Seneca, have been included here. The essential quality of the group is that of *prolonging* a movement. It differs from the Neo-Pythagoreans, Gnostics, and Neo-Platonists of the next section—with whom it overlaps in time—in that these express a *reorientation* of movement.

§7. Later Mediterranean Philosophy

Long before Greek philosophy was seen to be extinct—and with it I include Roman based on it: Lucretius, Cicero, Seneca—a set of new forces was at work undermining it. These were all essentially religious forces; and the term "undermining" is appropriate, because they did not so much try to sweep philosophy aside as to use it for their own ends, which, being religious, could not well be primarily intellectual. The strongest of these forces, in time, came to be Christianity, which, beginning on a wholly nonintellectual level, soon clothed itself, under John and Paul, more or less in the forms of Greek thought, and in the end used the weapons of Greek philosophy militantly against it. Contemporaneous with Graeco-Roman Christianity, however, the old pagan scheme of things was formally defended, as the names show, by Neo-Pythagoreanism and Neo-Platonism. But these were mystic and emotional cults, and at bottom they were religions also. They too, accordingly, used the old philosophy for fundamentally nonphilosophical ends, though they were outwardly friendly and compatible with it and had not the antagonistic Christian bias. Gnosticism, in the same period, may be described as a semiconscious endeavor to bridge Christianity to Greek philosophy by an intellectualized mythology.

In all these movements the new elements, like the ends, were not strictly philosophical, that is, abstractly intellectual; rather, they were emotionally religious: faith, salvation, vision. The late pagan philosophic cults as well as Christian apology therefore belong together, even though one was to die out and the other was to provide the basic religion for the Occidental civilization of the future and the Byzantine prolongation of Mediterranean civilization. They both at least looked ahead, and thereby stood in contrast to the dwindling trickle of Platonic and Stoic philosophizing.

The principal phases in this movement may be schematized as follows.

Non-Christian	*Christian*

1. Neo-Pythagoreans. Alexandria
25. Helleno-Judaism. Alexandria
150. Gnosticism. Syria, Egypt

                                              200. Apologists. Rome

                                              225. Early Fathers. Alexandria

250. Neo-Platonism. Egypt
300. Syrian Neo-Platonism

                                              375. Cappadocian Fathers

                                              400. Augustine, Western Empire

450. Athenian Neo-Platonism

                                              500. Greek Philosophers, Eastern
                                                        Empire
                                              525. Latin Philosophers, Western
                                                        Empire

These dates of course are merely central points of periods. In somewhat more detail, the most important personages, dates, and places group as follows.

Neo-Pythagoreanism. Alexandria. Nigidius Figulus, Roman, d. 45 B.C. Apollonius of Tyana in Cappadocia, fl. ca. 65 A.D., d. 97. Plutarch, in Boeotia, ca. 48–120.

Helleno-Judaism. Alexandria. Philo, ca. 25 B.C.–50 A.D.

Gnosticism. Syria and Egypt. Basilides, fl. 125 A.D. seq. Valentinus, fl. 136–165. Bardesanes, b. 153. Ophites, Pistis Sophia, to 3d cent.—Gnosticism of course can also be reckoned as Christian of a sort; though the Church fought it as arch heresy, and its aims are consistently different from Christian ones.

Apologists. Rome. Justin Martyr, ca. 90/100–166/7. Irenaeus, 140–202. Tertullian, 160–222/45. Minucius, d. ca. 200.

Early Church Fathers. Alexandria. Clemens, fl. 189–215. Origen, 185/6–232/54.

Neo-Platonists. Alexandria. Ammonius Sakkas, of Alexandria, ca. 175–242. Plotinus, of Lycopolis in Egypt, in Rome 25 years, 203/5–269/70. Porphyrius of Phoenicia, 232/3–304/5.

Syrian Neo Platonists. Iamblichus of Chalcis, d. 330/36.

Cappadocian Church Fathers. Basilius of Caesarea, 317–379. Gregory of Nyssa, 331–394. Gregory of Nazianzus, d. 390.

St. Augustine of Thagaste, Carthage, Rome, Milan, Hippo, 354–430.

Athenian Neo-Platonists. Proclus, 410/12–485.

Greek Christian philosophers. Dionysius Areopagita of Athens, mystic, probably last third of 5th cent. School of Gaza: Procopius, ca. 465–529.

Latin Christian philosophers. Martianus Capella, early 5th cent. Boethius (Christianity questioned), 470–525. Cassiodorus, 477–562. Isidor of Seville, d. 636.

Greece proper participated almost negligibly in these productions; Asia Minor, Syria, and Egypt, along with Rome, prominently. Alexandria is involved as the great city of the eastern half of the Empire rather than the intellectual center which it was in early Ptolemaic days. Alexandrian science and Alexandrian literature had flourished before 200 B.C., when such Greek philosophy as was still being produced clung chiefly to Rhodes and Athens on ancient Greek soil. In the early Christian centuries it was a cosmopolitan rather than Greek Alexandria—a Greek-speaking, Roman-ruled, half Christian, ethnically mixed Alexandria—which made its contribution to philosophy.

The five or six hundred years in question here obviously do not contain a coherent growth like that of earlier Greek philosophy proper, in which even the divergences stem from a central line of development. They include a series of diverse and often vehemently conflicting currents; currents, at that, aiming essentially either at a religion or at reconcilements of religion and philosophy. The whole Christian half, at least, of these endeavors would probably count for very little as philosophy if Christianity as an institution had not acquired so great and enduring an importance. There is therefore, naturally, no clear culmination on the Christian side. St. Augustine is no doubt the best known and most vivid figure. But if we take away St. Augustine the theologian and the personality, how much of a philosopher would we have left?

The pagan side is more heterogeneous, but it did produce at least one real growth pretty close to pure philosophy: Neo-Platonism, which had at any rate a beginning, and a culmination with Plotinus, and carried on more or less actively for two centuries or more.

After Augustine, what was left of philosophy upon its absorption into Christianity fell on evil days. The East retained at least a zest for subtlety and a passion for dispute; but in the West versatility and penetration died away with curiosity, and the chief desideratum became simplicity of content of thought. Witness the seven-arts compendium of Martianus Capella; witness the reduction of Euclid by Boethius, and his attempt to operate a philosophy by the distinction of multitudes from magnitudes. A program of elementary pedagogics was taking the place of a system creation. It was no longer a question of how great distances learning and thought could traverse, but of how narrow a compass they could keep alive in.

§8. Arab-Muslim Philosophy

I include here all Mohammedan philosophers as well as Jewish ones living in Mohammedan countries and writing Arabic. The criterion of cultural adhesion seems to be the use of this language. Yet only one of the more eminent men in the growth, and he the first one, Al-Kindi, was a pure Arab of Arabia by descent. The others were Persians, Turks, Mesopotamians or Egyptians, Jews, and, later, Spanish Mohammedans. Islam framed the movement, Arabic speech was its medium and cultural nexus. The word "Arab" is therefore appropriate in the same way that "Latin" is to contemporary western Christian civilization; but mediaeval Arab civilization has almost as little to do with Arabia as Latin with Latium.

It is easily apparent that Arabic philosophy consists, in time and place, of two movements. The first was general eastern, began as an absorptive growth about 800 and as a productive one around 850, culminated with Avicenna in the generation following 1000, and ended with Algazel's death in 1111. The second was Spanish-Moroccan and ran its course from 1100 to 1200, with the Spanish Jew Avicebron, a precursor around 1050, furnishing a temporal overlap with the earlier eastern pulse. Roughly, therefore, Spain began when the Orient ceased. The earlier or eastern growth was the less differentiated: its philosophy runs more on the one hand into theology, on the other into science. Apparently when Arab Mohammedanism turned into Arabic civilization, the impact of the Greek and other cultural material which it encountered was so heavy as to cause it to stagger for several centuries. More such material was absorbed than could be digested; hence metaphysics, optics, denominational theology, medicine, and alchemy were often pursued by the same men. Evidently the example of Aristotle was influential here. But where Aristotle spontaneously practiced his several activities, the Arabs struggled over the problem of their classification; the fact is symptomatic. They were more than mere cyclopaedists—their culture was probably too young for that; but they never got over an encyclopaedic approach. Philosopher and physician; historian and astronomer; mathematician and surgeon; historian and physician, are typical combinations; not to mention numerous polyhistors. Pure science, applied science, pseudo science tended not to get themselves segregated from one another, nor from philosophy and the *Geisteswissenschaften*. Everything was equally learning. All of which means, in the large, that a new, highly active, but still formative civilization absorbed such masses of material readymade from older civilizations that its powers of transmuting these had not come into complete activity.

The Spanish phase of Arab philosophy, probably because later, was more definitely philosophical, and had more influence on Latin philosophy. It falls in time mainly between European Early Scholasticism, 1075–1150, and High Scholasticism, 1220–1310. This fact is supplemented by another: that Early Scholasticism was essentially a French development, High Scholasticism an internationally West European one. Since Spain is also in western Europe, it is an almost inescapable conjecture that Spanish Arab philosophy was somehow related to Scholastic philosophy intrinsically as well as in space and time. That Averroës and his contemporaries influenced the High Scholastics is so well known as to be a commonplace; but could a subtler prior reverse current have flowed from Abelard's Early Scholastic contemporaries into Spain, so that all three unities (to borrow a phrase from dramatic criticism) were observed in the historic process? As for specific content, hardly so, since the Early Scholastics were less acquainted than the Mohammedan philosophers with the Greek sources from which they both derived. On the other hand, that such a current is not generally recognized means relatively little, because our histories of philosophy are written from the preconception of a continuous development from Thales to Kant, the Arabs being of interest chiefly as instruments which contributed to the Greek-Occidental continuity. Consequently, indirect influences, not manifest in transfer of content, would tend to be understressed or overlooked.

In any event, this is significant: Spanish Arabic philosophy flourished in the period when Mohammedan rule had passed from descendants of "cultured" Arabs into the hands of "fanatical" and "barbarous" Berbers, the Almoravides and then the Almohades, 1056–1269. Arab civilization is usually said to have reached its peak in Spain under the eighth and ninth Ummayad caliphs Abd al-Rahman III, 912–961, and Al-Hakum II, 961–976, when Cordova is said to have been the largest city after Constantinople, its "university" the center of Mohammedan learning, and its library to have contained 400,000 volumes. Now Spanish Arabic science began in these two culminating reigns with several Jewish, Christian, and Mohammedan physicians and with the astronomer Maslama, and continued for something like three centuries after them. But of philosophical activity there is not a trace until the Jew Avicebron, three-quarters of a century after the close of these reigns; and its main development in Spain lies between 125 and 225 years later, ending in fact only just before the final collapse of Mohammedan power under the advance of the Christian kingdoms of the peninsula. There is thus obviously a time gap rather than a conjunction between the Spanish Arab reigns of the so-called florescence of learning and the Spanish Arab philosophy—which does not prove the presence of Christian Scholastic "influences" in Muslim Spain, but does unbolt the door to the possibility that a connection of some sort existed.

Of course, Arab culture in Spain lagged temporally in all departments. Spain was conquered two-thirds to three-fourths of a century after Syria, Egypt, Mesopotamia, and Iran; and it lay on the margin of the Muslim world. Its great caliphs flourished a century and a half after Al-Mansur, Al-Rashid, and Al-Ma'mun. Its science began nearly two centuries later. Its philosophy also might therefore be assumed as "due" about as much later than eastern Arab philosophy as the interval actually was. But this meant that Spanish philosophy really began to be active when Arab civilization at large was already definitely declining. The point at which this general decline became manifest may be set at 1050; or, quite conservatively, between 1050 and 1100. The reference is primarily to general cultural vigor. By about 1100, for instance, France was producing more philosophy than the entire Oriental Mohammedan world; not to mention its Romanesque architecture and its dawning literature. Politically, the balance had probably shifted earlier. The consistent successes of the First Crusade just before 1100, carried on as it was under enormous difficulties of distance, leave little doubt that by then the Christian nations of the West were the stronger.

So here again Spanish Arabic philosophy fits in its time into the scheme of Occidental civilization as it does in its place. In the main the derivations of this philosophy must have been within the language and religion which defined its civilization. But as for time-space aspects, the Spanish philosophy is belated and remote enough to be almost outside the structural frame of Islam; and in the same respects it fits neatly into the framework of mediaeval Occidental growth. In brief, the principal or eastern Arab growth in philosophy was over by 1100, by which date also the Caliphate was long broken up and Mohammedan power was on the defensive against western Christian. From 1100 on, there were three successive philosophic developments in the Occident: Early Scholastic Christian, mainly French, 1075–1150; Spanish-Moroccan Mohammedan and Jewish, 1100–1200, under Berber, not Arab, rule; High Scholasticism, general west and central European, culminating

1220–1310. The Spanish growth therefore fits in its geography and period, contrary to its speech and religious affiliations, into an Occidental context. This fact suggests that the "causative" factors underlying this growth are to be sought in contemporary west-European general conditions of culture as well as in antecedent specific Islamic ones.

1. ORIENTAL ISLAM

Yahya ibn Batriq, early 9th cent. Translator of Greek philosophy.

Al-Nazzam, d. 845. Mu'tazilite theologian; latent creation.

Al-Jahiz, ca. 781–868/9, fl. Basra. Mu'tazilite theologian.

Dhu-l-nun, d. 859/60, from Upper Egypt or Nubia. Mystic forerunner of Sufism.

*Al-Kindi, early 9th cent., ca. 873, b. Basra of pure Arab descent, fl. Bagdad. Neo-Platonic Aristotelian; encyclopaedist.

Abdallah ibn Maymun, Persian b. Khuzistan, formed the Shi'a Isma'iliya secret sect with doctrine of number mysticism and microcosm-macrocosm.

Al-Ash'ari, 873/4–935/6, b. Basra of Arab family. Theologian; reëstablished Sunnite unity and orthodoxy.

*Saadia ben Joseph (Saadia Gaon), 892–942. B. Fayyum, fl. Sura, Babylonia. Jew, writing partly in Arabic. Jewish philosophy of religion.

*Al-Farabi, Alpharabius, ca. 870–ca. 950. Turk, b. near Farab, Turkestan, fl. Aleppo, d. Damascus. Neo-Platonist, syncretist, encyclopaedist.

Mutahhar ibn Tahir, fl. ca. 966. B. Jerusalem, fl. Bust, Sijistan. Encyclopaedist.

Al-Khwarizmi, fl. ca. 976. From Khwarism (Khiva). Classification of sciences; vocabulary of technical terms.

Ikhwan al-safa', "brethren of purity," secret association established at Basra ca. 983. Of their 52 treatises, 10 deal with metaphysics, 31 with science, mathematics, and logic, 11 with occult subjects.

Al-Baqilani, d. 1013. B. Basra, fl. Bagdad. Theologian, successor of al-Ash'ari; atomism of discontinuous time and motion.

*Alhazen, Ibn al-Haitham, ca. 965–ca. 1039. B. Basra, fl. Egypt. Scientist; greatest Arab physicist; commentaries on Aristotle.

**Avicenna, Ibn Sina, 980–1037. B. near Bokhara. Greatest "Arab" philosopher; modified Aristotelian.

*Algazel, Al-Ghazzali, 1058–1111. B. Tus, Khorasan, fl. Nishapur and Bagdad. Greatest Mohammedan theologian.

---

* Asterisks indicate eminence.

A thirteenth-century group of Arabic-writing Persians obviously represents a separate growth, and contains no first-rank philosophical figures: Al-Abhari, d. ca. 1263; Al-Katibi, d. 1277, astronomer also; Al-Qazwini, d. 1283, encyclopaedist. These belong to the same pulse as the Persian-writing poets Jalal al-din-i-Rumi, d. 1273, and Sa'di, d. ca. 1283.

2. Spanish-Moroccan Islam

*Avicebron, Ibn Gabirol, ca. 1021–1058. Jew, writing Arabic, b. Malaga, d. Valencia. First western Neo-Platonist; more influential on Christian than on Jewish thought.

*Avempace, Ibn Bajja, from before 1106 to 1138/9, b. Saragossa, lived in Granada, d. Fez.

Bahya ben Joseph, probably early 12th cent. Jew, writing Arabic; Neo-Platonist.

Avenare, Ibn Ezra, ca. 1089/92–1167, b. Toledo. Astrologer, grammarian, philosopher; translator from Arabic into Hebrew.

*Abubacer, Abu Bakr ibn Tufail (Thofail), 1100/10–1185/6; b. Guadix near Granada, d. Marrakush. Philosopher, physician.

**Averroës, Ibn Rushd (Roshd), 1126–1198; b. Cordova, d. Marrakush. Greatest western Arabic philosopher, perhaps of all Islam, but more influential on Christian and Jewish thought than on Mohammedan. Also important in medicine.

*Maimonides, Moses ben Maimon, 1135–1204, b. Cordova, d. Cairo. Physician, Aristotelian, and pious Jew, writing mainly in Arabic.

After 1200 there is only pseudo philosophy: e.g., Moses of Leon, ca. 1250–1305, possible author of the cabbalistic *Sefer ha-Zohar*.

§9. Occidental Philosophy

Western philosophy was produced in two great pulses. These ran their course among very nearly the same group of Romanic and Germanic peoples, but are separated by a definite gap in time, as well, of course, as by a thorough difference in content.

The earlier or Mediaeval philosophy on the one hand conducted itself within the frame set by the Church, and on the other leaned heavily on the thought of Mediterranean antiquity. It may fairly be said to have given to the patterns of Greek philosophy a reworking within its Catholic limits; but it began with these patterns and never wholly escaped their ban. It developed at a time when Christianity had long been firmly established, so that it could accept this religion as a foundation and largely pursue its own way within it. Thus it succeeded in carrying system creation much farther than the early or patristic Christians, who used philosophical concepts primarily as weapons in their battles of defense and propaganda. Still, mediaeval philosophizing began and ended by acknowledging the suzerainty of the faiths of the Church, and though at times it verged on the heretical its main current was orthodox and has ever since been proudly so recognized by the Church. This allegiance of course constituted a second inevitable limitation. That in spite of this double narrowing thirteenth-century European metaphysics succeeded in developing so rich and fine a system is proof that the impulses underlying it were genuinely philosophical in their nature.

Modern Occidental philosophy did not begin until the sense of a new world and civilization was fairly strong. It could therefore commence with new problems instead of those of Plato and Aristotle. Also, Christianity was a far weaker force; over half of western Europe it was a century since the Reformation had shorn it of most of its institutional power. God and the soul were still factors, but the mysteries and doctrines of established faith could be, and largely were, ignored. So far as a single generalization can be true, it may perhaps be fair to say that modern inquiry centered about the problem of how knowledge or understanding takes place.

Paralleling this difference in content and direction is the separation in time. Aquinas and Kant are more than five hundred years apart. There is a clear gap of half that length, from the later fourteenth to the early seventeenth century, in which not a single true system of philosophy was produced. This was the period of the Renaissance, humanism, the beginnings of science, the discovery of the New World, the Reformation. Far from being a time of intellectual slump, it was one of activity and curiosity. The metaphysical patterns of the Middle Ages no longer sufficed; but they had been carried to their inherent ultimate and exhausted. Philosophical thought had therefore to recommence. The gestation of its new set of patterns required two and a half centuries.

MEDIAEVAL

Mediaeval philosophy shows four phases, all but the last two discontinuous in time, and no two adhering to quite the same geography.

The emergent stage was scattering, with Erigena in the ninth century the principal figure. Early Scholasticism began two hundred years after him and lasted three-quarters of a century. After a lull of a couple of generations, High Scholasticism marked the third stage and culmination. It flourished for somewhat less than a century, from about 1210/20 to 1300/10. Occamism and Mysticism arose as High Scholasticism ended, and had a brief course of fifty or possibly seventy-five years, dying out during the second half of the fourteenth century. In content as well as time they form a typical terminal phase.

1. *Emergence.*—As an organized pulse of activity, the reality of this phase may be questioned. If it were not for John Scotus Erigena, about 810 to 880, one could almost speak of a complete void in Europe from the last of the ancient Latin philosophers to the first Scholastics. Erigena comes two centuries after Isidor and two before Anselm. The essential quality of his occurrence is therefore its isolation. He seems to represent an attempt of the feeble Carolingian Renaissance to draw to itself the best that the West then had; and this, in the intellectual field, was evidently what the longtime Christian, highly marginal Irish were producing. His origin from a never Romanized nationality justifies his historical placing with the future rather than the past, as the philosophers have recognized. This makes him an instance of a not uncommon phenomenon, namely, a precursor or initiator of growth who comes from the very periphery of the area in which the growth took place.

Erigena is an exact contemporary of Photius of Constantinople and the Arab Al-Kindi: their deaths occurred about 880, 897, 870. This is probably nothing but a coincidence which obtrudes because of the barrenness of the period in Europe. If there is any connection, it would seem to lie in the fact that, owing to the decline in the heart of the Roman Empire, the renascences and first new stirrings occurred beyond its former Latin-speaking boundaries.

2. *Early Scholasticism.*—The activity of this French phase revolves about the Nominal-Real issue. Empty as this problem seems now, the movement was active, vigorous, and definite. The main figures are:

Anselm of Canterbury, 1033–1109; b. Aosta in a French-speaking corner of Italy,
Roscellinus, b. ca. 1050 in Compiègne, d. after 1120.
William of Champeaux, ca. 1070–1121.
Abelard, 1079–1142; b. near Nantes.
Bernard of Clairvaux, 1091–1153; b. Burgundy.
Chartres school, ca. 1100–1150. (Bernard, Breton, fl. ca. 1117–1126; Thierry, brother of Bernard, d. ca. 1155.)
Gilbert de la Porrée, ca. 1076–1154; b. Poitiers.
William of Conches, ca. 1080–1154; b. near Evreux, Normandy.

It is evident that this development fell within the period 1075–1150/60. Also, it was overwhelmingly French. This is the more striking because France failed to participate prominently in the following phase of High Scholasticism, the culmination of which coincides closely in time with French culminations in literature, architecture, sculpture, and political institutions. In other words, philosophy ran well ahead of other national achievements in mediaeval France.

What is more, this Early Scholasticism is North French—the Seine and Loire basins, so far as birthplaces are concerned, and centering at the University of Paris. The time corresponds with that of the flowering of Romanesque architecture and sculpture in the Midi, 1100–1150; though the Provençal troubadour culmination was later, 1150–1220.

In short, Early Scholasticism was a North French growth a century ahead of most of the culminations of northern France, and more nearly contemporary with those of southern France.

3. *High Scholasticism.*—The period is from about 1220 or a little earlier to 1300 or a decade beyond. The movement be-

gan among Franciscans: Alexander of Hales, Grossetête, Bonaventura; and culminated with two Dominicans: Albertus and Aquinas. No wonder it was orthodox. The actual peak, as recognized by posterity generally as well as by the Church, is marked by the works of Aquinas, about 1265. This date falls just midway in the movement. Some place Duns Scotus rather than Albertus as the chief figure alongside Aquinas.

> Alexander of Hales, d. 1245; b. Gloucestershire, d. Paris. Franciscan.
> Robert Grosseteste, 1175–1253; b. Suffolk, chancellor of Oxford. Franciscan.
> Albertus Magnus, b. 1193/5 or later at Lauingen in Suabia, d. 1280 at Cologne. Dominican.
> Henry of Ghent, early 13th cent. to 1293.
> Roger Bacon, disciple of Grosseteste, ca. 1214–1292/4; b. Somerset. Franciscan.
> Bonaventura, 1221–1274; b. Bagnorea, in Papal State adjoining Tuscany. Franciscan.
> Thomas of Aquino, near Naples, 1225/7–1274; *1261–1265. Dominican.
> Ramón Lull, 1231/5–1315; Catalan, b. Majorca.
> Duns Scotus, ca. 1265–1308; b. probably in Berwickshire, perhaps in Ulster or England. Franciscan.

This is a strikingly international list. The heads are Italian and German; the British are most numerous; only the French, who carried the preceding phase alone, are unrepresented. Besides the two English Franciscan initiators, the series consists of a Suabian, a Fleming, an Englishman, a north Italian, a south Italian, a Catalan, and a Scot. Their close contemporaneity would perhaps hardly have been possible in a growth outside the supernational Church.

The men not of the first importance, likely to be omitted in a briefer compendium of the history of philosophy, show the same constellation:

> Michael Scot, d. ca. 1235; translator from Arabic.
> Petrus Hibernicus, fl. Naples ca. 1240–1242.
> Jean de la Rochelle, d. 1245.
> William of Auvergne (or Paris), ca. 1180–1249.

---

* The asterisk here, and to the end of §9, denotes dates of principal works.

Adam Marsh, d. 1257/8, b. Somerset.
Thomas of York, d. 1260.
Vincent of Beauvais, d. ca. 1264; encyclopaedist.
Petrus Hispanus, Pope John XXI, 1210/20–1277, b. Lisbon.
Ulrich von Strassburg, d. 1277.
Robert Kilwardy, d. 1279 in Viterbo.
Siger of Brabant, d. ca. 1281/4, fl. Paris.
Boethius de Dacia, Dane, fl. Paris ca. 1277.
William de la Mare, d. 1298.
Richard of Middleton, d. ca. 1300±.
Godfrey of Fontaines (near Liège), d. after 1303.
Giles (Aegidius) of Lessines (in Hainaut), d. 1304, or after.
Aegidius Romanus, ca. 1247–1316.

The mean of death dates is about 1277 as against 1282 for
the greater men; the mean "floruit" would thus lie around
1260. Franciscans outnumber Dominicans in about the same
ratio of two or more to one. As for national origin, the British
Isles are again definitely in the lead; France and the Netherlands somewhat better represented, Italy and Germany somewhat less, than among the greater men; but the significant
distribution is about the same.

British, 7 (English 5, Scotch 1, Irish 1); French, 3; Iberian, 1
(Portuguese); Italian, 1; German, 1; Danish, 1; Netherlandish, 3
(Flemish and Walloon, no Hollanders).

It is clear that Frenchmen did not hold philosophical leadership in this century, although the University of Paris unquestionably did, many foreigners studying or teaching there.
Northern Italy has but one representative in the major and
none in the minor list.

Because Scholasticism operated with a minimum of science
and within a given frame of theology, it seems arid or even
repugnant to most non-Catholic moderns. But its system in the
Thomistic formulation is rich, acute, integrated, and dignified,
and merely as an intellectual achievement it probably ranks
at least approximately with the systems of Aristotle and Kant.

By the Church, Thomism was embalmed. The Jesuit Suárez,
1548–1617, is reckoned a Scholastic in histories of philosophy;
and Aquinas' system is today the official philosophy of Catholi-

cism. As a creative or solidly constructive movement, however, Scholasticism was over soon after 1300 or 1310.

4. *Occamism and Mysticism.*—This stage is continuous with the last in time, but has traits characteristic of the terminal phases of culture growths. Occamism or Terminism is construable as a negativistic, skeptical reaction to the finished Scholastic system, and German Mysticism as another symptom of dissolution.

Terminists or Occamists
  William of Occam, English, 1299–1347/50, philosophical work
    done before 1323.
  Buridan, d. 1358/9.
  Nicholas of Oresme, d. 1382.
  Albert of Saxony, d. 1390.
  Minor German prolongation into the 15th cent.

German Mystics
  Eckhart, ca. 1260–1327/9.
  Tauler of Strassburg, 1300–1361.
  Suso of Constance, 1300–1365.

MODERN

Constructive modern philosophy occupies little more than the last half of the 560 years since mediaeval philosophy finished its accomplishments around 1380. Its coherent growth begins with Descartes in 1637. The long gap has already been mentioned. It remains to consider a few figures in this interval: Cusanus, about 1450; and Bruno, Bacon, and Boehme around 1600. Others mentioned in the books are humanists and refugee Byzantine scholars rather than philosophers.

Nicholas of Cusa, or Cusanus, born near Trier, 1401–1460/64, principal works 1440 and 1450, is one of the pioneers of modern science on account of his mathematics. It is therefore tempting to reckon him also one of the precursors of modern philosophy. In time, however, he stands much nearer the Scholastics. He lived only about a half century after the last Terminists, but two centuries before Descartes. His presuppositions are still mediaeval, his points of view often refreshingly modern. His place is clearer in the sequence of science than in philosophy.

Giordano Bruno of Nola, 1548–1600, and Francis Bacon, 1561–1626, have perhaps been overrated during the past century, not indeed as personalities and writers, but as philosophers. Neither of them evolved any considerable system. Both preached eloquently the method of science without attempting to do science. They are propagandists of a point of view which later became established. Their significance is as program formulators and active-minded individuals. They are surrogate rather than actual philosophers.

Jacob Boehme of Görlitz, 1575–1624, principal works 1612 and 1623, mystic and cobbler, is an expression of that strange streak of occasional childlikeness which runs through German civilization.

The incontestably philosophical development of modern Europe is that of the last three hundred years. It is much less international than was the mediaeval. In fact, it comes mainly in four successive pulses in as many countries: France, Holland, Great Britain, Germany. The British participation can justly be divided into two, English and Scotch. But this only increases the preponderance of the northwest European peoples. Italy has remained unrepresented. So are the marginal countries: Spain, Scandinavia, the Slavs. By the time these might have participated, as they did in science and the arts of the nineteenth century, modern European philosophy had spent its major force.

The four or five national pulses always abut and mostly overlap in time. There is thus a continuity of progress, in time as well as in thought content. However ethnic the phases, the growth is definitely a unit. There is a modern European philosophy as truly as an ancient Greek one.

Of the several national phases, the German is the latest, the longest, and—if general opinion so soon after the event is valid—the culminating one. Each nation made a major contribution only once. However, France returned twice to the task and England once, with fair success. I presume this means that France, having begun, has had the most time in which to try a repetition, and England the next most. The German movement, being long as well as late, was still in progress when these French and English revivals occurred. The Dutch, as a small people, could hardly be expected to produce more than once at their best.

Each major national movement has its climax coinciding quite closely with climaxes in other activities.

The relation to science shows this profile: Up to about 1700, association with science is generally close. Witness not only the precursors Cusanus, Bruno, and Bacon already mentioned, but also the Descartes group and Leibnitz with his calculus. About 1700, science and philosophy dissociate pretty thoroughly. This continues until the finish of the German culmination around 1820. Immediately thereafter philosophy begins a rapprochement. It leans on science or tries to use it for its own purposes. Witness Comte, Mill, Herbart, Spencer, not to mention later men. This is not an annexation of conquest by philosophy, but a sign of its exhaustion. It had achieved and filled the patterns within the frame it set itself at the beginning of the movement, and now it began to fall back on science.

France.—Modern philosophy, like modern mathematics, dates from the *Discours de la méthode,* 1637. Descartes, however, was only the most important figure of an extraordinarily brilliant group of contemporary Frenchmen. They are:

Mersenne, 1588–1648; *1630, *La Vérité des sciences.*
Descartes, 1596–1650; *1637. B. Touraine.
Gassendi, 1592–1655; *1647, *1649, *1655. Provence.
Pascal, 1623–1662; *1669, *Pensées.* Clermont-Ferrand.
Malebranche, 1638–1715; *1674–1675, *Recherche de la vérité.*
    Paris.

The last differs somewhat in direction as in time. The cluster reappears with some changes—Fermat and Desargues in place of Gassendi and Malebranche—as equally fundamental in the history of modern science. This is a notable as well as a highly concentrated group. Its activity falls within a scope of 40 or 45 years. The Midi as well as northern France is represented.

After a gap of two-thirds of a century, there comes a second French development, very different from the first or Cartesian one, and about contemporary with the Scotch growth. It may be said to begin with Voltaire's earlier work, 1731, and to end with Condorcet's, 1794, but most of it falls within three decades, 1746–1774. This is a loose-jointed, semipopular philosophy of enlightenment, easily followed by intelligent laymen. It is one of the few philosophical movements which quickly and directly influenced social and political activity. At least, nearly all historians so affirm, in discussing the French Revolution. Nothing comparable can be alleged of Aristotle, Aquinas, Descartes, or Kant. It is further characteristic that whereas the names of most of the associates of Descartes are found also in histories of mathematics, those of Voltaire recur in histories of literature. In fact, they constitute most of the eminent figures in French "eighteenth-century" literature. They may fairly be described as producing a hybrid between literature, social theory, and philosophy. The group possessed a series of sufficiently clear points of view; but, except for mechanistic materialism, it did not evolve a general system of the world or of understanding.

Montesquieu, 1689–1755. *1748, *Esprit des lois*. B. near Bordeaux.

Voltaire, 1694–1778. *1731, *Lettres philosophiques;* *1764, *Dictionnaire philosophique;* *1777, *Réponse au Système de la nature*. Paris.

La Mettrie, 1709–1751. *1748, *L'Homme machine*. Brittany.

Rousseau, 1712–1778. *1762, *Contrat social.* *1762, *Emile*. Swiss of Geneva.

Diderot, 1713–1784. *1746, *Pensées philosophiques*. Champagne.

Condillac, 1715–1780. *1754, *Traité des sensations*. Grenoble.

Helvetius, 1715–1771. *1758, *1772, *1774. Paris.

D'Alembert, 1717–1783. *1759, *Eléments de philosophie*. Paris.

Holbach, 1723–1789. *1770, *Système de la nature*. Palatinate German by birth.

Turgot, 1727–1781. *1774. Paris.

Condorcet, 1743–1794. *1794, *Progrès de l'esprit humain*. Picardy.

The nineteenth century in France is dominated by the vigorous, insistent figure of Comte, who essentially renounces philosophy for a reform program of science and progress. There is no group homogeneity, either in time or in direction of thought.

Saint-Simon, 1760–1825. *1821. B. Paris.
Comte, 1798–1857. *1830–1842, *Cours de la philosophie positive.* Montpellier.
Poincaré, 1854–1912. *1903. Nancy.
Bergson, 1859–1941. Paris.

Holland.—Spinoza, 1632–1677, born at Amsterdam, died at The Hague, *1663, *1670, *1677, is rather close in his work to his contemporary Malebranche, but stands almost solitary in Dutch philosophy. The Jewishness of his point of view is often referred to. He is undoubtedly the greatest Jewish philosopher in seven centuries. But equally important is the fact that his lifetime is the era of Dutch eminence in painting, literature, science, and economics. His continuity relation with Descartes and Judaism is indubitable and significant from one point of view; but so is his contemporaneity in Holland with Rembrandt, Huygens, and the East India Company.

Ambivalent too is the position of the "Occasionalist" Arnold Geulincx, a Fleming born 1625 in Antwerp, a professor at Louvain, died a Calvinist at Leyden 1669, principal work *Ethic,* 1665–1675. Like Malebranche, he represents "religious reaction against rationalism within the framework of Cartesian presuppositions." But he is the one eminent Netherlander in philosophy besides Spinoza, and his professorship at Leyden is more than an accident. The movement of culture in Holland at the time was active enough to draw into itself both Catholic and Jew.

Great Britain.—Scotchmen may fairly enough be included with Englishmen because their language is English. But there is a significant grouping as between the two nationalities.

English philosophy is often represented as an almost self-contained stream from Bacon to the present. As a matter of fact, it presents a main growth from about 1640 to 1730, with a clear peak between 1680 and 1710 coincident with the Newtonian florescence of science (1687); then a long gap, and a lesser phase afterward. Hobbes stands enough apart in time in the chief growth to keep him out of the climax and must evidently be reckoned a precursor. Hume, later than Locke and Berkeley, was born in Edinburgh, and fits with his Scotch group in time.

Hobbes, 1588–1679. *1642, *De Cive;* *1651, *Leviathan;* *1658, *De Homine.*
Cambridge School:
    More, 1614–1687. *1668, *1671.
    Cumberland, 1632–1719. *1672.
    Cudworth, 1617–1688. *1678.
Locke, 1632–1704. *1680–1690, *Essay concerning Human Under-standing.*
Shaftesbury, 1671–1713.
Berkeley, 1685–1753. *1710, *Principles of Human Knowledge.*
Deists:
    Toland, *1696.   Wollaston, *1722.
    Collins, *1713.   Tindal, *1730.

Hobbes was 63 when the *Leviathan* was published, Berkeley 25 at the appearance of his *Principles,* but lived forty-three years longer. These may be accidents of personality or conformations of individuals to the culture movement of their days.

The culmination of the Scottish development falls within the fifty-three years 1739–1792, that is, about seventy years later than the English, with something like thirty of interval since Berkeley. The major figure of Hume precedes the minor members of the group sufficiently to make the cluster somewhat asymmetrical; but this is due to Hume's producing earlier in life than his seniors Home and Reid. On the other hand, Beattie and Stewart, who were born considerably later, also produced in youth.

Hume, 1711–1776. *1739, *Treatise;* *1748, *Inquiry.*
Home, 1696–1782. *1762, *Elements of Criticism.*
"Scotch School":
    Reid, 1710–1796. *1764, *1785, *1788.
    Beattie, 1735–1803. *1760.
    Stewart, 1753–1828. *1792.
Brown and Hamilton of the next century are often included.

Adam Smith, 1723–1790, *1776, *Wealth of Nations*, is evidently to be reckoned with this philosophical burst. Besides which, the Scotch peaks in science and literature are essentially contemporary.

After the lapse of the greater part of a century, about when the Scotch school was drawing to a close, a second phase of English philosophy may be said to have begun with Bentham. This was more straggling than the first, and it has received less consideration on the Continent. So far as ends are concerned, it resembles somewhat the second and third French pulses; it is humanitarian, concerned with social problems and progress, unmetaphysical, dependent on science. Scotch activity now tended more to be drained into English. The second Mill perhaps marks such center of gravity as there was.

Bentham, 1748–1832. *1789.
Malthus, 1766–1834. *1798.
James Mill (Scot), 1773–1836. *1829.
Brown (Scot), 1778–1820. *1820.
Hamilton (Scot), 1788–1856. *1829.
John Stuart Mill, son of James, 1806–1873. *1843, *1848, *1861.
Spencer, 1820–1903. *1855–1876.

If now we consider the British developments jointly, this is the result:

English growth, Hobbes to Tindal, 1642–1730.
    Peak, Locke and Berkeley, 1680–1710.
Scotch growth, 1739–1792; with aftermath into the next century.
Nineteenth century, English and Scotch, 1820–1870.

It is evident that continuity is attainable only by tenoning the Scotch development into the English socket. This is legitimate enough where coherence is the aim of depiction, as in a history of the content of philosophy. But it is equally legitimate to recognize the segregations.

Germany.—German philosophy consists first of Leibnitz and second of the great burst that culminated around 1800. This latter is a neat case of cyclic development; but Leibnitz (1646–1716, *1695, *1714), as eminent in mathematics as in philosophy, does not fit into any movement in Germany, nor any outside. He has no predecessors, and no successors except Wolff, who systematized what Leibnitz failed to "present in a coherent system." This last deficiency may be a symptom of his anomaly. Another perhaps is the fact that Leibnitz, although born a Saxon and spending his life in Germany, wrote mostly in French. However, whatever the reasons, Leibnitz is an exception. He belongs with Copernicus, Kepler, and Goya: they are unplaced in a group.

The main German growth covers the hundred and twenty years from 1755 to at least 1875. Of these, about twenty-five may be assigned to growth, a scant forty to the climax, some fifty-five to decline, plus as much more as one likes to add for dissolution. The most important works of the greatest personalities in the movement—Kant, Fichte, Schelling, Schleiermacher, Hegel, Schopenhauer—were produced within the period 1781–1819. Of these six, four were born east of the Elbe, two in Württemberg. The curve of development for the entire movement is skew: the date of the *Kritik der reinen Vernunft* falls only a fourth as far from the assumed beginning as from the assumed end of the cycle. Kant's "first and second periods" cover the duration of the ascent. In fact, his first work dates from 1746.

The cycle, of course, corresponds closely in time to the florescences in German literature and music; less nearly to the nineteenth-century developments of German painting and science. Like the literature and music, the philosophy began late, compared with more westerly countries, but had a long development.

Precursor

Wolff, 1679–1754. Breslau. Systematist of Leibnitz, but of significance here as the creator of German philosophical terminology.

Formative stage

Mendelssohn, 1729–1786. Dessau. *1775, *1764, *1767, *1785.
Lambert, 1728–1777. *1761, *1764, *1771.
Lessing, 1729–1781. *1766, *Laokoon*.
Tetens, 1736–1805. *1776.
Kant's earlier periods, 1746–1766.

Culmination
   Kant, 1724–1804. Königsberg. *1781, *Kritik der reinen Vernunft;*
   *1783, *Prolegomena;* *1788, *Kritik der praktischen Vernunft.*

Followers and contemporaries
   Hamann, 1730–1788.
   Jacobi, 1743–1819. Düsseldorf.
   Herder, 1744–1803. *1784–1791, *Ideen zur Philosophie der Ge-
      schichte der Menschheit.*
   Goethe, 1749–1832. *1790, *Metamorphose;* 1808, *Farbenlehre.*
   Maimon, 1754–1800. *1790.
   Reinhold, 1758–1823.
   Beck, 1761–1842. *1796.
   Schulze, 1761–1833. *1801.

Greater epigones
   Fichte, 1762–1814. Oberlausitz. *1794, *Wissenschaftslehre.*
   Schelling, 1775–1854. Leonberg, Württemberg. *1795–1801.
   Schleiermacher, 1768–1834. Breslau. *1799–1803.
   Oken, 1779–1851. Bohlsbach. *1805, *1809.
   Herbart, 1776–1841. Oldenburg. *1806–1840.
   Hegel, 1770–1831. Stuttgart. *1807, *1812–1816, *1817.
   Schopenhauer, 1788–1860. Danzig. *1819, *Die Welt als Wille
      und Vorstellung.*

Decline
   Feuerbach, 1804–1872. Landshut. *1839–1866.
   Fechner, 1801–1887. Lausitz. *1860, *Psychophysik.*
   Marx, 1818–1883. Trier. *1867, *Das Kapital.*
   Hartmann, 1842–1906. Berlin. *1869, *Philosophie des Unbe-
      wussten.*
   Lotze, 1817–1881. Bautzen. *1874–1879. (Kantian renascence,
      infl. Windelband, Rickert.)

Dissolution
   Nietzsche, 1844–1900. Lützen. *1883–1887.

This German growth is easily the longest in modern philosophy, the culmination of which is generally considered to be
effected by the German peak. Certainly the subsequent nineteenth-century activities in France and England cannot be
rated as equal to Kant's. They compare more equally alongside
the contemporary German products of the decline.

The strength of the German movement is exemplified by
the influence of Marx. Although neither professionally nor

technically a philosopher, he was trained in German thought and developed an ideational system; so he may fairly enough be counted in. He came well along in the decline—nearly a century after Kant; yet he has been a tremendous international force.

On account of this largeness of the movement, it is tempting to extend it farther and include Leibnitz, and at the other end both Nietzsche and the successors of Lotze: Windelband and Rickert. There seems to be much underlying justification for such a view. In a larger sense I suspect it to be true. On the other hand, it is thirty-two years from Leibnitz's last work to Kant's first, and sixty-seven to the *Kritik der reinen Vernunft,* with nothing to fill the gap except toward the end. A void generation is too long a period to ignore. I have in too many other instances counted it as negatively significant; and therefore prefer to remain consistent in such accuracy of measurement as is possible in these matters, and leave Leibnitz without "normal" cultural context.

Summary.—The general course of modern Western philosophy, with reference to its national cycles, may be summed up in the following table, which selects the narrower culminations for emphasis.

International, presystemic	French	Dutch	British	German
1440–1450, Cusanus				
1575–1625, Bruno, Bacon				
	1630–1675, Cartesianism	1642–1658, Hobbes		
		1660–1680, Spinoza		
			1680–1710, English	
				1695–1714 Leibnitz
	1746–1794, Enlightenment		1748–1792, Scotch	
			1755–1780, Formation	
			1781–1819, Culmination	
	1820–1840, Comte, etc.		1820–1870 Mill, etc.	
			1820–1875, Decline	
			1875–, Dissolution	

In summary, the preliminary first stage of modern European philosophy was international, but without serious French participation. Then followed, in close succession, a series of definitely national phases, in the order: French, Dutch, English, Scotch, German—the latter mainly east German. This order is obviously one of progression from the more to the less highly civilized peoples. Not that the last necessarily remained inferior; but they were so, in general culture, when the philosophical movement started, and accordingly it reached them later. Spain, Italy, eastern Europe, and Scandinavia were not reached at all, at least not to a degree to release important productivity. Southern France, however, participated along with northern. France, also, owing perhaps to its early start, was the only country to develop two secondary phases. The general direction of movement was centrifugal; the culmination came literally at the farthest margin attained—at Königsberg. The German phase was also definitely the longest, and the only one in which several continuous subphases can be clearly distinguished.

§10. Indian Philosophy

For India, there is always a lack of reliable dates: the Hindus are notorious for having developed a great civilization without historical sense. Many Western writers have complacently accepted the situation; others have tried to distinguish temporal development in spite of the difficulties. All are agreed that most dates are derivable only indirectly and remain approximate and tentative.

However, two main periods of philosophical creativeness do emerge. The first of these centers around Buddha about 500 B.C. and in the Ganges Valley. The second is long, from about 100 to 1000 of our era, and was south as well as north Indian. In fact, the probable culmination, around 800, occurred on Dravidian soil, although the language of all Indian philosophy is Sanskrit.

While a religion was built around the teachings and personality of Buddha, he was a philosopher who taught a way of life.

His dates are 560–483/77, or, died in 543—after Thales, but more than a century before Plato. A slightly older contemporary was Mahavira, the founder of Jainism, a religion parallel in many ways to Buddhism, though the one has maintained itself until the present as a minor Indian sect and the other died out in India after spreading north and east to hundreds of millions of people. Around 600 is put the legendary figure of Kapila, the founder of the Samkhya philosophy, though the earliest extant Samkhya text is nearly a thousand years younger. There is no doubt that Buddhism, Jainism, and Samkhya as idea systems sprang from a common root. They all accept as given the specifically Indian concepts of *samsāra* or endless chain of rebirth, *karma* or moral causality, and *nirvāna*. Samkhya and Jainism are dualistic with respect to soul and matter— though matter is so psychically conceived that Samkhya might in the West be reckoned an idealistic system. Buddhism is monistic on this point. Nevertheless, in view of our knowing Buddhism as a practiced, codified, and more or less organized religion, and Samkhya as an intellectual scheme, the conceptual elements which they share are impressive and significant. The books usually say that Buddha was influenced by Kapila. Legend has him born at Kapila-vastu, "Kapila-abode." That the extant systematic formulation of Samkhya should have been made by 600 B.C. is scarcely possible. On the other hand, the native tradition of Samkhya as the oldest of the six orthodox Brahmanical systems has this foundation: the *Mahābhārata*, 200 B.C. to 200 A.D., is full of Samkhya—and Yoga—quasi philosophy or presuppositions. It is reasonably clear, therefore, that Kapila, Mahavira, Buddha are semilegendary personalities expressing the fact that at a certain era a set of highly distinctive, abstract, and fundamental concepts was developed, out of which grew, as time went on, a popular, monastic, and finally international religion, an important national sect, and the philosophy of an educated class. In much the same way, the Upanishads, which may date from the eighth century on, express the basic pantheism which was much later organized into the philosophically articulate system of Vedanta.

The time of these developments or first formulations was roughly the sixth century; the place, the environs of the kingdom Magadha on the lower middle Ganges—far from the Punjab scene of the Vedas. Old Magadha, with capital at Pataliputra or Patna in Bihar, flourished 640–470; later it underwent long vicissitudes, and flourished again under the Mauryas and the Guptas.

The second growth, from perhaps 100 to 1000, was that of logic and formal philosophy, and was again Buddhistic as well as Brahmanical. The Buddhistic development probably preceded, on the whole; but its achievements were appropriated and reworked for themselves by the Brahmans. The Brahman philosophical culmination occurred after Buddhism had ceased to be philosophically productive; in fact, at a time when Buddhism as an institution was already decaying in India. To a certain degree it would be correct to say that there was but one greater flow of later Indian thought, the differences between historic Buddhism and Brahmanism being in the main institutionally determined, by an organized and established religion and a privileged and entrenched caste respectively. As in the field of religion Sivaism and Vishnuism replaced Buddhism, Vedanta replaced Buddhist philosophy; and, with an extreme pantheism which denied the reality of everything but soul, became about as negatively simplistic in effect as atheistic Buddhist nihilism had been. Earlier Buddhism shared much with both Samkhya and Yoga; Buddhistic logic approaches the Nyaya system; Jainism and the Vaisesika system are both atomically dualistic. These resemblances are cited not from any desire to minimize the differences between the several currents in the stream of Indian thought. These are conceptually as distinct as those within Chinese, Greek, or European thought. They are cited to indicate that a primary segregation of conceptual systems in terms of historic religious institutions is likely to be misleading. If in the list that follows I have for convenience nevertheless kept Buddhist and Brahman contributions separate, it is with this reservation.

Buddhist Thought, 100–700 a.d.

Aśvaghoṣa. Contemporary of Kanishka (120–162, V. Smith).
Nāgārjuna, fl. 175–200; b. Vidarbha, in the south.
Āryadeva, pupil, fl. 200–225; also a southerner.
*Asanga and his brother *Vasubandhu, ca. 350; culmination of philosophic idealism.
Buddhapālita, 400–450.
Bhavya or Bhāvaviveka, 450–500.
Buddhaghosa, 450–500; b. Magadha; culmination of Singhalese Pali school.
*Dignāga, 450–500 (or 350–400 ?); southerner, b. Kanchi, fl. Andhra. Formal logic of Buddhism.
Sthiramati, contemporary.
Candragomin, ca. 600.
*Dharmakīrti, 650–700; b. Trimalaya; logician.

Brahman Philosophy, 100–1000 a.d.

Kaṇāda, 100–150. *Vaiśeṣikasūtras.*
*Jaimini, 150–200. *Mīmāṁsāsūtras.*
Gautama, 200–250. *Nyāyasūtra.*
*Iśvarakṛṣṇa, ca. 350. *Sāṁkhyakārikā,* earliest extant Sāṁkhya work. (*Sāṁkhyasūtras* late, perhaps ca. 1400.)
*Bādarāyaṇa, 350–400, or 400+. *Brahma-* (*Vedānta-*) *sūtras.*
Śabara(-svāmin), 400–450. *Mīmāṁsābhāṣya* (sūtra commentary).
Vātsyāyana, 400–450. *Nyāyabhāṣya.*
*Patanjali, 400–450. *Yogasūtra.* (Probably not the grammarian Patanjali, 2d cent. b.c.)
Praśastapāda, 450–500. *Vaiśeṣikabhāṣya.*
Maticandra, ca. 600. Vaiśeṣika: *Daśapadārthī.*
Uddyotakara, 600–650. *Nyāyavārtika.*
Prabhākara, 650–700. *Mīmāṁsā.*
Kumārila, 700–750; south. Mīmāṁsā.
Gaudapāda, 700–750. *Sāṁkhyabhāṣya;* Vedānta: *Māṇḍūkyakārikā.*
Vyāsa, 650–850. *Yogabhāṣya.*
**Śaṁkara, 788–820. B. Kerala, d. Kanchi, both in Dravidian south. *Bhāṣya* on *Brahmasūtras.* Culminating Vedantist work.
Mandanamiśra, 825. *Vidhiviveka* (Nyāya).
*Vācaspatimitra, 830–860. *Sāṁkhyatattvakaumudī; Bhāmatī* (Vedantist); *Nyāyavartikatātparyaṭīkā; Tattvavaiśāradī* (gloss on Vyāsa's *Yogabhāṣya*).

* Asterisks indicate eminence.

Padmapāda, 800–900. *Pancápādikā* (Vedantist).

Jayanta, 900. *Nyāyamanjarī* (encyclopaedia).

Bhāskara, 900–950. *Bhāṣya* on *Vedāntasūtras*.

Udayana, 980–1000. Nyāya and Vaiśeṣika works: *Kiraṇāvalī, Lakṣaṇāvalī, Tātparyaṭīkapariśuddhi, Kusamānjalī.*

Śrīdhara, 991. *Nyāyakandalī.*

The greater Buddhist productions in logic and metaphysics seem in the main to have been over by the year 500. Pretty closely contemporary is an earlier phase of growth of the six orthodox Brahmanical systems. This includes the sutras or highly condensed apothegmatic versions of the systems, and the first bhasyas or commentaries on some of them. From about 500 to 600 there seems to be a gap. Then come more bhasyas, supercommentaries, and expositions. In the native view all philosophers are only commentators. Sankara's Vedanta treatment is often reckoned as the final expression by Hindus, possibly because most Hindus are Vedantist. The many-sided Vachaspatimitra may perhaps be set alongside him as of similar magnitude. Their dates are given as 788–820 and 830–860, indicating the first half of the ninth century as culmination. Productive activity continued to about 1000; after that there seems to have been little new thought or expression.

The duration of this growth is two or three times as great as anything comparable elsewhere. Naturally, therefore, the growth falls under suspicion of being composite; but the nature of the Indian data has so handicapped historical presentation in the available literature that I venture no analytic resolution. Even the break in the sixth century is none too marked. Even though it appears in the shorter Buddhist as well as the longer Brahman list, there are Buddhist logics and Brahman bhasyas after as well as before the gap. The one system, the Samkhya, which seems to have produced no sutra in the earlier phase, and to have gone without during the second, made itself one much later, around 1400. When a culture operates in this fashion, the historian's task is difficult.

The first phase, the growth from 100 to 500, or at least its latter portion, coincides fairly in time with the prosperous

Gupta kingdom of Magadha, 320–490. This is also the period of literary culmination under Kalidasa. The second phase, 600 to 1000, has its beginning contemporary with Harsha, 606–647, who ruled over the last great Hindu kingdom which the north of India was to see. In the main, however, the second phase coincides in period with the florescence of the greater Dravidian kingdoms of the south, Pallava, Chalukya, Chola, from 550 to 1150, more or less. Sankara in fact was born in Dravidian territory. To be sure, it would be a forced interpretation to limit the Dravidian development too rigorously in time. Several of the Buddhist thinkers before 500 were southerners. Successful kingdoms existed in the south before 500 and after 1000. And certain art developments, such as bronze sculpture, climaxed there around 1400 or later. Nevertheless, Hindu philosophy may be said in large part to have received its final form in flourishing Dravidian realms, in contrast with its first growth on the middle Ganges, and the still earlier, pre-philosophical Vedic development on the upper Indus.

§11. Chinese Philosophy

China produced its philosophy in two pulses, under the Chou and the Sung. According to tradition, Lao-tse was born in 605/4; by 200 B.C., the great ancient philosophers were all of the past. This means that during little more than the last three Chou centuries China made her early contribution to philosophy. There followed more than a thousand years of scholarship and textual comment on the one hand, and of religious works on the other, until, about 1050, metaphysics again began to be produced for a century and a half.

CHOU PHILOSOPHY

An ancient anecdote has Lao-tse and Confucius meet; but it is doubtful whether originally "Lao-tse" was the name of a man or a book. Some have even rejected the authenticity of most of the book, now usually known as the *Tao-teh-king*. On the contrary, Confucius edited already existing works, compiled the annals of his native state, and taught, but wrote no philosophy: his Analects were put down by his followers, like the sayings of Jesus, long after his death, perhaps a century later. Nevertheless, the apocryphal episode of the meeting has historical significance. It expresses the fact that the two principal philosophies or "religions" or streams of thought of China, the mystic and the orthodox moral nonspeculative, began to crystallize simultaneously out of the older, unformulated matrix of the civilization. About two hundred years later, the Taoist Chuang-tse and the Confucianist Mencius are again contemporaries; and they are historical personages whose authentic writings we possess.

To the Destruction of the Books, 213 b.c.

Lao-tse, traditional date of birth 605/4 at K'u-hien near Ch'enchou in northern Kiangsu on the Hwai River. The person is legendary, but a book *Lao-tse,* now generally called *Tao-teh-king,* was in existence by at least the end of the fifth century. It is the concise expression of a mystic philosophy and the basic text of the Taoist system and religion.

Confucius, K'ung Fu or K'ung Kiu, 551–479, b. Tsou, in the old state of Lu in Shantung. Political and social moralist, emphasizing virtue of the ruler as automatic cause of prosperity; study especially of ancient ritual; altruism and self-conquest. Unoriginal as a thinker, but successful formulator of the national social philosophy, and subsequently canonized as primary figure of the official cult of China.

Mo-ti or Mo-tse, last half 5th cent., d. soon after 400; b. Lu or Sung. Universal love, *lien-ngai;* the individual conforming to the will of heaven emphasized over rites. First logic and dialectic.

School of divinity metaphysicians, doctrine in *Hi ts'e* appendix of *Yi-king,* toward 400. There correspond in the ideal and sensible worlds: the full and broken line, whose sum is *t'ai-ki,* the great pinnacle, to the substances *yin* and *yang,* whose sum is *tao;* the 4 pair-combinations of lines to formless, visible "ideas," *siang;* the 8 trigrams to bodies, *k'i;* the 64 hexagrams to the 11,520 beings and things, *wan-wu.*

K'ung-ki (or -chi) or Tse-sse, (great- ?) grandson of Confucius, alive after 400; author of *Chung-yung,* Doctrine of the Mean. Confucian ideas developed, with some Taoist influence: study enables men to conform wholly to their heaven-given nature and attain equilibrium and harmony.

The *Ta-hsüeh* or *Tai-hio,* Great Learning, is attributed to Tseng-ts'an and K'ung-ki. It is about contemporary with the last, but more straitly Confucian.

The *Lun-yü* or Analects (sayings, "logia") of Confucius were compiled in his school about 100 years after his death.

Yang-chu, or Yang-tse, mid-4th cent., at Lu, Sung, Wei. Pessimist, fatalist, nonaltruist; defender of passions as inescapable; destiny rules and wisdom so recognizes. Non-Confucian, nonmystic, some influencing by Tao.

Fa-kia, legalist school, second half 4th cent. in Ts'i, continuing into 3d. The fact of law is the fixed principle of good government in the unstable world.

Hwei-shi, or Hwei-tse, d. ca. 315; of and in Wei. Paradoxical dialectician seeking a metaphysical basis for Mo-ti's universal love in the infinity of space and time, in which alone is there the "identity" which constitutes the reality of the world, dissimilarities being human, subjective, illusory. Tao-influenced, but also of the Ming-kia or Nominalist school.

Chuang-tse, flourished toward the end of the 4th cent.; b. 330 ?; apparent references in his work to events of 316, 314. Born in eastern Wei. The most brilliant expounder of Taoist philosophy, and perhaps China's greatest writer of prose.

Yin-wen, fl. terminal 4th cent., in Ts'i. "Practical" Taoist, concerned with government by the "eight methods," and the "rectification of names."

Mencius, Meng-tse, 372–289; b. either in Lu or in adjacent Tsou, Chu. Confucian, combating Mo-ti and Yang-tse; ruler's altruism and justice reform the people; human nature good from Heaven; great man has "heart of little child."

Kung-suen-lung, fl. before 300 to 258 or after, at Wei, Yen, Chao. Paradoxical sophist, Zeno-like seeking the essential identity of things in infinite divisibility rather than in the infinity of space and time.

The *Siao-ts'iu-p'ien,* of the same period as the preceding, is a dialectic text of true and false propositions, a formal but not abstract logic.

Hsün-k'uang or Hsün-tse, ca. 315–235, born in Chao. Confucianist, nominalist, legist; also Taoist influence: the *ta-ts'ing-ming* or great-clear-pure condition of meditation and empty heart makes the holy man. Man's nature, *sing,* is bad, but the "artificial," *wei,* is built up by reflection under study, which leads to rites, justice, morality. Justice and rites necessary because of man's specific faculty of organizing society. Rectification of names is important even though names are conventional.

Han-fei-tse, pupil of last, d. 233 at Ts'in. Final form of legalist theories, with Taoist coloring. *Tao* is origin of all; when names and things accord, government is good. Two elements in man: celestial, senses; human, reflection and the passions desire and fear; these controlled by rewards and punishments. Ruler practices inaction, receives the credit of his ministers' work. Laws changeable but supreme, justified by their efficacy, *kung-yung*.

Lieh-tse, Licius. Work of about mid-3d (or 4th ?) cent.; the personage may be mythical. Taoist.

The doctrines of Lao-tse, Chuang-tse, and Lieh-tse form a coherent system of mysticism. Among them are: the goal is an inward emptiness which is beyond even vision and ecstasy, and is union with *tao,* the primordial fact, great mystery, unsoundable principle. *Yin* and *yang* are illusory modes of this substance; life and death are phases of their flux. The world is like juggler's play. Soul and matter are not distinguished, but intuitive knowledge and the perceived world are. The "realized" man, *chen-jen,* lives or rules by "not acting," *wu-wei.* Greater or less influence of these doctrines is apparent in several non-Taoists: K'ung-ki, Yang-tse, Hwei-tse, Yin-wen, Hsün-tse.

This is a very remarkable array. Besides the Confucian-Mencian and Taoist systems, which have survived, there are a number of quite diverse ones: those of Mo-ti, Yang-tse, Hwei-tse and Kung-suen-lung, Hsün-tse, besides the divinatory metaphysicians, nominalists, legalists, and dialectic sophists. The variety is as great as in contemporary Greece.

The period begins only about 550 if one accepts Lao-tse as historic, not until 500 if his treatise is later. It seems ended soon after 250, say by 230. The suppression and burning of the books in 213 probably was the tombstone rather than the headsman's ax of the movement. The duration of creative activity was therefore not far from three hundred years, with an error of not more than fifty one way or the other.

The localization of the growth was equally definite. Not only was China of the time smaller than it has been since; but nearly all the philosophers were born, and most of them flourished, in its eastern half, beyond longitude 114° or 115°. The participating states were primarily Ts'i, Lu, and Wei; secondarily, Yen, Chao, Sung, Ch'eng, Ch'u. Ts'in begins to be mentioned only toward 300, as a place visited by philosophers. In modern terms, this list is equivalent to a focus lying in Shantung with adjacent parts of Honan, Anhwei, and Kiangsu; or, geographically, the open lowland of the Yellow River stretching south toward the Hwai.

This great low plain, and not the middle course of the Yellow River or the Wei Valley, as often asserted, seems to have been the region in which early Chinese civilization—as distinct from ruling dynasties—developed. Here the Shang dynasty, superseded centuries before philosophy was born, already had its capitals; and presumably the population was densest, as it is now. Every geographical consideration speaks for this lowland, rather than Turkestan, as the presumptive locus of a developing culture. There appears to exist a sort of obsession that drives one authority after another to derive Chinese civilization out of inner Asia, or to have it originate as far inland in China as possible. That the Chou and Ts'in dynasties which successively—and briefly—conquered all China had their first seats in the lower and upper Wei Valley, respectively, lends only an illusory support to these views; as does the fact that imported elements of culture were likely to enter China by the Wei Valley. Neither temporary overlordships nor the point of entry of foreign culture material are fundamental to the problem of how and where a rich and distinctive civilization developed its characteristic forms; and for China the place seems to have been this eastern lowland. Philosophy, hundreds of years later, had its growth where the roots of the civilization were longest and deepest in the soil.

INTERVAL

When the Han dynasty suceeded the Ts'in in 206, feudalism remained suppressed, but scholarship soon came back into its own. The edict against books was revoked in 191, and in 124 the Emperor Wu Ti provided for the teaching of Confucianism and examinations for office. In short, a relation began to be established between a school of philosophy and the state, which was to prevail until the twentieth century. Nevertheless, or perhaps because of this relation, the Han period produced scholarly comment instead of new systems of thought. Taoism, protected and personally favored by a number of emperors, flourished, but as a religion rather than a philosophy, and toward the end of the Hans it had acquired enough institutional organization to develop a sort of papacy. Its thought tended increasingly toward astrology, alchemy, and occultism. Its greatest florescence perhaps occurred in the period surrounding the close of the dynasty in 220 A.D.

Buddhism succeeded Taoism. First officially recognized under the Hans, it became increasingly important after them, and enjoyed a culmination during the last two centuries of the Six Dynasties and the first century of the T'angs; about 400–700. It was in this period that the Chinese sects or schools of Buddhist thought were founded, some by Hindus, others by Chinese; that the famous pilgrims from Fa Hien to I Tsing brought back learning from India; that the twenty-eighth to thirty-second patriarchs of Buddhism lived in China. Under the later T'angs, Buddhism was alternately encouraged and persecuted by the government, but the questions at issue were the number, wealth, and influence of monasteries rather than ideas. At its best, Buddhism more properly contributed to Chinese thought than produced philosophy—as in general is expectable, by definition, from an established religion.

The later T'angs saw one attempt at philosophy by an orthodox Confucianist, Han Yü, 768–823/4; but his system is meager and without depth.

There is a very definite contrast between the Chou period on the one hand and the twelve hundred years from the first Hans to the beginning of Sung on the other. Toward the end of the earlier era, genuine and important philosophic thought arose out of a background of the uninstitutionalized, traditional, national cult religion. This thought completed itself, or at any rate ended, just about the moment that the old political order proved insufficient and was superseded by a more tightly organized one. From this time on, religion also became institutionally organized, and the history of systematized abstract thinking is replaced by a history of the competive fortunes of established religions, of religious doctrines, and of scholarly preoccupation with ancient ideas.

Confucian

Tung Chung-shu, 170–90, of Chihli; perhaps the leading Han Confucianist.

Liu Hsiang or Liu Tse-cheng, 80–9; Han descendant.

Liu Hsin, his son.

Yang Hsiung, 53 B.C.–18 A.D., of Szechwan.

Wang Ch'ung, 27–97, of Chekiang. Monistic materialist and negativist.

Ma Jung, 79–166.

Cheng Hsüan, 127–200.

Hsün Yüeh, 148–209.

Liu Shao, b. Chihli, fl. 224: *Hsiao-king,* classic of filial piety.

The foregoing and their associates may be said to have organized the scholarly tradition on which Confucianism was to rest.

Taoist

Huai-nan Tse, d. 122; Han prince and "alchemist."

Chi (or Hsi) K'ang, 223–262, of Anhwei; of the "seven sages of the bamboo grove"; alchemist.

Kuo Hsiang, d. 312.

Kuo P'o, 276–324; astrologer; founder or systematizer of geomancy, *feng-shui;* commentator on *Erh ya.*

Ko Hung, 4th cent.; wrote *Pao-pu-tse,* most important text of later Taoism.

Hsü Hsün, d. 374, of Yünnan.

T'ao Hung King, 452–536.

Buddhist schools or sects

Pure Land, founded by Hui Yüan, 333–416.

Ch'an Tsung or Meditation, Japanese Zen; from Bodhidharma (Ta Mo), patriarch who came to China in 527 (520).

T'ien T'ai, originated under Sui dynasty, 589–618.

Lü Tsung, founded by Tao Hüan, 595–687.

Tsi En, or Fa Siang Tsung, founded by Hsüan Tsang, 602–664.

Tsü She or Reality, based on *Vasubandhu* as translated by Hsüan Tsang.

Buddhist pilgrimages to India

Fa Hsien, 399–414.

Hsüan Tsang, 629–645.

I Tsing, 671–695.

SUNG PHILOSOPHY

Some fifty years after the Sung dynasty was enthroned, there began to be born a series of men who were thinkers as well as scholars and who developed a genuine philosophy, the Neo-Confucian or Hsing Li school of metaphysical nature philosophy. In their formal religious status they were Confucianists, but Buddhist and Taoist thought had by now been so far amalgamated into the common culture of China that it was possible for these men to be more than perpetuators or commentators and to evolve a genuinely new system, or series of systems. To the westerner, these systems seem to operate largely within the frame of the ancient Chou philosophy; but native opinion sees them as novel and constructive, and must be accepted as decisive. The period of activity of this growth was from 1050 to 1200. About half of this period falls into the "northern" or united Sung dynasty, half into the Southern Sung, when North China was lost to barbarians. The climax is regarded as provided by Chu Hsi, 1130–1200.

> Shao Yung, 1011–1077, of Chihli.
> *Chou Tun-i, 1017–1073, of Hunan.
> *Chang Tsai, 1020–1076, uncle of next, of Honan.
> *Ch'eng Hao (Ming Tao), 1032–1085, born at Lo-yang.
> *Ch'eng I (Yin Chuan), 1033–1107/8, his brother.
> The last four, with Chu Hsi, are the *wu tse,* or five masters of Hsing Li.
> The "socialist" reformer Wang An-shih, 1021–1086, and the greatest historian after Sse-ma Ch'ien, Sse-ma Kuang, 1019–1086, were contemporaries of these men.
> Su school, founded by Su Hsün (Lao Ch'üan), 1009–1066, of Mei-shan; and his son Su Che.
> Hu or Hu Hsiang or Hunan school, founded by Hu An Kuo (Wen Ting), 1074–1138, of Fukien; included his son Hu Kung; grandson Hu Chi-sui, contemporary of Chu Hsi; and others.
> Yang Shih, 1053–1135, of Fukien, pupil of Ch'eng I, master of Chu Hsi's father.
> Hsie Liang-tso, Lü Ta-lin, Yu Tso, other pupils of Ch'eng I.
> **Chu Hsi, 1130–1200, of Fukien.
> Lu Hsiang-shan or Lu Kin-yüan or Lu Tse-ching, 1140–1192, of Fukien.

After Sung.—In contrast to this constellation, later figures are scattering, and, with the exception of the first to be named, whose work ties to that of Lu Hsiang-shan after more than three centuries, they are primarily critics or scholars.

Wang Yang-ming, 1472–1528, of Chekiang.
Ku T'ing-ling, 1612–1681.
Yen Yüan (Si Chai), 1635–1704.
Tai Chen (Tung Yüan), 1722–1777.
Liu Feng-lu, 1775–1829, of Kiangsu.

In summary, Chinese system-creating philosophy, as distinct from religious thought and practical or near-philosophy, developed twice: toward the end of the Feudal or Chou period, between 550 or 500 and 200; and again, more briefly, between 1050 and 1200. The first is generally considered not only the fundamental but the larger production. It closely paralleled in time Greek philosophy. The second growth was about contemporary with the last phase of Arab philosophy in Spain and the earlier phase of Christian Scholasticism. Although the two Chinese growths occur in the same country and in the same language, they are a little farther apart in time than the Greek and the mediaeval Arabic-Latin philosophies.

§12. Discussion

The question now arises, What common features do the nine or ten major growths of philosophy which we have reviewed show in the forms of their growths or in their relations to the cultures of which they were part?

The answer must be mainly, None. That the contents of no two philosophic growths are ever the same is a commonplace. If they are related, one builds on the other, and if it attains to genuine productivity, it thereby goes beyond it, the finalities of the first being the foundations of the second. If they are unrelated and develop in ignorance of each other, like Chinese and Mediaeval philosophy, any convergences which they attain to are always incomplete, or restricted to isolated items. Much the same holds for their outward growth configurations.

It is true that most civilizations which have produced true philosophy have produced it in two growths or separate movements. By counting Oriental and Spanish Arabic philosophy as distinct, we have in fact unanimity in our five classifications: Chinese, Hindu, Greek, Arabic, and Occidental. But the relations between the two members of each pair differ in importance, duration, and interval. The Later Greek or Mediterranean growth, for instance, as typified by Plotinus, has been pretty unanimously judged by posterity as intrinsically more meager than the Earlier Greek one which culminated under Plato and Aristotle. In the Occident, on the contrary, Mediaeval Scholasticism would be generally ranked below Modern philosophy in the inherent or permanent or universal human values of its accomplishments. Upon Greek thinking the verdict of history has been: a great philosophy with an attempted revival; upon European: a great philosophy with a limited precursor. For China, the first growth has usually been ranked higher; for the Arabs, probably the second. A more or less equivalent degree of "irregularity" is pointed out, a few paragraphs below, as prevailing in the duration of and interval between the pair of growths in each civilization.

There is similar variety in the relations to religion. Mediaeval Western philosophy moved almost wholly within the confines of Church doctrine; Modern began outside this frame. The one was produced by churchmen, the other by laymen. Greek philosophy originated in a civilization on which religion rested lightly: its cults were discrete and unorganized, doctrine almost lacking, the unifying qualities largely aesthetic. From Thales on, the problem of adjustment to religion scarcely arose; and even when the patterns of the philosophy had been realized and its remaining vigor was channeled into a morality, this morality remained essentially free from normal religious accouterments. Probably this very fact goes to explain the rise of the religiomystic Neo-Platonic pulse five hundred years later. Greek culture did not contain enough of the religious component to satisfy a wider and less highly differentiated sphere of peoples. The result of this deficiency was the religious growths from among which Christianity finally emerged dominant. But Christianity was foreign enough to classical Greek culture to be accepted with reluctance by this; and Neo-Platonism was its compromise or defense formation: an emotional religious content in the old philosophic form. Gnosticism was an analogous reaction with a reversion to myth-making. The early Christians, on the other hand, aimed blindly and persistently at a thorough replacement of Greek thought. Living alongside it within the frame of Mediterranean civilization, they made their adjustment by wresting from it its dialectic method and enough of its concepts to fight it with apology and propaganda. Being interested in Christianity and not in philosophy, they achieved only a surrogate philosophy.

In India, philosophy and religion sprang from a common root and remained intertwined stalks. China, on the contrary, began and continued with a religion in which cult predominated. Rites, therefore, rather than doctrine, was the religious load which orthodox philosophy had to carry; and the principal countercurrent, Taoism, is differentiated fundamentally by the attempt to inject into its system the element of religious experience without cult. The Arabs, finally, had the advantage of a religion that originated among a people of meager culture and tradition and was therefore elementary in tenets and simple in cult, so that their philosophy found it relatively easy to develop freely within the framework of Mohammedanism. The handicaps of Arab philosophy were perhaps due rather to science; or, more exactly, they were the difficulties besetting a new civilization inheriting a vast ready-made body of science, learning, and thought.

The relations to science, which can be equally strangulatory of philosophical activity, are as diverse as those of religion. The Arabs represent one extreme. It is only among them that a great philosopher was also a great physician. China developed little science of her own, and her remoteness prevented importation from occurring except by slow and partial seepage. It was literary scholarship which rather was the incubus. India also developed little science of her own, and when it was brought into the country from outside, it was in reduced form, and philosophy, reinforced by religion, was already firmly established in the civilization. The Greeks began with philosophy and science almost undistinguished, but successfully differentiated them as they developed in friendly alliance. After Pythagoras, no eminent philosopher made any major contribution to science as such; nor vice versa. Plato's famous warning at the gate applies only to abstract mathematics; and at that it may perhaps be described as a gesture more than an enforced practice: his goal of the ideal lies on the mystic side of the horizon rather than on the empirical. Aristotle may seem an exception; but he was a philosopher who had no aversion to the empirical, and who extended his organizatory genius also over the field of science: primarily he assembled and ordered science. And when Greek philosophy was through with metaphysics, it became much more a series of moralities than a science. And yet the Epicurean system shows that the old attitude of sympathy toward science was retained.

Mediaeval philosophy had no problem in this respect. It was of the Church, in an age of scientific inactivity. Modern philosophy, on the contrary, fell in a period of scientific stir. It began later than modern science, and finished earlier. Its precursors made propaganda for science, and its founders, Descartes and his associates, produced science as well as philosophy. The same was true of Leibnitz a generation or two later. On the whole, though, beginning even with Descartes and increasingly later, there was a delimitation of spheres perhaps more definite than in Greek times. The sensible world was left to science; the supersensible was handled with discretion and a certain indirectness or remoteness; and the main activity of philosophy came to revolve about problems of how we know. It is only in the final nineteenth-century phase, of exhaustion after the culmination, that philosophy attempted to annex science, or to take refuge in it, according as one prefers to phrase it.

Also variable is the time incidence of philosophy, as is already obvious from the fact that it has often blossomed twice within a civilization. Occidental civilization had been forming for perhaps five centuries when Scholasticism began; the Arabic developed its philosophy within two. The other civilizations have origins too uncertain to allow of exact comparison. But the Greeks began to philosophize within three hundred years after they knew how to write; the Chinese, not for at least six hundred, and perhaps two or three times as long. Indian philosophy was perhaps earlier than Indian writing. Mesopotamia and Egypt wrote for several thousand years without producing a formulable philosophy. There evidently is no significant correlation in these matters; let alone, no law.

At one point there is some seeming concordance or tendency toward regularity: the duration of productive growths. In half the occurrences this runs not far from three hundred years.

Three hundred years, more or less
  Greek, 585–280 (or 230 ?).
  Chou Chinese, 550/500–230/213.
  Oriental Arabic, 800/850–1100.
  Mediaeval Western, 1080–1380.
  Modern Western, 1630–1875 (or 1580–1890 with Bruno and Nietzsche).
Shorter
  Spanish Arabic, 1050–1200. Sung Chinese, 1050–1200.
Longer
  Later Hindu, 100–1000 (= 100–500 and 600–1000 ?).
Uncertain or unmeasurable
  Earlier Hindu. Later Mediterranean.

The Earlier Hindu philosophy is too dateless to be used here. The Later has already been mentioned as inordinately long by all precedent, and it may break up into two periods of about 400 years each. Even if these do not whittle down farther, on fuller knowledge, they are not disconcertingly far from the 300-year value. Later Mediterranean philosophy is difficult to define because of its religious preoccupation, its Christian and non-Christian strands, and its lack of a marked culmination. Neo-Platonism from Ammonius, the teacher of Plotinus, to Proclus can be assigned a span from 210 to 460/85; and Patristic Christianity from Justin to Augustine, similar dates of 130/50 to 410/30; somewhat under 300 years each, and somewhat over if the two are taken together. I am hesitant in this definition; but the dates suggested seem the most reasonable.

To sum up, we have five instances of a duration of about 300 years—say between 250 and 350; another somewhat dubiously falling within these limits; one superficially much longer but possibly resolving into two growths of around 400 each; and two instances pretty definitely around 150 only; with one too ill-defined to be counted. This does appear to establish a basis for considering that some degree of uniformity exists. Of course the total number of instances is so small that no great reliance can be placed in the finding, unless comparable results emerge from investigation of other culture activities.

There is the possibility that the explanation of the seeming partial uniformity of span of growth lies at least partly in implicit elements of my definition of productive philosophy. Essentially what we are comparing is the highest-level, systematized, abstract thought of civilizations, such as the greatest of these have produced only once or twice, and some never. Obviously, for a civilization to enter into the comparison at all, it must be rich in cultural energy; and once this energy had risen to the level of philosophical formulation, it would expectably have a considerable area to overflow, and this overflowing would require a considerable time. (I speak in metaphors in default of the precise terms which have not yet been devised.) Nevertheless, even this narrower explanation involves the two assumptions of more or less equal volume or head of cultural "energy" to rise to the "threshold," and of more or less equal "area" within the chamber of "philosophy." There is no inherent reason why these two assumptions may not be sound. Many historians constantly make similar assumptions and let them obtrude incidentally from the background of their thinking. When they are self-consciously schooled, however, and impressed by the "uniqueness" of all historical phenomena, modern historians tend to refrain from such interpretations as being outside the proper sphere of the historian. They are of course right. As soon as norms are dealt with, history as a constituted present-day discipline ends. At the same time, that historians stop somewhere is no proof that there is nothing beyond. Nor does the fact that all historic phenomena possess the aspect of uniqueness make it impossible for them also to possess another aspect of partial uniformity. The real problem is what the facts really are: whether the phenomena are intrinsically similar often enough to be significant; whether the similarities are due to expectable accident, especially within rough measurement; or whether selection under unavowed definition of terms has forced a similarity. On these points I cannot judge, but submit my evidence.

As for interval between growths within the same civilization, there is certainly no indication of uniformity, as witness:

China, 213 B.C to 1050 A.D., 1250 years.
Greek, 280 (230) B.C. to 210 A.D., 450–500.
Western, 1380 to 1630, 250.
Arab, Oriental ends 1100, Spanish begins 1050, interval is −50.
Indian, uncertain, not more than 600, possibly considerably less.

The Arab instance is obviously of a somewhat different order from the rest in that it involves a much greater geographical shift. But the others are so highly variable as to put the possibility of anything like a norm quite out of the question.

This consideration arises as a consequence: Does the lack of uniformity in interval diminish the probability that the apparent tendency toward uniformity in duration of growth is real, that is, statistically reliable and not an accident of small series? The answer is: Yes, but not definitely. We understand so little about the behavior of culture that it is conceivable that there might be much more uniformity in growths when they occur than in the conditions which bring them about. I do not defend this interpretation. Expectability seems to me to be against it. But its possibility cannot be dismissed offhand. What we need in these domains is more analyzed knowledge, with a minimum of opinion.

Tending to throw doubt on the regularity of total productive span is the fact of some diversity of internal organization of the growths with respect to time of culmination, direction of geographical shifts, and nationality.

Both the Occidental movements progressed centrifugally—from France as the point of origin. Roughly, the shift in the Arab movement was the same; also in the Late Mediterranean, with Neo-Pythagoreanism, Neo-Platonism, Gnosticism, and Christianity originating in Egypt and Syria and spreading outward. The partial shift of Hindu philosophy from the Ganges to southern India is perhaps parallel. Greek philosophical productivity, on the other hand, began at one edge of the Greek world, spread around its peripheries, culminated at the center, and at the very end spread out once more.

As for culmination, this sometimes falls near the end: Aristotle, Avicenna, Averroës; sometimes fairly early in the second half: Kant, Aquinas; but never, where we are dealing with sure data, in the first two-thirds of the course of the growth. The difficulty is in deciding when the epigones of the decline are still producing new ideas and when they are merely recombining or reformulating them. For China and India it is difficult to reconcile native and Western judgment. Presumably, a Chinese scholar would give Confucius undisputed primacy, and rightly so as an expression of Chinese culture as a whole; and yet, purely as a philosopher, he must seem to westerners meager in comparison with half a dozen of his successors.

As for participating peoples, the Greek, Chinese, and probably the Earlier Indian philosophies were uninational; the Later Mediterranean, Muslim, both Occidental growths, and probably the Later Indian one were multinational—of course always within the confines of one major civilization. This matter is obviously an incident of the composition of civilizational wholes rather than of philosophies as such. What seems of more significance to philosophies is their speech medium. This is normally one: Dravidians wrote philosophy in Sanskrit; Persians, Turks, and Jews, in Arabic. The Roman Empire being bilingual, its philosophy came in both Greek and Latin. Mediaeval Western thought of course was wholly expressed in Latin; it is only in the Modern growth that a variety of languages was used and the succession of participating nations became marked. Until 1600, full-fledged systematic and original philosophy was propounded in only five languages: Sanskrit, Greek, Chinese, Latin, and Arabic.

Perhaps the broadest inference to be drawn from our data is the rarity and spottiness of philosophical creativeness, combined with the added fact that this spottiness is not randomly distributed but highly concentrated. The five civilizations reviewed flourished in four areas: China, India, the environs of the eastern Mediterranean (Greek and Arab), and western Europe. About 600 B.C., philosophical activity which the world since has recognized as fundamentally important began almost simultaneously in the first three of these. This makes three stretches of 2,500 years until the present in which philosophy has been recognized and appreciated and studied. Western Europe started late, but added at least 1,000 years more, bringing the aggregate to 8,500. Of these, a total of perhaps 3,200 years contains all the new philosophy, all the original ideas which were developed to the philosophic level. In other words, philosophy flourished during little more than a third of the duration of the civilizations in which it had become established as an activity.

Even this is too favorable a view, because too summary. In every instance, philosophical productivity occurred in only a fraction of the area of its civilization. Early Chinese means northeastern China; Indian, the Ganges Valley and, later on, southern India. While Greek philosophy bloomed, the regions of later Arab civilization were silent; and reversely later. Europe throughout is western Europe; and even within this, a succession of nations relieved one another most of the time. Even in the thirteenth century, when European philosophical production was most nearly international, France was resting. If we take into consideration the great civilizations that never produced any indubitable philosophy, those of Egypt, Mesopotamia, Persia, Japan, and still more if we include those cultures which are popularly called semicivilizations, it is apparent that the fraction becomes exceedingly small.

The diagram given overleaf represents these periods and areas of concentration. It also emphasizes the seemingly abrupt

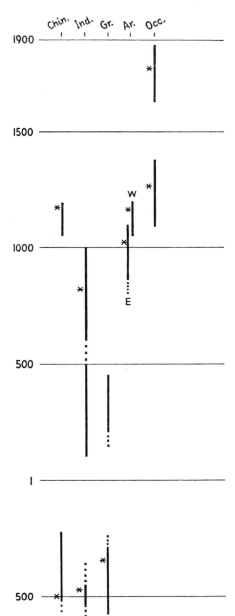

PHILOSOPHY

beginning of philosophy simultaneously in China, India, and Greece. This simultaneity has of course been frequently observed and discussed. Western scholars have examined the possibilities of sixth-century influences from India on Greece, and in the reverse direction. Some Chinese have extended the old legend of Lao-tse's disappearance in the west into a theory that he there founded Buddhism, which returned to China centuries later. To date, the actual evidence of connections is quite tenuous, not rising above the level of possibility, and is generally regarded as inconclusive. There is of course also the theoretical possibility that there had been at work supernational factors which we cannot as yet identify—factors operating in some unknown manner on human civilization as a whole. With such a view, we have touched, if not crossed, the borderline of pure intuition and faith. And yet it is legitimate to penetrate this hazy realm, at least briefly, to see if it contains indications of testable evidence.

A path is suggested by the diagram: namely, to compare the remainder of the course of human philosophy against the observed phenomenon at its beginning. If similar phenomena of contemporaneousness recur elsewhere in history, the case is proportionally strengthened for the supposition that sixth-century simultaneity was due not wholly to accident, but to factors operative in some sort of system or order which we do not yet recognize. And vice versa.

There is actually one other moment in which three of the five civilizations were producing philosophy: from 1050 to 1200. In fact, with the eastern and western Muslim movements held as distinct, the last half of the eleventh century must be reckoned as having contained four philosophical growths: the end of the eastern Arabic, and the beginnings of western Arabic, Christian Scholastic, and Chinese Neo-Confucian. But, except for the number of civilizations represented, there is little parallel to the sixth-century constellation. One of the later growths was in its culminating conclusion, two were second growths within the same civilization, the fourth the groping beginnings of a civilization the philosophical peak of which was not to be reached for 700 years. About all that these growths have in common is the fact that all of them are built in some measure on previous growths; this, however, is to be expected in view of philosophy's already having a history of over a millennium and a half in 1050. There is also certainly nothing evident in world history to point to the eleventh and twelfth centuries as a period which provided a setting or stimulus for widespread philosophical activity. In fact, India had only just completed its role and withdrawn permanently from the stage.

The counterweight of clusters are gaps; and of these there are two and perhaps three or four: the two centuries before and one after Christ; the sixth century after Christ, if the ultralong Hindu development in historic times proves to break into two pulses; the fifteenth and sixteenth centuries; and, for that matter, so far as we can judge, the present moment, the last half century. Again there is no visible reason, from the aspect of world history, why these universal suspensions should occur when they did—in the time of the gestation of Christianity, during the Renaissance, and among ourselves.

In fact, the diagram gives an impression that the distribution is random and does not follow any principle applicable to its totality. This is confirmed by quantitative analysis of the figure. Five civilizations are represented, each for 2,500 years, from −600 to 1900; total involved, 12,500.[1] The sum of minimum durations of active growths is 2,850; besides about 600 more doubtful years on the fringes. If we consider half of these doubtful durations to hold good, and count them in, we have a probable mean of 3,150[2] between the minimum of 2,850 and the maximum of 3,450. This is almost exactly one-quarter of the total dealt with. In other words, philosophy was being produced in one-fourth of the durations represented in the diagram. As there are five civilizations, the average number of philosophic growths active in all of them at any given moment would be one and a quarter.

[1] This is larger than the figure of 8,500 previously used, because in that connection reference was limited to areas (not civilizations) after they had once grown a philosophy.

[2] Of which the 3,200 previously mentioned is a rounding.

From this it follows that if we divide our total span of 2,500 years into 51 moments spaced 50 years apart, at the centuries and mid-centuries, we shall have 51 × 5/4 or about 64 occurrences of philosophic activity at these 51 moments. Next, it can be observed from the diagram how often two or three or more growths are active at the same moment, how often there is only one, how ofter all are quiescent. In the table here given I have entered in the second column the number of instances of each such type actually countable. As against this distribution there can be computed the frequency expectability of each combina-

Number of growths active simultaneously	Observed number of instances of each class	Expectability of frequency of each class in total of 1,024 instances	Frequency expectable in 51 instances
5	—	1	0.05
4	—	15	0.75
3	6	90	4.48
2	14	270	13.44
1	18	405	20.17
0	13	243	12.10
	51	1,024	50.99

tion—such as two growths, or no growths, active simultaneously—on a basis of random chance, comparable for instance to the relative frequency of the different combinations occurring among five tetrahedral dice, each with one marked side counted as successful or "active" when it fell face down. This expectable frequency is given in column three, and its conversion into 51 instances, corresponding to our 51 moments, in column four.

It is evident that the observed frequency and the theoretical chance frequency in the second and fourth columns coincide closely; nearly enough, at any rate, to preclude any serious possibility that the distribution of co-occurrences or simultaneities is due to anything more than chance. In other words, this time at least, the dice of history are not loaded, and there is no need to look farther for unknown deep-seated factors controlling an order of development holding for humanity in general, because there is no evidence of order. The co-occurrences are simply coincidences within the law of probabilities.

The idea that there is an underlying factor or set of factors determining the cultural history of humanity as a whole being therefore shown not to hold, this time at any rate, this idea may presumably be assigned to the class of concepts which spring from the undemonstrated assumption or article of faith respecting the "progress of humanity" which has been so increasingly powerful in the explicit and implicit thought of the Occident during the past century and a half.

Apart from this, the calculation has an incidental significance, as indication of the applicability of quantitative approach to problems in culture history. Not that the correspondence of observation to chance frequency proves my measures correct, since I might have obtained the same correspondence by drawing the diagram with eyes shut. But the correspondence does suggest that the judgments on which the measures are based are at least not formed with consistent bias; hence, that honestly endeavored estimates are of service, in default of exacter measures, for quantitative treatment. In fact, Galton showed this long ago; the present discussion merely reillustrates it in a somewhat new field.

Returning now from this arithmetical excursus, we may consider further the question why philosophical productiveness seems to be so rare. In itself, this fact may not seem remarkable, because it might be said that by definition full-fledged philosophy is a fruit that can ripen only when the civilization which bears it thrives under optimum conditions. But clearly it is not merely that a great civilization is in a flourishing condition. Europe in the fifteenth and sixteenth centuries was more populous, wealthy, and prosperous than in the thirteenth. It possessed far more knowledge, a greatly expanded technology including printing, a much wider and keener curiosity. And its civilization did flourish in other departments, as the Renaissance bears witness. The same holds for the Han and T'ang dynasties as compared with feudal China of the warring kingdoms; for the Maurya India of Asoka as against that of old

Magadha; in many ways—science and wealth, for instance—for Hellenistic Alexandria versus the Greece of Plato and Aristotle when Athens, Sparta, and Thebes were exhausting one another, deferring to Persia, succumbing to Macedon. Evidently it is more than florescence of a great civilization that is needed to produce philosophy. Such florescence of some sort is indeed a prerequisite; but there must be other factors which are responsible for the concentrations. Otherwise there would be productive philosophers more or less uniformly distributed throughout the flourishing periods and culturally advanced subareas of all great civilizations.

These factors which cause philosophy to be produced in bursts, though they may rest ultimately on other factors external to philosophy, must be in some measure internal to it. We have examined the historic relations of philosophy to religion and science and found them highly variable. Once philosophy springs from religion and remains intertwined with it, the next time, it arises without reference to religion; the third, it gets its start by liberating itself from religion. One philosophy ignores science throughout its course, one springs out of it, another diverges from it. The relations to more remote activities such as wealth, art, literature, government are obviously even more variable. In short, there are no constant conditions beyond a certain level of general cultural activity, which is expressed, however, in an endless diversity of ways. The principle of the uniqueness of historical happenings is vindicated. Hence it is necessary to fall back on internal factors, pertinent to philosophy itself, to understand its marked concentration or segregation in time and place.

What can such internal factors be? Evidently we can only attain to an approximation here. Of primary concern must be those influences which bring it about that when one individual succeeds in formulating a coherent series of abstract ideas which can be called a philosophic system, another and another follow in the same region, until an array of schools, an entire growth of philosophy, has developed. This really is the fundamental fact which our review has established; plus the complementary one that such a series of great thinkers does not go on indefinitely, but after a certain point positively ceases: they may be equally great thereafter, but they are no longer original.

Here it seems we have the key to such understanding as we can at present reach in these matters. Evidently the specific factors are superpersonal, but more limited than the factors maintaining the civilization as a whole, else the series of creative thinkers would go on as long as the civilization maintained a certain level of prosperity. They must, then, be essentially within the philosophy itself; and it is hard to define or describe them except in terms of what may be called patterns, or pattern systems. Apparently, when a given civilization breaks through to the philosophic level, it brings to this a particular body of knowledge, a particular group of religious assumptions, a particular set of social institutions. Out of these it develops something new: its particular system of philosophy. It does so by developing a certain set of thought processes; and these—or, if one prefer, their products—are what I call a philosophical pattern system. Such a system bears in itself certain specific potentialities, and also specific limitations, which enable it, even compel it, barring catastrophe from outside, to realize or fulfill itself to the terminus of these potentialites, but not to go beyond them. When the given set of potentialities is exhausted, the growth ends. Its products may be embalmed, or forgotten, or indefinitely restated and reshuffled; but there is no further growth until a thoroughly new set of impulses has arisen under new circumstances in another civilization, or in a well-separated phase of the same one. Because the forms and content of culture under which a pattern system arises are always particular, the philosophy is always unique also. Common to all philosophies, as we review them empirically, is their growth process, the fact that they represent a superindividual but prelimited pattern activity within the culture.

What the forces are that cause such activity within pattern systems, we do not know. We can call them cultural energy, for want of another label or better metaphor. Cultural energy would at bottom be psychic or physiological activity, but manifested through cultural channels and in cultural forms. For its specific quality we are therefore thrown back onto our culture patterns. It appears that it is through the objective, empirical, critical study of these that we can at present best hope to understand better what cultural energy is: they are its most, or one of its most, salient manifestations. And the characteristics of patterns, or pattern systems, are: first, their individual uniqueness even when similar in kind or genus; and second, an inner coherence or organization which tends to push them on to fulfillment and exhaustion and sets them a limit which is none the less real because we cannot foresee it.

This view is likely to be construed as savoring of the mystic, because of the element of predestination—even though limited and specific predestination—which it contains, and for its analogy to the phenomena of organic growth. I regret this, but cannot help it: the empirical phenomena, over and over again, and with really remarkably few exceptions, compel the conclusion that there are whole arrays of events in the history of culture which are objectively describable only in terms of the metaphors of "growth," "realization," "exhaustion," and "death," as our vocabulary today stands. I also believe that the phenomena themselves will sooner or later force acceptance of largely the same descriptive interpretation on everyone who is not deterred by a hyperscientific horror of analogy, metaphor, and the appearance of mysticism, greater than his interest in the substance of the phenomena. That the available vocabulary for discussing matters such as these is unfortunate must be admitted; but it is the fault at least as much of the past century of historians as of myself. I might coin new terms. I have on a previous occasion suggested "diaeta" as a technical term for a culture growth—without eliciting a response. But new words bring their own complications, not least of which are logical squabbles over definition; and I trust that the phenomena, if my observing of them is valid, will make the better impression for presenting themselves in a familiar if somewhat worn and wrinkled dress of terminology. The "rectification of names" has a way of taking care of itself if concepts are sound.

What holds of pattern systems in philosophy presumably holds for other departments of culture; and expectably, in some measure at least, for culture wholes. Evidently, something similar is going on also in such more trivial matters as fashion changes. Though these ripple along in an apparently endless continuity of surface changes, larger patterns underlie them; and these at times seem to exhaust themselves and crystallize into essential stability: the toga, for instance, or men's dress in the nineteenth century. Fashion, however, is in its nature the evanescent and superficial aspect of culture, just as on the opposite side subsistence economy is among the more solid, the physiologically and geographically conditioned parts of culture, and therefore expresses purely cultural processes, such as pattern formation, less sharply than do activities of the type of philosophy. We cannot here enter these bypaths with their vistas; and the following chapters will be concerned with culture growths of an order similar to that of philosophy.

We can now see why the question of the normal length of a philosophical growth cannot be very fundamental, though it may have a certain empirical interest. Strictly there can be no norm, because each growth, however similar to others, is particular. There can only be a mean, and a greater or less variability from this. With a high variability, the mean will presumably signify less; with a low, the inference follows that the course of the several particular pattern developments is likely to have been similar also in respects other than duration. The same holds for variability in position of culmination, in geographical shift of focus, or in other features. The case is similar to that of the business cycle in the modern industrial world. It is plain that every cycle is a particular and unique phenomenon, which however is also on the whole strikingly similar to other occurrences. Economists investigate very intensively the duration of cycles although they know well by now that no two will last exactly the same length of time, let alone having their beginning or end accurately predictable. They do derive from such measurement an average length, which is the first step toward ascertaining the variability of departure from it, which in turn is one of many features from which a more accurate and analytic description is built up, both of each particular cycle and of what they have in common, or of the degree to which they have traits in common or not. With this come statistical correlations to ascertain whether and in what degree various factors are or are not causally connected with cycles or their components. Compared with all this procedure, which quickly met approbation because it might be practically useful and was carried on with an elaborate technique, my simple attempts at measurement and calculation are humble enough. But their aim is the same: to formulate such norms as there may be, not as a product of law, but of complex factors never expressing themselves alike and yet ever with certain likenesses; and to undertake this formulation as one means toward more precise generalized description of the facts. I have expressly avowed that the variability of growth duration seems lower in philosophy than in most other activities of culture, and that the intervals between growths seem wholly irregular.

In the same way, it remains to be seen how much validity there may be to my preliminary findings of a tendency for the culmination to fall after the middle, and for the geographical shift to be centrifugal. There is admittedly no strict regularity in these matters; but knowledge of the degree and kind of variability is a preliminary to understanding better what is likely to have happened in each instance.

Finally, there is the fact that philosophic growths include more or less similar mystic, skeptic, dialectic, nominalist, or other analogous phases. I have tried to keep away from this aspect because it involves consideration primarily of philosophic content rather than historical configuration, and such consideration ought to be left to philosophers or qualified students of the history of philosophy. It is, however, an aspect which deserves consideration if those of time, place, culmination, and recurrence deserve it. I suspect that here, at least so far as philosophy is concerned, the explanation brings us quickly into psychology—not only cultural, but individual

psychology. We are probably dealing with temperaments ob-
truding into the cultural pattern. Skepticism seems deeply
ingrained in certain individuals. So are mystic proclivities,
which might be defined as impulses toward inward faith in a
unity between oneself and the world, and therefore between
the parts of the world. Mysticism and idealism share this quality—that their thinking is definitely tinged with feeling. The
dialectician may be said to have a temperament comparable to
the physiology of the man who prefers going on the gymnastic
mat to doing productive labor. And so on.

Now, whatever these temperaments are due to, whether
genetic factors or experiential conditioning, they seem to occur
in all civilizations, even primitive ones, and perhaps roughly in
the same proportion—relative, of course, to the "temperament"
of the culture. That is, in a culture whose thinking is essentially
along mystical lines, even the skeptical individual might seem
quite uncritical to us; in a skeptical one, the mystic is likely
to be pretty heterogeneous and half-baked. But they both will
be more skeptical or more mystic than the average of the culture. Now as a pattern system begins to unfold in a domain
such as philosophy, where some variety of opinion is of the
essence of the pattern, room will be found for expression of
the principal temperaments, always of course within the frame
of the pattern. The inwardly emotional, the negativistic, the
verbalistic, the combative find the opportunity to give their
personal reformulation of the pattern, and we have mystic,
skeptic, nominalistic, sophist schools. Historians have always
directed attention to the fact that these seemingly similar
schools in different philosophies are only superficially alike;
and rightly, of course, historically speaking; though psychologically the resemblances are probably well enough founded.
In short, the parallels of this type are grounded in individual
psychology; whereas the time-space-culmination resemblances
of pattern systems are phenomenally historical, and hold promise of being explicable psychologically, if they are explicable
at all, in terms of culture psychology, when we shall have one.

Chapter III

SCIENCE

Chapter III

SCIENCE

§13. General

SCIENCE IS often considered the antithesis of art in its quality of being cumulative. An art flourishes and withers away; the next one has to begin all over again; aesthetically we have not risen beyond the Greeks; but science, it is said, piles up and is progressive. In one respect this view must be granted, in spite of some definite scientific retrogressions. Perhaps the utility of science, as contrasted with the nonutility or aestheticism of the fine arts, is the principal reason: practical efficiency is a result of the one and not of the other.

Nevertheless, if we consider not the total mass of science gathered and retained by all cultures, but its new growths in particular cultures, these are seen to make their appearance in history just as intermittently and spasmodically as art. This fact will be substantiated by the evidence to be presented. The developments of growth of science accordingly seem to be due to, or limited by, factors of the same sort as those which bring about art growths.

In short, the essence of an art is not its content but its style, which by nature is noncumulative and limited in duration. The content of science is, or can be, cumulative, within or across cultures. But the style or form of science—that which is generally called the method, and through which alone it grows or progresses—is no more cumulative or perpetual than style in art. Hence, productive science is definitely cyclical as a phenomenon, contrary to the presupposition of most histories of science.

At least eight major civilizations have produced more or less notable additions to science. There will be considered first the three more familiar Western growths—the Greek, Mohammedan, and European ones, which are virtually the only ones treated in many histories of science. After that we shall take up, in geographical order from west to east, the sciences of Egypt, Mesopotamia, India, China, and Japan, which are less known and in part poorly datable. Where the material allows, I shall present the data on these relatively more fully than for the Western civilizations; not because they are intrinsically more important, but because in a comparative study they are equally significant and much less commonly known.

The line between science and philosophy is notoriously a doubtful one. Until little over a century ago, the term philosophy included what we now set off as science. In general, it is probably wisest not to insist on too sharp a distinction. But for our purposes it must be made. We may in fairness consider as philosophy those endeavors which aim primarily to build up a system of related ideas as such, with only secondary reference to factual observation. In science, however, this element of factual observation or experience is intrinsic and essential. Aristotle therefore is a figure in science as well as in philosophy; but Plato scarcely is, except as it were by contrast. Spencer supplements the thinness of his idea system by masses of data compiled from science, but does not use these for new scientific interpretation and so remains a philosopher.

A somewhat similar symptom is Francis Bacon, a philosopher whose philosophy consisted of making propaganda for the method of science while remaining uninterested in its actual achievements, or resistive to them, and averse both to mathematics and to systematic observation.[1] That scientists should feel kindly toward him is natural, but does not suffice to constitute him a scientist. His significance is as a symptom of the attitude of his age. The same is true of his earlier namesake Roger.[2] The criterion of a scientist, for our purposes, is specific, positive contribution to organized and interpreted knowledge.

---

[1] This strange attitude indicates a deep ambivalence, which perhaps finds another expression in his acceptance of bribes while in high social position.

[2] Apart from legendary achievements and his maintenance of a point of view, Roger Bacon's actual contributions to science, even for his own day, seem to evaporate to almost nothing.

Some doubt is also justifiable about the inclusion of personages of the type of Buffon, who might well be construed as a litterateur who had found in science a new vein of literature. He was successful because he lived in an age and land which prized polite enlightenment and urbane extension of knowledge. Still, Buffon dealt with factual data in an orderly way, and therefore is definitely entitled to a place in the history of science.

More important is decision of the question whether mathematics should be reckoned as part of science or a separate growth. Abstractly, one might incline to the latter view, because of the nonphenomenal control of mathematics. On the other hand, all science growths of which we have knowledge have used mathematics and have been intertwined with it, as might be expected in view of the widely held opinion that science is characterized by a quantitative approach. The reverse, incidentally, does not seem to hold. For instance, the Diophantine mathematics of the third century is unassociated, so far as is known, with any significant advances in concrete science; as are also the thirteenth-century Chinese and seventeenth-century Japanese developments of mathematics. All in all, however, a close association of mathematics and phenomenal science appears to prevail in history, so that in an empirical inquiry it is most useful to include mathematics in science.

Medicine also comes into question because it is an application, and, in the final analysis, an art. Actually a separation does not prove feasible.

Nevertheless, I have built as lightly as possible upon medicine; because the great figures in its history are, by and large, the able writers. The outstanding practitioners tend to remain legendary or subjective figures. The discoverers, when known, are primarily biologists. The great names in the history of medicine, in short, are of men who knew how to assimilate facts and opinions and to write books about them. In medicine, the reproductive constituent is definitely greater than in science. This is much as in history, where also the great historian rises above the ordinary one not so much in discovery or invention as by capacity for assimilation, judgment, and verbal expression. However, florescences in general science and in medicine tend to appear in company; hence they will be treated jointly, although without commingling.

Excluded from consideration are history, philology, the humanities, and the so-called social sciences. Great historians are always claimed as literary men. Philology resembles mathematics in its separateness and precision, and is therefore given a brief chapter of its own. Figures like Adam Smith and Marx I have reckoned as near-philosophers.

§14. Greek Science

The over-all length of time in which Greek-writing people were developing new concepts of science is from Thales to Diophantos and Pappos, 600 before Christ to 300 after. But more than a third of these nine centuries were unproductive of ideas and methods, so that the gross duration is misrepresentative. Segregation immediately shows a continuous growth of four to five centuries, from Thales to Hipparchos, say 585 to 120. After a long lull, there are two brief but important movements in Roman imperial times: those of Ptolemy and of Diophantos. Then follows permanent decline.

The data allow the convenient segregation of medicine from the rest of science, and its history will therefore be outlined separately and then refitted to the general course.

Philosophic phase, about 600 (585) to 440.—For a century and a half, Greek science and philosophy were scarcely differentiated. Thales, the first recognized philosopher, was also the founder of the beginnings of geometry and astronomy, by transfer and reworking of Egyptian and probably Mesopotamian products. Nearly all the men of this phase in the appended list were also philosophers, and most of the philosophers of the period could be reckoned as scientists in some degree.

Particularly interesting is the association of mysticism and science in Pythagoras and his followers. This appears to be

more than the individual accident of a split personality. Rather
it seems an integral association, characteristic of the culture at
the time. Greek mysticism was not vague, pantheistic, verbal,
aiming to subsume all formulations into one. It was precise
and phenomenal. It satisfied its emotional bent by finding
order and "harmony" in the variety of the world, not by denying the world or equating all its aspects. Hence the emphasis on
law; and hence too the fact that Pythagoras, the one unqualified pre-Platonic mystic in Greek philosophy, was also, almost
certainly, the greatest scientist in his period. It was evidently
his mysticism that made him see deep significance in his right-
triangle theorem, in the cord-length proportions of tones, in
the concept of a spherical earth. On the contrary, contemporaries whose intellects were less emotionally tinged took the
world's appearances less selectively, and when they tried to
interpret they fell back not on specific relations or "laws," but
on "principles" like water or air or four indefinite elements—
none of which can really be concretely related to the overwhelming mass of observable phenomena. Pythagoras's ultimate satisfaction may have been in the harmony of the spheres;
but it was the harmony of an astronomical system at least as
much as a poetic image.

The contrast is very marked with Anaxagoras, two generations after Pythagoras. The naïve, tangible first principles of
his Ionian predecessors could no longer satisfy him, and he
substituted Mind—thereby injecting a nonphenomenal but
nonrelational first cause into the phenomenal world. His curiosity was as wide-ranged as that of Pythagoras, but he had nothing to order it by. So he guessed that the sun was large, but the
earth flat, and went on to dissect brains—perhaps from a hope
that by so doing he would find out something about universal
Mind.

The Pythagorean universe seems a fantastic concoction, with
its central hearth, its counter-earth hiding the hearth from
sight, and the sun's orbit outside the earth's. But at least it is
a specific hypothesis, and a system; and it is not geocentric.
Stripped of its gratuities—the duplicate sun and earth,—it

stands nearer to what we believe than does the Ptolemaic theory. And all Greek systems of the universe are derived from it.

Like the philosophy from which it was not yet differentiated, this first phase of Greek science was peripheral Hellenic: Ionian, and then Italian-Sicilian. Toward the very end, its expounders began to settle in central Greek cities.

Pre-Alexandrian phase, 440–310.—This is the period of differentiation of science and philosophy. Perhaps the greatest and certainly the most influential scientist of the time is still a philosopher: Aristotle. But there are only three or four other hybrids, against twenty or more known scientists who played no role in philosophy proper. Essentially this phase is that of the disengagement of the two activities, as is evident from the number of new mathematical steps outlined in the list. By the end of the period, all but one of the Greek hypotheses of the universe had been promulgated: the central earth rotation of Ecphantos, a Pythagorean; the geocentric system with revolving spheres of Eudoxos, Callippos, and Aristotle; the geoheliocentric of Heraclides. The last Greek theory, the heliocentric of Aristarchos, was formulated early in the next period. In brief, all the productive avenues of classic Greek science had been entered upon: for instance, geometry, conics, theory of numbers in mathematics; though the ultimate destinations were not reached until the next phase.

The first great pulse of medicine, the Hippocratic, was contemporary with the earlier half of this period.

Geographically, the range of participation widens. Thrace, Pontos, Cyrene, even Massilia, are represented in addition to Italy-Sicily; Chios, Lesbos, the Cyclades, Aeolis, Cnidos, rather more prominently than Asiatic Ionia. The mainland of Greece begins to have representatives by birth; although relatively few. However, this last was true throughout the Greek course. In its whole history, not one scientist of the first rank, if we except those primarily philosophers like Plato, was born in nuclear Hellas. This is almost certainly a significant fact; though I do not venture to explain it. It does not hold in the same degree for literature, art, philosophy, or statesmanship.

The leading seat of activity was Athens, especially in the latter part of the period, after her political debacle; but at that not so predominantly as Alexandria led thereafter.

Alexandrian culmination, 310–120.—Two subphases are distinguishable, each of about a century: the climax proper, and its continuation.

Climax, 310–200.—Outwardly, this is marked by the passage of the center of activity from Athens to Alexandria; inwardly, by the culminating achievements, which remained final in their essentials, of Euclid, Archimedes, Eratosthenes, Apollonios. To these can be added other important names, such as Aristarchos and Conon; and the first systematic and exact observers in astronomy. This also is the great post-Hippocratic age of anatomical and physiological discovery in medicine.

Continuation, 200–120.—Greek science was now fully mobilized, but evidently it had already overrun most of the terrain which it was able to occupy with the equipment it had gradually forged for itself during the preceding centuries. In other words, its patterns were essentially saturated, so it proceeded to fill their remaining minor ramifications. Of this sort seems to be the new work on polygonal numbers, on the conchoid, spiric, and cissoid, on sphere segmentation, the fourteenth Euclidean book. The outstanding figure is Hipparchos, one of the world's most extraordinary observers. His exactness enabled him to discover the precession of the equinoxes, and drove him to take the first steps in trigonometry. On the theoretical side he achieved much less.

In this subphase probably fall the first applied mechanician, Ctesibios, and the first astrologically influenced scientist, Hypsicles—presages of what was to come.

Specially significant for the Alexandrian period as a whole is the final separation of science and philosophy. This was made the easier by the death of productive philosophy soon after what we have set as the initial date of 310. Hellenic science began to reach its peak at the moment that philosophy expired. The fact is notable in view of the intertwined birth of the two activities among the Greeks.

As for ethnic origins, the first non-Hellenes—or, if true Greeks in ancestry, then Hellenes born in non-Greek cities—appear in the Alexandrian period: sparingly, and from just beyond the margins of old Greek settlement, toward the end of the first phase—thus, Apollonios of Perga; more frequently, and from farther inland, in the second: Hipparchos of Nicaea, Crates of Mallos, Seleucus of Babylonia. Alexandria was overwhelmingly the focus of activity; but Syracuse, Rhodes, Pergamum participated vigorously; and during the second phase the preëminence of Alexandria was less outstanding. Athens was now devoting herself to perpetuation of her philosophic schools and contributed little to science.

Standstill of science, increase of knowledge, 120 B.C.–120 A.D.—This caption reasonably describes the next quarter millennium. It was a period of qualitative quiescence and quantitative growth. There were no new methods or points of view, except that toward the end of the age arithmetic began to disengage itself from geometry, and trigonometry from astronomy, as autonomous activities under Nicomachos and Menelaos. About the same time, alchemy followed its predecessor astrology and crept in. Applied mechanics reached its ancient zenith with Hero. It remained an affair of ingenuity much more than of economic or even technologic utility. The typical writings of the period are compendia of information, ranging from great encyclopaedias, mostly geographical, such as those of Strabo, Posidonios, and Marinos, to compact summaries of fields of science or excellent introductory manuals. In the appended list I have marked the principal names with daggers to indicate their significance, instead of with the usual asterisks for greatness of contribution.

By the beginning of this interval period, more than two centuries after Alexander, the whole eastern Mediterranean was Hellenized, and Greek the sole language of civilized society. The extension of Roman rule into the area during the period further entrenched Greek, which otherwise might have begun to recede before native reactions. The consequence was that Bithynians, Cappadocians, Syrians, Egyptians, and the like had the doors of Greek science wide open to them. The result shows in this part of the list: most of the birthplaces are not from old Greek cities or colonies, but from districts wholly barbarian until Alexander. Ethnically, then, this period is not really one of Greek science, but of the science of the cosmopolitan, Greek-educated, eastern half of the Roman Empire.

Accordingly, the Greek-educated but Latin-speaking western half of the Empire might also be counted in; and I believe it should be. I have kept it separate merely because two lists are more easily put together mentally than unscrambled once they are presented merged. Actually, what there was of Roman science falls precisely within our present phase, merely beginning a little later: 70 B.C. to 120 A.D. The same type of summary and of geographical encyclopaedia, of astrological tingeing of astronomy, appears in Latin as in Greek; and the same lack of new fundamental methods and concepts. Perhaps the principal difference is that Roman architects, engineers, and surveyors correspond to the Greek inventors of laboratory toys. Even the heavy participation of Hellenized barbarians in the Greek world has its counterpart in the frequency of provincials, especially Spaniards, in the Latin list.

In short, Greek science, which had set its patterns in the Greek city-states, carried them to full development in the world of Hellenistic kingdoms; and now when its growth, except quantitatively, had stopped, it was not so much any longer Hellenic science as a continuation activity of the half Greek, half Latin empire of Rome.

Ptolemaic codification, 120–170.—In the long peace of Hadrian and the Antonines, Claudius Ptolemy made the final, complete formulation of Greek astronomy and its subsidiaries. His own observations were less exact than those of Hipparchos, but he commanded more material for a longer period, and in geography his data, thanks to Marinos and many others, were infinitely more extensive. He made but one new discovery, that of the moon's evection; and he applied old principles throughout. His work is comparable to that of Justinian's jurists in law: immensely important because final for a long period, yet no more than a summation of the past; fundamental for a relatively unproductive future, but recapitulatory in its ideology.

The Ptolemaic systematization was the only great work of pure science in three or four Graeco-Roman centuries. But Ptolemy was the contemporary of Galen, who did a similar work in medicine—which evidently restores Ptolemy at least partly to normality as a cultural symptom. However, Galen was only the peak of a large and active movement in medicine, whereas Ptolemy stands much isolated.

Diophantine algebra, 250–300.—After nearly a century of apparently sterile interval, Diophantos and Pappos arose at Alexandria. The fact that they were virtual and perhaps exact contemporaries suggests that we are again dealing with a phenomenon of culture growth and not of inexplicable individualism. And yet the picture is perplexing. The mathematics of Pappos is essentially the old Greek mathematics in a somewhat altered dress. But the algebra of Diophantos is practically new, so far as we can judge; and it is advanced. It is at any rate thoroughly ungeometric, and therefore looks historically forward, not back. In that sense it is un-Greek, coming when it does, as Spengler has emphasized. Where culture configuration is concerned, nothing so fundamentally original has any business to appear so late in Greek civilization.

Two explanations are possible: that Diophantos was not Greek, culturally; or that he was less original and isolated than he seems. The first is Spengler's answer. But to connect the founder of algebra as a co-symptom with Christ and Mohammed, the Gnostics and Mani, astrology and alchemy, is a remote proceeding: it takes us pretty well beyond phenomena as handleable evidence. And whatever Diophantos's ancestry and religion—which we ignore,—he wrote in Greek in a Greek city and his work was accepted and embodied by Greek civilization.[8] The alternative, that he was not really an isolated phenomenon, is hard to prove or even to examine without

---

[8] Spengler's retort is that Greek civilization of 250–300 was no longer Greek but Magian-Arabian. In the sense that it was no longer Euclidean, that is true; but, after all, objective relations cannot be wholly disregarded.

considerable technical equipment in mathematics, in Greek, and in the history of the time. The best I can do is to suggest the following, which is only an incomplete explanation.

Fundamentally, Diophantos may be viewed as a symptom of the strength of the Greek culture movement. Long after Greek civilization attained the essential limits of its growth, it remained vigorous enough to produce new impulses. Ptolemy and Galen in the second century are such shoots; Diophantos and Pappos, others in the third. More specifically, Diophantos may perhaps be partly accounted for by the preponderant addiction of classical Greek mathematics to the geometric approach, which prevented other methods from coming into their own until geometry and its derivations were exhausted. Arithmetic remained particularly retarded because of the inadequate calculatory symbolism: the Greeks had made some progress in the theory of numbers while their ordinary arithmetical operations were still below the level of a modern schoolboy's; and some proficiency in this regard seems almost prerequisite to algebraic thinking. By the end of the first post-Christian century, however, arithmetic and trigonometry began to disengage themselves increasingly from long-stationary geometry; and with them probably the beginnings of algebra. Whether there are enough actual evidences or clues of such predecessors of Diophantos in algebra to "account" for him, at least partially, is again a highly technical and special problem. The interpretation, which I suggest rather than press, really involves two premises: first, that a genuinely great civilizational growth does not die easily or rapidly; and second, that an overweighting in one direction may bring partial compensation later, especially after the potential of the culture has been lowered by geographical spread and social mingling. Both these premises seem reasonable. Diophantos, in short, on this view, would represent a late counterbalance to earlier high specialization of pattern. With this tentative explanation, I leave him: he is admittedly a difficult phenomenon.

Definitive decline, 300 and following.—After Diophantos and Pappos, there is no question that Greek science failed to achieve any further growth. It even went backward, evidently under a weakness impulse to simplify itself even at the cost of ignoring data. Witness Proclos's denial of the equinoctial precession, and his suggestion that the planetary orbits touch. There is really no exact terminus to the retreat. I carry the list down to 500 because from about then onward the Christian-Byzantine reconstellation of the Greek-speaking world was complete, even to the formal breaking of links with the past, as in the closing of the Academy at Athens.

THE GREEK LIST

Philosophical phase, 600 (585)–440

*Thales of Miletus, ca. 624 (640?)–548+. Founded abstract geometry from Egyptian empiricism; inscribed right triangle; eclipse cycles (solar prediction, 585); loadstone (and amber electricity ?).

Anaximander of Miletus, ca. 610–ca. 545. Obliquity of ecliptic(?); gnomon; map.

Cleostratos of Tenedos, second half 6th cent. Zodiacal signs; eight-year intercalary cycle.

**Pythagoras of Samos, fl. ca. 532, d. Metapontum, Magna Graecia, 497/6. Geometry (Pythagorean theorem, etc.) and theory of numbers ($\sqrt{2}$ incommensurable); mathematical theory of music; earth a sphere. Genuine scientific discovery and strong mysticism associated. The work of Pythagoras and of his school for a century later are not differentiable with certainty (see Philolaos).

Hecataeos of Miletus, ca. 550–ca. 475. Geography; improved map.

Parmenides of Elea, Magna Graecia, first half 5th cent. Earth spherical, central in spherical finite universe, five-zoned.

Anaxagoras of Clazomenae, ca. 499–ca. 428, fl. Athens, d. Lampsacos. Sun a burning meteorite (stone, "larger than Peloponnesus"); moon like earth, its light reflected; earth and planets flat; animal dissections, including brain. Genuine curiosity associated with dogmatic guessing.

Empedocles of Agrigentum, ca. 490–ca. 435. Four elements; corporeality of air; skin respiration; blood flux is respiratory rhythm; ear labyrinth.

Philolaos, prob. of Magna Graecia, fl. (at Thebes ?) ca. 450 ±. Perhaps the first Pythagorean writer: his own theories and the older oral school doctrines are not differentiable. Antibody, earth, moon, sun, five planets, sphere of stars revolve about central fire hidden from us by antibody. Regular solids; harmonic progression: 6, 8, 12 (cube).

Pre-Alexandrian phase, 440–310

*Hippocrates of Chios, fl. Athens ca. 450–430. Quadrature of lunes; duplication by mean proportionals; geometrical text, including reduction and letters in figures (?).

Oenopides of Chios, younger than Anaxagoras. Geometric constructions. Obliquity of ecliptic (?); "great year" of 59 years of $365\frac{22}{59}$ days.

Hicetas of Syracuse, Pythagorean younger than Philolaos. Earth rotates on axis (?).

Meton, fl. Athens 432. Solstitial observations, length of seasons; Metonic cycle, 19 years = 235 lunations.

Hippias of Elis, the sophist, fl. ca. 420. Quadratrix curve for angle trisection.

*Democritos of Abdera, ca. 460–ca. 370, fl. ca. 420. Pyramid, cone volumes $\frac{1}{3}$ prism, cylinder. Anatomical and sense-physiology inquiries. Mechanistic atomic theory (with his teacher Leucippos): vacuum and indestructible atoms differing only geometrically.

Antiphon, contemporary of Socrates. Quadrature of circle by doubling sides of inscribed polygons (beginning of exhaustion method).

Bryson of Heraclea, Pythagorean, contemporary of last. Same plus circumscribed polygons.

Theodoros of Cyrene, fl. Athens end 5th cent., Pythagorean, teacher of Plato. $\sqrt{3}$, 5, 6, 7, ... 17 irrational.

Ecphantos of Syracuse, Pythagorean, early 4th cent. Earth rotates at center of universe

Plato of Athens, ca. 428–348/7. Geometric definitions; rule for squares sum of two squares; mean proportionals: 1 between squares, 2 between cubes.

Theaetetos of Athens, fl. ca. 380. Theory of surds; discovered (?) two regular solids, wrote on all five.

Leon, between Plato and Eudoxos. Geometrical text; insistence on diorism or limitation of solution.

*Archytas of Tarentum, Pythagorean, fl. first half 4th cent. Solid geometry; cube duplication, with first double-curvature curve. Arithmetical, geometric, harmonic progressions distinguished. Theoretical mechanics.

*Eudoxos of Cnidos, ca. 408–ca. 355. Twenty-seven geocentric spheres. Spherical lemniscate (hippopede); proofs of geometric

discoveries; method of exhaustion; proportions of incommen-
surables.

Thymaridas of Paros, prob. first half 4th cent. Prime numbers;
flower of Thymaridas; method of solving a linear equation
system.

Xenocrates of Chalcedon, ca. 397–ca. 314, Platonist. Combina-
torial analysis.

*Menaechmos, fl. mid-4th cent. Discovered conic sections; cube
doubling.

*Callippos of Cyzicos, b. ca. 370, fl. Athens. System of 34 spheres.
Season length and Metonic cycle rectifications.

**Aristotle of Stagira, 384–322. System of 55 spheres. Estimate of
earth's size. Law of lever. Sound is air vibrations. Meteorology.
Wide anatomical and biological inquiries and observations.

*Heraclides of Heracleia on the Pontos, ca. 388–ca. 315/10. Geo-
heliocentric system (cf. Tycho Brahe): earth rotates daily; sun,
moon, planets revolve around it, except Mercury and Venus
around sun; stars fixed; universe infinite.

Speusippos of Athens, nephew of Plato, fl. 348–339. Prime, etc.,
numbers; geometry.

Dinostratos, younger brother of Menaechmos. Quadratrix used
for circle squaring.

*Theophrastos of Eresos, Lesbos, ca. 372–ca. 288. Botany. Works
on stones, meteorology, senses, physiology.

Pytheas of Massilia, fl. ca. 330. Navigator to Britain, etc.; measured maximum height of the sun.

Theudios of Magnesia, fl. second half 4th cent. Editor of Academy's text of geometry.

*Aristoxenos of Tarentum, fl. second half 4th cent. Mathematics;
harmonies; theory of music.

Dichaearchos of Messina, fl. second half 4th cent. Geography.
Mountain height measures; earth circumference estimated at
300,000 stades; sun influence on tides.

Eudemos of Rhodes, fl. ca. 320. Geometry; esp. history of
mathematics.

Autolycos of Pitane, Aeolis, fl. ca. 310. Mathematics. Astronomy:
moving spheres, risings and settings.

Alexandrian culmination: climax, 310–200

**Euclid, fl. in Alexandria probably under Ptolemy I (323–285)
and mainly after 300; but later estimates are also given, to as
late as fl. 250. (Cf. Autolycos and Aristaeos). Synthesis and
carrying on of existing geometry. Theory of numbers; geometrical optics.

Aristaeos the Elder, fl. ca. end 4th cent.; collaborator with Euclid and Apollonios (*sic*). Regular solids; solid loci of conics.

*Aristyllos and Timocharis, fl. Alexandria beginning 3d cent. Principal star observations before Hipparchos.

*Aristarchos of Samos, fl. ca. 280. Heliocentric hypothesis; stars immensely remote; computation of size and distance of sun, moon: results poor, method sound.

**Archimedes, "of" Syracuse, ca. 287–212. Geometry of measurement: areas and volumes of curved figures by integration instead of exhaustion; spirals; $\pi > 3^{10}/_{71}$, $< 3\frac{1}{7}$; volume of cone, hemisphere, cylinder as 1, 2, 3; cubic equations, some by intersection of conics. Statics: lever, center of gravity, hydrostatics.

**Eratosthenes of Cyrene, ca. 273–ca. 192, fl. Alexandria. Prime-number "sieve"; cube-duplication instrument. Earth circumference calculated from latitude and distance measures of Syene and Meroë: 252,000 stades (= 24,662 m. ?). General geography, including map projection. Chronology. Literary history.

**Apollonios of Perga, Pamphylia, b. prob. ca. 262, fl. Alexandria second half 3d cent., younger than two last. Conic sections: the fundamental work, going far beyond Menaechmos, Aristaeus, Euclid, Conon. Originated astronomical epicycles (and eccentrics).

*Conon of Samos, d. young before 212. Conic intersections; astronomical observations in southern Italy, Sicily; records of Chaldaean eclipse observations.

Alexandrian culmination: continuation, 200–120

Ctesibios of Alexandria, fl. most likely not far from 200, but date uncertain within wide limits. Applied mechanics; invention of hydraulic organ, clock, force pump, etc. (?).

*Hypsicles, fl. prob. in Alexandria early in 2d cent. Book xiv of Euclid; polygonal numbers; arithm. progressions; astrology.

Crates of Mallos, Cilicia, fl. Pergamum first half 2d cent. Terrestrial globe. First Greek grammar.

Seleucos of Babylonia, fl. ca. 150, perhaps at Seleucia. Last positive advocate of Aristarchos's heliocentric system.

Nicomedes, fl. prob. in 2d cent. Mathematics: conchoid, use of quadratrix.

Perseus, also of 2d cent. Spiric curves.

Zenodoros, 2d cent. Isoperimetric plane surfaces; volume of sphere $>$ all solids of equal surface.

Dionysodoros of Amisos, Pontos, prob. of 2d cent. Sphere division by plane in given ratio, by parabola-hyperbola intersection. Tores.

Diocles, prob. 2d cent. Cissoid and cube duplication; burning mirrors; same sphere division.

**Hipparchos of Nicaea, fl. Rhodes third quarter 2d cent. Greatest astronomical observer of antiquity, at Rhodes and Alexandria 161 (146?)—127; discovered precession of equinoxes (from older observations, incl. Chaldaean; 14ˢ short); founded trigonometry (table of chords, natural sines). Position and magnitude catalogue of 850+ stars. Celestial globe. Applied epicyclic and eccentric theories. Computed moon distance and diameter (about 10 and 23 per cent excessive), tropical year (6ᵐ 26ˢ over), synodic month (0.6ˢ too long). Stereographic projection.

Standstill of science, increase of knowledge, 120 B.C.–120 A.D.

Philo of Byzantium, fl. prob. end of 2d cent. Applied mechanics, inventions.

Artemidoros of Ephesos, fl. ca. 104–100. Phys. geogr., distances.

Theodosios of Bithynia, fl. about the turn of the century. Spherics (older geometry), star positions, universal sun dial.

†Hero of Alexandria, probably a native Egyptian; most likely early first century, but date much in dispute. Applied mechanics and mathematics, semipopular. Siphons, fountains, presses, steam and automatic contrivances; surveying; areal and volume formulas: triangle area $= \sqrt{s}\,(s-a)\,(s-b)\,(s-c)$, where $s = a/2 + b/2 + c/2$; first- and second-degree algebraic solutions.

†Posidonios of Apamea, Syria, ca. 135–ca. 51. Philosophy, history, geography, astronomy; encyclopaedist. Earth measurement, inferior to Eratosthenes; sun distance and size estimate, superior to Hipparchos and Ptolemy. Both sun and moon cause tides; spring and neap tides.

Geminos of Rhodes, fl. prob. ca. 70. Introductory scientific summaries of mathematics and astronomy.

Cleomedes, prob. 1st cent. Astronomical summary; refraction.

†Strabo of Amasia, interior Pontos, 63–20+ A.D. Geographical encyclopaedia, astronomical aspects slurred.

Xenarchos of Seleucia, Cilicia, contemporary of Strabo. Criticism of Peripatetic astronomy.

Pseudo-Democritos, 1st or 3d (?) cent. A.C. Earliest extant Greek alchemy.

Periplus of the Indian ocean, sailor's manual, prob. second half of 1st cent. A.C.

†Nicomachos of Gerasa (prob. in Arabia Petraea), fl. prob. end of 1st cent. A.C., at any rate between 30 and 150. Introduction to arithmetic as an autonomous discipline; theory of numbers.

---

† For significance of daggers, see text, p. 104.

†Menelaos of Alexandria, fl. in Rome, 98, similarly separated trigonometry from astronomy in his *Spherics*. Astronomical observations; specific gravity.

†Marinos of Tyre, prob. not far from turn of century, predecessor of Ptolemy. Geography, latitude-longitude map of world.

Ptolemaic codification, 120–170

Theon of Smyrna, fl. ca. 127–132. Platonist. Mathematical compilation: arithmetic separate from geometry, similar to that of Nicomachos but independent.

*Claudius Ptolemy, b. Egypt, fl. (observed) 127–151 in Alexandria, d. after 161. *Megale Syntaxis,* or *Almagest:* final summary and encyclopaedia of Greek astronomy, based largely on Hipparchos; observations poorer, but more numerous (1,028 stars); eccentrics and epicycles; evection of moon (new); plane and spherical trigonometry, with table of chords by half degrees. *Geographike Hyphegesis* equally fundamental or final; facts based largely on Marinos; orthographic and stereographic projections; parallels and meridians so named. *Optics* (by Ptolemy?) contains experiments on refraction.

Interval, 170–250

Achilles Tatios, fl. end 2d or in 3d cent. Commentator on Aratos.

Diophantine algebra, 250–300

*Diophantos, fl. at Alexandria prob. second half 3d cent.; put also at various dates from ca. 250 to ca. 325, but prob. anterior to next. Founder, essentially, of algebra, especially of indeterminate analysis (equations up to fourth degree solved in rational numbers); but also determinate equations (linear up to 4 variables, quadratic, 1 cubic). Symbols for unknown quantity, negative quantities, second, third, fourth powers.

Anatolios, fl. at Alexandria, 269 at Laodicea, Syria. Manual of arithmetic; Egyptian reckoning; Easter.

*Pappos, fl. at Alexandria prob. under Diocletian (284–305). Systematic summary of previous Greek geometrical mathematics, including new explanations and some new propositions.

Zosimos of Panopolis, Egypt, fl. end of 3d cent., possibly early 4th. Alchemy, mysticism.

Definitive decline, 300–500

Serenus of Antinoöpolis, Egypt, 4th cent. Mathematics, on cylinder and cone sections.

Theon of Alexandria, fl. ca. 365–372 and under Theodosios (378–395). Edition of Euclid; commentary on Ptolemy. Multiplication, division, square root of sexagesimal fractions.

Hypatia, daughter of last, d. 415. Commentaries on Diophantos, Apollonios, Ptolemy.

Synesios of Cyrene, b. ca. 370/75, fl. ca. 410, d. before 415? Alchemy.

Proclos, 410–485, b. Byzantium, studied Alexandria, Athens, d. Athens. Neo-Platonist. Commentary on Euclid; cinematic construction of curves. Introduction to Hipparchos-Ptolemy contains: denial of precession of equinoxes; successive planetary orbits touch at maximum and minimum distances; epicycles = eccentrics.

Julianos of Laodicea, fl. 497–500. Astronomy, astrology.

GREEK MEDICINE

The growth curves of medicine run fairly parallel to those of pure science in the Greek world, with some interesting variations of emphasis.

It seems sufficient to recognize only one pre-Alexandrian phase, because medicine as an empirical art did not go through a first stage of nondifferentiation from philosophy. It began somewhat later, in the preserved record: toward the end instead of with the beginning of the sixth century. Its "father" was Alcmaeon, an Italian Greek, almost inevitably influenced by Pythagoras if he was not his formal disciple. Next appeared figures from Sicily, Crete, and Thrace; and these led directly to the schools of Cnidos and Cos at the southwest corner of Asia Minor, the latter culminating in Hippocrates. There was a Dorian-Aeolian cast to the whole development which contrasts with the Ionic aspect of philosophy and pure science. Hippocrates, whose "floruit" appears to have been during the later Peloponnesian War, say 420–400, was perhaps a greater genius than any Greek pure scientist up to his time, and even beyond. He was certainly less superseded by his successors than any mathematician or astronomer.

The schools of Cos and Cnidos continued to flourish until the rise of Alexandria: there seems no break in time. Rather was Greek city-state talent drained off to the Egyptian metropolis after about 310. Great names now crop up again: Herophilos and Erasistratos. The direction is somewhat dif-

ferent: the beginnings of specific anatomy and specific physiology tend to take the place of general clinical medicine. These
men were of course contemporaries of Euclid, Archimedes,
and Aristarchos; but the medical burst seems to have ended
a generation the earlier; and to the second or continuation
subphase of Alexandrian science, that of Hipparchos, medicine presents little counterpart.

On the other hand, there was some medical activity during
the first part of the long noninnovating, post-Alexandrian, pre-
Ptolemaic period of science: namely, in the last pre-Christian
century. There are no very great names; but the Empirical
school flourished and the Methodical and Atomic sprang up.
The foci seem to have been Bithynia and Tarentum.

I have already mentioned that Galen and Ptolemy were contemporaries. But Galen forms part of a larger and more illustrious company; and it was active longer: from about 50 to
about 200. Besides the schools which originated in the previous
period, there now were the Pneumatic, Eclectic, and Dogmatic. The differences, where they did not lie in practice, seem
to have referred to the underlying philosophies; they were
preferential rather than objectively scientific. Still, they indicate intellectual interest and activity. Just wherein Galen's
greatness lay is a little difficult for the layman to define. It was
probably in his qualities of physician as such. As a scientist it
seems difficult to rank him above Herophilos and Erasistratos.
But then, much the same may be said of the relation of Ptolemy
to Hipparchos.

Besides Galen, the most illustrious physicians of the period
were Rufus, Soranos, and perhaps Aretaeos. These were all
from Asia Minor. So were a good half of the remainder. It is
a curious list of birthplaces: Pergamum, Ephesus, Nicomedia,
Phrygia, Pamphylia, Cilicia, Cappadocia—the rest scattering
or unknown.

Asia Minor, in fact, is persistently associated with medicine.
The Hippocratic period climaxes at Cnidos in Asia Minor and
at Cos just off its shore; the Alexandrian, with Herophilos
from Chalcedon; the mid-Hellenistic, at least half in Bithynia;

the present one draws from all over the peninsula; and the best-known of the successors, Oribasios, is from Pergamum.

It is also notable that no Latin appears in the roll of honor of ancient medicine, in spite of the fact that the practical aspects of the subject might be thought to have appealed to the Roman and Romanized temperament; in spite of the fact also that Asclepiades, Rufus, Soranos, Galen, and others flourished part of their lives at the imperial capital. Of Latin writers on medicine, Celsus was essentially a compiler, Caelius a translator.

On review of the whole course of Greek medicine, we can probably segregate it into two main growths. The first extended continuously from Alcmaeon through Hippocrates to the great Alexandrians, from about 510 to 240, or, counting a generation more of presumptive but unrecorded successors, to 210—a round three centuries. This was a Greek movement, by Greeks only. The later growth also ran for three centuries, from about 100 B.C. to 200 A.D., but with a sag around its second quarter and with its climax in the fourth. This growth was Hellenistic-Anatolian.

The degree of parallelism of Greek pure science and Greek medicine is illustrated by the following table, which reads upward.

	Science		*Medicine*
250–300	Diophantine algebra		
170–250	. . . .		
120–170	Ptolemaic summary	50–200	Galenic
120–120	. . . .	25–50	. . . . . .
		100–25	Mid-Hellenistic
200–120	Alexandrian continuation	240?–100	. . . . . .
310–200	Alexandrian climax	310–240?	Alexandrian
440–310	Pre-Alexandrian	440–310	Hippocratic
585–440	Philosophical	510–440	Pre-Hippocratic

THE GREEK MEDICAL LIST

Hippocratic medicine, about 510–310

*Alcmaeon of Crotona, toward end of 6th cent., younger contemporary (disciple?) of Pythagoras. Father of Greek medicine. Optic nerve, trachea, brain as seat of mind.

Empedocles of Agrigentum, ca. 490–ca. 435. (See General Science.) Founder of medical school of Sicily.

Herodicos (or Prodicos) of Selymbria, Thrace, fl. ca. mid-5th cent., teacher of Hippocrates. Diet.

Diogenes of Apollonia, Crete, ca. mid-5th cent. Vascular system; heart.

**Hippocrates of Cos, b. ca. 460, d. old at Larissa, Thessaly.

*Euryphron, of the school of Cnidos, Caria, contemporary of Hippocrates.

Hippocratic treatises on fractures, dislocations, generation: early 4th cent. (with interpolations nearly a century later).

Polybos, of the school of Cos, son-in-law of Hippocrates, fl. early 4th cent.

Philistion of Locroi, school of Sicily, fl. early 4th cent.

Diocles of Carystos, Euboea, fl. first third 4th cent. Dogmatic school; fusion of schools of Cos and Sicily.

Chrysippos of Cnidos, fl. ca. 365. Cnidian and Sicilian schools.

Hippocratic treatises on anatomy, heart: mid-4th cent.; the latter with Sicilian influences.

Praxagoras of Cos, fl. 340–320.

Mnesitheos of Athens, pupil of last, fl. prob. last quarter 4th cent.

Alexandrian medicine, about 310–240

**Herophilos, b. Chalcedon, fl. Alexandria under Ptolemy I (323–285). Pupil of Praxagoras. The greatest Greek anatomist.

**Erasistratos, b. Ceos ca. 304, fl. Alexandria ca. 258/7. Founder of physiology; in anatomy, second only to Herophilos.

*Eudemos, fl. Alexandria in mid-3d cent. Anatomy.

Interval

Serapion, fl. Alexandria prob. first half 2d cent. Founder of Empirical school.

Mid-Hellenistic medicine of the first century B.C.

Demetrios of Apamea, Bithynia, fl. ca. 100±. Obstetrics.

Asclepiades, b. ca. 124 in Prusa, Bithynia, fl. also in Rome. "Atomic" and mechanistic medicine, neglecting anatomy.

Heraclides of Tarentum, fl. ca. 75. Greatest Empiricist; pharmacology.

Glaucias of Tarentum (?), contemporary of last, also of Empirical school.

Themison of Laodicea (which one?), fl. ca. mid-1st cent., disciple of Asclepiades. Founder of Methodical school.

Ammonios the Lithotomist, fl. Alexandria prob. second half 1st cent. B.C.

Imperial Hellenistic or Galenic medicine, about 50–200

Athenaeos of Attalia, Pamphylia (?), fl. in Rome mid-1st cent. A.C. (under Claudius and Nero, 41–68). Founder of the Pneumatic school.

Pedanios Dioscorides of Anazarbos, Cilicia, mid-1st cent. (41–68). Encyclopaedia of materia medica.

Demosthenes Philalethes, fl. in reign of Nero (54–68) near Laodicea, Phrygia. Ophthalmology.

Claudios Agathinos of Sparta, fl. second half 1st cent. Founder of the Eclectic or Episynthetic school, out of the Pneumatic. Disciple of Athenaeos.

Archigenes of Apamea, Syria, fl. at Rome under Trajan (98–117).

Heliodoros, probably Egyptian, also at Rome under Trajan. Pneumatic surgeon.

*Rufus, Rhouphos, of Ephesus, fl. at Rome and in Egypt under Trajan (98–117). Next to Galen, the greatest post-Christian physician of antiquity, especially in anatomy: sensory and motor nerves, lens, oviduct.

Marinos, fl. Alexandria early 2d cent. Anatomy. He was the teacher of Kointos (Quintus), who in turn taught the teachers of Galen.

*Soranos of Ephesus, fl. Rome under Trajan-Hadrian (98–138). Anatomy. Gynaecology. Methodist school.

Antyllos, fl. first half 2d cent. Pneumatic school.

Menodotos of Nicomedia, fl. prob. mid-2d cent. Empirical and Skeptical schools.

*Aretaeos of Cappadocia, second half 2d cent. Eclectic with Pneumatic leanings. He is distinguished for his excellent clinical descriptions.

**Galen, 129–199, b. Pergamum, fl. there and at Rome. Systematic unification of Greek medicine—anatomic, physiological, clinical. A broad personality, at once observer, experimenter, teleologist, dogmatist, deductive reasoner, and encyclopaedic in his knowledge.

Marcellinos, fl. 2d cent. or later. Eclectic with Dogmatic tendencies. Pulse.

Aftermath, 350–400

Oribasios, ca. 325–ca. 400, b. Pergamum. Medical encyclopaedia.

Philagrios of Epirus, fl. Thessalonica second half 4th cent. Observer. Spleen.

Posidonios, brother of last, also an observer. Psychiatry, brain diseases, brain-function localization.

§15. Roman Science

There is little to add about Roman science beyond what has already been said. Such as it is, it falls into the brief period of Roman cultural greatness. Its span, about 70 B.C. to 120 A.D., coincides almost exactly with that of Roman literature, except for beginning later. This is hardly surprising, since Roman scientists, when they were not engineers, were men of letters, not inquirers into the unknown.

Besides fitting into Roman culture history, however, the Latin list also fits in a way into Greek. It falls wholly into the long Greek standstill from 120 to 120. While Greek science was scarcely yet dead but certainly stagnating, Roman was at its little peak; and the two just about equaled each other in achievement. When Greek activity revived with Ptolemy and again with Diophantos, there was no stir of Latin counterpart: the center of intellectual activity, for a while seemingly in equipoise between East and West after the exhaustion of the pure Hellenic growth, had returned to the Greek-speaking world. This wavering and swingback of the balance seem typical of the relation of "Greece" and "Rome" in the larger unit of Greek-Roman or Mediterranean history.

In the list, I add a few names from the post-Constantinian Latin world; not because the contributions to science are of any consequence, but because the geography and subjects represented are typical.

THE ROMAN LIST

Roman science: 70 B.C.–120 A.D.
  Varro, 116–27. Encyclopaedist.
  Lucretius, 98/5–55, the poet and philosopher.
  Figulus, fl. 59, d. 44. Neo-Pythagorean philosophy. Astrology.
  Agrippa, 63–12, in charge, and Balbus, chief engineer, of survey of the Empire.
  C. Julius Hyginus, b. Spain, fl. Rome, 28 B.C. seq. Polygraph.
  Vitruvius, fl. prob. under Augustus, 31 B.C.–14 A.D. Architecture, engineering, technology.
  Manilius, fl. ca. 14 A.D. Astrology.

Celsus, fl. under Tiberius (14–37). Encyclopaedic compilation, including excellent summary of medicine.

Pomponius Mela, b. Spain, fl. ca. 43. Summary of descriptive geography.

Pliny the Elder, 23–79. Encyclopaedia of natural history.

Columella, b. Spain, fl. near mid-1st cent. Agriculture.

Frontinus, ca. 40–103. Engineering.

Balbus, fl. under Trajan (98–117). Surveying.

Hyginus, fl. same reign. Surveying.

Latin science of the Western Empire, 325–500

Firmicus Maternus, b. Sicily, fl. 334–337. Astrology.

Caelius Aurelianus of Numidia, fl. prob. ca. 440. Best Latin medical writer after Celsus; translator of Soranos.

Victorius of Aquitania, fl. 457. Easter canon = Metonic 19 years $\times$ $4 \times 7 = 532$ years.

Martianus Capella of Madaura, Africa, fl. Carthage ca. 470. Encyclopaedist.

§16. Greek and Roman Relations

The history of Greek science, including medicine and Roman productions, may be recapitulated as follows.

There were two main periods. One may be called Greek: the other, Greek-speaking Imperial Roman, or Graeco-Roman; Roman Greek would perhaps be the best epithet. I avoid the term Hellenistic in the present connection because with its 600-year range it overlaps ambiguously.

Pure Greek science lasted between four and five hundred years: 465 by my reckoning, if one wishes to be exact. It began with a phase of nondifferentiation from philosophy, a century and a half long; went on, without a break, to one not quite so long, of disengagement from philosophy and setting of its fundamental patterns; culminated, almost exactly coeval with the third century, under Euclid and his successors, at Alexandria in a Hellenic-Macedonian kingdom on foreign soil, when philosophy had finished its course; and spent another scant century in its final phase of chinking crevices and adding scattered pinnacles. This was what may be called a normal growth, simple in its curve.

The second period, intrinsically much less great, is less simple: in its time configuration, in its ethnic constituents, and in resting on the first. It begins about the time the Hellenistic kingdoms crumbled before the expanding power of Rome. For a quarter millennium, knowledge increased, but there were no new ideas and almost no new methods. In this long, ideologically sterile interval, Romans were able to compete on about even terms with Greeks. Then, however, the increase of knowledge and general cultural faculties forced, or at least permitted, some attempts at genuine productivity; and as soon as these began, the Latins dropped out: all the later activity was by speakers of Greek, of probably highly mixed ethnic ancestry. The first constructive impulse, represented by Ptolemy and Galen, was essentially repetitive of the past, but on the basis of the wider knowledge that had accumulated and with some new methods, such as trigonometry. The second or Diophantine impulse involved a new ideology, but was limited in scope and proved stillborn. The over-all duration of these revivifications, including medicine, was about 250 years; but the pure-science activities were confined to two separated half centuries, about 120–170 and 250–300. After 300, there was no further growth, and by the fifth century retraction was evident, probably in knowledge and certainly in thinking.

This second period, then, is a period only in the conventional chronological sense. It is not the growth of a set of interrelated culture patterns. Rather it is the sequelae of such a growth, which had been great enough to live on long after it completed itself. The vitality of the first growth was sufficient to produce a subsequent final astronomical codification, and to send up the new shoot of Diophantine algebra from the root system of its decaying trunk; but this shoot could not struggle through to independent survival.

As for the ideology of the first or true growth, while perhaps the outstanding characteristic of this growth, in world-history perspective, is its first complete freeing of science from magic, it seems that this liberation began to be accomplished precisely through association with a conscious element of mysticism.

Hellenic science at any rate, if not philosophy, was enabled to attain its ultimate high rationality perhaps more as a result of Pythagorean mysticism than of Ionian naïve rationalism and undirected observation, paradoxical as the statement may seem; and of course with the proviso that the mystic elements were discarded as soon as they had served their function of directing attention to problems of law.

§17. Arab-Mohammedan Science

This growth is Arab in the sense that its medium almost throughout was the Arabic language; but only part of its product was due to men who were ethnic Arabs. It was prevailingly Mohammedan, but included a considerable number of Jews and Christians. Arabic science must accordingly be understood as that science which developed in the major culture characterized by dominance of Arabic speech and Mohammedan religion, but which was participated in by men of several faiths and especially of many nationalities, using Arabic as the language of learning as west Europeans used Latin.

As in philosophy, there are really two movements within the Arabic growth of science. They were well separated geographically, and nearly so in time. The greater and earlier movement was in the East; the second, in Spain and Morocco. The first began about 750 and was in full swing soon after 800, culminating before 1050. The western growth begins only about 950, does not become active until about 1000, and climaxes between 1000 and 1200. The two movements are thus some two centuries apart, in their beginnings and peaks. They overlap because each lasted more than two hundred years.

North Africa was a rather feeble link between eastern and western Islam. A few scientists were born or flourished in Tunis; but of those of greater importance, as indicated by the stars before their names in the lists that follow, not one originated between Egypt and Morocco.

Both movements began earlier and ended later than the philosophical developments which accompanied them. This is especially clear for the greater eastern movement. Thus Arabic science parallels modern Occidental science: both enclose within their time limits a somewhat briefer growth of philosophy.

The eastern and western Mohammedan science growths being in the main disparate phenomena, they will be taken up separately.

EASTERN ARABIC SCIENCE

The basic list is given a few pages farther on. Since most historical accounts are either sketchy or devoted to special aspects, I have compiled chiefly from Sarton, omitting however the background and fringe of science, as defined at the outset of this chapter. Up to about 850, but in general not beyond, the principal translators have been included, because Mohammedan science had to get its start by assimilating what Greek-Hellenistic and Indian science had left. The arrangement is, so far as possible, chronological. But death dates are unfortunately more frequently given than birth dates, and when both are lacking there remains only the "floruit," and this is often either indefinite or defined by a reign or external event. I have, however, united in a single chronological list, contrary to Sarton, the men of all departments of science.

The most relevant inferences, for our purposes, can be drawn from a briefer table (see overleaf), consisting of the starred and double-starred names in the main list on pages 127–131, below.

It will be seen that in this list of 21 there is not one Arab born in Arabia. There is one Egyptian, no Syrian. Thirteen of the 21, or 11 out of 19 if the epigonoi are disregarded, are from the Iranian plateau or the oases north of it: Merv, Bokhara, Khiva, Ferghana. I do not know to what degrees this Russian Turkestan area was at that time peopled respectively by Iranians and by Turks; but its culture had long been Iranian. Nearly all the other distinguished men are from Hira, Basra, Bagdad, Harran; that is, Mesopotamia, which was Semitic-speaking at the time of the Mohammedan conquest. In short, something like nine out of ten of the most eminent Muslim

Man	Origin	Born	Flourished	Died	Fields
Jabir (Geber)		.....	776	.....	Alch.
		I. Opening: To 813			
		II. Main Period: 813–1048			
A Al-Khwarizmi	Turkestan.	.....	813–833	850	Math.
Al-Farghani	Turkestan.	.....	By 833	861+	Astr.
Al-Kindi	Basra.	.....	.....	873	Philos., var. sci.
Ibn Ishaq	Hira.	809/10	.....	877	Medic.
B Al-Razi	Persia.	.....	.....	923/4	Med., phys., alch.
Al-Battani	Harran Sabian.	Bef. 858	.....	929	Astr., math.
C Al-Sufi	Persia.	903	.....	986	Astr.
Ibn 'Abbas	Persia.	.....	.....	994	Medic.
Abu-l-Wafa'	Persia.	940	.....	997/8	Math., astr.
Ibn Yunus	Egypt.	.....	.....	1009	Math., astr.
Al-Karkhi	Bagdad.	.....	.....	1019/29	Math.
Al-Sijzi	Persia.	951	.....	1024	Math.
Ibn 'Isa	Christian.	.....	1000–1050	.....	Med. (ophthalm.)
Ibn Sina	Turkestan.	980	.....	1037	Philos., medic.
Al-Haitham	Basra.	965	.....	1039	Optics
Al-Biruni	Turkestan.	973	.....	1048	Geogr., math., etc.
		III. Close: After 1048			
Omar Khayyam	Persia.	1038/48	1074/5	1123/4	Astr., math.
Al-Khazini	Turkestan (Greek).	.....	1115–1122	.....	Physics
		IV. Epigones: After 1150			
A Al-Tusi	Persia.	1201	1240	1274	Astr., math.
B Ulug Beg	Turkestan.	.....	1437	.....	Astr.

men of science—exclusive of Spain[4]—originated in the region of modern Iraq, Persia-Afghanistan, and Turkestan. Syria, Arabia, Palestine, Egypt, North Africa are very sparsely represented in comparison.

The disproportion is not quite so excessive among the less illustrious, the unstarred names of the longer list that follows. For about 60 of these the origin is given. They classify as follows: Syria and west, including a few Arabians, 10, mainly after 900; Iraq, 5; Persia and Turkestan, 30; Jews, 5, chiefly before 900; Christians, 10. Among Muslims, the proportions for Iraq and east-north as against Syria and west-south are as 5 to 2; and this in spite of the Fatimite florescence in Egypt. Iranians evidently contributed about half the total: any possible subtractions on account of Turks in the Persia-Turkestan group would be made up by the addition of Persian Nestorians.

I do not know what this distribution means. Its causes are presumably multiple. But this fact is perhaps significant: the division between the areas of higher and lower productivity in the times of Mohammedan science corresponds with the eastern frontier of intensive Hellenization and of the Roman Empire. Greek science drew recruits from Asia Minor, Syria, Egypt, but few or none from Mesopotamia and Iran. Christianity spread solidly as far as the Empire extended; beyond, it was a minority sect, or the heretical Nestorian one. In short, there appears to be an old culture cleavage at work here: the Mediterranean lands against those to the east, Greek-Roman-Christian civilization against Parthian-Sassanian-Zoroastrian. It was in the soil of the latter that Islamic science grew most flourishingly, though the bulk of the content which it assimilated to operate on was Greek. How this curious constellation happened to come about must be left to those better informed to explain; but the facts certainly reveal a problem.

With respect to time, the limits of the growth are evidently around 750 and 1125 or 1150. This means that about a century elapsed after the Arab conquest of Syria, Egypt, Mesopotamia,

---

[4] The proportion would remain at seven-tenths or eight-tenths with Spain-Morocco included.

and Persia before Mohammedans had assimilated enough
Hellenistic science to begin to make some independent progress with it. The beginning of the period of greatness about
coincides with the reign of Al-Mamun, 813–833. After him,
the Caliphate began to decline, soon broke up, and was finally
superseded by the Seljuk Turk sultanate in 1055. This date,
or the reign of the founder of the new dynasty, Tughril Beg,
1037–1063, or the death of Al-Biruni in 1048, conveniently
marks the end of the main phase of Muslim science. Its greatest
heights were not reached until around 1000 or after, when political disintegration had been progressive for nearly two centuries. A few names mark the downward course of the next
seventy-five or a hundred years. By 1150, if not before, continuous development was ended. What followed was spasmodic.

The main period, say 813–1048, seems to fall into three divisions, on the basis of the clustering of the greater names. I
have marked these A, B, C in the briefer table. The first, A,
shows a clustering of deaths from 850 to 877; the third, C, from
986 to 1048. Between is more than a century, B, with only two
first-rank men, whose deaths fall midway. The numbers involved are too small to prove that a dip or wavering occurred
about the middle of the growth; but they suggest it.

Two subsequent brief spurts occurred: the Maragha observatory and tables of Al-Tusi in the late thirteenth century,
and the Samarkand observatory and star catalogue of Ulug
Beg in the early fifteenth. Both of these were institutional en-
terprises supported by Mongol princes, successors respectively
of Hulagu and Timur. They indicate that interest in astronomy and capacity to prosecute it were being maintained somewhere in the world of Islam; but they are not evidences of
sustained productivity, they are only flashes. Essentially, they
seem to indicate that Mohammedan science was great enough
to retain some vitality long after it had ended.

A few observations regarding content may be appropriate.

The movement was built on long-finished Greek and mature
Hindu science. It did not originate as part of a philosophy. In
fact it preceded philosophy, and philosophers became promi-

nent chiefly toward the end. The most active scientific development was over before Spanish Mohammedan philosophy began. Medicine was intertwined more closely than philosophy with the pure scientific movement. This bent is perhaps related to the interest in alchemy. The most original contributions of the Mohammedans were definite progress in trigonometry, some in algebra, empirical observations and technical devices in chemistry and optics, good observations and tables in astronomy. Their science was intelligent, open-minded, acquisitive, interested in accuracy, practically competent, but weak in creativeness or theory. It tended toward encyclopaedic and undifferentiated approach. There is no strong indication that interest shifted from field to field as time went on. Astrology and alchemy were possibly somewhat more strongly emphasized in the early than in the late part of the growth. The importance of astrology versus scientific astronomy was no greater than in mediaeval Europe; perhaps less.

EASTERN MOHAMMEDAN SCIENCE—FULL LIST

Ibn Bakhtyashu, d. 771, fl. ca. 765 at Jundi-shapur and Bagdad. Nestorian Persian. Medicine.

Al-Naubakht, d. ca. 776/7, Persian. Astronomer, engineer.

Ibrahim al-Fazari, d. ca. 777. Astronomical instruments, calendar, astrology.

Ya'qub ibn Tariq, prob. Persian, fl. Bagdad ca. 767–778, d. ca. 796. Sphere, arc of $3° 45'$ or its sine, tables from the siddhantas. Hindu-influenced.

*Jabir ibn Haiyan, Geber, fl. ca. 776 at Kufa. Most famous Arabic alchemist. Sulphur-mercury theory of metals; preparation of As and Sb ex sulphides, of basic lead carbonate; also, it is said, HNO_3, HCl, KOH known.

Muhammad al-Fazari, son of last, d. ca. 796/806; transl. siddhantas from Sanskrit ca. 772/3.

Al Batriq, d. ca. 796/806. Transl. Hippocrates, Galen, etc.

'Umar ibn al-Farrukhan, b. Tabaristan, fl. Bagdad, d. ca. 815. Astron., astrol., architect, transl. from Persian.

Mashallah, Messahala, d. ca. 815/20, Jew. Astronomer, astrologer, surveyor.

Al-Fadl, son of Al-Naubakht, d. ca. 815/6. Astron., astrol., translator from Persian.

Al-Asma'i, 739/40–ca. 831, b. and d. at Basra. Pure Arab. Domestic animals, anatomy.

Al Ma'mun, caliph 813–833, provided for degree measurements, observatories, etc.

Sahl al-Tabari, Jew of Tabaristan, early 9th cent., first transl. *Almagest* into Arabic.

Jibril ibn Bakhtyashu', Nestorian, d. 828/9. Medicine.

Yahya ibn Abi Mansur, Persian, d. ca. 831. Astronomer at Bagdad.

Sahl ibn Bishr, Jew, fl. Khurasan first half 9th cent. Astrology, algebra.

Ahmud al-Nahawandi, fl. at Jundi-shapur by 803, d. ca. 835/45; astronomical observations and tables.

Al-Hajjaj ibn Yusuf. 829/30 transl. *Almagest;* also Euclid; prob. at Bagdad.

Al-'Abbas, fl. 829–833; astronomical observations at Bagdad and Damascus; commentaries on Euclid.

'Ali ibn 'Isa al-Asturlabi, fl. Bagdad and Damascus ca. 830–832. Astronomer, instrument maker, degree measurer.

Al-Marwarrhudi, of Marrud near Merv, fl. Damascus 832/3. Astronomy.

Salmawaih ibn Bunan, Nestorian, d. 839/40. Medicine.

*Al-Khwarizmi (whence Algorism), b. Khwarizm, Khiva, fl. under Al-Ma'mun, d. ca. 850. Fuser of Hindu and Greek arithmetic, algebra, trigonometry, astronomy, geography.

Ibn Masawaih, Mesuë Major, Christian, b. Jundi-shapur, fl. Bagdad, d. 857. Medicine.

*Al-Farghani, Alfraganus, b. Transoxiana, fl. by 833, living 861. Influential astronomer: precession. distance, and diameter of planets, diameter of earth, etc.

'Ali al-Tabari, fl. 850. Son of Sahl al-Tabari. Medicine, etc.

'Utarid, 9th cent., author of oldest known lapidary.

Sanad ibn 'Ali, of Jewish birth, d. after 864. Observatory; tables; specific gravity.

Habash al-Hasib, fl. Bagdad, observed 825–835, d. 864/74. Hindu-type "tested" and abbreviated astronomical tables; introduced "shadow" (tangent).

Sabur ibn Sahl, d. 869, Christian, fl. at Jundi-shapur. Medicine: antidotes.

*Al-Kindi, Alkindus, b. Basra, d. ca. 873, pure Arab. *Philosopher (q.v.) and scientist: mathematics, physics, music, medicine; also astrology; but alchemy he considered imposture. Four books on Hindu numerals; translations from Greek.

Al-Mahani, b. in Kirman, Persia, fl. ca. 860, d. 874/84. Math., astron.

*Hunain ibn Ishaq, Joannitius, 809/10–877. B. Hira, fl. Jundi-shapur and Bagdad. Nestorian. Medicine; and especially trans-lations of higher standard. Assisted by his nephew Hubaish ibn al-Hasan.

Abu Ma'shar, Albumasar, b. Balkh, Khurasan, fl. Bagdad, d. 886. Highly influential astrologer.

Al-Dinawari, ca. 815/25–895 Persian, b. Dinawar, fl. there and Ispahan. Astronomy, botany, history.

Thabit ibn Qurra, b. at Harran 826/36, fl. Bagdad, d. 901. Math., astron., medic., transl. Theory of trepidation of equinoxes.

Ahmad ibn Yusuf, Egyptian, fl. in Egypt, d. ca. 912. Math.: similar arcs, proportions.

Al-Nairizi, from Shiraz, d. ca. 922. Math., astron.; best work on spherical astrolabe.

*Al-Razi, Rhazes, b. at Ray, near Teheran, fl. Ray and Teheran, d. 923/4. Medicine: "greatest mediaeval clinician"; physics (specific gravity), alchemy.

*Al-Battani, Albategnius, b. before 858 at Harran, d. 929. Muslim of Sabian family. Greatest astronomer of his time. Observed and calculated 877 seq., more accurately than Ptolemy. Sine, tangent, cotangent.

Ibn al-Adami, around 900. Astronomical tables.

Ishaq al-Isra'ili, d. ca. 932; Egyptian Jew, fl. and d. in Qairawan, Tunis. Medicine, philosophy.

Ibn Amajur, fl. ca. 885–933; from Farghana, Turkestan. Astron-omer; one of the best Mohammedan observers.

Abu Kamil, Egyptian, fl. prob. early 10th cent. Mathematician, carrying Al-Khwarizmi's algebra farther.

Ibn Serapion, geographer, fl. in Mesopotamia early 10th cent.

Ibn Rusta, fl. ca. 903; Persian. Geographer.

Ibn al-Faqih, fl. ca. 903; Persian, born in Hamadhan. Geog-rapher.

Abu Zaid, fl. ca. 920; Arab, from Siraf. Geographer.

Sinan ibn Thabit, son of Ibn Qurra, d. 943, fl. Bagdad; con-verted Mohammedan. Medic., math., astron.

Ibrahim ibn Sinan, son of last, 908/9–946. Math., astron.; com-mentaries on conics and an almagest; quadrature of parabola.

Al-Hamdani, d. 945/6; Yemenite. Geogr., astron., antiquities of Yemen.

Al-Mas'udi, before 912–ca. 957; b. Bagdad, d. Cairo. Geography, history.

Al-Istakhri, fl. ca. 950; from Persepolis. Geography.

Ibn Hawqal, fl. ca. 943–977. Geography.

Abu Ja'far al-Khazin, d. 961/71; b. Khurasan. Mathematics.

Al-Qabisi, Alcabitius, fl. ca. 955–967. Astrology.

Ahmad al-Tabari, Persian, fl. ca. 970. Medicine.

Al-Tamimi, b. Jerusalem, fl. Egypt ca. 970–980. Materia medica.

*'Abd al-Rahman al-Sufi, 903–986, b. in Ray. Astronomy: *Book of the Fixed Stars.*

Ibn al-A'lam, d. Bagdad 985. Observational astronomy.

Al-Saghani, of Saghan near Merv, fl. Bagdad, d. 990. Math., astron., instrument maker.

Abu-l-Fath, fl. prob. ca. 982; Persian from Ispahan. Mathematics.

Al-Muqaddasi, b. Jerusalem 947/8, fl. in Fars 985/6. Geography.

Abu Mansur Muwaffak, fl. in Herat 968–977. Pharmacology: K_2CO_3, Na_2CO_3, CuO, As_2O_3, Sb, H_4SiO_4, $2CaSO_4H_2O$. He wrote in Persian, not Arabic.

Al-Kuhi, fl. Bagdad ca. 988; from Kuh, Tabaristan. Mathematics, astronomy.

Al-Baladi, fl. Egypt before 990. Medicine.

*'Ali Ibn 'Abbas, d. 994; b. Ahwaz, southwestern Persia, of Zoroastrian family. Medicine.

* Abul-l-Wafa', 940–997/8; b. Quhistan, fl. Bagdad. Among greatest of Mohammedan mathematicians (trigonometry); astronomer; one of the last translators from Greek.

Abu Sahl al-Masihi, 959/60–999/1000; Christian from Jurjan, east of the Caspian. Medicine.

Al-Khujandi, d. ca. 1000; from Transoxiana; fl. at Ray. Astron., math.

Ibn al-Jazzar, Algizar, d. 1009, fl. Qairawan, Tunis. Medicine.

Al-Qumri, fl. prob. ca. 1000; from Qum, Jibal. Medicine.

Abu Nasr, fl. 1007/8. Math. (trigon.).

Ibn al-Husain, soon after al-Khujandi. Math.: "fixed geometry."

**Ibn Yunus, Egyptian, d. Cairo 1009. Astron., trigon.; ca. 990–1007, Hakemite tables.

Masawaih Al-Mardini, Mesuë the Younger; from upper Mesopotamia, fl. Bagdad, d. Egypt 1015. Christian. Pharmacology.

*Al-Karkhi, b. and fl. Bagdad, d. ca. 1019/29. Arithmetic, Diophantine algebra.

*Al-Sijzi, ca. 951–ca. 1024; from Sijistan. Mathematics: geometry.

Kushyar ibn Labban, Persian of Jilan, south of the Caspian, fl. ca. 971–1029. Trigon., astron.

'Ammar, Canamusali, of Mosul, fl. Egypt early 11th cent. Ophthalmology.

*'Ali ibn 'Isa, Jesu Haly, prob. Christian, fl. Bagdad first half 11th century. Ophthalmology.

Al-Nasawi, Persian of Nasa, Khurasan, fl. ca. 1030, wrote in Persian and Arabic. Mathematics, calculation (decimal fractions).

Al-Kathi, fl. Bagdad 1034. Alchemy.

**Ibn Sina, Avicenna, 980–1037, b. near Bokhara. *Philosophy, *medicine (*Qanun*), math., astron., physics.

**Ibn al-Haitham, Alhazen, ca. 965–ca. 1039; b. Basra, fl. Egypt. *Optics, physics, astron., math., medicine.

Ibn al-Taiyib, Abulpharagius Benattibus, d. 1043/4. Nestorian, fl. Bagdad. Medicine.

**Al-Biruni, 973–1048; Persian, b. Khwarizm (Khiva), d. prob. Ghazna. *Geogr., astron., *math., philosophy.

Abu Sa'id 'Ubaid Allah, d. 1058. Medicine.

Ibn Butlan, Elluchasem Elimithar, d. ca. 1063, fl. Bagdad, Antioch. Christian. Medicine: tables of health.

'Ali Ibn Ridwan, ca. 998–1061/7; b. near and fl. in Cairo. Medicine, astrology.

Zarrin Dast, fl. 1087/8. Persian, writing in Persian. Ophthalmology.

Ibn Jazla, Bengesla; Christian, converted to Islam 1074, fl. Bagdad, d. 1100. Medical synopsis.

Sa'id ibn Hibat Allah, d. 1101/2, fl. Bagdad. Medical synopsis, physiology, philosophy.

Al-Ghazzali, 1058–1111, Persian, b. and d. at Tus, Khorasan, fl. at Nishapur, Bagdad. Astronomy, *theology.

**Omar Khayyam, ca. 1038/48–1123/4, the Persian poet, b. Nishapur. Math. (in Arabic), astron., calendar (1074/5), physics.

*Al-Khazini, Greek of Merv, fl. 1115–1122. Physics.

Aftermath

Yaqut, ca. 1179–1229, b. Rum. of Greek parentage. Geography.

Ibn al-Suri, 1178/9–ca. 1242, b. Tyre. Observational nonmedical botany.

Al-Jazari, fl. 1181/2–1205/6 at Amid on Tigris. Applications of mechanics.

*Nasir al-din al-Tusi, 1201–1274; Persian writing Arabic and Persian. Math. (trigon. as an end, not means), astron. (Ilkhan tables, Maragha observatory).

Al-Katibi, d. 1277; Persian writing Arabic. Astron. at Maragha; philos.

Al-Qazwini, 1203/4–1283; Persian writing Arabic. Encyclopaedist.

WESTERN ARABIC SCIENCE

As already noted, western or Spanish Arabic science begins two centuries later than eastern. Its career is also briefer. In 1212 Mohammedan power was broken at Navas de Tolosa, and in the following forty years the southern half of the peninsula, except Granada, passed into Christian hands. The decline was therefore abrupt. The Moroccan Berbers evidently made some effort to carry science on, but their effort is without much significance.

Spanish Mohammedan science was a smaller product than eastern. If we except Abubacer, Averroës, and Maimonides, who were physicians as well as great philosophers, there is no name of the first magnitude, and only a handful of the second. In European culture history western Arabic science looms disproportionately large because of proximity and lateness. Spain was the most important place of transmission of both Arabic science and philosophy to Europe.

The lag of philosophy behind science was more pronounced in Spain than in the East, amounting to nearly two centuries.

The period of glory of Arab rule in Spain was under the eighth and ninth Ommayad caliphs, ʿAbd al-Rahman III and Al-Hakam II, 912–976. It was under them that science got under way in Spain; but in a fairly modest way, with emphasis chiefly on medicine. It flourished in the troubled century that followed; but about half its total productivity occurred after 1090, when political control passed from cultured Arabs to Berbers, the Almoravides and Almohades. Of course, the language of science remained Arabic.

Of nearly 30 names in the list that follows, it will be seen that 2 are of Christians, 5 of Jews. This makes the total proportion of non-Mohammedans about the same as in eastern Islam; but there the Christians exceeded the Jews.

In philosophy we have seen some warrant for affiliating the Spanish Mohammedan growth with the Christian mediaeval one as well as with the eastern Mohammedan. Such a relation hardly holds for science, because when Spanish Arabic science ended in the thirteenth century, there was no real movement of science in Europe for it to integrate with. The Alphonsine tables were a step in this direction, but their follow-up did not occur for two centuries.

WESTERN MOHAMMEDAN SCIENCE—FULL LIST

Rabi' ibn Zaid, fl. 961. Spanish Christian, writing Arabic. Astrology.

Hasdai ibn Shaprut, ca. 915–970/90; Jew, b. Jaen, fl. Cordova. Medicine.

Arib ibn Sa'd, fl. at Cordova before 976, of Christian origin. Medicine, history.

Ibn Juljul, fl. 982 at Cordova. Medicine.

*Maslama ibn Ahmad, "of Madrid," fl. Cordova, d. 1007 or earlier. Math., astron., occultism. "Earliest Hispano-Muslim scientist of importance."

*Abu-l-Qasim, Abulcasis, b. Zahra' near Cordova, fl. Cordova by 976, d. 1013. "Greatest Muslim surgeon."

Ibn al-Samh, 979–1035, fl. Granada. Math., astron.

Ibn al-Saffar, fl. Cordova, d. Denia 1035. Math., astron.

Ibn Abi-l-rijal, Abenragel, Alboacen; b. Spain or North Africa, fl. Tunis ca. 1016–1040. Astrology.

Al-Karmani, ca. 976–1066, b. Cordova, d. Saragossa. Math., surgery.

Ibn al-Wafid, Abenguefit, of Toledo, 997–ca. 1074. Medic., pharmacology.

Ibn Said, 1029/30–1070, b. Almería of Cordovan family, fl. Toledo. History, astronomy. Good observer.

Al-Zarqali, Arzachel, ca. 1029–1087, from Cordova. Astronomy. Best observer of his time.

Al-Bakri, fl. Cordova, d. very old in 1094. Geography.

Abraham bar Hiyya, Savasordo, d. 1136±, fl. Barcelona, Provence. Astron., math. in Hebrew.

*Jabir ibn Aflah, Geber, of Seville, d. 1150±. Astron., trigon.

*Ibn Zuhr, Avenzoar, 1091/4–1161/2, b. Seville. Greatest western Muslim physician.

Al Idrisi, 1099/1100–1166, b. Ceuta, Morocco. Geography.

Ibn Ezra, Avenare, ca. 1089/92–1167. Jew, b. Toledo. Philos., astrology, grammar, translations.

Al-Mazini, 1080/81–1169/70, b. Granada. Geography.

Benjamin of Tudela (in Navarre), fl. ca. 1160–1173. Jew, writing in Hebrew. Geography.

Ibn Tufail, Abubacer, 1100/10–1185/6, b. Guadix. *Philos., medic.

Ibn Rushd, Averroës, 1126–1198, b. Cordova. *Philos., medic.

Maimonides, 1135–1204, b. Cordova. *Philos., medic.

Al-Bitruji, Alpetragius, pupil of Abubacer, b. at Pedroche, near Cordova. Astron.

Abu-l-Abbas al Nabati, 1165/72–1239/40, b. Seville. Botany.

Ibn al-Baitar, b. near Malaga, d. Damascus 1248. Pharmac., botany.

Al-Hasan al-Marrakushi, fl. in Morocco ca. 1229–ca. 1262. Good compilation on trigonometry, gnomonics, astronomical instruments.

Ibn al-Banna, ca. 1256–1321±, b. Marrakush. Calculation.

§18. Occidental Science

The science of modern Europe is international, but examination of its national strands reveals a number of interesting phenomena, so that it will be profitable to defer consideration of the Occidental movement as a whole until the components have been reviewed separately. Some of the outstanding facts of national participation are: sharply defined second growths; an early, loosely configurated, but important growth in and about Germany, followed by a long pause; a very surprising tardiness, on the whole, of French participation; limitation of major Italian activity to the late Renaissance; the British development late as compared with Italy but earlier than the French, and in two main pulses only briefly separated; the Netherlands and Switzerland manifesting growth in concentrated periods, Scandinavia less so; Spain consistently inactive.

In general, the national growths in science coincide with, or follow closely on, periods of national florescence in other branches of civilization, as might be expected. This fact, however, makes it almost impossible to present the nationally viewed data—and they obviously deserve attention in so international a civilization as that of Europe—in the framework of the sequential developments of the larger whole. For instance, on the basis of first appearance of scientific activity in the West, Germany would have to be considered first. But this would mean that recent German science, which does not begin until the nineteenth century, was reviewed before Italian, French, and British, all of which began long before the nineteenth century. If we follow the order of latest or highest culminations, Germany is reached only toward the end of the series, and its early phase, which is initiatory for all Europe, would be presented after the subsequent Italian, French, and British growths. The historians of science have not been keenly conscious of the dilemma, because they were interested in the progress of science rather than in its phenomena of growth in culture, and have therefore dealt with developments in Europe as a whole rather than with national participations. For our purposes, however, component developments are as important as comprising ones. Seeing no way of seriating the nations satisfactorily on a chronological basis, I shall therefore not make the attempt, but will take up the several nations in a roughly geographical order: from Italy via France to England, then to Germany and marginal countries; leaving the integration into the European time-whole for separate consideration later. This very awkwardness of presentation will at any rate help to emphasize the important fact that Occidental civilization, and Occidental science in particular, are, in comparison with most other great civilizational growths, ethnically heterogeneous and therefore both complicated and unique.

It remains to state how European science is to be delimited. Soon after 1200 there appear as two sporadic phenomena Fibonacci and Nemorarius, who may be looked upon as precursors but are too isolated to be included in the great development that was to follow. The growth proper begins about 1450, with Cusanus and the mathematicians who succeeded him; has been continuous since with only one brief and partial lull; and is not yet ended. The cycle therefore is of five hundred years plus as many more as the future may add. On account of the unsatisfactoriness of strictly contemporary evaluations, the formal record is ended, wherever possible, by 1900. This is unfortunate for a movement still in vigorous growth, but better than entering controversial and prophetic fields.

Cusanus is also, according to some, the first figure in modern philosophy. But again he is construed as the last of the mediaevalists. In science, he clearly looks forward; in philosophy, forward and back. This fits with the fact that in science he is followed by successors, in philosophy by a gap. In other words, modern European science began earlier than modern philosophy. This is evident also from the time of appearance of the first very great individuals, indicative of the respective patterns taking on definite configuration: Copernicus precedes Descartes by a century. Since philosophy ended with the nineteenth century and science is still in blast, the growth of modern philosophy is not only briefer, but entirely enclosed, in time, by the associated growth of science. The same holds, incidentally, for space, as expressed by ethnic participation. Scandinavia, Russia, America have produced scientists but no philosophers of the first order.

With this orientation, let us proceed to the separate national examinations.

ITALY

Science raises its head in Italy almost at the same time as music—the end of the first quarter of the sixteenth century, when painting and sculpture were just beginning the descent from the zenith, and literature was entering the last phase of its great period. Pacioli in 1494 had sounded a prelude. Galileo obviously marks the peak. By 1670 the configuration was over. It was thus a late Renaissance growth—in current historical terms, Baroque. A second, separate, late eighteenth-century development was much feebler.

The great period shows four successively overlapping phases; in turn, chiefly of mathematics, of anatomy, of physics, of biology. The third phase is obviously an outgrowth from the first; the fourth, from the second. It is difficult, however, to see much immediate relation between mathematics and anatomy, either in specific objective or in method; nor do the third and fourth phases have much in common beyond association in time and area. The case is therefore evidently one of two parallel and nearly simultaneous growths, one mathematical-physical, the other anatomic-biological in concern; much as in Greece, India, and Islam, mathematics-astronomy and medicine rose and flourished almost concurrently. The Italian medical growth is, however, distinctive in that its eminence lies much less in clinical aspects than in its emphasis on the strictly scientific foundations of the art of medicine.

That mathematics precedes the other sciences within a cycle is a phenomenon that we shall see repeated in several other national growths—though by no means all. An intimate association of mathematics with philosophy is familiar from Greek history, and from Cartesianism. It also holds for Restoration England. Italian philosophy, however, ended in 1274 with the deaths of Aquinas and Bonaventura. The antecedents of the Italian mathematics of the second quarter of the sixteenth century—at least in terms of total configuration—are the German mathematics of the predecessors of Copernicus.

As for anatomy, Italy was famous since the Middle Ages for its teaching of medicine at Salerno and Naples. One of the founders of Italian anatomical science, Eustachius, in fact was born near Naples. No doubt, interest in the subject was flourishing in 1540, when Vesalius was made professor at Padua. But Vesalius was a Belgian; and the event parallels the calling of his countryman Willaert to Venice in 1527, and the origin at that time of the first recognized Italian "school" of musical composition. Also, there are the Belgian painters who visited Italy in the sixteenth century and brought Italian influence home.

The culmination of the whole 1520–1670 cycle ought, because of Galileo's eminence, to coincide with his individual peak of creativeness. Such a peak is by no means as evident in Galileo's life as in Newton's or in the careers of perhaps most scientists. His two most famous books were published when he was an old man of 68 and 74. His astronomical observations are earlier. They produced a strong impression. But they resulted from an application of the Dutch invention of the telescope, and show an inquiring spirit rather than profound originality. Some personally lesser man would certainly have

turned a telescope on Jupiter within a very few years if Galileo
had not done so in 1610. Galileo's most fundamental and distinctive contributions in physics, on gravitation, force, mass,
inertia, and sound, seem to have been made chiefly before 1600.
This would make the course of the main Italian development
symmetrical.

GREAT PERIOD, 1520–1670

Precursor

Pacioli or Paciuolo, ca. 1450–ca. 1515. Tuscany. 1494, *Summa,* of
mathematics.

Mathematics, 1520–1560

*Tartaglia (Fontana), 1506–1559. Brescia. 1537–1556.
*Cardano, 1501–1576. Pavia. 1545, *Ars Magna.*
Ferrari, 1522–1565. Bologna. 1543.

Anatomy, 1540–1570 (1610)

**Vesalius, 1514–1564. Belgian, to Italy 1540. 1542.
*Fallopius, ca. 1523–1562. Near Modena. 1548.
*Eustachius, d. 1574. Near Naples. 1563.
Fabricius, 1537–1619. Acquapendente. 1603.

Physics, astronomy, mathematics, 1560–1650

Della Porta, 1543/5–1615. Naples. 1558/60, *Miracles of Nature;*
1589, *Natural Magic.*
Guidubaldo del Monte, Ubaldo, 1545–1607. Pesaro, 1577 seq.
Cataldi, d. 1626 at Bologna. 1597 (1613), *Mathematics.*
**Galileo, 1564–1642. Pisa. Before 1600 (1583, 1589, 1592), falling
bodies, mass-force relation, sound vibrations, "written 1592,"
published 1634 as *Scienza mechanica;* 1632, *Dialogue;* 1638,
Two New Sciences.
*Cavalieri, 1591/8–1647. Milan. 1632, logarithms in astronomy;
1635, indivisibles.
*Torricelli, 1608–1647. Faenza. 1640–1644, mathematics, barom-
eter

Biology, 1580–1670

Cesalpino, 1519–1603. Arezzo. 1583, *De Plantis;* 1601, *Ars Me-
dica.*
Asellio, 1580–1626. Cremona. 1622, lacteal vessels.
Malpighi, 1628–1694. Near Bologna. 1660–1661, capillary circu-
lation; 1669, silkworm; 1670, plant anatomy.
Scilla, 1639–1700. Messina. 1670, fossils.

The birthplaces are north Italian, with a sprinkling from
the Two Sicilies. Venice, Florence, Rome are not included.

After the Renaissance or Galilean flare of Italian science had burned down, there were ashes for two generations. Then, about 1740, a second and much less productive growth began, to last for something like seventy years. Its greatest personage is without doubt Lagrange, born in Turin in 1736, when this city had for more than four centuries been part of Savoy. He lived a large part of his life in France, and usually is considered a Frenchman. He certainly fits with contemporary compeers in France better than in Italy. The efforts of the other eighteenth-century Italians were diverse in direction, and, while of importance, nevertheless neither specially profound nor systematic. The whole movement, apart from Lagrange, has a slight flavor of dilettantism. Galvani's discovery was a domestic accident; and both his name and Volta's have remained embedded in the terminology of electricity with a little of the same kind of merit in relation to fundamental performance as Amerigo Vespucci's in geography. Avogadro's contribution is significant, but was long overlooked.

A curious fact is the relatively late period in life at which a considerable proportion of Italian scientists made their contributions. This may be the accident of a small series.

Late eighteenth century, 1740–1830, centering 1770–1810
  Lazzaro Moro, b. 1687. Friuli. 1740, deposit and lift of strata.
  Spallanzani, 1729–1799. Scandiano, Modena. Regeneration of parts. 1768–1777.
**Lagrange, 1736–1813. Turin. To France. 1755, calculus of variations; 1776, stability of orbits; 1780, libration of moon; 1788, *Mécanique analytique*.
  Galvani, 1737–1798. Bologna. 1789.
  Volta, 1745–1827. Como. Ca. 1800, battery and pile.
  Piazzi, 1746–1826. Ponte in Valtelline. 1801, discovered first asteroid; 1803, 1814.
 *Avogadro, 1776–1856. Turin. 1811, molecular comp. of gases.
  Nobili, 1784–1834. 1826, animal electricity.

SWITZERLAND

Switzerland is too small a country to produce any wholly independent growth, especially in a subject like science. Its contributions could in fact be mostly divided between those of

France and Germany without great violence to the systematic fit of the facts. Yet they deserve separate consideration also.

An early and modest Swiss development of science, which produced Paracelsus and Gessner, falls soon after the military and political expansion of the confederacy culminating about 1513, and coincides in time with the Zwinglian[5] movement, some attempts at painting, and Erasmus at Basel.

The main Swiss growth falls largely into the eighteenth century. It got under way at least as early as the approximately contemporary French growth, and most of a century earlier than the German one. In fact, the German part of the Swiss growth was over before the modern growth of science in Germany itself began. German-Swiss and French-Swiss scientists made their contributions separately in time, in the main the former preceding. But the two pulses adjoin and are evidently only phases of one bilingual movement.

The eighteenth-century growth came toward the end of a long period of political quiescence and institutional petrifaction, which terminated, before the movement of science had quite spent itself, in the temporary—and only—dissolution of the country's independence under the pressure of French Revolutionary ideas and Napoleonic arms.

It is plain that the Swiss eighteenth-century growth is no mere accident of the clustering of birth years of half a dozen men of science, since it is contemporaneous with a similar growth in literature, education, and social theory, of which the evidences are Bodmer, Gessner, Rousseau, Lavater, Pestalozzi, who died between 1783 and 1827. The two intertwined growths obviously form part of the European eighteenth-century "Enlightenment," to use current historical parlance; and this also proceeded in a period of political quiet and equilibrium ending in violent rupture and reconstitution. What is peculiar to the main Swiss development, however, is that it began after two preceding centuries of national peace, during much of which France and Germany were in activity or turmoil.

---

[5] The more important Calvinistic development at Geneva is obviously also a symptom, although Calvin was a Frenchman of Picardy.

It is also to be noted of Swiss science that after a beginning with mathematics it specialized definitely on natural history instead of experimental science.

Early sixteenth century, 1530–1550

Paracelsus, 1493–1541. Einsiedeln. 1530.

Gesner, Gessner, 1516–1565. Zurich. 1542, catalogue of plants; 1551, *Historia Animalium.*

"Eighteenth century," 1730–1840

*Bernouilli,[6] Jacob, 1654–1705. Basel. Mathematics, 1689–1704.

*Bernouilli, John, brother of Jacob, 1667–1748. Mathematics, 1691–1697.

Bernouilli, Daniel, son of John, 1700–1782. Groningen. 1738 seq., gas molecules, mathematical physics, hydrodynamics.

**Euler, 1707–1783. Basel. 1736 seq.

Haller, 1707/8–1777. Bern. 1743, muscle contractility; 1748, comparative anatomy. Also a noted poet.

Bonnet, 1720–1793. Geneva. 1745, entomology; 1754, botany; 1762–1773, palingenesis.

De Saussure, 1740–1799. Near Geneva. 1779, 1790, geology.

De Candolle, 1778–1841. Geneva. 1813, 1824, natural classification of plants.

Agassiz, 1807–1873. Motier, Neuchâtel. 1833, 1839, 1840, palaeontology, ichthyology, glaciation.

It is evident that the German-Swiss contribution was made mainly before 1760; the French-Swiss, after 1760, persisting well into the nineteenth century. The German-Swiss development thus had no chronological counterpart in Germany, as already mentioned; the French-Swiss one, on the other hand, might well be construed as an integral portion of the eighteenth-nineteenth-century science of France.

It is only fair to add that Swiss science did not become extinguished in 1840, as the more recent names of Forel, b. 1848, and Jung, 1875, evidence. Proportionally to its population, Switzerland still rates high in scientific productivity, in comparison with its neighbors. But it has produced no great constellation in the past hundred years.

---

[6] The family originally was Flemish, but moved to Frankfort, and afterward to Basel.

FRANCE

The history of science in France is simple and definite, compared with that of Britain and Germany.

The beginnings were late, as in so many French postmediaeval activities of culture. The mathematician Vieta, 1540–1603, came a half century after the Italians Cardano and Tartaglia and more than a century after the Germans Peurbach and Regiomontanus. Otherwise there was little until about 1630.

Then suddenly the mathematics of Descartes, Pascal, Fermat, Desargues and several contemporaries flashed brilliantly but briefly. Several of this group were also distinguished philosophers. Their nonmathematical contributions to science were much more limited.

By 1660 this movement was over. There followed a century of relative sterility.

Not until about 1760 did France begin to contribute importantly to general science. The ensuing century produced the work of Laplace, Legendre, Cauchy, Lavoisier, Coulomb, Ampère, Gay-Lussac, Fresnel, Carnot, Lamarck, Cuvier, Geoffroy Saint-Hilaire, and a host of others. The Savoy-Italian Lagrange joined them. It is significant that the work done ranged over all fields of science. It would be invidious to rank any century of science in any country higher than this great French century, either in number of great names or in total importance of contributions.

From about 1830, however, and more clearly by 1850, a decline is manifest. All the men just named were born before 1800. Of those born after that year, Galois, Hermite, Leverrier, Fizeau, Bernard, Pasteur are perhaps the most distinguished; and it seems fair to estimate that they do not quite equal the earlier generation. Pasteur, indeed, has an enormous popular reputation, perhaps because the practical value of his discoveries has made him a convenient symbol of science for the layman. Yet, like Koch, he excelled in well-applied tenacious energy rather than in creative profundity.

After possibly 1860, or certainly 1870, this great growth may be considered as ended. To leave national sensibilities un-ruffled, I remark again that we are discussing relative attain-ments; and I am not arguing against historical continuity. It would be incredible that so saturatedly civilized a people as the French should suddenly and completely cease taking part in the flow of science. But England and Germany with some of the bordering countries have loomed far larger in the new science produced in the past two generations than has France. In the fields of atomic structure, relations of the elements, rays, quantum theory, relativity, genetics, for instance, leader-ship has belonged to these other nations. How the post-1870 science of Britain and Germany is to be rated in comparison with the pre-1870 is difficult to judge, on account of our in-volvement in it. For France there can scarcely be legitimate hesitation. Its major configuration in science essentially fin-ished about 1870.

Pre-Cartesian, to 1630
Belon, 1517–1564. Dept. Sarthe. 1553, 1555, natural history.
La Ramée (Ramus), 1515–1572. Cuth, near Soissons. Mathe-matics.
**Vieta, Viète, 1540–1603. Poitou. 1579–1595, mathematics.
De Caus (Cauls, Caux), 1574/6–1626/30 ? Normandy. Engineer.

Cartesian mathematics, physics, philosophy, 1630–1660
Gassendi, 1592–1655. Champtercier. 1631, first planetary transit.
**Descartes, 1596–1650. Touraine. 1637.
Desargues, 1593-1661/2. Lyons. 1636, 1639.
**Fermat, 1601–1665. Montauban, near Toulouse. 1629 (1642), 1637, 1643.
*Roberval (Personier), 1602–1675. Near Senlis. 1636.
*Pascal, 1623–1662. Clermont-Ferrand, Auvergne. 1640–1663.

Intervening century, chiefly physics, 1660–1760
Picard, 1620–1682. La Flèche. 1669–1671, longitude measure-ment.
La Hire, 1640–1718. Mathematics. 1673–1685.
Varignon, 1654–1722. Caen. 1687, *Nouvelle Mécanique*.
Sauveur, 1653–1716. La Flèche. 1700–1713, acoustics.
Réaumur, 1683–1757. Rochelle. 1722–1742; 1731, thermometer.
Du Fay, Dufay, Du Faye, 1698–1739. Paris. 1732, positive and negative electricity.

Great period, 1750/60–1860/70

Biology

B. de Jussieu, 1699–1777. Lyons. Natural system of plant classification, largely unpublished.

Buffon, 1707–1788. Montbard in Burgundy, 1749 seq., *Histoire naturelle*.

Bonnet, 1720–1793. Swiss, from Geneva. 1745–1773.

*Lamarck, 1744–1829. Picardy. 1801–1822; 1809, *Philosophie zoologique*.

A. de Jussieu, 1747–1836. Lyons. 1778–1789, *Genera Plantarum*.

*Cuvier, 1769–1832. Near Besançon. 1812, *Ossements fossiles;* 1817, *Règne animal*.

*Geoffroy Saint-Hilaire, 1772–1844. Etampes, Seine-et-Oise. 1818–1822, *Philosophie anatomique* (homologies); 1828.

Bichat, 1771–1802. Thoirette, Jura. 1798–1801, comparative anatomy.

*De Candolle, 1778–1841. Swiss, from Geneva. 1824, natural classification of plants.

Bernard, 1813–1878. Dept. Rhône. Internal secretions.

*Pasteur, 1822–1895. Dôle, Jura. 1859, 1863 seq.

Geology

De Saussure, 1740–1799. Swiss, near Geneva. 1779, 1790; glaciation, etc.

Haüy, 1743–1822. Saint-Just. 1801–1822; mineralogy.

Chemistry

Rouelle, 1703–1770. Normandy.

**Lavoisier, 1743–1794. Paris. 1772–1794.

Barthollet, 1748–1822. Savoy; studied at Turin.

Gay-Lussac, 1778–1850. Haut Vienne. 1808/9, gas combination in multiple volumes.

Berthelot, 1827–1907. Paris. Organic chemistry.

Mathematics and astronomy

*D'Alembert, 1717–1783. Paris. 1743–1756.

**Lagrange, 1736–1813. From Turin. 1755–1788.

**Laplace, 1749–1827. Normandy. 1783, long inequality of Jupiter; 1799, *Mécanique céleste*.

*Legendre, 1752–1833. Paris. 1783–1826.

*Cauchy, 1789–1857. Paris. 1815–1820.

*Leverrier, 1811–1877. Saint-Lô. 1845–1875. Discovered Neptune; meteorite and planetary orbits.

Galois, 1811–1832. Near Paris. 1828–1830.

Hermite, 1822–1901. Dieuze, Meurthe. 1855–1882.

Physics

> Coulomb, 1736–1806. Angoulême. 1776, torsion balance; 1779.
> Biot, 1774–1862. Paris. Polarization. 1802–1833.
> Malus, 1775–1812. 1808, polarization by reflection.
> Ampère, 1775–1836. Lyons. 1822, 1826, electrodynamics.
> Arago, 1786–1853. Estagel. Polarization, induction.
> Fresnel, 1788–1827. Broglie. 1815, refraction; polarization.
> Carnot, 1796–1832. Paris. 1824, thermodynamics.
> Fizeau, 1819–1896. Paris. Ca. 1850, velocity of light.
> Foucault, 1819–1868. Paris. 1851–1855, velocity of light.

THE NETHERLANDS

The Netherlands development of science in the sixteenth and seventeenth centuries shows two phases. The peak of the Belgian growth, which we may consider marked by Vesalius and Mercator, falls before the revolt against Spain. The Dutch cycle begins after the revolt. The shift of residence by Stevinus from Bruges to Leyden in 1583 thus is significant. The Dutch climax may be reckoned as attained with Huygens, the contemporary of Spinoza and Rembrandt. By 1700 the Dutch movement was definitely on the decline; soon after, it died in quietude.

As in painting, there was not really a Belgian and a Dutch growth of science, but a single Netherlandish one, with Walloon and Flemish-Dutch ethnic elements contributing together, like French and German in Switzerland. As in the arts, the earlier center of development lay in the southwest, now Belgium. Holland took the lead after the southwestern provinces returned to Spanish allegiance. Whether the sense of freedom and initiative engendered in the seven northeastern provinces by their tenacious revolt was the cause of their sudden spurt in science and art, appears to me more than dubious. It is the type of interpretation which explains by invoking something seemingly simple, but actually psychological and therefore outside the frame of history. It seems sounder to assume merely that the religious and political revolt, the economic upswing, the aesthetic, scientific, and philosophic growths, were functions of one another.

In any event, there was no abrupt migration of science from Belgium to Holland. Soon after about 1580, the focus shifted from the Spanish to the rebellious provinces, but the former continued with declining activity. That they continued less long than in painting with Rubens and Van Dyck is perhaps because great painting was much older and more firmly established in the Netherlands than productive science.

The Belgians in their sixteenth-century primacy tended to lose scientists abroad—Vesalius and Stevinus; the Dutch, from before the turn of the century onward, to attract them—Stevinus, Van Ceulen, Girard. To this phenomenon there are parallels in music, painting, and philosophy.

While the Dutch were the first to produce both telescopes and microscopes, it is in accord with their national character as generally represented that for the most part[7] they left discoveries with the former to Galileo and others, but excelled as microscopists.

Netherlandish science is one of the earliest in Europe—almost coeval with Italian, well ahead of British, nearly a hundred years ahead of French, definitely preceded only by early German, which it survived by well over a century. One may therefore suspect that its roots are intertwined with those of German science, but that it continued to flourish when this fell upon evil days and suffered a check to its growth.

In spite of the essential homogeneity of the growth, it will be convenient to group its manifestations into Belgian and Dutch, so far as possible. It will be noted that there appears to be an arrest of nearly a generation in the middle of the Dutch development, just before Huygens.

BELGIUM

*Gerhard Mercator (Kremer), 1512–1594. Rupelmonde, Flanders. Mathematical geography, 1569.

**Vesalius, 1514–1564. Brussels, to Italy in 1540. Anatomy, 1542.

Ortelius, 1527–1598. Antwerp, probably of German extraction. *Theatrum Orbis Terrarum,* 1570.

*Stevinus, 1548–1620. Bruges, to Holland in 1583. Mathematics, statics, hydrostatics, navigation, 1585–1599.

---

[7] Huygens is the one conspicuous exception.

Van Roomen, 1561–1615. "Dutch," but published in Antwerp. Circle quadrature, etc., 1593–1599.

Van Helmont, 1577–1624. Brussels. Physics, chemistry ("gas"), 1624.

Vernier, 1580–1637. Mathematics (vernier), 1631, Brussels.

Gregorius à St. Vincentio, 1584–1667. Mathematics, 1647, Brussels.

HOLLAND

Ludolph van Ceulen, 1539–1610. Hildesheim, Germany, to Leyden. Circle quadrature ca. 1596.

*Stevinus, 1548–1620. From Belgium, which see.

Van Drebbel, 1572–1634. Alkmaar. Physics, ca. 1621.

Zacharias (Jansen) and Lippershey, spectacle makers in Middelburg, by 1609 were competing in the claim for priority of telescope manufacture.

Snellius, 1581/91–1626. Leyden. Mathematics, 1617–1627.

Girard, ca. 1595–1632. Prob. Saint-Mihiel, Lorraine. Algebra, in French, publ. Amsterdam in 1629.

Vlacq, d. ca. 1635. Logarithms 20,000–90,000, 1628.

**Huygens, 1629–1695. The Hague. Mathematics, pendulum, undulatory theory of light, ether, polarization, 1657–1690.

*Leeuwenhoek, 1632–1723. Delft. Discovered protozoa, 1673, bacteria, 1683.

*Swammerdam, 1637–1680. Amsterdam. Blood corpuscles, 1667; insects, 1685.

Boerhave, 1668–1738. Near Leyden. Chemistry, 1701–1732.

During the past hundred years, Belgium and Holland have again contributed successfully to European science. There is little indication of specific national growths. The revival is rather part of the wave of international European activity, in literature and in art as well as science, which toward 1830 began to spread from the major European countries, and especially France, to the minor and peripheral ones. Belgium appears to show a definite little peak by 1850, Holland a half century later, repeating the greater sequence of three hundred years before. The precedence may be due to greater susceptibility of Belgium to French influence than of Holland to German, coupled with the fact that modern French science ran fifty or so years earlier than German. But this explanation should be held with reserve, because of similarly situated

Switzerland, which we have seen to begin synchronously with France and earlier than Germany, and with its French-written growth of science ending just about when the Belgian began.

MODERN BELGIUM AND HOLLAND

Quetelet, 1796–1874. Ghent. 1845. Probability.

Schwann, 1810–1882. Neuss, near Düsseldorf. To Louvain, 1838, Liège, 1848. Cell theory, 1839.

De Vries, 1848–1935. Haarlem. Mutations, 1903.

Van't Hoff, 1852–1911. Rotterdam. To Berlin, 1896. Physical chemistry, 1874 seq.

GREAT BRITAIN

Apart from some halting pre-Elizabethan precursors, modern science in Britain began around 1600 and has continued since, with a definite dip in the first half of the eighteenth century. There are thus two growths, one from 1600 to 1700, culminating in Newton; the other from 1750 to the present.

The first growth was later than the Italian and earlier than the French one of the time, and about synchronous with the great gap in Germany between Kepler and Leibnitz. It coincides most nearly with the Dutch movement. As it approached its culmination under Newton, it was easily the most important activity of science of its day in Europe, or for that matter in the world.

It came in two pulses, which I have called Jacobean and Restoration. These were briefly but definitely separated in time by the Civil Wars. However, the second phase began to be in evidence before the end of the Protectorate. It was therefore the prolonged unsettlement of the internal war that temporarily suppressed a flow of activity which otherwise would have been continuous. The end of the movement came suddenly about 1700. By grace it might be extended a decade, to include some of Newton's and Halley's later works. On the other hand, an argument in favor of 1690 as the real close, everything subsequent representing merely momentum, would not be altogether unjustified. The ideas and methods characteristic of the growth were essentially all developed during the reign of Charles II. The designation "Restoration" is therefore happier than it might at first seem. The fact that Newton lived to be 85, and that the full text of his *Fluxions* was not published until nine years after his death, in 1736, ought not be warped into a construal of continuity with the post-1750 science of England. The inner or activating climax of the growth was the *annus mirabilis* of 1665, when Newton conceived the principles of gravitation and calculus.

As a time configuration, this movement coincides almost exactly with English music, which also died abruptly about 1700. But music remained dead, whereas science started afresh in a half century.

The interval of slump was real. The single figure of note in the interregnum was a Scotchman. The emphasis of the time was on "politeness"; which, earlier developed in France than in England, had perhaps contributed to the premature ending of the great Descartes-Fermat growth. Dryden and Pepys seem still compatible with a Newton, but not so Pope and Addison, who wanted a compact, finished world governed by well-bred good sense.

That the interregnum was profound though short is indicated also by the miscellaneous origin of the participants when British science began producing again after 1750. The list that is appended includes nine names as probably the most distinguished for activity in the eighteenth century. These nine consist of one German, one American, three Scotchmen, one Frenchman of Scotch ancestry, one Englishman born in Savoy, one Yorkshireman, one Londoner. The home-bred Englishman born between 1665 and 1765 was evidently resistive to science. The difference is marked in contrast with those born after 1765 and coming to activity from 1800 on. Englishmen proper then make up four-fifths of the list, and draw English-Irish and Jews in their train. The Scotch, contributing about the same absolute number as before 1800, have become a small minority: and there are no foreigners at all.

The pre-1700 and post-1750 growths are also shown to be separate by the distinctiveness of their directions and hence their patterns. The glory and strength of Jacobean-Restoration science was its mathematics and physics. The later eighteenth century began with chemistry and with observational astronomy, geology, and zoölogy. In the early nineteenth century the chemistry became quantitative, physics once more flourished with new problems—electricity, thermodynamics,—and new sciences were launched: evolutionary biology, anthropology, biometrics. Only mathematics lagged: Cayley and Sylvester are modest contributors alongside the giants of the Continent.

This second movement which began around 1750, synchronously with one in France, is still in full activity, whereas the French growth substantially ended two generations ago. The modern German development continues active like the British; but it began a half century later. The British growth is therefore considerably the oldest extant. It is nearing its bicentenary, which no other European national growth has yet attained. Needless to say, it is also a great cycle, with Davy, Young, Dalton, Faraday, Lyell, Joule, Kelvin, Darwin, Tyndall, Galton, Maxwell, to name only those whose work was done, or well started, by 1875.

The list ends at this point, 1875, because contemporary and near-contemporary greatness is difficult to judge. I am under the impression that after 1875 there is a sag in the curve, but that this picks up again around 1900. Still, it is the generation before the last which is often definitely superseded and therefore looks dwarfed. The great figures surviving into the present generation sometimes still loom personally large while the innovators of the day are emancipating themselves from them; or again, once superseded, they seem to shrink fast and unduly; but more than two generations back the serenity or oblivion of history begins to prevail.

For related reasons I have refrained from starring and double-starring the most eminent names in the second list. However, there is presumably one, or a cluster of two or three, that outshines the rest, and is critical for the culmination of the growth and hence for its whole configuration. Who is the Galileo, Descartes, Huygens, or Newton of the last two British centuries? The one name the world at large would single out by overwhelming majority is that of Darwin. Also in such matters the verdict of the world, as expressed by history, is to be accepted as presumably near the truth. And the three-quarter century since the *Origin of Species* is an appreciable bit of history. And yet one may hesitate. That Darwin's name is a household word is due to the fact that the nonscientific world of his day and since has wanted to believe in evolutionary progress. This had become a desired but assumed major premise. Darwin appeared to give this premise scientific cachet. Scientifically, however, he produced a series of hypotheses, of which natural selection was the most important, none of which has science yet confirmed or disproved: one may suspect that they are unprovable. Such direct evidence as there is for organic progressive evolution has been brought by palaeontology; and upon the mechanisms to which the Darwinian hypotheses relate, palaeontology is silent. As an expression of the general ideology of his time, and an influence on it, Darwin unquestionably rates full first magnitude. So much must be conceded to the world's verdict. But as for Darwin the scientist, only the perspective of the future can decide whether he is to rank higher or lower than his contemporary, Mendel. The case is somewhat parallel to that of Marx, whose influence on the thought and actions of men has been of the greatest, and whom one would yet deny a place among the great philosophers.

MID-SIXTEENTH-CENTURY PRECURSORS

Recorde, 1510–1558. Pembrokeshire, Wales. 1540/42, arithmetic; 1557, algebra.

Turner, ca. 1520–1568. Northumberland. 1551, *History of Plants*.

Wotton, 1492–1555. Oxford. 1552, *Differences of Animals*.

FIRST GREAT MOVEMENT, 1600–1700

Jacobean phase, 1600–1640

*Gilbert, 1540/44–1603. Colchester, Essex. 1600, *De Magnete*.

Harriot(t), 1560–1621. Oxford. 1610, sunspots, Jupiter's moons; 1631, mathematics, but negative and imaginary roots still rejected.

*Napier, 1550–1617. Edinburgh. 1614, logarithms.

Briggs, 1561–1630/31. Yorkshire. 1624, logarithmic tables.

*Harvey, 1578–1657. Folkestone, Kent. 1628, circulation.

Oughtred, 1573/5–1660. Buckinghamshire. 1631–1648, algebra, trigonometry.

Horrocks, 1619–1641. Toxteth, near Liverpool. 1639, transit of Venus.

Restoration phase, 1655–1700

*Wallis, 1616–1703. Kent. 1656, *Arithmetica Infinitorum;* 1676 (1685), *Treatise on Algebra.*

Neil, 1637–1670. 1657, measure of parabola $y^2 = x^3$.

Wren, 1632–1723. Wiltshire. Architect; 1658, measure of cycloid.

Sydenham, 1624–1689. Dorset. 1660, medicine.

Hooke, 1635–1702/3. Isle of Wight. 1660–1678, microscopy, cellular structure, earth measure.

*Boyle, 1626/7–1691. County Waterford, Ireland. 1661–1666, gas compression, air, hydrostatics, chemistry.

*Barrow, 1630–1677. London. 1665–1670, geometry, optics.

Gregory, ca. 1638–1675. Scot. 1667–1671, mathematics.

Nicholas Mercator, 1620–1687. Holstein, Germany. 1668, *Logarithmotechnia.*

Grew, 1628–1711. Coventry. 1672–1701, microscopic plant anatomy.

Mayow, 1643–1679. Cornwall. 1674, physics.

*Halley, 1656–1742. London. 1676–1705, astronomy.

Ray, 1628–1705, Essex; and Willughby, 1635–1672, Warwickshire. 1677 seq., plant structure, animal classification.

**Newton, 1642–1727. Lincolnshire. 1687, *Principia.* Newton's fundamental ideas came to him in 1665, but were elaborated much later. The *Methodus Fluxionum* was composed, or begun, in 1671, but published in full only in 1736, with partial presentations in 1693, 1704, and 1711. He discovered the dispersal of light in 1671, published his *Optics* in 1704. Since his results became partly known to colleagues by word of mouth or letters, the formal dates of his published works are misleading.

Woodward, 1661/5–1727/8. Derbyshire. 1695, minerals and fossils.

INTERVAL, 1700–1750

De Moivre, 1667–1754. Frenchman, to England. 1707, binomial theorem; 1718, doctrine of chances.

Maclaurin, 1698–1746. Argyllshire, Scotland. 1719/20, 1742, mathematics.

SECOND GREAT MOVEMENT, FROM 1750 ONWARD

Eighteenth-century chemists

Black, 1728–1799. Bordeaux, of Scotch and Irish ancestry. 1754–1774, CO_2, latent heat.

Cavendish, 1731–1810. Nice. 1766, H; 1784, H_2O.

Rutherford, 1749–1819. Edinburgh. 1772, N.

Priestley, 1733–1804. Yorkshire. 1772, N_2O_2; 1774, O.

Later eighteenth century, various

Hutton, 1726–1797. Edinburgh. 1788 (1795), *Theory of the Earth*.

Hunter, 1728–1793. Lanarkshire, Scotland. Comparative anatomy.

Maskelyne, 1732–1811. London. 1774, density of the earth.

Herschel, 1738–1822. Hanover, Germany. 1781, Uranus; star catalogue.

Rumford (Thompson), 1753–1814. Massachusetts. 1798, friction heat.

Nineteenth century

Davy, 1778–1819/20. Cornwall. 1799–1815, physics.

Young, 1773–1829. Somersetshire. 1801, interference; 1817, undulatory theory.

Wollaston, 1766–1828. Norfolk. 1802, dark lines of spectrum.

Dalton, 1766/7–1844. Cumberland. 1808, atomic theory, multiple proportions.

Smith, 1769–1839. Oxfordshire. 1815, geological map of England.

Faraday, 1791–1867. Near London. 1821–1855, electromagnetism, electrolysis.

Lyell, 1797–1875. Kinnordy, Scotland. 1830, *Principles of Geology*.

Owen, 1804–1892. Lancaster. 1833–1866, comparative anatomy.

Sylvester, 1814–1897. London; Jew. Mathematics.

Cayley, 1821–1895. Richmond, Surrey. Mathematics.

Joule, 1818–1889. Near Manchester. 1843, mechanical equivalent of heat; 1847, velocity of H particles.

Hooker, 1817–1911. Suffolk. 1844–1893, systematic botany.

Kelvin (W. Thomson), 1824–1907. Belfast, of Scotch father. 1852, dissipation of energy.

Wallace, 1822–1913. Monmouthshire. 1853–1889, zoölogy.

Huxley, 1825–1894. Middlesex. 1857–1877.

Darwin, 1809–1882. Shrewsbury. 1859, *Origin of Species*.

Lister, 1827–1912. Essex. 1860–1867, antisepsis.

Tylor, 1832–1917. Near London. 1861–1881, anthropology.

Huggins, 1824–1910. London. 1862, stellar spectroscopy.
Tyndall, 1820–1893. County Carlow, Ireland. 1863–1873.
Galton, 1822–1911. Duddeston, near Birmingham. 1864–1889, biometrics, heredity.
Maxwell, 1831–1879. Edinburgh. 1871, *Theory of Heat;* 1873, *Electricity and Magnetism.*
Crookes, 1832–1919. Lóndon. 1875–1879, radiation, gases.

SCOTLAND

In the preceding list and discussion, Scotland has been included with England. I now present the Scottish names separately. They make a fairly steady trickle for three centuries, with a concentration of births between 1725 and 1750, that is, of activity in the later eighteenth century. This is the period of Scotch greatness in other departments of culture: philosophy and literature.

If the sample is sufficiently representative, Edinburgh loomed far larger in Scotland, as a birthplace for intellectual talent, than London in England, at all times.

SCOTTISH EXTRACT FROM BRITISH LIST

Napier, 1550–1617. Edinburgh.
Gregory, ca. 1638–1675.
Maclaurin, 1698–1746. Argyllshire.
Hutton, 1726–1797. Edinburgh.
Black, 1728–1792/9. (Bordeaux, of Scotch and Irish ancestry.)
Hunter, 1728–1793. Lanarkshire.
Rutherford, 1749–1819. Edinburgh.
Lyell, 1797–1875. Kinnordy.
Kelvin, 1824–1907. Belfast, of Scotch father.
Maxwell, 1831–1879. Edinburgh.

GERMANY

The history of German science is unusual. It begins earlier than that of any other European country; shows a second pulse contemporary with the beginnings in Italy and Belgium; then enters on a quarter millennium which is of low level but punctuated by a great name or so; and finally starts on its modern florescence a half century later than Britain and France. The configurations thus are aberrant, and in part blurred.

About the middle of the fifteenth century, nearly five hundred years ago, three German mathematicians flourished close together in time. Cusanus, a west German, also one of the first postmediaeval philosophers, recognized, in effect, negative powers as values, marking a milestone in European algebraic conception. Peurbach and Regiomontanus, from the southeast and center,[8] contributed to the tool-science of trigonometry. This is no great absolute showing; but it stands quite alone in the Europe of its day. These three Germans came a century and a half after Fibonacci and Nemorarius, who typify mediaeval mathematics. They preceded Pacioli by a quarter century, and Pacioli is a precursor rather than a member of Italian Baroque science.

The next phenomenon is mid-sixteenth century. From about 1540 to 1560 there flourished the botanist Fuchs, the mathematicians Stifel and Rhaeticus, the metallurgist Agricola—giving a fair sample of science as a whole. The movement was about synchronous with the pre-Galilean phase of Italian anatomy and mathematics. Half the names are those of Saxons, countrymen of Luther.

Copernicus, the glory of Poland, fits into this second German growth, and nowhere else. He was born of a German mother, in the German city of Thorn, in the lifetime of Regiomontanus, whose tables he used in his work. His *De Revolutionibus* was published by Germans in adjacent Germany at a time of scientific activity in Germany. As a historical Slavo-German, he has a setting, like almost all other great men; as a product of pure Polish science, he is a gem without a matrix. It is true that his life falls in a period of flowering of Polish nationality. But this flowering produced no other scientist, beyond his teacher Brudzewski, 1445–1497. As a Pole he is "unexplained," that is, essentially unassociated; much as would be Leonardo born in the France of his day, or Beethoven in England. I realize that his culture-historical interpretation as German, even with explicit admission of his literal nationality, may be construed as an attempt to rob Poland of her

[8] From Königsberg in Franconia, not Prussia.

one ewe lamb." But in terms of cultural configuration I see no alternative: he fits German science, and that only.[10]

To guard against misunderstanding, I state explicitly that I do not regard Copernicus as fitting well into the German development of 1540 to 1560. But he fits better there than anywhere else.

In any event, with reference both to the fifteenth- and the sixteenth-century development, we are evidently dealing with a growth which is considerably of the German marches. Frontier phenomena are recognized in the history of nationalistic vigor. But they do seem rare, and unexpectable, in the history of so definitely civilized and organized an activity as science.[11] Possibly the explanation lies partly in the fact that within Occidental civilization Germany has always been somewhat of a frontier country, as she has certainly been a decentralized one.

German science of the Late Mediaeval–Renaissance period is evidently connected with a contemporary German technological development, of which book printing is the most famous exemplification. From the eleventh or twelfth century on, Italy had definitely led Europe in the number of inventions, technical adaptations or acceptances, refinements, and new economic devices. The list is a long one: universities, Arabic numerals, the word "million," spectacles, table forks, chimney hearths, canal locks, silk reels, perhaps paper manufacture, banks, insurance, double-entry bookkeeping, pawnbroking, paper money. About 1500, the Italian productivity ended; it had been unaccompanied by strictly scientific productivity.[12] Meanwhile, Germany had entered on a similar career. The beginnings of this perhaps go back to twelfth-century mining

[9] Especially in view of my own patronymic; which, however, seems to be a Germanization of a Slavic, probably Wend, original. I have been unable to consult Prowe's full work on Copernicus, so cannot say whether it is objective or colored by Germanophile bias. Apparently resented in Slavic quarters, it is accepted as final in German encyclopaedia biographies, ignored in the French, mentioned without comment in English ones.

[10] As a man of genius *per se*, with no reference to science, Copernicus in his time is a true son of Poland, which was then in florescence; and I have so credited him in the section on that country.

[11] Though Greek science began on the frontiers of the Greek world.

[12] But compare Leonardo da Vinci's designs, sketches, and strivings.

developments in the Harz and Erzgebirge. A wider mechanical enterprise is visible around 1400, and continues until 1550 or a trifle later. The innovations include zinc, perhaps cast iron, iron stoves, printing, etching, domestic clocks and watches with steel springs, treadle on spinning wheel, mine railways, perhaps bullion extraction with amalgam,[13] graphite pencil. From 1450 Germany was abreast of Italy, from 1500 to 1550 ahead of any European country in inventing.[14] Then the movement suddenly came to an end. The time coincidence with the science growth is exact, and connection indubitable.[15]

After the early mathematicians and the Copernicus-Stifel-Agricola constellation, follow more than two centuries—about 240 years, to be exact—which contain two names of very high eminence, but rather few of even second magnitude and little if any crystallization or trend. Kepler, who discovered his laws in 1609–1619, and Leibnitz, calculus in 1684, stand remarkably isolated. Bürgi the Swiss, who invented logarithms as early as Napier but was too little impressed by his discovery to publish it, Guericke the burgomaster with his horse-pulled hemispheres, Stahl of phlogiston, Werner the controversial Neptunist, Goethe the poet, make a medley, thin, and disorderly system for the two great peaks to arise from. Herschel, German by birth, went to England at 21, where he fits into a company. Primarily an observer, he might never have been a great astronomer in Germany, with no great telescope to operate. Like him, Van Ceulen, Nicolas Mercator, Glauber, Sylvius, and Wolff, in the two preceding centuries, went abroad—often to Holland—for the encouragement they evidently did not find at home.

As for Leibnitz, we have already found him the most refractory of philosophers to place: and he fits German science no better than German philosophy of his period. Kepler might be joined with Copernicus and Tycho to form a century's triad

---

[13] Usually attributed to Spaniards in the New World in 1557.

[14] As England began to forge ahead about 1600 or soon after.

[15] Two qualities characterize this German technological growth: many of its inventions, including printing, have to do with metals; none of them relate to commerce or finance. The interest was mechanical and artisan, not capitalistic.

of northeast European astronomers anomalous for their national isolation; but to designate them outright as an aberrant group with its own special laws of perturbation would be only a metaphor.

Science was certainly not dead in Germany from 1560 to 1800, but it clearly was languishing. Kepler and Leibnitz were evidently men who were able to rise to full greatness over an environment which long paralyzed all others. My fundamental thesis is that history shows that this does not ordinarily happen; that cultural greatness, as distinct from individual or psychological superiority, is a function almost wholly of cultural configuration. But with these two men, as in a measure with Copernicus and Tycho, the hypothesis breaks down. There is no use equivocating about it.

All that I can claim is that these four exceptions form a large fraction of the total number of prominent exceptions in history—Goya is one of the few others—and that they occur in or just beyond the borders of Germany within a span of two hundred years in the abstract domains of mathematics-astronomy and philosophy. This localization does form the exceptions into a quasi constellation of their own. In other words, there was one time and place in the world when normal configurations failed to form.

What influences brought about this unique but evidently real suspension of the usual configuration formation? One can rule out the Thirty Years' War: three of the four aberrant figures preceded it. Rather is this war, so supremely and devastatingly senseless for its period, to be construed as a product of the anarchy of German culture, of its lack of structure and configuration at the time. This much is clear: during the first half of the sixteenth century, Germany produced several nearly synchronous brief constellations: in science, painting, humanism, the Reformation. About the time of the Peace of Augsburg, 1555, these all ended, and a long period began in which Germany developed to fruition no pattern in any department of civilization. Music was first to emerge from the paralysis; then literature and philosophy; finally, science, painting, and politics, in that order; and all the earlier of these activities were carried to great heights.

To return to our science in the interregnum, the list that fol-. lows does reveal one hint of organization: a break in births of three-quarters of a century, from 1660 to 1733. Before 1660, the minor births trickle along at an average 15-year interval, with no interval greater than 30 years. After the 73-year gap, they come considerably thicker. Wolff, Herschel, Werner, Chladni are therefore probably to be looked upon as precursors of the great group that was soon to follow them. It is probably significant that two of them still went abroad.

About 1800 began the growth of German science which still continues. Its most striking feature, because we are likely to forget it, is its lateness. France, Switzerland, England, Scotland, Sweden all got their modern science into active flow a half century earlier. Even within Germany, philosophy, music, and literature were at full apogee when Gauss in 1799 sounded the reawakening of German science—as so often, with mathematics.

In importance, this growth obviously ranks with the modern French and British ones. It would be difficult to award preëminence among the three. Beginning latest, the German growth might be expected to continue longest; perhaps to be in the lead today. Most neutrals evidently think so. As for France, we have seen that its high configuration definitely ended about two generations ago. As between Britain and Germany, I doubt whether a discrimination for so near a period as that since 1875 is possible without more controversy than proof.[16]

One phenomenon seems clear in the more modern growths of science: they do not manifest the sharp focus of a single outstanding personality, like the developments that culminated in Copernicus, Galileo, Descartes, Huygens, Newton. As to the several primacies of these earlier men, there would scarcely be dispute. Yet if one were to name Lavoisier as the one great figure of modern French science, there would certainly be pro-

[16] But see the Nobel Prize evidence below, p. 166, note 17.

test. Darwin might be singled out for England because his work carried the widest influence outside of science. Apart from what he touched off in this respect, who would venture to say that Darwin's strictly scientific contribution was greater than that of Dalton, Faraday, or half a dozen other British contemporaries? And for Germany it would be more difficult still to select a center for the constellation since 1800. There is no one outstanding name that is familiar on the street and in the household; unless it is that of Einstein—still living and therefore difficult to appraise against the measure of the figures of the past.

Perhaps it is shortness of perspective that interferes with our judgment here. But the world has not hesitated to pass practically unanimous judgments with respect to Kant in philosophy and Beethoven in music within only a slightly longer span. It seems therefore that it is a characteristic of modern science as compared with that before 1750—and with most other highly specialized activities of culture—to be relatively deficient in sharp culmination of salient personality.

Mid-Fifteenth-Century Mathematics

*Cusanus, 1401–1464. Kues near Trier. Algebra. Also of some importance as a philosopher.

*Peurbach, 1423–1461. Linz. Edited Ptolemy's *Almagest* with tables of natural sines.

*Regiomontanus, 1436–1476. Königsberg, Franconia. 1464, *De Triangulis;* 1475, tables.

Mid-Sixteenth-Century Development

**Copernicus, 1473–1543. Thorn, Poland; German mother; Czech grandfather; Polish teacher in astronomy. 1529, *Commentariolus;* 1543, *De Revolutionibus.*

*Stifel, 1486/7–1567. Esslingen, Saxony. 1544/9, *Arithmetica Integra:* negative coefficients; anticipation of four-dimensional space.

*Agricola, 1494–1555. Glachau, Saxony. 1550 (1556), *De Re Metallica.*

Fuchs, 1501–1565. Wendingen, Bavaria. 1542, *Historia Stirpium.*

Rhaeticus, 1514–1576. Feldkirch, Vorarlberg. 1540 seq., mathematics.

SCATTERING, 1560–1800

Van Ceulen, 1540–1610. Hildesheim; to Holland. 1596, circle quadrature.

Bürgi, 1552–1632. Lichtensteig, Switzerland; to Cassel. (1620, logar. tables.) Bürgi appears to have evolved logarithms as early as Napier, but failed to publish.

Pitiscus, d. 1613. Silesia. 1600–1613, mathematics.

**Kepler, 1571–1630. Weil, Württemberg. 1609, laws 1, 2; 1619, law 3; 1628, Rudolphine tables.

Von Guericke, 1602–1686. Magdeburg. Ca. 1650, air pump; 1672, frictional electricity.

Glauber, 1604–1668. Karlstadt; to Amsterdam. Iatrochemist.

Sylvius, 1614–1672. Hanau; to Leyden. Chemistry.

Nic. Mercator, 1620–1687. Holstein; to England. 1668, *Logarithmotechnia*.

Becher, 1625–1682. Speyer. 1669, chemistry of combustion.

**Leibnitz, 1646–1716. Leipzig. 1684, differential calculus.

Stahl, 1660–1734. Anspach. 1702 seq., phlogiston.

(A long gap occurs here in births.)

Wolff, 1733–1794. Berlin; 1766 to St. Petersburg. Anatomy, physiology.

Herschel, 1738–1822. Hanover; 1759 to England. Astronomy.

Goethe, 1749–1832. Frankfurt. 1790, *Metam. der Pflanzen*.

Werner, 1750–1817. Ober-Lausitz. 1774 seq., Neptunist geology.

Chladni, 1756–1827. Wittenberg. 1787 seq., acoustics.

PERIOD BEGINNING ABOUT 1800†

Mathematics and astronomy

Gauss, 1777–1855. Brunswick. 1799 seq.; pure mathematics, mostly before 1820.

Bessel, 1784–1846. Minden. 1818–1837; first stellar parallax.

Schwabe, 1789–1875. Dessau. 1837 (1843), sunspot cycle.

Encke, 1791–1865. Hamburg. 1819 seq., comet calculation, planet masses.

Jacobi, 1804–1851. Potsdam. 1829–1846, elliptic functions.

Weierstrass, 1815–1897. Ostenfelde, Westphalia. Mathematics.

Riemann, 1826–1866. Near Dannenberg, Hanover. 1854, non-Euclidean system.

Physics and chemistry

Seebeck, 1770–1831. Reval, Esthonia. To Nürnberg, 1812, then to Berlin, 1821, thermoelectricity.

---

† Incomplete: the list is carried up to about 1875. No stars are assigned.

Fraunhofer, 1787–1826. Straubing, Bavaria. 1814/15, 576 dark lines.

Wöhler, 1800–1882. Near Frankfurt. 1828, synthetic urea.

Liebig, 1803–1873. Darmstadt. 1832–1853.

Bunsen, 1811–1899. Göttingen. 1841–1861. Spectrum analysis, etc.

Mayer, 1814–1878. Heilbronn, Württemberg. 1842, conservation of energy.

Helmholtz, 1821–1894. Potsdam. 1847–1863.

Clausius, 1822–1888. Köslin. 1850, thermodynamics; molecular theory.

Kirchhoff, 1824–1887. Königsberg. 1859–1860.

Kekulé, 1829–1896. Darmstadt. 1861, 1867.

Biology

Humboldt, 1769–1859. Berlin. 1807–1827, 1845–1858.

Treviranus, 1776–1837. Bremen. 1802–1822.

(Von Baer, 1792–1876. Esthonian "Russian," in Russia. 1828–1837.)

Weber, 1795–1878. Wittenberg. 1817–1851, sensory physiology.

Müller, 1801–1858. Coblentz. 1826–1840, physiology.

Fechner, 1801–1887. Gross-Särchen. 1831–1873, psychophysics.

Schleiden, 1804–1881. Hamburg. 1842, 1846, cell theory, botany.

Von Mohl, 1805–1872. Stuttgart. 1853, protoplasm.

Schwann, 1810–1882. Neuss near Düsseldorf. 1839, cell theory. 1838 to Louvain, 1848 to Liège.

Dubois-Reymond, 1818–1896. Berlin. 1846–1884. Physiology.

Virchow, 1821–1902. Köslin, Pomerania. 1858 seq., pathology.

Mendel, 1822–1884. Heinzendorf, Austrian Silesia. 1865.

Haeckel, 1834–1919. Potsdam. 1862 seq.

Wundt, 1832–1920. Neckarau. 1862 seq., psychology.

Weismann, 1834–1914. Frankfurt. 1864–1896.

Kühne, 1837–1900. Hamburg. 1878, enzymes.

Mach, 1838–1916. Turas, Moravia. 1863–1885, psychophysics, physics.

MARGINAL NATIONS

In general, the peripheral nationalities did not enter seriously into Occidental science until after 1800 to 1830. Much as in music and painting, a desire to participate in what the leaders of western Europe were doing began to stir in that generation, and bore various fruit in the century after. Like music and painting, science has therefore been rather widely international during the past hundred years, as compared with the preceding centuries during which creative productivity tended to be confined to two or three or four peoples at any given time.

The only exception to the rule that European nationalities other than those so far considered did not contribute to science before 1800 is provided by Scandinavia, where Sweden shows a definite and Denmark a doubtful national florescence.

Denmark.—The most famous Danish scientist is Tycho, successor of Copernicus and predecessor of Kepler, and like them he is difficult to fit into a configuration. His one countryman-contemporary of note is the mathematician and physician Finck; which does not make much of a constellation. Moreover, Tycho was born in the Swedish province of Scania, then Danish in its allegiance. How far it was Danish in culture, I am not in a position to say: its speech presumably was Swedish.

Nearly a century later, Roemer the physicist and Steno the biologist form another pair finding mention in the histories of science.

Finally, there is a trickle of important names since 1800—probably about as many as Denmark could expect on a basis of its proportionate population in Europe.

Norway.—Poorer, less populous, more remote, Norway has mostly depended on Denmark, culturally as well as politically, for nearly a thousand years. Her most distinguished man of science is probably the mathematician Abel, 1802–1829. He brackets with the Dane Oersted, 1777–1851, who flourished in physics about 1820.

Sweden.—The fundamental importance of Linnaeus in descriptive biology leads to expectability of a contemporary constellation in Swedish science. It exists: Celsius, Bergmann, Scheele, Retzius, notable contributors to physics, chemistry, and botany, were born between 1701 and 1742; Linnaeus, in 1707. Another famous name can, in fact, be added: Swedenborg, born 1688, who, until his break into mysticism at the age of 57, was a competent mineralogist.

This configuration is confirmed by the nearly contemporary culmination of Swedish literature. This was in growth while the science culminated, and reached its peak a generation or two after. On the other hand, the period of Swedish politico-military success ended shortly before the science growth got under way: collapse at Poltava, 1709, *Systema Naturae,* 1735.

During the nineteenth century Sweden contributed to science much like the other small north European nations—Danes, Norwegians, Scotch, Belgians, Dutch, Swiss: fairly steadily, with definite frequency of eminence considering population size, but without burst or peak.

Poland.—Besides Copernicus, the recently deceased Mme. Curie provides the one famous name in Polish science. We have already linked Copernicus with the largely east German configuration of the sixteenth century. Nationalistically he is intelligible enough as a Pole. He was born and educated under Casimir IV, 1447–1492, who gave Poland access to the Baltic and under whom Ostoróg the humanist flourished and the first printing press was set up at Cracow in 1474. He worked out his system in the reign of Sigismund I, 1506–1548, the "first humanist king," who married a Sforza and built himself a Renaissance palace. Poland was at her cultural height: her literature culminated under Kochanowski, 1530–1584. It is only that she was too far from the centers of Western civilization to participate in science as a nation. Copernicus as a man of genius is an expectable and fitting product of his country. The specific astronomical bent of his genius, however, expressed itself as part of a growth which happened to be otherwise German. His binational parentage is thus historically significant rather than a mere biographic accident.

Russia.—Two pulses appear in Russian science. The first is signalized particularly by two Baltic Germans from Esthonia, Seebeck and Von Baer, and by a Russian mathematician, Lobachevsky. The birth dates are 1770 to 1793; the period of productivity, about 1820–1840. The second pulse followed some thirty years later, and is represented by Mendeleyev, Mechnikov, and Pavlov, born between 1834 and 1849. This is a respectable showing for a country so late in westernizing. The two pulses come unusually close together. Possibly the break between them is the result of accident of distribution in a small series: a full history of Russian science might fill the gap. However, if the configuration was really single, it is not quite usual either: a group of the importance of the Russian one, and productive for a century, might be expected to contain one overtowering personality. At least, such was the rule in western Europe up to the eighteenth century, to which nineteenth-century Russia might expectably conform, in view of its general retardation.

Other Slavs.—The Czechs and southern Slavs have had no scientific growths of note identified with their nationalities. Czech-Moravian science, like Hungarian and Austrian proper, was essentially drained off into German until World War I. It was usually written in German.

Hungary.—The Magyars contributed to the foundation of non-Euclidean geometry with Bolyai in 1832.

Spain and Portugal.—Spain has never had a distinctive development of science since Arab-Moorish days, but of course for different reasons from those affecting the Slavs. In fact, no clear reason appears in the external relations of the country or in the general European situation. The Spanish national culmination lasted until about 1650–1680 in several activities, such as literature and painting, by which time the other Western countries had each experienced a scientific growth or had one well under way. The causes must therefore be internal, and probably related to those which inhibited the development of a Spanish philosophy since Scholasticism.

It is one of the ironies of history that the one Spanish scientist generally mentioned in the handbooks, the anatomist Servetus, was burned at the stake with the aid of Calvin.

Italy and the Netherlands.—We have already seen that both Belgium and Holland reëntered the field of science with tolerable distinction during the nineteenth century, evidently as part of the wave then spreading over Europe. The secondary Italian growth, on the other hand, ended about then, and falls mainly into the second half of the eighteenth century. It is therefore contemporary with, and probably related to, the Swiss, French, and British developments that began around

1750. It is rather remarkable how little science of the first importance Italy has produced in the last hundred years

United States.—It is also curious how little science of highest quality America has produced, not only up to 1875, but, if we continue the record, to the present day. There is no country in which more time is devoted to scientific pursuits, or a fraction of the money. There is none in which science in the abstract rates higher with the common man. In technological invention America has long claimed preëminence for herself, and even if we discount all claims heavily in a subject as controversial and difficult to judge as this, there is no doubt that the American record in practical inventiveness is extremely high. In the private opinion of American scientists, when they are discussing informally among themselves, or going abroad to study, and not when they are making a public address in which a measure of national patriotism is usually in order, they tend to cede general preëminence to Germany, allow precedence in some fields to England, in a few perhaps to Russia or Scandinavia, in none, probably, to France, as compared with their own country.[17] On the whole this ranking would probably be fairly well accepted in Europe, unless Europeans in general are even more polite to us than they appear to be.

---

[17] The Nobel prizes confirm this judgment. In Physics, Chemistry, and Physiology-Medicine, 1901–1937 (*World Almanac,* 1938), the number of nationals receiving awards during 1901–1918, 1919–1937, and 1901–1937 respectively was:

Germany	18	20	38	Sweden	3	3	6
Great Britain	8	14	22	Denmark	1	3	4
United States	3	11	14	Switzerland	2	2	4
France	9	4	13	Seven others	5	5	10
Holland	5	3	8		—	—	—
					55	65	120

Germany, here, includes five Austrians. The assignment of nationality is evidently by citizenship or residence, not by birth: the Curies are counted as French, Carrel as American, etc. If prizes rather than persons are summated (there sometimes are double and even triple awards in one year in one field), the German lead is more accentuated: Germany, 33.3; Britain, 16; U. S., 10.5; France, 11; Holland, 6.2; Sweden, 5.5; Denmark, 4; Switzerland, 3.5; others, 7; total, 97.

As between pre-1918 and post-1918, the most notable changes are the American rise from 3 to 11, the French decline from 9 to 4; these accord with what is said in the text concerning the two countries. The period difference between Britain, 8–14, and Germany, 18–20 (without Austrians, 17–16), is probably more indicative of temporary postwar conditions in a victorious and in a beaten country than of any long-range overhauling of German science by British.

However, with all this standing achieved by 1935, America as yet seems to have produced no men of really first rank, no general initiative and directive leadership, acknowledged as such in Europe. A few exceptions rise to mind, as in regard to genes and cosmic rays.[18] But these are in fields which are highly specialized or which lend themselves with particular effectiveness to public exploitation since science has become news in the public press. In any event, they are of most recent date, and therefore particularly difficult to evaluate against events in historical perspective.

A fair judgment perhaps would be that America seems on the verge of a period in which she will bid for leadership in science, possibly seize it. However, there are bids that fail; and predictions are outside the scope of this book. We can justifiably say that the tide of important scientific production in America is rising, and that it has risen high; and we may, if we wish, hope that it will soon come into full flood. But the fact remains that certainly not up to 1875, nor even 1900, perhaps not up to the present moment, has America produced any scientific geniuses of fundamental creative significance equal to those of several European nationalities.

DENMARK

Tycho Brahe, 1545/6–1601. Knudsthorp in Scania, Sweden, then Danish. 1576, Uraniborg observatory.

Finck, 1561–1656. South Jutland. 1583, mathematics.

Steno (Stensen), 1638–1687. Copenhagen. 1657, salivary duct; 1669, fossils.

Roemer, 1644–1710. Aarhuus. 1676, velocity of light.

Oersted, 1777–1851. Rudkjöping, Langeland. 1820, magnetic current deflection.

Bohr, 1885. 1913, atomic structure.

NORWAY

Abel, 1802–1829. Findoe. Theory of elliptic functions.

[18] And J. Willard Gibbs, 1839–1903, is occasionally singled out. But it may be suspected that European estimates of him are like the occasional European admirations of Walt Whitman or Jack London—based tacitly on a special standard for non-Europeans.

SWEDEN

Rüdbeck, 1630–1702. Westerås. 1649 (1653), lymphatics.

Olaus Celsius, 1670–1756. Upsala. 1745, *Hierobotanicon*. Flora of Upsala.

Swedenborg, 1688–1772. Stockholm. Mathematics, mining, anatomy to 1745, then mysticism.

Anders Celsius, 1701–1744. Upsala. Physics, astronomy. 1742, centigrade thermometer.

Linnaeus, 1707–1778. Småland. 1735 (–1768), *Systema Naturae;* 1753, *Species Plantarum.*

Bergmann, 1735–1784. West Gothland. 1761, CO_2, solubility, weight, "elective affinities."

Scheele, 1742–1786. Stralsund (then Swedish). To Gothenburg and Upsala. 1775, O; also Cl, Mn, Ba, NH_3, HCl, HF.

Anders Retzius, 1742–1821. Christianstadt. 1779–1791, botany.

Berzelius, 1779–1848. Linköping. Chemist; 1818, blowpipe.

Arrhenius, 1859–1927. Wijk. 1884–1908, astrophysics.

POLAND

Copernicus, 1473–1543. Torun. 1529, *Commentariolus;* 1543, *De Revolutionibus.*

Mme. Curie, 1867–1934. Warsaw. 1898, polonium, radium.

RUSSIA

Wolff, 1733–1794. German, to St. Petersburg, 1766. Anatomy, physiology.

Seebeck, 1770–1831. Reval, Esthonia; to Germany. 1821, physics.

Von Baer, 1792–1876. Esthonia. 1828–1837, embryology, human ovum.

Lobachevsky, 1793–1856. Nizhni-Novgorod. 1829, the first non-Euclidean geometry.[19]

Mendeleyev, 1834–1907. Tobolsk, Siberia. 1869, periodic law.

Mechnikov, 1845–1916. Kharkov. 1883 seq., physiology.

Pavlov, 1849. Ryazan. 1897 seq., physiology.

There might be added the mathematicians Zhukovsky, b. 1847; Kovalevskaya, 1850; Lyapunov, 1857.

SPAIN

Servetus, 1509–1553. Tudela or Villanova. Anatomy.

---

[19] This was about contemporary with, and independent of, the Hungarian non-Euclidean geometry of the Bolyais, probably originated by F. Bolyai, 1775–1856, executed by his son John, 1802–1860, published 1832–1833.

§19. The General European Course

When we summate the several national European developments, a somewhat new picture results.

First of all, obviously, the total course is much longer than
any one national growth. The earliest positive productions
can be put around 1450. Activity is still in intense flux today.
It would be rash to say of Occidental science that it is finished
or in a state of disintegration of its patterns, as there is warrant
for saying of Occidental philosophy, music, art, and literature.
The part of the span actually completed being almost 500
years, the total duration may be guessed as anywhere from
six centuries up—certainly a long growth of activity.

It would be difficult to decide whether the peak still lies
ahead or has already been passed. An answer even by analogy
is problematical because science possesses a cumulative content which is lacking in philosophy and the arts. The science
of our day, bulking larger and fuller than that of previous
centuries, must inevitably impress us as superior. However,
it is the forces at work that count. And we are too close to these
to estimate them with confidence. For all we can tell, Einstein
may be a greater Newton; or, on the other hand, his corrector
and commentator. The theories of relativity, atom structure,
quantum, entropy, a finite universe, may be solid achievements which carry science to new heights of its own and at the
same time enable it almost to substitute for philosophy. On
the other hand, they may represent an inflation of theory for
its own sake, and be a symptom of strain presaging collapse.
It is interesting at times to follow reflections such as these. But
a pinning of conviction to any one view would carry us beyond
the realm even of limited predictability into that of prophecy.

A second feature observable in the course of Occidental science as depicted in the diagram (see overleaf) is the sag in
the first half of the eighteenth century. The depression is not
very deep; but it seems indubitable. No major European nationality was in culmination, or even definitely in the ascendant

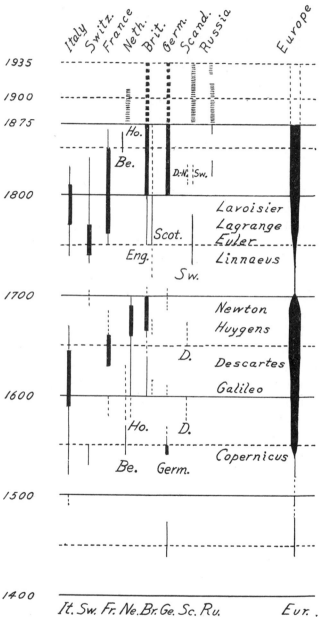

OCCIDENTAL SCIENCE

phase, in its science during this generation or two from 1700 to 1750. It might be argued that the period was merely the accidental moment in which the half-dozen national waves happened to coincide in being in trough. But the change of direction observable after fuller activity is resumed, around 1750, suggests that the lapse is significant.

Sixteenth- and seventeenth-century science is primarily concerned with obviously mechanical problems. Its culminating formulation is gravitation. It measures and calculates, but largely with the instruments of daily life. It achieved a dependable instrument of time measure, independent of observation of the heavenly bodies, only just before its close. It used the telescope and microscope to enlarge its horizon of knowledge, but hardly at all to support its system of interpretation.

Post-1750 science grappled with apparently qualitative aspects until it subjugated many of them. Hence chemistry for the first time became an organized discipline, and within fifty years had put itself on a quantitative basis. Hence, too, the successful interest in electricity. The systematic classification of the organic world is another phase of the same unconscious program. This led at least to organized conception of the field and its problems, and later to the quantitative interpretations of physiology and genetics. Usable instruments of measure were developed out of what before had been rude makeshifts or toys or devices for demonstrating a principle: the clock, the thermometer and barometer, the microscope and telescope; then the galvanometer and spectroscope. In consequence, whole new areas of nature could be investigated with a sense of problem instead merely of curiosity. We must not hastily infer that the instruments were the cause of the discoveries; but they were requisite to their solution. If we must choose, it was rather the direction of trend of the movement as a whole which produced the instruments, or the recognition of their utility. The setting up of the metric system less than fifty years after the newer science got under way is probably no accident, but a symptom of the elevation of the measures of specialized science above the immemorial ones of daily life.

Experiment, too, was infrequent and simple before 1700; increasingly important after 1750.

The older wave manifested itself first, strangely enough, in Germany; next in Belgium and, for a somewhat longer time, in Italy. Then it passed to France, briefly, concentratedly, but was rather devoid of substantial content—a philosophy or method of science rather than science itself, and hence largely mathematical. To be exact, Holland and Britain had begun to be active earlier, if anything, than France; but, more concerned with content, they progressed more slowly and climaxed later. The crest of the whole wave was reached in England. Newton evidently exhausted the possibilities of the phase. The chronological record indicates a sudden stoppage of endeavor within a decade or two of the *Principia,* as if thereafter only problems in process of solution had been completed and no new ones undertaken.

Apart, then, from a century of preparation, unproductive except in some sharpening of the tool of mathematics, and a few closing years of disengagement, the older Occidental science is essentially comprised between Copernicus in 1543 and Newton in 1687. The former lived just long enough to inaugurate a period; the latter, for forty years after its close.

The later or post-1750 wave was international, but remained north European.[20] It showed almost simultaneously in France, Britain,[21] and, on a smaller and briefer scale, in Italy, Switzerland, and Sweden. The two little countries, in fact, preceded, for Euler and Linnaeus were pure scientists, while Buffon, also born in 1707, was half a literary man. Britain too seems to have got under way slightly earlier than France, with half a dozen distinguished men born before 1740 while France had only two or three besides the Italian Lagrange. But once launched, the French movement was characteristically rapid. Before the Revolution it was in full swing with Laplace, Lavoisier, and

---

[20] Nearly half of the French scientists listed for 1760–1870 were born in Paris; none of those for 1630–1660. Reference is to those eminent in mathematics, astronomy, physics, and chemistry. In biology the provinces contribute all, and the Midi its fair proportion.

[21] Now England and Scotland, whereas the Newtonian movement was almost wholly English.

others, whereas the British school did not come into maturity until about 1800. The French movement also was virtually over by 1860 or 1870, while the British has carried on, with a possible minor depression in the late eighteen hundreds, to the present. Germany was late: her period begins about 1800, and has continued, without any apparent sag, to the present. Russia followed soon after, and finally Holland and Scandinavia participated, as junior members of a large partnership, as it were, rather than with separate firms. France is the only Catholic country that contributed importantly in this second phase of the larger cycle.

The two waves within Occidental science also differ in their relations to philosophy and religion. The relations of the earlier with philosophy were much closer: Cusanus, Descartes, Pascal, Gassendi, Leibnitz are examples.[22] In the second, not one important scientist is of consequence as a philosopher; nor vice versa.[23] The earlier wave also had no quarrel with religion. Copernicus was a priest, and Newton was genuinely pious. Where there was antagonism, it was on the side of the Church as a strict and jealous parent: science sought no quarrel. The second wave, on the contrary, was signalized at its very outset by the firing of La Mettrie's philosophical gun, *L'Homme machine,* 1748: the ammunition was scientific indeed, but its hostile mark was religion. His attempt has been repeated since, most often perhaps by those who loved science little but hated religion much, though also by occasional quarrel-lovers among scientists. On the whole, post-1750 science has gone its way quite independently of religion, and it is the latter which has felt on the defensive when relations were strained. Innumerable modern individual scientists have adhered to established religion. But they mention the Creator in parentheses or perorations, if at all.

Allied to this change was one of popular attitude. Until Newton, the scientist was believed to be doing something special and apart, to be practicing a kind of curious, irrele-

---

[22] Mainly mathematicians in science, but not wholly so.

[23] Except D'Alembert. Herbart, with his ambivalence toward metaphysics, is hardly a true exception: his psychology was prescientific.

vant, secret calling. His work, to the layman, was hardly distinguishable from astrology and alchemy. All this dropped away quickly after 1750. Science was now believed to be of interest to anyone of intelligence, and of benefit to the whole world. In recent generations this trend has become so strong that today science is almost a religious fetish to a large part of the world.

The existence of these two waves or pulses within the Occidental configuration redescribes the curious diversity of length of the relatively sterile periods in England, France, and Germany: a half century, a full century, more than two centuries, respectively. Germany participated early in the first wave, late in the last, hence had the longest interval. England terminated the first impulse, was among the initiators of the second, hence escaped with the shortest interregnum. But of course this explanation does not answer the question why the two peaks in each of these countries came when they did. This problem can be approached only through a consideration of the several national culture histories and of international developments in the total field of culture.

§ 20. Egyptian and Mesopotamian Science

The development of science in the ancient Near East is obviously of fundamental importance in the history of this subject, because whatever is pre-Greek, whatever the Greeks and their heirs built on, originated there. But this field cannot be treated satisfactorily in the present connection, because the available data do not suffice, with one possible exception, to show "normal" growth developments. Our picture is static, or of successive stations, rather than continuously formative. There occurred certain extraordinary persistences in Egypt and Mesopotamia. Of course, the systems which crystallized so remarkably must have had also their time of growth; but in general this is where the record fails us. Apparently, formative periods were sometimes very short in these civilizations in comparison with the little-altering durations that followed. The history of masonry architecture in Egypt seems an apt example. But for science the data on the corresponding growth phases are, as is to be expected from the nature of archaeological evidence on science, rarer and insufficient. We must therefore confine ourselves to a brief statement of existing knowledge on the nature and age of the several blocks of ancient Near Eastern scientific attainment.

In Egypt, as in most ancient civilizations, science was developed principally in three directions: astronomy, mathematics, and medicine.

Egyptian astronomy was normatively calendrical in objective; and having satisfactorily attained this end, it seems to have developed no further interests. It scarcely dealt with the moon, planets, or eclipses. Its calendar freed itself from all the complications and provocative stimuli of lunar months by adopting a purely solar year, with completely artificial but practically convenient months. This was a great achievement, but not calculated to produce further astronomy in an age which could hardly yet be expected to practice science purely for its own sake. Moreover, this establishment of the solar calendar took place, according to conservative historians, in 4241 B.C., the earliest known date in human history, but therefore also one about the antecedents of which little would be known.[24]

Egyptian mathematics is a highly individualized product. Lamentably deficient geometrically, it had developed as its specialty a peculiar and elaborate system of operating with fractions. The object of this system was to reduce fractions not to a common denominator but to a common numerator, and that, except for $\frac{2}{3}$, always 1. This method, in which the Egyptians were definitely skillful, seems to have become an end in itself. In fact, as a means toward other mathematical purposes, it is usually awkward, and in complicated situations

---

[24] Eduard Meyer's original computation of 4241 looks watertight, but the result is being increasingly doubted by authorities. The date just is too early: about a millennium before political unity, masonry, and writing! It is a question of seeming demonstration from evidence as against a growing feeling of contrary perspective.

prohibitively so. The result is that while the Egyptians did not hesitate to multiply fractions and attempt equations at times, they seem to have picked favorable problems in which their method happened to work readily. At least, such is my interpretation.

We have fairly adequate knowledge of this arithmetic from four ancient manuscripts. Three of these are actually from the twelfth dynasty in the nineteenth pre-Christian century. The fourth is of Hyksos period but professes to be a copy of a twelfth-dynasty original. Four much later papyri, from Roman to Coptic times, continue to use the ancient methods—this in the country of Euclid and Ptolemy. We have therefore a mathematics that remained stationary for twenty-five hundred years: other than that, we know nothing of its history. It may have originated in a great sudden burst shortly or long before the twelfth dynasty, or have developed gradually; there is no present means of knowing.

In medicine, the situation is similar. There are several manuscripts, from the eighteenth to the thirteenth centuries, which consist of chaotic lists of prescriptions. One other, the Edwin Smith papyrus, of late Hyksos or early New Empire date— within the same time range—is of fundamentally different character. Two of its three parts are frankly magical: to turn away the wind that brings pestilence, and to change an old man into a young one. The third part is an orderly, wholly objective, anatomical and surgical treatise, resting on considerable sound knowledge unmixed with magic. It is evident that Egyptian medicine comprised, in the same period, three almost unrelated strands, pharmaceutic, magical, and anatomic. But the story of its development is again unknown to us.

In Mesopotamia, we encounter from Sumerian times, in the third millennium, a system of measures and weights, and of numeration and calculation, which may have been old then and which remained essentially fixed. It is unrelated to the Egyptian, its primary basis being sexagesimal. The measures of length, area, volume, weight are or became integrated; as in our metric system. This integration, especially of the weights, may be secondary; but it is notable. The unity-numerator fractioning of the Egyptians is lacking: the sexagesimal base made the dealing with fractions of measures by the common-denominator method almost automatic, at least for ordinary purposes. Written numeration is with symbols for 1 and 10, repeated up to 9 and 5 times respectively. But for 60 unity is written; and again for 3,600; also for $\frac{1}{60}$ and $\frac{1}{3600}$. This is a true position-numeral system: 4,096 is written simply 1-8-16; that is, $1 \times 3,600$, 8×60, 16×1. There is even a sign for zero. But it is used only between the sexagesimally developing units, not within them, nor in external position in the whole number: 60 is expressed by 1, not by 1-0, $\frac{1}{60}$ also by 1, not by 0-1. There are also special signs for 600, 3,600, 36,000, 216,000. The numeration might be described as a mixture of the Arabic, Roman, and special methods applied to a sexagesimal base diluted by a decimal one.

In spite of its empirical tempering of a logical plan of high order, the Babylonian system is remarkable. It illustrates the importance of measure systems and number-representation systems in the development of conceptual mathematics. It is obviously wholly unrelated to the Egyptian system. Its revolution around 60 is as unexplained as the Egyptian numerator equating. And unfortunately we know no more of its development than of its origin.

In geometry there is the usual pre-Greek deficiency. The inscribed hexagon was known; but not the Pythagorean proposition as a formulated theorem. Instead of $h = \sqrt{(a^2 + b^2)}$, the first-dynasty Babylonians around 2000 B.C. made choice of two arithmetical formulae: $h = a + 2b^2a/60^2$, and $h = b^2/2a$.

Astronomy was thoroughly different from the Egyptian. Instead of being concerned with timekeeping as an end, and considering essentially only the sun and its relation to the celestial sphere, it recorded time mostly as a means of dealing with heavenly events treated as presages or determinants of human fortunes. Hence Mesopotamian astronomy throughout had an astrological tinge, which Egyptian lacked. All astrology, in whatever part or period of the world, seems in fact to be reared directly on Mesopotamian foundations. The Egyptians sought fixity, and having found this, remained content in it and ignored other phenomena, in the main. But the Sumerians and their Semitic successors, concerned with omens, were interested much more in change; hence their interest was directed to the moon and planets as well as the sun, and the fixed stars were used chiefly as a background against which observations and calculations could be carried on. The calendar was lunisolar, with all the attendant complications. Particular attention was paid to eclipses; the attempt to predict these involved observations, not only of period, but of position; and so the ecliptic—the path of the eclipses—was discovered, measured into the zodiacal constellations, and the synodical revolutions of the planets were established. A great fund of quantitative observations was thus gradually built up, such as Egypt, uninterested in change, and therefore in prediction of the variable, did not attain. On the other hand, Mesopotamia, under the obsession of its celestial-human causality assumption, scarcely developed astronomy where it did not serve other ends. It did not concern itself with the absolute distances of the heavenly bodies, only incidentally and hesitantly with their relative ones, not at all with any scheme of physical mechanism.

Some preserved documents go back to third-millennium Sumerian dynasties. The great mass are from after 750—from the last century and a quarter of Assyria, from Chaldaean Neo-Babylonia, and from Persian and Hellenistic times to the second century. Many of these are copies of older documents; but we do not know always which, and rarely how old the originals were. We do know that the ecliptic was recognized in Sargonian times, around 2800; the cycle of zodiacal signs may or may not be much later. So with the 360 degrees of the circle, planetary retrograde movements, the varying heights and lengths of the visible ecliptic, the "Kaksidi" period of 361 sidereal months equaling 334 sidereal lunations; and with the instruments: clepsydra, gnomon, and polos—a hollow hemisphere with a ball or stylus at the center, perhaps the ancestor of the armillary sphere. All these were recognized or employed in the late period between 747 and 111: their discovery or invention may have been late also. There definitely was progress until 200; but hardly enough record is preserved to build a measurable configuration of growth.[25]

§ 21. Indian Science

As so often in India, some crucial dates are highly uncertain. Also, history of connections with the outside world is almost lacking, so that evaluations are difficult: a given mathematical achievement, if original, may argue creativeness of a high order, but if imported from the Greeks, nothing more than a degree of intellectual receptiveness. A satisfactory history of science in India cannot yet be written.

One thing, however, is clear: the science of India, like that of China, Egypt, and Mesopotamia, consists almost exclusively of two interests: one mathematical and astronomical, the other medical. It will serve clarity to consider these two separately.

The *Śulvasūtra* or "cord rules" of Apastamba are an interesting geometry-arithmetic evolved around the Pythagorean theorem. Unfortunately, estimates of the age of the work are both indefinite and far apart: eighth to seventh century for

---

[25] Olmstead gives the following developmental steps. Eight-year month-intercalation cycle, by the third Ur dynasty (ending in 2183). Star-sighting pole and water clock, twelfth century. Nineteen-year cycle of intercalation, 747 under Nabu-nasir of Babylon; the first eclipses quoted by Ptolemy date from this time. Definite prediction of lunar eclipses, shortly before 668. Textbook on planetary appearances or cycles, 577. Also in the Chaldaean period, discovery of the saros or 18-year period of eclipse repetitions. Preserved ephemeris tablet, 523. About 490, the astronomer Nabu-rimanni, Strabo's Naburianus: true time of new and full moon; maximum and minimum diameter of moon's face, more accurate than Ptolemy and Copernicus; sun's mean motion; inequality of the seasons; sun and moon perigee. Under the Seleucids and perhaps the Parthians, Babylonian astronomy achieved its final and greatest triumphs. Apart from eclipses, astrology played little part in this late development, which was observational and calculatory. Astrology entered civil life only after Alexander. (A. T. Olmstead, *Am. Jour. Semitic Languages*, Vol. 55, 1938).—There is strong indication here of a long, slow development finally coming into a genuine culmination of true science; its roots wholly in Mesopotamian soil, the climax reached after Babylonian independence was finally lost; almost certain influence on Greek astronomy; some Greek influences on it to be suspected, but less evident.

the older portions, fifth to fourth for the remainder; 322 B.C.; between 500 and 1 B.C.; between 500 B.C. and 200 A.D. Apastamba may have been preceded by Baudayana and followed by Katyayana. While the *Śulvasūtra* contains a generalized statement of the Pythagorean theorem, it consists for the most part of specific problems like finding a square which is the sum or difference of two squares, or transforming a rectangle into a square of equal area; and of formulae expressing the theorem in a series of integral numerals: not only 3-4-5 and several of its multiples, but 5-12-13, 8-15-17, 12-35-37, 15-36-39 (= 5-12-13), this last being put into first place, perhaps as the highest attainment. There is a passage dealing with a trapezoidal altar of bases 30 and 24 and altitude 36 and its contained right triangles. This passage has been construed as geometric in purport; but the dimensions, including the half bases, of the altar lead easily to expressions of all the just-mentioned numerical values. It therefore seems legitimate to infer that this altar was famous and sacred precisely for all that it "contained"—much like a magic square. While the *Śulvasūtra* is probably post-Pythagorean in date, the specific formulae are almost certainly non-Greek and of native origin. Whether they are old empirical numerical findings from which the geometric theorem was subsequently generalized, or whether they are specific Hindu arithmetical applications developed out of the theorem, is less clear. In short, we have here, whatever its origins, a genuine Hindu mathematical production; but unfortunately we cannot date it, except as being considerably older than all other extant Hindu mathematics.

Next in age are the five siddhantas, the *Paitāmaha, Vāsiṣṭha, Sūrya, Paulíśa,* and *Romaka.* These are Hindu versions of Greek astronomy and mathematics, especially trigonometry (with sines instead of chords), plus prescientific native elements. Direct Greek influences are increasingly evident in the five treatises in the order named. They also seem to derive from different Greek sources. At least the *Romaka-* (Roman-) *siddhānta* is almost certainly based on Ptolemy or Greek sources later than Ptolemy. On the other hand, the siddhantas are cited in India in 505 A.D. This roughly delimits their range, and Sarton's estimate of the first half of the fifth century as the date of their composition—or at least the central point of the composition of the series—seems reasonable enough.

Next follow three mathematician-astronomers within a century and a quarter:

Āryabhaṭa, fl. 499, b. 476 near Pataliputra, systematizer of the siddhāntas, especially the *Sūrya*. But he held that the earth spun on its axis, a view rejected by later Hindus. His mathematics includes: quadratic and indeterminate first-degree equations; summation of arithmetical series; tables of sines and versed sines; π value 3 and $177\!\!/\!_{1250} = 3.1416$.

Varāhamihira, fl. ca. 505, b. near Ujjain, d. 587? Summary of the five siddhāntas, plus astrology. Āryabhaṭa is quoted.

Brahmagupta, b. 598, fl. ca. 628 at Ujjain. Work based largely on the *Sūryasiddhānta* and Āryabhaṭa. Adds indeterminate equations of the second degree; permutations and combinations; cyclic quadrilaterals; volume of pyramid frustum; $\pi = \sqrt{10}$.

These three names evidently mark the culmination. There follow several others of eminence spaced a century or two apart.

Mahāvīra, fl. ca. 830? in Mysore in southern India. His mathematics is fuller but perhaps more elementary than that of Brahmagupta. New elements are: three types of quadratic equations, but without imaginary roots; geometric progression; division by a fraction by inversion multiplication; ellipses (inaccurate, but not dealt with by any other Indian).

Śrīdhara, b. ca. 991, fl. ca. 1020. Compendium of arithmetical calculation and measures. Clear use of o: $n \times 0 = 0$; but no division by o.

Bhāskara, 1114–1178, fl. 1150. His astronomy is essentially a clear exposition of that of the *Sūryasiddhānta*. His mathematics includes: division by o; minus times minus gives plus, times plus, minus; quadratic equations with only positive roots genuine, a few types of cubic and biquadratic, also indeterminate of two first degrees; cyclic method of solving two Pellian equations; π, from 384-polygon, $= 3927\!\!/\!_{1250}$ or $754\!\!/\!_{250} = 3.141666\ldots$; letters for unknown quantities suggested; some trigonometry.

The important innovation of position numerals by a symbol for zero seems still—or again—in dispute as between Hindus and Arabs. Whatever the ultimate outcome of this difficult problem, it appears that the first Hindu use of zero falls between the sixth and ninth centuries—which accords either exactly or fairly with the period of culmination.

The greater works of Indian medicine fall into two eras, one traditionally contemporary with Buddha, the other with the mathematical-astronomical peak.

In the days of Buddha there are said to have taught: Ātreya at Taksasila or Taxila in the far northwest, and his younger contemporary Suśruta at Kasi or Benares in the heart of the Ganges Valley, the latter's school tending to emphasize surgery—hernia, caesarean, lithotomy, cataract. Suśruta's *Saṁhitā* is preserved, but the true date of the text may be much later than its traditional one.

Caraka, born in Kashmir, fl. under Kanishka, ca. 120–162, wrote a compendium based on Agniveśa, pupil of Ātreya.

The Bower Manuscript, ca. 450 A.D., contains two medical tracts in which Suśruta is quoted.

Vāgbhaṭa, ca. 625 ?, Buddhist, forms a triad with Ātreya and Suśruta.

Vāgbhaṭa the Younger, a similar treatise.

Mādhavakara, eighth or ninth century.

Vṛnda, successor, contemporary, or the same person as the last.

With all the lack of rigorous chronology, it is clear that the major productions of Indian science fall chiefly into one certain and one earlier but undefined period.

This earlier period is the traditional era of the great rival schools of medicine, contemporary with the founding of Buddhism, Jainism, philosophy, and philology, in and about the sixth or fifth pre-Christian century. Whatever the historicity of this period, it no doubt was subsequently felt as the great golden age of the past. For this very reason sanctified or revered works may have been falsely ascribed to it. However, a sound historic intuition may underlie much of the legend. When subsequently India first comes into the light of history, it is with an accumulation of highly distinctive cultural values so great that it seems at least one major growth of civilization must have preceded. Such a growth may well have lasted several centuries rather than only one or two. It is certainly within possibility that the *Śulvasūtra* mathematics, or Panini's grammar, or the great traditional physicians, may actually have been genuine products of such a movement; as tradition alleges.

The second and more certain period, both in mathematics-astronomy and in medicine, quite evidently culminated in and around the sixth Christian century, with a gradual tapering off. About 800, the Dravidian south began to participate or lead. Roughly, the time is that of the second half of the great swell of systematic philosophy from 100 to 1000, which we have seen reason to assume consisted of two phases from 100 to 500 and 600 to 900. If these phases are real, the science developments would approximately fill the dip between them. The period of best science is also close to the culminations in literature under Kalidasa around 450, and in sculpture.

This later Hindu science was derivative from Greek science, and intrinsically less original than the first; but it was reworked into a national product.

§22. Chinese Science

Science in China is only partly comparable with science in the Mediterranean and Occidental spheres. It has tended to consist of technology on the one hand and of scholarship on the other. Observation, except for practical utility, inclined to be casual and summary, and experiment was nearly lacking. Geometry was never systematically developed: mathematics began essentially arithmetically and developed toward algebra. The bent of Chinese civilization from the earliest times known to us was toward an interest in human behavior and relations, rather than toward the physical world or abstract relations. Nature was something to be taken for granted, dealt with, or enjoyed aesthetically, but hardly to be curious about. Astronomy seems to have been practiced primarily for calendrical purposes. The physical sciences were little developed except in their technological aspects; the biological ones remained rudimentary. Medicine went on without a sound foundation in observational anatomy, and hence its concern with symptoms and remedies was easily invaded by magical notions, or satisfied with arbitrary systems.

It is significant that the Chinese have made many important inventions, but not one major scientific discovery. They have sought a way of life, but neither an understanding nor a control of nature beyond what was immediately useful. They are of course not abnormal in their attitude: most cultures have done the same. It is, with minor exceptions, only the few civilizational growths that have at one time or another been under the influence of Greek example which have really tried to develop science further; and these only transiently. Even the Hindus would presumably have been little affected if Greek mathematics and astronomy had not furnished fuel to their passion for the abstract *per se*. This passion the Chinese did not share to any notable degree. They were eager enough to reason about living, about the relations of men; but much less so about the relations of quantities or things.

For the last two thousand years the history of Chinese science is well dated. In fact, this is the longest continuous record in the history of science. Farther back, data are scanty. There are the usual legendary attributions of origins to emperors of the third millennium before Christ and to the stock figure of Prince Chou Kung of the incipient Chou dynasty. Our actual acquaintance with Chinese science previous to the Ts'in unification rests upon a few works rediscovered or reconstituted early in the Han period within a generation or two after the destruction of the books, or upon comments later in Han times on similar works which have since become lost. This body of knowledge with which the record opens quite likely contains some elements imported into China from the west, but we know neither the time nor the route of their transmission. Essentially, then, our story is that of growth from this given status of 200 B.C.—development from within and under foreign stimulus.

The productive outside influences were three. First came Indian science, in the wake of Buddhism and culminating around the seventh century. Next, Arab—or better, Mohammedan—influence, especially with the Mongol conquest in the thirteenth century, effective notably in astronomy. Finally, in the seventeenth century, the Jesuits introduced much European science. Toward all three influences the Chinese attitude seems to have been the same: neither resistive nor enthusiastic, but impartial and ready to accept demonstration. The periods of greatest original productivity seem not directly related to the periods of heaviest importation either positively or negatively. Evidently the Chinese assimilated foreign science into the organism of their own, and the periods of heightened activity of this were due to causes which are still obscure.

The story is clearest for mathematics, on which Mikami has an excellent memoir; upon this the following is based.

To Han-Wei inclusive, or 265 A.D.—The two oldest works, apart from two numerical magic squares in the *Yi-king*,[26] are the *Chou-pei* Mathematical Classic and the Nine-Section Arithmetic. These represent the mathematical heritage, of unknown but no doubt varying age, with which the Han Chinese began. They include: the Pythagorean theorem; circle-squaring with $\pi = 3$; computations of the distance and orbit of the sun; distinction of odd and even numbers; operations with fractions, including a rude method of division, in effect by multiplication after inversion; extraction of square and cube roots; distinction of positive and negative numbers; problems in alligation; linear, simultaneous, and quadratic equations. The geometry is computative rather than demonstrative, and gives formulae for the areas of triangles, rectangles, trapezoids, circles, segments, sectors, and the volumes of prisms, pyramids, wedges, cylinders, and cones. The triangle is correctly determined from its altitude, not side; but the segment and sector have curious rule-of-thumb approximations; and of course the error in the gross assumption for the value of π runs through all curved-figure computations.

It is clear that this was an advanced arithmetical mathematics, weak or uninterested on the side of theory. Its recognition

---

[26] The *lo-shu* is the familiar square adding to 15 in each direction. The *ho-t'u* is somewhat similar but does not add up, and contains two extra 5's (for 10?).

of negative numbers, root extractions, perhaps its complete familiarity with fractions, are evidently due to the use of calculatory apparatus. This was not the later *suan-pan* wired-frame abacus, but, as nearly as I can understand the references, a system of laying rods of two colors, for positive and negative, in columns and rows. This of course was the equivalent of a position-numeral system, and no doubt explains the computatory faculty of the ancient Chinese as compared with their Mediterranean contemporaries. It is unfortunate that we do not know the successive stages by which this arithmetic was built up prior to 200 B.C. It contains some curious limitations. For instance, while roots were extracted by a process apparently very similar to that in use among ourselves, the absence of a decimal point seems to have blocked the Chinese completely if a number's root was not integral, and they knew no better recourse than to divide the remainder by the root in hand, so that the square root of 105 would come out $10\frac{1}{2}$.[27] Obviously, the interest was in a sufficiently accurate result, not in any principle. Nevertheless, the Nine-Section Arithmetic represents more than a random set of practical rules: it is a body of fairly systematically organized understanding.

The *Chou-pei,* which is primarily astronomical, contains an interesting passage in which the distance of the sun is given as 16,000 Chinese miles (*li*?) south at the summer solstice, and 135,000 at the winter solstice, at points where verticals cast no shadows; the difference of 119,000 being doubled for the distance it is to the north at midnight, gives 238,000 for the diameter of the sun's orbit in summer and twice that in winter, the respective orbits being three times ($\pi = 3$) as great.

The Nine-Section Arithmetic was reconstituted by Chang Ts'ang, who had held office under the Ts'in dynasty and died more than a centenarian (!) in 152 B.C.

Another work is the mathematical classic (*Suan-ching*) of Sun Tzu, attributed to the Ts'in period but containing references which if authentic mark it as not earlier than Later Han.[28] Its math-

[27] What they made the root of 115 is not stated in my sources, and was perhaps evaded by the texts themselves. The point is the more interesting because the Nine-Section Arithmetic does not shrink from attempting roots of fractions.

[28] References to the cities of Changan and Loyang, and to Buddhistic writings, Buddhism having been first "recognized" in 65 A.D.

ematics omits certain features of the Nine-Section Arithmetic, and contains little that is not given there, except for indeterminate equations with only one answer indicated. The side of a square is to the diagonal as 5 is to 7: a typical ungeometric but effective simplification.[29]

Sun Tzu's book, in connection with measures, also gives several densities, which are, in comparison with the actual ones: iron, 7.2 (7.8); copper, 8 (8.94); lead, 11.4 (11.4); silver, 16.8! (10.53); gold, 19.2 (19.4).[30]

Hsü Yüeh, fl. ca. 200 A.D., wrote the *Su-shu Chi-i.* He refers to *chu suan,* jewel or ball arithmetic, which may or may not be a reference to the wired-frame abacus later called *suan-pan.*

In astronomy, a definite progress seems discernible during Han times:

Lo Hsia Hung about 104 B.C. designed a celestial cupola which was cast in 59 B.C.

Chia K'uei, fl. 89–101, is said to have added the ecliptic to the celestial sphere (?).

Chan Heng, 78–139, born in Nanyang, set a celestial hemisphere over the equatorial plane. He recognized 5 planets, 28 solar mansions, 124 ever-visible and 320 named stars; explained the origin of the physical universe; is said to have devised a seismograph; and used $\pi = \sqrt{10}$. It is not known if this value is native.

Liu Hung, fl. ca. 196, pointed out that the equator was not the ecliptic, the solstitial points were not fixed, the year not exactly $365\frac{1}{4}$ days.

Lu Chi, ca. 200, made a celestial map.

Activity in both mathematics and astronomy continued through the troubled period of the rival three kingdoms, or most of the third century.

Wang Fan, ca. 229–after 264, a Buddhist in the southern Kingdom of Wu, made a celestial sphere instead of previous hemispheres, with the equator and ecliptic differentiated. His value of π was $142/45 = 3.1555\ldots$

---

[29] For the area of a circle three formulae are given, all following from the simplification of π to 3: $c/2 \times d/2$; $3d^2/4$; $c^2/12$. The Nine-Section Arithmetic adds a fourth: $cd/4$. No one of these formulae refers to the radius. It is clear that the interest is in a process yielding a computable result, not in any principle.

[30] They are given, in terms of weight units per cube-measure units, as 6, 7.5, 9.5, 14, 16, which I have multiplied by 1.2 for readier comparison with the accepted densities. There is no indication of any consideration of displacement: rather do blocks of the substances appear to have been cut to measure and weighed in the balance.

Liu Hui, in the northern Kingdom of Wei, wrote in 263 the *Hai-tao* or Sea-Island Mathematical Classic, dealing with fairly complicated problems of distances, with two factors to be obtained. An algebraic manipulation of some kind is suggested, but only specific methods of solution are given, not principles. The value of π is found by successively inscribing polygons of 6, 12, 24, 48, 96, 192 sides, and is put at $157/50 = 3.14$, with recognition of being too small.

Pei Hsiu, 224–271, first developed the principles of cartography.

The Tsin dynasties, 265–420, were a period of slump in scientific productivity.

Period of 420–740.—These three centuries, on the contrary, witnessed much new activity, both of native Chinese development and of Indian stimulus. This is the time of the brief Early Sung, Ch'i, Liang, Ch'en, and Sui dynasties, and the first century of T'ang. The era of the short-lived dynasties was one of political instability, and is usually described as a time of discord and unsettlement, from which the country did not emerge into prosperity until the T'angs. As a matter of fact, most of the scientific progress was accomplished under these little-esteemed dynasties, and the first T'ang century seems to have gone on under the momentum then attained, plus direct import from India. The latter two-thirds of T'ang and most of the also "glorious" Sung period, were scientifically sterile.

Ch'ien Lo-chih about 436 devised a celestial sphere which was moved one Chinese "degree" each day.

Ho Ch'eng-t'ien about 443 asserted that the solstices should be determined by observation.

Wu, who lived under the Earlier Sung dynasty (420–477), gave π as 3.1432+.

Tsu Ch'ung-chih, 430–501, born in Fanyang, was an able mathematician and astronomer, apparently in advance of his age. He is also one of a number of Chinese of various periods credited with inventing a south-pointing vehicle and a self-propelling boat. His treatise *Chui-shu* on calendrical theory was distinguished for the minuteness and elegance of its processes, and was adopted by the T'angs for official examinations; but before long it was little understood, then disused, forgotten, and finally lost. Tsu calculated the value of π to lie between 3.1415926 and 3.1415927, and hence set it at $355/113$. This remarkably accurate value appears to have been wholly unknown to the Greeks, Hindus, and Arabs, and to have been rediscovered in Europe only in 1585. In fact, it went out of use in China until Mongol times, and $22\frac{2}{7}$, which Tsu had given as the inaccurate value of π, came to be known as the accurate one.

Chen Luan, fl. ca. 566 in North China, was profoundly read in Buddhism, but his *Wu-ching* or Five-Classic Arithmetic is a commentary on Hsü Yüeh of Later Han times. Certain of his problems of computing unmeasurable distances depend on geometric factors for solution; and he attempted indeterminate equations, of a "hundred hens" type, but with only one answer for each.

Hsia-hou Yang, of the same period but a little later—he refers to Chen,—wrote a Mathematical Classic based at times on the Nine-Section Arithmetic and at times on the *Wu-ts'ao* of the Han period.

Chang Ch'iu-chien, probably of the second half of the sixth century, appears to have been the greatest mathematician of the period subsequent to Tsu. His "Classic" particularly stresses fractions. He divides $6,587\frac{2}{3} + \frac{3}{4}$ by $58\frac{1}{2}$ and has it come out as $112\frac{437}{702}$. He gives his method, which is multiplication after inversion of the divisor; but, characteristically for Chinese mathematics, he does not enunciate the formal principle involved. This method was used in India by Mahavira about 830, but was not known in Europe until the sixteenth century. In essence, however, the method was already to be found in the early Han or pre-Han Nine-Section Arithmetic. Chang deals also with compound proportions; arithmetical progressions; one geometric progression (successive halving); and gives three answers to a "hundred hen" indeterminate equation, though his "rule" is merely factual for the case. In computing the area of a segment, and in not dealing with remainders in square-root extractions, he is still on the basis of the Nine-Section Arithmetic. To a nonmathematician and non-Sinologist like myself, it seems fair to rate Tsu as the original and profound genius of his era's growth, and Chang as its most important general representative.

Wang Hsiao-t'ung, fl. 623 seq., wrote a *Ch'i-ku* Mathematical Classic, most of which is preserved, in which he gives twenty problems, including some cubic equations. For instance, in a right triangle, the product P of the two sides is $706\frac{1}{50}$, the "surplus" S of the hypothenuse over the longer side is $30\frac{9}{60}$; to determine the lengths of the sides, an equation is used equivalent to $x^3 + \dfrac{Sx^2}{2} - \dfrac{P^2}{2S} = 0$, which is solved by a process similar to the extraction of cube roots. The rules for arranging and computing the equations are given, but not the method of constructing them. These cubic equations represent the limit attained by the growth of Chinese mathematics.

Astronomy, which appears to have been rather stagnant for a century, developed again during the first T'ang century, chiefly, however, through Hindus or Indian-trained Chinese. This was also the century of the last great Chinese Buddhist pilgrims to India. There were four official T'ang astronomers named Chü-t'an, Chinese for Gautama, and hence Indians. At least some and perhaps all of these wrote their computations instead of using calculatory pieces. Written calculations in China are not reported again until more than a half millennium later, in the thirteenth century, and then also by foreigners.

Chü-t'an Chüan made a calendar in 618.

Jen-chün, fl. ca. 626, Taoist astronomer.

Chü-t'an Lo: calendrical and astronomical official.

Li Shun-feng, fl. 664: history of astronomy, comment on mathematical works.

Chü-t'an Hsi-ta (Siddharta), fl. about first quarter of 8th cent. Constructed a calendar based on the recognition of 360 instead of $365\frac{1}{4}$ degrees, with 60 minutes to the degree; and wrote an astrological work for 713–741. His astronomy seems to have been little understood by the Chinese and was lost.

I-hsing, or Chang Sui, 683–727, a Chinese Buddhist versed in Sanskrit, in 727 composed a calendar found by trial to be more accurate than any previous or contemporary one. He used the *t'ai-yen* method of indeterminate analysis.

Chü-t'an Ch'ien, astronomical official after 700, unsuccessfully attacked I-hsing's calendar.

Later T'ang and Sung, 740–1240.—These five centuries of great literature, painting, scholarship, and, toward the end, of philosophy, produced little in science.

Chia Tan, 730–805, completed in 801 a map of China, 30 by 33 (Chinese) feet, scale of 100 *li* to the "inch" (which would mean that 6,000 miles were included); and a gazetteer of itineraries.

Li Chi-fu, 758–814, military map north of Yellow River and gazetteer.

Ch'en Huo, 1011–1075, of Ch'ien-t'ang, an able astronomer, dealt also with the problem of a wedge composed of casks, this being the first Chinese attempt at the summation of a progression. His formula that an arc equals its chord plus twice the squared sagitta divided by the diameter represents at least an effort to go beyond his predecessors.

Chou-ts'ung, fl. 1065; astronomer, who wrote a history of the calendar.

Su-sung, fl. 1092: astronomical treatise with celestial maps; constructed an orrery.

In 1137 two stone maps were engraved, in squares of 100 *li;* north was on top. Another is from ca. 1193.

Fan Ch'eng-ta, 1126–1193, geographer.

Terminal Southern Sung and Mongol, 1240–1320.—This truly great period of Chinese mathematics, which produced half a dozen illustrious men, and an original system of algebra, is remarkable for its brevity. Its important productions fall actually into less than sixty years, from 1247 to 1303. It is an equally remarkable fact that this is the period when the harassed Sung dynasty, long confined to southern China, was tottering under Mongol blows to end in 1279, the Mongols being already in control of the North. Nor can the growth be imputed to influences brought in with the Mongol invasion, since South and North China both participated; also because the Mongols had scarcely come in control of the whole Empire, with peace and material prosperity setting in, when in a few decades the scientific movement ended. It is quite evident that this mathematical growth was determined in large part by factors below the threshold of conventional history and but little related to political and economic conditions. Nor does it seem to be connected with the Sung philosophy, the period of which was 1050 to 1200; except perhaps indirectly, somewhat as Han science followed after Chou philosophy.

On the other hand, the Mongol period affords parallels of originality in literature and art. The Chinese novel and drama are usually said to have been established under this dynasty; and its painting, while mostly deprecated, shows considerable vigor, freshness, and novelty. Some of these phenomena have puzzled historians, who have had recourse to such suggestions as the improbable one that the Chinese drama was derived from a native Mongol drama. What seems much more likely is that new semipopular currents, developing below the surface in science, literature, and art, were checked by the fine but backward-looking classic scholarship and traditionalism of the Sungs, until, when the fabric of this was disrupting, they poured forth vigorously under the new political and social order. The Sung philosophy, however original, was still the work of literati operating within the frame of the old culture; its name of Neo-Confucianism is therefore not without appropriateness. But the drama and novel have never been admitted into classic Chinese literature; and of Chu, the greatest of the mathematicians, we hear that he led the life of a wanderer, teaching crowds of pupils, instead of being promoted to high office.

From its first preserved beginnings, the "celestial-stem algebra" of this Late Sung–Early Mongol period contained new elements. One was the symbol zero, in its circular form. This may have come early or late in the course of the preceding five unproductive centuries, from the Arabs of the southern sea route, or directly from India, or from the Muslim-influenced peoples of the northern land route. With the zero, position numerals were written and decimal fractions handled, but the symbols themselves were derived from the old calculating pieces, and the computations were made with such pieces. Positive and negative quantities were at first written in red and black, to correspond to the colors of their calculating pieces; but, this being impracticable in printed books, word characters for positive and negative were added, or a diagonal line drawn through the last digit of a negative number. Whether the *suan-pan* frame abacus was also in use is not certain. The existence of division tables such as were later employed with it suggests that it was; as do the names of treatises from the preceding two centuries: *Pan-chu Chi, Tsou-pan Chi.* Chu's triangle of powers, which he gives as something known, is a list of binomial coefficients. These the Arabs had known since the end of the eleventh century; two hundred years seems time for knowledge of the coefficients to have reached China and become established. Finally, the most characteristic feature of this whole Mongol-period Chinese mathematics, the "celestial element," appears, like the zero, in the earliest extant works of the school as if it were something familiar. The growth thus quite evidently had a developmental phase of which we possess no direct record.

The *t'ien-yuen* or celestial-element or monad method employed unity as representative of the unknown. This seems to be its fundamental feature. Whether it is the essential conceptual characteristic of the method, or more of an extrinsic manipulative one, I am insufficiently conversant to decide. At any rate it resulted in an algebra or quasi algebra which reached results comparable to ours but with a different technique and in a wholly diverse dress. Centuries later, when it had become practically forgotten in China, it was taken up in Japan and developed much farther.

Ch'in Chiu-shao, of the Southern Sung monarchy, wrote his *Su-shu,* or *Su-hsiao,* in 1247. It contains 81 problems, none of them simple. He uses the *t'ai-yen* method of indeterminate analysis, developed, as he says, by astronomers: such as I-hsing, no doubt. He also uses the celestial-element method; and his zero is the first extant Chinese occurrence. He extracts the fourth root, and deals with equations containing powers up to the tenth. His method of extracting the roots of equations is similar to Horner's method of 1819 for the approximate solution of numerical equations. He always makes the absolute term of an equation negative—in which he was followed by all subsequent Chinese mathematicians, and which is compared to Harriot's (1560–1621) making all significant terms stand on one side. For the area of a scalene triangle he uses the Heronic formula: the square root of $s\,(s-a)\,(s-b)\,(s-c)$, where s is half the sum of the sides a, b, c. Uncorrected Chinese defects in Ch'in's work are: the absence of decimal fractions; the remainder in a root extraction still merely divided by the integral part of the root; π variously taken as 3, or $\sqrt{10}$, or $22\frac{2}{7}$, the last now being called the accurate value. He explains his process of solution much more fully than his methods of converting his problems into algebraic constructions.

Li Yeh, ca. 1178–ca. 1265, born in Luan-ch'eng, lived first under the Chin and then the Mongol dynasty in North China, but appears to have known nothing of Ch'in. His principal work is the Circle-measurement Sea-mirror, *Ts'e-yüan Hai-ching,* of 1248. He also wrote in 1259 the *I-ku Yen-tuan.* He uses the celestial-element method similarly to Ch'in, but with emphasis on the algebraic construction of an equation from the given data, the method of solution being skimped. For negative quantities he uses the diagonal cross line instead of color or a word character.

Liu I, who was born in Chungshan and flourished about the middle of the century, taught Yang Hui, who credits certain of his methods to him.

Yang Hui, born in Ch'ien-t'ang, wrote between 1261 and 1275 in the collapsing Sung monarchy. He does not employ the term "celestial element," nor mention Ch'in or Li Yeh; his work appears to have been wholly independent of theirs. He gives formulae for the summation of arithmetical progressions; solves linear equations with four and five unknown quantities; was evidently able to operate with decimal fractions, though he does not formally explain the method; and divides with a division table such as was later used with the abacus.

Chang Yu-chin, whose date is unknown except that he lived under the Mongol dynasty, wrote the *Ko-hsiao Hsin-shu,* a calendrical-astronomical work with a mathematical part in which Tsu's $355/113$ is rediscovered or revived as the best value of π.

Chu Shih-chieh probably represents the apogee of native Chinese algebra. He published in 1299 a textbook, Mathematical Study Introduction, *Suan-hsiao Chi-meng,* and in 1303 a more important work, the Four-element Precious Mirror. The Introduction was forgotten in China, where it was restored only in 1839 from a Korean reprint of 1660; but it had got into Japan, where it exercised great influence in the seventeenth century when mathematical studies finally awoke in that country. The Mirror also became lost in China, but was rediscovered in 1802. Chu's work contains no reference to his predecessors Ch'in, Li Yeh, or Yang. He extended the celestial-element method to four quantities by using four elements: heaven, earth, man, thing. The second and third of these he states to have been used previously by mathematicians whom he names but who are otherwise unknown. It was Chu who gave the binomial coefficients in the form of an arithmetical triangle to the eighth power. He did not, however, recognize more than one root to an equation. His work appears all to have been done with calculatory apparatus.

Astronomical development seems to have been foreign-influenced.

Kuo Shou-ching, 1231–1316, born in Hsing-tai, in 1280 constructed the best Chinese calendar, but after Western models. He appears to have been the first Chinese to deal with spherical trigonometry, with which of course Mohammedan science was familiar.

Period of 1320–1600.—In mathematics, this was a time of ebb, without evidences even of assimilation from Mohammedan sources; in astronomy, Mohammedan influences prevailed. The Mings in 1368 established a *hui-hui* or Mohammedan astronomical board alongside the Chinese one. The Jesuits around 1600 found these astronomers still at work. They calculated on a slate, that is, in writing; recognized our degrees and minutes; and used an intercalary day instead of month.

T'ang Shun-chih, 1507–1560, dealt with circle measurement, arcs, and sagittae.

K'u Ying-hsiang in the mid-sixteenth century wrote a Classified Details in the Sea-mirror (of Li Yeh), but, evidently no longer grasping the celestial-element algebra, he evaded the difficulties in the book he was commenting on, and thus helped make the method unintelligible. It was not reunderstood by the Chinese until after they had learned European algebra.

Ch'eng Tai-wei in 1593 published the *Suan-fa T'ung-tsung*, which contains the oldest known picture of a *suan-pan* or *soroban*-type abacus.

By historians of government and art this period of the Mings, 1368–1644, "the last great native dynasty," is reckoned as one of relative florescence, especially during its earlier part.

European influence, 1600–1720.—The Jesuit influence in China on mathematics, astronomy, cartography, and many branches of technology was enormous. It is plain that the Chinese were in the main receptive; and having so much to learn, it is natural that they developed little original productivity. The import may be approximately dated from the visit to Peking in 1601 of Matteo Ricci, known as Li Ma-tou in Chinese. It is essentially complete in the *Su-li Ching-yün* of 1713, a work of composite authorship under the guidance of the great and long-lived Manchu emperor K'ang Hsi. This includes accounts of both native and adapted European algebra with letters, the latter method being known as *Chieh-ken-fang;* logarithmic tables without theory; π correct to nineteen decimals.

From 1720.—After the Jesuit influence ended, the Chinese were left to themselves. Works of European science ceased being translated into Chinese until the mid-nineteenth century, and their scholars could not read European languages. It speaks well for the vitality and stability of Chinese civilization that for the century and a half between Jesuit and modern Occidental influencing they groped ahead from their uncompleted education. It was not a period of great productivity, but they made unaided progress, revived some of their old native mathematics, and increasingly integrated it with the European which they had begun to learn. Significant in this connection is the complex but interesting story of attempts to deal with the nine formulae attributed to the Jesuit Jartoux, 1670–1720, known to the Chinese as Tu Te-mei. It is not impossible that the Chinese themselves evolved these theorems. At any rate, they succeeded in analyzing them.

Mei Ku-ch'eng, graduated in 1715, grandson of Mei Wen-ting, 1633–1721, in his *Ch'ih-shui I-chai* concluded that European and celestial-element algebra were fundamentally similar, and therewith brought the latter back into honor. He published three of the Jartoux formulae.

K'ung Chi-han, descendant of Confucius in the sixty-ninth generation, republished ancient mathematical works.

Ming An-t'u, a Manchu, work published posthumously in 1774. He explained Jartoux's nine formulae. These as a series were unknown in eighteenth-century Europe; one, for the square of an arc, was first published there in 1815, but is given by Takebe Kenko in Japan in 1722. Mikami quotes Hayashi as therefore believing that Ming established the nine formulae. At any rate, his are the first definitely analytical studies, in the European sense, in China.

Li Juan, 1773–1802, wrote Equations Theory, *K'ai-fang Shuo*. He appears to have been the first Chinese to recognize the existence of more than a single root in equations; a fact, however, which the Japanese had discovered in the seventeenth century. It was he that rediscovered and republished Chu's Precious Mirror of 1303.

Yüan Yüan in 1799 published Biographies of Astronomers and Mathematicians.

Chu Hung, graduated 1802, soon after calculated π to forty decimal places, twenty-five of which are correct; ellipse rectification.

Tun Yu-ch'eng, 1791–1823, analyzed the Jartoux formulae independently of Ming An-t'u's analysis.

Hsiang Ming-ta, 1795–1850. Circle and ellipse.

Hsia Luan-hsiang, 1823–1864. Exact root extraction of equations.

Tseng Chi-hung, d. 1877, π correctly to 100 places.

This development is meager alongside that of contemporary Europe, from which it stems; but in view of the premature interruption of the connection, eighteenth- and nineteenth-century Chinese mathematicians must be credited with productivity. If we knew nothing about the seventeenth-century influencing, we should probably rate the period as one of rather flourishing originality.

Medicine and biology.—The scientific deficiencies of Chinese medicine have already been mentioned: notably the lack of anatomical foundation. It did develop specific features of its own, such as acupuncture, and interest in the spleen. Its periods of relative activity, inferable from the works preserved as listed by Sarton, are the following:

1. *Later Chou,* perhaps lapping over into Early Han
   Pien Ch'iao, or Ch'in Yüeh Jen, a legendary figure of perhaps the early fifth century B.C., said to have been born in Chihli and to have flourished in the state of Cheng, "wrote" the *Nan-ching.*
   The *Nei-ching Su-wen,* attributed to the legendary emperor Huang Ti, may date from the fourth century.
   The *Pen Ts'ao* or herbal or materia medica of the legendary Shen-nung seems more or less of the same age.
   Shun Yü-i, b. ca. 216, work lost.

2. *End of Han, Three Kingdoms, Tsin, 175–325*
   Chang Chung-ching, or Chang Chi, end of 2d cent. Dietetics and fevers.
   Hua T'o, prob. fl. ca. 190–265. Surgery, etc.
   Huang Fu or Shi An, fl. under Chin (Tsin), ca. 215–282. Acupuncture.
   Wang Shu-ho, fl. under western Chin, 265–317. Pulse.

3. *Pre-T'ang and Early T'ang, 500–775*
   T'ao Hung-ching or T'ung-ming, 451–536. Materia medica. Also Taoist alchemist.
   Ch'ao Yüan-fang, fl. ca. 605–609. Theoretical medicine.
   Li-chi or Ying Kung soon after 650 officially revised the materia medica (*pen ts'ao*) for the T'angs.
   Su Kung a few years later again revised it.
   Sun Sse-mo, d. 682; recipes; Taoist medicine.
   Wang Tao, fl. ca. 752; comprehensive treatise on medicine.
   Wang Ping, fl. ca. 761; commentary on the *Nei-ching.*

4. *Sung*

Wang Wei-te, fl. ca. 1027; acupuncture.

P'ang An-shih, fl. ca. 1090; fevers.

Sung, Tz'e, fl. 1241–1253: *Hsi-yüan-lu,* or instructions to coro-
ners, still in use.

The time relation of these periods of activity to those in
mathematics and astronomy is as follows:

Mathematics, Astronomy	*Medical works*
...?	−500 to −150
−200 to 265	
	175 to 325
420 to 740	500 to 775
	(960 to 1280 ?)
*1240 to 1320	?
	?
(1720 to 1880)	?

Apparently the courses of the two activities had no more
than partial relation.

General or systematic biology hardly existed in native
China. Its place was taken by compilatory books written by
scholars on subjects of special interest. Some such are:

On tea, by Lu Yü, d. 804.

On bamboo sprouts, by Tsan-ning, fl. ca. 988.

On li-chih nuts, by Ts'ai Hsiang, ca. 1011–1066.

On crabs, by Fu Kung, fl. 1059.

On peonies, by Wang Kuan, fl. ca. 1070.

On rice and silk culture, by Lou Shou, fl. ca. 1150.

On oranges, by Han Ch'an-chih, fl. 1178.

On chrysanthemums, by two authors of the early twelfth century,
and by Fan Ch'eng-ta, the geographer, 1126–1193.

These are really scholarly and belletristic encyclopaedia articles written as monographs. They express the same tradition as
the famous twelfth-century works on antiquities (the *Po-ku-
t'u-lu*), jades, coins, and families, and are allied to the encyclopaedias which began to be written in the same Sung periods.
Their interest is literary or humanistic, and at best only incidentally biological.

Summary.—Especially in mathematics, for which the data have been well analyzed, and apparently along with it in astronomy, it is clear that Chinese scientific productivity was definitely concentrated into periods. The first two of these periods, centering respectively around the beginning of our era and five centuries later, were of some length: from three to five centuries each. The third, in Mongol times, was sharply accentuated but brief—less than a century for its recorded span. A fourth, derivative from European science, is probably to be recognized as centering around 1800. On the whole, these cycles of Chinese success in science fit rather badly with the generally accepted periods of national prosperity and florescence. The first and third begin very soon after the completion of philosophical growths. The second is roughly contemporary with the basic development of native philology, and like it seems to have its roots at least partly in Indian influences which came as a by-product of Buddhism. These matters will be touched upon again in their wider relations when the history of Chinese national civilization is considered.

In contrast to all other growths of which we have knowledge, the periods of productivity of medicine and of general science coincide rather poorly in China: probably because medicine remained nonscientific to an unusual degree.

§23. Japanese Science

Japanese science, apart from technological aspects, seems to have had only one pulse of growth, and that confined to mathematics. Its history is remarkable.

Until 1600, mathematics in Japan depended on that in China, but was much in arrears. There was in fact nothing that could be called a science. In the pre-T'ang and Early T'ang period Japan made enormous imports of culture from China; but not of mathematics. Having only just assimilated writing, Buddhism, the Confucian classics, the art, and many institutions of China, Japan was presumably not yet ready to absorb the Chinese pure science of the time, unrelated to life as this must have seemed. A little later, when Japan might have been ripe, Chinese scientific activity had become dormant for five hundred years. The Late Sung–Early Mongol productivity in China again went by without causing a contemporary ripple in Japan. Three hundred years later, however, the Japanese took up this celestial-element algebra of China, and developed it brilliantly. Most curious of all, they did this after they had had contacts with European nations and Christian missionaries had been in the land during the sixteenth century. Their mathematics began to flourish about the time they isolated themselves from the world. There is no trace of European influence in it; and they reached back into what China had forgotten while she was learning from Europe, in order to make their own start. The growth, far spent by 1868, soon succumbed under the systematic self-Europeanization of Japan

Nevertheless it would seem that the birth of this mathematics immediately after the two generations of exposure to European civilization cannot be a nonsignificant coincidence. The materials with which the development began were wholly Sinitic; but Europe provided the ferment, or at least the catalyzer, to start the process. This is made probable by two analogous developments of the period from 1622 to 1868: in art and drama. The art represented by Hokusai's prints is certainly Sino-Japanese and not Occidental; but it also certainly represents a new direction in Sino-Japanese art: a plebeianization, as it has been called, and a fresh vigor. This very lack, in some degree, of the most highly specialized qualities of Sino-Japanese art is what commended Hokusai to the first Europeans who became acquainted with Japanese art; since a complete alien is almost inevitably a vulgarian in his relation to the finer essences of a culture. Similarly, the genuine drama that began after 1600 and culminated under Shikamatsu about 1700 was very different from the established traditional, ritualistic, narrowly formalized No drama: far broader in subject and method, of more genuinely universal interest, emotional, often crude, and—from the aristocrat's standpoint—thoroughly bourgeois. The resemblance of Shikamatsu to Shakespeare has been noticed, and the possibility of his deriving from European drama has been discussed. But there seems to be neither historical nor internal evidence sufficient to establish a connection. Mathematics could hardly evoke so wide an appeal as pictures and plays; but the post-1600 mathematics was also of the people: it became an interest of commoners and rare aristocrats; it did not flourish under court patronage, nor develop into part of a gentleman's standard education.

In short, it looks as if in all three activities contacts with the Occident were too light and brief to allow any important or traceable borrowing of Western culture material, but that they did suffice to act as a stimulus resulting in distinctive internal changes and new productions still within the framework of the established culture as a whole. This finding obviously touches on an aspect of culture history of broad theoretical import. It indicates that connections may be influential even if they leave no direct record; and that while close resemblances of specific elements of culture are necessary to establish proof of borrowing, transmission, or diffusion, especially where documentary evidence of the act of importation is lacking, analytic comparison merely of elements will not exhaust the answers to problems, especially when these seem to result negatively. There remains a possibility that subtle stimulus influences can express themselves indirectly, or invisibly, within the patterns of the influenced rather than the influencing civilization. Evidently the old and vexed question of the dependence of Greek science, philosophy, and art on Mycenaean, Egyptian, and Asiatic, and of Hindu on Greek, are of this order. Many of the Greek developments beginning about 600 can certainly not be "derived" from outside; and yet the Greeks, and with them most historians, are almost certainly also right in believing that Greek civilization was not wholly a unique miracle of spontaneous internal generation. There were external influences, and they were all-important, though they can perhaps never be wholly discovered because of the equally important transmutations into other patterns, and the stimulation of new pattern developments which they set into operation.

JAPANESE MATHEMATICS

*Mori Kambei. *1600 (?), 1628, is credited with introducing, and
certainly popularized, the Chinese *suan-pan* abacus calculation—*soroban* in Japanese. "A multitude of pupils crowded
around him."

Yoshida Koyu, 1598–1672. *1627, pupil of Mori.

Imamura Chisho and Takahara Kisshu, fellow pupils with Yoshida; together, the Sanshi or three honorable mathematicians.

In 1658, Japanese edition of Chu's Introduction of 1299, long
lost in China, was published. The celestial-element method,
t'ien-yuen-shu, was called *tengen jutsu.*

Sata Seiko, *1666, recognized multiplicity of equation roots.

**Seki Kowa, 1642–1708. *1674 seq. The "father" and "Newton"
of Japanese mathematics. Established first the *yendan* and
then the *tenzan jutsu* or Japanese algebra. Both were carried
on in writing up to the calculations, which in the *yendan* were
always and in the *tenzan* sometimes performed with apparatus.
The *tenzan* was taught secretly and not published until 1769.

Miyagi Seiko, *1695, full treatment of equation of 1,458th degree.

Nakane Genkei, 1672–1733.

*Takebe, 1664–1739, *1710–1720, *1722, *yenri* or circle measurement or principle by analytical considerations (π to forty-one
figures, correctly).

Matsunaga Ryohitsu, *1739, further *yenri.*

Lord Arima, 1714–1783.

*Ajima Chokuyen, 1739–1798. *1774, *1781, *1794. His use of
the circle principle resembled the operation of integration
within two prescribed limits.

Fujita Sadasuke, 1734–1807. *1779.

*Aida, 1747–1817. *1785 seq.

Wada Nei, 1787–1840. *1822.

1844, first logarithmic tables printed in Japan by Koide.

1868, all schools closed.

1877, Society of Mathematics includes old Japanese as well as
modern mathematicians.

Hagiwara, 1828–1909, *1878, last of the line.

It is evident that the main development was from 1600 to
1800, with its peak toward 1700 under Seki. The movement
went on through the nineteenth century, attaining certain
higher specializations; but apparently the men born after 1750

were less "great," or had fewer fundamentals left to discover,
than their predecessors. The individual ages at which outstanding achievements were produced in the instances listed are:
29, 32, 35, 35, 38, 45, 50 (delayed? 10 years after 1868), 58. Evidently the growth phenomena of this mathematical development, strange as it stands out in culture history, were normal
by the precedent of developments in other lands and times.

   Though they are of only indirect bearing on problems of
configuration, I add some statements condensed from Mikami,
the principal authority on the subject, since so little is generally known about this interesting chapter in the history of
science.

   Japanese mathematics was not cultivated by the government; it was entirely the science of the people. It was treated
as an art or branch of natural history; hence imperfect induc-
tion was used. Especially at first it was semisecret, and much of
it was taught but not published; and there were rival schools
in the literal sense. The development throughout was alge-
braical, not geometric, and without feeling for the need of
demonstration. When geometric theorems were arrived at
other than algebraically, it was intuitively and without means
of testing their correctness. Subjects which were investigated
were the ellipse, cycloid, epicycloid, ovals, catenary, sections
and intersections of cylinders; ignored were: conic sections,
parabola (known but not studied), hyperbola (probably unknown). Circle measuring was done with inscribed squares
and their derivatives, not with hexagons and rarely with circumscribed polygons. (These limitations are strong internal
evidence confirming the independence of Japanese mathematics from direct European influences.) In integration, "folding
tables," *jo-hyo*, were used. Logarithmic tables were known
from the Chinese *Su-li Ching-yün* of 1713, but not studied
until the end of the eighteenth century and rarely used in the
first half of the nineteenth. There existed a contemporary
astronomy derived from the Dutch, but no Occidentalist
(reader of Dutch) is known who was also a mathematician.
After about 1750 a tendency was evident to seek equations of as

low a degree as possible instead of high ones; before long there was a related impulse in the word-formulated rules expressing formulae, leading to a mania for shortening statements, as an end in itself. (This is of interest as an exemplification of the deep-seated passion of Japanese civilization for parsimony of form—form that is finished, elegant, compact, simple, pared down, suggestive, and as nearly freed from content, or relation to crude reality, as possible.) There is said to be extant a *soroban* abacus of 1444–1448.

§24. Conclusions

The most important inference which can be drawn from the foregoing analyses is that science does not differ essentially from other creative activities of human culture and is produced in irregular pulses, cycles, or intensive bursts of growths. On account of its accumulative nature, this fact, though patent enough, is often overlooked or denied. It is true that there is a large measure of accumulation in science, as in certain other departments of civilization—invention, technology, general knowledge. If one is specially interested in continuity, as most moderns are, because of the satisfaction of seeing themselves as the summation of a long series of progresses, much continuity is certainly to be found. It is, however, specifically to be noted that continuity is a proper quality only of the results of scientific activity. The activity itself is discontinuous. The process of producing new science is highly intermittent. It gathers momentum, develops energy and speed, falls away, ends, remains dormant for periods that are sometimes extremely long. It runs a course like a fever. In short, its activity is cyclic; substantially as cyclic as that of the nonaccumulative, supposedly untrammeled arts.

The nature and relations of the principal growths in the datable periods of civilization are diagrammed herewith. It is evident that the general character of the configurations is much like those of philosophy, although differing greatly in detail, and sometimes without apparent relation between them.

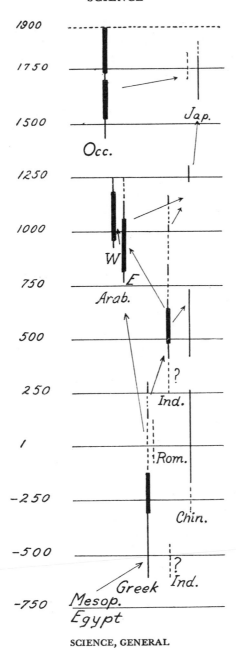

SCIENCE, GENERAL

The total duration of the major cycles is not uniform. We have: Greek, —600 to 300; Mohammedan, 750 to 1250; Chinese, —200? to 740; Occidental since 1440; in other words, 900, 500, 940+? 500+ (unfinished) years. However, these figures denote frames within which a more or less coherent development occurred. In no cycle was the development continuously single. The Mohammedan growth took place in two separated regions and in periods which only partly overlapped. The other growths were all interrupted by one or more definite slowings or stoppages. The longest continuous activity—of growths already completed—does not exceed 500 years, and many are much shorter.

It appears that the duration of culminating phases is also fairly variable:

Greek, 310 to 120: 190 years.
Indian, before 499 to after 628: 130–175 years.
Second Chinese, 420–740: 320 years.[31]
Third Chinese, 1240–1310: 70 years (mathematics only).
Eastern Mohammedan, 810–1050: 240 years.
Western Mohammedan, 950–1200: 250 years (probably less).
First Occidental, 1540–1700: 160 years.
Second Occidental, since 1730: 205+ years.

This does suggest that a movement of science which becomes important tends to maintain itself at genuinely high level for something over a century, at least, and not infrequently up to twice that span.

The diagram allows a rough computation analogous to that already made for philosophy. From —600 to 1900 there are 51 half-century moments. These become 255 for five areas: western Europe, the Greek world, the Mohammedan world or Near East including Iran and Turkestan, India, China-Japan. These five exhaust the known areas in which serious and datable progress has been made in science. Egypt, Mesopotamia, and southern Mexico–Guatemala are too uncertain in the chronology of their achievements, as distinct from what they preserved, to be usable in a reckoning. Egypt and Meso-

---

[31] Probably to be reduced.

potamia in any event are already included in the Near East.
Now the number of active moments is:

Occident 10
Arab–Near East 10
Greek 13
India 8
China-Japan 23
                                  ——
                                  64

Sixty-four is just one-fourth of 255. The proportion might
be increased somewhat by counting seven Spanish-Arab moments as Western,[32] and about as many more Greek moments
as happening actually in Egypt or Asia; though for the latter
some deduction ought also be made for contemporary inactivity in the old Greek world. At best, however, we can bring the
total up to only about 78, or 30 per cent. In other words, in
those regions in which science has ever been active at all, it
has been in a state of activity less than a third of the time, perhaps not over a quarter.

Moreover, our five regions cover only a fraction of the habit-
able globe. Also, many times science is actually developing
only in a part of a region which we have counted as a whole.
In the West, for instance, there has been only one moment
in 500 years—the generation beginning in 1800—when Italy,
France, Germany, and England were synchronously in high
active productivity. All the foregoing shows how really rare
actual creativeness in science has been in human history.

There have been two periods when science was making no
progress anywhere in the world: from 300 to 400, and from
1310 to 1440.

There have been several times when productivity was going
on in only one region: among the Greeks from −500 to −300;

---

[32] This assumes that because Spain is in Europe it is to be reckoned as Western.
However, since Christian Spain never produced any science, the Iberian peninsula could alternatively be construed as forming part not of the Occident but
of the North African–Near East area. Such an allocation yields a better historical
fit for Spain in science and philosophy, but less good for other aspects of
civilization.

in China from −120 to 120, from 650 to 740, and again from 1250 to 1310; in the Arabic-writing world apparently part of the time from before 800 to about 1240—whenever India was intermittently inactive.

Nowhere do three regional sciences clearly flourish contemporaneously.

All these findings closely parallel those already made for philosophy.

Our results definitely dispel the doubts, raised in the beginning of this chapter, concerning the proper inclusion of mathematics and medicine in science. Wherever these activities belong logically, historically they belong in science: their growth curves fit those of science. This is especially clear for mathematics. Practically every scientific development began with mathematics; some, especially in India and China-Japan, never got beyond it. The Greek and Arab cycles are somewhat aberrant from the rest in that astronomical and other interests are prominent alongside mathematics from the beginning. In the West, not only the general European course but the German, Italian, Swiss, French, English, and Scotch commence with mathematics.

For medicine the correspondence is also convincing, though not quite so close, largely on account of the imperfect historical fit of medicine to science in China. The reason for this exception seems to be that Chinese science consisted largely of mathematics, Chinese medicine of a mixture of folkways and literature.

As for external relations of science, that with philosophy is, as expectable, the closest. But the relation is quite variable.

Phase	Science	Philosophy
Greek I	−600 − −120	−600 − −270
Greek II	120 − 170	
Greek III	250 − 300	200 − 450
Arab, E.	800 − 1250 (1150)	850 − 1100
Arab, W.	975 − 1250 (1200)	1050 − 1200
Western I		1080 − 1380
Western II	1440 − (incompl.)	1630 − 1880

Phase	Science	Philosophy
Indian I	ca. 500	ca. 500
Indian II	400 – 650	100 – ·1000
Chinese I		−550 – −230
Chinese II	−200? – 260	
Chinese III	420 – 740	
Chinese IV		1050 – 1200
Chinese V	1240 – 1310	
Japanese (VI)[33]	1600 – 1850	

In general, China seems to have taken up science after she got through doing philosophy; the other civilizations, to have developed them more or less simultaneously but never exactly so.

Science longer, at one or both ends: Greek I, E. Arab, W. Arab, Western II.
Philosophy longer: Indian II (science in a philosophic sag?).
Philosophy without science: Western I (and Chinese I, IV).
Science without philosophy: (Sino-Japanese II, III, V, VI).[34]

So far as a generalization can be made, it seems fair to say that in India philosophy was the more deeply rooted, determining, and tenacious; that in the three civilizations to the west science was at least the more durable; and that in China science began after philosophy finished. This last relation might also be construed as having obtained once in the Occident: Scholasticism ended about 1380, European science began around 1440.

As for the relation to religion, it is more difficult to generalize, because religion is a much more variable and less definable set of cultural activities than philosophy. In general, the relations would seem to be slight, as is expectable from the fact that religion is first of all a set of cult practices, and, so far as it contains a theory, this is in a plane that usually intersects only

---

[33] The phases here numbered I, II, etc., are neither those previously called first, second, etc., in science, nor those similarly called in philosophy. The Roman numbering applies only to this comparative table. Thus Greek III is the third Greek pulse of science, but the second of philosophy.

[34] Greek II could also be added, but I am reckoning it as a recapitulation or codification of Greek I.

distantly with the plane of scientific theory and phenomena. Most civilizations except our own have had little consciousness of a clash between religion and science: the Mohammedans and Greeks only occasionally, the Chinese not at all, and the Hindus in fact rather tending to identify them. Even in our civilization, the conflict has been magnified since science, in the two last scant centuries, has at times asserted absolute preeminence, in imitation of the Church in the days when European science was young.

More profitable and fundamental is the problem of the time and inner relations of science to national and cultural florescences in general. On the whole it would seem that the periods of science tend either to coincide with, or somewhat to follow, the periods of culmination in national success or the arts. Examples of delay are:

> Greek science, culmination begins −310; virtual loss of independence, −338.
> Eastern Arab, peak begins ca. 813; last great caliphs 786–833.
> Western Arab, science begins ca. 960 or after; great caliphs, 912–976.
> Italy, science growth begins 1520, art at zenith 1530.
> England, initial phase Jacobean, culmination Restoration; literature, Elizabethan-Jacobean.
> Germany, modern phase begins 1800, literature and music at peak 1800–1815.
> Holland, peak 1660–1690, political culmination about 1650; Rembrandt died 1669, Spinoza 1677, Huygens 1695.

This last is almost a case of synchronism. Other instances of near-coincidence are:

> Roman science, −70–120, almost simultaneous with literature, but averaging a little later.
> France, first pulse 1630–1660, in the earlier half of the upswing usually designated after Louis XIV.
> France, second pulse 1750/60–1860/70, centering at the zenith of Napoleonic success and one to two decades before the Romantic overturns in literature and art.

There is danger of overstraining instances like these, which probably do have some generic significance, into a pseudo

law. There are enough contrary instances to make it necessary
to guard strictly against this, with respect both to political-
nationalistic and to aesthetic achievement. Thus, the Swiss
nationalistic climax around 1500 was followed by a very modest little scientific—or pseudo-scientific—spurt. The great Swiss
science of the eighteenth century began in a period of dry rot
of institutions which led to a national collapse while the science still continued to flourish. Spain culminated politically,
as well as in literature, drama, painting, and sculpture, without ever having any growth of science. The time coincidence
of English music and earlier English science is very exact, yet
cannot well be more than an accident, so far as specific relation
of the two is concerned; and the Restoration, when both culminated, was certainly not a period of national glory. In nearly
all such cases there probably are underlying connections within the configuration of the national culture as a whole. But
this is a quite different thing from positing a direct connection
with nationalistic—that is, politicomilitary—success. There
have been, and presumably will continue to be, such nationalistic culminations without allied culminations in science or
some other branch of civilization; and vice versa.

China shows an unusually bad fit of scientific pulses to the
recognized periods of national prosperity. The imperfection
of fit is great enough to raise suspicion that these periods have
been constructed only partly with objectivity, and in accordance with some schema of Chinese national-culture evaluation
which has been accepted in our books without much testing.

Chapter IV

PHILOLOGY

Chapter IV

PHILOLOGY

§25. The Nature of Philology

PHILOLOGY[1] is perhaps the least of the activities treated here, but as a subject of investigation it has the virtue of definiteness. I shall restrict myself so far as possible to grammar, namely, that part of philology which deals with the structure of language. Phonetics also properly belongs here, but in general has been much involved with problems of orthography. Lexicography I deliberately disregard, so far as possible, in the present connection. Etymology[2] or word-formation cannot properly be dissociated from grammar in most languages, but dictionary-making generally springs from an animus and interest quite different from those that impel the discoverers of grammar. It deals primarily with the content of language, as distinct from its form or structure. It requires industry, patience, erudition, an accumulative sense, but less insight and imagination than are needed for original investigation in grammar.

Structure is of course something that is always present in language, and almost equally without exception its speakers are virtually unconscious of it until they are taught. The dis-

---

[1] Usage of the terms Philology and Linguistics varies. Many modern scholars define Linguistics as that which has to do with sounds, grammar, and lexicon, while Philology includes Linguistics plus the study of products of speech, such as literary history and criticism. I do not quarrel with these definitions; but in this work I am not concerned with the history of literary history and criticism; and I do find it necessary to distinguish the analysis of a particular language from the comparative and general study of languages. By "philology" I therefore mean here the analytic study of the sounds, words, and forms of any *one* language, such as Greek; that is, its phonetics, grammar, and dictionary. By "comparative philology" I designate the study of a group of *related* languages, in practice most often the Indo-European, that is, Sanskrit, Greek, Latin, Germanic, etc., viewed comparatively. By "linguistics" I mean the inductive study of human languages generally, the concern with speech as such, but through the medium of any and all particular languages.

[2] In the general or popular sense, not its technical philological one.

covery of this structure, or grammar, is in many ways comparable to the discovery of physiology, most of the processes of which are also operative within us without our being ordinarily aware of them; except that the essential limits of what can be discovered are more readily reached in grammar than in physiology.

There is no indication that any recognition of grammar beyond casual glimpses was ever attained by a people that had no writing. Moreover, it is probable that no people, except such as borrowed a philological technique ready-made from others to apply it to their own speech, ever discovered grammar until after they had a literature the text of which was canonical or classical. It seems usually if not always to have been the desire for textual purification or standardized preservation of an accepted literature that led to philological commentary; and only after this had been in vogue for some time did interest in grammar for its own sake, as a problem of the discovery of forms, awaken. Just so, medicine, or attempts at medicine, preceded physiology; and counting, measuring, and reckoning, mathematics for its own sake. Again pretty universally, once grammar has been discovered, it tends to be given a place in education for its supposed practical or applied value, which is probably insignificant for all except the professional scholar. On the other hand, there is of course a very real intellectual discipline in learning to deal with abstracted form; and this value of grammar has been and still is for the most part overlooked in popular estimation.

Another feature of philology is that, like mathematics and physics, it can be made to prove or disprove itself. An inadequately founded "rule" promptly runs foul of the facts of language, and is then reformulated until it either fits all the facts or is supplemented by another rule. There is, theoretically, no remainder left unaccounted for. Grammar is therefore a precise science, not an approximative one. Except for logic, it is accounted the most rigorous of the disciplines in the humanities.

Obviously, there are limits to what can be learned about

the forms of any one language, and with systematic inquiry these limits are rather soon reached. The course of development of pure philology, apart from lexicography and practical applications to orthography, prosody, or style, is therefore fairly brief, normally. Or, more exactly, the growth is a struggle to substitute conscious recognition of structure for unconscious use of it—a process that is groping at first, but then proceeds more rapidly until the forms of the language have been essentially determined and definitely formulated; whereupon, the inherent patterns of the material having been exhausted, preoccupation with philology becomes repetitive, didactic, or merely learned without new ideas. In the main, what concerns us here is the placement in time of developing philologies within their national cultures, and their relations to other creative activities of these cultures.

It appears that grammar was independently discovered only twice in human history, in India and in Greece, and so nearly at the same time as to suggest a possible connection and an ultimate single origin, though no historic relation is as yet traceable. All other philologies, including the Chinese, have probably been influenced by one or another of these two, if not outrightly derived from them. The latter eighteenth century saw the beginning of growth of systematic comparative philology, which was a novel undertaking in human culture. But comparative philology was not a wholly Occidental achievement. It got its impetus from the discovery by Western scholars of the long extant and highly perfected native Indian philology.

§26. Indian Philology

Sanskrit grammar appears to have been developed earlier than Greek, though the usual uncertainty of Indian dates forbids any dogmatic judgment. It was also carried to greater fineness. It was a pre-Christian development in northern India.

Yāska wrote the only pre-Pāninian treatise which has survived, the *Nirukta*, an etymological commentary on the Vedas, with at least part of the grammatical terminology of Pāṇini. The date of

Yāska is usually set either between 700 and 500, or in the fifth century B.C. The language he treats is more archaic than any other non-Vedic Sanskrit. He knew all Vedic Samhitas, most of the Brahmanas, some of the Upanishads.

**Pāṇini is probably the greatest name in philology. He was born at Shalatura, near modern Atak, in extreme northwest India. The most usual estimate of his date is 350 B.C.; Winternitz, however, holds to some probability of his having lived in the fifth century, when Buddhism was not yet important. His mention of Yavanānī, Ionian writing (or female slave), seems to preclude his having been earlier than the late sixth century. However, Vincent Smith favors a date not later than 600, and Goldstücker the eighth century. Pāṇini names Yāska and Śaunaka as predecessors. His rules refer to a form of speech nearer to that of the Brahmanas, Upanishads, and Sutras than to Vedic speech. His work is the *Aṣṭādhyāyī*, or Eight-Sections. It is really the end product of a philological development, because it takes the rules for granted and teaches the exceptions. It uses formulaic abbreviations, and everything, even logical order, is sacrificed to ultracondensation. Even the lists of Sanskrit roots, and of words falling under the same grammatical rules, are presupposed as known.

Kātyāyana is definitely later than Pāṇini: his grammar refers essentially to classical Sanskrit. His *Vārttika* is a supplement to parts of Pāṇini rather than a commentary on him.

*Patañjali's *Mahābhāṣya* is primarily a commentary on Kātyā-yana, but contains also extensions and critical examinations of Pāṇini. The stage of Sanskrit dealt with is about the same as Kātyāyana's; but some interval must have elapsed, because Patanjali names previous commentators on Kātyāyana. The work is written in true dialogue style. The generally assumed date for Patanjali is the second century B.C., and surely not later than the first post-Christian century, says Winternitz; Sarton gives fl. B.C. 185 seq. or 144–142 in northern India.

Essentially, this concludes the history of native Sanskrit philology. What follows is repetition or preservation, or discussion of Panini rather than inquiry into Sanskrit. The fundamental and great period of Sanskrit philology is thus comprised between 500 and 100 B.C., with its peak probably around 350, but with the possibility that both beginning and culmination of the growth were somewhat earlier. The general era therefore is that of Kapila, Buddha, Mahavira, and the first Indian

mathematics and medicine. This high development of so abstruse and self-conscious an activity as philology at so early a
time remains perpetually astonishing. It suggests the existence
of a vast historic lacuna in our knowledge of more ancient
India—a great realm which we can hope to see in part explored
by archaeology alone.

What followed the main growth can be briefly indicated by
a few selected mentions.

Sarvavarman, probably ca. 300 A.D., wrote the *Kātantra,* an
elementary grammar which shows some attempts to depart from
Pāṇini. It was used in Kashmir and eastern Bengal, and by later
Pali and Dravidian grammarians.

Candragomin, about 600, composed a commentary to Pāṇini,
that is, a Sanskrit grammar, which had wide vogue in Buddhistic
lands, Nepal, Tibet, Kashmir, and Ceylon.

Bhartṛhari, d. 651/2, wrote the *Vākyapadīya,* a commentary to
Pāṇini, but dealing with the philosophy of language, or linguistics
as such, rather than with philology or grammar.

Jayāditya and Vāmana wrote the *Kāśikavṛtti,* an excellent and
clear comment on Pāṇini, which quickly became a textbook—it
took five years to master. The Chinese pilgrim, I-tsing, who probably learned his Sanskrit from this book, gives Jayāditya's death as
not later than 661/2.

The contemporaneity of the last three works suggests a secondary peak; which would nearly correspond with the sixth-century
one of Indian general science.

About 1625, Bhaṭṭojī Dīkṣita issued the *Siddhāntakaumudī,* a
rearrangement of Pāṇini by topics logically grouped, Pāṇini, who
wrote for grammarians, having neglected this convenience in his
ardor to achieve compactness.

The Paninian system was ultimately extended from Sanskrit
to Prakrit and Pali. The oldest preserved Prakrit grammar is
the *Prākṛtaprakāsa* of Vararuchi, of unknown date. It treats
Prakrit as derived from Sanskrit. Pali was first grammatically
analyzed, so far as we know, by Kachchayana, who handled it
as an independent language. His date is very uncertain: he
lived later than the fifth century, but possibly not until the
eleventh. He was followed, from the eleventh and twelfth centuries on, by a series of grammarians in Ceylon and Burma, Pali

being the language of the canon of the Hinayana or Lesser
Vehicle of Buddhism in Ceylon and, later, Burma, Siam, and
Cambodia.

§27. Greek Philology

Greek philology seems to have been somewhat slow in reaching
its zenith; or perhaps we merely know the course of development more fully than in India. The first symptoms of interest
come in the fifth century; the earliest preserved grammars are
from the second centuries B.C. and A.C.

Stage of philosophers
>   Protagoras of Abdera, the sophist, ca. 485/80–411/10, distin-
>   guished genders and certain modes and tenses.
>   Aristotle distinguished three parts of speech.
>   Chrysippos of Soli, the third head of the Stoic school, ca. 280–
>   208, is said to have improved certain grammatical definitions.

Stage of editors
>   *Aristophanes of Byzantium, ca. 257–ca. 180, librarian of the
>   Museum at Alexandria, 195 seq. Textual criticism, with sys-
>   tematization of punctuation and accent, lexicography, recog-
>   nition of grammatical analogies.
>   Aristarchos of Samothrace, ca. 220–145, successor of Aristophanes
>   at the Museum. Commentator; recognized eight parts of speech.

Stage of grammarians
>   *Crates of Mallos in Cilicia, flourished at Pergamum, visited
>   Rome in –168, Stoic, geographer, and philologist. Wrote what
>   appears to have been the first formal Greek grammar, no
>   longer extant.
>   *Dionysios Thrax, so named after his Thracian father, born ca.
>   –166, pupil of Aristarchos, fl. at Alexandria and Rhodes. His
>   *Techne Grammatike* is the earliest extant Greek grammar, and
>   the basis of later and Latin ones.

Stage of grammarians, lexicographers, etc.
>   Didymos, ca. 65 B.C.–ca. 10 A.D., fl. at Alexandria. Commentary,
>   lexicography, grammar.
>   Pamphilos of Alexandria, fl. ca. 50 A.D. Rare words.
>   Pamphila, fl. at Epidauros under Nero (54–68). History of
>   literature.
>   *Apollonios Dyskolos, fl. at Alexandria under Hadrian (117–138).
>   "Systematized Alexandrian grammar"; "inventor of syntax."
>   Aeolios Dionysios, fl. under Hadrian. Attic lexicography.

Nicanor, fl. at Alexandria, probably under Hadrian. Distinguished eight varieties of punctuation.

*Aeolios Herodianos, son of Dyskolos, in Rome under M. Aurelius. Wrote *Katholike Prosodia,* 21 books on quantities, accentuation, breathings, enclitics. He and his father are accounted the foremost philologists of the Imperial age.

Phrynichos, fl. 161–192 in Bithynia. Atticist lexicographer.

Julius Pollux (Polydeukes) of Naucratis in Egypt, fl. in Athens under Commodus (180–192). Atticist lexicographer.

Late stage

Orion of Thebes in Egypt, fl. ca. 421 at Alexandria, then at Constantinople. Etymology.

Hesychios of Alexandria, fl. prob. 5th cent. Largest Greek lexicon of antiquity.

The greatest scholarship is generally attributed to Aristophanes. For our present specific purposes, however, when we are concerned with philology as such, and recognize grammar as the core of this, the culmination must probably be sought in Crates and Dionysios. As the former's work has perished, it was evidently soon superseded by the latter's, and the zenith may be dated about 125 B.C. This is after the close of creative activity in Greek philosophy, science, and poetry; in fact, it appears to be the latest of all Greek culminations.

There was a second peak two hundred and fifty years later, under Dyskolos and his son. This seems related to the preceding much as the astronomy of Ptolemy was to that of Hipparchos. In each case the later men possessed a fuller accumulation of knowledge and were therefore better able to formulate a definitive system, but operated mainly with the ideas and methods of their predecessors. The difference was that between Greek Alexandria and the Antonine empire.

It is notable that the sharp definition of grammar was attained by men whose mother tongue, or at any rate their ancestral one, was other than Greek: a Cilician and a Thracian. This is almost certainly no accident. The Hellenized alien would be more conscious of the Greek language than the Hellene, and perhaps at an advantage in abstracting its forms. It is even more notable that these educated barbarians concerned themselves only with Greek grammar, never, apparently, comparing it with other tongues. We do not even any longer know their Cilician and Thracian languages. It was the written language of perfected civilization, and only that, which became the subject of philology. Language or languages as such the Greeks seem to have developed no interest in. The same of course holds for other philologies until after 1700.

It is a question of interest why it was only the Hindus and the Greeks who originated grammatical inquiry. They shared the following circumstances: a system of wholly nonideographic, consonantally phonetic writing, to which they added their own vowel signs; and the possession of this since a few centuries only—long enough, perhaps, for the nicer problems of orthography to be still alive, and yet neither so new as to leave the basic manner of writing uncertain nor so old as to have crystallized writing into something fixed and independent of speech. The alphabets themselves were quite diverse: the Greek derived immediately from the Phoenician, with only minor alterations and retaining the same order of the letters; the Hindu, at second or third hand, so much altered that the channel of derivation is hard to trace and has been disputed; and the symbols were thoroughly reclassified and reordered. In fact, the order of the letters in the Sanskrit alphabet could have been devised only after systematized phonetic observation of the language. It is also true that both Greek and Sanskrit are Indo-European languages; but it would be hazardous to assume that this had any effect on the development of philology other than through a certain pressure exerted on writing by the character of the Indo-European languages in the direction of vowel-sign invention, as compared with Semitic. A partly ideographic or phonetically imperfect syllabic system of writing like Egyptian or Cuneiform would presumably present serious obstacles to the development of an analytic attitude toward actual or spoken language.

As to possible connections of origin between Hindu and Greek philology, the known gradual development of the Greek activity and the apparently indicated priority of the Hindu by a century or two seems to put transmission almost out of question. If there were connections at all, they were indirect—common stimuli rather than outright learning.

§28. Latin Philology

After the Romans ruled the Mediterranean world, and Latin became the civilized language of half this world, a grammar was in order and was constructed on the Greek model with only such modifications as were necessary. The Romans themselves were making efforts in this direction in the last pre-Christian century; the systematization took place about the middle of the first century after Christ, apparently at the hands of Romanized foreigners. The grammars most used in the Middle Ages were composed several centuries later.

> M. Terentius Varro, 116–27, born at Sabine Reate. Husbandry, botany, and *De Lingua Latina.*
> Caesar is said to have coined the term ablative.
> Verrius Flaccus, fl. ca. 10 B.C. Encyclopaedic lexicography and grammar.
>
> Q. Remmius Palaemon, born at Vicenza evidently of Greek ancestry, fl. 35–70. The leading teacher of his day, who, with Probus and Pliny, fixed the main outlines of Latin grammar in his *Ars Grammatica,* the first schoolbook.
> M. Valerius Probus, fl. in Rome ca. 56–88, born in Beyrut.
> Quintilian the rhetorician, ca. 35–ca. 95, born at Calagurris in Spain, fits into the period of Palaemon and Probus.
>
> Aelius Donatus, fl. at Rome about the mid-4th cent.
> Priscianus, born at Caesaria in Mauretania, fl. at Constantinople ca. 512, wrote a grammar that remained popular in the Middle Ages.

§29. Chinese Philology

The Chinese language has a minimum of a grammar. It is written by an elaborate ideographic system. Conditions accordingly were the worst possible for the origination of grammatical philology, and on the other hand some sort of categories became desirable by which the numerous written symbols could be classified or arranged—to furnish an equivalent for an alphabetic order, for instance. Inevitably, therefore, Chinese philology became something different from that elsewhere.

The first achievement was the classification of characters according to their "radicals," that is, their common ideographic elements, making possible an orderly dictionary. This step was taken in Han times, about 100 A.D. The result, however, remained primarily a classified lexicon of stroke symbols, only indirectly of words.

Next came a pronouncing dictionary, having regard to the phonetic quality of spoken words. The whole set of Chinese writing made this an awkward task, and it was not attempted till a hundred and fifty or more years later than the symbol classification, almost certainly under the stimulus of Indian writing, which had become known through Buddhism. This religion had now had governmental recognition for two centuries, and was about to enter the period of greatest activity of its sects, philosophies, and propaganda in China.

Two hundred years more, and the Chinese discovered that their language had tones. This apparently simple and fundamental discovery was not made until two thousand years after they possessed a writing, and a thousand after they had scholars. It might not have been made then, if the learning of Sanskrit for religious purposes had not made them phonetically self-conscious. This consciousness spread; in or by T'ang times, alternation of tones became one basis of Chinese prosody.

The next century saw the first systematic dictionary in which ideographic radical, pronunciation, and tone were all considered; and soon afterward came the first in which the basis of organization was phonetic, by rhymes, with regard also to tones.

This whole development had taken 500 years; that part of it which involved phonetics, between 300 and 350 years, from about 270 to 601. Thereafter there were larger lexicons and finally encyclopaedias, but no important new methods. Phonetics, which in most languages is a sort of gateway to structure, is in Chinese the core of its philology, owing to the near-lack of formal grammar. Two facts seem specially significant. Chinese philology, as distinct from orthography, evidently got its start from Hindu stimuli; and its development of basic approaches falls in the four centuries of short, local, and competing dynasties between Han and T'ang which are generally described as a period of confusion and breakdown. As a matter of fact, other activities of Chinese culture, such as plastic art and science, had or began their florescence in this same era, which is evidently undervalued by historians on account of its lack of material and political stability.

Hsü Shen, b. in Honan, d. 120 A.D. Wrote, about 100, *Shuo wen* (*Ch'ieh tsu*), dictionary of 10,500 characters classified under 540 (ideographic) radicals.

Sun Yen, or Sun Shu-jan, b. in Shantung, fl. prob. ca. 270. Introduced into lexicography the method of *fan ch'ieh,* "spelling"— or, better, pronunciation, that is, indicating the initial and final sounds of words by two other characters.

Shen Yo, 441–513, b. in Chehkiang. Differentiated and explained the tones, in a lost work called *Sse sheng,* "Four Tones." The discovery has also been attributed to Chou Yung of Honan, of the same 5th cent.

Ku Yeh-wang, 519–581, b. in Kiangsu. His *Yu p'ien* is a dictionary organized under radicals, with the *fan ch'ieh* and tones first systematically applied.

Lu Fa-yen and Yen Chih-t'ui in 601 prepared the *Ch'ieh yun,* the first extant phonetic dictionary, classified under 204 rhymes, with tones considered.

This was revised in 1011–1013 by Ch'en P'ong-nien.

In 1039 appeared the phonetic dictionary *Chi-yün* of 52,523 characters, by Sung Ch'i (or Hui An) and collaborators.

§30. Japanese Philology

Motoori was the founder of Japanese grammar, in 1779.[3] Japanese scholars generally believe this to be an autochthonous development. However, its growth commenced more than two

---

[3] See chapter on Literature.—This is the usual statement. But in Upton Close, *Behind the Face of Japan,* 1942, p. 39, I find the following: "In 1593 ... Ieyasu in his castle at Nagoyu under Mt. Fuji was discussing Japanese rhetoric with the Jesuit Rodriguez, pitting him for amusement against Buddhist and Confucian scholars. This ended with Rodriguez, under encouragement from Ieyasu, creating Japanese grammar. Before word-minded Europeans came to Pacific Asia

centuries after Europeans came into the land; and even during
the period of rigid isolation and exclusion there was a group
of Japanese scholars of things Western. That no Latin or Dutch
grammar should have reached them is inconceivable; that it
might have taken a century, more or less, for such a model to
have stimulated one of the small group into applying a parallel
effort to the Japanese language seems within the range of probability. It is therefore likely that we have here a case of idea
diffusion: the suggestion of the goal, of the possibility of the
undertaking, came from outside; the specific working out was
native. Internal evidence of the accomplishment ought to yield
a definite answer to the suggested hypothesis. It may be an
accident or it may be significant that in the thousand years
before European contact so culturally advanced a people as
the Japanese made not even a beginning of grammatical
analysis of their speech. Chinese stimulation seems out of the
question because China had no model to supply.

§31. Arabic Philology

Arabic philology developed rapidly after the contact of Mohammedanism with civilization. The reputed "discoverer" of
Arabic grammar was adult at Mohammed's death; vowel points
and prosodic formulation were soon added; and the systematic
presentation of grammar was essentially completed before 800.
The philological growth was consequently much faster in getting started than Arab science or philosophy; in fact, it had
run the originating part of its course by the time science and
philosophy were beginning to pass from the assimilative to the
productive stage. This is rather remarkable in view of the fact
that Greek precedent was of relatively little direct service to.

---

neither Chinese nor Japanese literati had bothered with that pseudoscience."
On account of the war, my Japanese colleagues are not available in California
for consultation, as this passage is being set in type in 1944. Close's statement
sounds somewhat dramatized and simplificatory; but, so far as authenticable, it
would confirm and merely push back the date of my suggested foreign stimulation. From 1593 to 1779 seems a long interval for an idea pattern to be dormant
and then germinate "spontaneously." But Chinese algebra slept even longer
in Japan.

grammarians of so different a language as a Semitic one. The Arab possession of an actively flourishing poetry and oratory before Mohammed may have been an influence; or, more broadly, the strong and successful verbalizing quality of all specific Arab civilization, ancient and modern, which has been recognized by themselves in contrast with other nationalities. Moreover, the first Arabic philologists, and a fair proportion of the later ones, were of Arab ethnic stock; with time, the share of Muslims of non-Arab origin increased. Whatever the causes, the contrast is sharp with Greece and China, where philology developed much more slowly, and later than philosophy.

The Greek stimulus may have been transmitted via Syriac. According to Sarton, vowel and diacritical signs were introduced into Syriac by Jacob, Bishop of Edessa, ca. 633–708; the Arab invention is ascribed to Al-Hajjaj, ca. 663–714. But the interval is short: so brief that Syriac priority is not inferable with complete certainty. At any rate, the sudden Islamic development may have been the specific ferment which launched the two cognate Semitic languages into problems of orthography and grammar about simultaneously. The Syrians, with centuries of exposure to and participation in Greek civilization, would expectably make more rapid progress at first. Later, the priority seems to have been Arabic. Thus the system of Arab grammar was essentially achieved by Sibawaihi, 755–795. The Syriac philologists mentioned by Sarton are Hunain, ca. 809–877, grammar and lexicon; Bar Bahlul, later 10th cent., dictionary; Elias of Tirhan, d. 1049, grammar by the Arabic method; Barhebraeus, later 13th cent., same. Whatever the origins, then, Arabic philology grew more rapidly and set the model for Syriac as for Hebrew.

In any event, the evolution of the first grammar of a Semitic language represented genuine originality. Greek philology could provide the objective and some conceptual tools; but everything else had to be created. The rapidity of the Arabic development is therefore notable. The very magnitude and freshness of the task probably stimulated unusual energy. This presumably received further impetus from association with and sanction by a young and fervent faith: philology theoretically served the better understanding of the Koran, which might not be translated out of Arabic.

Abu-l-Aswad, ca. 606–688/9, fl. at Basra, traditional discoverer of Arabic grammar.

Al-Hajjaj ibn Yusuf, ca. 663–714, soldier, grammarian, and founder of Wasit near Basra. The invention of vowel marks and diacritical points for consonants is ascribed to him; at any rate, is attributable to his period. Syriac may have provided the example, as discussed above.

Khalil ibn Ahmad, ca. 720–791/2. B. in Oman, fl. at Basra. Grammarian, lexicographer, formulator of Arabic prosody.

*Sibawaihi, ca. 755–795. Persian, pupil of last; at Basra, Bagdad, Shiraz. His Arabic grammar is the earliest systematic presentation and is essentially complete. Like other Iranians and Turks and Jews of this and several following centuries working in philology, science, or philosophy, he wrote in Arabic.

Jehuda ben Qaraish, Jew, b. in Tahort, North Africa, fl. about the turn of the 8th to 9th cent., wrote, in Arabic, on the interrelation of several Semitic languages. This led to nothing systematic but is an interesting anticipation of comparative philology.

Ibn Qutaiba, 828/9–ca. 889, Iranian, b. and fl. at Bagdad. First leader of the grammatical school of Bagdad, which succeeded the rival ones of Basra and Kufa.

Hunain ibn Ishaq, 809/10–877, b. Hira, fl. Bagdad. Syriac grammar and lexicon.

Hamza, Persian, fl. ca. 961 at Bagdad. Etymology of homonyms and grammar.

Ibn al-Qutiya, b., fl., and d. (in 977) at Cordova. Verb conjugation. Apparently the first Spanish Arab philologist of importance, two centuries later than the fundamental Oriental Arab philologists, but a century to two earlier than the Spanish Arab philosophers.

Al Jauhari, d. 1002. Persian, born in Farab, Turkestan, fl. at Nisabur, Khorasan. Arabic dictionary, arranged in the alphabetic order of the final letters of the stem.

Ibn Jinni, 941/2–1002, son of a Greek slave, fl. at Mosul and Bagdad, attempted the philosophical treatment of language.

It is evident that while the first work was by Arabs, the fundamental formulations toward the end of the eighth century were participated in, if not chiefly made, by non-Arabs. After 800 no Arab from Arabia contributed anything of prime importance. After the same date there occurred a proliferation into refinements of conjugation, larger and better organized dictionaries, and attempts at both a comparative and a philosophical study of speech.

§32. Hebrew Philology

Hebrew grammar was worked out by Jews in Mohammedan countries, writing chiefly in Arabic, some two centuries later than Arabic grammar had been formulated, namely, about 950 to 1050; with Spain and Morocco leading in productivity.

Sahl ben Mazliah, b. 910 in Jerusalem. Grammar and dictionary.

Menahem ben Saruq, b. at Tortosa, fl. Cordova second half 10th cent. Complete dictionary, in Hebrew, of the Old Testament, with grammatical comment.

David ben Abraham, from Fez, fl. same half century. Dictionary, in Arabic, included remarks on derivation and grammar, and comparisons with Arabic.

Dunash ben Labrat, b. at Fez of Bagdad family, fl. at Sura, Fez, Cordova. New Hebrew prosody founded on the Arabic; rival of Menahem; their quarrel ushered in the "golden age" of Hebrew philology in Spain-Morocco.

*Hayyuj, ca. 950–1000†, b. at Fez, pupil of Menahem, fl. at Cordova. "Father of scientific Hebrew grammar." His work was translated into Hebrew 1050–1150.

*Ibn Janah (Rabbi Marinus), b. 985/90 at Cordova, d. at Saragossa. "Greatest Hebrew philologist of the Middle Ages." Translated into Hebrew 1150–1200.

Samuel Ha-Levi, 993–1055, b. Cordova, fl. Malaga, Granada. Wrote chiefly in Hebrew. Grammar.

§33. Linguistics and Comparative Philology

With the rise of vernacular literatures, especially in Europe, grammars of vernacular languages began to be worked out, for the most part on the Greek-Latin model. These represented applications of old ideas to new material, and while they are often important from the point of view of national consciousness and development, they may be passed over here as too diverse to be considered as a coherent growth. The eighteenth

century saw the origin of two currents of thought, following
different channels but related since they were comparative in
interest, that is, no longer concerned primarily with the establishment of a canon or absolute standard of correctness for one
language considered as given and perfect.

One of these growths is Linguistics, or the empirical science
of language on the basis of descriptive study of particular languages the world over. In spite of the injection of some philosophizing, its approach has never ceased to derive from a curiosity
akin to that of biological natural history. Beginning with a
primarily factual productivity toward the end of the eighteenth
century, it got well under way in the nineteenth, primarily
in the hands of Germans, and is still in active flow.

> P. S. Pallas, 1741–1811; b. Berlin, to Russia. Siberian travels
> including linguistics.
> Hervás y Panduro, 1735–1809; b. Horcajo, Spain; *1784–1805.
> J. C. Adelung and J. S. Vater; *1806–1817, *Mithridates.*
> Wilhelm von Humboldt, 1767–1835; *1836. He represents the
> same type of interest and ability in the "Geisteswissenschaften"
> as his more famous brother Alexander in the "Naturwissen-
> schaften."
> O. Böhtlingk, 1815–1904; *1851.
> H. Steinthal, 1823–1899; *1861.
> W. Wundt, 1832–1920; *1900.
> Friedrich Müller, 1834–1898; *1876–1888.
> G. von der Gabelentz, 1840–1893; *1891.
> H. Sweet, 1845–1912, Englishman; *1900.
> F. de Saussure, 1857–1913, Swiss; *1915.
> F. Boas, 1858–1942; German, to America; *1911.
> O. Jespersen, Dane, 1860–1943.
> N. I. Marr, Russian, 1864–1934.
> N. Finck, 1867–1910; *1905, 1910.
> W. Schmidt, 1868——; *1926.
> E. Sapir, American, b. Germany, 1884–1939.

The other growth is that which has appropriated the name
of Comparative Philology. Its activity is much narrower, its
techniques much more definite. It differs from earlier philologies in that it concerns itself with more than one language and
does not aim to set up a canon, but proceeds historically. It

differs from Linguistics in that its interest does not extend to all aspects of all languages, but lies in working out the historically demonstrable or supposedly demonstrable changes which have occurred in a group of languages which are obviously related historically, that is, are of common descent. Theoretically there are thus as many "comparative philologies" as there are families of languages; and there actually exist Semitic, Finno-Ugric, Bantu, Malayo-Polynesian, and several other comparative philologies, some fairly well developed, some in their beginnings. Actually, the movement began with Indo-European and has been some eight- or nine-tenths concerned with it. There has also been a considerable inclination to restrict consideration to languages that are historically documented. The relation to orthodox "history" is therefore somewhat like that of linguistics to culture history or natural history. An important difference from history, however, is that the phenomena of language, perhaps because their causative factors lie for the most part in the unconscious level, present a high, even if sometimes complex, degree of regularity in their "laws" or "shifts." This regularity has been seized upon by philologists, and a technique has been erected upon it which is more rigorous than that of any other discipline in the humanities and social studies. Modern philology in principle does not consider a demonstration as valid until it is documented by evidence that is both objective and exhaustive. This rigorous standard is the triumph of philology, and gives it a genuine significance in the history of culture far greater than its content-results, which are not only necessarily technical but essentially narrow. As a matter of fact, Indo-European philology is concerned almost wholly with changes in the forms of words and grammatical elements. The meanings are disregarded so far as possible, and so, largely, are causative factors, relations to psychology, and problems of broader interrelationships within the field of language, all of which obviously do not lend themselves to the discovery of rigid regularities.

The particular method used consists of the reconstruction of the hypothetical original mother tongue, the "Primitive" or

"Ur" Indo-European, for instance, not as end in itself, but as a starting point for the differentiating changes that have taken place. Naturally, inquiry proceeds reciprocally here: further comparative analysis of historical languages modifies the formulation of the hypothetical original one, and as this becomes more correct, more exhaustive explanation of the derivations becomes possible. The result is a self-correcting but closed system; where this begins to have relations with other systems, or other fields of knowledge, the proper method of "philology" ceases. The principal impingement which philologists were slow to discountenance has been on the side of philosophical psychology and logic; partly because of the ancient Greek precedent, partly because most nineteenth-century German philologists grew up in an atmosphere saturated with Kant and Hegel.

The actual beginnings of comparative philology, however, or at least its prolegomena, were not German but English; and its true foundation was the Sanskrit philology of Panini more than two thousand years before. Since the seventeenth century there had been at least a trickle of interest in the empirical historical comparison of the Germanic subdivision of Indo-European. Then, in the eighteenth, there began to come knowledge from India of Sanskrit; and, soon after, of the rather closely related Old Persian speech. Sanskrit arrived in Europe with the prestige of an immemorially ancient language, and accompanied by a grammar more perfectly worked out by the Hindus than that by the Greeks for Greek, or by Latin and European imitators for their tongues. Comparison and new stimulation followed, in an age of enlightenment, and comparative philology was born. An Englishman, William Jones, was its founder; within a generation the Germans dominated it, at the very period in which their natural science was swinging into its full stride and their philosophy was still in culmination. There is no doubt, however, that it was the grafting of the ancient Hindu philology on the European stock which immensely stimulated, if it did not produce, the new growth. The sharpness of technique, for instance, which is the

hallmark of modern philology had been more nearly attained
by Panini than by Greek grammarians.

Franciscus Junius, 1589–1677/8; b. Heidelberg, to Holland and
England; *1665, comparative Germanic.

G. Hickes, 1642–1715; Yorkshire; *1689, *1703, same.

Sir William Jones, 1746–1794, *1786.

Rasmus Rask, Dane, 1787–1832, *1818.

Jakob Grimm, 1787–1863, *1819 seq.

Bopp, 1791–1867, *1816, *1833 seq.

Diez, 1794–1876, *1836 seq., Romance.

Pott, 1802–1887, *1833 seq.

Zeuss, 1806–1856, *1853, Celtic.

Miklosich, 1813–1891, *1852 seq., Slavic. (B. in Slavic Styria,
wrote in German.)

O. Böhtlingk, 1815–1904.

Schleicher, 1821–1868, *1861.

F. Max Müller, 1823–1900; b. Dessau, to England; *1859 seq.

Whitney, American, 1827–1894, *1867, *1874.

Leskien, 1840–1916, *1876 seq., Slavic and Baltic.

J. Schmidt, 1843–1901, *1872, wave theory.

Paul, 1846–1921, *1880. Psychologizing most developed.

Verner, Dane, 1846–1896, *1876.

Brugmann, 1849–1919, and Delbrück, 1842–1922, *1886 seq.

And others essentially or actually contemporary.

Distinct as Linguistics and Comparative Philology are, they
deal partly with the same and always with similar material, and
their curves run parallel in time and geography. They can
therefore be culture-historically construed as two currents of
the same stream. The one is impelled by scientific curiosity, and
even now struggles inadequately with a vast body of phenomena. The other roots in historical attitude and scholarly
tradition, and has developed an astonishingly sharp method,
but has narrowed its problems until much of its pursuit often
seems as purely intellectual and sterile as the playing of chess.
It has shown considerable inclination to remain wholly self-
sufficient. Whether the two currents will approach and integrate into a larger one probably depends on how much strength
remains in each and in the Occidental civilization of which
they are part.

§34. Summary

So far as is known, philology had two independent origins, in India and in Greece, the Indian being apparently the somewhat earlier as well as more intensive activity. It is almost indicated to suspect some historic connection between these two first growths, but none whatever has been uncovered. From these two developments all other national philologies are derived by imitation or transfer: the Indian stimulating the Chinese; the Greek stimulating the Latin, Arabic, Hebrew, and more recent West European language treatments. Invariably it was a written and avowed "language of civilization," usually serving as the medium of a standardized religious canon,[4] that was made the subject of philological study; other languages were ignored. The application of philological analysis to European vernaculars came when these were felt also to be languages of civilization with rights of national autonomy. The transfer of Indian philology to Chinese, and of Greek to Arabic, involved problems calling for some originality. The other transfers were mainly applications of an old method to somewhat new but similar material, and were generally characterized by a minimum of originality of conception. It is in the nature of the case that there could not well be successful recurrences of philology so long as each growth was unilingual.

A new type of development began in the terminal eighteenth century with General Linguistics and Comparative Philology. Into the birth of these there entered several factors: a widened horizon of curiosity associated with geographical exploration and colonial conquest; the parallel vernacular grammars of Europe, which sooner or later invited comparison; and specifically, acquaintance with ancient Sanskrit and its acute, ready-made philology. From the junction of the Indian, Greek, and Occidental streams, Linguistics and Comparative Philology were produced. Until this time, philological development had

---

[4] Among the Greeks the Homeric poems took the place of purely religious texts, and in China it was the Classics, compiled by "philosophers," that functionally filled the place of a Bible or canon.

not been unitary: it now became so. Or rather, it should have
become so, it would logically seem; but Linguistics and Comparative Philology are not yet properly integrated. In the
growth of the former, a natural history-interest predominated;
and while the goal was scientific, the route has been descriptive.
Comparative Philology, on the other hand, began with a definite historic interest, but has been largely deflected into analysis of process of change, though within a strictly limited historic
field. It has also remained quasi-national rather than objectively comparative, in spite of its name: a kin-group of languages was substituted for one language as the object of study.
The result is that Comparative Philology, moving from history
toward science, is not quite either; while Linguistics, beginning with scientific intent, has found progress slow and has
shown some inclination to attempt historic problems. The two
movements are therefore considerably intertwined, and constitute complementary historic growths. This is shown also by the
simultaneity of their dates.

The following little table recapitulates the more important
developments the world over:

Philology	Period of Activity	Peak
Indian	−500? − −100?	ca. −350?
Greek	−450 − +200	−175 − −125
Latin	−100 − +500	+25 − +75
Chinese	100 − 650+	500 − 600
Arabic	650 − 1000	ca. 790
Hebrew	950 − 1050+	1000 − 1050
Linguistics	since 1780	
Comparative Philol.	since 1780	

As there cannot well be a notable second phase or growth of
any one individual philology, at least hardly so until general
linguistics shall have developed rather fundamentally new concepts, this list differs somewhat from the summarizing tables or
diagrams for other cultural activities. It is really almost a table
of diffusion—diffusion not of culture content or material, but
of a culture method or pattern.

Chapter V

SCULPTURE

Chapter V

SCULPTURE

WITH THE fine arts we come to that group of civilizational activities in which periodicity has always been recognized as a characteristic phenomenon and emphasis on the modern idea of cumulative progress has been difficult for historians to maintain.

Obviously, sculpture and painting often occur in association, and are then likely to stand in a relation of intimate interinfluence. However, their consideration here will be consecutive, on the basis of simplicity of presentation. Problems of relation will be more clearly defined if taken up later. There have been sculptures without known equivalent pictorial art: Mesopotamian and Gothic, for example. Painting has sometimes continued to flourish and develop long after plastic art was producing no new qualities, as in China and Japan; but no important growth of painting has occurred which was clearly unassociated with sculpture in its development.

As we are less concerned with tracing the direct and indirect connections between different sculptural developments than in the growth features characteristic of each, the order of treatment is almost immaterial. A natural and unobjectionable sequence is that of the sequence of beginnings: Mesopotamia and Egypt, the Greeks with their Roman sequel, India and Indonesia, China with Japan as an outgrowth, western Europe.

§35. Egyptian Sculpture

Egypt offers the classic example of cycle in the strict sense. It is no wonder that Petrie based his *Revolutions of Civilization* on the history of that country, and took its sculpture as his point of departure. However, a cycle must be distinguished, so far as possible, from a growth. It is with the latter that the present work mainly deals. A cultural growth consists of the development, fulfillment, and often persistence of a set of definite, qualitative patterns in some one or several associated activities of culture: indeed in the whole of a culture, in the fullest cases. The Italian Renaissance is an excellent type example. A cycle, on the other hand, is a wave or pulse within a growth or civilization. It is a recurrence of development after temporary suspension. It takes place within the framework of a set of patterns. The patterns may change somewhat from cycle to cycle within the civilization; but they change less than they remain constant. If they are reconstituted fundamentally, we have a new growth. Civilizational cycles are thus much like the business cycle, which is a series of alternating repetitions of relatively successful and unsuccessful activity within the economic or industrial pattern of one civilization.

It is plain that ancient Egyptian civilization is a growth—in the main a single growth of more than three thousand years. Within this growth occurred a series of pulsations of prosperity and misfortune; but after each such cycle there was a return to the patterns of the preceding pulse, as closely as possible and on the whole remarkably closely. This fixity of anchorage to its system of basic patterns has always been recognized as characteristic of Egyptian culture. Only, the concept of fixity has then tended to be transferred to the civilizations of Asia—presumably for the simple and self-centered reason that they too are non-European—where it applies very much less.

It is also characteristic of Egypt that its prosperity cycles in the different activities of culture tended to coincide to a quite unusual degree. A definitely successful dynasty regularly meant military expansion, accumulation and diffusion of wealth, notable building operations, high-grade sculpture, painting, and often literature. Even writing, scarab inscriptions, the quality of industrial utensils, stonework, and tombs improve. So regular, on the whole, is the concordance of the several curves that evidently they are all only functions of one underlying factor or group of related factors. How far this factor was predominantly political or economic, or something less easily namable that is adumbrated by the term "psychologic," is an interesting and important problem. It is a problem that seems to have a real relation to the problem of the modern business cycle. Not that the basis of the Egyptian cycle need have been primarily economic. It may just as well be that our familiar industrial cycle is economically expressed rather than economically produced. We are economic-conscious in this age and would therefore tend to see chiefly the economic aspects of the phenomena even if these were secondary. I am only outlining a parallel which suggests a problem that as yet has no answer.

The history of Egyptian sculpture, then, is roughly also the history of the florescences of Egyptian civilization as a whole; except that some other activities began earlier and some later. Briefly, good sculpture was produced in Dynasties I, IV or V, XII, XVIII, and XXVI. Between these, it was less in quantity and inferior in quality; but the kind or type varied only within an astonishingly small range.

Dynasty I, after about 3315.[1]—There is a little sculpture, including some in the round, of fair aesthetic value, far better than anything predynastic, but with the characteristic Egyptian pattern still not wholly realized.

Dynasties IV–V, 2840–2540.—After a rise in Dynasty III, about 2900, sculpture in IV and V comes to a peak never thereafter surpassed in Egypt. Some books carry the period from IV through VI, which would prolong it until about 2475. Petrie puts the culmination in IV, Eduard Meyer and Steindorff definitely in V, Maspero seems noncommittal. It may be suspected that some of the finest statuary—like, perhaps, the Sheikh-el-Beled, for example—was found early in the development of Egyptology and can no longer be dated accurately. We shall probably not be far wrong if we define the peak by the transition from Dynasty IV—that of the greatest pyramids—to Dynasty V; which would be around 2680.

Dynasty XII, 2000–1788.—After a long impoverishment, improvement is manifest in Dynasty XI (2160–2000) and culminates in XII.

---

[1] The Meyer-Breasted chronology is followed, although the most recent tendency is to have Dynasty I begin about 3000, with shortening of the interval between Dynasties VI and X.

Dynasty XVIII, 1580–1310.—Dynasty XIX continues until 1200, often with colossal pieces, but the art culmination falls in XVIII under Amenhotep III, 1405–1370, according to Eduard Meyer, as compared with the period of most successful conquest under Thutmose III, 1480–1450. Amenhotep IV (Ikhnaton), 1370–1352, made the famous monotheistic reform, which was accompanied by a new sculptural manner. This manner lasted only as long as the religious overturn, but left occasional traces of influence into the beginning of the next dynasty. Characteristic of the Ikhnaton school are a softening of the contours, a mixture of graceful effeminacy and partial realism, new attitudes and proportions. There is a substitution of new conventions for old, not a doing away with convention. The style expressed itself better in relief than in the round, and perhaps best of all in painting. Some see in it the effect of the king's insistence on truth, whereupon the sculptors transferred peculiarities of his individual physique to all their human representations. Maspero, on the other hand, construes the movement as due largely to temporary favor given the provincial school of Hermopolis, active since Dynasty XII, over the royal studios of Thebes.

Dynasty XXVI, 660–525.—Often called the Egyptian renaissance, the art of this time was more nearly a successful resuscitation, especially of Fourth Dynasty traits of detail. I speak of traits because essentially there was only one Egyptian style. Execution was often excellent in this period, and the time was not wholly lacking in features recognizably its own, such as careful head modeling and a degree of individual characterization of faces.

The forms of Egyptian sculpture were adhered to through nearly a millennium longer, often with slovenliness and ignorance and sometimes with foreign hybridization in Roman times, but surviving until the population became Christian.

The intervals between wave crests run about 600, 800,[2] 500, 800 years. Petrie, using a much longer chronology, now generally abandoned, reckons 650, 1,300, 1,900, 950, respectively.

---

[2] Or 500 by the shorter count now coming into vogue.

§36. Mesopotamian Sculpture

Mesopotamian sculpture travels in a less firmly cut channel than Egyptian. It is also much less abundant. The highest point of which we have knowledge does not occur until just before the collapse of Assyria, in the seventh century, when Egyptian sculpture was undergoing its third renascence and the Greeks were already struggling in the awkward phase of their art.

I treat Sumerian and Semitic productions as part of a single biethnic development, much as scholars usually have found it necessary to treat the civilization as a whole. Hittite and Elamite sculpture could be included, and for that matter Achaemenian Persian.

The period of the Royal Tombs at Ur, which may be estimated at not far from 3500 or 3200,[3] shows a surprisingly developed metallurgy, including well-modeled bulls and bull heads. Most of the woodwork has disappeared, and stone sculpture seems to be absent. There are some scattering stone heads, busts, and relief stelae from Erech, Lagash, and other Sumerian city-states during the next five centuries, but none equal to the "predynastic" Ur metalwork in aesthetic quality. In general, earlier Sumerian stone sculpture hardly emerges from the stage of semi-ineptness. The lapidary's seals are now and then carved somewhat more skillfully, perhaps. But they also do not rest on any great art.

The Sargonic age of Semitic Akkad, around 2750, has yielded the Naram-sin stele, a stone relief composition. This is a meager remnant, in quality as well as quantity, to represent the sculpture of the greatest kingdom which Mesopotamia had yet produced.

A half millennium of mature Sumerian florescence—its final stage—followed before the next Semitic overlordship. Now at last, in the times of Gudea at Lagash and of Ur-engur at Ur (respectively to and from ca. 2475), and probably also at Erech and other cities, a genuine stone sculpture developed. The

---

[3] Recent estimates tend to make the period later by some centuries.

pieces preserved are few, and perhaps never were many; but some of the heads show control of technique, poise, and a certain nobility, although not yet devoid of archaism. A temple-scene relief on a steatite vase, evidently undated, possesses composition, posture, motion, and even some sweep of drapery; much of its line is almost reminiscent of early Greek work, rather than of Mesopotamia. Except possibly for the Royal Tombs metalwork—and this does not deal successfully with the human figure—the late Sumerian stone carving represents the sculptural peak of the Mesopotamian area during two thousand years. Withal it is a modest peak, compared with Egypt's.

The important Semitic Hammurabi dynasty of Babylon proper, around 2100, seems to be without preserved statuary, except the relief of the famous Code; and this represents a heavy retrogression. We hear from time to time in Mesopotamian history of the carrying away of god statues by conquest, and of their recapture, even to and from Elam, so sculpture of some kind was continuously made; but the practice of the art cannot have been very frequent. The stonelessness of the lower Mesopotamian plain may hardly be considered a serious factor, because there is no indication of a high-grade plastic art in wood or metal. Moreover, Assyria and Elam, and the desert adjoining Mesopotamia proper, possessed rock. Clay was perhaps too common a material to tempt the sculptor or his patron. Ceramic ware turned wholly plain and utilitarian by the Sargonic era, and went on century after century practically without change. The pottery art was therefore unlikely to provide the sculptor with stimuli.

A thousand nearly barren years follow Hammurabi—in Kassite Babylonia, nascent Assyria, Elam, and the Anatolian Hittite realm. The Elamite work shows some proficiency in metal and ivory, but little feeling of style; the Hittite is both hybrid and awkward.

The later Assyrian period from Ashurnazirpal to Ashurbanipal, 884 to 626, has given us most of our preserved specimens of Mesopotamian sculpture. These consist of both statues and reliefs, as well as half-round figures of winged man-lions and other composite monsters and some work in ivory and metal. The reliefs are easily the best. The work really was produced in two pulses: under Ashurnazirpal, 884–860, and his successor Shalmanezar II, 860–825; and again in the final great period of the Assyrian conquest and empire, which began after 750 and lasted until the fall of Nineveh in 612 or 606. There is a gap of a century between the two phases; but a glance at the earliest and latest work shows that it all belongs to one style. When sculpture resumes in the second pulse under Sargon II and Sennacherib, 722–682, the reliefs show increased freedom of line, both in human and animal attitudes. The high point, however, is not reached until Ashurbanipal, the last great ruler of Assyria, 668–626, whose reign ended only two decades before the complete collapse of the empire and nation. It is from his day that the spirited hunting scenes date, including the famous galloping horses, pack animals, wounded lions, and fleeing wild asses. Here at last, at the very close, we have, in spite of some persistence of mannerism, especially of musculature, sculpture that is real art. But it is only a flash, in time; and the high quality is limited to the portrayal of animals. It is evident that Assyrian sculpture followed the fortunes of empire, as Egyptian sculpture had done earlier.

In spite of its internal improvement, Assyrian art was not a self-contained growth, but a segment of Mesopotamian art. Many of its motives and techniques were old. The extraordinary superanatomical limb musculature which it delighted in is not the sort of thing an incipient art groping to seize form would be likely to hit upon, but rather a highly specialized convention inherited ready-made.

The Neo-Babylonian Empire, 607–538, continued something of the last relief style in its skill of handling animal form, but with less expression and motion: and transferred it to enameled brick

The Achaemenian Persians both at Persepolis and Susa carried on the late Assyrian and Neo-Babylonian motives and techniques, though with discernible change of style, and, as time went on, with some infiltration of Greek influences. Their formal decorative sense was strong, and ornament for its own sake often intruded into representation. Directness and a certain simple chastity characterized the expression of this art; but its inherited ingredients were too diverse to blend into a wholly successful and independent new manner.

It is obvious that Mesopotamian sculpture does not equal Egyptian. It surpasses it at one point only: expression, especially in animal form. And expression of emotion is what Egyptian art consistently avoided. The human body was something the Sumerians, Babylonians, and Assyrians scarcely knew what to do with. They left most of it clothed, but showed the cut instead of the lines of the drapery. The limbs mainly afforded an opportunity for stencil-like application of an artificial pattern of internal structure. The faces, like the postures, were generally lifeless. It is true that Egyptian sculpture is also consistently stiff. But it never seems heavy; and it is always pleasing, and at its best has durable charm. Neither serenity nor charm can be found in any Mesopotamian work; nor for that matter, repose, except for some examples of Late Sumerian and again Persian work. The final achievement of all Mesopotamian sculpture is in the depiction of fear, pain, and death agonies. Is it coincidence, or significant of the civilization of Assyria, that this is her contribution to art?

As for time, area, and nationality, we have this, in summary. The history is somewhat sparse but fairly continuous for three thousand years, from the undated Royal Tombs of Ur to after 500. In all this long span there is no evidence of Egyptian influence, except for a while in the Hittite hill lands beyond Mesopotamia. The first beginnings known to us are Sumerian, and already characteristic for the whole era and area. The Semites, whether of Akkad, Babylon, or Assyria, contributed nothing of importance until the very end. The centuries of their dominance were in general centuries of recession of sculpture. The Sumerians reached their peak about 2475, slightly before the middle of their last period of autonomy from 2650 to 2225. Some sixteen hundred years later the Semites of Assyria set going a real art, endowed with some of the titanic, convulsive energy of their empire. This sculpture, pictorial rather than statuesque, grew for two hundred and fifty years, climaxing just before the sudden and complete collapse of Assyrian rule. The art did not die with Nineveh, but passed over to the inheriting Chaldaeans and Iranians, among whom it persisted, in quieter and more monumental or at least more decorative form, for two or three hundred years. Here, then, we can recognize a "normal" rise-and-fall growth of about five centuries. Before that, our record is too spotty to allow of much inference; except that it is clear that whether the period was one of city-states or of empires, the achievements of sculpture were dependent on military and political successes. Not that these necessarily brought art in their train: witness the aesthetic poverties of Sargon and Hammurabi. The art evidently ran on more or less continuously, but humbly or limited to artisanship; until now and then—but not always—victories, dominance, and governmental organization helped it into a flowering. The parallelism of courses is less regular than in Egypt; just as Mesopotamian sculpture adheres through its fluctuations mainly to certain motives and devices, but Egypt to a single and precisely defined style.

§37. Sculpture in the Greek World

The earliest fine art on Greek soil was by the non-Hellenic people who carried the prehistoric Aegean civilization. I omit this art from intensive consideration not because it was non-Greek, but because its sculptural remains are scant and their dates only estimates or conjectures. Mainly, the Minoan sculpture of Crete was *Kleinkunst;* so was the Mycenaean of the mainland, except for the lions of the Cyclopean gate of Mycenae. The periods of art florescence were Middle Minoan III, Late I, Late II in Crete, corresponding approximately to Early and Middle Mycenaean on the mainland, perhaps 1700/1600 to 1400/1350. Around perhaps 1250 the last Late Minoan period, and Late Mycenaean, ended; from which date there is a gap of six centuries to the inception of Greek plastic art.

Greek sculpture proper arose earlier than Greek painting, culminated earlier, and lasted longer, besides giving birth to a more vigorous Roman daughter.

The first crude beginnings in stone are about 650, or a little later. To define the peak presents certain difficulties; but it falls between 450 and 323, probably near the beginning of that span. The end of creative growth came not before 150, and is generally considered to have stretched well beyond that. The duration thus was five centuries and up, the curve of growth skew, with a more rapid rise than decline.

Until Salamis, 480, everything is still obviously archaic, although the recognized difference between Early and Late Archaic, 625–550 and 550–480, is striking. The earlier work is childlike, often to the point of being ludicrous. The later Archaic, though still stiff and encumbered, shows control of line, and sometimes attains dignity and the beginnings of charm. However, the works definitely manifesting these qualities can with fair certainty—nearly all dates being conjectural— be assigned to the latter half of the "Late Archaic," say post-520. These again can be united without violence, though progress was by now rapid, with the products of much of the so-called Transitional period of 480–450. This regrouping also avoids certain difficulties connected with the beginning of the following or Great period. In other words, choice of the Battle of Salamis as a dividing point has mainly the advantage of familiarity, plus the convenience of dating certain important archaeologic pieces from Attica as surely before or after the Persian invasion. So far as sculpture is concerned, 480 seems to fall in the middle rather than as the end of a phase. That the moral effect of the victory upon the Greeks was enormous is not doubted. But the implication that it was *per se* significant for sculpture is, like all similar interpretations, to be met with suspicion, as being either simplistic or due to a habit of seeing cultural history through the eyes of political history.

If we set back the beginning of the Great period a decade or a decade and a half from the mid-point of the fifth century, the whole work of Phidias and Polyclitus may be included therein. The change that was undergone around 465–460 might be defined as follows. Before then, archaism was dominant, however great the purity or grace of form, as in the Delphi Charioteer or the Ludovisi Throne. For a generation or so after the turning point indicated by 465–460, there was essential liberation from archaism; though Phidias, and still more Polyclitus, are sometimes charged with retaining traces of archaism. The turning point also leaves room for the occasional stronger archaism still later; for instance, in some of the Parthenon metopes, 447–432: they represent a more conservative stream persisting actually contemporary with the peak of Phidias.

Phidias was still working in 430, Polyclitus in 420. There is no name or known product comparable to theirs until Praxiteles, born about 380, or flourished about 370–340, according to different versions: in other words, a half-century interval. It would be unjust to speak of a recession; rather it might be called a resting period; at any rate, it was such so far as the appearance of supreme genius is concerned. With Praxiteles, the whole tone is changed. The serene but silent majesty of Phidian form is replaced by serene loveliness. The feeling has changed to a more feminine one. Youth is emphasized as against agelessness. Expression has come into its own; and technical dexterity is at its pinnacle. In Scopas, expression is more pronounced, and of stronger emotions. If we add Lysippus, younger than Praxiteles by two and than Scopas by perhaps three decades, we come to the last of the very great names. His association is with Alexander; and while he outlived him, we can close his career, and the Great period, not far from 320, or at any rate about 310.

There seems to be general consent that the Great period constitutes an integral unit of quality as compared with what there was before and after. However, we cannot take its chronological mid-point, say the decade around or following 400, as the culmination, because the greatest names fall well before and after. The choice must be made between the generation of Phidias and that of Praxiteles, centering about eighty years apart. This is not easy, and decision is likely to be made on respective preference for profundity or beauty, for sheer form or for form plus expression. Most ancients, and most moderns, seem to have found more of the very highest qualities in Phidias; and we shall abide by their verdict.

With Alexander's conquests Greek sculpture became established over the eastern Mediterranean world, before long as far east as Turkestan and India. In time, Hellenized non-Greeks participated. Pergamum, Ephesus, Rhodes—in or just off Asia Minor—harbored the leading schools in the last two and a half centuries B.C. Hand in hand went a stylistic diffusion, a proliferation into new and diverse subjects and manners: genre, landscape, vehement expression of pathos and anguish alongside seeking after calmness, the superheroic as well as the familiar, even return to deliberate archaism. These are typical breakdown symptoms. The characterizing patterns of the art had been achieved, but momentum remained, and spent itself in variously seeking new subpatterns, and straining or recombining or perpetuating the old ones. The geographical extension is not to be construed as the cause of the stylistic dilation, because the latter is a common phenomenon when there is no Alexandrine conquest. It is true that some arts as they approached or entered their dissolution phase have experienced a geographical spread—nineteenth-century Europe offers a striking parallel in sculpture, painting, music, and literature. But in these cases the late spread in space and the internationalization seem a symptom and integral part of the history of the growth, rather than a cause of its deterioration.

Periods are difficult to define after 320/10. The products of each generation were diverse, and where literary records or inscriptions are lacking, there is often great variability or vagueness in time attribution—much more than in the centuries of formative growth of the art. Until around 200, a more or less tempered realism prevailed, and something of the restraint of the great period was retained—enough, on the whole, to be dominant in spite of the growing expressionism. Then for about a century both vehemence and realism increased, in the main. Until at least about 150, as in the Pergamum friezes, the working out of a residuum of the potentialities of the old patterns continued. Around 100, there was a conscious reaction toward and imitation of the past, though instead of serenity it chiefly attained repose, and instead of nobility, dignity; while a countercurrent aimed at more exaggerated action, emotion, and musculature, and emphasized story over form—as in the Farnese Bull and the Laocoön.

By about the beginning of the Christian era the growth may be counted as substantially over. The best sculpture made for a century or two thereafter was Roman portraits. In the provinces and in the East, sculpture of some sort was produced in abundance, sometimes not wholly lacking in taste, and with constant minor modifications of manner and subject, but on a level, essentially, of skilled artisanship. What before had been a stream, had become a standing expanse of gradually subsiding level.[4]

The Greek course may be summarized thus:

650/25–525/20, Incipient: ineptness still prevailing over control.
525/20–465/60, Late Archaic:[5] control predominates, though not complete; the pattern objectives are evident, but not yet attained.
465/60–420, First Phase of Great Period, and Culmination: liberation from the confinement of archaism, except in patches; full control.
420–370, Second or Plateau Phase of Great Period: divestment of last shreds of archaism.
370–320/10, Third Phase of Great Period, with Second Peak: widening of the scope of the patterns, and technical perfection.
320/10–ca. 200, First Stage of Decline: appearance of aims and mannerisms incongruent with the fundamental patterns of the growth.

[4] No formal list of names is added: we know more of the works than of the sculptors, and the attributions are often uncertain. This seems especially true for the decline. The Victory of Samothrace has been dated all the way from 322 to 31.
[5] Beazley and Ashmole call the time to 520, Early and Middle Archaic; 520–480, Late Archaic; 480–450, Early Classical. I was not aware of their classification until after this section had been written, and am gratified at the confirmation which it gives to 525/20 as a turning point, and to the great or classical phase beginning before 450. In spite of their eminent authority, I remain somewhat dubious of 480 as the milestone at which the great turn comes: I suspect the familiar landmark of Salamis has been moved into the field of art.

Ca. 200–ca. 100, Second Stage of Decline and Beginning of Dissolution: growing internal strain upon the patterns.

Ca. 100–ca. 1, Third Stage of Decline and Predominance of Dissolution Tendencies: extreme dilation of patterns, with exaggeration and distortion; on the other hand, endeavors to restore the past, even to archaism, and to enforce repose; between and surrounding these conflicting tendencies, indiscriminate eclecticism that is, operation without commitment to pattern.

Ca. 1 A.D. seq., sculpture a functioning civilizational institution but no longer an aesthetically creative growth, except for Roman true portraiture.

The geography of the sculpture growth is similar to that of several other Greek activities in evincing a peripheral beginning; notably in Ionia and the Aegean islands, plus Athens, but also in Sicily. Dorians were represented rather strongly alongside Ionians; the two seem to have largely developed the male figure and musculature, the female figure and drapery, respectively.

In the Late Archaic, the Greek mainland took the lead, with one center in Attica, the other Dorian in the Peloponnesus, especially at Argos, Sicyon, and Aegina. On the whole, these remained the focal points through all three phases of the Great Period, with Athens drawing sculptors to itself as well as producing them. Thus Phidias was an Athenian, Myron a Boeotian who worked in Athens, Polyclitus a Sicyonian at Argos. Much the same holds for the next century: Praxiteles an Athenian, Lysippos at Sicyon, Scopas probably a Parian working in the Peloponnesus and Caria rather than at Athens. Cretans, Cypriotes, Eleatics are mentioned alongside these; but Ionia and Sicily are now missing.

In the Hellenistic periods of decline, Greek culture as well as speech had become essentially uniform, the old rooting in localized tradition had grown feebler, dialect affiliations no longer kept the civilization polychrome. Asia Minor, including the off-shore island of Rhodes, soon contained the most active centers of sculpture, as already mentioned; but the Peloponnesus continued to produce sculptors into the second century, and Athens to the end.

§38. Roman Sculpture

Roman sculpture grew gradually out of Greek, and to define when it became Roman is difficult, especially as most of the sculptors seem to be unknown. Pasiteles, who flourished in Rome in the early first century, was an Italian Greek who had become a Roman citizen. His pupil Stephanos still worked in the Greek style. It is at the turn of the era, in the reign of Augustus, that we seem to get the first typically Roman subjects, and the Roman emphasis on portraiture, though the feeling and handling are still prevailingly Greek. From then on, there was growth for about a century, to a peak usually set as occurring under the Flavian emperors, or in the decades just before 100 A.D. The art is fundamentally Greek, of course, but with characteristic emphases and virtues of its own: realism, sometimes aesthetically inappropriate in landscape and depiction, but genuinely excellent in the character delineation of portraiture; by contrast, a strain of abstract allegorizing; undercutting for light-and-shade effects; and in scenes, an effect of distance by varying height of relief—a device handled with some skill, but essentially a trick. Claudius to Trajan, say 40 to 120, is the good period, with the culmination around 70 to 100.

With Hadrian came a Greek revival; that is, the proper Roman growth, brief as it was, had spent its main force and now tried to draw sustenance from its parental root stock. This, and not the Graecizing of Hadrian or the deification of Antinoüs, led to a new, softer line, an indecision both of form and expression, a simplification of composition by omissions. A formal return to a more Roman manner under the Antonines did not help: the work now seems vacant of sculptural meaning. Some authorities wait until the end of the Antonines, 192, before admitting definite degeneration; others give the round date 150, allowing only an occasional good portrait thereafter. By the time of Constantine, in spite of some retention of technical control, the art is pitiful in comparison with its past,

The specific Roman contribution of realistic portrayal seems to have been founded in the custom of preserving impression masks of ancestors' faces for cult purposes. It appears to be the first successful and genuinely individual portraiture, in the modern sense of the words, in the history of art.

§39. Byzantine Sculpture

The Byzantine revival in the age of Justinian expressed itself in architecture and mosaics more than in sculpture.

The second revival under the Macedonian emperors produced a sculpture of perhaps as high quality as was possible within its very restricted frame: it was overwhelmingly religious; it completely avoided large sculpture in the round, limiting itself to miniatures or to essentially pictorial low relief: and it did its best work in a precious material, ivory. Within these narrow limits, however, Byzantine carving of the tenth and eleventh centuries shows taste, reserve, some sense of beauty of form, and extraordinary technical perfection. The beginning of this sculpture in miniature is ascribed to the later ninth century; the end, to the Latin Empire in 1204; but already in the eleventh century the art had begun to freeze into repetitiveness. The climax may therefore be inferred as having lain not far from 1000; perhaps somewhat before, almost certainly not later.

§40. Indian Sculpture

There exist fairly continuous data on the history of Indian sculpture for twenty-two hundred years. We know nothing of the beginnings of the art in the peninsula, which, to our eyes, springs forth ready-made, and equipped with surprising proficiency, under the great Asoka, 273–232. The record ever since is largely archaeological and therefore incomplete. Hence the story leaps from province to province with seemingly greater variety than is likely to have characterized the actual events. Finally, there is little agreement upon the time when the cul-

mination was attained. Smith seems to waver between the
Asoka and the Gupta period—250 B.C. and 450 A.D. Ferguson
gives the palm to Amaravati, 200 A.D., Havell to Elephanta
around 700–800; while the Gandhara art of the early Christian
centuries—about contemporary with Amaravati, though from
the opposite end of India—has been the most discussed in recent
decades, and sometimes highly rated, on account of its Hellenistic incorporations and central and east Asiatic influencings.
In part, judgments differ presumably because Indian art is so
different from Western that it is difficult for westerners to feel
their way into it. In part, however, the character of Hindu
sculpture itself may be at fault: it shows no sharp climax, as
Greek or Italian sculpture do, but tends to progress over an
undulating plateau for long periods, like the Egyptian. Perhaps
for this reason, too, the art of distant colonies among barbarians, in Champa, Cambodia, and Java, rises nearly to the level
of that of the motherland.

Maurya sculpture is represented by carvings on the capitals
of monolithic inscribed pillars erected by Asoka in a wide reach
of districts in northern India. This sculpture is clean, decisive,
controlled, but the known examples portray chiefly animals.
There appears to be some Persian influence, especially in the
capitals; but nothing that suggests Greek influence. The best-
preserved specimen is the lions from Sarnath.

Post-Maurya, 200–1 B.C., is characterized by sculptured stone
railings surrounding stupas. There is more representation of
the human figure than under Asoka, but a continuation of
reliefs in floral medallions or rosettes. The principal sites are
Bharhut (with an inscription of Sunga dynasty, 185–173);
Bodh-Gaya; and Sanchi; in that order of time; with Sanchi the
finest. The region is south of the Jumna: possibly an accident
of preservation.

Kushan period, about 1–200 A.D.: represented at Sarnath on
the Ganges, and especially at Mathura on the Jumna north of
the principal sites of the last period, of which it is an evident
continuation. The first representation of Buddha as a person,
or of a Bodhisattva, appears, dated 80 A.D., and there are more

scriptural and fewer Jataka scenes represented than in immediate post-Maurya times. There also is some Jain sculpture.

Amaravati, 150–250, lies on the lower Kistna or Krishna, in Dravidian India. Notable are the railing—with an Andhra inscription of 150–200,—stupa slabs, and Buddha statues with accentuated formalized drapery.

Gandhara, 1–400, on the northwest frontier: Taxila, Peshawar, the Kabul Valley, western Punjab beyond the Jhelum. Outright Hellenistic influence, though in varying degree; and, through Turkestan, influencing of China and Japan. Numerous Corinthian capitals, a few Ionic. The culmination is assumed to have fallen between 50 and 200; but all internal dating is problematical, resting on the assumption that the more Hellenistic pieces are the earlier, those less so, the later. However Greek-derived the art forms, the subjects are always Indian and always Mahayana Buddhistic, and include many and varied representations of Buddha. This is a vigorous art; eclectic or hybrid, but not deficient in originality; yet without deeper rooting in a set of inner patterns. It appears to have left little if any influence on any subsequent native sculpture, and from the point of view of India was evidently a frontier phenomenon.

Kushan, Amaravati, and Gandhara sculpture were partly contemporary, and were the last wholly Buddhistic arts of India.

The *Gupta* dynasty at Patna, 320–490, has given its name to the Gupta period of sculpture, the dated monuments of which, however, begin only around 400. The region is once more the Ganges drainage; Delhi, Mathura, Udayagiri in Bhopal, Deogarh, Allahabad, Rajgir, Mankuwar, and Sultanganj in western Bengal. This is the first sculpture to represent Brahman as well as Buddhist subjects. The first four-armed Sivas appear, and the first Buddhas with large decorated nimbuses. Metal statues—of copper, not bronze—are made successfully. Monolithic pillars, still surmounted by lions, are again erected: the dates of a series fall between 456 and 528. The preserved pieces of this period are not very numerous—much fewer, for instance,

than those of the Gandhara school—owing to intensive exposure of the area to subsequent Mohammedan iconoclasm. The
art is on the whole reposeful, controlled rather than vigorous,
apparently entirely free from any Hellenic influences, the
execution finished and technically competent.

The Gupta age is the time of great literature and great
mathematics, though the latter lagged somewhat. Politically,
disasters broke before 500 with an invasion of White Huns
and the following century was one of disorganization. A large,
firmly ruled kingdom did not reëmerge in northern India until
Harsha, 606–647; but was the last important native one there—
in fact, it collapsed with his death. There seem to be no sculptures attributed to Harsha's reign, and fewer to the sixth
century than the fifth. As the third is also without examples,
400–500 may be set as the known period of florescence, possibly
continued to about 600.

I am inclined to regard the Gupta products as marking the
climax of all Indian sculpture: not only because of the synchronism with other cultural peaks, but for reasons of intrinsic
quality. This is not an art which makes a strong impress at
first sight. It lacks architectural setting and the weight of
masses. It is unrelieved by Mediterranean strains, is sufficiently
Indian—with occasional animal-headed and multiple-armed
figures—to seem very strange, yet lacks the shock of overwhelming barbaric exaggeration. Still, it possesses restraint and finish,
and its classic quality grows on acquaintance. What it most
lacks, perhaps, is outright charm.

Another reason for postulating Gupta as the culmination of
Indian sculpture is its approximate balance of Buddhist and
Brahman interest. Earlier art is wholly Buddhist; later, prevailingly Brahmanical, except in peripheral regions like Bengal
and Ceylon. We have seen in philosophy how Indian intellectual activity was not so much Buddhistic at one time and
Brahman at another as inclined to be at its best when the two
strains stimulated each other. Buddhism, on the whole, was
the originating as well as more human element: as it certainly
showed in its art. Brahmanism was not only more given to

ritual, but more repetitively, almost insanely, addicted to formalism as an end. It thereby succeeded in giving sharper form and system to the great but somewhat diffuse and anarchic ideas which Buddhism mainly evolved. As expressing thought, each certainly complemented the other, and Indian ideology may fairly be construed, in the rough, as the product of the continuous interaction of the two tendencies or currents. All through Indian history, cultural success seems to have been best achieved when the pair of forces of which the two "religions" are one expression were most nearly in complementary balance. It is in this sense that the Buddhistic-Brahmanical bilaterality of Gupta sculpture is perhaps of significance.

With Gandhara art counted in, we have to this point a continuity of sculpture somewhere in India: as Gandhara goes into decay around 400, Gupta rises into bloom. With Gandhara ruled out as being of the frontier and semiforeign, there is an apparent gap, just before Gupta, since the Kushan sculpture of Mathura ends about 200 and the Dravidian of Amaravati by 250. However, this is more likely a break in the record than in the actual history. As a style, Gupta art ties closely to these two; and it may have been well on its way by 300.

The *Cave* or rockhewn temple sculpture succeeded the Gupta from about 550 to 800. It is characteristically west Indian, mainly from south of the Vindhyas-Nerbudda. Among the principal sites are Ajanta (better known for its painting), Bagh in Gwalior, Badami in Bijapur, Aurangabad, Ellora, and Elephanta in Bombay Harbor—perhaps roughly in that time sequence. The center of this distribution evidently was the Chalukya state, which fell before the Pallava kingdom of Kanchi near Madras in 642. Pallava cave and rock sculpture of the seventh and eighth centuries, as at Mamallapuram (Mavalipuram) and near Trichinopoly, is a southern variant. Ajanta, Bagh, Aurangabad are Buddhist; the others, Brahman. The hewing out of native rock conduced to colossal effects; but also at times to lack of simplicity in composition—generally a weak point in Hindu sculpture. Eight-armed Sivas now appear. The best pieces are considered to be at Ellora and Ele-

phanta. At any rate, Brahman works now surpass Buddhist
ones in quality as well as number.

The *"Late Mediaeval"* period runs from 800 to perhaps 1300
in the north, indefinitely longer in the south. Its products on
the whole seem difficult to separate from those of the subsequent six centuries which bring us to the present. Apparently
this means that sculpture settled into essential repetitiveness
around 800 or soon after. Certainly no one has singled out the
following eleven centuries, nor any one phase of them, as a
high point of Indian art. Mohammedan domination probably
contributed to this lower level; but the decline, or crystallization, of sculpture took place long before this pressure was
serious—two centuries before in the most exposed regions, half
a dozen in the more remote. However, the art, like many
mature ones, did not die readily. It experienced a number of
resuscitations, or survivals, of fair quality. Thus, even toward
the northwest, there is the temple sculpture of Khajuraho in
Bundelkhand around 1000, and of Mount Abu in Rajputana
of about the same period and again two centuries later. In
Bihar and Bengal the Pala dynasty maintained itself and a
respectable if not notable Buddhist art—the last one on the
mainland of India—from about 775 to 1193. The best products
are from around 800, and none too good in comparison with
the Gupta work of the same region. Farther south, in Orissa,
around the mouths of the Mahanadi, a Brahman state held out
against Mohammedanism until Mughal times, and carved some
remarkably vigorous horses and elephants at Konarak, in the
mouths of the Mahanadi, as late as 1240–1280. In the far Tamil
south, the Cholas of the eleventh century—under two able
kings, 985–1035, at Trichinopoly and Tanjore—rivaled the
Pallava work of several centuries before. Vijayanagar, somewhat more northerly and inland on a southern affluent of the
Kistna, was a powerful kingdom for two centuries until 1565,
and produced simple stone reliefs full of vigorous action, as well
as cast statues which though stilted possess a suave grace. Somewhere in or near this Dravidian region, too, was evolved the figure of the four-armed, cosmic-dancing or *nataraja* Siva, which,

though done over innumerable times in copper or brass, was a genuine plastic concept to create. Its main fault has been the strict adherence given the type; hence the authorities vary in their dates for its invention, and for the best-executed examples, between pre-eleventh century and fifteenth to seventeenth.

Whatever the sources of its original stimuli, Indian sculpture has run in a long native development, essentially uninfluenced from outside. The course has also been a relatively timeless one, even and slow, with its alterations gradual: no fundamental changes of direction, no lapses or intermissions of moment, no strongly marked culmination. If, as seems reasonable, we accept the fifth century as such peak as there was, we have six and a half known centuries before this, and at least ten after it, in which some creativeness was still active. This is a continuous duration so long that perhaps we ought to expect rather little vertical profile.

COLONIAL INDIAN SCULPTURE

In the countries adjacent to India by land—Afghanistan, Pamir, Turkestan, Tibet, Assam, Burma—Indian culture influences were carried largely in association with Buddhism. This religion, universal in its ends, tended to further the hybridization of Indian and local nationality. Indian art exerted a powerful influence in these countries, but it did not, on the whole, remain pure. Moreover, Buddhist art, like Buddhist doctrine, aimed at the mass of the population more than at the courts, which on the whole were best able to foster the highest aesthetic developments.

On the other hand, in southern Farther India—the remoter portion, beyond the Malay Peninsula—and in Java, countries accessible by expeditions in ships instead of by pilgrims on foot, Hindu culture established itself much more purely. It brought Brahmanism as well as Buddhism. The natives were backward, illiterate, and apparently in tribal societies. Here Hindus set up kingdoms instead of seeping into functioning ones. At times Sanskrit was the language of royalty and decree. Art began to flourish at the new courts. Mass production was directed at building up capitals, or temples under royal edict, rather than at manifolding objects for distribution to the innumerable host of the pious. This was in the Indian spirit; and the arts transplanted overseas prospered and reached peaks of aesthetic achievement not attained by those in the inland countries touched by Indian civilization.

The difference is marked between Java and Sumatra. The latter is nearer: it should have been and presumably was colonized or infiltrated first. It contained a large kingdom, Shri-vijaya, which in the main preceded and for a time dominated those of Java. But Java has preserved Boro-budur, and temples, reliefs, and statues in several other parts. Shri-vijaya apparently had neither sculpture nor permanent architecture, and we scarcely even know the precise site of its capital in the vicinity of Palembang. It was Buddhist; Java, Brahman and Buddhist. No doubt further factors entered into the difference, as also in the other countries marginal to India. But they are likely to have been associated with the sectarian difference: the sort of society set up by the immigrants, for instance. The Brahmans became kings; or if not, they may have come with Kshatriyas, and these in turn with following and retinue. Thus, little replicas of India were aimed at and established, where the natives were impressed and coöperative, or overawed or conquered.

The result was that apparently from about the third post-Christian century on—before rather than during the Gupta age,—Hindu states began to spring up around the nearer shores of the South China Sea. By the sixth century probably—when the Gupta dynasty at home had collapsed,—these were producing works of art. The great period of sculpture in colonial India is comprised between about 800 and 1200, when the level in the motherland had definitely sunk. The movement continued with some vigor for a few centuries longer in spots.

Champa.—On the eastern coastal plain of Indo-China was Champa, one of the realms whose beginning seems to go back to two or three hundred years after Christ at the latest. The capitals were first Indrapura near Tourane, then Vijaya or

Chaban, close to latitudes 16° and 14° respectively. The kings had Hindu names; Sanskrit was more or less spoken at their courts; the vernacular of the dominant population seems to have been a Malayo-Polynesian, not a Mon-Khmer or Sinitic language; at least such is the prevailing view of the authorities, though opinions differ. Brahmanism and Buddhism were both introduced; Brahmanism the earlier. Mison has a seventh- to eighth-century Sivaite temple; Dongduong, a ninth-century Buddhistic one. The architecture is of brick. In 988, twenty years after the Annamese of Tongking freed themselves from long centuries of Chinese domination, they pressed southward against the Cham sufficiently to cause the removal of the capital to Binh-Dinh. The threat of Annam continued, and later had added to it that of Cambodia from the inland side. Toward 1200 the Cambodians several times defeated Champa, and at least once installed a viceroy. However, Champa went on; and when in the fourteenth century the capital at Chaban near Binh-Dinh was again menaced by the Annamites, temples were built farther south, around latitude 12½°. The end did not come until 1471, when Chaban fell to Annam. At that, the Cham nationality had maintained a state for full twelve centuries.

The record of Cham sculpture is much briefer. Four periods or phases are recognized by Parmentier, their names apparently taken from architectural stages: Primary or Primitive, Cubic, Classic, and Derived. The first two, in architecture, seem to represent two stylistic strains which were at least partly contemporary. In sculpture, to judge by the dates assigned to particular pieces, the Primary art was that of the seventh and eighth centuries, the Cubic that of the ninth and tenth. A few specimens with attribution earlier than 600 are chiefly decorative architectural sculpture. The best pieces yet discovered are attributed to the two Primary centuries, or to the first of the two. The art of the two Cubic centuries manifests a certain half-sinister power, as if artists bred in a tradition of high sculpture had set out to imitate Polynesian idols; but the work no longer attains the quality of the Primary style. The

Classic and Derived phases are described as definitely schematized, meager, and uninspired: the reproduced examples are
few, perhaps because of the very inferiority. Down to 1000, at
least, the subjects are purely Indian and Brahmanistic: Siva,
Ganesa, Apsaras, lions, *makaras,* female dancers. The treatment, however, is distinctive: there was without question an
original Cham style: direct, controlled, both simpler and less
voluptuous than the Indian. This evidently reached its peak
in something between one and two centuries after it emerged
as a style willing to attempt the human figure. It retained some
vigor for two, perhaps three centuries thereafter; then dragged
on, lifeless, for two more—there is a relief dated 1157,—perhaps
considerably longer. The peak may perhaps be estimated to
have come not later than 800, perhaps as early as 700. The
history of the art has been called the history essentially of a
decadence. The sculptural decline was well under way before
the state was on the defensive toward its neighbors.

Cambodia.—The Khmer empire of Cambodia began its
career about the same time as Champa, with what the Chinese
called Funan around the mouths of the Mekong, and Chenla,
farther upstream. Both were traditionally founded by Brahmans married to native princesses or goddesses. There were
struggles for hegemony, in which Chenla was victorious and
emerged, between 550 and 600, as historic Kambuja or Cambodia. Up to 650 the sequence of kings is known; then follow
a troubled and obscure century and a half. In 802, an able and
long-lived monarch, Jaya-varman II, restored the power of the
state and fixed its center in the region of the northwest end
of Tonle-sap, the great lake. About 900, under Yaso-varman,
Angkor definitely became the capital, with the occupation of
the palace-city of Angkor Thom. The temple of Angkor Vat
was begun around 1090, completed perhaps by 1130–1140.
The last great king—and the first Buddhist one—was Jaya-
varman VII, 1182–1201. He temporarily conquered Champa
and ruled Siam and the northern Malay Peninsula, perhaps as
far as Pegu. With him, great architectural constructions ended,
as well as conquests: before 1300, the Siamese were invading

and devastating Cambodia proper. After that date, inscriptions are scarcer, and reigns and events less accurately known. Probably about the mid-fifteenth century, Angkor was abandoned and Cambodia became a remnant state, when not a vassal or a puppet one.

We can thus recognize five Cambodian periods: a traditional one of at least three centuries; a formative but historic one from about 550 to 802—inscription dates go back to 604; a period of greatness, from 802 to 1201; one of defense and decline for two centuries and a half; and finally another four of shadow existence until the French protectorate. The second and third periods are those of sculpture.

Religion, so determinative of art, was Brahmanistic in the formative and great periods: Sivaism predominating, Vishnuism secondary. The kings and ruling class were Brahmans, or reckoned as such; grammar and the Indian sciences flourished; inscriptions were in pure Sanskrit or in Khmer; around 900 a new script, of north Indian origin, came into usage alongside the older south Indian one. Integrated with this Hindu culture were native strains such as the matrilineate and human sacrifice. About 950, Buddhism seems first to have become flourishing; not until 1182 was there a professed Buddhist king. All this Buddhism was Mahayana, with its infusion of Brahman ideology, absorption of Brahman deities, and use of Sanskrit. This older Khmer Buddhism, which is first mentioned in 665 with reference to an event two generations earlier, was not in conflict with Brahmanism, and was partly assimilated to it: it performed sacrifices! Only after the great period, and beginning in the thirteenth century, did Khmer Buddhism gradually adopt the Pali canon from Ceylon by way of Pegu and Siam, become Hinayana, and finally supplant Brahmanism. The notable art and architecture, whether Brahman or Buddhist—and a considerable fraction was the latter,—were therefore thoroughly Indian in inspiration, not the expression of an international art as in central and north Asia.

Four periods are recognized in sculpture and architecture: Pre-Angkor, Angkor I, Angkor II, post-Angkor. The Pre-

Angkor phase extended from the sixth century through the eighth and probably the ninth. Angkor I is roughly the tenth century; Angkor II, the eleventh and twelfth. Post-Angkor is after 1200: the name implies not the abandonment of Angkor, but that great construction there had ceased.

Pre-Angkor was contemporary with Cham sculpture and, like it, direct, rather severe, restrained—not far beyond archaism, but definitely out of it. There is little movement, but considerable poise, in the full-round standing figures, and dignity without harshness in the faces. The characteristic Indian voluptuousness has been got rid of to a surprising degree, as in Champa. The two styles are distinguishable, but as local variants of one set of impulses and expression.

Angkor I seems to represent a recession in quantity and quality. Perhaps architectural activity had temporarily diverted sculptural interest.

Angkor II is the period of the famous Khmer-type heads with the subtle "Angkor smile" half playing over a physiognomy of profundity and repose, and of large, crowded scenes in low relief. The latter differ notably from the Javanese reliefs. The background is completely filled, there is more sense of mass movement, less Indian sensuousness and less tenderness, more pictorial and less sculptural quality. The dates are also later than in Java. Angkor II is undoubtedly a great art: Indian-derived, but not Indian-dominated. It probably reached the highest peaks of Colonial Indian sculpture.

Post-Angkor, as represented by reliefs of probably the fourteenth century, has sunk. The human figures are mediocre, relief runs into wealth of decorative detail.

In summary, Cambodian art has a history of at least eight centuries, from say 550 to 1350, perhaps longer. A first peak was reached somewhere around 700; a second and greater one, about 1100, possibly a little later.

Siam.—The valley of the Menam is the heart of Siam. The early history is ill defined. The lower Menam was originally Mon-speaking, that is, ethnically related to Khmer Cambodia; the upper valley may already have been Thai, that is, Sinitic. In the thirteenth century the Thai pressed their power southward, and, not far from 1290, shook off the Cambodian overlordship and took from it the lower Menam and upper Malay

Peninsula. The capital was now at Sukothai; in 1350, or according to other reckonings about 1460, it was transferred to Ayuthia, in the lower Menam Valley, the old Mon country. From this time on, Thai speech gradually replaced Mon, which is now confined to Burmese Pegu. The Thai kings were, and their subjects became, Buddhists of the Lesser Vehicle, Ceylonese, or Pali canon. In brief, an independent and flourishing Siam arose as Cambodia waned. The shift was not only of political power, but also of ethnos and religion: from Mon-Khmer to Thai dominance; and from Brahmanism with a secondary current of Sanskrit Mahayana, to Pali Hinayana Buddhism. The Thai were evidently too far inland, and therefore too belated, to have become saturated with Brahmanical culture to the same degree as the coastal Cham, Khmer, and Mon.

Siamese sculpture was therefore later than Cambodian, on the whole. Half-a-dozen or more phases of it have been recognized, associated with districts and periods—in part somewhat dogmatically associated, I suspect. There are a few specimens which may go back to the seventh century, at any rate seem to be pre-Angkor in time; but they are inferior qualitatively to contemporary early Cham and Cambodian specimens. They are attributed to the Malay Peninsula and to Prapatom near the Menam mouth—districts on the sea and accessible to Indian ships. The finest Siamese sculptures are assigned—I cannot judge how authoritatively—to the tenth, eleventh, twelfth, and perhaps thirteenth centuries. This would make them contemporary with the two Angkor periods; and they certainly show strong Cambodian relations, although a distinctive non-Khmer physiognomy with narrow convex nose was also evolved. Direct Indian influences and mannerisms are not strong in the best work, nor is cultish expression.[6] All in all, Siamese sculpture at its peak gives the impression of having been a healthy but

---

[6] In this remote and difficult field I have had to proceed more subjectively than usual. Selecting what seem to me the finest specimens in the magnificent corpus of Salmony's *Sculpture in Siam*, I find the following attributions for them: Plates 14, 15a, 18: "Sawankolok, X–XI centuries"; Pls. 21–22: "Lopburi, IX–XIII"; Pls. 39, 41–43, 45: "Pitsanulok, XII." Lopburi is on the lower Menam, Sawan-

provincial derivative and variant of Cambodian. The large-scale relief is lacking; the finest specimens known are heads in the round.

After the thirteenth century, Siamese sculpture retains considerable form and finish, but little spirit or urge.

Sumatra.—The realm of Shri-vijaya in Sumatra began in perhaps the sixth or seventh century, and for more than a hundred years preceding 860 dominated all but eastern Java. It maintained influence or possessions in other islands much longer, and was finally destroyed by Madjapahit of Java only in 1377, about the time Malacca was being founded by the Arabs. It does not enter into the history of art.

Java.—Java traditionally received Hindu immigrants in the early Christian centuries. The authenticable political growths were roughly between 700 and 1000 in the central part of the island, in a state legendarily known as Mataram; and from about 1000 until the overthrow by the Mohammedans in 1478 or thereabout, in the east end of the island, with a partial cultural survival until today in Bali. The Mataram inscription dates found fall between 732 and 928. The earlier central Javanese kingdom was mainly Buddhist, but also Sivaite; the later eastern one, Brahman, except for a secondary Buddhist influence, about the middle of its course, from southernmost India. More accurately, east Java held three successive states. The first emanated from mid-Java, and had Airlangga as its greatest ruler, in the eleventh century. The second was at Toemapel and Singasari in the thirteenth century. The third was the kingdom of Madjapahit, which lasted from (1293) 1328 to 1478.

Central Javanese art runs from the eighth to the tenth century. A Buddhist temple at Kalasan and monastery at Sari were founded in 779. The great Boro-budur stupa, with 500 Buddha

kolok and Pitsanulok upstream. Pl. 6, "Prapatom, VII–X," must also be included, although the nearly closed eyes suggest the later styles so strongly as to make a guess of century X seem far more likely than VII. Le May's *Concise History of Buddhist Art in Siam*, 1938, which was published after the present chapter was written, recognizes an U-T'ong style, a Khmer-Thai transition of about centuries XIII–XIV, in the vicinity of Ayuthia.

figures and 1,300 reliefs, is generally dated around 800 or 850; the Sivaite temples of Prambanam, toward 900; the Plaosan Buddhist monastery, in the tenth century.

East Javan art is mainly post-Airlangga and pre-Madjapahit. Its flourishing period seems to have begun somewhat before 1200 and ended somewhat after 1300. It is therefore roughly contemporary with the Singasari kingdom; although some of the most important productions, like the Panataran temples, the largest on the island after Boro-budur, seem to be associated

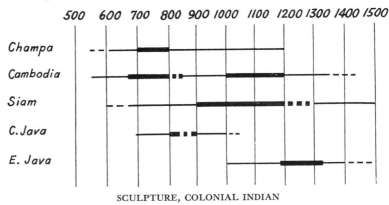

SCULPTURE, COLONIAL INDIAN

with the remnants of Airlangga's empire. The art is Sivaite and Vishnuite; at Singasari itself, Buddhistic.

The two periods differ stylistically about as might be expected. The later, dealing with Indian gods, is more specifically and formally Hindu. It also shows, in its finer pieces, superior finish of workmanship. On the other hand, the Boro-budur sculpture is more spontaneous and original. The somewhat coarse stone used does not allow really fine execution. It was perhaps chosen because it worked easily and quantity of production was part of the program.

Summary.—The diagram above illustrates the principal currents of Colonial Indian art. It is evident that the florescences came in two pulses, one centering around 800, the other at about 1200, the mainland tending to precede these dates somewhat, Indonesia to lag behind them. Cambodia and Java apparently experienced two pulses, but in Java the second came in a new district. In the main, Brahman religion and cult preceded in dominance on the mainland and tended to be superseded by Buddhism; the island development, the reverse. The most Indian of all the sculptures was the latest, that of thirteenth-century east Java. The first sculpture of genuine merit in this Colonial Indian world dates from perhaps 550 to 600, as compared with an estimated culmination of Indian art around 400–500. The Colonial beginnings thus evidently overlapped the end of the Gupta period, but the average lag of the earlier Colonial florescences behind the Indian one was around three centuries. The later pulses, around 1200, appear at their best to outrank qualitatively anything produced in India for three or four centuries preceding. In every instance the Farther and East Indian sculptures were wholly derivative from India; but except for the final Javanese phase, each developed a true style of its own on the spot, almost certainly in the hands of natives. The term Colonial in the present connection therefore refers to the cultural paternity of the area rather than to masses of transplanted colonists. The local arts were Malayo-Polynesian, Mon-Khmer, and South Sinitic growths under Indian stimulus.

§41. Chinese Sculpture

Sculpture has long ranked lower than painting in China. We know the names of few sculptors, but of thousands of painters. Sculpture involves vigorous use of the hands, and savors of artisanship. Chinese painting, however, is allied to calligraphy—the Chinese use the same brush with similar strokes,—and this in turn is part of education, the hallmark of social status. A scholar or official would not model, carve, or cast; but even emperors painted. The associations of painting were with the literary tradition of Confucianism; those of sculpture, very considerably with Buddhism. Up to perhaps the great persecution of 845 it seemed as if Buddhism might yet capture all levels of culture in China as it did in Japan. Thereafter it became the religion of the uneducated, nonruling class. By the same ninth century, sculpture had run its course in China.

Pre-Han, to 200 B.C.—No true sculpture is known from the Shang, Chou, or Ts'in dynasties,[7] though there are seemingly authentic literary records of bronze statues from about 500 on: for instance under Kou-chien, from 495 to 465 prince of Yüeh south of the Yang-tse in Chehkiang; and at the grave of Shih Huang-ti—twelve musicians and twelve giants—in 209. But few large figures of metal ever long survived the melting pot in China, where coinage was of bronze or baser alloys; and none from these early times. Stone sculpture seems not to have been practiced: the age was one of bronze. In fact, in vessels the Shang-Chou period surpassed all later ones. Their form and ornamentation show a highly developed style. It is indeed one of the great decorative styles of the world: monumental, at once rich and severe, mature, profound. Allied technologically to sculpture, this art in ritual utensils evidently was the surrogate of sculpture for a long aniconic age of early China. With the Han period the vessels lose their distinctive quality: they are simpler without corresponding gain. But as they decline in virtue, sculpture emerges.

Han, 206 B.C.–221 A.D.—Except for reliefs, sculpture is still sparse; and rude. The earliest datable piece seems to be the stone horse of Ho Ch'ü-ping in Shensi, 117 B.C. The animal is done with little skill of form, the prostrate barbarian with less. Other figures, of men or animals in bronze, are little better. The one Han sculptural manner which is fairly developed is the stone grave reliefs. The known ones are nearly all in the two separated provinces of Shantung and Szechwan; the dated ones fall between 87 and 171, in other words about the second century after Christ, in the decline of the posterior Han dynasty. The active participation of Szechwan, far in the west up the Yangtse, is surprising in view of the inclusion of this district in historic China only just before the Hans: it evidently accepted Sinization with enthusiasm, just as it became the refuge of the Hans when these fell, and during the next thou-

---

[7] This statement is no longer accurate. Archaeological excavations made since 1934 have shown that there was stone sculpture in Shang times, in a decorative style similar to that of Shang bronze vessels. See H. G. Creel, *The Birth of China*, 1937.

sand years it several times seems to have been in advance of the country in characteristic Chinese developments, such as block printing and paper money.

The Szechwan Han sculpture differs from that of Shantung in a tendency to greater roundness, as well as other particulars. The Shantung reliefs are now well known, and are in a definite style. This, according to some of the authorities, represents the transfer of painting to stone carving. I question this judgment. Even on allowance of exaggeration of the block silhouette effect in the rubbings usually reproduced, the art is clearly one of line, which would gain little by color. However, as we know nothing of earlier painting and next to nothing of earlier or contemporary sculpture, the origin of the relief style remains wholly obscure; just as it left no known direct successor. This art is too representative, and for a primitive style too successful in telling a story, to be a very great one. But it is vigorous, animated without vehemence, truthful to life, skillful in proportions. Its outstanding convention is almost complete adherence to pure profile. But within this frame human figures are surprisingly varied in posture and free in movement, the horses spirited; the compositions are simple and decorative, for a narrative delineation. There is little if anything non-Chinese in these Han reliefs; and surprisingly little similarity to any later Chinese sculpture or painting.

Three Kingdoms, Tsin, Wei, Six Dynasties, 221–589.—These nearly four centuries of partial or total conquest and continuous division of the empire—all China was united only from 280 to 302 under the foreign Tsin—are generally pictured as a time of retrogression between the glorious Han and T'ang periods; evidently because nationalistic Chinese historians so see it. As a matter of fact, the T'ang achievements in sculpture, painting, literature, philology rest on innovating progress made during these politically turbulent preceding centuries; in science, in fact, the main growth was pre-T'ang. The period also was that of the introduction and greatest influence of Buddhism. This had begun to seep in in Han times, but poured its main flood into China during the following four centuries.

In short, this period of minor dynasties was the one in which the characteristic patterns of historic Chinese culture were for the most part originated, to undergo their full development under T'ang and ultimate refinement under Sung.

Most of the sculpture of the period has perished, except in the northern Buddhist grottos or rock temples; and their art, wholly religious and mass-produced, is far inferior to what Japan has preserved of Chinese-produced or Chinese-inspired sculpture from the end of this and the early T'ang period, while China herself has lost her statuary of bronze, wood, and lacquer. The beginning dates of the principal grottos are:

366, Tun-huang, western Kansu, by Chinese priest Lo-tsun.
455, more at Tun-huang.
455, Yün-kang, near Ta-t'ung-fu, northern Shansi, old home of the Wei dynasty; mainly 471–516.
Ca. 500, Lung-men, near the capital Lo-yang; also 642 and after.
526, T'o-shan, near Ch'ing-chou, in Shantung; again ca. 590.
531, Kung-hsien, near Lung-men, in Honan.
532, Li-cheng at Tsi-nan-fu in Shantung.
After ca. 550, Hsiang-t'ang-shan at Wu-an-hsien, Honan, and Tz'ŭ-chou, Chihli.
584–600, Yü-han-shan, Lung-tung, Fo-yü-ssŭ near Tsi-nan-fu.
Ca. 600, Yün-men-shan, opposite T'o-shan, Shantung.
589–618, T'ien-lung-shan, Shansi; until ca. 888.
589–618, Ling-chüan-ssŭ, Honan; into T'ang.
After 618, Tun-huang, Kansu.
After 618, Kuang-yüan-hsien and Chiu-ching in Szechwan.
Ca. 730, 360-foot rock Buddha at Chia-ting-fu.
Ca. 750, Nan-kan-shan near Pa-chou, Szechwan.

Probably a full half of the development, and most of the best quality of work, fall into Sui and T'ang; but the sculpture is a unit growth irrespective of dynasty. Much of the votive rock sculpture is dated. Gandhara and central Asiatic influences are evident; but style and execution are nearly always characteristically Chinese.

The religious stimulus and example that underlay this Buddhistic development probably did not all come into the North from Turkestan. South China may have received direct influencing from Farther India and perhaps India by sea. Literary records tell of statues of Buddhas and Bodhisattvas by 266; again, with preserved inscription, in 320; of Amitabha about 366; of Avalokiteshvara, the prototype of Kwanyin, in 408; of Manjusri in 420, the first and two last being in South China.

The one outstanding name is Tai Kuei, who died about 395. He devised the *chia-chu* technique of building up free-standing statues of lacquer and cloth over a frame. The resulting figure was light, portable, and at the same time durable. Several examples from only two or three centuries later have been preserved in Japan. It is characteristic of the Chinese attitude that Tai Kuei's name appears to have been preserved as an inventor rather than as a great sculptor.

A low-relief stele set up in 524/5 at what is now T'ai-ming in Chihli illustrates the change since the terminal Han times four centuries before. Animation has been replaced by repose, vigor by control; composition, ornament, even a measure of perspective, have superseded the older simple profile realism of line. The horses still paw and arch their necks, but decoratively, not with the pull of motion. The carving is as typically Chinese, in the sense of the China we know, as the Han work is proto-Chinese.

Non-Buddhistic work seems to be represented chiefly by conventional animals lining the approach to the Southern imperial tombs near Nanking, of 453, 493, 549, 559.

Sui and T'ang, 589–907.—In the first half of the T'ang dynasty, Chinese plastic art reached its zenith. If certain attributions are correct, the brief Sui dynasty, 589–618, must be included in the period of greatness. After about 750 there is a falling off, both in quality and quantity of work. Pious work continued to be done in the grottos; but the masterpieces are non-Buddhistic grave figures—for emperors, of avenues of attendants and animals in stone; for others, exceedingly lifelike and charming smaller pieces of pottery. Of the former, there are, near Si-an-fu, examples for emperors who died in 649, 683, 691, 716, 805. Of these the 683 set is rated the best; but T'ai Tsung's six war horses in relief (649) have immediate appeal even without acquaintance with Chinese style. Begun before the Emperor's death in 637, they are better in design than in execution. The terra-cotta grave figurines developed from pre-Sui models, but are probably for the most part to be set down as T'ang, on the basis of costume studies. The horses are genuinely noble, the women full of grace.

It looks as if the apogee of Chinese sculpture could be set not far from 700.

Five Dynasties, Sung, and Later, 907 seq.—The later T'ang falling-off continued. Sculpture, Buddhistic or secular, tended to become repetitive. It aimed essentially at decorative effect, rather than either religious sentiment or freely conceived natural form. The Ming dynasty (1368–1644) tomb-avenue animals maintain a genuine monumental quality; but the tradition of such rows was then a thousand years old, and it is hardly expectable that they could surpass or even equal the best of their predecessors. There are Sung and Mongol cast-iron statues; but this technique goes back to at least 557. Post-T'ang plastic art never disintegrated or even seriously deteriorated in execution. It did lose the impulse toward new motivation or feeling of intensity.

Summary.—Chinese sculpture has a one-growth history, which becomes definite with the introduction of Buddhism. Shang-Chou bronze vessels are decoratively plastic to a high quality, and the Han stone reliefs represent the beginning of what might have become a vigorous art. Around 200 A.D., Buddhism entered the country actively and brought an established tradition and manner of sculpture and painting. Under the impetus of this introduction, Chinese sculpture developed, gradually working up to its culmination about 700, when at least certain of its strains had freed themselves of foreign elements and religious domination, and even the Buddhistic work had become thoroughly Chinese. Thereafter decline set in, contemporary with that of the Buddhist religion in the culture. Both maintained a place in the national fabric, but on a level of acceptance as semiplebeian, fairly dissociated from the more guarded values of the culture, and continuing century after century without important change of intensity or direction.

Painting, which early achieved association with Confucian scholarship and officialdom instead of popular Buddhism, remained esteemed and lived much longer than sculpture.

§42. Japanese Sculpture

Japanese sculpture was a great art from 600 to 1300. Wholly dependent at first on China, it surpassed this by 900, when Chinese sculpture had begun its decline, and before 1200 it had become wholly emancipated. Chinese tomb sculpture was never accepted in Japan, where motives remained wholly Buddhistic. In fact, there was no wholly secular sculpture until after 1300, when religious work had become repetitive and other carving was merely decorative.

As in China, the career of sculpture was much briefer than that of painting, although their beginnings in Japan were contemporary. The climax, by native reckoning, was reached around 1200 and the decades immediately following; in painting, in the decades just before 1500. This is the gap between Early Gothic and Leonardo, in European terms. Moreover, painting lived on through a long, respected old age, whereas sculpture was dead within a century of its culmination. Perhaps, apart from the association with calligraphy and aristocratic techniques in China, one reason for the early ending was the exclusive association with Buddhism. In China, non-Buddhistic tomb sculpture survived after Buddhistic sculpture decayed. However, it is not wholly clear why Japanese plastic art failed to find an outlet in other subjects after its one-sided addiction had staled; unless it is due to a difference in initial attitude of the two nations toward the Indian religion.

Buddhism came into China when writing was much more than a millennium old, and not only a formal philosophy but a whole idea-system had been formulated. There was even a definite art style. This well-rooted civilization was rocked, and fertilized, by Buddhism; and enormous chargings of the culture are due to it. But the religion never dominated China. It was alternately tolerated and favored, encouraged and persecuted; and after 845 it settled, in the main, into being a plebeian religion with some proliferations of influence upward; a religion of numbers rather than of quality, of which the official cults took little cognizance.

Early Japan, however, was uncivilized except for work in iron. The first importation of Buddhism followed that of writing by little more than a century: 405 as against 522. Another seventy-five years, 594, and the emperor ordered a temple and images in every province. Less than a century later, in 685, Buddhism was made the state religion. The native Shinto had no literature and no philosophy: its first records were written after Buddhism was part of the government. Its cults went on, its deities were given a place as incarnations of Buddhist ones. Japan's first idea of art was Buddhistic: for centuries all art served the religion. Moreover, it may be questioned whether a seeking after the higher civilization of China brought Buddhism into the country, or the reverse: the latter seems a possible interpretation, and at least a probable factor.

At any rate, it was only about 1400 that art ceased being the servant of religion in Japan. By that time sculpture had exhausted itself, and painting started on a new career, mainly secular.

This may be the reason why around the middle of the eighth century Japanese sculpture was more Indian than Chinese was. The one nation welcomed, the other half resisted, the newer influences from the land of Buddha. Yet there seems no record of communications between India and Japan except through China.

It is also a fair question whether at that time the plastic art of Japan is not to be reckoned as superior to that of China. In view of its being derivative, and Chinese sculpture being still close to the culmination of its whole career in this very period around 750, the question is of some moment. If answered affirmatively, the daughter art rose to the greater height, both in a briefer time and ultimately. It is difficult to be sure, because so little T'ang sculpture has been preserved in North China, and practically none in the South, compared with what

stands intact in Japanese temples. Also, the Japanese are perhaps still inclined to be overrespectful to their teachers.

One thing must probably be admitted for all periods: the
superior finish of Japanese execution. The line may be charged
with much or little meaning, but it is clean. Rough or crude
surfaces, materials inadequate to the sculptor's conception, are
not tolerated.

Possibly connected with this quality is a curious fact. Alone
of all great plastic arts, Japanese sculpture makes practically
no use of stone. Up to the Heian era, when Kyoto became the
capital in 794, bronze and lacquer were the leading materials,
with clay perhaps third; after that date, wood almost crowded
out all others, only bronze continuing to be used rarely. The
cast iron of China and Korea seems not to have been employed.

I am inclined to divide the course of Japanese sculpture into
two major periods at the same point when wood came: the
abandonment of Nara in 784 or occupation of Heian-Kyoto
in 794. This division is not recognized as primary in the books
I have consulted; but it does seem to mark a change in direction and spirit; and the change in material may be a symptom.

Through the Nara period, sculpture retains suggestions of
archaism but aims at profundity. As the Japanese say, the figures and faces express sagacity and fortitude but are deficient
in mercy and compassion. Their repose is that of a great god,
their serenity dark and superhuman. With the Heian period
the bodies and heads become plump, rounded, soft; and while
the excess of this quality was in time lost, and the fullest characterization achieved, it is then the characterization of men,
not the calm brooding of divinities.

I offer this judgment of two main phases or periods for what
it may be worth; venturing it because there seems as yet no
settled Occidental tradition in the matter, all opinions being
individual.

At any rate, the growth would seem to have had two peaks:
the first in the Nara or Tempyo era, between perhaps 710 and
760; the second in the Kamakura period, in the half century
beginning at 1200. The outward culminations might be con-

strued as being marked by the two gigantic bronze Daibutsus—
that of Nara, 752, sixteen meters high, several times destroyed,
and preserved only in restoration; and that of Kamakura, 1252,
fourteen meters, still intact. The former comes in a time of
flourishing bronze casting; the latter in one of wood carving,
two generations after a Chinese founder had to be imported
to repair or recreate the ruined Nara colossus. The interval is
an exact half millennium—too long a time for the two events
to belong to the same continuous curve of growth.

The question is, which rose the higher; which was the peak
of the entire development of 700 or more years. The Japanese
are not in doubt, and most westerners seem to follow them:
they name the later or Kamakura age. This answer should
perhaps be accepted, in a study like the present one. But I
cannot free myself from doubt of its ultimate soundness. I
feel the Nara art as the greater by world-wide and timeless
standards. Perhaps I am influenced by a personal predilection
for a slight remnant of archaic flavor. On the other hand, I am
conscious of an equal resistance to predominating religious
motivation in art; by which, however, the earlier Japanese
sculpture is undoubtedly dominated. I shall therefore state
such reasons as seem to support my feeling, and leave judgment
to the future.

The eighth-century art excels in depth, the thirteenth in intensity. The former aims at ideal type, the latter at characterization. The earlier one operates in several materials and
techniques, the later essentially in only one, and this—wood
carving—a material and technique in which the greatest sculpture of no other nation has been produced. The Japanese
judgment of their own art deserves the heaviest respect. But so
does that of the world, when it shall have had time to form a
mature judgment. And this time has hardly yet come: it is only
fifty years ago that Hokusai was hailed in many Western circles
as the Japanese painter *par excellence*—because he was extraordinarily vigorous and clever, lacking in nobility, and somewhat
European-influenced. That the highly individualized Kamakura semiportraits of priests and abbots evoke a readier appeal

in the Occident than the serene Nara Buddhas, Amidas, Kwannons, and Yakushis, is rather to be expected. The Japanese
predilection is rather to be explained by the fact that the Kamakura sculpture is a national art, without Chinese counterpart,
whereas the Nara art followed Chinese and Korean models and
traditions, in fact was only a half century to a century removed
from the days when it was executed by immigrants or their
immediate descendants. On the other hand, Japanese pride
ought also to find a proper satisfaction in the circumstance that
the ancestors in so short a time equaled and perhaps surpassed
their foreign teachers. In brief, neither Japan nor the Occident
has any particular ground for bias in either direction.

When viewed as are parallels in other growths, there are certain difficulties or abnormalities in either interpretation. In
one alternative the birth, in the other the death, is unusually
sudden. Our first extant examples are from 600, the earliest
work definitely by pure-blood Japanese begins around 650,
the first great period runs from about 700 to 750, the second
from 1200 to 1250, after 1300 there is no longer anything notable. In the one case the prolongation after the climax is unduly great; in the other, the slowness of the climb. A couple of
unquestionably low-level centuries in the middle would help.
But there seems to be no authority who recognizes such a dying
away and rebirth; like most European literatures, the art is
always treated as a continuum. Yet an art requiring six centuries to climb to its pinnacle ought hardly, except by catastrophe from without, outlive itself in one more. A rapid youth,
with the vitality of greatness clearly shown in a long persistence
and late renaissance, seems historically more expectable.

In any event, it is clear that we are dealing with a growth of
magnitude, duration, and two climaxes.

To 650.—Suiko period, 552–646
  To nearly 600, imports from Korea and then China, or work by
    imported sculptors.
*Tori, probably part Chinese, grandson of the Chinese Shiba
    Tatto, bronzes in the Horyu-ji, 606, 607, 623; perhaps also
    wooden Kwannon attributed to Shotoku.

Wooden Lokapalas, probably by Oguchi and Tokuho, apparently of Chinese descent.

Other works, of wood or bronze, dated 628, ca. 650, 651.

*650–800.—Hakuho, 646–710, and **Nara (Tempyo), 710–784*

Sculptors Japanese.

Ca. 665, introduction of *kanshitsu* lacquer-and-cloth technique.

Bronzes, dated ca. 670, 681, *717, and the great Buddha of the Todai-ji, 752.

Lacquer, ca. 733 (four-armed), 750, 750, 750, 760.

Clay, ca. 750, 750.

Quasi portraits of priests who died 728, 758, 763, 773, made of lacquer or paper presumably soon after their deaths.

The heaping-up of dates as the middle of the eighth century is approached is conspicuous. This is also the period of most evident Indian resemblances.

800–900.—Early Heian or First Kyoto period, 794–889

Wood replaces other materials. Fewer productions preserved. Kwannons predominate.

No artists known; sculptures attributed to the priests who instigated their manufacture.

Swelling, soft, sensuous figures.

This looks like a period of relaxation.

900–1000.—Earlier Fujiwara period, 889–(1069)

Continued use of wood, mostly joined pieces.

Ca. 890, semirealistic figures of the emperor Ojin, his wife, and his mother, who later became gods.

Few extant products. Probably an interval period.

1000–1175.—Later Fujiwara and Heike periods, (1069)–1192

Ca. 1000, Kosho, employed by court.

*Jocho, his son, d. 1057, established the Shichijo-bussho from which all later ateliers sprang.

Chosei, 1010–1091, his pupil, founded the Sanjo-bussho.

Enkwai, fl. 1069.

Genzo, fl. 1074, 1093.

Kwaiken, fl. 1127.

Kyojin, fl. 1148, 1182.

Jiga, fl. 1156.

Chojun, fl. 1170.

Keison, fl. 1184.

This is evidently a period of growth leading to the next. It is described as a time of increasing national consciousness in literature and art.

1175–1300.—Kamakura shogunate, 1192–1336
> 1183, Ch'en Ho-ch'ing reintroduces bronze in restoring Nara Daibutsu, but wood continues to prevail.
>
> *Kokei, fl. 1171, 1188 seq., counted founder of the Kamakura style.
>
> **Unkei, fl. 1203 seq., "son" of last, the greatest sculptor of Japan.
>
> **Kwaikei, fl. 1190–1219, pupil of Kokei, often esteemed the equal of Unkei.
>
> *Tankei, *Jokei, Koben, "sons" of Unkei. The first in his day was rated equal to his father.
>
> Koyu, fl. 1251.
>
> *1252, the Kamakura bronze Daibutsu.
>
> Koen, "grandson" of Unkei, fl. ca. 1260.
>
> Zenzo, fl. ca. 1288.
>
> This is a period of realism.
>
> From 1300, there was a return to the Fujiwara manner; in other words, the burst was spent.

1300 seq.—Ashikaga, Interval, and Tokugawa shogunates, 1336–1868
> Buddhistic sculpture inferior; secular: architectural and decorative.

§43. Middle American Sculpture

Regretfully I omit consideration of Maya-Toltec-Aztec sculpture, one of the world's major art developments. In spite of a surprisingly exact internal chronology for part of the Maya development, the absolute dates are still in dispute for this period. For the Toltecs, assumed dates vary by centuries. For the Aztecs proper we have a good chronology for a century preceding the Conquest in 1521, a fair one for another century, a contradictory maze beyond. The majority of so-called Aztec works of art cannot even be brought into validated relation with such chronology as we possess. The customary classification of Mexican sculptures into Toltec and Aztec has been made without real definition of the criteria of the two alleged styles. Variants may be provincial, temporal, or stylistic—they are mostly not discriminated as such. While there undoubtedly was an influence from the region of the Valley of Mexico on the late Maya of northern Yucatan around 1200, we do not really know that this was Toltecan; nor has the concept Toltec much generally accepted defined meaning other than pre-Aztec, that is, pre-1325. The famous stucco pyramid at Uaxactun in the Guatemala lowland, which is unquestionably early, shows sculptures which are construed as proto-Maya, no doubt correctly. But they are also construable as proto-Toltec, perhaps with equal warrant. The minor local cultures, such as Zapotec, Totonac, Xochicalco, float almost completely free in time. In short, a temporally integrated picture of the whole development from Guatemala to the Valley of Mexico—which was almost certainly a connected growth from a single source—has not yet been achieved.

We do know this: The finest Maya sculpture is found at sites which bear inscribed ninth-cycle dates in the native time reckoning. As Americanists transcribe these, they run from something after 9.0.0.0.0. to a little after 10.0.0.0.0. A cycle consists of 400 360-day years—something over 394 of our years. Within the major part of one such cycle we know that the florescence of Maya sculpture was consummated. Eighth-cycle executions are less developed; late Maya sculpture—when the long cycles had gone out of use—is definitely inferior or decorative, though the architecture held its own. We know further that the sculpture began to rise to its heights in the 98–99 years from 9.10.0.0.0. to 9.15.0.0.0., and attained them chiefly in the next 98–99 from 9.15.0.0.0. to 10.0.0.0.0., plus a few decades longer. The trouble is that we cannot translate this native calendar into the Christian one or any other that correlates with it. Three theories of chronology are actually advocated by as many groups of Maya specialists and astronomers. One puts the crucial 9.0.0.0.0. in 176 A.D.; another, about 260 years later; a third, 520 years later. Ten or fifteen years ago, the 176 A.D. correlation seemed fairly on the way to general acceptance. Since then, favor has veered somewhat to the next later one. Whether the gap from 10.5.0.0.0. to the period of Mexican influence on the Maya around 1000 begins at 620 or at 880 obviously makes considerable historical difference.

I think it will be evident why the data do not lend themselves to adequate treatment under the plan of this book. On

the other hand, when once the chronology, "empires," nationalities, and styles shall have been extricated from their present
uncertainties, there can be no doubt that Middle America, and
Peru too, will offer a large contribution to culture history. It
will be doubly important because, so far as we can tell at present, the American growth occurred in essential isolation from
the historically interconnected ones of the Old World, and
therefore provides. as it were, a unique balance or control to
these as an aggregate.

§44. Occidental Sculpture

It is usual in histories to treat Western sculpture as an essential
unit, as a European production, with successive characteristic
stages: Romanesque, Gothic, Renaissance, Baroque, Rococo,
Neoclassic, Modern; and to consider the national growths as
subdivisions or variants of these stages: Romanesque sculpture
in France, in Italy, in Germany, etc. Gothic, for instance, is
said to begin about 1200 and to continue to 1500, when it is
followed by the Renaissance, except in Italy, where the Renaissance has to be set back to 1400. With 1600 the Renaissance
passes into the Baroque; and so on.

There is no question that each of these stages or phases represents something real, a genuine and peculiar aesthetic quality
or direction. Nevertheless, each European stage is also a national, often provincial growth; and its distinctive national
character is blurred by its being conceived chiefly as a European phenomenon. On the side of art, the Renaissance is
wholly Italian and overwhelmingly Tuscan in its beginnings
and in the formation of its characteristic patterns. Its typical
antecedents can be traced far back of 1400 in the peninsula. It
was a fully characterized growth, in Florence, by 1400; and it
reached its peak, there and for Italy, so far as both sculpture
and painting are concerned, by 1525. Of course its recognition
and influence became greatest only at the peak, and persisted
thereafter. It is therefore true enough to speak of the sixteenth
as the Renaissance century—of Europe: that was the period

when the patterns evolved by the Renaissance dominated consciousness and affected the greatest number of human beings. But it was also the period when the distinctive Renaissance patterns were being stretched to extravagance and rupture, or when their unique and high quality was being dissolved away by repetition. The Renaissance movement in France, Spain, Germany was on the whole a poor thing, however humanizing; whereas in Italy it was one of the great achievements of humanity. And the Renaissance had little result in quality of production in the transalpine countries until they were able to unlearn the education which it gave them. Historians of art have become so taken up with the continuity of their narrative as a whole, and with tracing an interconnecting web of specific influences within this, that they tend to relegate to the background the story of the development of the quality of patterns. This story begins to take on sharper outlines as soon as it is organized on the basis primarily of area or nationality, and of time within this framework.

Occidental sculpture grew out of the pitiful soil of so-called Carolingian art, which was little better than a childish substitute for art. It grew in two growths. The earlier was French; substantially uninfluenced by Classical Antiquity, but ecclesiastical; and architectural in origin. It was promptly adopted in most of western Europe, though with varying degrees of success; and culminated in the thirteenth century or perhaps about 1300. The second growth was Italian, with at least some roots in ancient Mediterranean civilization; it was less chained either to Christianity or to buildings; it began to attain its distinctive forms only after 1400, and ceased improving them soon after 1500. Its influence abroad took place largely after it was qualitatively deteriorating at home. Its outside influence was therefore on the whole constructive of content but inhibitive of quality, except where a larger national growth already under way enabled a national sculpture, as in Spain, to arise out of the flood of Renaissance debris. And the Renaissance persisted in its effects for three hundred years after it had passed its peak.

Sculpture and painting did not march hand in hand in Europe. The earlier or Gothic growth was unaccompanied by any serious development of painting. The second or Renaissance growth rose probably somewhat less high than the associated painting, and outside of Italy it remained more restricted in time and space. Nations whose aesthetic development was retarded, like England and Holland, never developed a genuine sculpture, probably because the Renaissance movement had spent its vitality before they were ready to tap it.

Like painting, sculpture took on a new direction in the post-Napoleonic period under French leadership. This movement became international, extending even to the peripheral countries of recent civilization. Its qualities of revolt and dissolution were less prominent than in painting, and came later to the surface. This movement is construable as an attempt at a third European growth.

The Italian growth has a very different configuration from the French, in spite of occasional early and pervasive later influences between them. The Italian growth was a single great wave. It can be traced back nearly to 1100. It ran a course in one direction, to its culmination in the Florentine Renaissance and its crest in Michelangelo. It produced great masters, like Bernini, even in its decadence; and it remained Italian in a continuous configuration, to Canova in 1800. In France, on the other hand, along with the persistence of certain national qualities, three successive phases of sculpture must be recognized, namely: the Romanesque-Gothic of national origin; the Renaissance-Baroque of Italian initiative and aims; and the Modern, in which France again took the lead. Other countries varied in having their sculpture in one wave or more. Where there was one only, this was briefer than the Italian, and stimulated either by the Italian or the French movement.

FRANCE

French sculpture, like the mediaeval architecture to which it was accessory, and like European literature, began in southern France in the eleventh century and culminated in northern France in the thirteenth. The best Romanesque sculpture falls between 1075 and 1150; the High Gothic, from 1200 to 1325. After that comes the diffuse, less and less characteristic Gothic, until 1500, or later in spots. This was no longer so definitely dominated by France: it was a sort of Hellenistic stage of Gothic. Rather remarkable is the rapidity with which each new phase in the development of Gothic spread to adjacent countries.

Romanesque.—Languedoc is usually given preëminence: Moissac (1115?–1150?), Toulouse, Soaillac.—Burgundy ca. 1120–1130 rivals Languedoc in influence: Cluny, Vézelay, Autun.—Provence: Arles, after 1150, less fine, "more Roman."—Auvergne: Clermont-Ferrand, Conques.—Poitou: Poitiers, Angoulême, Saintes, Aulnay.

Early Gothic.—Like the cathedrals, the Gothic sculpture originated in and about the Île de France. That at Chartres, 1140–1165, is still transitional or pre-Gothic. The finest Gothic sculpture is generally considered to be that at Paris, Saint-Denis, Amiens, Reims, Bourges, Bordeaux, executed between 1200 and 1325. It tended toward increasing control, simplicity, idealism, and repose; definitely "classic" quality is ascribed to it. It coincided closely in time and geography not only with the great associated cathedrals, but with the growths in North French literature, music, and royalty during the thirteenth century.

Later Gothic.—During the first half of the fourteenth century there was a change from essentially architectural sculpture to separate devotional statues and tomb figures, and increased interest in realism. With this came a mounting participation of Netherlanders. Since early in the century a colony of Flemish artists had been active in Paris. From 1360 to 1403 the ablest of these, André Beauneveu, was at work. The tendency toward realism also appears Netherlandish, both at this time and for centuries later. On the other hand, there was no contemporary great school of sculpture within the Netherlands. Even later the Flemish carvers of Brussels and Antwerp worked chiefly in wood and in what today would be called skilled shop production. Historians of art seem fairly agreed that the fourteenth-century French sculpture is essentially to be credited to France even though executed largely by Flemings and Walloons. This is a situation in need of further elucidation; though it evidently parallels what happened in music, with the "Gallo-Belgic" school in the lead about this time. However, the musical phenomenon is more nearly "normal," in that a supposedly early purely French school of the twelfth and thirteenth centuries was succeeded by the Gallo-Belgic, after which the Netherlanders were supreme, with only occasional Frenchmen participating, until after 1500. In sculpture there was no such complete passing of leadership into the Netherlands.

The same anomaly holds for the remarkable Burgundian school active around Dijon in the decades before and after 1400. The known masters are Jean de Marville, a Fleming, died 1389; Claus Sluter, a sculptor of true genius and a Dutchman, who died perhaps in 1406; and his nephew, Claus de Werve, died 1439. Holland was then, and long afterward, so backward as compared with Belgium in art, music, literature, manufacture, and trade, that it seems astonishing the greatest sculptor of his day in northern Europe should have been a Dutchman by birth.

It can only be concluded that an unusual situation had arisen as between France and the Netherlands: the French were finished, for the time being, after their great initiating burst; the Netherlanders had learned enough from them to take over the lead; but conditions were such that those of them who stayed at home remained high-grade artisans, while those who went to France could become artists. The specific factors seem to have been that Paris and Dijon provided princes' courts, the Netherlands a postmediaeval bourgeois environment.[8]

Provincial France remained more French, and was characterized by the "Détente," a relaxation, or perhaps rather

---

[8] The same situation is repeated a little later in painting. Clouet, the greatest sixteenth-century painter of France, came of a Netherlands family but painted in a French manner.

refusal, of the realism and expressiveness associated with Netherlandish participation in sculpture. The beginnings of this style are traced to about 1400 on the Loire. Its culmination lay between 1450 and 1525, and in Touraine. It is represented at Tours, Solesmes, Nantes, Bordeaux, Champagne, even in Burgundy after the Dijon school had run its course. The leading exponent is Michel Colombe, who was born in Brittany about 1430, was active at Tours by 1473, and died 1512/19.

The Détente was not a great phase of sculpture, but it achieved a certain restrained loveliness. It was Gothic in that it knew no roots but ecclesiastical Gothic art, and was seemingly uninfluenced by the Renaissance, that is, by Italy. But it was a very different "Gothic" from the architecure-dominated Gothic of the thirteenth century—nearer both ancient and modern standards in its aims, much more truly sculptural. It is a fair question, accordingly, whether the culmination of pre-Renaissance French sculpture is more properly to be set in the thirteenth or in the fifteenth century; whether the earlier work, if considered detached from the overwhelmingly impressive cathedrals to which it is ancillary, would be rated superior, or even equal, to the products of Sluter and the Détente. I bow in this question before the opinion of the critics and historians. Moreover, their verdict in favor of the thirteenth century fits with the peaks of literature, music, and statehood in that time. But so far as sculpture alone is concerned, the French configuration would be simpler if we could regard the thirteenth century as the formative period, in which the art was still unliberated in its proper jurisdiction.

The argument might be carried farther, and Colombe, the master of the Détente, be united with Goujon and Pilon, the first and greatest exponents of the Renaissance in France, to form a culmination superior to that of the siècle Louis XIV. The duration of this crest would be from about 1460/70 to 1580/90. This interpretation suffers from the weakness that the period is rather long for the number and rank of masters included in it; and from the further one that the time is not

an eminent one in other fields of French culture. Again, therefore, I do not press the point of view, but merely remark that
the conventional classification of Colombe's sculpture as
Gothic and Goujon's as Renaissance would be of little force
against the suggested interpretation if otherwise this carried
sufficient conviction.

Renaissance, Baroque, Rococo, and Neoclassicism.—After
Colombe, there are almost three hundred years of French sculpture under Italian precedent if not dominance, without a great
school or even a great name, except perhaps the earliest in the
list, Goujon. They are centuries of court artists. The Italian
influence is rarely complete. Something distinctively French,
sometimes for better and sometimes for worse, is almost always
recognizable. But there is no genuine national growth; only
the successful cultivation of a foreign-born art which polite
society had come to accept.

Richier, ca. 1500–1567, of Lorraine. Active there, not at court.
*Goujon, b. ca. 1515 probably in Normandy, d. before 1568 in
Italy.
Pilon, 1535–1590, of Paris.
Prieur, ca. 1540–1611.
Franqueville, ca. 1550–1615. Italianized Netherlander.
Sarrazin, ca. 1588–1660.
Fr. and Mich. Anguier, 1604–1669, 1612–1686.
Puget, 1622–1694, of Marseilles. Away from court; in Italy.
Girardon, 1628–1715.
Coysevox, 1640–1712.
Nic. and Guill. Coustou, 1658–1733, 1677–1746, nephews of
Coysevox.
Bouchardon, 1698–1762.
Lemoyne, 1704–1778.
Pigalle, 1714–1785.
Falconet, 1716–1791.
Caffieri, 1725–1792.
Pajou, 1730–1809.
Clodion, 1738–1814.
Houdon, 1741–1828.
Chinard, 1756–1813.
Cartellier, 1757–1831.
Chaudet, 1763–1810.

There are two slackenings in the stream, each of about 50 years in the series of birth dates: from 1540 to 1588, with only the foreigner Franqueville; and from 1640 to 1698, in which there fall only the brothers Coustou, who without their uncle Coysevox would probably not have attained to distinction. These breaks may be accidents of a small series, or significant. If we allow thirty years for a sculptor to come into his own, Sarrazin, born 1588, would reach maturity in the Richelieu-Mazarin period; Coysevox, 1640, be the last sculptor born in time for most of the reign of Louis XIV. Significance of the breaks is suggested, but can hardly be stressed. On the whole, what is impressive is the continuity of the flow with so uniform a level of achievement through successive phases of style.

Nineteenth-century French sculpture.—This obviously corresponds to the synchronous movement in French painting and literature. Though it bears less label of "revolt" and "romanticism," Rude and David were called innovators. Most important, the growth is genuinely French: Italian influence, even indirect, is wholly lacking. Even the last and rarely acknowledged great-grandchild of the Renaissance, Canova's neoclassicism, had passed away.

Rude, David, and Barye may not impress us today as artists who launched a great movement. Yet, the growth which they initiated is a considerable one, for it includes one master perhaps of first rank: Rodin. His dates, 1840–1917, indicate the last third of the century as the culmination. The other birth dates, with the group of initiators set apart by a generation, confirm: they cluster around Rodin's.

Rude, 1784–1855.
David (d'Angers) , 1788–1856.
Pradier, 1790–1852.
Barye, 1796–1875.
Fremiet, 1824–1910. Nephew of Rude.
Carpeaux, 1827–1875.
Dubois, 1829–1905.
Falguière, 1831–1900.

Chapu, 1833–1891.
Dalou, 1838–1902.
*Rodin, 1840–1917.
Mercié, 1845–1916.
Bartholomé, b. 1848.
Maillol, 1861.
Bourdelle, 1861.
Bouchard, 1875.

THE NETHERLANDS

Two facts characterize Netherlandish sculpture from beginning to end. The first is an intimate relation with France,
largely of dependence but at times of reciprocation. The second is the predominance of Belgium over Holland, in early
as well as modern times. There never was a true Dutch school
of sculpture. Whenever in the following paragraphs the word
"Netherlands" is used, it therefore means Belgium, unless the
contrary is specified. As between Walloons and Flemings, the
Romance and Germanic halves of Belgium, the Flemings seem
to have been pretty consistently somewhat more productive in
sculpture, until the nineteenth century, when the balance becomes equal, or shifts in favor of the Walloon element, if the
personal names are ethnically significant.

These facts suggest that language has been a fairly indifferent
factor so far as nationality in the Netherlands is concerned. It
is the Germanic Flemings who show more active relations with
France than the Romance Walloons, but the Germanic Hollanders who show least, in sculpture.

In the Romanesque and earlier Gothic periods, the Netherlands produced, or at least have left, little sculpture, and that
dependent on and inferior to the French. After about 1370,
with the best architectural Gothic sculpture over, the Belgians
became more prominent, with small figures, often of everyday
life, made of wood in shops, sometimes for export. Also, Tournai specialized in "epitaphs," and Antwerp and Brussels in
retables. Jan Borreman of the latter city, active about 1479–
1522, is perhaps the most distinguished worker in the movement, which in quality was scarcely more than mediocre. On
the other hand, it must be remembered that Paris and Burgundy, from 1360 to 1440, had their best sculpture executed
by Netherlanders: Beauneveu, Jean de Marville, Sluter, Claus
de Werve;[9] who added something of French taste and at times
a certain nobility of idea to their Flemish realism.

Belgian sculpture continued, without ever rising to a serious

_____

[9] Cf. Nicolaus Gerhaert of Leyden, died 1487, active in Germany.

peak, into the eighteenth century, irrespective of whether its stimulus was Gothic, Renaissance, or Baroque. Quite evidently there was a definite sculptural tradition, such as Holland lacked.

These are some of the better-known names: Du Broeucq, 1500/10–1584, who studied in Rome; Mone and De Vriendt, also under Italian influence; Colyns de Nole of Cambrai, ca. 1520–1601; Giovanni Bologna, 1524–1608, permanently to Italy; Gerhard, ca. 1545–1620, and De Vries, 1560–1627, both of Holland but active in south Germany; De Keyzer, 1565–1621, the only Dutchman in this series to remain at home;[10] Duquesnoy (Il Fiammingo), 1594–1643, to Italy; Quellin, 1609–1668, of Antwerp; Faydherbe, 1617–1697, of Malines; Verhulst, 1624–1698, also of Malines, active chiefly in Holland; Delcour, pupil of Bernini, 1627–1707, at Liège; Van Geel and Van Hool at Antwerp; Verhaegen, 1701–1759.

During the eighteenth century, the Belgian level of production seems to have sunk while a tradition kept alive. After independence and the French so-called romantic flare-up around 1830, Belgian names reappear in histories of sculpture. The principal are, in the order of their births: Geefs, 1805; Fraikin, 1817; *Meunier, 1831; Van der Stappen, 1843; De Vigne, 1843; Vinçotte, 1850; Lambeaux, 1852; Charlier, 1854; Braecke, 1859; Lagaë, 1862; Rousseau, 1865; Minne, 1867. There are enough here to constitute a real school. Meunier is reckoned their primate. His sculptured laborers, though somewhat in the sentiment of Millet, also suggest the old Flemish predilection for themes of subbourgeois life. Meunier was slightly anterior to Rodin, but Geefs and Fraikin followed Rude and Barye by about two decades. A partial historic dependence on France is therefore indicated; but the movement seems a genuinely national one.

GERMANY

As usual, the German pattern of development is for the most part unconformable to that of the remainder of Europe, and not clear-cut in terms of itself. Germany has never produced a

---

[10] It will be noted that all the Dutchmen in this list reached their thirtieth year between 1575 and 1595, while Holland's independence was being established; whereas there is a gap of seventy years about this time in the Belgian part of the series. Significant, or accident of few cases?

top-rank sculptor; naturally, the configuration of its nine hundred years of sculpture tends to lack sharpness.

Three early pulses seem recognizable: one in the eleventh century; another in the thirteenth; the third around 1500. These represent respectively, and with allowance for some lag of art behind dynasty, the Othonian and Hohenstaufen periods, and the time of Luther and Dürer. During the last four centuries, it is difficult to see anything like genuine swells or troughs in the history of German sculpture. As in painting, there certainly was no marked crest around 1800, when music, philosophy, and literature culminated.

Really remarkable, however, is the fact that Germany was the first country of Europe west of Byzantium to attain to any sculpture at all, beyond the Carolingian imitations and ineptnesses. The bronze cathedral doors of Hildesheim, cast in 1015, are pre-Romanesque. They are separated from the South French growth in time, in space, and in style. The usual explanation of the art of which they are the peak is that it is Byzantine in origin, owing to the Byzantine relations of the Ottos, such as the Greek wife of Otto II. The insufficiency of this explanation lies in the fact that the Hildesheim art is not Byzantine in style, but original. A craving for show and a growing feeling for delicacy, certain technical processes, perhaps some motives, may be derivable from Constantinople. But the essence of the art, its style, is distinctive and apparently autochthonous. The marvel is that it should have arisen at this time in northern Germany. Italy, France, even the Netherlands, would be more expectable; but their first real styles came later.

The following explanation is suggested in terms of national growths.

About the year 1000, Denmark, Poland, Hungary, Russia, in a measure Bohemia, all rose to a national crest. This was of fairly brief duration; but while it lasted it brought political centralization, Christianity, a degree of prosperity, and a national consciousness—national in contrast with what previously had rather been ethnic. In none of these countries was there a corresponding upturn in the aesthetic and intellectual levels of culture sufficiently marked to get above the threshold of history. The nations were too new for that. What they did in this period was to find civilization and to accept its first outward stages with enthusiasm.

Now, in a rough parallel, this is what happened in Saxon Germany part of a century earlier. In the last quarter of the eighth century, the Saxons were conquered by Charlemagne and definitively Christianized, after stubborn resistance. They were the last Germans to come into the fold of the Carolingian kingdom and the Church; once in, they evidently developed vigorously. In 919, on the extinction of the Carolingian line and the death of the elected Conrad of Franconia, the Frank nobles of Germany chose Henry, Duke of Saxony, to be king, as best able to keep Germany in order and to resist the Hungarian menace. His successors reigned for a century, Otto the Great, 936–973, being the most distinguished. It looks as if this Saxon peak were the counterpart of the Scandinavian, Slavic, and Hungarian ones, except for being earlier; and this precedence would be expectable for a German people receiving its Christianity and civilization from a long-Christianized other German people, as compared with Scandinavians and Slavs. Being in the ascendant about a century after their conquest by Charlemagne, while the Franks were by comparison declining, and the Alemanni-Suabians, Bavarians, and Thuringians being all longer within the pale, so to speak, the Saxons came into leadership among Germans. With the recognition of their dynasty, the East Frankish kingdom passes into the German one.

Apparently, as so often, this newly civilized Saxon nationality developed energy in a variety of directions; and one of these was sculpture. From somewhere, bronze founding and goldsmithing had come in; Carolingian and, a little later, Byzantine models were available; and out of these materials the Saxons created a new style. This found its fullest expression about a century after the Saxons assumed political leadership, about a half century after their dynasty was at its apogee; but this degree of lag is hardly disconcerting. The Othonian style was not confined to the Saxony of the time; but it found its best expression there, and continued until French Romanesque influences came into Germany and mingled with it. Essentially Othonian art is in metal and not architecturally conditioned; Romanesque is definitely architectural.

Othonian
    Cologne, cross of Gero, 970.
    Gernrode, stucco, 1000.
    Hildesheim, bronze doors, 1015, Easter column, ca. 1020.
    Basel Antependium, 1020.
    Cologne, wooden doors, ca. 1050.
    Augsburg, bronze doors, ca. 1050.
    Merseburg, bronze grave slab, ca. 1080.

Romanesque
    Magdeburg, bronze grave slab, 1152.
    Brunswick, lion, 1166.
    Novgorod, bronze doors, 1150–1175, cast in Magdeburg.
    Gnesen, Poland, doors, 1180–1200.
    Hildesheim, baptismal font, 1220.

The monuments usually classed as Romanesque are so designated here. It will be seen that nearly a century separates them from the Othonian ones. They differ, it would seem, by embodying concepts and motives which can be traced back to southern France; but, reciprocally, Othonian elements persisted into the German Romanesque, especially in Saxony.

In fact, Othonian, Romanesque, and Gothic strains overlap. Compare the Hildesheim font, 1220, which still carries much of the Othonian handling; the "Romanesque" Jonas of Bamberg, 1230; the Gothic sculptures at Bamberg, 1230–1240, and at Naumburg, 1250–1260. Evidently the differences between the styles, however real aesthetically, are rather technical when viewed in relation to national development. Incidentally, this very Gothic of Bamberg and Naumburg is considered the best Gothic sculpture that Germany produced—highly characterized, expressive, and yet dignified. Next best, perhaps, is that of Strassburg, 1276 and after, and adhering more closely to French models. It is rather remarkable how avidly and quickly central Germany seized on the Gothic sculpture of France and yet gave it a new twist.

The second German peak, Gothic or Hohenstaufen, may therefore be put about 1250.

With the fourteenth century, the east and north of Germany recede, and Nürnberg, Würzburg, Ulm occupy the proscenium. The development tends gradually to a climax in Nürnberg in the first decades after 1500. This is the moment, and city, of Dürer. It is also the decades of the culmination of Renaissance painting and sculpture. Naturally, some influences came into Germany from the greater Italian growth. They absorbed and blended, however, and seem not to have altered the configuration of events. Stoss, Krafft, Riemenschneider are classed as Gothic sculptors; Vischer as Renaissance but half Gothic; Dauher and Flötner as Italian-influenced; and yet they are all essential contemporaries. Evidently the aesthetic strands were interwoven to a unity of place and time much like the Saxon, Romanesque, and Gothic strains in the thirteenth century.

> Nicolaus Gerhaert of Leyden, d. 1487; at Trier, Strassburg, Vienna.
> Jörg Syrlin, ca. 1430–1491, of Ulm.
> Erasmus Gresser, ca. 1450–1526+, at Munich.
> Adam Krafft, 1455/60–1509, of Nürnberg.
> Veit Stoss (German? Pole?) at Cracow 1477–1496, at Nürnberg 1496–1533.
> Peter Vischer, 1460–1529, of Nürnberg.
> Adolf Dauher, ca. 1460–1523/4, of Ulm.
> Tilman Riemenschneider, 1468?–1531, at Würzburg.
> Konrad Mett, active ca. 1500, of Worms.
> Peter Flötner, ca. 1485–1546, perhaps Swiss, at Nürnberg.
> Hans Dauher, ca. 1485–1538.
> Peter Vischer the Younger, 1487–1528.

By 1550 this third thoroughly German growth was over, and much of German sculpture fell into the hands of Belgians and Hollanders for a century: Colin, 1527/9–1612, of Malines; Gerhard, ca. 1545–1620, a Dutchman active at Munich and Augsburg; De Vries, ca. 1560–1627, of The Hague. Some Italian influence came back into south Germany after the Thirty Years' War.

There were enough German sculptors in the three centuries since 1600, as the following list shows; but they do not seem to constellate significantly in eminence. Possibly Dannecker, Schadow, and Rauch might be elevated above the rest; or the contemporaries of Begas, Hildebrand, and Klinger; but there would be no general agreement on any selection. Nor have any important innovations come out of this series of German sculptors. European leadership has remained in Italy or France, as in painting and in architecture. The Germans have certainly tried harder than the English to produce something new in sculpture in these last three or four centuries, but with not much more success.

Degler, d. 1637. Bavarian; wood.
Münstermann, d. ca. 1639, of Oldenburg.
Permoser, 1651–1732, at Dresden.
Schlüter, 1664–1714, at Berlin.
Donner, 1693–1741, at Vienna.
Wagner, 1730–1809, at Würzburg.
Messerschmidt, 1732–1783, Swabian at Vienna.
Dannecker, 1758–1841, at Stuttgart.
Schadow, 1764–1850, at Berlin.
Rauch, 1777–1857, at Berlin.
Zumbusch, 1830–1915, Westphalian in Austria.
Begas, 1831–1911, at Berlin.
Wagmüller, 1839–1881, at Munich.
Tilgner, 1844–1896, Austrian.
Hildebrand, 1847–1921, b. Marburg.
Maison, 1854–1904, at Munich.
Klinger, 1857–1920, at Leipzig.

Are the three crests of German sculpture around 1000, 1250, and 1500 only pulses of one larger, essentially mediaeval growth? Possibly. And yet the period seems unduly long for a development that never became one of the greatest. What is common to all three phases is a certain originality, manifest in the time precedence of the Saxon over the Romanesque movement, as also in the German transformation of French-derived Gothic. This originality, or at any rate independence, on the contrary, is just what has been lacking in German sculpture since 1550.

ITALY

As already mentioned, Italian sculpture has a long, single-curve history. During the early part of this history, until about 1400, it resisted transalpine influence tenaciously; after 1500, it influenced all transalpine countries for three centuries. In other words, Italy alone in Europe largely evaded becoming Gothic, and in return gave Europe the Renaissance which it had created instead.

The Italian "Romanesque" of the books is Lombard and South Italian art before 1250. The Lombard sculpture of 1100–1150 is of uncertain origins: local or Carolingian or South of France. The doubt is due partly to its crudity. Master Guglielmo and his pupil Niccolò are mentioned at Modena and Ferrara about 1117. Milan and Pavia, nearer Provence, had ruder work. After 1150, some influence of Languedoc is generally admitted. Benedetto Antelami was active at Parma and Modena following 1178; and Lombard sculptors spread to Tuscany, especially Pistoia and Lucca: 1166, ca. 1200, ca. 1250 are some of their dates.

Southern Italy learned from Byzantines, or copied antiques, until 1250. Monte Cassino imported Greek craftsmen from Constantinople in 1066. Barisanus put up bronze cathedral doors at Trani about 1175; Bonanus at Pisa 1180, at Monreale 1185; the best of the type are perhaps those at Benevento, from the early thirteenth century. In Sicily and Campania there was a school of marble sculpture which directly and frankly imitated antiquity, under Frederick II, 1215–1250; much as his poets imitated troubadours.

If this is Italian Romanesque, Italian Gothic sculpture is the movement which flourished at Pisa, or radiated from it during the next century and a half. The paternity, however, was not Gothic French, but the South Italian classic tradition. Nicola d'Apulia, 1205/15–1278/80, became Nicola Pisano with change of residence, and founded the school.

Giovanni Pisano, ca. 1250–ca. 1328, son of Nicola.
Arnolfo di Cambio, ca. 1232–ca. 1302, pupil.

Andrea di Ugalino, "Pisano," ca. 1270–1348, at Florence; influenced by Giotto.
Andrea Orcagna, d. ca. 1376, follower of Giotto.
Tino di Camaino, d. 1337; at Siena, Pisa, Naples.
Lorenzo Maitani, at Siena, Orvieto.
Nino Pisano, active 1342–1368.
Giovanni di Balduccio, from Pisa, at Milan 1339.
Andriolo Santi, d. 1377, Pisan influence to Venice.
Apparently without Pisan connection: the Campionesi, a family or group from Lake Lugano, active at Bergamo, Milan, Verona until about 1400 or after.

Up to this point, everything is pre-Renaissance, by the usual classification. This is true in the sense that the characteristic patterns of the developed Italian Renaissance had not yet been found. On the other hand, the pre-1400 sculpture of Italy is also not French or Byzantine. It sustained Romanesque, Gothic, and Byzantine impingements, and was somewhat influenced by them. But it tenaciously resisted acceptance of these styles as wholes: resisted them in spite of its own poverty and weakness. This resistance, it would seem, was due to the strength of native impulses which were working toward something different and greater, and which finally broke through as the Renaissance. Viewed as Romanesque or Gothic art, this early Italian sculpture is both surprisingly mediocre and heavily atypical. Viewed as the still somewhat uncharacterized formative stage of the Renaissance, it is equally mediocre, but at least not atypical. It is true that we cannot with much profit speak of divergence from a type not yet emerged. Yet as a proto-Renaissance stage, this sculpture forms a continuum in time and geography, and in background of speech and general civilization, with Renaissance Italy; but a discontinuum in everything save time with Gothic France. The requirements of the principle of historic continuity seem better met by the interpretation here advanced than by the usual art-history classification in terms of pan-European stylistic periods. No one tries to force Russia or Byzantium into the Romanesque-Gothic formula. Why should not Italy be allowed to have been exempt, if the preponderance of facts points that way? As for the Romanesque and Gothic

and Byzantine art currents which flowed into Italy, the significant historical fact is not that they reached the peninsula, but
that in the main it refused to assimilate them.

Here we resume our review of the sculptural developments
in Italy.

Just about 1400, Florence took the lead in sculpture, as it
had previously taken it in painting, and not only kept it for
more han a century, but reached the undisputed peak of Italian and all Western sculpture. Ghiberti, Donatello, Della Robbia, Verrocchio, Michelangelo mark the culmination. After
1480, lesser men were born, and their work began to tend toward the colossal, the strained, or the mannered: 1510–1530 is
the period when this change became visible: even Michelangelo was not exempt from the new tendencies and did much
to establish them. "Renaissance" and "Baroque" largely signify
respectively the upswing and the decline of the Florentine-
Italian growth—the decline being also the period of the spread
over much of Europe.

Florence
   Nanni di Banco, ca. 1373–1420.
   *Lorenzo Ghiberti, 1378–1455. "Initiates the Renaissance" or
      "essentially Gothic," say different critics.
   *Donatello, 1385/6–1466.
   *Luca della Robbia, 1400–1482.
   Bernardo Rossellino, 1409–1464.
   Agostino di Duccio, 1418–1481, pupil of Donatello.
   Antonio Rossellino, 1427–1478.
   Desiderio da Settignano, 1428–1464.
   Mino da Fiesole, 1430/31–1484.
   Antonio Pollaiuolo, 1432–1498.
   Andrea della Robbia, 1435–1525.
   *Andrea del Verrocchio, 1435–1488.
   Benedetto da Maiano, 1442–1497.
   Baccio da Montelupo, 1469–1535.
   *Michelangelo, 1475–1564.
   Niccolò Tribolo, 1485–1550.
   Jacopo Tatti Sansovino, 1486–1570. After 1527 to Venice.
   Baccio Bandinelli, 1493–1560.
   Benvenuto Cellini, 1500–1571.
   Giovanni Bandini (dell' Opera), 1540–1599.

Siena
  Jacopo della Quercia, 1365/75–1438. At Bologna 1425.
  Lorenzo di Pietro, ca. 1412–1480.
  Antonio Federighi, ca. 1420–1490.

Lombardy and Emilia
  Niccolò da Bari (dell' Arca) , ca. 1440–1494; Bologna.
  Amadeo (Omodeo), 1447–1522, of Pavia.
  Cristoforo and Antonio Mantegazza.
  Guido Mazzoni, 1450–1518; Modena, France.
  Antonio Begarelli, ca. 1479–1565; Modena.
  Giovanni di Bartolo (Rosso), d. after 1541; of Florence, to
    Verona.
  Giovanni Bologna, 1524–1608; naturalized Belgian of Douai.

Venice
  Bartolomeo Buon, from Florence; active ca. 1382–1442.
  Antonio Rizzo, ca. 1430–ca. 1500.
  Pietro Lombardo, ca. 1435–1515; Tullio, 1455–1532.

Rome
  Antonio Filarete, ca. 1400–ca. 1469.
  Andrea Bregno, 1421–1506; Lombard.
  (Mino da Fiesole, 1430/31–1484; Florentine.)
  Giovanni da Traù, Dalmatian.
  Andrea Sansovino, 1460–1529.

Naples and Sicily
  Francesco Laurena, ca. 1425–ca. 1502; Dalmatian.

Of men born after 1550, there is no longer any question:
they exemplify the Baroque, that is, the flamboyant, facile,
overrich, and mannered phase of the Renaissance. The outstanding individual was Bernini of Naples, 1598–1680, probably one of the most talented of all sculptors, who sometimes
rose above his style. Place of birth now no longer counted
heavily as in the days of city-states. The shift to Naples probably is significant chiefly of drying up of talent in the north.
The Italian tradition continues to Canova, contemporary of
Napoleon, leading neoclassicist, and greatest European sculptor of his day. Or, if one wishes, one may see in him the sculptural representative of a secondary peak of florescence which
Italy manifested in several spheres of culture toward the turn
of the century.

Girolamo Campagna, 1550–1626.
Pietro Bernini, 1562–1629.
Stefano Maderna, ca. 1576–1636.
Pietro Tacca, 1577/80–1640?
François Duquesnoy (Il Fiammingo), 1594–1643.
*Giov. Lorenzo Bernini, 1598–1680.
Alessandro Algardi, 1602–1654.
Ercole Ferrata, 1610–1686.
Giacomo Serpotta, 1656–1732.
Pietro Bracci, 1700–1773.
Giuseppe Franchi, 1731–1806.
*Antonio Canova, 1757–1822.

Nineteenth-century sculpture in Italy shows some wavering of direction, and some foreign influences, as of Rodin on Rosso. There is little indication of concentration.

| (Bartolini, b. 1777.) | Vela, 1820. | Rosso, 1858. |
| Duprè, 1817. | Gemito, 1852. | Bistolfi, 1859. |

Summary.—The course of Italian sculpture is simple and long. It lasted from 1100 to 1800, climaxing about 1500. Its growth exactly parallels that of Italian painting, in time, in participating provinces, and in purity of ethnic expression. If the beginning seems earlier than that of painting, this is evidently because stone survives better. Both arts are genuinely autochthonous. As growths, they cannot be derived from either Byzantium or mediaeval France. Some elements from both these civilizations were accepted during the formative period. But the forces at work in Italy were fundamentally resistive to import; and what was borrowed was promptly transmuted. By 1400, a national and great style had been worked out, which developed further for over a century and attained the indubitable peak of all Western sculpture. The highest attainments were the product of Florence; not merely predominantly as in painting, but overwhelmingly. It was by being uncompromisingly national, even provincial, that Florence—or Italy—succeeded in achieving the greatest sculpture of Europe. There is also no parallel, in that continent, of any nation achieving a unitary cycle of sculpture, single in its trend and smooth in its contour, of a duration even approaching seven hundred years. With the growth still able to produce a Canova around 1800, it is no wonder that, after the end finally came, Italian sculpture lay fallow while other nations were sending up lesser and briefer shoots.

SPAIN

Spain was the last country of Europe to attain a national school of sculpture; namely, in the seventeenth century. Till 1400, Spanish sculpture was under French influence, then till 1550 under Flemish-Burgundian, with Italian tending to supplant this after 1500. To the Italian immigrants there soon were added Spaniards who had studied in Italy. About 1600 a group of Andalusians established an art which had sufficiently freed itself from the weight of the Renaissance, which worked chiefly in wood, and which was genuinely Spanish. This sculpture did not reach the heights of the great painting and great drama of Spain, but was very nearly synchronous with them. And like them, when it was done it was dead.

French influence, "Romanesque and Gothic," 1080–1400
  To 1300, chiefly Burgos, León, Compostela.
  1300–1400, rest of the Iberian Peninsula.
Flemish-Burgundian influence, "Gothic," 1400–1550
  Janín Lomme, of Tournai, 1416 in Pampeluna.
  Pere Johan de Vallfongona, 1426 at Tarragona, 1445 Saragossa.
  Damián Forment, ca. 1480–ca. 1541.
  Felipe Vigarni, d. 1453, Burgundian.
  Lorenzo Mercadante, Breton, Burgundian influence.
  Gil de Siloé.
  Pedro de Milán, Burgundian school.
  Juan de Arfe, of Flemish or German family.
Italian influence, "Renaissance," 1500 seq.
  Domenico Fancelli, 1469–1519. To Avila, Granada, Seville.
  Pietro Torrigiano. To Seville, 1526.
  Leone Leoni, 1509–1590; Pompeo Leoni, d. 1610.
Spaniards trained in Italy or influenced by it, 1500 seq.
  Bartolomé Ordóñez, pupil of Fancelli.
  Alonzo Berruguete, ca. 1486–1561; pupil of Michelangelo.
  Juan de Juni, ca. 1507–1577.
  Gaspar Becerra, ca. 1520–1570.

National school
  Gregorio Fernández (Hernández), ca. 1567–1636. Valladolid.
  *Juan Martínez Montañés, ca. 1564–1649. Seville.
  *Alonso Cano, 1601–1667. Granada.
  *Pedro de Mena, 1628–1688. Granada.

ENGLAND

England hardly needs separate treatment. There never was a genuine growth of sculpture in Britain. Norman architecture both Romanesque and Gothic, used little accessory sculpture; and without a model, the English seemed never to get started. Their best productions are on the Wells façade (1220–1250) and Westminster transept (ca. 1250). The time is right, but the product meager; meager both in quantity and quality, even as compared with that of Germany, which was also dependent on France at this period. The fact is the more glaring because in mediaeval architecture England showed definite originality. It may have anticipated France in the first use of intersecting independent ogival arches, usually regarded as the basal characteristic of the Gothic order. At any rate, England evolved its own variant styles of both Romanesque and Gothic building; and they are styles which in general opinion can fairly vie, on almost even terms, with those of France, and reached higher attainments than any in Germany. Buildings, after all, have a use and present problems of engineering, but statues deal with pure form; and for the latter, English culture never appears to have been able to develop much real interest. Painting, it is true, finally worked up to a respectable climax in the eighteenth century. But scarcely a ripple extended to sculpture.

MODERN PERIPHERAL COUNTRIES

In painting, literature, and music a new direction, often of much vigor, appears in nearly all European countries at dates varying from about 1800 to 1860, in relation to distance, but averaging around 1830. This took the form of a so-called romantic reaction against classic, neoclassic, and lingering Renaissance-Baroque-Rococo tendencies. It was most definitely expressed in France, perhaps because there these tendencies were more firmly entrenched than in Germany. But in literature both Germany and England, and in music Germany, had become romantic before France. It is rather clear, therefore, that the movement as a whole was not intrinsically French in origin, as mediaeval literature, architecture, and sculpture had been in the main. In certain of its spheres, however, notably painting and sculpture, as of course in the political field, the innovations took place in France; and the whole movement was best focused in that country. Essentially, the romantic movement seems to have been international European, as is evidenced by the rapidity of its spread, which extended even to marginal nations that had never before participated in the creative activities of Europe.

This movement, which was not merely a romantic surge in the arts, but was intertwined with other powerful currents such as democracy and industrialism, is difficult to analyze or resynthesize, both because it presents a number of unique features to which history holds no close parallel, and because of its nearness. In fact, we are still more or less in it. It clearly unleashed much aesthetic energy, but this is not easily appraised, and is therefore best dealt with summarily.

In sculpture the most successful hearth of revolt was France; and there too the highest achievement was apparently attained, under Rodin. In certain respects, however, the whole movement is Hellenistic: its wide dispersal, the participation of wholly new nationalities, the diversity of stylistic currents, the leaning toward realism and subsequent reaction toward the primitive, the lack of any organized peak. In few of the countries involved was any high level of creativeness achieved. Some of the better-known names are listed, not because it is likely that many of them will still be familiar a few centuries from now, but because their aggregate, in its national and temporal distribution, parallels the corresponding distributions in painting, music, and literature.

France
    See list under that country, beginning with Rude, 1784, or
        Fremiet, 1824.

Netherlanas
See list already given, beginning with Geefs, 1805.

Germany
See previous list, beginning with Zumbusch, 1830, and Begas, 1831.

Italy
See previous list, beginning with Bartolini, 1777, or Duprè, 1817.

Spain

Bellver, 1845.	Blay, 1866.
Querol, 1863.	Clará, 1878.

Scandinavia
(Thorwaldsen, 1770, Dane. Neoclassic.)
Sinding, 1846, Norwegian, to Denmark.
Vigeland, 1869, Norwegian.
Milles, 1875, Swede.

Slavic peoples
Troubetskoy, 1866, Russian.
Metzner, 1870, Czech.
Meštrović, 1883, Yugoslav.

England

Stevens, 1817.	Gilbert, 1854.
Watts, 1817, primarily painter.	Drury, 1859.
Foley, 1818, Irish.	Frampton, 1860.
Brock, 1847.	Wood, 1871.
Thornycroft, 1850.	Epstein, 1880, American.
Ford, 1852.	

United States

Greenough, 1805.	Niehaus, 1855.
Powers, 1805.	Adams, 1858.
Crawford, 1813.	Taft, 1860.
Brown, 1814.	Dallin, 1861.
Rimmer, 1816.	Grafly, 1862.
Palmer, 1817.	Barnard, 1863.
Ball, 1819.	MacMonnies, 1863.
Story, 1819.	Bartlett, 1865.
Rogers, 1825.	Pratt, 1867.
Rinehart, 1825.	Gutzon Borglum, 1867.
Ward, 1830.	Solon Borglum, 1868.
Milmore, 1844.	Anna Hyatt, 1876.
Warner, 1844.	Aitken, 1878.
*Saint-Gaudens, 1848, Irish, of French father.	Fry, 1879.
	Manship, 1885.
French, 1850.	Malvina Hoffman, 1887.

The longer lists for England and the United States do not imply a correspondingly greater importance. Not wisning to discriminate among near 'and actual contemporaries, I have used a work of reference which, happening to be American, no doubt weights the Anglo-Saxon contribution unduly.

§45. Summary for the West

Except for a local and somewhat primitive preliminary in Low Germany around 1000—seemingly autochthonous but possibly Byzantine-influenced—European sculpture of merit originated in southern France in the eleventh century. By 1200, leadership had passed from the Midi to the environs of the Seine basin; and characteristic quality was maintained till after 1300. The surrounding countries, Spain, Italy, Germany, the Netherlands, England, were all invaded by the Romanesque-Gothic sculpture, but with widely different results. England did very little with the imported style. Germany, at least in spots, seized it avidly and developed it rapidly and with certain modifications; in fact, passed its peak more quickly than France. Italy reacted selectively; it accepted, as it were, under pressure, having as yet nothing much of its own to oppose. In the Netherlands the art flourished while it declined in France, until, around 1400, Netherlandish artists were achieving a brief peak of Late Gothic under French patronage in France. At this moment Italy found the pattern for which it had evidently been groping for several centuries, and Ghiberti ushered in the undeniable Renaissance.

From then on for four centuries Italy maintained unchallenged primacy, with Donatello and Verrocchio in the fifteenth century, Michelangelo in the early sixteenth, Bernini in the seventeenth, Canova in the final Renaissance phase of neoclassicism around 1800. The influence on the rest of Europe was overwhelming. In Germany a modest national development which had regrown out of Gothic divested of its architectural attachments, and had come to its best by about 1500, was obliterated within a half century. An analogous French growth, the Détente, culminating about the same time, was also swept away. On the whole, however, the Renaissance growth produced little sculpture of high merit outside of Italy. Only in Spain does it seem to have helped stimulate a brief national school into success: in the time of Bernini—but also of the great Spanish painters. In France, in its first onrush, the Renaissance can register to its credit the sculptor who is probably the greatest of his nation in several centuries: Goujon, who died less than four years after Michelangelo. But after him the Italian influence, now become Baroque, resulted in pretentiousness more than in intrinsic value. In Germany, the Netherlands, England, sculpture in the Italianate centuries was colorlessly mediocre or worse.

Finally, soon after 1800, about the last years of Canova and in the maturity of his Danish pseudo-successor Thorwaldsen, the romantic revolt was launched in Paris, and France took the leadership away from Italy. She also produced the greatest sculptor of late times, Rodin; but the movement came in days of internationalism, and France exercised hegemony rather than dominance.

During something over eight hundred years, accordingly, Occidental sculpture was primarily French half the time, Italian the other half. France led during the formation and the epilogue; Italy produced the middle period and culmination. The other nations which participated creatively at all—Spain, the Belgian Netherlands, Germany—are all adjacent to these two. Those more remote, Holland, England, Scandinavia, the Slavic lands, played no part at all in the fundamental activity of setting or even of developing patterns. Their role was passive and imitative—at any rate until the late nineteenth-century era of dissipation.

This makes Occidental sculpture essentially a Latin product. And this fact in turn is perhaps associated with another: that sculpture has on the whole had less prestige in western Europe than painting—a relation by no means universal or to be taken for granted. For both Italy and France it might be argued that sculpture had achieved equal greatness with painting over the centuries. At any rate, the tendency is to regard the two arts as substantially abreast, and as counterparts. But in Spain, Germany, both the Netherlands, Great Britain, the attainments of painting definitely outrank those of sculpture. Art, unqualified, means first of all painting. It is unquestionably the expression more characteristic of West European civilization as a whole. Not that Germanic-speaking Europe consciously resisted or depreciated sculpture because it was Romance in origin. But sculpture, having taken its forms in Romance Europe, molded them Latin enough in character for the Germanic nations to be unable to do much with them. Or possibly sculpture is, in its nature, less adaptable than painting to progressive reformulation. At any rate, nothing comparable to the Dutch transmutation of Renaissance painting into a new great and national style occurred in sculpture anywhere in Europe. The Germans certainly were eager to take over Gothic sculpture from the French. They lost no time in adopting it; but they were through with their little culmination before their masters: evidently the art was something they could modify but not carry farther.

§46. Discussion

The usual diagrammatic presentation of the several growths is appended (see p. 310). Owing to the nature of its materials, sculpture has a longer historical record, for its most important manifestations the world over, than any other of the high developments of civilization: more than five thousand years.

For the first half of this enormous span, however, sculpture of high-level aesthetic value was being produced only in a limited area in the Near East: within a nearly unchanging set of patterns, though not continuously of one quality, in Egypt; with considerably less fixity of system and style and much more intermittently, in Mesopotamia; and rather briefly, toward the end, in Crete and the Aegean.

As the middle of the last pre-Christian millennium began to be approached, this old and monotonous story swerved its

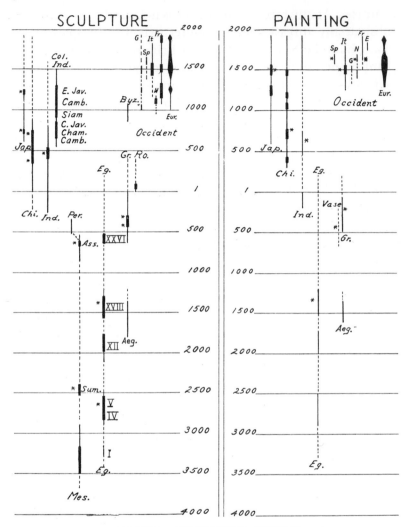

SCULPTURE AND PAINTING, GENERAL

course rather suddenly. In the seventh century, Mesopotamian sculpture lifted itself to its final brief culmination in Assyria, and Egyptian began to experience the last of its several real revivifications. Before the next century ended, both of these were essentially dead; but on the one hand the Persians, and on the other and much more successfully the Greeks, were producing new growths. Two or three hundred years more, and India had begun; within another like interval, the Chinese to the east and the Romans to the west. India and China reached their respective climaxes shortly before and shortly after 500 A.D., in round numbers; but meanwhile had propagated daughter offshoots in Farther India—mainland and island—and in Japan, at the very limits of the growing *oikumene* of higher civilization. The opposite periphery, in western Europe, became sculpturally active much the latest, after India and China had run their course and Indonesia and Japan were approaching the end of theirs. The first pulse of Occidental sculpture, the Gothic, coincides in its peak exactly with the greatest but last century of notable Japanese sculpture, the thirteenth. By 1500, when the European growth as a whole culminated, there was no longer a single other important sculpture alive in the world. It was the first time in two thousand years that there had not been two or three flourishing simultaneously. And the concentration took place at the very edge of the civilized world.

Obviously, this is also the outline of the history of higher civilization in accentuated form. In no other domain is the picture so sharp: the early prolonged narrow localization at the eastern end of the Mediterranean; the sudden collapse there, coincident with the spread of activity to both sides; the more rapid and brilliant development on the west, but at no great distance from the old center; the slower but much more enduring gradual spread eastward to the Pacific; and as this reached its geographical terminus and began to slacken in strength, the birth and flowering of a new set of impulses on new soil more westerly than ever before.

Of course, certain qualificatory corrections to this outline picture are necessary, as for every grand summary in the field of history. In strictness, an argument can be made against the generalization that the Occidental growth had occurred wholly on more westerly soil than any before. After all, Roman sculpture, though overwhelmingly dependent on Greek, also produced certain new values of its own, however limited and transient, and produced these chiefly on Italian soil. And in the Occidental growth, the component which reached the highest values and marks the culmination of the whole was again Italian. On the other hand, the frame of this growth, its incipient and final phases, were French, and there was genuine though minor participation in Spain, the Netherlands, and Germany. Hence with the Occidental development at least half transalpine, and the Roman one wholly derivative from the Greeks, it seems fair enough to speak of a westerly shift toward the peripheries as between the ancient or Mediterranean and the more modern European growths. And yet, their overlap or repetition on Italian terrain must almost certainly have significance as an evidence of the continued operation of factors not visible on the surface of the current of history. Beyond these, there is the little flowering of Etruscan sculpture five centuries before the Roman rise—rather insignificant in values attained, but possibly more than a mere coincidence wholly unconnected with the Florentine surge two millennia later.

In this connection also, the tenth- and eleventh-century Byzantine florescence is not to be wholly overlooked. This can hardly be construed as anything but the last flutter of the Aegean-Greek-Roman configuration. Though Christian and miniature instead of "Classical," it originated among Greeks speaking Greek on Greek soil. At the same time it is contemporary with the first stirrings in the Occident, and this again is probably more than mere coincidence. Reference is not so much to Byzantine seeds directly sown in Othonian Germany and in recently Byzantine South Italy—their germination is perhaps even more problematical than their sowing. Again it is a question mainly of undercurrents suggested by the time-space relation of the grand configurations. After all, Constantinople of 1000 was in Europe and was Christian. Viewed from one standpoint, its art is to be seen as the final phase of Greek art at its hearth; from another, as one of several concurrent symptoms, scatteringly European in their first frame, though persistent only in southwest Europe, which mark the beginning of a new growth constellation.

There is also this to be considered, in the centrifugal movement of sculpture out from its original Mesopotamian-Egyptian hearth: as the center became vacant, its older civilizations, the Hellenistic and Iranian as well as the locally native, became replaced by Mohammedan civilization, which forbade representation. Which of these phenomena is cause, and which is effect? The problem is fair, and not easily soluble. If one likes specific causes, one can see sufficiency in the Islamic prohibition, to account for a thousand years of dearth. On the other side are two considerations. The first is that native sculptures were dead in the region long before Mohammed, and the Hellenistic sculpture had ceased creating new positive values— in other words, was prolonging a heavily deteriorated existence for six centuries before. There was thus already a marked trough of performance when Islam imposed its prohibition. The new religion merely went farther in a direction already established. Secondly, if Mohammedanism had impinged on a culture containing a vigorous impulse toward representative culture, it is at least problematical whether it would have succeeded in thoroughly suppressing this, or whether an accommodation would have taken place. It would be going too far to name the aesthetic decay as the specific cause and the Mohammedan taboo as its direct effect; as always in such cases, it is probably wisest to view two such associated phenomena as joint products of underlying forces.

Such underlying forces, it must be admitted, are vague and elusive things, and dealing with them at all breeds suspicion of subjectivity and mystic inclinations. It is legitimate to try to look deep and discern in dim outline an x which is perhaps more potential than the specific a and b factors or causes floating on the surface; but it is sterile to deal only with such an x, or to resolve everything into an x number of x's. If we are really to understand, the presumption that there is an x at work must be followed up either by some approach to a definition of it, or by the expression of x as a relation or function of the specific a and b factors. Such an expression or definition, it seems, is given, at least incipiently, by the recognition of growth configurations. What the forces in these configurations really are, is still almost wholly obscure. But the time, space, and value characteristics of the configurations are phenomena, thoroughly objective and approximately measurable. They can be dealt with scientifically as behavioristic manifestations. It does seem fair that the point of view here maintained should at present be judged less by what it leaves unresolved, much as that is, than by the standard of what it contributes to the larger organized description of phenomena and to the awareness of problems.

Some consideration can well be given to the matter of recurrences of florescence on the same soil. Egypt is the striking example, and the fluctuations of its sculpture are simply the fluctuations of its whole culture, so far as we can judge.

In the Two-River Lands, where a single civilization prevailed equally long, although the dominant nationality changed gradually from Sumerian to Semitic, and unrelated Elamites and Indo-European Hittites also participated, sculpture has a much less consistent history. It was a less important means of expression of the culture, and less intimately and strongly interwoven with its other activities. There were certain traits that persisted, as in the treatment of eyebrows and drapery, but no sharply fixed canon comparable to that of Egypt. In short, Mesopotamia developed an intermittent succession of related styles while Egypt early found one style and then adhered to it. The best early Sumerian and later Elamite work known is metallurgical; late Sumerian sculpture attains its peak, so far as we know, in stone carving in the round of human heads in repose; late Assyrian, in essentially pictorial reliefs of animals in action. If it were not that these sculptures are all emanations of a single civilization with essentially uniform cults, script, architecture, measures, and economic and legal system, they might be rated as disparate growths. But the low uniformity seems to be due less to ethnic diversity than to the fact that sculpture constituted a smaller and more loosely attached pattern within the pattern system of the civilization, than on the Nile. Possibly this is why the art culmination was not attained until the very end of the civilization's life.

The Aegean-Hellenic-Roman-Byzantine configuration is roughly like the Mesopotamian in ethnic diversity, shifts of center, and stylistic differentiation of the separated phases of productivity. Representative art, however, occupied relatively more of the attention of the civilization from Late Middle Minoan times on. At any rate, this can be maintained in view of the fact that the Cretan-Mycenaean culture was a smaller and poorer one than the Mesopotamian, but its art at least equal. For the Hellenic phase the integration is even more valid, as the simultaneous association of sculpture with architecture, cult, athletics, funerary practices, and coinage shows. While it is true that the art did not begin to grow until shortly before 600, this is very soon after the beginning of the whole truly Hellenic movement. Homer is only two centuries older, and Homer is still transitional between Mycenaean and historic Greek culture. For Hellenic sculpture accordingly, it is evident that we have a rather early development within the specific Hellenic culture, and a long retention, but without revival, unless the minor contributions of the Romans in portraiture be construed as a very secondary one. The Byzantine renaissance around 1000 is a renaissance within Imperial and Christian Byzantine culture.

The Occidental growth is distinctive in being multinational from first to last. This holds as well for the civilization as for its sculpture—in fact, somewhat more for the civilization as a whole. As for the course of sculpture, its salient and unique feature is the competitive struggle for hegemony of influence between France and Italy, the one dominating beginning and end, the other rising higher in the middle. In a remote way the configuration is parallel to that in the political field between

Sparta and Athens. The roles of Spain and Germany, in sculpture, might even be seen analogous to those of say Argos and Thebes, politically; with England corresponding perhaps to Thessaly.

India and China seem to be one-pulse, nonrepetitive growths, except for their extensions into new soil and foreign nationality in Colonial India and Japan, which we have treated as separate movements. In Japan, however, there is indication of two peaks, Nara and Kamakura, in the eighth and thirteenth centuries, though without interruption of continuity of flow. The two crests seem to represent respectively the complete mastery of an imported art heavily charged with nonnational religious feeling, and the fullest expression of the same art after it had largely replaced the religious feeling by characteristically national secular interests, though retaining formal adherence to the religion. The relation to religion is somewhat parallel to that of Gothic versus Renaissance art in Europe.

Colonial Indian art in Java seems also to show two crests, but I am incompetent to analyze their configurative relations adequately.

Chapter VI

PAINTING

Chapter VI

PAINTING

THE INTRINSIC relation of painting and sculpture and the reasons for treating the two separately have been touched on in the introduction to the chapter on sculpture. The relation of the configurations of the two arts is discussed at the end of the present chapter. The order of treatment of the several growths is the same as for sculpture.

§47. Egyptian Painting

In ancient Egypt the fortunes of painting followed those of sculpture. Relief carving united the two arts. Being mostly very low-raised, or later sunk, its sphere was essentially two-dimensional, the bounding line all-important. Painting, with a few exceptions, laid its colors on in flat areas without shading or toning, like the color masses which accentuated relief work. Linear quality thus is the strength of both arts. They might in fact be considered a unit as against statuary, except that this and relief were tied together by their material and type of manual execution.

At any rate, Egyptian painting flourished and decayed when sculpture flourished and decayed. If there is a difference, it is only that in statuary the very highest point of Egyptian sculpture must probably be set in the Fourth or Fifth Dynasty, with the Eighteenth a close rival; whereas in painting, primacy seems to be considered to belong to the Eighteenth and Nineteenth. The reason for this difference may be, in large part, that the more perishable art has been preserved better from the later period. It should be observed, it is true, that the Twenty-sixth Dynasty "renaissance" appears to have left almost no painting and no notable reliefs. However, this was a brief period, compared with the New Kingdom of Dynasties XVIII–XIX, and a far less notably prosperous one.

As already stated under Sculpture, the new or Amarna style associated with the "madness" or "reform" of Ikhnaton toward the end of Dynasty XVIII in the fourteenth century was much more fully expressed in relief than in statuary, and perhaps best of all in painting; perhaps because a revolutionary break was more quickly accomplished in the more fluent medium. The part played in this transient change by royal patronage is evident. Not so clear is the distribution of emphasis among several influences that have been alleged: an already latent, intrinsically aesthetic impulse toward innovation; political or social demand for alteration, in whatever direction; the dragging into official favor and status of the divergent provincial school of Hermopolis as part of the program of breaking the religious dominance of Thebes; or the seeping in of Aegean influences during preceding centuries.

In any event, the Amarna school did not break fundamentally with Egyptian tradition. It substituted certain somewhat new interests and manners for the existing ones, but within the framework of historic Egyptian convention. The attitude of figures toward each other—in other words, the composition—was freer, more enterprising, imbued with charm, and seemingly full of promise for future development. On the other hand, the clean, decisive, controlled line of standard Egyptian art gave way to contours that were soft and proportions that were at once effeminate and at least as artificial as the old ones. Actually no distinctly greater realism was attained: only a shift in the qualities in which realism was sought. Given an unhampered course of a century or two, the new style might conceivably have advanced into a new art growth. But historically this seems unlikely. The innovation began by giving up too many of the virtues of the ancient art: not only its fundamental quality of line, but its seizing of monumentality, of dignity and unceasing grace of proportion. At bottom, the Amarna style appears to be a symptom of pattern saturation, a first attempt at dissolution. This interpretation is confirmed by the fact that the reform came in the generation immediately following the one in which New Kingdom standard art culminated: the culmination under Amenhotep III, 1405–1370, the reform under Amenhotep IV (Ikhnaton), 1370–1352. The strength of the basic patterns of Egyptian civilization is shown in the fact that it was able to throw off this danger of disintegration, in art as well as in religion, and, resuming its established way, to die peacefully of senile atrophy more than a thousand years later.

§48. Greek Painting

The ancients are said to have rated their painting as highly as their sculpture. Our knowledge of its history, however, depends entirely on their judgments, since no masterpiece has been preserved. Most of what we possess is excavated coffin portraits from Egypt, some Italian remains, chiefly Pompeian house frescos, and an occasional "copy," like that of Alexander's Battle in mosaic.

That painting of respectable quality was being done in quantity in Imperial times is clear from Pompeii. But the Romans as well as the later Greeks seem to have regarded great painting as something that had ended in early Alexandrian days—much as we look back to the zenith of the Renaissance. The period of the masters thus was brief compared with the entire duration of the art—between two and three centuries out of eight or ten. We have therefore a situation like that of Greek and most modern growths of drama, in which great quality was attained very quickly, maintained for a span, and then succeeded by a long, undistinguished continuation. In other terms, once the patterns of the art were conceived, they were rapidly realized and exhausted.

How far Greek painting was derived from vase painting does not seem clear. It is certain that vase painting was earlier, and had attained essential mastery of outline representation of the human figure before any painting known to us began. Red-figured Attic vases commence about 540–525 B.C., more than fifty years before Polygnotus. The first painters as such therefore began with an inherited tradition of control and purity of line. Their problem was to add modeling, light and shade, perspective. We first hear of shadows about a generation after Polygnotus. Perspective was never completely attained, but more adequately so than is sometimes said. It simplified its problems by tending to take somewhat of a bird's-eye view, as in Sino-Japanese art. Landscape came into its own in Alexandria; it is doubtful if it ever wholly freed itself from human figures and the story they told, though these elements did become subsidiary. Encaustic painting seems to have developed about the middle of the fourth century: its invention is ascribed to both Pausias and Aristeides. It was the Greek equivalent of our oils: wax applied with a hot tool. It no doubt relieved flatness and helped the attainment of realism. The coffin portraits of Greeks made in Egypt by Greeks in the first two Roman centuries are naturalistic and encaustic.

Attic school
  *Polygnotus of Thasos, fl. 470–455, older contemporary of Phidias.
    Assisted by: Panaenos of Athens, brother of Phidias, and
    Micon of Athens.
  Agatharchos of Samos, contemporary of Alcibiades; originally
    a scene painter.
  Dionysos of Colophon.
  Timarete, daughter of Micon.
  *Apollodorus of Athens, end of 5th cent.; "skiagraphos."
Ionian school
  *Zeuxis of Heracleia, fl. ca. 420–390; light and shade.
  *Parrhasios of Ephesus, fl. 399.
  Timanthes of Cythnus, rival of last.
Theban-Attic school
  Nicomachos of Thebes, fl. 360.
  Aristeides of Thebes, pupil of last; encaustic.
  Euphranor of Corinth.
  Nicias of Athens, fl. ca. 340–300.
Sicyonian school
  Eupompos; contemporary of Parrhasios.
  Pamphilos, his pupil; Macedonian?
  Pausias, pupil of Pamphilos; encaustic.
  Melanthios, contemporary of Apelles.
Time of Alexander and the first Ptolemies
**Apelles, probably from Colophon, possibly Ephesus or Cos;
    trained at Sicyon; painter of Alexander.

*Protogenes of Rhodes, contemporary.
Theon of Samos.
Antiphilos of Alexandria..
Aetion of Alexandria.
Helena, daughter of Timon.
Peiraiikos; genre, shop scenes.
Preserved in mosaic copy: Alexander-Darius battle.

School of mosaic at Pergamum
Sosos founder, later 3d cent.

Later Greek painters
Timomachos of Byzantium, early 1st cent.; or, fl. ca. 200?
Laia (Lala) of Cyzicus, woman, fl. 180–150?
Preserved copies: Achilles in Skyros, Omphale, Telephos, Dionysian initiation, Orestes and Pylades, landscape scenes from the *Odyssey*, still life at Pompeii.

Roman painters
Fabius Pictor, fl. ca. 300.
Pacuvius, fl. ca. 200.
Metrodorus.
Serapion.

Roman, 100–1 B.C.
Sopolis.
Dionysius.
Antiochus Gabinius.
Ludius, ca. 20 B.C.

Pompeian fresco styles (after Mau)
Incrustation, to 80 B.C.
Painted Architectural, to 1 B.C.
Ornate or Candelabra, to 50 (70) A.D.
Intricate or Fantastic, 50–79 A.D.

I have listed the "schools" as they are usually given. The older Attic is really Ionian in origin, but centered in Athens. In the Ionian school, Zeuxis presumably had predecessors, perhaps for a century. The Theban-Attic and Sicyonian schools seem to have been about contemporary; in fact, all four so far mentioned evidently overlapped, as Apelles did with the Sicyon group. Beyond Apelles, most books have a way of treating everything Alexandrian as if it constituted a timeless unit. It may be guessed that the most-named men worked before 200, perhaps before 250. The little Roman lists really mean nothing, except that as early as the Punic or perhaps Samnite Wars there were Romans or Romanized foreigners painting for Romans, no doubt in the Greek manner. The essentially Greek style held on into Christian times. The several Pompeian manners are listed as a sample of interior-decoration fashion changes in the Graeco-Roman world during the century before and that after Christ. The paintings proper on the Pompeian walls seem pretty generally to be in the "Alexandrian" manner. This probably means that the style was essentially completed in the time of the immediate successors of Apelles.

The ancients reckoned Polygnotus as the first great painter, and Apelles as the greatest—the Phidias of his art. This means that the interval from the first emergence out of obscure beginnings to the zenith was 150 years; probably less rather than more. Another 100 years may have been used for the completed art to ramify into all its specialties and channels: landscape, genre, portraits, miniatures, mosaic. After that there is no evidence of anything really new. However, an interest in painting, a professed admiration for the masterpieces of old, and with it a certain purity of taste, remained vivid, probably at least to the age of the Antonines in the west and longer in the east.

This means that while Greek painting climbed to its summit steadily and fairly fast—somewhat more rapidly than Italian painting from Giotto to Raphael,—it then remained, except for changes of fashions, apparently level, but actually slowly descending, for a period several times as long. Perhaps Renaissance painting would have had the same indefinitely protracted fate if Italy had been a world to itself, instead of part of a Europe in which her own achievements stimulated other countries to produce new patterns, which in time superseded the Italian ones even in Italy. The Mediterranean world was too predominantly Greek in its aesthetics for such foster children to dispossess their mother, who therefore grew peacefully older and weaker. Even Christianity limited the Greek patterns and debased their execution, rather than supplanted them. We also hear of nothing in the Greek world comparable to the Sung and Ming renascences after the T'ang peak in China.

In summary, the significant time points seem to be:

475, known emergence as an autonomous art.
325, culmination.
To 250 (or 200?), extension of motives and subjects, probably also of technique.
After 250 (or 200?), geographical extension of the art, fashion variations, no fundamentally new achievements of importance. This plateau phase lasted several centuries.

The beginning and peak fall later than in sculpture, the maturation is more rapid, the spreading out into stability or slow deterioration apparently also more rapid. There seems to have been no Roman painting comparable to Roman sculpture in degree of quality and semi-independence.

The internal geography is somewhat unusual. Ionian representation predominates, at the beginning and at the peak. However, it is active mainly outside of Asiatic Ionia, whose prosperous days were over when painting was launched as an art. About half the pre-Hellenistic painters were mainland Greeks. These appear all to have been from Athens, Thebes, Corinth, or Sicyon. Of these four cities, the first three were old and thriving centers of pottery manufacture and painting. Fourth-century Sicyon flourished in sculpture as well as in painting: Lysippus and Apelles were contemporaries. The two Theban painters belong to the generation following Epaminondas and Theban political hegemony. The Peloponnesus proper, Sicily, and Greek Italy seem never to have participated prominently. That Apelles's Ionian nativity was no sporadic accident is indicated by the fact that his greatest rival, Protogenes, was a Rhodian.

VASE PAINTING

That there probably were extremely important relations between Greek painting and Greek ceramic decoration can hardly be denied. We also possess an excellent history of the vase art, based on innumerable preserved examples, now nearly all datable within a couple of decades. I have kept this development out of the previous discussion, though aware of its intrinsic pertinence, because we know so little of Greek true painting at first hand, or otherwise than through the literature, that statements on its relations to ceramic painting must be inferential. As to the greater art, we do have at least the judgment of the Greeks that Apelles represented its culmination. We do not seem to possess their opinions on how Polygnotus and Apelles were related to the vase painters of Corinth and Athens. This relation can only be reconstructed by comparison of literary statements and a few surviving copies, on the one hand, with almost no statements, but a mass of extant originals, on the other. Such a reconstruction is the fair and proper task of the historian of Greek art, but too special for use here. It seems better to outline separately the history of Greek vase drawing.

From 900 to 700, roughly—Homer's time,—is the period of Geometric vase painting, Attic *par excellence*. Small representative scenes are included in the ornamentation, but the figures are angular, ill-proportioned, awkward. About 700, or soon after, scenes begin to be represented, especially in Crete, with definitely more spirit, movement, and control of line; decorative ornament remains, but fills spaces instead of being primary. During the same seventh century, in which sculpture also made its beginnings, three other styles developed: the East Greek or Ionian-Rhodian, the Corinthian, and the Attic. The East Greek style remained Oriental and decorative in its drawing: rows of animals among floral motives, rosettes, and other abstract ornaments. Story was scarcely attempted. The Proto-Corinthian style keeps to well-controlled, precise ornament, but separates it spatially from scenes of human action, which, however, tend to the repetitive: the essentially decorative sense of the whole is never lost. Shape, color, and pattern harmonize into an effect of quiet but extraordinarily high charm. After about 600, Proto-Corinthian ware turns into Corinthian, which loses some of its best qualities, probably under factory production, but at times attempts realistic depiction of action, the human figures being now black. Seventh-century Athenian ware goes in for action of story. The representation is definitely vigorous if crude. Other parts of the vessel are covered with pure ornament, which is carried out loosely, as if feeling for it were beginning to dissolve. Toward 600 the black-figured manner is ready to emerge: pure ornament recedes, the names of the actors begin to be written in, the story factor is thrust increasingly forward.

After 600, black-figure treatment definitely displaces outline in all styles, which now assimilate somewhat. The black-figuring is probably of Corinthian origin, but the new styles perhaps owe most to the older Attic, especially in variety of figure and posture, freedom and vigor of composition, emphasis on story. This means that the Asiatic Ionians had yielded the essence of their old style, and were patently on the decline. The Corinthians held on somewhat better. New local manners develop alongside the Attic: the Chalcidian in Euboea, the Laconian or Cyrenaic. By about 550 the Attic ware was the best and the most successful.

The black-figured manner continued until 500 and after but around 530 was challenged by the red-figured—reserved or negative painting,—which within a generation surpassed and virtually displaced the older tradition. This was an Attic innovation; and from now on Athenian supremacy was unchallenged. In fact, other painted ware was almost crowded out. Athenian red-figured provided the peak of all Greek vase painting between 490/475 and 425. The first half of this period excelled the second: 460 may be estimated as the moment of apogee. By 400, decline is manifest, and, in spite of a partial revival in the decades around 360, continued until painted ware died out around 300. Monochrome or pressed ware took its place.

The last center to develop was southern Italy. Here painted-vase manufacture sprang up in derivation from Athenian, while Athens was entering on its decline.

Representative vase painting thus lasted four centuries among the Greeks: from 700 to 300. The culmination around 460 was after the middle of the total span. The end came just about the time that Greek fresco and panel painting attained its summit.

The connection of painting with vase painting is clarified by the time configurations of the two. Around 460, the growth of painting suddenly begins with a notable master. This is the very point in time at which vase painting, having developed for several centuries from geometric decoration through curvilinear ornament to representation, finally reached its apogee in delineation of the human figure in action. At the moment that vase painting, limited to line and mass in one medium, could go no farther, painting branched out from it by entering new media and adding rounding or shading of figures and color variety. The minor art thus launched the greater one already half formed and equipped; no wonder itself declined.

In one respect, Greek vase painting is unusual. It began at least as early in mainland as in colonial or peripheral Greece. For once, the Ionians cannot be said to have initiated or even taken a distinctive early lead. Within a century both they and the Cretans were outclassed. Before another century, Corinth and Chalcis were displaced by Athens—a generation or two before Marathon. Athens alone achieved the culmination and began the decline. Only after decadence was definitely under way did Italiote Greece join in the art. This localization is unique in Greek culture history.

In this connection coins may be mentioned, though of course they are really a branch of relief sculpture. The finest Greek coins, perhaps the most beautiful ever struck, are Dorian and Ionian from Sicily, from 475 to perhaps 400. Now and then a Lucanian or west Peloponnesian issue nearly equaled the many of Syracuse, Agrigentum, Himera, Leontini, Naxos, Katana. Athens, Corinth, the rest of Greece, and Ionia were obviously satisfied with much humbler products. For Ionia the reason is evident: she was in aesthetic and economic decline when coinage began to achieve quality. For Athens and the rest the reason is not so obvious. Possibly the attitude of Athens in this matter was like that of nineteenth-century Italy, France, Germany, England about postage stamps, in which they long complacently allowed Russia and South America to surpass them aesthetically.

§49. Indian Painting

Painting and sculpture seem to have their courses nearly abreast in India, but as usual the preserved record of the former is far less complete. If it were not for the rock temples—the so-called caves—of Ajanta, we should possess only occasional hints of Indian painting until modern times. At that, there are more gaps than chapters in the story of what was presumably a continuous development. Everything earlier than 800 which we know of is in fresco, and is Buddhist or perhaps occasionally Jain in subject.

Post-Maurya period, 200–1 B.C.—This is represented at the Jogimara cave, south of Mirzapur, Central Provinces, and in grottos IX and X at Ajanta, west India. The preservation is imperfect, the pictures have been reproduced only in part: but the style, though recognizably different in detail, is already essentially the classic one of Ajanta.

For some four centuries of our era there seem to be no data.

Ajanta period, 450–750, corresponding to the later Gupta and earlier rock-temple periods of sculpture: Sigiriya in Ceylon, 479–497; Bagh in Gwalior, probably 550–650; Ajanta other than caves IX and X, 500–750, probably for the most part 550–650. This is a skilled, animated, even rapid art, mundane far more often than spiritual, in spite of its Buddhistic subject matter. The range is from large frescos crowded with a hundred figures to decorative panels containing a single person or animal. Perspective is nearly lacking, modeling fair, foreshortening met without fear, the postures free and extremely varied. The grand or deep is not often attempted and perhaps never well realized, but liveliness, charm, activity—with a range from almost restlessness to easy repose—are constant qualities. It is a definitely pleasing art, far more flowing than the contemporary sculpture. The stroke is accurate and easy. The one Ceylon series has a narrower range than Ajanta, stylistically and in subject, and specializes in delicate feminine grace, but obviously belongs in the same current.

This growth of painting is perhaps too worldly to be one of the great arts of history, but it is certainly one of the most spontaneous and delightful.

A long lacuna of eight centuries follows. There have been preserved some examples of tenth-century and later Pal palm-leaf pictures and fifteenth-century book illustrations from Gujarat, and while these indicate that painting of some kind continued always to be practiced in India—as indeed would be assumable,—they chiefly are evidence of the mannered elegance or formalism and aesthetic softness of the schools of the interim. If there was high-class painting executed in India in these eight hundred years, it remains to be discovered.

Mughal and Rajput painting, since 1550, is Persian-derived, Indian in subject and execution and, from soon after 1600 on, European-influenced. The Mughal was a court art, which flourished best under Akbar, Jahangir, and Shahjahan in its first hundred years, but continued for nearly two centuries longer. Most of the work is on paper in tempera. Emphasis is on line, which is sharp, firm, yet delicate. Portraits convey individual character exceedingly skillfully; group compositions, landscapes, perspective are all attempted without hesitation. The Rajput school of the seventeenth and eighteenth centuries seems to be Mughal-derived, and is certainly closely related. It specializes more on esoteric and purely Indian themes, such as the loves of Krishna and personifications of the modes of music, and is less cosmopolitan, realistic, and vigorous, but possesses a definite, almost femininely light style of its own, at once somewhat classic and provincial. It can hardly be a direct historic descendant of Ajanta art, but approximates it in certain qualities. Mughal and Rajput painting are scarcely intense enough in their endeavors to have risen to a place among the supremer arts of the world; but within the limits of their patterns they have attained to highly competent execution and much charm. Their impression on first acquaintance is likely to be that of an Occidental art, on account of their European components; but much of their style and all their content is Indian.

While there are more gaps than positive data in the long history of Indian painting, it does seem reasonably certain that the art has been cultivated in the peninsula for something more than two thousand continuous years. The finest examples of which we know fall between 450 and 750. It thus seems fair to make a tentative assumption of a peak for the whole movement somewhere in the neighborhood of 600. This would yield a span of 800 years—possibly more—for the antecedent development, and of nearly 1,000 for subsequent decline; until, with Persian and European stimulus, a renaissance took place which culminated around 1600 and persisted a couple of centuries.

§50. Chinese Painting

I approach Chinese and Japanese painting with certain misgivings. The literature on the subject is abundant, the dating good; but the two related arts move in so narrow a compass that I find it extremely difficult to feel my way into them far enough to make internal comparative judgments of quality. Not that any individual appraisal can begin to take the place of the collective appraisal of history; but, in matters of art especially, a mere recording and averaging of the opinions of others, unreinforced by spontaneous emphatic reactions, savors of externality: a certain kind of needed inner reliability seems lacking. In all the art growths previously considered, though my acquaintance with most is at best only moderate, some such conviction of the values involved has been present. In fact, at several points I have had a sense of bowing my personal sentiments before the more general ones. Not so with East Asiatic painting. For it, I evidently possess a blind spot: the work of the great masters seems difficult to distinguish from that of the rank and file: the differences are subtly elusive. I am therefore also unable to form an opinion upon which of the Western historians and critics have possessed the faculty of genuine aesthetic discrimination of Far Eastern painting, and which of them have merely followed the dicta of the Chinese and Japanese authorities. In any event, it is these dicta, as summarized by European writers, on which the present section is built. Fortunately, there has long existed much highly cultivated opinion on art, and careful writing of its history; in Japan as well as in China.

However great as an art, Chinese painting is characterized by certain limitations or negations, which at once narrow its compass and heighten its refinements or subtleties. Lacking, or extremely undeveloped, are: individual portraiture, representations of the nude human body or of subjects even remotely erotic, direct shadows, modeling by values. On the other hand, perspective, though bird's-eye, is present; and distance, atmosphere, and landscape are all old and important elements. The basic qualities are perhaps these two: drawing from memory instead of model, which inevitably encourages decorative, so-called rhythmic, aspects; and emphasis on quality of stroke. "Brush strength" is the painter's highest virtue in native opinion. The stroke must be free, bold, direct, continuous. "Stroke" seems the most appropriate word, because of the varying breadth and density of the mark of the brush, as compared with "line" in sculpture or etching. Much Chinese painting is in fact sketchily impressionistic rather than linear, in the literal sense. Yet fundamentally it is a linear, not a pictorial art. The outlines are drawn in first, except in one minor heretical tradition; and paintings merely in ink are frequent and are regarded as highly as colored ones. In fact, color is often sparingly applied; and throughout, the unused background is left untouched. All told, restraint not exuberance, control not striving, are the keynotes, in matter and manner.

Stroke, brush, ink, paper or silk as materials, are common to painting and writing, and the two arts have grown up intertwined, in mutual influence. Calligraphy is the full sister of painting in Chinese opinion.

Some sort of painting was practiced at least in later Chou times (to −255), though we know no specimens. The later Han grave reliefs have been considered as transpositions of paintings into stone; but if so, the style of the time was thoroughly different from that which we encounter in actual pictures two or three centuries later. The Han period (−206−+221), however, invented brush, carbon ink, and paper, the prerequisites of historic Chinese painting, which was evidently developed early in the Han-T'ang interval, the four politically unsettled centuries from Three Kingdoms to Sui inclusive (221–618), in which Chinese sculpture and later poetry also grew up. Around 350, Wang Hsih-chih introduced one-stroke writing; and a century later, Lu T'an-wei transferred the technique to painting. Still a hundred years later and we hear of enormous imperial collections of paintings: connoisseurship and patronage were evidently in full bloom.

There is preserved to us what is at least an ancient and faithful copy of the work of a painter from about 400: Ku K'ai-chih. It is remarkable how thoroughly this early specimen is already done in the style of all later painting: only the landscape element is not represented. We must conclude that for a full millennium and a half one unbroken tradition or manner has ruled Chinese painting: that this has constituted a single growth.

In native opinion, the culmination of this growth came under the T'angs (618–907). Wu Tao-tsu, who flourished around 750, is reckoned the greatest master of the dynasty, and inferentially of all China. According to later critics, he excelled in line, not in value shading. Many other high reputations are on record for the period. Unfortunately, nearly all T'ang paintings in China had already perished toward the end of the Sung dynasty. Japanese treasure houses have preserved a few examples or ascriptions. How far the T'ang supremacy rests on unbiased comparative judgment or on assumed superiority of ancient times might be hard to decide.

With the Five Dynasties (907–960) and Sungs (960–1278) new tendencies appear—in the status of the art and the feelings with which it deals, apparently more than in its manner or execution. On the one hand there are governmentally founded academies, and emperor painters; on the other, a cultivated-person movement, that is, an exaltation of the mandarin amateur over the professional painter, and emphasis on painting as the subjective expression of individuality. Mood rather than form became the objective, especially in the Southern school which finally dominated. In most growths, these manifestations would be construed as symptoms that decay had set in, or at least that the full classic phase had been left behind. But in so specialized an art as Chinese painting it is possible that they represent the ultimate realization. To later ages Sung pictures have represented an ideal inspiration; yet, with the T'ang works no longer in existence, they may merely have inherited the place of influence of these. Li Lung-mien, from Anhwei, died 1106, is generally rated the greatest Sung master. It is significant that his friend Su Tung-p'o, died 1101, who specialized in painting bamboo, was also the greatest calligrapher of the age. Mi Fei, died 1107, was the leading painter and calligrapher in the South. This certainly looks like a genuine constellation.

About the time of the tenth-century Five Dynasties, remote interior Szechwan had been important in painting. With the Sungs, the lower Yangtse Valley—Anhwei, Kiangsu, Chehkiang —came into the foreground, especially of course under the later or Southern Sungs (1127–1278); but the local accentuation continued through the Mongol and Ming periods.

After Sung, a somewhat new stream was injected into North Chinese painting by the Mongol interest in horses. The Ming period (1368–1644) is divided by about the year 1500 into two nearly equal halves, the first ranking as superior, apparently both in direct rating by the Chinese and in the incidence of the high lights. Thus Shen Chou of Kiangsu, the greatest Ming master, 1427–1509; and Tai Wen-chin, the most gifted non-gentleman professional painter, fl. ca. 1450. By the end of Ming, there began to be European influence, and this continued and increased under the Manchus (1644–1912), without, however, seriously deflecting the current of native tradition. The outstanding figure perhaps is Wang Hui, 1632–1717, whose work period coincided almost exactly with the long reign of K'ang Hsi, 1662–1722.

European writers differ in their rating of post-Sung painting. To some it is merely epigonal in quality. Others have the

Chinese themselves appreciating their Ming painters essentially as much as the Sung, and esteeming the Ch'ing ones highly. Without controlling Chinese literature, it is impossible to decide what the native opinion is or whether it concerns itself with rankings, other than indirectly. It is quite likely that the Chinese, like the historians of most literature, are more concerned with the continuity of their art, and the minor changes of direction within it, than in positive and comparative qualitative ratings. As already said, I cannot even add a subjective judgment in which I have any personal sense of reliance. Taking into consideration such expressions of opinion as there are, I am inclined to consider as warranted the setting of a peak in middle T'ang times, around 750, and a gradual, somewhat pulsating decline thereafter, the art, however, being extremely slow to exhaust itself.[1] After the T'angs, the pulses appear to coincide fairly well with times of dynastic prosperity; before, they do not. In fact, the development of Chinese painting, sculpture, and poetry forges ahead through a long period of governmental turmoil and adversity in war.

For the course as a whole, two comparisons suggest themselves: with Chinese sculpture, and with Egyptian art.

Sculpture and painting in China grew up side by side, and under Buddhist influences, and culminated contemporaneously. Then, however, they diverged. Sculpture rapidly deteriorated into repetitive artisanship or decorative mannerism, whereas painting maintained high virtues, and struggled to new expressions, for a thousand years. The difference is conditioned by the attitude of the culture: sculpture involves labor of the hands, whereas painting is allied through calligraphy with classic literature, Confucianism instead of Buddhism, and the cultivated official class.

The resemblance to Egyptian art is in the long persistence within one set of patterns, after early culmination, and a conse-

---

[1] Fenollosa, *Epochs of Chinese and Japanese Art,* gives a quality diagram for painting. His Chinese profile is characterized above all by a huge surge culminating in T'ang times and declining rather steadily since; his Japanese, by five brief curves almost equal in duration and height, the one toward 1500 exceeding the others only slightly.

quent looking back to the past. The difference lies in the fact
that Egyptian art, perhaps because it was largely plastic, apparently held artisan status, and was dependent on materials,
labor, and supply of wealth. Thus in times of national prosperity and a successfully strong government the art promptly
improved; with exhaustion, it deteriorated. However high
some of its aesthetic qualities, Egyptian art was primarily workmanship, and this rose and fell with economic fluctuations.
Chinese painting required no materials, tools, or outlays but
those of a simple scholar, and therefore flowed in a qualitatively
far steadier stream as long as classic literary learning and self-
cultivation remained among the primary ideals of the culture.

Chou, Ts'in, and Han, before 221 A.D.
    Ca. 300 B.C., apparent references to frescos of historical subjects.
    Ca. 250, reference to paintings of dogs, horses, and demons.
    220, invention of brush for writing.
    120, references to portraits of individuals.
    105 A.D., invention of paper.
    87–171 A.D., preserved stone reliefs, more or less representative of
painting.

Brief dynasties, including Sui, 221–618
    By ca. 250, first Buddhist temples, pilgrimages, translating
Hindus, statues.
    *321–379, Wang Hsih-chih, greatest Chinese calligrapher; intro-
ducer of "one-brush" writing, with varying intensity and breadth
of continuous stroke.
    Ca. .395, Tai Kuei died; painter, sculptor, inventor of lacquer
statuary.
    *Ca. 400, Ku K'ai-chih. Preserved in the British Museum: a silk
roll, with eight scenes on women's virtues: at least a faithful copy,
possibly the original.
    *Ca. 450, Lu T'an-wei, under the Liu Sung, 420–479, transferred
the "one-brush" or single sweeping shaded stroke style from writing
to painting: *i-pi-hua.*
    *Chang Seng-yu, under the Liang emperor Wu Ti, 502–550, also
in South China, painted Buddhist subjects in "Indian style," with
value tones.
    554, Yüan Ti, Liang emperor of the South, himself a painter,
burned most of his collection of 140,000 (!) rolls of paintings in
evacuating his capital to the northern barbarian conquerors.

Ts'ao Chung-ta, under the Northern Ch'i, about 550, is one of the few northern painters mentioned. He was a barbarian, Chinese-trained.

610, frescos in the Horyuji Kondo, at Nara, Japan. Some Japanese attribute the present Kondo to 708–714, the original one having been burned. In that case the painting was probably done by Japanese. If the date of 610 is correct, the frescos were almost certainly made by Chinese or Korean artists. They are said to be more Indian in manner than known Chinese T'ang paintings.

T'ang, 618–907, and Five Dynasties, 907–960

*Yen Li-pen, ca. 600–673, portraits and historical subjects. Great est early T'ang painter.

*Li Ssŭ-hsün, 651–716, imaginative landscape in elevated style.

*Wang Wei, 698–759, also a poet, lyrically felt landscape expressive of mood, often without color. These two men have been made into the founders of the later so-called Northern and Southern schools of landscape; they are precursors of two directions. Wang Wei was himself a North Chinese.

**Wu Tao-tsŭ, ca. 700–760, from near K'ai-feng, Honan, recognized as the greatest T'ang painter, and by implication therefore of all Chinese history. Equaled by the two preceding in landscape; unequaled in historical and portrait painting and Buddhist subjects.

Han Kan, ca. 720–780, excelled in doing horses.

Pien Luan, ca. 800, specialist in flowers.

Li Chen, ca. 800, accounted of the second rank, is of historic importance because five pieces of his work, brought to Japan in 806 by Kobo Daishi, the first Shingon patriarch, are preserved in the Toji in Kyoto.

Kuan-hsiu, 832–912, of Szechwan, first painter of Arhats.

Shih K'o of Szechwan, d. 919. Two specimens are preserved to the present day.

*Huang Ch'üan, of Szechwan, mid-tenth century. Superb flower painter. Real founder of the later Sung Academy. First to paint in the *wu-ku-hua* or boneless manner, use of color without previous outlining, which was followed by Hsü Ch'ung-se and in the next century by Chao Ch'ang, but which never became orthodox.

At Nanking in the Five Dynasty period were Tung Yüan, noted for landscapes of mood; the monk Chü-jan, considered his equal, and noted for the perfection of his painting equipment; Hsü-hsi, flowers.

Li Ch'eng, at K'ai-feng (Lo-yang), d. 967, represented the Northern school of landscape of form rather than of mood.

"Northern" Sung, 960–1127

Huang Chü-ts'ai, first president of the Academy at K'ai-feng (Lo-yang).

Chao Ch'ang, ca. 1000. Flowers.

Kuo Hsi, ca. 1050. Frescos, distances, and winter.

Chao Ta-nien, teacher of Hui Tsung. Landscape.

*Su Tung-p'o, 1036–1101, greatest Sung calligrapher and poet; painter especially of bamboo. One of the first representatives of the *wen-jen-hua* or cultivated-person movement, which emphasized the painter and the expression of his personality rather than the painting.

**Li Lung-mien, d. 1106, friend of last, sometimes reckoned as the greatest genius of Chinese painting after Wu Tao-tzŭ of T'ang times. He was a gentleman and official, not a professional artist. His range of subjects was wide.

Kuo Jo-hsü, theoretician of the *wen-jen-hua* movement.

*Mi Fei, 1051–1107, greatest southern painter of the period, was also a notable calligrapher.

Hui Tsung, emperor 1101–1126, was also an able painter.

Southern Sung, 1127–1279

Ch'ou Chun, from Szechwan.

Li Ti, from Yünnan; head of Academy.

*Ma Yüan and *Hsia Kuei, fl. ca. 1190–1225, form, with Yen Hui of the next dynasty, the Ba-Ka-Gan trinity of the Japanese, who have preserved much of their work. Highly lyric, suggestive landscape, consisting of a partial foreground with sketchy bits of background.

*Mu-hsi, 1181–1239? Of the Liu-t'ung-ssŭ school, Ch'an- (Zen-) influenced.

Liang K'ai, said to have resigned from the Academy to study with Mu-hsi.

Yüan or Mongol, (1259) 1279–1368

Yen Hui, mentioned above under *Southern Sung,* better known in Japan than in China.

Ch'ien Shun-chü, b. 1235, and Wang Jo-shui, his pupil.

*Chao Meng-fu, 1254–1322.

Kao Ko-kung, ca. 1250–1330, reckoned as successor of Mi Fei in the Southern school.

*Huang Ta-ch'ih, 1269–1354, Wu Chen, 1280–1354, Ni Tsan, 1301–1374, and Wang Meng, d. 1385, form a group of Southern-style masters whose work had the ideal of expressing the artist in all his moods. They were from Chehkiang or near it, and were all "dilettanti" or nonprofessionals.

Ming, 1368–1644, Ch'ing (Manchu), 1644–1912
*Shen Chou, 1427–1509, of Kiangsu. Greatest Ming master, marking the triumph of the Southern school.

Tai Wen-chin, fl. ca. 1425–1450, most gifted Ming professional painter. Of Chehkiang, founder of Cheh school.

*Wang Hui, 1632–1717, of Kiangsu, probably the best Ch'ing painter.

§51. Japanese Painting

The same deficiency of personal-feeling qualification runs through this section as through the preceding.

The painting of Japan is derivative from and partly dependent on that of China, but, like its sculpture, must not therefore offhandedly be assumed to have been less great. As in China, the course of the art was a long one, though a little less so: from 600 to the present. Also as in China, painting climaxed later than sculpture and far outlived it. The peak was almost coeval with that of Italian Renaissance painting; perhaps a generation earlier.

The record of preserved works, however, differs in China and Japan; and in the latter's favor. In thirteen consecutive centuries there is not one from which authenticated examples of Japanese painting are lacking; whereas in China the entire earlier period, including perhaps the culmination, is known through literary records, or by Japanese reflections, rather than by extant specimens; much as in sculpture.

The Suiko period, 552 to 646, is known by Buddhistic frescos in the famous Horyu-ji temple at Nara, painted almost certainly by Chinese or Koreans or their part-Japanese descendants, but done on the spot, if the assigned age of 607/610 is authentic. They may date from a century later, in which case the painters were Japanese.

In the Hakuho and Nara eras, 646 to 784, painting was active. In 701 an official atelier was established to provide Buddhist temple pictures. There are extant works from about 733, 735, 772, thought to be by Japanese artists but more or less representative of T'ang art. One of them consists of long rolls or *makimonos* of painted narrative—a manner in which the later

Japanese painting was to attain some of its greatest secular achievements, although in this period the stories were still wholly Buddhistic.

The early Heian period, 794 to 889, witnessed the first turning away from exclusively religious preoccupation. The governmental bureau of painters had its staff reduced, and then was united with the lacquerwork shop, but this was the counterpart of a development of painting of lay subjects: landscapes, flowers, portraits, historical scenes. Two great names have come down to us, though none of their work has been preserved: Kawanari and Kanaoka. The first was of Korean descent, a professional artist but also a gentleman of the court. The second has been called the Wu Tao-tzŭ of Japan. An extant example of the period is the famous Red Fudo; the chances that religious pieces in the temples would not perish with the centuries were always somewhat better. It is a composition which combines the expressions of a childlike simplicity and tremendous intensity.

The three centuries of the Fujiwara and Heike periods, 889 to 1192, should probably be divided between two phases. Native reckoning puts a division at 1069. My own guess would be that for painting the mark could be set somewhat earlier in the eleventh century. Buddhistic pictures were made by, or at any rate ordered by and attributed to, priests of aristocratic lineage, such as the famous Eshin, the apostle of Amida Buddhism, 942–1017. However much or little these influential dignitaries did or did not paint with their own hands, their appreciation of art, and zeal for it, were active. The first named middle-class priest-painter, Kyozen, appears toward the end of the second phase of the period. Secular art is represented by the *Yamato-e,* "Japanese painting," now using the long rolls for scenes of national, historic, novelistic, or satiric interest, and developing a high power of composition, especially of groups or masses of people, sometimes in intense activity. Motomitsu (ca. 1090), Toba (1053–1140), and Mitsunaga (second half of the twelfth century) were among the high lights in this development, during the last century of the period.

The Kamakura age, 1192 to 1336, carried the Fujiwara tendencies farther. Religious pictures began to substitute semiprofane for wholly sacred subjects. Portraits were fairly common, and well-characterized, at least by non-Occidental standards. Both these drifts are evident also in the sculpture of the period. Numerous rolls—of the life of Genji, of Michizane, of the priest Ippen, of the Heiji revolt, highly varied in character—develop the narrative *Yamato-e* style to its highest. Kamakura painting and sculpture both are nationally Japanese in interest and motivation, and as free from Chinese influence as their ancestry permitted.

The Ashikaga shogunate, 1336 to 1574, brings a new direction and manner. These were Chinese inspired; but the Japanese reckon this period the culmination of their painting. Cult pictures, as well as carvings, continued to be made, but possess no claim to serious aesthetic value, in comparison with the past. Fine art and religion became definitely divorced by about 1300. The difference was that painting had developed a vigorous secular branch by 1100, whereas sculpture never wholly freed itself from its Buddhistic involvement, and died when the old aesthetic-religious impulses waned. In painting, the narrative *Yamato-e* style also declined, though held in esteem until 1500.

The new or *Kangwa* style of Ashikaga times was influenced by Zen, but since this Buddhistic sect was subjective instead of cult-interested, the effect accentuated the impulse away from the old devotional art. At that, the Zen factor was perhaps largely an incident of the Chinese source of the new movement. This was the determining influence. Yet it was not the China of their day, nor of a generation or two before, from which the Ashikaga Japanese drew their stimulation, but that of the Southern Sungs of the twelfth and thirteenth centuries. As it was about 1400 before the new style got under way, and nearly 1500 before it attained its climax, the Japanese were about two centuries or more behind their teachers. When Sesshu traveled in China, he found no contemporary art of interest—only paintings of the past, and nature. Like the South-

ern Sung, the Ashikaga style is impressionistic, lyrical, given
to preference of black-and-white over color, and especially to
effects of ink-density gradation. The favorite subjects are
atmosphere, landscape, animals, vegetation—in a word, nature
rather than man; and above all, mood.

Actually, there seems to have been something of a dip in
achievement during the fourteenth century. The best *Yamato-e*
productions were almost all made before 1300. The first real
master of the so-called Zen style was Mincho, 1352–1431. Then
followed a true constellation:

Josetsu, ca. 1375–ca. 1450, priest.
*Shubun, fl. mid-15th cent., pupil of Josetsu, master of the next
    five.
Sotan, 1398–ca. 1485.
Noami, ca. 1405–1485.
Jasoku, d. 1483.
**Sesshu, 1420–1506. Often regarded as the greatest of all Japanese
    painters, at any rate in landscape.
Masonobu, 1454–1550?, least of the five.
Geiami, 1432–1485, son of Noami.
*Soami, ca. 1460–1530, son of Geiami.
*Motonobu, 1476–1559, son of Masonobu.
*Sesson, alive in 1572, greatest of Sesshu's successors; priest.
Chokuan, d. ca. 1600.
Togan, end of 16th cent.
Tohaku, 1537–1610.

Here, with biographical dates available, we have a configuration like those of the Renaissance: even to the characteristically long lives of painters—averaging 76 years for the eight best
authenticated. Also by precedent it is reasonable to assume the
culmination of the whole movement to have fallen in the span
of fully mature power of the greatest individual; which would
put it in the second half of the fifteenth century, perhaps not
far from 1460–1470; say at about a third of the total course from
1400 to 1600.

The distinctive quality of this movement is concentration,
or retraction, as one prefers. Limitation of subject, by preference to nature; minimum of strokes; suppression of color;

reduction of emotion to a single mood—everything tends to extreme specialization. One wonders whether an art with so deliberately narrow an aim can really be the climax of thirteen centuries, no matter how supreme its expertness. However, contraction of objective and technique has generally been typical of Japan: in sculpture, literature, science, evidently in music, manners, and clothing also. The national genius seems to feel itself happiest and most successful in a strait dress, and when operative with subtle touches. Nowhere else would the greatest painters have limited themselves to a half-expressed landscape, a wave or a brook, a snow-covered tree or bough, a sprig or a lone bird, and contemptuously suggested the human figure, if admitted at all, by five strokes. Even the specialized Chinese prototypes mostly seem saturated, solid, and human by comparison. Still, an art must be judged first by its own standards; and therefore the Japanese presumably judge soundly in rating the Ashikaga art as their peak.

The interval from 1574 to 1603 is partly still Ashikaga, partly Tokugawa in style. The Tokugawa or Yedo shogunate, 1603 to 1868, divides into an Earlier and a Later period. The division is usually set at 1716, or at the end of the Genroku era, 1688–1703—a sort of Postwar Prosperity decade and a half. So far as painting is concerned, the significant turning point possibly comes somewhat earlier. It is a question of when vigorous plebeian styles for the first time came into their own alongside withering patrician ones—or bourgeois and aristocratic, if one prefer. Naturally there was considerable overlap. Thus Moronobu, who stood for the new order, died in 1694, but Korin, representing the old, in 1716, and his brother Kenzan not till 1743. The matter is further complicated by the Japanese grouping into physical schools with succession of master and pupil, which persisted as new stylistic tendencies developed. All in all, the Tokugawa era makes the impression of an age of dissolution of patterns. On the one hand there is a clinging to a great past style the heights of which can no longer be attained; on the other, experimentation in a variety of new manners—decorative, realistic, popular, Chinese, European-influenced.

Early Tokugawa, 1603–1703 (1716)

Kano school, decorative representation. *Eitoku, 1543–1590; Sanraku, 1559–1635; Sansetsu, 1589–1651.—Koi, d. 1636; *Tannyu, 1602–1674.—Black on white: Yusho, 1533–1615; Yusetsu, his son, 1598–1677.

Tosa school, also claiming to revive the *Yamato-e*. *Mitsuoki, 1617–1691.

Kwoetsu school. **Kwoetsu, 1557–1637, greatest genius after Sesshu; calligrapher. Sotatsu, d. 1643. *Kworin, 1655–1716. Kenzan, his brother, 1663–1743.

Ukiyo-e, genre or social-life style, founded by Matabei, 1568–1650. *Moronobu, d. 1694, made this style bourgeois.

Later Tokugawa, 1703 (1716)–1868

Lower-class Ukiyo-e style, further popularized when wood-cut prints became polychrome about 1765: Choshun, 1682–1752; Harunobu, 1718–1770; Sharaku, d. 1795; Kiyonaga, 1752–1815; Utamaro, 1754–1806; Hokusai, 1760–1849; Hiroshige, 1797–1858; Kuniyoshi, 1798–1861.

Bunjingwa, the Chinese *Wen-jen-hua* or cultivated-person style, introduced by Gi Nankai, 1677–1751: Buson, 1716–1784; Taigado (Taigwa), 1723–1776; Noro Kaiseki, 1747–1828; Buncho, 1763–1842; Chikuden, 1777–1835; Kwazan, 1793–1841.

Kwoetsu-Kworin tradition: Shiko, 1683–1755. Hoitsu, 1761–1829.

Manchu dynasty Chinese style, containing some European influence: introduced at Nagasaki, 1731–1733, by Shen Nan-p'in. Japanese: Kien, 1706–1758; Kuma Hi, 1712–1773; Soshiseki, 1716–1780; Jakachu, 1716–1800.

Maruyama school, with direct European influencing, not evident to a naïve Western eye: *Okyo, 1733–1795; Rosetsu, 1755–1799; Shijo branch school: Goshun, 1752–1811; Keibun, 1799–1844.

The average duration of life is less than in the Ashikaga period, but still sufficiently high: Early Tokugawa, 72 for eleven; Later, 63 for twenty-four. The decrease is consistent: Ashikaga, youngest death among eight at 53, next at 70; Early Tokugawa, at 47, next at 61; Later, 44, next at 45. Three explanations suggest themselves: the earlier data are partly unauthentic and exaggerated; or one did not ordinarily attain renown as a painter in the earlier times until of advanced age; or the average length of life, either in the profession or in the Japanese population generally, decreased.

All in all, Japanese painting makes the impression of a continuous and unified configuration through thirteen hundred years, growing gradually for a long time, possibly halting or even receding somewhat in the fourteenth century, culminating toward the end of the fifteenth, and branching into numerous smaller channels after the sixteenth. Its peculiar features are the slowness of growth and the specialization of the climax. These traits are perhaps the consequence of the fact that the entire higher civilization of Japan was a derivative one, and derivative through a single channel. There were no conflicting stimuli, except such as might develop internally. Very gradually the art freed itself from its Buddhistic and Chinese trammels in the Fujiwara age and attained a national character in the Kamakura thirteenth century. But in the isolation of the country the motives it could nourish itself on were limited. With all its supreme qualities in certain directions, its range was too narrow to attain the high rank of universality. This effort therefore relaxed; and after a fourteenth-century interval of indecision, a new taproot was sent out into the one available foreign soil, that of China. That this nourished itself on a style then two centuries old in China rather than on a contemporary one is probably due to the fact that the Japanese, now with centuries of ultracultivation behind them, no longer were eager and indiscriminate imitators. They evidently selected the Southern Sung style because it contained qualities they had long trained themselves to value: subtlety, concentration, refinement, indirection of expression. Sculpture failed to find such a style in China and therefore withered after the Kamakura age. The Zen flavor to the Late Sung painting rather helped it in Japan, which was much more consciously Buddhist than China. At the same time the Buddhist association proved no incubus, because already through the whole of Kamakura times the shogunate of art had been exercised over the empire of religion. The Ashikaga *Kangwa* movement lasted two centuries—a long period for so specialized a style, and indicative of its intensity and vitality. Then came breakup, as indicated by the conflict of impulses: decorative and realistic, Chinese, European, and native; colored and black; aristocratic and lower-class; ancient and modern. That in this chaos of disintegration all quality was not lost, and some new virtues were discovered, evidences the strength of the traditional patterns which had been gradually built up during the previous millennium. The entry of the bourgeois element is probably a most important symptom. Though temporarily indicative of the dissolution of old standards, it is likely to be significant for the future in long perspective.

§52. Occidental Painting

The national strands in European painting are tangled. Often the story is simplified for the telling by organization in terms of international period concepts like Renaissance, Baroque, Classicist, Romantic, and by then considering each country repeatedly as a subtopic under these heads. There can be no legitimate quarrel with this procedure, but it will not serve the purposes of the present work. In an inductive analysis, each nationality must first be examined in terms of its own history, and only then should the synthesis be made for international Europe. This makes the story unwieldy and slow, and full of episodes of little broad bearing. On the other hand, the contrary procedure of beginning with the general currents would result in overemphasis on these and obliterate many nationally significant events. I must therefore ask the reader's patience; or, if his interests be only general, recommend that he turn at once to the summary at the end of the section.

The order of presentation will be, as nearly as possible, that of the time of first developments of importance.

As for relation to sculpture, it need only be said in anticipation that while Gothic sculpture is without counterpart in true painter's art, the sister activities, when viewed as European wholes, show roughly parallel developments and synchronous culminations in the same countries in both the Renaissance and the nineteenth century. It is true that Giotto painted in the terminal period of best Gothic sculpture; but I reckon him into the Renaissance configuration, Gothic sculpture into the mediaeval one, for reasons to be discussed later.

§53. Italian Painting

Italian painting is a single movement lasting from the mid-thirteenth to the mid-eighteenth century, and culminating in the decades immediately following 1500. Its growth curve is therefore essentially symmetrical. It is also one of the longest national movements of any kind in Occidental civilization. No other national growth in painting or music approaches it in duration. This length of life and the greatness of Italian painting are evident functions of each other.

The whole course of Italian painting is also a Renaissance product, if one understands the Renaissance not as a rebirth, still less as a revival of antiquity; also not as a European event except by repercussion; but as a national growth—the only one experienced by Italy in seventeen hundred years. This growth happens to root in the period of High Mediaevalism and to end in that of Enlightenment. It is therefore mediaevally, scholastically, Gothically colored at the beginning, and somewhat sentimental or violent, enlightened, and modern at the close. But these are incidents of Italy's being in Europe. They are traits, like its early Byzantinism, that the Italian growth had to, and did, rid itself of, or which it could not resist accepting to some degree when it became feeble. The culmination in the High Renaissance, from about 1500 to 1530, is at once wholly unmediaeval and wholly unmodern in every quality; and also wholly Italian, that is, noninternational.

For this reason, the old question need not specially concern us here of how far the origins of Italian painting were due to Byzantine or north-European Gothic or other influences. For the same reason, there is no need to dispute with the historians of art who make the Renaissance begin with Ghiberti in sculpture and Masaccio in painting shortly after 1400. It did begin then, if "Renaissance" means that part of the movement which had definitely freed itself from High Mediaeval influences. It did not begin then, if, as in the present connection, we construe the whole Italian growth of painting as "Renaissance" because mainly it is both postmediaeval and premodern and culminates in the admitted High Renaissance—in other words, represents Italy in her florescence.

The provinces of Italy involved are, however, of our concern. The beginnings lie in Tuscany: first scatteringly, in Arezzo, Pisa, Lucca, Siena, Florence; then, about 1300, settling down to a predominance of the two latter under Duccio and Giotto; and, after about 1350, of Florence alone. Reference is to centers of activity, the so-called "schools," not to birthplaces of artists. The handicraft nature of painting brings with it an apprenticeship ordinarily learned only in a painter's shop. Hence the site of residence becomes important, and a well-established center tends to draw in men born elsewhere. However, in the main the members of a school are natives, if not of the city, at least of its environs or of neighboring districts. There are enough instances to the contrary for the places of nativity to build up a somewhat different story; but this is less complete, because of considerable gaps or vagueness in knowledge. The artists' names are no safe guide. Antonello da Messina was born in Messina though he worked in Venice; Niccolò Pisano was an Apulian who distinguished himself in Pisa. Leonardo, born in Florentine territory, was essentially a Florentine. He spent twenty-two years—about 1485–1499 and 1506–1514—in Milan, where a local school of some merit was in existence. This of course he at once eclipsed; and what is usually called the "school of Milan" consists of followers and imitators of Leonardo. The pre-Leonardo current of the school derived from Venetian-influenced Padua, where Foppa of Brescia had studied under Squarcione; whereas in Milan Foppa trained Borgognone da Fossano. The earlier and later periods of the "Milanese" school are thus quite different in direction, and its unity is in one sense artificial. However, no other arrangement or grouping seems more feasible: if a painter is classed according to the masters or traditions which influenced him, he often belongs to several schools. So the conventional arrangement has almost perforce to be retained.

A list of the earlier local growths follows.

Arezzo
  Margharitone, 1216–1293.
  Spinelli Aretino, 1333–1410.
  Lorenzo di Bizzi, fl. 1370–1409.

Pisa
  Giunta, 13th cent.
  Campanna, 14th cent.
  Francesco da Volterra, fl. ca. 1370.
  Avanzi, 14th cent.

Lucca
  Deodati, fl. 1288–1310.

Siena
  Guido, fl. ca. 1281.
  *Duccio di Buoninsegna, ca. 1260–1340.
  Simone Memmi (Martini), 1284–1344.
  Lorenzetti, d. 1348.
  Taddeo di Bartolo, 1362–1422.

Florence
  Cimabue, ca. 1240–1300.
  *Giotto di Bondone, 1266–1337.
  Taddeo Gaddi, ca. 1300–1366.
  Orcagna, ca. 1308–1368.
  Giottino, 1324–1396.
  Fra Angelico da Fiesole, 1387–1455.

Orvieto
  Puccio, fl. 1364.

About 1400 there occur both an enlargement of style and a geographical spread. The "Gothic" character of the work of Giotto's successors is replaced by the first work showing the beginnings of typical Renaissance qualities. Control of perspective and some attention to light values develop. Masaccio "initiates the Renaissance" in Florence. He is a contemporary of Van Eyck, under whom the great development of Netherlands painting begins. In Italy, Florence has and keeps the lead. Siena is secondary, but maintains a continuous tradition, and finally has a great painter as head of its school in Sodoma, a contemporary of Michelangelo and Raphael. Umbria begins to participate about 1400. Then Melozzo, Perugino, and Pinturicchio there are close contemporaries of Signorelli, Botticelli, and Leonardo in Florence. Finally Raphael emanates from Umbria in the decade of Michelangelo and Del Sarto in Florence. Farther north, Bologna and Ferrara constitute minor centers. Across the mouth of the Po, Venice, Padua, and Verona are all active through the fifteenth century. Of the three, Padua is the earliest to establish a flourishing school; Venice probably the last: there is no high-class Venetian painting before 1460, no first-rank master active until 1500. By that time the Paduan movement is finished, the Veronan still flourishing but producing no new growth: Paolo Veronese moved the school to Venice. Both Padua and Verona became subject to Venice in the course of the fifteenth century, which may be the cause of the transference. Vicenza, Brescia, and Bergamo, which also became Venetian-ruled although more distant to the east, each had a school, all three of which were late, that is, becoming of consequence only around 1500, and brief, ending by 1550–1570. The peak at Venice fell from 1500 to 1550, but the movement was far from spent then.

Up the Po, in Milanese territory, Cremona and Parma participated with Milan. Cremona was the earliest and least important center of the three: its school was active by 1450. Milan got under way soon after, with imported talent: Foppa of Brescia from Padua, Borgognone his pupil, Leonardo from Florence. Leonardo of course overshadowed everyone else, and Milanese work from 1500 to 1560 is all influenced by him. The school of Parma essentially is Correggio plus his followers.

Farther east still, in Savoy and Genoa, painting never got beyond the second-rate. Turin had a minor school around 1500; Genoa, not until the decadence.

It is significant that Rome and the whole southern half of Italy had been wholly unproductive so far. It was only when the culmination of painting had been reached, about 1500, that Rome entered, as a court influence to draw established talent to itself.

The zenith I compute to have lasted from 1500 to not beyond 1550, except for the late work of occasional long-lived masters like Michelangelo and Titian. In fact, 1540 is surely a better terminus. In that year Michelangelo was 65, Sodoma 63, Titian 50 or older; Leonardo, Raphael, Correggio, Del Sarto, Giorgione, Palma were dead since six to thirty years.

If the question is approached from the side of birth dates, 1530 appears as probably an even truer turning point than 1540. The painters who show symptoms of decadence—strain, desire for effect, mannerism of violence instead of awkwardness, loss of definite line—begin to be born almost exactly at 1500. Before that there are none who can be called decadent—though Correggio, 1494, foreshadows what is to come. Those born after 1500 all are decadent in greater or less degree.[2] This does not mean that no great painters were born after 1500, but that their greatness was already tainted. This holds for Tintoretto, 1518, and still more for the meretriciously infected Veronese, 1528. I realize that, especially concerning these Venetians, this is not the opinion of all historians of art; but it is of some; and it seems impossible to concentrate attention on the qualities that mark inner or essential decline and not find them in these men.

On the basis of our usual criterion that thirty to fifty is the period of most men's best productivity, and thirty certainly the age by which it generally becomes characterized, 1530 would mark the point at which the new generation, destined to initiate the decline, became active participants alongside the surviving older masters; 1540 would see them in the majority; 1550, wholly in control except for a few rugged giant survivors like Michelangelo. Reference in this connection is of course wholly to quality of style, not to activity of production or interest in painting, which, if anything is to be said of them, continued to increase.

It is plain that the various local schools found themselves in a different position when the culmination was entered about 1500. Some of the smaller ones, like Padua and Umbria, ended then. Florence, which had been flourishing actively for a full two centuries, began to decline soon after. Painting in Venice,

---

[2] Moroni of Brescia, 1510–1578, comes nearest to being an exception, but his strength is in portraits.

less than a century old in 1500, and just beginning to come to its full strength, ran on vigorously, however inferior the style, till nearly 1600. The causes of this variability are twofold, at least. First, the degree of maturity of each school was a factor, as just indicated for Florence and Venice. Second, there was a strong tendency for larger centers, especially capitals, to absorb smaller ones. Rome particularly, which hitherto had produced no painting at all, began to drain off talent from Florence, Umbria, and in some degree from elsewhere. Padua and Verona became absorbed into Venice. This process was of course the counterpart, and largely the result, of what had been going on in the political sphere—the gradual consolidation of innumerable independent city-states into some fifteen larger ones, among which Savoy, Milan, Venice, Florence, Rome, and the Two Sicilies were predominant.

But the essential unity of the Italian growth is clear from the fact that the phases of the whole apply rigorously to the several parts of local movements. Padua may end just before the culmination, Florence attain it and then break, Venice live on through and past the great period, Rome begin with it, Naples commence only in the decline—the quality of each school, in spite of some local excellence or mannerism like color in Venice, is fundamentally that of its time in terms of the whole Italian development. That is why the year 1500 as the turning point for birth dates is after all so significant. For the understanding of the complete history of Italian painting, the schools must be known and dealt with; for recognition of the outline course of the national growth, they may almost be ignored, so strongly does the larger configuration dominate and include the provincial ones.

Siena

Giambono, fl. 1430–1470.

S. and D. di Pietro, 1406–1481, 1410–1480.

Matteo di Giovanni, ca. 1435–1495.

Benv. di Giovanni, 1436– ca. 1517.

Pietro di Domenico, 1457–1501.

Fungai, 1460–1516.

Pacchiarotti, 1474–1540.

*Sodoma, 1477–1549.

Peruzzi, 1481–1537.

Beccafumi, ca. 1486–1551.

Florence
Masolino, ca. 1383–1447.
Andrea del Castagno, ca. 1390–
1457.
Uccello, ca. 1396–1475.
*Masaccio, 1401–1428.
Domenico Veneziano, fl. 1438,
d. 1461.
Filippo Lippi, ca. 1412–1469.
Benozzo Gozzoli, 1420–1498.
*Pollaiuolo, 1429–1498.
*Verrocchio, 1435–1488.
*(Signorelli, 1441–1523. See
Umbria.)

*Botticelli, 1446–1510.
*Ghirlandaio, 1449–1494.
**(Leonardo da Vinci, 1452–
1519; to Milan.)
*Lorenzo di Credi, 1459–1537.
Filippino Lippi, 1460–1504.
Piero di Cosimo, 1462–1521.
Fra Bartolommeo, 1475–1517.
**Michelangelo, 1475–1564.
Franciabigio, 1482–1525.
*Andrea del Sarto, 1486–1531.
(Bronzino to Dolci, see below.)

Umbria (and Umbro-Florentine school)
San Severino, fl. ca. 1400.
Ottaviano Nelli, fl. 1410–1434.
Piero della Francesca, 1423–
1492.
*Melozzo da Forli, 1438–1494.
*Signorelli, 1441–1523. (See
Florence.)

*Perugino, 1446–1524.
Pinturicchio, 1454–1513.
Timoteo Viti, 1469–1523.
**Raphael, 1483–1520. (To
Florence and Rome.)

Bologna
Vitale, fl. ca. 1320–1345.
Dalmasii, fl. ca. 1376–1410.

Francia (Raibolini), 1450–
1517.

Ferrara
Galassi, d. 1473.
Cosimo Tura, ca. 1420–1498.
Cossa, 1430–ca. 1483.
Costa, 1460–1535.

Dossi, 1479–1542.
*(Palma Vecchio, ca. 1480–
1528. To Venice.)
Mazzolino, 1481–ca. 1530.

Venice
Lorenzo Veneziano, fl. 1357–
1379.
Jacobello del Fiore, fl. 1400–
1439.
Negroponte.
Jacopo Bellini, ca. 1400–1464.
G. and A. Vivarini, fl. 1440–
1470.
*Giovanni Bellini, 1428–1516.
*Antonello da Messina, ca.
1444–ca. 1493.

*Carpaccio, ca. 1450–ca. 1520.
Alvisi Vivarini, ca. 1450–
ca. 1503.
*Carlo Crivelli, fl. 1468–1495.
*Cima da Conegliano, fl. 1489–
1517.
*Giorgione, ca. 1477–1511.
*Palma Vecchio, ca. 1480–1528
*Lorenzo Lotto, ca. 1480–ca.
1558. (See Bergamo.)
Pordenone, 1483–1539.

Venice (Continued)

*Sebastiano del Piombo, 1485–1547. (Also at Rome.)

**Titian, 1490 (1477)–1576.

Paris Bordone, 1500–1570.

*Tintoretto, 1518–1594.

*Paolo Veronese, 1528–1588.

Palma Giovine, 1544–1628.

Padua

Gentile da Fabriano, ca. 1360–1450.

*Squarcione, 1394–1474.

Foppa, d. 1492; to Milan.

*Mantegna, 1431–1506.

Verona

Turoni, fl. 1360.

Altichiero, fl. 1375–1380.

Pisanello, 1380–ca. 1455.

D. Morone, b. 1442.

Liberale, 1451–1536.

Torbido (Il Moro), fl. 1486.

Bonsignori, 1455–1519.

Giolfino, 1465–1518.

F. Morone, 1473–1529.

*Girolamo dai Libri, 1474–1556.

Melone, fl. 1515–1520.

Morando, 1486–1522.

Bonifazio da Verona, ca. 1491–1540.

*(Paola Veronese, 1528–1588; to Venice.)

Vicenza

Montagna, fl. 1484–1517.

Buonconsiglio, d. 1530.

Brescia

Civerchio, fl. 1495–1540.

Mocetto, fl. 1514.

Romanino, 1485–ca. 1566.

Moretto, 1498–ca. 1566.

Savoldo, fl. 1540–1548.

*Moroni, 1510–1578.

Bergamo

*Lorenzo Lotto, ca. 1480–ca. 1558. (Or "Venetian.")

Previtali, ca. 1480–1528.

Garofalo, 1481–1559.

Milan

Foppa, d. 1492. From Padua.

Buttinone, fl. 1484.

Zenale, d. 1526.

Borgognone da Fossano, ca. 1445–1523, fl. 1490–1520.

**Leonardo da Vinci, 1452–1519. From Florence.

Solario, ca. 1460–1530.

Bernadino de' Conti, fl. 1498.

*Beltraffio, 1467–1516.

Salaino, fl. 1519.

Oggione, 1470–1549.

Sesto, ca. 1475/80–1524.

Luini, ca. 1475–1533.

Gaudenzio Ferrari, ca. 1481–ca. 1545.

Melzi, 1493–1568.

Bramantino, fl. 1529.

Lanini, 1508–1578.

Cremona

Oriolo, fl. 1449–1461.

B. Bembo, fl. 1455–1478.

Tacconi, fl. 1464–1490.

G. Bembo, fl. 1524.

G. Campi, 1500–1572.

Parma
   Araldi, 1465–1528.   Mazzuola brothers.
   *Correggio, 1494–1534.   Parmigiano, d. 1592.
   Ludovico da Parma.
Turin
   Macrino d'Alba, fl. ca. 1500.

The decline need not be lingered over. The Papal court
tried to gather in the fruits that had ripened in northern Italy
independent of it, and succeeded; but in the moment of gathering they began to decay. The effects are visible even in some of
the later work of Raphael, short-lived as he was—his large-scale,
crowded, ambitious attempts already show something of the
mechanically shallow vigor of his successors. Only a titan like
Michelangelo seemed able to resist the influences of both court
and years. Venice succeeded in running out its main course.
Florence, with its old-established and strong tradition, also
continued, but with its inevitable falling off accentuated by
the sapping by Rome. Bologna became important, mainly with
men born 1550–1590. Naples came into activity last, as in
music; and, like Rome, drew part of its strength from non-
Italians whom it had gathered to itself.

Finally, in the eighteenth century, an afterglow shone over
Venice, with Tiepolo, Guardi, and Canaletto. Part of their
work is as modern—at least Rococo—in its quality and nature
as it is Renaissance; perhaps more so. That, however, they
belonged historically to the Renaissance configuration is shown
by the fact that after them comes the great dearth which is the
expectable sequel to a great growth—at any rate in a polyphonic
culture such as that of the Occident.

Italy in the nineteenth century is barren of any painting
which has European significance. It is outranked not only by
France which has the lead, but by Spain, England, Holland—
perhaps even by Germany and America.

Florence
   *Bronzino, 1502–1572.   Zuccaro, 1542–1609.
   Daniele de Volterra, 1509–   Allori, 1577–1621.
      1556.   Da Cortona, 1596–1609.
   Vasari, 1512–1574.   *Dolci, 1616–1686.

Bologna

Fontana, 1512–1597.
Procaccini, 1520–ca. 1591.
P. Tibaldi, 1527–1596.
Paserotti, 1540–1595.
Calvaert, 1548–1619, from the
   Netherlands.
Lod. Carracci, 1555–1619.
Ag. Carracci, 1557–1602.
*Annibale Carracci, 1560–1609.
*Guido Reni, 1575–1642.

Albani, 1578–1660.
Lanfranco, 1580–1647. (Born
   in Parma; imitator of
   Correggio.)
*Domenichino, 1581–1641.
*Guercino, 1590/91–1666. (See
   Rome.)
Minor men with birth dates
   to about 1657.

Venice

See above (pp. 353–354) and
   below.

Genoa

Cambiaso, 1527–1585.
Sorri, 1556–1622.

Pelegro, 1617–1640.

Rome

**(Michelangelo, 1475–1564.)
*(Sodoma, 1477–1549.)
**(Raphael, 1483–1520.)
*(Sebastiano del Piombo,
   1485–1547.)
Penni (Il Fattore), 1488–1528.
Imola, 1490–1549.
Treviso, 1497–1544.
*Giulio Romano, 1498–1546.
Mantovano, fl. ca. 1532.

Tassi, 1566–1642.

Arpino, 1567–1640.
*Caravaggio, 1569–1609. (See
   Naples.)
Viola, 1576–1622.
Feti, 1589–1624.
*Guercino, 1590/91–1666.
Berretini (Cortona), 1596–
   1669.
Sassoferrato, 1605–1685.
Maratta, 1625–1713.
Giordano, 1632–1705. (Also
   to Naples.)

Naples

(Solario, 1382–1455.)
(Simone Papa, b. 1455.)
*(Caravaggio, 1569–1609, in
   Naples 1606–1609.)
Spada, 1576–1622.
Manfredi, ca. 1580–1617.
Stanzioni, 1585–1656.

*Ribera, 1588–1656. (Spaniard.)
Vaccaro, 1598–1670.
Della Battaglie, 1602–1660.
*Salvator Rosa, 1615–1673.
Giordano, 1632–1705. (See
   Rome.)
Solimena (Ciccio), 1657–1747.

Venice

*Tiepolo, 1696–1770.
*Canaletto, 1697–1768.
Longhi, 1702–1762.

Guardi, 1712–1793.
Piranesi, 1720–1778.

§54. Netherlands Painting

Netherlands painting rivals French for the longest history in Europe, next to Italian, of sustained excellence. But the configuration is quite different from the Italian. It begins later and it ends earlier; yet still more marked is the abruptness of its beginning around 1400, and the sudden totality of its eclipse, so far as notable quality is concerned, by 1700. The Van Eycks rise almost without warning, so far as the record goes; and Rembrandt, Teniers, Ruysdael, and their contemporaries all die almost simultaneously and without successors.

In fact, it is the current custom to exalt most highly the masters at the two ends of the period. This implies a double-peak curve for the growth as a whole. There is nothing theoretically impossible in such a configuration. Indeed, put in terms of a fifteenth-century culmination, a sixteenth-century dip, and another culmination in the seventeenth century, the history, while unusual, would have nothing abnormal about it. What does seem unlikely is that great masters should arise out of nothing, be followed by increasingly inferior descendants for four or five generations, and that from these again still greater masters should derive, to die off without successors worth mentioning. The last phase of this development is indubitable fact. The first one might be doubted, on account of the scantiness of available records; though if there had been any very notable predecessors of the Van Eycks, it seems a reasonable belief that we ought to have heard more of them. I am unable to judge this matter decisively. I am also not clear whether sixteenth-century Netherlands painting is best construed as an actual recession, or as a plateau of arrest which merely seems to dip because of the contrast with the contemporary marked florescences in Italy and Germany. What is sure is that the total configuration is of a widely different character from the Italian one.

Another question concerns the relation of the Dutch school to the "Flemish," or in modern terminology Belgian, school in the seventeenth century. The two are usually kept apart by historians and critics. However, Rembrandt was only thirty years younger than Rubens, eight than Van Dyck, and actually older than Teniers, while Hals was senior to all these except Rubens. So far as time goes, there was therefore essential contemporaneity. As for nationality, all three of the Belgian masters were Flemings, and therefore differing only dialectically in speech from the Hollanders. The difference of Rubens and Van Dyck from the Dutchmen is in subject and style of work. But this does not hold for Teniers, who stands closer to Rembrandt, and as for Brower, he is assigned sometimes to one and sometimes to the other national movement. There is not much more difference, probably, between the Flemish and Dutch schools than between the Florentine and Venetian. As for a Netherlandish configuration, the two are thus best considered together.

Indeed, the custom of separate treatment is evidently due to the fact that from the time the seven United Provinces turned Protestant and independent, the political fortunes and nationalism of Belgium and Holland diverged increasingly. Before then, in spite of the bilingualism of the Walloon and Flemish-Dutch elements, there was only the Netherlands. To insist heavily on the split is an undue projection backward in time of a largely recent dualism.

It is true that the great phase of Dutch painting fits neatly in time with Dutch military and naval success, expansion, commercial supremacy, and the peaks in literature, philosophy, and science. There is thus considerable legitimate reason for keeping Dutch painting separate from "Flemish." But the accord gained on one side is in large part lost on the other. The Rubens school has counterparts only in Belgian industry, music, and science, and the culminations of these fall somewhat earlier.

To do justice to both sides of the doubtful argument, I shall present the lists in double column, kept contemporary so far as typography permits.

As already said, the origins of Netherlands painting are fully as obscure as the Italian ones. The suggestions sometimes made of Byzantine influences in Germany seem quite farfetched. There does seem to have been some influence from Cologne in the latter fourteenth century just before the Van Eycks. Yet this does not explain much, both because the origin of the Cologne school is itself obscure, and because Cologne from its position was almost as much Netherlandish as German.

French students claim a larger share for France, and perhaps at bottom more justly, although their specifications seem thin. They aver the union of Flanders and Burgundy in 1384, which made Flanders French; and that it was only the ensuing disasters of the French kingdom which instituted Dijon instead of Paris as the temporary art capital of France. However, Burgundy was only qualifiedly French in the fourteenth and fifteenth centuries: at any rate, antinationalistic rather than nationalistic. Then too, the known artists of note of the period, both in Burgundy and France, were all Flemish-Dutch immigrants or imports: the sculptor Claus Sluter, a Hollander; the "painters" Bandol of Bruges, Broederlam of Ypres, Malouel from Guelderland, Paul of Limburg. This scarcely speaks for French priority.

It seems rather that what happened was the parallel of events in other fields. In the thirteenth century, northern France, especially the Île de France and adjacent counties, was supreme not only in music, but in literature, architecture, and sculpture. The Netherlands, Walloon and Flemish, participated belatedly as marginal provinces. We may perhaps assume—though this is hypothesis only—a similar French superiority in painting, which then was as yet represented chiefly by book illumination and window-glass staining. During the fourteenth century, French productivity in all these activities waned, that of the Low Countries, especially the western and southern Netherlands, increased. This is merely an instance of the familiar phenomenon of a culture growth passing from the original focus or hearth to the peripheries as the hearth burns itself out. The process is either authenticated or generally accepted for French-Flemish music, sculpture, architecture, and literature. It is no rash theory, in the absence of documents, to assume the same for painting. By about 1400, when picture painting had come into its own, supremacy had definitely passed to the Netherlands: certainly in music and sculpture; and at least relatively in literature and building. At any rate, France was then on an ebb tide as compared with 1300, the Netherlands on the flood. Already before 1400 the Flemings had begun to achieve superiority, with their Broederlams and Malouels. That these left home was because there was higher demand for their talents at courts, whether in Dijon, Bourges, or Paris, than in their native bourgeois society.

The next event is the appearance of the Van Eycks, just after 1400—their predecessors, who were drawn to Burgundian and French soil, belonging roughly to the close of the preceding century. The Van Eycks now paint real pictures, and for Flemish cities—Bruges and Ghent—instead of for dukes and kings; and therewith Netherlands art is "born." That is, it is launched on its career as an indubitable Netherlandish development no longer claimable for either France or Germany. This development, then, is after all not so abrupt in its beginning as it is often represented; and it fits nicely into a broad current of culture which is well authenticated. Its general course is strikingly parallel to that of music, at any rate until about 1500.

After that century-turn, both Flemish musicians and Flemish painters began to go to Italy: but the former to teach, the latter to learn. Italy, having been until then without an art music, was receptive and, starting fresh, initiated a great musical growth which continued while the Netherlandish one ran its course and died. But in painting Italy had the older and stronger tradition, and it was the Flemings who returned home staggered by the impact, and floundered for a while—in their sixteenth-century arrest or sag—until they could assimilate the overwhelming Italian influences and start fresh on a broader scale, with larger patterns; while Italy, self-contained, glided into decadence.

The relation of Italian to Netherlands painting can thus be approximately defined. There seems nothing common to the two growths in origin, other than a remote joint mediaeval ancestry—a before-picture-painting stage; and the lineage from this to the Italian beginnings is none too clear. The Van Eycks certainly seem uninfluenced by anything Italian. The same is true of Van der Weyden, though he painted in Ferrara in 1449 and visited Rome in 1450. On the other hand, the oil process of the Van Eycks, whatever it was, stirred the Italians to admiration. Antonello da Messina, ca. 1444–ca. 1493, who had learned it in Flanders, introduced it in Venice. As a Sicilian, he was almost as much a foreigner to the one as to the other. His style is obviously Flemish, perhaps more than Italian. One fifteenth-century Fleming went to Italy and became Italianized: Justus or Jodocus of Ghent, who in 1474, nine years before the birth of Raphael, completed for Urbino a Last Supper, ordered by a public subscription which included among its contributors the reigning duke. Obviously he was looked upon as a master. Nor does he seem to have returned to the Netherlands, as a pupil who had profited from his masters would presumably have done. Hugo van der Goes, who died in 1482, painted on order in Ghent the Portinari altarpiece for Florence. These incidents make a clear record of Flemish giving rather than receiving until at least 1480, possibly longer.

About 1500, the current reversed. Quentin Massys, born at Louvain in 1466, founder of the school of Antwerp, is still free from Italian influence. Gossaert-Mabuse, of Maubeuge, born only four or six years later, is reckoned the first Netherlands painter to feel the Italian Renaissance. A journey to Italy in 1513 ruined his Flemish manner. He was then over forty. Van Orley, twenty years younger, went farther in his Italianization. Then follow Coxcien, born 1499, Jan Massys, 1509, Floris, ca. 1517, Vos, 1513 or 1531, Van Veen, 1558. To these must be added Calvaert, 1540/48, who founded an academy of teaching in Bologna which competed with that of the Carracci. The Dutch fell under transalpine sway later, and more lightly, than the Flemings proper. Cornelis Corneliszoon, Lastman, Bloemaert, born about 1562–1565, and the Crabeths and Honthorst, about 1592, are the chief examples.

From this it is clear that until around 1480 the Netherlands influenced Italy; subsequent to 1513, Italy the Netherlands. The turn presumably coincides with the beginning of the Renaissance culmination. It was the Italians of the formative generation or two before this culmination who were ready to absorb from the northerners. It was the Italians of the very zenith by whom the Netherlanders were dominated.

Of course not all Flemish painters became Italian imitators. The native tradition continued active also, though more or less influenced by absorptions; until Rubens was able to give painting a new and vigorous impulse on a broadened but still fundamentally Flemish basis.

In any Netherlandish, especially Belgian-Netherlandish, achievement it is always of interest to consider the part played by the Romanic and Teutonic elements, the Walloon and Flemish proper, who have so long kept themselves distinct while yet jointly maintaining a nationality. In music we found the contributions seemingly in balance. In painting, the Flemish element was definitely in preponderance, somewhat at first, overwhelmingly later, even within the Burgundian-Spanish or Belgian Netherlands; with Holland added, the disparity would be even greater. Some French authorities claim the Van Eycks as French, that is, Walloon, on the basis of an epithet "Gallicus." They were born at Maaseyck in Limburg, which the maps make Flemish-Dutch soil. I cannot adjudicate the evidence. If the Van Eycks were really Walloon, we should have, with them and Van der Weyden of Tournai, whose native name was La Pasture, an essentially Romanic beginning for the Netherlands development, which would accord well enough with the hypothesis that it first grew out of an extension of mediaeval French influences. If the Van Eycks were true Flemings, the whole development was primarily Flemish, with the Walloons playing an honorable secondary part at first and a less important one later.

As for the various Netherlandish "schools," they scarcely are such except in the literal sense: that is, ateliers in which young men learned from a master and came under his personal influence. There are definable centers of activity, which on the whole are situated in the more flourishing towns of the moment. In the beginning these were definitely western: Ypres, Bruges, Ghent, Tournai; then Louvain. From about 1500 on, under Massys, Antwerp became the Belgian focus, to remain such to the end, with Malines and Liège playing a quite subordinate role, Brussels perhaps an even lesser one. In Holland, Haarlem, Leyden, and Amsterdam were centers from the beginning and to the end. Gouda, Utrecht, Dordrecht, and Delft come in a little later, all but Gouda to continue. Essentially the Dutch "schools" are therefore synchronous, and their significance is technical. They do emphasize the intensely localized, unmetropolitan character of Dutch civilization; even though the seven centers enumerated all lie close together in the depressed "hollow-land" part of the country.

Pre-Van Eyck

Hennequin (Jehan) of Bruges,
  fl. 1370–1377.
Jehan de Hasselt at Courtrai,
  fl. 1373–1386.
Jean Bandol of Bruges, court
  painter of Charles V of
  France, 1337–1380.
Melchior Broederlam of Ypres,
  in Burgundy ca. 1390, fl.
  1383–1409.
Paul of Limburg, illuminated   Malouel of Guelderland, in
  Book of Hours, before 1416.   Paris ca. 1400.

Fifteenth Century

*Hubert van Eyck, 1366–1426,
  b. at Maaseyck, Limburg;
  to Ghent.
*Jan van Eyck, 1381/90–1440,
  y. br., to Bruges.
Robert Campin, at Tournai,
  ca. 1400 seq.
*Rogier van der Weyden (de La
  Pasture), ca. 1399–1464, b.
  at Tournai; pupil of last.

(Dierick [Thierry] Bouts at
  Louvain: Dutch.)

Dierick Bouts, 1399/1400–
  1475, of Haarlem, to
  Louvain.

Hubert Stuerbout, fl. at
  Louvain ca. 1447–1449.

Petrus Christus, b. near
  Ghent, in Bruges 1444,
  living in 1472.

(Jehan Clouet ["Cloet of Brussels"], b. ca. 1420, prob.
  Dutch, to France.)

Simon Marmion, ca. 1425–
  1489, (of Amiens) at
  Tournai.

Albert van Oudewater, fl. at
  Haarlem 1467–1480.

Jacques Daret, pupil of Van
  der Weyden at Tournai.

*Hans Memling, d. 1494, prob.
  German, to Bruges.

Justus (Jodocus) of Ghent, to
  Italy, fl. at Urbino, 1468–
  1474.

(Hugo van der Goes, at Ghent:
  Dutch.)

Hugo van der Goes, of Zealand, to Ghent, d. 1482,
  fl. 1465–1475.

(Gerard David at Bruges:
  Dutch.)

Gheeraert David, ca. 1460–
  1523, b. Oudewater, 1483
  seq. in Bruges.

Jean Prévost, from Mons, at
  Bruges 1494–1529.

Jerome van Aeken (Bosch), fl.
  at Hertogenbosch 1493, d.
  1518.

SIXTEENTH CENTURY

*Quentin Massys (Metsys),
  1466–1530, b. Louvain,
  founded "school" of
  Antwerp.

Cornelis Engelbrechtsen,
  1468–1533. At Leyden.
  Studied at Bruges?

Jan Gossaert (Mabuse), 1470–
  1532, of Maubeuge; Italian
  influence, to Antwerp and
  Utrecht.

Jacob Corneliszoon, of Oost-
  Zaandam, fl. at Amsterdam
  1506–1530.

Jean Bellegambe, 1490–1542,
  of Douai.

Jan Mostaert, 1474–1555/6.
  At Haarlem.

*Joachim de Patinir, at Ant-
  werp and Bruges, perhaps
  pupil of G. David, d. 1524.
  Landscapist.

Jan Sanders, of Hemessen, in
Antwerp 1524–1548; imit.
Massys and Italians.

Bernard (Barendt) van Orley,
ca. 1490–1542; to Brussels;
Italian influence.

Lucas van Leyden, 1494–1533.
At Leyden.

(Marten van Veen, to Ant-
werp: Dutch.)

Marten van Veen, 1494–1574
Of Heemskerck. To Ant-
werp and Haarlem. Italian
influence.

Lancelot Blondeel, 1496–
1561.

Jan Schoreel (Schoorl, Scorel),
1495–1562, b. Schoorl, to
Haarlem, Amsterdam,
Rome, Utrecht.

(Marinus Claeszoon, to Antwerp: Dutch.)

Marinus Claeszoon van Rom-
erswalen, 1497–ca. 1566. Of
Zealand. Follower of
Massys.

Hendrik Metten Bles, b.
Dinant, pupil of Patinir,
d. Liège ca. 1550.

Michael Coxcien (van Cox-
cyen), 1499–1592, b.
Malines, pupil of Orley,
to Brussels; Italian influence.

Lucas Gassel, b. Helmont,
Liège; d. Brussels, ca.
1560.

Lambert Lombard, 1505–
1566. At Liège. Italian influence.

(Pieter Aartzen, at Antwerp:
Dutch.)

Pieter Aartzen, 1507–1572. Of
Haarlem, to Amsterdam
and Antwerp.

Jan Massys, son of Quentin,
ca. 1509–ca. 1575. Antwerp.

Pieter Porbus the Elder, ca.
1510–1584. At Gouda.

Frans van Vriendt (Floris),
1517/18–1570. Pupil of
Lombard. Antwerp. Italian
influence.

*Antonij Mor (Moro), 1518–
1588. At Utrecht and
Brussels, and international
career.

(Willem Key, at Antwerp,
Brussels: Dutch.)

Willem Key, ca. 1520–1568, of
Breda. To Antwerp and
Brussels. Pupil of Lombard.

Pieter ("Peasant") Breughel
the Elder, ca. 1525–1569.
Antwerp.

Martin (de) Vos, 1531–1603.
Pupil of Van Vriendt
(Floris). Antwerp.

Frans Porbus the Elder, 1540–
1584. Antwerp. Son of
Pieter Porbus of Gouda.

(Adrian Key, at Antwerp: Adrian Thomas Key, 1544–ca.
Dutch.)   1590. Of Breda, to Antwerp.

Denis Calvaert, 1548–1619.
School of Antwerp; to
Bologna.

Paul Bril, 1556–1626. Ant-   Hendrik Vroom, 1556–1664.
werp. Landscapist.   Sea painter. (Amsterdam.)

Otto van Veen, 1558–1629.   Cornelis Corneliszoon, 1562–
Antwerp.   1638. At Haarlem. Italian
                                  influence.

Pieter ("Hell") Breughel the   Pieter Lastman, 1562–1649.
Younger, 1564–1638.   At Leyden. Teacher of
Antwerp.   Rembrandt. Italian influ-
                                  ence.

                                  Abraham Bloemaert, 1565–
                                  1647. At Utrecht. Italian in-
                                  fluence.

Jan ("Velvet") Breughel,   Van Mierevelt, 1562–1641. At
1568–1625. Antwerp.   Delft.

Frans Porbus the Younger,   Paul Moreelse, 1571–1638. At
1570–1622. Antwerp.   Utrecht.

CULMINATION

At Antwerp   ### In Holland

**Rubens, 1577–1640. Born in
Siegen, Westphalia, of
Flemish parents, to
Cologne, to Antwerp
age 10.

Frans Snyders, 1579–1657.   Jan van Ravesteyn, 1580–1665
                                  (1573–1657?) Haarlem.

Gaspard de Crayer, 1582–   *Frans Hals, ca. 1584–1666.
1669.   Haarlem.

Cornelius de Vos, 1585–1651.

Jacob Jordaens, 1593–1678.

*Van Dyck, 1599–1641:

*Adriaen Brower (Brauwer),
1606–1638. B. Oudenarde,
studied at Haarlem, to Antwerp 1631.

Jan Fyt, 1609–1661.

*David Teniers (the Younger),
1610–1690/94.

Jacques d'Arthois, 1613–1665.
At Brussels.

Gonzales Coques, 1614–1684.

Pieter van der Faes (Lely),
1618–1680. (B. Westphalia,
to England.)

Jan van Goyen, 1596–1656/
66. Leyden.

Jan Wynants, 1600/15– ca.
1679. Haarlem.

Albert Cuyp, 1605(20)–ca.
1691. Dordrecht.

(Brower, studied with Hals),
1606–1638. Haarlem, to
Antwerp.

**Rembrandt, 1607–1669. Of
Leyden, to Amsterdam
1631.

*Gerard Ter Borch (Terburg),
1608–1681. Haarlem.

*Adriaen van Ostade, 1610–
1685. Haarlem.

*Gerard Dou, 1610/13–1675.
Leyden.

Aart van der Neer, 1619–1683.
Amsterdam.

Philip Wouwerman, 1619–
1668. Haarlem.

Willem von Aelst, 1620–1679.
Delft.

Aalbert van Everdingen,
1621–1675. Amsterdam.
Norwegian landscapes.

Paul Potter, 1625–1654.
Haarlem.

Jan Steen, ca. 1626–1679.
Haarlem.

*Jacob Ruysdael, ca. 1628–
1682. Haarlem.

Bartholomeus van der Helst,
1630 (1612)–1670.
Haarlem.

*Pieter de Hoogh, 1630–1677
(1632–1681). Delft; to
Amsterdam.

Ludolf Backhuysen, 1631–
1708. Amsterdam. Marines.

Nicholas Maas, 1632–1693.
Dordrecht.

Jan van der Meer (Vermeer),
1632–1675. Delft.

Antonij Frans van der Meulen,
1634–1690. Brussels, to
France.

Willem van der Velde (the
Younger), 1633–1707. At
Amsterdam.

Frans Mieris (the Elder),
1635–1681. Haarlem.

Melchior Hondekoeter, 1636–
1695. Utrecht.

*Minderhout Hobbema, 1638–
1709. Amsterdam.

Gabriel Metsu, 1630/40– ca.
1667/69. Amsterdam.

(Sir Godfrey Kneller, 1646–
1723. German, trained in
Amsterdam. To England.)

The Dutch culmination comes to a close with startling rapidity. Hals and Rembrandt died in 1666 and 1669. By 1685, a century after Hals's birth, Terburg, Ostade, Dou, Ruysdael, Helst, Hoogh, Metsu had followed. In 1700 there survived only Hobbema and a few others; by 1710 these were gone. The principal reason for the finish was that births of superior talent ceased at 1640. The abruptness is accentuated by the fact that the older masters lived longer than the later ones. So far as the often uncertain dates allow calculation, the average age attained by the Dutch painters in the list above who were born between 1580 and 1610 was between 67 and 71; only one of the ten failed to reach 60. Of seventeen born 1619 to 1640, the average life was barely 55; only three attained 70; and these are the ones that lived into the first decade of the next century.

Belgian-Dutch painting of the nineteenth century is noted in §59 (pp. 395–396, below).

§55. German Painting

Great painting ended in Germany by 1550. This is a sort of counterpart of England's producing nothing before 1750. The latter fact may be construable as due to England's being until late a barbarian frontier in representative art—she never did attain to distinctive sculpture. But it is remarkable that Germany, once having had a great art of painting, and continuing ever since to try to paint, achieved so little in the period around 1800 in which she led Europe in philosophy, music, literature, and, soon after, in science.

The one German growth in painting is again remarkable for beginning almost as early as the Italian one, remaining uninfluenced by it,[3] culminating simultaneously almost to the identical decades, but then dying away rapidly and completely. The swift disappearance is probably the most easily understood phenomenon of the cycle. Just because Italian and German painting reached their climax synchronously in adjacent countries, they were bound to come into competitive conflict: and it was the lesser art that succumbed. That it crumbled away at the contact indicates how much more deep-seated and powerful a set of impulses underlay Italian painting.

The first growth on German soil of picture painting, in the sense here used, centered in Cologne. The beginning goes back almost to the lifetime of Giotto, was the earliest notable development north of the Alps, antedates the Van Eycks by one to two generations, and is held to have contributed to the formation of the Early Flemish school. The peak, a century later, probably falls on Lochner, about 1450. The Cologne school was not a great growth, but a well-defined one. Like Siena as compared with Florence, it remained too much steeped in religious sentiment ever to become a free art; but it broke the way for Nürnberg and Augsburg.

After Cologne, it is usual to distinguish schools of the Middle

---

[3] Directly uninfluenced, of course. Both are parts of the same greater European movement.

Rhine, Upper Rhine, Suabia, Franconia, and Saxony. Of the two on the Rhine, the Upper was the stronger. Associated with it were a group of German Swiss, whom I list separately below though they include no great masters, because of their symptomatic significance in Swiss national development. The Suabian school had two centers, Ulm and Augsburg, the latter more important. The Franconian was primarily of Nürnberg, though Regensburg also participated, and Kronach produced the man who by going to Wittenberg founded, or rather constituted, the Saxon school.

The tract of highest productivity was Suabia and Franconia from Ulm to Nürnberg, within the northern half of the Bavaria of recent centuries. This is a small area, about the size of Tuscany. The relation of the rest of Germany to this area of concentration, in degree of development or quality of product, was much like that of the rest of Italy to Florence about 1450.

Practically all the centers that participated in German painting were free cities: not only Nürnberg, Augsburg, Ulm, but also Regensburg, Nördlingen, Strassburg, Colmar, Basel. The art was in no sense a court art; it seems to have flourished largely without relations even to the nobility or prelates.

The concentration in time is equally strict, apart from Cologne, which was a somewhat separate and earlier growth. Of the painters whose work possesses some individuality, perhaps only two, Schongauer and Pleydenwurff, died before 1500. The others were born between 1460 and 1505; the majority evidently between 1470 and 1500. In the double decade 1510–1530, which can be selected as marking the crest, the following were active: Dürer, Holbein, Cranach, Grünewald, Grien, Zeitblom, the elder Holbein, Burgkmair, Wolgemut, Altdorfer, Süss, Beham, as well as some of lesser name; in fact, those whose work did not overlap these twenty years did not amount to much. By 1550/60 the whole movement was over.

The sudden and complete withering of a more than respectable growth which had produced at least two world masters of the first rank, is astounding even if intelligible. The readiest explanation seems to be the one already offered: eclipse by the still greater Italian growth which culminated at exactly the same moment. At any rate, Italian supremacy appears to account for the lack of German epigones. The Reformation might be alleged as an interference with painting. But the Reformation itself produced no great churchmen in the generation after Luther. And in German science there was a similar stoppage after about 1560. In short, German creativeness in all directions seems to have been pretty well spent around the middle of the sixteenth century. Either this more general condition, or Italian overshadowing, or both, seem to be at the root of the abrupt ending of German painting.

It is a problem whether without the Italian overshadowing German painting might have continued to develop. It certainly lacked important qualities of contemporary Italian art: suavity, smoothness of form, a certain largeness of swing. The Germans never got over wrestling with irrelevant detail, even when they aimed at something bigger. This obsession perhaps hampered Holbein the least, because he was a portraitist; but it shows everywhere in Dürer and the others. Possibly, left to themselves, the Germans might have worked out into a greater freedom—though something of the impulse has stayed with their painting to the present day. But at any rate, the qualities which they lacked came provided in Italian art, and were probably easier to accept ready-made than to struggle toward independently.

PERIOD OF PRODUCTIVITY

Cologne

Various anonymous, ca. 1320–1350.
Wilhelm von Herle, active 1358–1378.
Wynrich von Wesel, act. 1397–1417.
Lukas Moser, act. 1431.
Stephan Lochner, act. 1430–1451.
Master of Liesborn in Westphalia, act. ca. 1465.
Master of the Life of Mary, act. 1465–1490.
Master of the Lyversberg Passion, act. 1463–1480.
Master of the Bartholomew altar, ca. 1490.
Master of St. Severin, ca. 1500.
Bruyn, 1493–1556.

North Germany
  Bertram, from Minden, active at Hamburg 1370–1390.
  Master Francke, act. at Hamburg ca. 1425.
  Notke, at Lübeck, ca. 1440–1509.

Upper Rhine
  Schongauer, 1440/45–1488/91; b. Kulmbach; at Colmar.
  Grünewald, active 1503–1529.
  Baldung Grien, 1476/80–1545; of Gmund; at Freiburg, Strass-
    burg.

Suabia, Ulm
  Multscher, active 1427–1467.
  Schüchlin, d. 1505.
  Zeitblom, act. 1484, d. 1518.
  Schaffner, ca. 1480–1541; act. 1508–1535; Italian influence.

Suabia, Augsburg
  Hans Holbein the Elder, ca. 1460–1516/25, act. 1490 seq.
  Burgkmair, 1473–1531.
  Breu, ca. 1480–1537; Swiss.
  *Hans Holbein the Younger, 1497–1541/3; to Basel, after 1526
    in England.
  Amberger, ca. 1500–1561.

Franconia, Nürnberg
  Pleydenwurff, active 1451–1472, d. 1495.
  Wolgemut, 1443–1519.
  Stoss, 1445–1533; sculptor also.
  Traut, act. 1477?, 1505–1520.
  *Dürer, 1471–1528.
  Süss, of Kulmbach, ca. 1476–1522; also to Cracow.
  Altdorfer, ca. 1480–1538; Regensburg.
  Schäuffelein, 1490–1539.
  H. S. Beham, ca. 1500–1550.
  Pencs, ca. 1500–1555.
  B. Beham, 1502–1540.
  Hirschvogel, 1503–1553.
  Solis, 1514–1562.
  Ammann, 1539–1591, of Zurich, 1561 to Nürnberg.

Saxony
  *Cranach, 1472–1553; from Kronach, Franconia, to Wittenberg.

Swiss
  Witz, d. 1447, active in Basel and Geneva.
  Fries, act. 1487–1518; Freiburg.
  Herbst, act. 1492–1500.

Breu, ca. 1480–1537; to Augsburg.
Manuel (Deutsch), 1484–1531; Bern.
Urs Graf, 1485–1529; Solothurn; 1512 to Basel.
Asper, 1499–1571.
Stimmer, 1539–1584; Schaffhausen; to Strassburg.
Ammann, 1539–1591; Zurich; 1561 to Nürnberg.
Bock, act. ca. 1560.
Maurer, 1558–1614.

There is little to say about the period of sterility and new effort from 1550 to 1900. Painting went on, of course, continuously, only it lacked distinction in the eyes of the world. The most frequently named figure is Mengs, 1728–1779, who is sufficiently commonplace. Italian influence, which was certainly strong at least in the beginning of the period, cannot be held overly responsible, for seventeenth-century Netherlandish, French, and Spanish painting all grew to florescence after, or through, emancipating themselves from Italian influence.

PHASE OF STERILITY

Goltzius, 1558–1617.
Rottenhammer, 1564–1623; b. Munich.
Elsheimer, 1578–1620; b. Frankfurt.
Sandrart, 1606–1688; b. Frankfurt.
Lely, 1618–1680; to England. (See Netherlands.)
Kneller, 1646–1723; to England. (See Netherlands.)
Roos, 1655–1705.
Denner, 1685–1749.
Dietrich, 1712–1774.
Tischbein, 1722–1789.
Chodowiecki, 1726–1801; b. Danzig.
Mengs, 1728–1779; b. Aussig, Sudeten Bohemia.
Füssli, 1741–1825; Swiss of Zurich; to England as Fuseli.
Angelica Kauffmann, 1741–1807; Swiss.
Carstens, 1754–1798; Dane.

The last four or five are peripheral Germans, or Germans by courtesy. From 1723 to 1783 there was no unqualified German-born who attained even to third rank in painting. These were the sixty years in which Kant, Goethe, Schiller, Mozart, and Beethoven were born.

The nineteenth century, being nearer, is harder to judge in perspective; but if it produced a swell in German painting, this was a slight one. Cornelius and Overbeck brought about a "revolution" nearly synchronous with that of Géricault and Delacroix; but, for all its excitement, the effects were mild. And where the Frenchmen originated their revolt in Paris, the Germans had to go to Rome for inspiration. Incidentally, it is characteristic that during the two centuries or more of French leadership in painting, the Germans, while paralleling in their art activity nearly every change of direction occurring in France, have refused to study in Paris or to admit direct influence from there, but until recently have consistently turned to Italy.

The strongest nineteenth-century native painter produced in Germany is probably Menzel, born in 1815. Second perhaps is the portraitist Lenbach, 1836. Both are highly skilled rather than profound. The greatest genius, and certainly imagination, are possibly those of Boecklin, 1827, a Swiss. If he be counted as German, we have in the trio the nucleus of a constellation, around which predecessors like Cornelius, Overbeck, Begas, Kaulbach, contemporaries like Piloty, Knaus, Feuerbach, and successors such as Makart, Liebermann, Stuck make a symmetrical group. The peak would come about 1850–1870, nearer to that of German science than of literature or music.

The growth, however, is not a notable one, especially as a revival after nearly three hundred years of second-rate performance. Comparison may fairly be made with France because nineteenth-century French painting also failed to produce a single genius of the very first rank. German nineteenth-century painting does not equal French, either in the number of able painters or in the quality of their work. Also, there is no concentration of birthplaces. The schools of Munich, Bonn, Berlin, were spots of encouragement and congregation rather than of painters' origins.

As for the fact that the literature which centered around 1800 had no adequate counterpart in painting, it is well to remember that the painting of 1500 was accompanied by a literature little better than third-rate.

Cornelius, 1783–1867.
Overbeck, 1789–1869.
Schadow, 1789–1862.
Begas, 1794–1854.
Schnorr von Carolsfeld,
   1794–1872.
Schwindt, 1804–1871.
Kaulbach, 1805–1874.
Lessing, 1808–1880.
*Menzel, 1815–1905.
Hasenclever, 1818–1853.
Piloty, 1826–1886.
*Boecklin, 1827–1901; Swiss.
Knaus, 1829–1882.

Feuerbach, 1829–1880.
Defregger, 1835–1921.
*Lenbach, 1836–1904.
Marées, 1837–1887.
Thoma, 1839–1924.
Makart, 1840–1884; b.
   Austria.
Leibl, 1844–1900.
Uhde, 1848–1911.
Corinth, 1850–1925.
Hodler, 1853–1918.
Stuck, 1863–1928.
Klimt, 1867–1918.
Slevogt, 1868–1932.

§56. French Painting

French painting was late in beginning to have a history. The first native-born individual substantiated by paintings is Fouquet, 1410/15–1480/85, more or less midway in time between Van der Weyden and Memling, although he himself had been in Italy, and seems to have toned his essentially French portraiture by Italian rather than Flemish influences. Before him and in his day, there certainly were Flemish influences and Flemish painters in France and Burgundy: Paul of Limburg and his brothers, Malouel their uncle, Broederlam, the first Clouet from Brussels. Apparently there was the same situation as in sculpture and music: France dependent on Belgium in the fifteenth century. The difference from sculpture is that there is no record of any great thirteenth century of painting in France to serve as the first flux for the later Flemish reflux. Gothic two-dimensional art was in glass in church windows, or miniature illumination of books. It was not picture painting. This greater technique appears to have been essentially post-High Mediaeval in transalpine Europe. It formed in the fourteenth century, when France was receding and the Netherlands advancing, and hence became a Flemish art in its origins. On

this Flemish art the contemporary French leaned, and from it
they borrowed painters for their courts, until after 1400. What
during the fifteenth century they themselves ventured to undertake in the new art was portraits. They scarcely attempted
scenes as the Flemish had done since the Van Eycks, and the
Florentines a century earlier. Such strength as early French
painting possessed lay in these portraits, which they did with
sincerity and competence. Beyond them, they evidently remained timid and constrained.

Toward 1500, and for some decades afterward, there are a few
names or extant examples of French painting: Froment, of Avignon, active 1461–1476; Perréal, painter to Louis XI, fl. 1490, 1497;
Bourdichon, ca. 1484, 1508; Corneille, of Lyon, fl. ca. 1540; *François Clouet, the last and ablest of the family, ca. 1500–1572.

These somewhat hesitant tentatives, however, were more or
less overpowered by the example of Italians imported by Francis I, especially Primaticcio and Dell'Abbate of Bologna and
Rosso of Florence; temporarily also, Leonardo and Del Sarto.
This "school of Fontainebleau," however, disconcerted rather
than remodeled French painting. Most of the Italians were not
of the greatest themselves; they were supported by the court
rather than by public interest, which remained apathetic; and
French talent long continued to receive more spontaneous
recognition in Italy than Italian superior skill received in
France. The leading Frenchman to be influenced by Italy was
Cousin, 1500–1589, born near Sens, painter, sculptor, architect, glass painter, miniaturist. Others, later, were Dubreuil,
died 1604; Dubois, 1543–1614, a Fleming; and Fréminet, 1567–
1619. Antoine Lenain, 1568–1648, oldest and perhaps ablest of
a family of portrait and lower-class genre painters, stands somewhat apart.

So far, the Italian influence in France had produced neither
a definite French school, a good imitation of the Italian, nor a
great genius. It was only after 1600, when French painters went
of their own accord to Italy, drank deeply of its stimulus, but
remained French, that superior talent began to appear. There
is a notable group whose birth dates fall between 1590 and 1620.

It was initiated by Vouet, who studied under Caravaggio and Guido Reni, and who taught Lesueur, Lebrun, and De Lahyre. It includes Poussin and Claude, who spent respectively most and much of their adult life in Rome. Altogether it is probably the greatest group of painters France has produced, unless one chooses to except the nineteenth century. Lebrun has little to satisfy modern standards; but that he bent his talent to satisfy the taste of Louis XIV's court does not deprive him of talent— no more than Molière. It is true that the greatest of the group, Poussin and Claude, escaped from the presence of this court; but they were Frenchmen nevertheless, and fall within the group's period of concentration.

Incidentally, if we allow 30 to 50 as the normal age of originality, the births from 1590 to 1620 yield 1620 to 1670 as the span in which the new contributions of the group were made. Much the longer part of this art pulse, in other words, falls into the time of Louis XIII, Richelieu, and Mazarin; only a minor fragment of it into the majority of the Grand Monarch. As with literature, Louis XIV captured the renown of a productivity which largely preceded him.

The crest
*Vouet, 1590–1649.
Perrier, 1590–1656.
Callot, 1593–1635; of Nancy; engravings.
Louis Lenain, 1593–1648.
*Poussin, 1594–1665; b. Andelys, Normandy; in Italy 1624–1640, 1642–1665.

Blanchard, 1600–1638; Venetian-style rival of Vouet.
Le Valentin, 1600–1634.
*Claude Gelée (le Lorrain), 1600–1682.
Philippe de Champaigne, 1602–1674; born in Brussels.
Nicolas Mignard, 1605–1668.
Mathieu Lenain, 1607–1677.
De Lahyre, 1606–1656.
*Pierre Mignard, 1610–1695.
Dughet, 1613–1675; brother-in-law of Poussin.
Bourdon, 1616–1671.
*Lesueur, 1617–1655.
*Lebrun, 1619–1690.

Of the decline
  Lefèvre, 1633–1673.
  Van der Meulen, 1634–1690. Fleming, b. Brussels.
  Monnoyer, 1634–1693/9.
  De Lafosse, 1636–1716.
  Bon Boulogne, 1640–1670.
  Jouvenet, 1644–1717 (1646–1708).
  J. Parrocel, 1648–1704.
  Santerre, 1650–1717.
  Verdier, 1651–1730.
  Louis Boulogne, 1654–1733.
  Largilière, 1656–1746.
  Rigaud, 1659–1743.
  Martin, 1659–1735.
  Desportes, 1661–1743.
  A. Coypel, 1661–1722.

Some minor and provincial names, mostly from the culmination, are:

  Bosse (etcher) 1602–1676; H. and Ch. Beaubrun, 1603?–1677,
1604–1692; P. Patel, 1605?–1676; Errard, 1606–1689; Louis de
Boulogne, 1609–1674; Nocret, 1612–1672; L. and H. Testelin 1615–
1655, 1616–1675; Courtois (le Bourgignon), 1621–1676.
  Lyon: J. Stella, 1596–1657; Gérard Audran (engraver), 1640–
1703; Claude Audran (painter), d. 1684; *Touraine:* Mosnier, 1600–
1656; Vignon, 1590–1670; *Lorraine:* Deruet, d. 1642.

This French culmination in painting is almost exactly contemporaneous with the Spanish and Dutch; essentially so with
the Flemish—about two decades later, but mainly overlapping;
and corresponds in time with Guercino, Sassoferrato, Rosa,
and Dolci. With this Italian group at least it can certainly bear
comparison in quality. It is clear that good painting was more
international in this period than ever before. As compared
with 1500, only Germany had dropped out, while Spain and
Holland had come to participate, and Italy included Rome
and Naples instead of being limited to Tuscany-Lombardy-
Venice. In fact, painting about 1500 had flourished in a narrow
strip of Europe: essentially the ancient Lotharingia—from the
mouth of the Scheldt up the Rhine (including the Main to
Nürnberg) and in Italy barely to Rome. In 1640 all western

Europe painted with interest and success, except Germany which was through and England which had not begun. And in none of these West European nationalities was painting wholly a court art—not even in France, which was the most centralized: perhaps the very best French work was being done on Italian soil.

For the first time, then, with France participating on even terms, painting had become a nearly pan-West European institution. This is evidenced also by the simultaneous rise of landscape *per se* as a subject: Claude, born 1600, Rosa 1615, Ruysdael 1628, Hobbema 1638. At the same time, what is called a healthy nationalism was much more active than any conscious international attitude. Rubens and Velásquez, Rembrandt and Poussin, influenced each other scarcely at all. Only between France and Italy, and more distantly between Belgium and Italy, were there relations.

The resolution of the antithesis of contemporary internationalism and separatist nationalism seems to be this: Italian painting was the great painting of Occidental civilization. When it rushed to its splendid climax in 1500 and the next few decades, it stamped itself on all Europe. It killed German painting; staggered Belgian; and almost swamped the struggling French art. Both these last had to recover themselves and find a national basis before they throve again; and Dutch and Spanish painting were born precisely through the act of filtering themselves clear of the Italian influence; without which, on the other hand, they would presumably never have been conceived.

With this underlying interrelationship, it is not strange that the several growths also died simultaneously—ended their main phase about 1670 or 1680, and became extinct a generation later. Spain and Holland, which were definitely epigonal to Italy, finished completely then. So did the Flemings, who had begun independently of Italy but had entered their culmination only after a half century of Italian influence. Italy herself was well on the downgrade in 1640–1650—since a full century, in fact, she had been traveling on momentum of the past. By

1700, she too was finished. Thereafter she produced only the eighteenth-century Tiepolo-Canaletto school of Venice, which is stylistically fairly far from the Renaissance, and includable only because the amplitude of the Italian growth is great enough to take it in. This leaves only France. And France was ready to go on after 1710. Here, then, is evidently a phenomenon of another kind.

What seems to have happened is that, early in the eighteenth century, France attempted to find, and essentially succeeded in finding, a level of permanent, established, relatively conscious civilization. One element of this was enlightenment as an aim; another was stability; another, limitation. The sort of impulses that had produced Gothic cathedrals, pre-Raphaelite painting, Elizabethan drama, spontaneous growths out of nothing, were renounced. Change there was to be; indeed must be, for savor and piquancy; but it was the change of mode in a court or metropolis. And every enlightened or gracious activity was to go on: there was an accorded place for it, whether it were science, painting, sculpture, music, opera, poetry, or prose. Only, none of them attempted to soar to the sky. What underlay this new attitude, it is difficult to say; but it originated chiefly in France and was more or less adopted in the rest of western Europe. Evidently the French under Louis XIV had a sense of having themselves attained to something, rather than of something having happened to them; and this they set out to keep. But what they aimed to keep was not so much the attainments as the activities which had led to attainment. Continued novelty of some sort therefore was an essential in the new program; and Byzantinism was successfully avoided.[4]

Such a point of view in a civilization must make for continuity rather than great pulsations. It must be exceedingly favorable to talent; it may cramp genius. It is a commonplace that such is the aim of French civilization in the past two hundred years. Even the earthshakings of Napoleon and Hugo were but a titans' revolt, after which the rule of the talented gods went

---

[4] It is from this time on, in the beginning of the eighteenth century, that the modern urban attitude seems to date, of thinking of oneself as belonging to a period rather than an area, according to the significant distinction of Tarde.

on. It is, I believe, evidence of the depth of the forces making for pulsation that the French, with all their intent and setup to the contrary, were nevertheless unable wholly to avoid experiencing pulsations. And yet, they smoothed them down remarkably. The profile of accomplishments in French literature, music, sculpture, as well as painting, since 1700, is one of continuous undulations rather than of sharp valleys and crests.

In painting, after the undistinctive decline from the culmination of 1620–1670 to the later years of Louis XIV, the Watteau-Boucher-Fragonard tradition sets in as characteristic of Rococo after about 1710. But alongside it there are painters of the bourgeois like Chardin and Greuze; representatives of the *grande peinture* like Van Loo; and a series of portraitists. Then follow the Classicists, anticipated by Vien and headed by David. After a generation, Gros and Ingres vacillate; and after another decade or two, Géricault and Delacroix initiate the Romantic school. This last happens to coincide with a real pulse: a cluster of men born, the most notable, between 1790 and 1830, the remainder until 1850. But here again there is enormous diversity: Vernet, Corot, Rousseau, Millet, Meissonier for instance. The common factor of "Romanticism" is not so much anything positive as a being different from Davidian Classicism. Soon after 1830 begin the births of the founders of the Impressionist or Luminarist school, Manet and Monet. Contemporary with them, however, are late-comers in the Romantic manner, like Carolus-Duran and Bastien-Lepage. It looks therefore as if Impressionism, although undoubtedly novel in its aims, represented, historically, a phase of the 1820–1880 culmination, and not a separate pulse.

In fact, it seems that there was not even a minor culmination in French painting between the early Louis XIV culmination and that of the nineteenth century, although for the intervening hundred and fifty years France produced enough painters of ability to lead and influence Europe. Since 1700, every notable new movement in the art has emanated from France.

Apart from subject matter, the most distinctive feature of Watteau and the Rococo style was its deliberate breaking down of line. To be sure, the purely linear type of painting began to end with Raphael's and Titian's later work, at the peak of the Renaissance. And certainly Velásquez and especially Rembrandt went much farther. But however much they subordinated or merged line, it always remained at least implicit. Watteau, however, destroyed line as incompatible with his aims, replacing it by his characteristic fuzzy, textile-tatter effect. The same manner promptly appeared in the two nations which in his day were still painting successfully: Italy in the last rays of its Renaissance sun, and England in its newly born art. This in spite of the fact that Canaletto and Guardi did Venetian canals, and Gainsborough, portraits. All of them were born after Watteau.

Similarly, David led the Classic movement for Europe, Géricault and Delacroix the Romantic,[5] Manet the Impressionist. Paris had become the place in which a young painter learned his art—as it still is.

To summarize, France has produced worthwhile painting without interruption since 1450, rising twice to definite culminations, each with its greatest men grouped, by their births, into a span of thirty to forty years. The one crest is early or pre-Louis XIV, the other immediately post-Napoleonic. Both crests coincide pretty closely in time with crests in other activities. On the whole, however, France, in comparison with other European countries, has the history of her painting, like that of her other arts, marked more by continuity than by swells. She painted for nearly two centuries without notable results: partly under Flemish and then Italian influence, partly in her own, hard, sincere, modest manner. This long training contrasts vividly with the suddenness of the onset of the art in Italy, Belgium, Holland, and England, as Giotto, Van Eyck, Hals, and Reynolds testify. But, except for Italy, and in a measure Belgium, the others, and likewise Spain and Germany, had their brief day of glory and were done; whereas France went on. Indeed, at the very moment when her Louis XIV

---

[5] Subject to the qualification of German essential synchronism, as mentioned above, and literal precedence, as discussed below.

culmination ended, she assumed the leadership of European painting and maintained it—to, and through, and beyond her second culmination, until today.

In Occidental painting, accordingly, Italy held the lead from the beginnings until past 1600, say 1610 or 1620. Then followed a scant century in which a number of nations rivaled one another in fairly even balance. Thereafter, from about 1710 on, the superiority as well as the dominant influence belonged to France. It may be questioned whether the period of Italian supremacy with Leonardo, Titian, Raphael, or the time of international balance between Rubens, Rembrandt, Poussin, and Velásquez, is to be accorded primacy. But the world has never been seriously in doubt that both these periods produced greater painters than the two centuries of French leadership, even during the nineteenth-century culmination. After all, the hegemony of France was initiated under Watteau; and, in the widest perspective, it began only in the afternoon of the day of the art.

FRENCH PAINTERS SINCE 1710

Rococo

Gillot, 1673–1717, master of Watteau.
Raoux, 1677–1737.
Watteau, 1684–1721.
Lancret, 1690–1743.

Pater, 1695–1736.
Natoire, 1700–1777.
Boucher, 1703–1770.
Fragonard, 1737–1806.

Bourgeois subjects

Chardin, 1699–1779.
Jeaurat, 1699–1781.

De la Porte, 1724–1793.
Greuze, 1725–1805.

Portraitists

Tournières, 1668–1752.
Grimou, 1680–1740.
J. B. van Loo, 1684–1745.
Nattier, 1685–1766.
Tocqué, 1696–1772.

H. Drouais, 1699–1767.
De Latour, 1704–1788, pastels.
Duplessis, 1725–1802.
F. Drouais, 1727–1775, son.

Landscape

J. Vernet, 1714–1789.

Lantara, 1739–1778.

Grande peinture, battles, etc.

De Troy, 1679–1752.
Lemoyne, 1688–1757.
Ch. Parrocel, 1688–1752.

N. Coypel, 1692–1734.
Lépicié, fl. 1765, d. 1784.
C. van Loo, 1705–1765.

Grande peinture, battles, etc. (Continued)

A. van Loo, 1718–1785+.   Le Prince, 1733–1781.
Casanova, 1730–1805.

"Classicists"

Vien, 1716–1809.   Prud'hon, 1758–1823.
Lagrenée, 1724–1805.   Lethière, 1760–1832.
Doyen, 1726–1806.   G. Drouais, 1763–1788.
Robert, 1733–1808.   Girodet, 1767–1824.
De Marne, 1744–1829.   Isabey, 1767–1855.
Vincent, 1746–1816.   Gérard, 1770–1837.
David, 1748–1825.   Gros, 1771–1835.
Valenciennes, 1750–1819.   Guérin, 1774–1833.
Regnault, 1754–1829.   Ingres, 1780–1867.
Vigée-Lebrun, 1755–1842.

"Romantics," born before 1830

Sigalon, 1788–1837.   Millet, 1814–1875.
H. Vernet, 1789–1863.   Chintreuil, 1814/16–1873.
Géricault, 1791–1824.   Meissonier, 1815–1891.
Robert, 1794/5–1835, Swiss.   Daubigny, 1817–1878.
Scheffer, 1795/7–1857/8,   Chassériau, 1819–1856.
   Dutch.   Courbet, 1819–1877.
Corot, 1796–1875.   Frère, 1819–1886.
Delaroche, 1797–1856.   Fromentin, 1820–1876.
Fleury, 1797–1830.   Rosa Bonheur, 1822–1899.
Delacroix, 1798–1863.   Cabanel, 1823–1889.
Decamps, 1803–1860.   Gérôme, 1824–1904.
Huet, 1804–1868/9.   Puvis de Chavannes, 1824–
E. Isabey, 1803/4–1886.   1898.
Diaz, 1808–1876, Spanish   Bouguereau, 1825–1905.
   ancestry.   Moreau, 1826–1898.
Daumier, 1808–1879.   Maillot, 1826–1888.
Flandrin, 1809–1864.   Breton, 1827–1906.
Troyon, 1810–1865.   Baudry, 1828–1886.
Marilhat, 1811–1847.   Stevens, 1828–1906, Belgian.
Dupré, 1811–1889.   Henner, 1829–1905.
Rousseau, 1812–1867.

Later "Romantics," born after 1830

Doré, b. 1832.   Constant, 1845.
Bonnat, 1833.   Bastien-Lepage, 1848.
De Neuville, 1836.   Gauguin, 1848.
Carolus-Duran, 1837.   Detaille, 1848.
Regnault, 1843.   Dagnan-Bouveret, 1852.
Lhermitte, 1844.

Impressionists, etc.

Pissarro, b. 1830.
Manet, 1832.
Degas, 1834.
Fantin-Latour, 1836.
Sisley, 1839.

Cézanne, 1839.
Monet, 1840.
Renoir, 1841.
Mary Cassatt, 1843, American.

Later

Van Gogh, 1853, Dutch.
Seurat, 1859.
Toulouse-Lautrec, 1864.

Matisse, 1869.
Picasso, 1881, Spaniard.

§57. Spanish Painting

The history of Spanish painting has a simple profile. It begins humbly by 1450, perhaps soon after 1400, under Flemish and Italian tutelage, leans increasingly on Italy, begins to produce respectably by 1550, continues to train itself in Italy until about 1600 when it attains independence and maturity culminates from 1620 to 1660, falls off rapidly till 1690, and then is dead. Goya, a century later, is a brilliant comet without an orbit, and Spanish participation in nineteenth-century European painting is secondary and late.

The one great period of Spanish painting is an obvious part of the general effervescence of Spanish nationality; but, with sculpture, is the last activity to culminate within that growth. It is almost exactly synchronous with the seventeenth-century climaxes of painting in France, Belgium, and Holland. These also derived largely from Italy, which at the time had probably been surpassed and certainly equaled by them, though it still enjoyed the prestige of the preëminence which it had once indisputably held. Belgium and Holland, like Spain, lost their great art by about 1700, whereas France at the same time prepared to enter into a second, more or less continuous phase of productivity. German painting was over and English had not yet begun when Spanish flourished.

A double relation thus characterizes Spain's peak in painting. On the one hand, it fits into the configuration of the general Spanish national climax; on the other, into that definite

Baroque phase of European art which occurred when painting, having passed its European climax in Italy of the High Renaissance, broke, almost a century later, into a series of concurrent national climaxes.

Provincially, three foci are recognizable in the Spanish growth. Perhaps the earliest, and certainly the least national, was that of Valencia and Barcelona, in other words, east Spain, or the urban centers of the kingdom of Aragon with its old dynastic relations to Sicily-Naples. Valencia was the real seat of the school, and Italy remained its training ground. The Valencian master whose life falls into the period of greatness of Spanish painting, Ribera, left Spain to live in Naples just as the national culmination commenced.

The real Iberian focus was Andalusia, and especially its greatest city, Seville, which had been Christian and Castilian for two centuries (since 1248) when we can trace the first beginnings of Spanish painting, and for four centuries when this painting reached its crest. In Seville a definite and progressing school flourished from about 1540 on, which produced Roelas, Herrera, Zurbarán, Velásquez, and Murillo, and maintained itself successfully even after national life centered increasingly in Madrid.

The so-called Castilian school was not really such: it lacked a focus. Toledo was prominent, and so was Madrid later on account of the court. But of the greater names, Coello was probably a Portuguese in origin, Theotocopuli a Greek, Velásquez a Sevillian; and of their predecessors, Berruguete and Morales were connected with Valladolid and Badajoz.

I add the principal Portuguese names. They are neither important nor well-concentrated, but suggest a grouping centering somewhat earlier than that of Spain, in line with the respective national crests of the two countries.

Valencia-Catalan: Valencia unless otherwise stated
    Iacomart, ca. 1410–1464. Flemish and Italian style.
    Dalmán, 1428–1481?, fl. 1445? Catalan? Barcelona? Valencia?
       School of Van Eyck.
    Vergos, d. 1495. Barcelona.

Vermejo, active ca. 1500. Andalusian, of Cordova, at Barcelona.

*Juanes, 1507/23–1579. Studied in Italy.

*Francisco de Ribalta, 1551/5–1628. Studied in Italy.

*Ribera ("Spagnoletto"), ca. 1588–1656. Pupil of Ribalta; in Naples after 1616.

Juan de Ribalta, 1597–1628. Son.

Espinosa, 1600–1680. Pupil of Ribalta and studied in Italy.

Andalusia: Seville unless otherwise stated

Machuca (Granada), Castro, Merzal, Borgona, Núñez, Fernández, Guadalupe, active ca. 1440–1530.

Vargas, ca. 1502–1567/8, studied in Italy, introduced oil, "founder" of Seville school.

Pedro Campaña (Pieter de Kempeneer), b. ca. 1503 in Brussels, studied in Italy, to Seville before 1548.

Becerra, 1520–1570, Andalusian (Granada?), worked in Castile. Studied in Italy.

Céspedes, 1538–1608, of Cordova, studied in Italy.

*Roelas, 1558/60–1625. Style based on Tintoretto.

Pacheco, 1571–1654. Teacher and father-in-law of Velásquez.

*Herrera el Viejo, 1576–1656.

Juan del Castillo, 1584–1640. Teacher of Murillo.

*Zurbarán, 1598–1662/4. Pupil of Roelas.

*Velásquez, 1599–1660. To Madrid 1623.

*Cano, 1601–1667, of Granada. Sculptor and architect also.

Antonio del Castillo, 1602/3–1656/67. Battle painter.

Moya, 1610–1660/66, of Granada. Pupil of Van Dyck in England.

Gómez, ca. 1617–ca. 1690. Assistant of Murillo.

*Murillo, 1618–1682. At Madrid 1642–1645.

Herrera el Mozo, 1622–1685. Son: to Italy; to Seville on father's death; to Madrid 1661.

Valdés Leal, 1630–1691.

Palomino, 1653–1726. Pupil of Leal; historian of art.

Tobar, 1678–1758.

Castile: Toledo, Madrid, etc.

Rincón, 1446–1500. Toledo.

Pedro Berruguete, d. 1500/06. Flemish and Italian style.

*Alonso Berruguete, ca. 1480–1561. Studied in Italy; to Valladolid 1520.

*Morales, 1509/10–1586. Badajoz and Toledo.

*Sánchez Coello, ca. 1515 (1531)–1588/90. Probably Portuguese (Santez Coelho).

*Navarrete (El Mudo), 1526–1579. Studied in Italy, probably with Titian.

*Theotocopuli (El Greco), 1547/8–1625. Born Crete; to Venice; in 1570 at Rome; by 1577 at Toledo.

Pantoja de la Cruz, 1551–1609. Pupil of Coello.

Cuevas, 1568–1635.

Tristán, 1586–1640. Follower of El Greco.

Collantes, 1599–1669. Landscapes.

*Velásquez, 1599–1660. Born and trained in Seville, to Madrid 1623. To Italy 1629–1630, 1649–1651.

Mazo, 1602/15–1667. Madrid. Pupil and son-in-law of Velásquez.

Pareja, 1606–1670. Follower of Velásquez.

Juan de Toledo, 1611–1665. Madrid.

Carreño de Miranda, 1614–1685. Velásquez influence.

Arellano, 1614–1676.

Cerezo, 1635–1673/75/85. Madrid.

Claudio Coello, 1623/24/30/35–1693. Madrid.

Portugal

Vuno Gonçalves, active 1450–1471.

Vasco Fernandes, act. 1506/12–1541/3.

Francisco de Olanda, act. 1549.

Santez Coelho, act. ca. 1550–1590. (See Castile.)

Vasco Pereyra, act. 1588.

José d'Alvelar, act. 1639–1656.

Diego Pereira, d. 1658+.

The thoroughness of the collapse is proverbial, and rivals that of Dutch painting. As in Holland, the great men died all at once. Around 1625 the older generation had gone: Roelas, El Greco, Ribalta. Thirty to forty years later, from 1656 to 1667, died Ribera, Herrera, Velásquez, Zurbarán, Cano. Only Murillo remained, till 1682; and by about 1690 his lesser successors were being buried. After 1700, foreigners painted at the court.

Goya, 1746–1828, is an inexplicable phenomenon. Enough erratics like him would wreck the point of view underlying my approach in this volume. However, Goya is isolated in manner as well as in time, place, and genius. A contemporary, friend, and fellow student of David in Italy, he painted like a modern instead of a neoclassicist. The case is the more strange because, in general estimation today, Goya was perhaps the greatest European painter of his day.

Modern Spanish painting, like every other, is of course part of an international movement. It comes rather late, roughly fin-de-siècle instead of mid-nineteenth century.

Fortuny, b. 1838.	Zuloaga, 1870.
Sorolla, 1862.	Picasso, 1881. To Paris.

§58. English Painting

About 1670, says Spengler, there occurred the definitive victory of music over painting in Occidental culture. Granted, with the inevitable qualifications, the substantial truth of this statement, it is nevertheless open to one flat contradiction of history. England, which had a real music until 1700, has had none since; and, ·wholly without a painter's art before, began to produce her one notable lineage of painters in the eighteenth century.

The case of England shows that a great culture, or a nation carrying a worthwhile share of a great international civilization, can go indefinitely long without achievement in particular activities. Apart from some meager mediaeval sculpture— and this much less distinctive than the associated architecture— England managed to get on very comfortably for century after century without any representative art. A picture was a likeness; and so rudimentary were English tastes that for a long time the only likenesses that interested them were likenesses of themselves. There was an aristocracy able to pay; and Holbein, then Rubens and Van Dyke, still later Lely and Kneller, made their living from it. They did not, in these hundred and fifty years, stimulate many native efforts; nor did Englishmen go to the Netherlands or Italy to learn. One bought portraits of himself from foreigners as under the Stuarts one began occasionally to collect pictures, and from the eighteenth century on one imported musicians: Handel, Gluck, Weber. Lely's and Kneller's parallel careers illustrate the status of painting and the contemporary orientation of these societies. Both men were born in Germany, professionally shaped in Holland, knighted in England.

How lacking England was in sense for what painting really is, is shown by the fact that Hogarth, 1697–1764, a satirist illustrator, still often passes as the father of English painting. An individual of high originality and verve, he was about as remote from a tradition of what painting aims at as Dickens was from being a poet. He is the ancestor of Cruikshank and Tenniel rather than of Gainsborough and Turner.

English art painting formally began in 1752 when Reynolds returned from Italy at the age of twenty-nine and became fashionable for his portraits. It is the only national school in Europe that began with portraiture and kept its strength therein. The other great figure, Gainsborough, born 1727, is almost contemporary; so is Romney, 1734. A generation later, but in the same vein, come Raeburn the Scot, born 1756, Hoppner, 1759, Lawrence, 1769, in the last of whom a certain facile if still charming meretriciousness gives evidence that the movement had already become decadent. The activities, of course, run thirty to sixty years later than these birth dates.

Landscape, the other forte of English painting, came up mainly as portraiture went down. The one earlier figure is Wilson, 1714–1782, who painted Italian landscapes after Poussin, Claude, and Rosa. The more original artists are Crome, born 1768/9, Turner, 1775, Constable, 1776. Of these the most purely native in manner, Crome, is also considered the least. Constable painted somewhat in the manner of Hobbema, Turner frankly in competition with that of Claude. These resurrections across the Channel after a hundred and a hundred and fifty years are a strange phenomenon. They suggest that English art at its best was by no means nourishingly rooted in a soil of English tradition. At that, Constable and Turner were men of genius—the latter dazzlingly if theatrically so—and with Reynolds and Gainsborough constitute a fairly brilliant constellation. Its period of activity was about ninety years: from shortly after 1750 to somewhat before 1850.

For Turner this must also be said: he was the only British artist who penetrated successfully into the realm of imagination, one of the few who even ventured beyond the visibly real.

Also, he embodies the strange contradiction of expressing the feelings of Claude with the technique of the Impressionists, and is thus at once a resurrection and an anticipation. If he is the greatest figure of the English configuration, as seems probable, he thus reveals a certain artificiality or stimulated quality, a shallowness of rooting in time and native soil, as characteristic of this English growth.

Within the period 1750–1840 there also fall the best of the rather mediocre British genre painters, Morland, born 1763, and Wilkie, 1785—the latter, with Ramsay and Raeburn, of interest as one expression of a Scotch florescence which showed itself in several other cultural activities of the time.

The Pre-Raphaelites—Hunt, born 1827, Rossetti, 1828, Millais, 1829—with Watts, 1818, and Burne-Jones, 1833, fall outside the greater English period. In spite of sincerity, much feeling, and some skill, they could not shake off mannerisms of subject and treatment. The group is separately constellated in its birth dates, but was beginning to produce as the older group ended, and so must be considered a pulse within the one larger British growth. It is also of interest to compare these men with their exact French contemporaries. The Frenchmen originated new manners; the English, new themes.

How weak the molding influences of English art tradition were at best, is shown by the eccentric products and careers of Fuseli, born 1741; Blake, 1757; and Haydon, 1786—from whom, incidentally, the career of Turner differed more in its success than in balance. In Italy, Spain, France, or the Netherlands these men would either have been channeled into becoming successful painters, or would not have been rated as artists. Blake was a genius who achieved remarkable poetry as by-product to designs which are a hybrid of painting, engraving, and illustration, and which mix noble lines with ineptness and banal platitudes in a manner suggesting that Blake himself did not feel the difference. Like most English painters, but to an exaggerated degree, he had his subjects looming larger in his consciousness than his expression of them: a condition perhaps least unfavorable to pure portraiture.

Earlier American painting is an adjunct to British. Copley and West were portraitists, of the generation of Gainsborough and Romney, who spent most of their adult lives in England. West succeeded Reynolds as president of the Royal Academy. Stuart, who stayed in America, was a portraitist of the generation of Raeburn and Hoppner. It is of interest that the portrait tendency showed itself in America almost as early as in Great Britain. Copley and West quite fitted into the English school, but hardly got their start from Reynolds: they came too soon after him.

A century later, Whistler and Sargent also settled in England from America, though they were not English in tradition.

THE ENGLISH LIST

(Lely, 1618–1680. Born Van der Faes in Westphalia, trained in Haarlem, to England 1641.)

(Kneller, 1646–1723, b. in Lübeck, studied in Amsterdam, to England 1675.)

Thornhill, 1676–1734.

*Hogarth, 1697–1764.

Portraitists

Ramsay, 1713–1784. Scotch.

*Reynolds, 1723–1792.

*Gainsborough, 1727–1788.

Romney, 1734–1782.

Copley, 1737–1815. American, to England.

West, 1738–1820. American, to England.

Stuart, 1755–1828. American, trained in Scotland and by West.

Raeburn, 1756–1823. Scotch.

Hoppner, 1759–1810.

Lawrence, 1769–1830.

Landscapists

Wilson, 1714–1782.

John Crome, 1768/9–1821.

*Turner, 1775–1851.

*Constable, 1776–1837.

Cotman, 1782–1842.

Genre

Morland, 1763–1804.

Wilkie, 1785–1841. Scotch.

Landseer, 1802–1873.

Eccentric
  Fuseli, 1741–1825. Swiss from Zurich.
  Blake, 1757–1827.
  Haydon, 1786–1846.
Pre-Raphaelite, etc.
  Watts, 1818–1904.
  Ford Madox Brown, 1821–1893.
  Hunt, 1827–1910.
  Rossetti, 1828–1882. Italian, b. England.
  Millais, 1829–1896.
  Burne-Jones, 1833–1898.
Expatriate Americans
  Whistler, b. 1834.
  Abbey, 1852.
  Sargent, 1856.

§59. Nineteenth-Century Painting in Marginal Countries

As in sculpture, literature, music, and science, so in Occidental painting: a number of countries began for the first time to participate successfully during the nineteenth century. Many of these growths were connected with a revived national self-consciousness; but this in turn implied the acceptance of an international standard of civilization. However locally colored or patriotically motivated, therefore, these national schools ran more or less parallel and contained common elements. One of these elements, generally, was the setting up of the work of the country then predominant in painting, namely France, as a standard. Now as French painting entered a new phase, its "Romantic Revolt," with élan about 1820, it would be expectable that the other nationalities, especially the newcomers, would take their inspiration from this phase, and follow it in time. One or the other of these things, and often both, did actually happen.

It seems desirable, accordingly, to review these nineteenth-century developments comparatively, for countries which have, as well as those which have not, a previous recognized history of painting.

France.—As already shown, the new movement began with men born following 1790, and its greatest achievements were from men born by 1830, although the growth continued after them.

Germany.—The German movement is a little earlier than the French. This is surprising in view of the undoubted superiority of French painting both before and after the "Romantic" revolution. But the dates all run one way: Cornelius born 1783, Overbeck and Schadow 1789, Veit 1793, Schnorr 1794, as against Géricault 1791 and Delacroix 1798. Similarly, Géricault's "Raft of the Medusa," which is considered as inaugurating the Romantic school, was exhibited in 1819; but the German "Nazarene" group was forming in Rome soon after 1810, was doing fresco in the Prussian consulate in 1816, and Cornelius was back in Munich with official status in 1819. Two interpretations are possible.

First, the dates can be accepted at face value, and priority be accorded the Germans, the new movement, however, becoming of international significance only when the French, the recognized leaders of European painting, took it up a few years later. In other words, in French and international opinion, events did not happen until they happened in Paris; and with some measure of truth. In support of this interpretation is the fact that the poetic and dramatic "revolution" of which Hugo is the symbol occurred in France something like forty years after its counterpart in Germany; and somewhat similarly in music.

Second, a claim might be made that the German priority was more apparent than real, owing to the French inclination to recognize traditions and overturns. Up to 1819, David's Classicist school was dominant. In that year, its authority was challenged, and an art quarrel became the talk of Paris and the civilized world. However, the change had for some time been preparing. Gros, born in 1771, and Ingres, 1780, while conventionally counted as members of the Classic school, are admitted not really to form part of it, but to be in some ways Romantic precursors. With them reclassified in the new movement, the priority of birth dates would go to France. In other words, there was no room in France for a group of obscure aspiring young men to reform art by silently launching a pietistic revival in Rome. One school or party was in power until another overthrew it, as it were, by an interpellation or barricades. The date of the challenge, if successful, marked the new regime, irrespective of how long the overturn had been preparing.

I shall not try to assign superior weight to one or the other of these interpretations. They are not essentially in conflict.

In any event, however, the early "Romantic" Germans were not the best painters of the movement which they initiated. Its peak came a generation later, with Menzel, Boecklin, Lenbach, born 1815–1836. This fact puts at any rate the center of gravity of nineteenth-century German art definitely later than that of French.

England.—The Pre-Raphaelite cluster closely parallels the German Nazarenes, in group program and brotherhood sense, in religious feeling, and in cult of fifteenth-century Italian art. The English seem, however, to have come to their attitudes independently, without having been influenced by the Germans; and their time was a full generation later. Ford Madox Brown, Hunt, Rossetti, Millais, Burne-Jones were born from 1821 to 1833. Watts, who was perhaps the leading English painter of his day outside the school, was born in 1818. His synchronism makes 1815–1835 the significant birth period of English painters of the century, the Pre-Raphaelitism of the majority remaining rather an incident, from a larger historic point of view.

Belgium.—This little country also had its renaissance. In fact, it was one of the earliest in Europe, treading close on the heels of those of Germany and France—about a decade after the latter, and of the same duration, 1800–1840 for births, or 1830–1890 for the productive period. This meant that the older men were nearly thirty when Belgium became independent. The historians recognize in their work the persistence of some old Flemish traits, but on the whole its character is modern, of course.

Wappers, 1803.
Wiertz, 1806.
Gallait, 1810.
Leys, 1815.
De Groux, 1825.

Alfred Stevens, 1828; to
    France.
Alma-Tadema, 1836; to
    England.
Henri de Brackeleer, 1840.

Holland.—The sister country underwent a similar renaissance, beginning about two decades later, and briefer.

(Ary Scheffer, 1795; to France.)
Jongkind, 1819; pre-Impressionist; to France.
Joseph Israels, 1824; Jew.
Mauve, 1838.
The three Maris, 1837–1839.
Van Gogh, 1853; to France.

Austria.—Makart, b. 1840 in Salzburg, is the outstanding figure, if one chooses to detach him from the Germans.

Hungary.—Munkácsy, 1844, is Makart's Hungarian counterpart.

Russia.—Of a number of Russians, Verestchagin, 1842, is easily the best known in Europe, whether through merit or choice of subjects.

Sweden.—Zorn, 1860, has become the most widely known, and therefore probably represents rather fairly such crest as there was.

Italy.—Segantini, 1858, is the representative of modern Italian art most often chosen as illustrative in the books.

Spain.—Fortuny, 1838, French-inspired, is most often mentioned in the books, but Sorolla, 1862, Zuloaga, 1870, Picasso, 1881, seem to form a cluster—the last constellation to arise in Europe.

Mexico.—Orozco, 1883, and Rivera, 1886, mark the latest of all groups yet over the horizon. With all discount for enthusiasm which their work has aroused on account of nonaesthetic propaganda in some of its subject matter, there can be no question of their representing, with their contemporaries,[6] a genuine growth.

---

[6] Orozco, born 1883; Goitia, 1884; Montenegro, 1885; Rivera, 1886; Atl, 1887; Rodríguez Lozano, 1896; Ruiz, 1897; Siqueiros, 1898; and others since 1900.

United States.—Second-rate as North American painting has generally been rated, it is nevertheless of some interest because its brief history shows at least two or possibly three pulses.

The first is that of a series of men most of whom were born in the Colonies and went to England, or, a little later, were British-born but settled in America. This "American" growth is therefore still essentially English.

Copley, 1737; to England.
West, 1738; to England.
Peale, 1741; pupil of both.
Stuart, 1755; American, British-trained, returned to America.
Trumbull, 1756.
Jarvis, 1780; Englishman, to America.
Sully, 1783; same.

The last two are somewhat lesser lights. Without them, the births all fall within two decades.

Then follows a long, barren period, with only the inventor of the telegraph, Samuel Morse, 1791, and the German immigrant Leutze, 1816.

The second growth is that of Americans born between 1825 and 1856. The dates fall into two clusters, with a dozen nearly empty years between. This gap is too short to be of certain significance; but it may have meaning, since the men before it average probably higher in ability than those after.

Inness, 1825.	Chase, 1849.
Whistler, 1834.	Abbey, 1852.
La Farge, 1835.	Brush, 1855.
Vedder, 1836.	Sargent, 1856. B. Florence.
Homer, 1836.	Alexander, 1856.
Mary Cassatt, 1843.	Cox, 1856.

Whistler, Sargent, and Abbey went to Europe to live, but they went to a more congenial atmosphere, not as provincials forced to migrate to the metropolis for a career. Cassatt similarly identified herself with France and was accepted there.

Since these groups were born, more than eighty years have passed. Many more Americans have painted since than were at work then; yet not one American painter has arisen, in the forty or fifty years available for him to come to maturity, who is generally rated the equal of at least several of the men in the list. There can be little doubt, accordingly, that Inness, Whistler, and Sargent represent, however modestly in comparison with the great of Europe, a true culmination, and that since them American art has been in a qualitative depression.

Comparison.—When now we draw the threads together, a plan eventuates as follows, in terms of *birth dates*[7] of the men who mark the several national peaks.

1790–1830, France (continuing with less force for another generation).
1800–1840, Belgium.
1815–1840, Holland, Germany, England (the German movement perhaps began before the French, but certainly culminated later).
1825–1855, United States.
1840–1850, Austria, Hungary, Russia.
1855–1865, Sweden, Italy.
1860–1880, Spain.
1880– ——, Mexico.

In short, France led, Belgium followed on her heels; then came the three Germanic nations Holland, Germany, England. The United States, without being in the least Pre-Raphaelite, followed England much as Belgium did France. Then came the turn of the central and east European nations, Austria, Hungary, Russia; still later, the extreme north and south of Europe, Scandinavia and Italy, one probably retarded because of lack of tradition and the other because of lingering presence of an old established one. Last of all in Europe came Spain, resistive as usual to modernization; and following this, much as the United States followed England, Mexico. The pattern is one of radiation from center to peripheries. What is chiefly of interest is that it was a quickening of artistic productivity that spread, irrespective, on the whole, of the content or style of the art.

———
[7] Birth dates give the sharper definition, because one man is at his zenith at 30, another at 50, and both are likely to be at the height of their repute at 70, if they live till then. For the period of productivity, 30 to 50 years can be added. Thus, Belgium, births 1800–1840 = florescence 1830–1890.

§60. The Occident as a Whole

The following pages aim to express the configurative story of painting for Occidental civilization as a whole. Many of the ideas have of necessity been set forth already in connection with national developments and relations. At the cost of some repetitions, it seems desirable to outline as well the total or pan-European growth as a composite unit.

Painting in Europe arose later than sculpture as an autonomous and competent art. Roughly speaking, the whole Mediaeval or Gothic phase was absent. The growth began in Italy, and was essentially a Renaissance one—Renaissance-Baroque-Rococo—plus a nineteenth-century counterswing episode of Romanticism. The Middle Ages produced chiefly church windows and book illuminations, plus apparently some crude frescos. However important these may have been as a foundation for painting—like ceramic decoration in Greece,—they were not a full painter's art in our sense.

It is true that Duccio and Giotto worked around 1300, when Gothic sculpture was only just beginning to pass its very highest point. Nevertheless the transalpine sculpture of that day was the end product of a development then more than two hundred years old; the Italian painting, the beginning of a two-hundred-year upgrowth. That it was genuinely a beginning is shown by the fact that it is still obscure what Giottesque art developed out of. Its Byzantine strains, while no doubt actual, are rather tenuous and do not suffice to explain the phenomenon. Of course one of the lessons of history is that the birth of a new pattern system is among the things which, broadly speaking, it never does succeed in demonstrating the reasons for. Granted this generalization—and it seems substantial even though it appear dogmatic,—the difficulty which historians have had in "accounting" for Giotto is due precisely to his marking the inception of a new pattern system.

It is true that Giotto is still very mediaeval as compared with his successors a century later. Every European of 1300 was

necessarily mediaeval. Dante expressed certain aspects of mediaeval civilization better than anyone else. But he is also the
initiator of the Renaissance growth of Italian literature. Both
men were of their day. But they were also Italians; and because
the mediaeval culture system rested lightly on Italy—lightly
and with constant encountering of resistance—and Italy was
therefore quickly able to shake off mediaeval patterns and
evolve the more congenial Renaissance ones as a substitute,
Giotto and Dante can and must be reckoned among the founders of the Renaissance growth. Across the Alps, on the contrary,
mediaevalism was felt as a positive achievement, not as a fetter,
and hence two centuries later France and Germany and England and Spain were still struggling to extricate themselves
from Gothicism. With all his technical advance and personal
greatness Dürer is still far more mediaeval than Giotto in many
aspects of subject, type of feeling preoccupation, and pattern
mannerism. He never really achieved the cardinal Renaissance
virtue of direct simplicity; and this is already strong in Giotto.

For these reasons, then, we may count Giotto into the
Renaissance growth, and have this, and therewith true painting
in Europe, begin with his immediate predecessors of 1250–
1300. I say "Renaissance growth," which is defined primarily
by certain phenomena in space and time and secondarily by
phenomena of content or direction, as distinct from "Renaissance," where the emphasis is on direction and quality with
the space-time delimitation only incidental. They are overlapping but distinct concepts. If one wishes to make the Renaissance proper begin with Masaccio in painting as with Ghiberti
in sculpture, soon after 1400, that is no doubt correct enough;
but reference is then to something else than the culture-growth
configurations which we are here trying to trace.

There is one other origin of painting in Europe: about the
lower Rhine. Originating possibly in Cologne by 1350, it rose
to genuine achievement in the Netherlands with Van Eyck and
his successors, from about 1400 on, and, spreading up the river
through southwest Germany, led to the Dürer culmination
just after 1500. Both these related growths were independent of

Italy. In fact, as has been shown, they were influencing rather than influenced, so far as Italy was concerned. They constitute the only non-Italian growth or growths of moment which Europe produced.

When the Italian growth in 1500 entered the two or three decades of its highest culmination, it was with sculpture abreast of it. Michelangelo, at almost as high a peak in one art as in the other, expresses the identity of their zeniths. Of the two growths, the one in painting has probably been accorded, usually, a slight superiority whenever comparison has been made. This accords with its longer consecutive development. Sculpture of a sort, it is true, was being made in Italy a century or more before we have any paintings. But this early phase was one of floundering. A forward movement did not get under way until Ghiberti; whereas in painting the development was more continuously consecutive from the beginning soon after 1250.

Almost immediately after 1500, the Renaissance began to spread over western Europe. The effects were nationally diverse. The German growth, which perhaps had run its main course, was wiped out without any lingering aftermath. The Flemish one was pretty thoroughly but not completely Italianized for nearly a century, but continued. In Spain, France, Holland the Italian influence was absorbed, gradually assimilated, and finally, around 1600 or a little later, reconstituted into a national school in each country. These flourished brilliantly for about two generations. The same thing happened about the same time in the Spanish Netherlands—Belgium— except that here there had been a previous national history, whereas in the three other countries painting, previous to the flood out of Italy, had been rather insignificant except for some effects of Flemish influence. Of the four countries, France and Belgium, the two nearer, remained somewhat more directly under Italian tutelage. Spain and Holland, slightly more remote, worked out two more definitely characterized styles, in which the fundamental High Renaissance component had been so well digested and worked over as to be nonapparent at first sight. All four of these national styles culminated from a hundred to a hundred and fifty years after their Italian mother style—at the zenith of what is called the Baroque. How oscillating this concept of Baroque is, other than when it means merely post-High Renaissance and Italian-derived, is shown as soon as Velásquez, Poussin, Van Dyck, and Rembrandt—almost exact contemporaries—are bracketed.

In Spain, France, and Holland the seventeenth-century growths of painting are all associated with general national culminations. They fit completely into curves of national growth. At the same time they fit equally into the general configuration of Occidental painting: Italy, the chief originator, reaching the highest point of the whole movement soon after 1500, the three peripheral nations following with somewhat lesser peaks a century later. It is neat how the smaller national cycles of painting integrate at once with national cycles in activities other than painting, and equally with the larger general European or international Occidental cycle in that art. It would be difficult to imagine a more complexly organized yet more unifiedly functioning system or machine than history has somehow devised in this case.

By 1700 all these national schools except the French were gone. In France, successful painting went on, through the development of the Rococo manner, with Watteau its first great exponent. The essence of this manner I would construe as an attempt to modify the established patterns by skillful breaking up of formal line, and even of the light values which during the preceding century had largely replaced line in interest without wholly crowding it out. On the side of content the characteristics were frivolity as expressed in fashionableness, and emphasis on mood. There had been some leanings in the direction of all these traits during the seventeenth century. But it was the Rococo manner that made them consciously salient characteristics.

All this time, of course, Italy had been carrying on. Painting there did not end with Raphael or Michelangelo. The century or so following is that of Veronese, Carracci, Caravaggio, Reni,

Domenichino, Guercino, Salvator Rosa, Dolci, who form a typical decline sequence. In the eighteenth century there was even some backwash from France: Canaletto's technique is Rococo, while his contemporary Tiepolo's conceptions are still emotionally strained Baroque.

A curiously belated phenomenon is a British growth which began out of nothing about 1750. Qualitatively English in little more than its dominant limitation to realistic subject matter, it was more Rococo than anything else in manner, but was also influenced by seventeenth-century French and Dutch land-scape—altogether a strange hybrid. Culture-historically it seems to represent this: England, until then devoid of any vital repre-sentative art, had finally become sufficiently civilized, in its general relation to continental Europe, to feel the need of such an art. In producing it, she dipped nominally into Italy for inspiration, more into contemporary France for technique and note of modernity, but also into the seventeenth century for models—all the time not venturing far into what still seemed, except to Turner, the cloudy realm of imagination. The growth, which while not of the greatest was yet much above insignificance, thus looks like a catching-up or overtaking en-deavor on entrance into a wider international society. In litera-ture a similar effort had been begun more than a half century earlier with the Restoration, but it remained an episode, be-cause in poetry and drama England already possessed estab-lished national patterns.

Around 1800, the European situation was this. The last pulsation of the Italian growth which had culminated three centuries before was just over. In Germany, the Netherlands, Spain—except for the erratic genius of Goya,—painting was low-level: between constellations. England was still undergoing long-retarded growth, but was without influence or recognition on the Continent. Only in France was painting an established and successfully functioning institution, though without great-ness. Then, in the immediate post-Napoleonic decades, came a conscious movement, the "Romantic Revolt." Probably mak-ing its first actual stirrings in Germany, it broke through to importance and success in France, where there was a tradition of skilled painting, and spread in a rapid contagion over the whole continent, even to areas like Russia wholly untouched before, and to the Western Hemisphere. In its general time-space configuration, in the quick succession of little local growths which it set off like a string of firecrackers, and in its shallow rooting in national soil at a time when avowed political nationalism was developing more strongly than ever before, this movement has close parallels in sculpture, music, literature, and science. As an event in total Occidental civilization, it is essentially a dissolution phenomenon; as the name "Revolt" appropriately suggests. This is shown in painting by the rapidity with which, after a first phase of attempted and fairly successful constructiveness, new manners, each more extreme than the last, were evolved; until, before long, nothing but atmosphere, or archaisms, or form unrelated to reality, or completely personalized mood, was left as the goal of each current in the movement. This was evidently an attempt first to replace, next to stretch, then to burst, and finally to explode patterns. The movement began with a desire to substitute new patterns for those at the moment in vogue—the Neoclassic moribund phase of the Renaissance growth. This was easy enough; but, the satisfaction of rupture having been experienced, the process was continued, with increasing acceleration, until it had been applied to all patterns as patterns, and a novel kind of chaos had been achieved. It was a century of probably unparalleled disintegration from within, and is evidently not yet ended.

Well, the Renaissance growth, which is the Occidental growth in painting, had lived for more than five centuries, was three beyond its zenith, and was outlived anyway. Whether it followed one of the more usual courses—of crystallizing into repetitiveness, or gradually sinking to a level of clumsy tastelessness, or perishing in a catastrophe from without—or this original and dramatic course of suicide by progressive internal disintegration, presumably does not matter: in any case the outcome is the same. The alternatives suggest the choice between mummification, abandonment, burial, or cremation of

a corpse. The way followed has been at least novel, and illustrative of the rich variety of the history of human culture.

What has just been said of the course of nineteenth-century
painting applies with practically the same force to sculpture;
except that this was a little slower in attaining the equivalent
degree of disintegration. The greatest French Romantic paint-
ters—and France is decisive because it was in the lead—were all
born before 1830; Rodin, the peak in sculpture, in 1840.

Chapter VII

DRAMA

Chapter VII

DRAMA

§61. The Nature of Drama

WHILE the drama is almost invariably too integral a part of literature to be left out, acted plays contain so definitely added an element to what is merely written that a separate consideration seems worth while even at the risk of partial repetition beyond.

Under drama in the full sense of the word I include only types of plays which are actable and have been repeatedly performed, and which at the same time possess a fixed text of literary value. Plays like *Faust* or Shelley's *Prometheus* are therefore at best on the borderline, although undoubtedly great literature. On the other hand, though in most forms of genuine drama passages or even whole plays may be in prose, all the growths of drama to which the consensus of history has accorded greatness rest on a foundation of verse. This poetic criterion is not of my subjective choice, but empirically enforced by the world's opinion. A dramatic growth which is wholly in prose may produce excellent and stirring plays, but they have never been generally accounted as of the greatest.

The following must be excluded: plays in which the religious element, or the merely spectacular, or song or music or dance, or pantomime predominates over the actable literary text. Without such exclusion there simply is no limit to be drawn to the subject in consideration, and configurations lose their character. There is no denying that miracle plays and operas and ballets and pageants are related to the drama, that they often are ingredients of it and have influenced it; but from the point of view which governs the present inquiry, there is no course but to omit them.

The order of treatment will be chronological: Greek and Latin; Sanskrit; Chinese and Japanese; Occidental European.

§62. Greek Drama

The Greek drama is too familiar to need much discussion. It is one of the stock examples of "cyclic" or concentrated growth, being recognized as such by the later ancients themselves.

Two well-known traits of this growth may, however, be recalled. The first is the consistent distinction between tragedy and comedy, owing to their diverse religious or ceremonial associations and literary rootings. They never were blended, although there was some assimilation in poetic form. The distinction was maintained as long as there was a Greek theater, and was taken over not only by the Romans but largely by the Italians and French. In Spain and England, on the other hand, where a national drama grew up less influenced by ancient Mediterranean tradition, the segregation of tragedy and comedy is somewhat artificial, many plays falling between or partaking not quite of the nature of either. The same holds true in India, China, and Japan.

The second distinctive feature is the intensive localization of the Greek growth. Both tragedy and comedy were Athenian in development and achievement—even in decline. Such writers as were not Attic by birth became so, for the most part, by residence or citizenship. This Athenian preponderance does not hold at all for nondramatic literature, especially poetic. It also does not hold in sculpture, painting, science, or philosophy, in spite of eminent Attic participation in most of these activities. Nor is the local dominance a mere function of the time of the birth of the drama—the period when Athens was beginning to unfold her growth: for the periods of painting and philosophy were almost identical.

The two principal non-Athenian dramatic currents were in comedy. One was early, mid-fifth century or pre-Aristophanic, and Dorian Sicilian. Here Epicharmus and Sophron were representatives of gnomic comedy and the prose mime. The other was late: three of the five most prominent writers of Middle and New Comedy were born in Greek Asia. The greatest,

Menander, was the nephew of Alexis from the Athenian colony of Thurii in Italy. Here, then, is an instance of centrifugal tendency toward the end; but Athens still remained the recognized center. Within another century, however, Latin comedy was being produced which, though frankly imitative, was no doubt as good as any contemporary Greek plays.

The summary that follows is designed to show the time relationship of tragedy and comedy. A fuller list of names is included under Literature (p. 505).

TRAGEDY

(Arion of Lesbos, to Corinth, ca. 625; invented the satyr chorus.)
Thespis of Athens, *534.
Choerilus of Athens, *500.
Pratinas, Peloponnesian Dorian, to Athens, *500.
Phrynichus of Athens, *494.
**Aeschylus of Athens, *485.

**Sophocles of Athens, *456.

**Euripides of Athens, *440 (b. 485 or 480).
Ion of Chios.
Achaeus of Eretria.
Agathon of Athens, *415.

COMEDY

Epicharmus of Cos, to Sicily, gnomic comedy in Doric; invented plots; possibly no chorus, *480.
Sophron of Syracuse, mimes in rhythmic prose, *440.

OLD COMEDY

Chionides of Athens, *460 (480 seq.).
Magnes of Athens, *460.
Cratcs of Athens, ca. *450.
Cratinus of Athens, *448/4.

Pherecrates of Athens, *430.
Eupolis of Athens, *415.
**Aristophanes of Athens, *415 (ca. 444–380.)
Plato of Athens, *405.

MIDDLE COMEDY

Antiphanes of Asia Minor, *368.

TRAGEDY (*Continued*)

COMEDY (*Continued*)

Alexis of Thurii, *354 (or
*348).

*Diphilus of Sinope, *337.

NEW COMEDY

*Philemon of Soli, *320; d.
262!

**Menander of Athens, *302
(342–291); nephew of
Alexis.

Lycophron of Chalcis (also
epic poet), *280. Member
of the Pleiad group of seven
Hellenistic tragedians.

(Plautus, Terence.)

Till first century B.C., tragedies written.

(Mimes and pantomimes.
Greek and Latin.)

In the time of Lucian, ca. 165
A.D., only the great three
still acted, without chorus.

Third century, only Euripides acted.

Another classification unites the Middle and New Comedy
as New contrasted with the Old or Aristophanic. These two
were quite distinct in content and form. The Old Comedy used
a chorus; was thoroughly lyrical in parts, lampooning and
ribald in others; and mingled caricature of particular persons
with satire of political situations and mythological buffoonery.
The New Comedy dispensed with the chorus and, while still
in verse, scarcely attempted poetical feeling. It dealt with
imaginary, almost abstract personages, omitted myth, politics,
and abuse, was civilian and timeless, and satirized types of
human nature. The difference is at least as great as that between
Shakespeare and Molière. The New Comedy remained an
internationally imitated model for more than two thousand
years; the Old died, where it was born, within a century. Yet
Aristophanes is today reckoned as greater than Menander; and
the ancients themselves seem to have inclined to the same judg-

ment, at any rate in literary value. Menander's plays might and did hold the stage indefinitely, while the contemporary and personal content of Aristophanes's put them beyond the range of successful popular appeal within a generation. This thorough change in the character of Greek comedy no doubt accounts for its possessing two peaks barely a century apart. At that, the whole growth is comprised within two hundred years.

Tragedy merely developed and then underwent no more material changes. Hence its course was even briefer: scarcely a hundred and fifty years, if we except the Hellenistic literary revival. The culmination falls between 485 and 405, or probably 490 and 410. The mid-point would be about 450, or before the birth of Aristophanes.

§63. Latin Drama

Latin drama was born with Latin literature, but died much earlier. It attained to successful achievement within a generation after the first written play was produced in Rome, and it had offered its best in less than a century more. It ran on for perhaps two hundred years longer, but tragedy became a non-dramatic literary activity, while comedy altered into non-literary farce, mime, and pantomime. When the rest of the literature—poetry and prose—culminated in the two last generations before the birth of Christ, the drama, as living plays having also literary value, was well in its decline if not moribund.

This brevity of span appears as a nearly constant characteristic of the life history of the drama the world over. But the particular causes that visibly account for the brevity vary widely. Hence it becomes a question whether these specific causes are not merely apparent; or at any rate merely precipitating or partial; and whether there is not in the nature of the drama something which we have not been able to isolate or analyze out, but which nevertheless is real because it predestines any growth of great drama to unusual short-livedness. Such at least seems the empirical indication of most of culture history to date.

Some of the particular characteristics of the Roman drama viewed as a configuration are the following. It is wholly Greek-derived and Greek-dependent—more so than the literature, which at least developed a native vehicle of expression in the satire, and in the epic, lyric, essay, and history rose to achievements not far inferior, on the whole, to those of the Greeks, and surpassing them now and then in some regard. When the Roman drama began, Greek tragedy had been living on its past for a century and a half, and Greek comedy for about two generations.

Latin tragedy clung to Greek mythological and legendary themes throughout. It could hardly have risen to much force of originality so long as it remained in this bondage of content. The earliest Latin tragedian was the Greek Andronicus, whose first play, a translation, was performed at Rome in 240. The greatest, in general Roman estimation, was Accius, born about 170; Cicero was inclined to prefer Pacuvius, born fifty years earlier. In the time of Augustus, the *Thyestes* of Rufus and the *Medea* of Ovid shared the highest repute, but as works of literature rather than stage plays. Toward the time of Nero, Seneca wrote his rhetorical tragedies. If they were acted at all, this was only as an incident to their being read. The fact, however, probably contributed to their being preserved: they are the only Roman tragedies extant. This in turn led to their being taken as models in the Renaissance, especially in Italy, and with pernicious effect, because no nascent drama could hope to flourish by beginning where a former one ended in senility. Of course, the concept can also be reversed: if Italian Renaissance drama had possessed genuine viability, it would never have leaned on Seneca, or would promptly have discarded him.

Roman comedy rose even more rapidly than tragedy: Plautus was born only thirty years after Andronicus; Terence, another sixty-odd years later; Caecilius, a Gaul, about halfway between them. The plays of Plautus and Terence, incidentally, are the only Latin comedies preserved to us. Of the two, Plautus was the more vigorous dramatist, Terence the more finished writer.

Caesar's judgment of the latter as a halved Menander is not only
the verdict of the modern world, but also refers to the complete
derivation of the growth from the Attic New Comedy of just
before 300—a hundred to a hundred and fifty years earlier. The
comedy of Plautus and Terence is *fabula palliata*—the characters wearing Greek dress and bearing Greek names. In short,
the imitativeness was complete and unconcealed.

Immediately after Terence, the *fabula togata*, with Latin
characters, perhaps first attempted by Naevius some fifty years
before, displaced the *palliata*. It prevailed about two-thirds of
a century, with Titinius, Afranius, and Atta as its leading
exponents. It did not surpass, nor apparently equal, the frankly
Greekish *palliata* of Plautus and Terence even in Roman estimation. It was in turn displaced by the *fabula Atellana,* an
ancient popular farce, supposedly of Etruscan origin and using
only a few stock characters with Etruscan names, but developed
in Oscan Campania. This was brought into literary form by
Novius and Pomponius soon after 100. Here was at last a
product of the soil, and as a starting point to be transcended
might have had possibilities. But genuine dramatic originality
was evidently too feeble in Italy, or the time was too late, and
the *Atellana* did not develop. It lingered into the early days of
the Empire, but in the main was supplanted in favor within a
half century by the *mimus,* a burlesque or farce with inter-
spersed song but without masks, and therefore with women
taking women's parts. The language, however, remained verse.
The leading authors were Decimus Laberius, a Roman knight,
and Publilius Syrus, a slave from Antioch, around 50 B.C. In
Imperial times the pantomime gradually crowded out the
mime, and the circus in the end displaced this.

In short, what began as a valiant effort to transplant and
equal the Hellenic drama withered into farce, then trans-
formed into show, dance, and song, and was crowded out of
existence by spectacles of sport. Modern parallels are not far
to seek.

On the contrary, Greek drama was dead long before the
circus was introduced.

§64. Sanskrit Drama

The Sanskrit drama is post-Christian. The earliest references to seemingly true plays with literary text are from the first century, and Buddhistic. The first preserved fragments are from the next century. They are frankly Buddhist in content; they are almost the only known Buddhist plays in the history of the Sanskrit drama. The full record opens with the thirteen plays of Bhasa, around 300 or a little later. One of these was reworked into the famous *Little Clay Cart*, also known as *Vasantasena* in some European versions, by Sudraka, at some unknown but presumably not much later period This is perhaps the most dramatic of all Indian plays, by Occidental standards. A century more and India's greatest poet is reached, who is also her greatest dramatist, Kalidasa, author of *Sakuntala, Urvasi*, and *Malavika and Agnimitra*. His most probable florescence is either about 400 or 450.

Two centuries later followed King Harsha; and a century later, Bhavabhuti, ranked second to Kalidasa by the Hindus, and a powerful poet, though lacking in dramatic vigor. From here on, for perhaps two centuries, follow the epigonoi, such as Bhatta-Narayana, and Rajasekhara, who flourished around 900. Thereafter the literary level is lower, in native as well as European opinion, though Sanskrit plays have continued to be written, and occasionally performed, until the twentieth century. This long continuance of form, content, and language, but with diminished vitality, has parallels in other civilizations, though not often for so long as the thousand years in this instance. The parallels suggest an inherent dramatic short-livedness as the cause of the falling off in India, rather than any moving away of living speech and custom from the forms in which the drama crystallized. The latter explanation certainly does not hold, because the Indian drama at its highest, like Indian literature, was never written or spoken in a vernacular, Sanskrit having been for about two millennia a literary or cultural language.

In summary, the documented growth lasted about 600 years, from the second to the eighth century, with its culmination near the middle or perhaps a little earlier. After another 200 years of subsidence, a level of mere continuance or essential repetition of the classic drama was reached; during which, however, other dramatic or semidramatic forms came up, such as the puppet-shadow play, farce, and monologue. At that, the 600 years of Indian florescence constitute a longer term than is found in any other language or civilization;[1] in line with the unusually slow-moving progress of Indian culture generally. The period coincides fairly closely with those of highest productivity in sculpture, painting, science, and philosophy, except for the protohistoric phase of the last.

Kalidasa is associated with Ujjain, and his principal successors Harsha and Bhavabhuti, as well as Rajasekhara, with Kanauj. Both cities lie in mid-northern India, some 600 and 300 miles respectively west of the Gupta capital Patna. Other than this, the localization of the Sanskrit drama does not seem to be documented.

Chronologically, the Hindu drama stands solitary in a long void. By the birth of Christ, Greek drama and its short-lived Latin daughter were dead. Toward 1300, the Chinese began producing plays, and then, from two to four centuries later, two groups of peoples littoral to the Atlantic and Pacific: the West European nations and the Japanese. In the more than thousand intervening years the only drama of literary merit that grew up in the world was that of India.

The problem of the derivation of the Sanskrit theater from the Greek is still in dispute. The one specific evidence cited for connection is the Sanskrit name of the backdrop (not curtain): *yavanika,* "the Ionian" or Greek or Western, "partition" being understood. This is slight foundation for a structure of proof. The best arguments yet advanced are for a connection with the popular and semiliterary Greek *mimus,* which flour-

---

[1] China is only technically an exception, because Chinese drama was never fully recognized as classic and seems to show no clear growth configuration or peak; in short, remained semi-subthreshold to the accepted cultural ideals of the nation.

ished in the Mediterranean world after classic tragedy and comedy were moribund. For this the time too fits more closely. The whole question is as elusive as those of the relations of Greek and Hindu sculpture, painting, science, and philosophy: actual proof is chiefly absent. Whatever first stimulations from outside there may have been, there can be no serious doubt that in the historic consciousness of the Hindus their theater developed as a national institution and that it possesses even to us a wholly national character.

The themes are primarily love, heroism, and intrigue. There is almost no tragedy; and comic passages are relatively sedate. Both prose and verse are employed, and Prakrit as well as Sanskrit. The latter is the language primarily of kings and heroes; Prakrit, of women and the lower classes. The Prakrit, however, is not so much a true vernacular as the literary form of one or another vernacular. Like the contemporary literature, accordingly, the Sanskrit literary theater was never really popular in its appeal, but a consciously artificial production by and for a cultivated class—a sort of court drama.

The definite Buddhist participation in the earliest stages of this drama, and the almost complete ignoring of this religion toward and after the culmination of the growth, are a phenomenon to which we have encountered partial parallels in sculpture, painting, and philosophy, and which must therefore be reckoned as a pervasive trait of Indian civilization. It has little to do, in this case, with the gradual decay of Buddhism in the peninsula, since the religion was still flourishing when the theater reached its peak on a Brahmanical foundation.

Origins and Culmination

Aśvaghoṣa, probably of the second century A.C., is known also as a narrative poet. Three fragments of Buddhistic dramas were discovered in 1911 among manuscripts from Turfan. One of these is directly ascribed to Aśvaghoṣa. The form is already that of the classical drama: the *vidūṣaka* buffoon appears, prose occurs alongside verse, Prakrit beside Sanskrit. The Prakrit is of an older form than in other preserved plays. The subject of one is the conversion of Sariputra to Buddhism.

*Bhāsa was known only from native literary references until the discovery in 1910 in Travancore of manuscripts of twelve and a half of his plays. His date cannot be much earlier than 300, nor later than 350. He is therefore about a century earlier than Kālidāsa. Nine of the plays, running from one to seven acts, are heroic *nāṭakas* taken from the *Mahābhārata* and *Rāmāyaṇa* as already developed substantially to their present form. The four less heroic *prakaraṇas* contain comic scenes, the *vidūṣaka,* and more Prakrit and prose. Of these, the *Dream-Vāsavadattā,* a love play, is considered Bhāsa's best. The incomplete *Daridracārudatta* seems to be the basis of Śūdraka's more famous *Little Clay Cart.* Bhāsa was an ardent Vishnuite.

*Śūdraka's date is wholly unknown, but he may have been pre-Kālidāsa. His one known play is the *Mṛcchakaṭika* or just mentioned *Little Clay Cart,* also called *Vasantasenā* in translation, after the heroine, a noble courtesan. This is a reworking and elaboration of one of Bhāsa's dramas. The *Clay Cart* is in Western eyes the dramatically most vigorous Indian play; but the author's Sanskrit is not perfect. Buddhist influences are discernible, but the play is not Buddhist.

Viśākhadatta probably lived in the early fifth century, more or less contemporary with Kālidāsa; but possibly not till the eighth or ninth. His *Mudrārākṣasa* deals with *nīti,* the political art, and the conflict of two prime ministers.

**Kālidāsa is in Hindu estimation the greatest poet, his plays his greatest works, and the *Śākuntala* his greatest play. His dates, according to Winternitz, were either ca. 350–420 or ca. 390–460, corresponding to floruits of about 390 or 430. The latter corresponds with Vincent Smith's assignment of his dramas to the reign of Kumaragupta, 413–455. He is believed to have been a native of the city of Ujjain or its district. Besides the *Śākuntala* he wrote *Vikramorvaśīya* and *Mālavikāgnimitra.* While primarily an unrivaled poet, Kālidāsa is both effective and delicate as a dramatist also. He is still occasionally acted in India.

Second Phase

*Harṣa or Harsadeva, the last great native king of northern India, who ruled at Kanauj from 606 to 647, or two hundred years after Kālidāsa, wrote, or had written in his name, three love plays on the model of the *Mālavikāgnimitra.* Why the two intervening centuries were barren, or, if not, why nothing has been preserved from them, is obscure. One of the three dramas, the *Priyadarśikā,* contains a play within a play. The *Nāgānanda* is mainly a love story

for three acts, a dramatized Buddhist legend—with Brahman gods
—for two more; in line with the king's vacillation between Buddha,
Siva, and sun worship.

*Bhavabhūti, at Kanauj about 730–740, is the last great figure.
By Indians he is ranked second to Kālidāsa. A poet excelling in
pathos and grandeur, he stands lower in dramatic skill and humor.
Of his three plays, the *Mahāvīracarita* and *Uttararāmacarita* deal
with the hero of the *Rāmāyaṇa,* with respectively heroic and pathetic emphasis; the *Mālatīmādhava* is a love play. They were
probably more successfully read than acted, as so often in Sanskrit
literary drama.

EPIGONES AND LATER

Bhaṭṭa-Nārāyaṇa took the material for his *Veṇīsaṁhāra* from
the *Mahābhārata.*

Rājaśekhara lived around 900 in Kanauj. Two of his "plays" are
outlines of the whole *Mahābhārata* and *Rāmāyaṇa,* respectively;
two others are love comedies, one of them wholly in Prakrit. Rājaśekhara occasionally uses rhyme, supposedly under the influence
of popular vernacular poetry.

Murāri, whose time probably falls between 1050 and 1135, wrote
the *Anargharāghava.*

Bhāskarabhaṭṭa: *Unmattarāghava.*

Jayadeva: *Prasannarāghava.*

Mahādeva, a south Indian, in the first half of the seventeenth
century, wrote the *Adbhutadarpaṇa* in ten acts.

SHADOW PLAYS, ETC.

Mahānāṭaka or great play, already cited by 850, exists in two
versions, both only semidramatic and in strophes, and is based on
the *Rāmāyaṇa.* It was evidently recited to the accompaniment
either of silent acting or shadow puppets, and is similar to the text
of Javanese shadow plays.

Subhata's *Dūtāngada,* from the *Rāmāyaṇa* and performed 1243
in Gujarat, is explicitly a shadow play.

Rāmakṛṣṇa of Gujarat, post-twelfth century, wrote the *Gopāla-
kelicandrikā.* This is characterized as a descriptive idyllic mystery
play dealing with Krishna the herdsman, and probably recited to
pantomime.

Vyasa Śrirāmadeva, in the first half of the fifteenth century, wrote
shadow plays on episodes taken from the *Mahābhārata* and the
Rāmāyaṇa.

§65. Chinese Drama

The Chinese traditionally do not reckon their drama—or their novel—as a genuine part of literature, because it is composed in spoken instead of classical written Chinese, or at best in a form somewhat approaching the latter. The drama has accordingly not entered into their formal literary histories, on which ours ultimately rest, and the story of its development is therefore imperfectly known. Native tradition derives the dramatic art from the "pear orchard" training school for music, song, and dance of the T'ang emperor Hüan-tsung, 713–755; and attempts have been made to carry the paternity back to mimetic dances referred to in the pre-Christian Chou writings. All such expressions, however, are only potential materials, not a drama as such, and the explanations therefore fail to illuminate the real problem. Giles's derivation of the Chinese drama from the inner Asiatic nomads seems fantastic.

The essential known facts seem to be these:

There is one preserved Sung-period play, the *Hsi-hsiang-ki,* the *Story of the Western Pavilion* (or *Monastery Cell*), in 16 acts or scenes, by Wang Shi-fu. Presumably this is late Southern Sung, 1127–1279 (or 1260).

The Yüan or Mongol-dynasty period, 1279–1368, is generally accepted as the time of florescence. Eighty-five writers of 564 plays are known: 100 of these have been brought together in a collection which forms a sort of standard repertory. They are usually in four, rarely in five acts. Song is less prominent than in earlier or later times, and mostly restricted to one of the leading characters. The personages are designated in the text, and no doubt in the selection of acting parts, by stock names such as young hero, old hero, white-bearded servant, comedian, plotter, but announce their individual names on their appearance. Some of the most highly rated plays are:

Dream of the Goldpieces, by K'iao Mong Fu.

Autumn in the Han Palace, by Ma Tung Li.

Pavilion on the Stream, and *Tu Wo's Sorrow,* by Kuan Han K'ing.

Rain under the Wutung, by Po Jen Fu.

The Slave of His Wealth.

Intrigues of a Maid.

The Mysterious Box, anonymous.
Circle of Chalk, by Huei Lan Ki.
The Orphan of Chao, by Ki Kiün Siang.

The last two are best known in the West because they have long been translated, but are said not to be among the plays rated highest by the Chinese.

Of early Ming times is the *P'i-p'a-ki* or *Story of the Lute,* in 24 scenes, first performed in 1404. At least four names are given for the author: they agree only in the family designation Kao. This play has probably the highest native repute of all Chinese dramas; shared possibly by the *Hsi-hsiang-ki.*

Subsequent drama is generally reckoned inferior.

The meanings of titles, authorship, and time of composition are given with considerable variation in the several European writers who have treated the subject. For instance, the two famous pieces cited above, on the authority of Grube, as respectively Sung and Ming, are included by Wilhelm as Yüan. As a layman, I presume that the collection of the hundred famous pieces was made some time after the Yüan dynasty and given a title referring to this period because this was the traditional age of moving plays, and not because of any attempt at critical or historical accuracy; much as we might use terms like "Restoration" or "Elizabethan" somewhat loosely in titles of anthologies. As for the date and authorship of particular dramas, the recorded information may be hearsay or conflicting. Evidently Yüan came to be conventionally associated with drama as Chou with classics, T'ang with poetry, Sung with postclassic philosophy. As a generic verdict, this time association is no doubt sound, though quite likely far from exact. We may accordingly set the main growth of the Chinese theater as from about 1200 to 1400 or 1450.

Some of the peculiarities of this drama are: its being nonclassic in native estimation, and composed in nonclassic language; the mixture of prose dialogue and sung verse, with orchestral accompaniment; the complete or virtual absence of scenery, properties, and masks, but sumptuous costuming; and its continued popularity, with relatively little change of form, during seven hundred years.

§66. Japanese Drama

The Japanese drama experienced two histories. The earlier is that of the *No* plays, occasional, restrained, semireligious, aristocratic, of Ashikaga times, and culminating around 1400. The second is that of the puppet and true theater, which was bourgeois, began after 1600, culminated around 1700, and has continued. There seems to be no connection between the two developments, nor can either be traced to an origin outside Japan. Chinese drama is a century older than the *No,* but there is little similarity other than the fact that acting and song occur in both. The true and the puppet theater originated in a time of both Chinese and European influence, but again no specific relation is traceable. On the other hand, Chikamatsu, who expresses the culmination, wrote only fifty to a hundred years after Shakespeare, Lope de Vega, and Molière—about the same interval as that by which the Japanese *No* followed the Mongol-period burst of the Chinese theater. It is difficult to believe that these are only accidental coincidences, especially since true drama is a relatively rare culture phenomenon. Both the Japanese growths therefore were perhaps stimulated by idea transmissions, as distinct from diffusions of specific culture contents or forms. It was merely knowledge of the fact that a theater could exist which was imported, it would seem. The receiving civilization became conscious, in spots at least, of a potentiality which had been realized elsewhere before; and then proceeded to achieve this potentiality out of its own materials and in its own way. Hence there is nothing tangible in the historical record which the historian can cite as evidence of an "influence" or connection; and he renders, correctly enough, a negative verdict. In all occurrences of this type, accordingly, we have from one point of view a spontaneous generation or cultural creation *ex nihilo;* from another, an origin possibly due to contact stimulation. It is date-place concordances or sequences which suggest and at times almost establish stimulation diffusions or concept transmissions otherwise elusive.

Concept transmissions resulting in seemingly independent inventions or growths are perhaps clearest in the mechanical field. Porcelain making was discovered in Europe as the result of conscious experiment to reproduce porcelain imported from China. The invention of block printing and type printing in the West may be due to a similar transfer merely of idea or example; though the lag is so great, and the interposed Mohammedan barrier apparently so intact, as to leave grave doubt. Excellent instances, fully documented, are the Cherokee invention of writing by Sequoya, and the contemporary one among the Vai of West Africa, both due to recognition of the value of writing and a smattering knowledge of the alphabet which, however, resulted in the formulation of much more elaborate syllabaries. In the chapter on Philology the Chinese discovery of tones has been cited as the probable result of Chinese exposure to Buddhist-carried philology of Sanskrit, though this is a toneless language.

And in the drama itself, is not the Elizabethan theater an analogous case? It is not a miracle play or mystery, not a masque or pageant, not a copy of Plautus and Seneca nor of Trissino's imitation of these, but an indigenous formulation with its own forms and content. And yet, if there had existed no knowledge whatever in England of the ancients and the Renaissance Italians, can one be sure, or even believe, that the Elizabethan drama would have grown up when it did?

The Japanese *No* or *Sarugaku no No* is a lyrical dance melodrama, Shintoistically and Buddhistically colored or charged, and usually culminating in a theophany, possession, or appearance of the spirit of a hero. There are two acts, the second consisting of the dance-and-song recital of the spirit or deity; two or three mask-wearing actors and a chorus; and the theme is bound to a shrine, sacred spot, or more or less sanctified personage. Of plot in the ordinary sense there is almost none, except in the narrow range indicated. The dialogue begins in prose; the verse is of *imayo* type, an alternation of 7-syllable and 5-syllable lines; and consists largely of a skillful tissue of citations of poetry—an exceedingly specialized type of drama.

The full development of the *No* occurred at the hands of Kwan-Ami Kiyotsugu, who died about 1384 (or 1406), and of his greater son Se-Ami Motokiyu, ca. 1363–1444 (or 1455). The peak can therefore be set near 1400. Of 260 *No* plays which are still performed, nearly all date from the Ashikaga period, according to Wilhelm; or according to Aston, of the 235 pieces in the most complete collection, 15, 93, and 22 are attributed to Kwan-ami, Motokiyu, and the latter's son-in-law, respectively, and nearly all the 105 others are of the fifteenth century. After the sixteenth century, *No* ceased being written. Of *kiogon* or farce-interludes between *No,* more than 200 have been preserved. The only actors taking part in these are two clowns.

The Japanese theater proper, *kabuki,* and the puppet show, *ayatsuri joruri,* began about 1600, and their history is coextensive in time with that of the Tokugawa shogunate, 1603–1868. The courses of the two forms ran closely parallel, although the theater grew out of song and dance, the marionette show out of rhythmic narrative spoken or sung by one reciter. The great Chikamatsu wrote for both, but with preference for the puppets, where there were no actors to encroach on the author's text. Until around 1725, the puppet play had perhaps the higher development, especially in Osaka. For a generation thereafter puppet plays were performed also by actors. Then the theater gradually prevailed over the puppets, with Yedo-Tokyo as the center. The peak had come under Chikamatsu, whose best period is put at 1703–1713, exactly a century after Shakespeare's. A minor culmination fell in the first quarter of the nineteenth century, under Tsuruya. In contrast with the *No,* devised for aristocrats, both the *joruri* and *kabuki* were plebeian, or as we should say, bourgeois: samurai did not attend. Also, the plays were secular, and of two main types, *jidai-mono* and *sewa-mono,* which might be called romantic-historical and civilian-domestic in theme. The plot most often revolves about the conflict of *giri* and *ninjo* or social order and subjective impulse—institution and personality. Chikamatsu's plays are mostly in five acts, and prevailingly in verse.

Ca. 1600, *joruri* story recitations, originally rhythmically marked by fan beating, began to be accompanied by the three-string *samisen* and by puppets, *ayatsuri*. Then new stories were used.

1603–1607, O Kuni, a runaway priestess, presented erotic songs with dancing in Kyoto, the actors inverting their sex. This was the origin of the *kabuki*. It was followed by separate men's and women's companies, associated with prostitution. Earlier plots were mostly comic; gradually, pieces of several acts were developed.

1624, puppet play introduced at Yedo.

1629, women's companies forbidden.

1655, men's companies regulated. Women's parts by men. Until Meiji, such actors wore women's clothes off-stage also.

1664, first enactment of one full play after another in the same performance.

1685, Takemoto Gidayu, 1651–1714, founds the Takemoto-za puppet house in Osaka, performing Chikamatsu's plays.

**Chikamatsu Monzaemon, 1653–1724, begins writing in 1685 (1686), for Gidayu in 1686 (1690); best period, 1703–1713/15.

*Ki no Kaion, ca. 1663?–1742, wrote 1699–1723 for the Toyotake-za, the rival puppet theater of Osaka.

*Takeda Idzumo, 1688–1756, fl. 1746–1748 (!) with collaborators.

Chikamatsu Hanji, 1725–1783.

Namiki Sosuke, fl. ca. 1742.

The puppet theaters flourished until the second half of the eighteenth century.

Later drama, mostly *kabuki,* in Yedo-Tokyo:

Sakurada Jisuke, 1730–1802.

Namiki Gohei, b. 1747, fl. 1777–1795.

*Tsuruya Namboku IV, 1755–1829, fl. 1813–1825.

Kawatake Nokuami, 1816–1893, fl. 1862 seq., only slightly under Western influence.

§67. Occidental Dramas

ITALY

Italy was the first European country to produce formal, literary, nonreligious plays; but it was also the only major and highly civilized nation which failed to accomplish a genuinely successful dramatic growth. The Italians pioneered, others carried through to full achievement.

Several factors appear to be involved in this result. First of all, in 1515, when Trissino produced his *Sofonisba*, the first regular tragedy of postclassic Europe, the Renaissance was at the very mid-point of its zenith in painting and sculpture, and past it in literature. Other Western literatures mostly evince a definitely High Mediaeval and a definitely Early Modern phase, with an interval between. The great pulse of Italian literature falls in this very interval. It is mediaeval at one end, premodern at the other, in European terms: 1300 to 1575 is its period. The drama therefore was born too late in the life cycle of the containing literature for much chance of vigorous development. Most dramas coincide with the peak of the literatures which contain them, as is shown by the fact that some of the greatest poets or writers of the literary growth are also playwrights, or playwrights only, in Greece, India, England, Spain, France, Germany, and smaller countries. The high century of letters in Italy, the fourteenth, was evidently too early for a real drama in Europe. The sixteenth, when Europe was beginning to be ready, was too late for a new development to succeed in Italy. The result is that Italy was able to disseminate fruitful dramatic influences in retarded Spain, France, and England while her own efforts never reached full fruition.

Another element in the situation is the failure of the various ingredients of a potential full drama to integrate in Italy. The literary example of the ancients, the miracle-mystery of the Church, the idyllic pastoral dialogue, the court pageant or masque, the crudely farcical or blood-and-thunder representations for the vulgar public—these strains never united successfully in Italy as most of them blended in Spain and England, and some of them in France, into a new and greater product. The imitation of Seneca and Plautus remained one thing, the pastoral another. Neither bore much relation to existing national life. Soon after 1550 the *commedia dell'arte* of improvisation grew up. This was vigorously popular enough; but it continued to aim low, not even achieving a literary text; and its addiction to fixed or stock personages limited its emphasis to situations and kept it from achieving individual characterization. The result was that Italian drama remained restricted to two or three more or less formal or decorative types of literature, whereas the essence of full drama obviously is the representation of life, subjectively as well as objectively.

Where such representative impulses were strong, as in Spain and England, and in Aristophanic Athens, history, national and other, or the particular events of contemporary life, were drawn into the subject matter of the drama. Where they were weaker, as in France, tragedy tended to content itself with themes of antiquity, and comedy with types or manners. In Italy the impulses were weaker still, and the essentially undramatic delineation of idyllic and pastoral situations, or of other nonrealistic situations, continued prominent.

These several factors—the time as such, and place in the course of the literature; the nonintegration of components; the feebleness of reality-representation impulses—are of course also interrelated as functions of one another, in Italy.

As the Italians produced the first regular tragedy of Occidental civilization, they also produced the first opera: Rinuccini's *Dafne* in 1594. This is due in part to Italian leadership in music at the time; but perhaps also to the fact that the pastel-shaded, decorative, nonrealistic text of Italian drama lent itself readily to hybridization with music. The idyllic theme of the first opera is almost certainly significant. It would have been more difficult to create a new musical form on librettos by Lope de Vega or Shakespeare.

A second Italian attempt to achieve a national drama, in the Risorgimento of the later eighteenth and early nineteenth centuries, was fundamentally no more successful than the first. Goldoni converted into written form a comedy which for two hundred years had traveled on improvisation. In spite of considerable success, the effort came too late for the founding of a new great growth. Alfieri's tragedies were propagandist on behalf of Italy, liberty, and enlightenment. It is one thing for a people to reflect in its drama consciousness of an achieving national greatness; another, to use the drama as an instrument to bring about the greatness. In proportion as the instrument is effective, the drama is likely to fail of greatness in its own right, in the nature of things human.

To 1580

Comedy, of modernized Plautus-Terence type

†Ariosto, 1474–1532: five comedies, 1503 seq.
Dovizi, 1470–1523: *Calandria*, 1513.
†Macchiavelli, 1469–1527: *Mandragola*, 1513 (1520).
†Aretino, 1492–1536: five comedies; also tragedy *Orazia*.
Also Cecchi, Firenzuola, Grazzini.

Tragedy

Trissino, 1478–1550: *Sofonisba*, 1515, in unrhymed hendeca-syllabics. Also an epic writer.
†Aretino, as above.
Giraldi, 1504–1573: *Orbecche*. Seneca influence.

Pastoral and dell'arte

†Tasso, 1544–1595: *Aminta*, pastoral, 1573.
Guarini, 1538–1612: *Pastor Fido*, pastoral.
Commedia dell'arte, originating ca. 1550, gradually supplants written comedies.

1580–1750

Rinuccini: 1594, *Dafne*, first opera.
Martelli, 1655–1721: imitations of French tragedies, in Alexandrines.
Maffei, 1675–1759: *Merope*, 1713, classical.
Conti, 1677–1749: influence of Shakespeare; precursor of Alfieri.

1750–1850

Goldoni, 1707–1793: comedy.
Alfieri, 1749–1803: tragedy.
†Foscolo, 1778–1827.
†Manzoni, 1785–1873: historical tragedies, 1817, 1822.
Niccolini, 1781–1861: romantic drama, political and historical.

AFTER 1850

D'Annunzio, b. 1863.

In spite of the great names in this list, it is obvious that there is not a dramatist of the first rank among them; also, that no

---

† The dagger denotes that the primary contribution was nondramatic.

great type of drama was produced, in the sense that such types were evolved in Athens, Spain, France, and England. There is also no clear-cut configuration of growth such as is patent in these countries. The history is one of four hundred years' wandering among patterns, without concentration on one pattern and consequent culmination. It seems reasonable to believe that the parallelism of contrast with the other national developments is more than coincidence; that the respective absence and presence conjointly of dramatic genius, of great dramatic type or pattern, and of culminating configuration, are but facets or functions one of the other.

SPAIN

The Spanish drama was slow in forming. From Encina's first religious pastoral to Lope de Vega's thirtieth year was an exact century: 1492–1592. The peak is first-half seventeenth century, with Lope, Castro, Tirso de Molina, Alarcón, Calderón, Rojas, and Moreto, whose deaths all fell between 1635 and 1681. By 1670 these were all dead except Calderón. The four who are probably greatest, Lope, Tirso, Alarcón, and Calderón, were born in 1562, ca. 1572, ca. 1580, and 1600. The first three died in 1635, 1648, and 1639; and Calderón ceased writing profane plays when he took orders in 1651. After that date, decline was accomplished within two decades.

The growth curve thus is skew, and peculiar in that its peak comes late. If we mark the culmination by its mid-point in 1625, there were 133 years preceding, only 45 following. Even if drama proper be made to begin only with Rueda instead of Encina, at least three-quarters of a century must be allowed before 1625.

This slowness of development was perhaps due to Italian influence, which had to be assimilated and overcome before a national theater could arise. This Italian influence manifested itself both in pastoral themes and in plays of intrigue. With Italian imitations came classic ones, for a time. It seems to have been only around 1590 that the Spanish theater definitely acquired its full characteristics.

The general course thus is similar to that of French drama, which also groped in different directions before finding itself. However, the French were somewhat later. The formal beginning was not till 1552; Hardy, the equivalent of Rueda as the founder of a popular, fully dramatic theater, was born only just before the latter died—1560 and 1565, respectively; and the great period was not initiated in France until 1636 with Corneille's *Cid*. In fact, Molière's and Racine's work falls after 1660. The two growths accordingly are roughly parallel and overlap in time, but the Spanish is the earlier. Such influencing as there was, was also from Spain to France.

England began later than both the Latin countries, but came to its climax, 1600 to 1615, and out of it, more quickly. On the other hand, dramatic vitality in Britain was not spent with the climax, but continued for nearly a century after. In Britain there was little Italian or classic precedent to be worked out of, and the native pattern set very rapidly.

The essential fact, however, is the near-coincidence of the culminations of the three great growths:

English, 1600 to 1615, or, if one will, 1590–1625.
Spanish, 1590 or 1600 to 1650.
French, 1630 to 1680.

The three are not derivative one from the other: the Spanish influence in France was moderate, and the English and Spanish theaters seem scarcely even to have known of each other's existence. Nor are the three growths common in period because of common derivation from Italy; for the Italian drama never was realized, the Spanish and French began to flower only when they forgot the Italian attempts, and the English was only half aware of them.

We accordingly have here a very definite configuration of similar activity, of equivalent achievement value, in the three contiguous countries of western Europe, at virtually the same historic moment, and without adequate specific causal connections to account for the parallelism. It seems incredible that there should have been nothing but chance coincidence at work. Therefore it is incomplete to explain Shakespeare, Lope, and Corneille, as culture-historical phenomena, in terms merely of late sixteenth-century British, Iberian, and French culture, respectively. But specific extranational derivations and the tracing of specific influences are also obviously incomplete as explanations. We are thus left confronting a configuration which is a fact and almost certainly a highly significant fact, but of which we do not know the meaning in causal terms. This seems the moral of the case: that we do not know precisely how the concatenated phenomena came to be concatenated.

Juan del Encina, 1468/9–1533/4, b. Salamanca. 1492, first nativity or religious pastoral.

Celestina, 1499 and 1502, attributed to Fernando de Rojas, authorship questionable, probably in Salamanca. Dialogue novel or book prose drama.

Torres Naharro, of Estremadura, d. ca. 1530. Italian-influenced plays of intrigue in *jornadas* (acts); collection published in 1517; influence on Lope via Cueva.

Gil Vicente, b. 1460/70?, Portuguese, fl. 1502–1536; 44 plays, part in Castilian.

Delgado: 1524, *Lozana andalusa.*

Saa de Miranda, 1496–1558, Portuguese of Coimbra; 2 comedies, lost tragedy.

Lope de Rueda, d. 1565, author, actor, and director of a wandering troupe. Italian imitations and comic *pasos.* "Father of the Spanish drama."

Alonso de la Vega, subsequent director.

1579, 1582, founding of permanent theaters in Madrid; Seville and Valencia had preceded.

Juan de la Cueva, in Seville, ca. 1580 seq., 14 plays; themes novelistic, classic, modern events, Spanish legend.

Cristóbal de Virués, in Valencia, classical drama *Elisa Dido* with chorus.

Cervantes, 1584, tragedy *Numancia* published; dramatically a failure.

**Lope de Vega Carpio, 1562–1635, Asturian b. in Madrid. *1590 seq.

Colleagues and competitors of Lope at Madrid: Antonio Mira de Amescua, from Cadiz; Juan Pérez de Montalván; Luis Vélez de Guevarra, from Ecija.

Guillén de Castro y Belvís, 1569–1631, in Valencia: *Mocedades del Cid.*

*Tirso de Molina (Gabriel Téllez), 1570/72–1648, b. Madrid;
   1620, *Cigarrales de Toledo* published.
*Juan Ruiz de Alarcón y Mendoza, ca. 1580–1639, b. in Mexico.
**Pedro Calderón de la Barca, 1600–1681, Asturian b. in Madrid.
  Francisco de Rojas Zorilla, d. 1661: *Del rey abajo ninguno.*
  Agustín Moreto y Cabaña, 1618–1669: *Desdén con el desdén.*

The beginnings are west Iberian: Salamanca, Estremadura, Portugal. The relation of Portugal to Castile was in some ways like that of Scotland to England, but as a precursor rather than belated follower. Camoëns precedes Cervantes by a generation, and Vicente and Miranda were pre-1550. Later in the formative period of the drama, Seville and Valencia were most active. Madrid, which became the capital in 1560, took the lead a few decades later, and was the seat of the culmination. Lope and Calderón were Asturians born in Madrid. Of their two contemporaries who perhaps equaled them as playwrights though not as poets, Tirso was also a Madrileño, and Alarcón one of the very few Spaniards born in the New World to achieve eminence.

Nineteenth century.—A minor dramatic impulse flared in Spain in the nineteenth century. While this produced no great master, it resulted in a vigorous school which would perhaps have had international influence if Spain were not regarded by Europe as only half participating in contemporary Occidental civilization. The configuration is interesting because the movement was able to realize itself only after the romanticists had been successful in Paris. Then, from 1834 to 1837, half a dozen romantic and historical dramatists burst forth in Madrid. Several of them had been or were exiles or resident in France. Their ages at the moment of first success were 47, 44, 41, 31, 25, 23; their birth dates, from 1787 to 1813. The older were obviously held back until Paris had made the time ripe for them; the younger could begin in youth. The growth was, however, no merely imitative one: much of its content and quality was Spanish. Also, Bretón, who wrote comedy which lay outside the romantic damming and break-through, began to function ten years earlier than his tragic contemporaries.

An aftermath, after an interval of 15 years in the birth dates, is provided by Ayala, Tamayo, and Echegaray. The two former mark a bending from romanticism to realism but are still specifically Spanish. Their work was substantially done before 1870. Echegaray, their contemporary, did not produce until after 1870 and dealt with social problems which were being felt internationally.

Martínez de la Rosa, 1787. *1834, *Conjuración de Venecia.*
Saavedra, 1791. *1835, *Don Alvaro (La fuerza del sino).*
Zárate, 1796. *1837, *Carlos II (El hechizado).*
Bretón de los Herreros, 1796. 1824 seq., comedies.
Hartzenbusch, 1806. *1837, *Amantes de Teruel.*
Larra, 1809. *1834, *Macías.*
García Gutiérrez, 1813. *1836, *Trovador.*

López de Ayala, 1828. *1851 seq.
Tamayo y Baus, 1829. *1853 seq.
Echegaray, 1832. *1874 seq.

ENGLAND

England is universally considered to have reached the greatest heights of any European drama in the works of Shakespeare. Its drama has also the sharpest historic configuration. This configuration is marked by a sudden birth, an exceedingly rapid rise to a culmination as brief as it was high, a continuance on a lower level of quality, a later attempt at revivification by modification of the pattern, and the complete collapse of this final impulse almost at the moment of its realization. Thereafter the theater continued as a permanent Anglo-Saxon institution, but the drama, definable as a successful integration of successful performance and genuine literary quality, was dead. As in English music, which ended contemporaneously, there was not even a minor subsequent growth. Twice it seemed as if a new birth were about to take place: through Sheridan and Goldsmith around 1775, and through Wilde and Shaw toward 1900. But neither impulse included more than a handful of participants, lasted very long, or rose above the level of prose. Also it is significant that all the successful activity in these half starts was by Irishmen; just as the last playwright in the final phase of the great growth, Farquhar, was the first Irishman to appear in English literature Significant of what? Of the fact that by 1700 the patterns of great English drama were exhausted, for Englishmen: the part-alien Irish still had a chance to find in them something new.

Scotland, by the way, never produced even a second-rank playwright. In Elizabethan-Restoration time she was too provincial, puritan, and anti-English; in her eighteenth- and nineteenth-century period of bloom and acceptance by England, the latter had no drama for Scotland to contribute to.

Within the great period, the formative or groping stage lasted only from 1550/60 to 1580. It is marked by Sackville and Norton's *Gorboduc*, 1562; *Ralph Roister Doister*, 1552, published 1566; *Cambises*, 1569; *Gammer Gurton's Needle*, 1563?, published 1575.

Around 1580 the specific Elizabethan drama constituted itself in the hands of Lyly, followed immediately by Peele, Kyd, and others. By 1587 Marlowe introduced blank verse; two years later Shakespeare was writing; in 1597, Jonson. By 1600, the rapid rise was complete: let us say 1601, when by the classification of the older critics Shakespeare passed from the second to the third of his four periods. The beginning of the climb is strictly coincident with the beginning of significant nondramatic literature: Lyly, *Euphues*, 1578; Spenser, *Shepherd's Calendar*, 1579; Sidney, *Arcadia*, 1580.

The culmination is clearly comprised in the fifteen years between 1601 and 1616. Thus, Shakespeare's two last and greatest periods, 1601–1613 (died 1616); Jonson's best plays, 1598–1614; Webster's, 1612, 1616; Beaumont and Fletcher's *The Knight of the Burning Pestle*, before Beaumont's death in 1616.

After 1616 equally rapid decline is manifest. Jonson, Fletcher, and others who continued, produced inferior works. Of newcomers, the best were Massinger, from 1620, and Ford, flourished 1629–1634: one is feeble as a dramatist, the other overstrained. In 1642 the Civil Wars closed the theaters for eighteen years.

The Restoration drama, 1660–1700, is physically separated from the Elizabethan-Jacobean by these eighteen years. It is also usually contrasted with it, as being French-inspired, licentious, and concerned with manners. The contrast is genuine, but as of phases within one growth. There was French influence, in comedy situations and in the temporary rhyming of "heroic" tragedy. But Shirley and Davenant formed a bridge from the pre-Civil War stage; Shakespeare was acted and his renown was high; Dryden, while trying to improve and outshine him, never got away from imitating him; the licentiousness quickly took a characteristically direct and brutal turn which would have offended Molière and the court of Louis XIV, but not an Elizabethan audience. In short, there were dissipation and dissolution symptoms in the Restoration drama and, because of these strains, novelty and French example were clutched at; but the strains presupposed the basic persistence of the old pattern. As a matter of fact, after a generation the Restoration drama finally achieved a coherent and distinctive pattern of its own in the comedy of manners of Congreve, only to have this wither immediately. Congreve was born in 1670, did his best play in 1697, his last in 1700; Jeremy Collier's attack on the theater came in 1698. That one clergyman's blast should by itself have sufficed to wilt a flourishing school of drama seems a somewhat naïve belief. It implies at least that this drama was a brief, frail flower. The growth can be extended a decade beyond Congreve by the inclusion of Farquhar, who flourished in 1699–1707, or after Collier's attack; but who, as already noted, can also be construed as the first of the Irish heirs and epigones.

The names and dates are given under English Literature. The earlier birth dates begin in 1553/4 with Lyly, cluster thickly from 1558 on, and end within less than a generation, in 1584–1586, with Beaumont, Massinger, Rowley, and Ford; beyond whom there was no one born, except the minor figure of Shirley, 1596, to produce with even semidistinction before the closing in 1642. Two things are clear: Shakespeare, 1564, was born well before the middle of the great cluster; and all pre-Restoration births were Elizabethan, in fact within the first two-thirds of Elizabeth's reign, although the culmination was definitely Jacobean. These figures reëmphasize the rapidity of the rise and climax attainment of this unusually great growth. However, the compensating principle that really high developments are rarely altogether brief is supported by the prolongation of the growth—after a subsidence and its forcible suppression by rebellion and despotism—for almost a century after the peak, to a final end in a lesser but incontestable burst.

FRANCE

The predrama or near-drama had a history of full three hundred years in France: from the High Mediaeval thirteenth to the post-Mediaeval sixteenth century. Reference is not only to religious miracles, mysteries, and moralities, but to profane comedies, farces, and *soties:* Adam de la Halle's *Jeu de la Feuillée*, 1260, *Pathelin* of the fifteenth century. Neither of these currents seemed able to develop into a full literary drama.

Jodelle of the Pléiade, 1532–1573, wrote the first specific or regular tragedy in French: *Cléopâtre*, in 1552. This was on the Senecan model and was Italian Renaissance-stimulated. The time coincides with the end of the mysteries, the acting of which ceased in 1548. Jodelle also wrote the first regular comedy, *Eugène*. He introduced the Alexandrine into the French theater. A step farther along were Larivey, 1540–1611, in comedy, and Garnier, 1545–1601, in tragedy with chorus. Hardy, 1570–1631, represented a temporary reaction toward vigor and irregularity: rapid movement of plot, no unities, lack of literary quality. He first popularized the drama with all classes.

The great triad were born between 1606 and 1639, and flourished from 1636 to 1677, while the drama of Spain was in its sunset and that of England long past its supreme phase. The period was that of Richelieu, Mazarin, and the early years of Louis XIV's self-rule; and was almost exactly coincident with the culminations in painting, philosophy, and science—averaging perhaps a decade later.

The classic French drama is genuinely national in that it achieved its own spirit, form, and tradition in spite of what it drew from Spain and Italy. Its salient quality is restrictiveness or limitation: the personages, situations, themes, sentiments, words excluded are infinitely more numerous than in Spain or England. This quality is more or less evident in all French products of the period. Once in its self-imposed frame, the French spirit of the time flowed powerfully enough. But other nations, once they had got over their mode of upper-stratum imitation of Louis Quatorze, have always felt the frame as too narrow.

The classic unities typify the situation. It was because they enforce limitation on a freedom which may become disorderly that the seventeenth-century French liked them, not because they were classical. Indeed, the French were very little interested in seizing the spirit of classic antiquity, and wisely enough. They did borrow some of its rhetorical plumes, and its limiting rules, following the Renaissance Italians' drawing on the Latin imitation of Greek literature. Molière, of course, is less hampered than the tragedians, either because of greater genius, or because he began as an actor, or because comedy needs no plumes. At that, his resemblance is to the denationalized, Hellenistic Menander and his Roman successors; whereas Shakespeare, though knowing nothing of Aristophanes, is the latter's kin.

Rather unusual is the paucity of lesser lights contemporary with the great three. Rotrou is the only one whose name has any familiarity; and this hardly extends beyond his name. This fact is perhaps another expression of restrictive tendencies: Corneille, Molière, Racine formed the canon and this was promptly closed.

As might be expected, the successors were handicapped: Regnard, born 1655, and Marivaux, 1688, in comedy, least so; but Crébillon, 1674, has sunk to a fame of semicontempt. Even Voltaire, had he done nothing but his plays, would hold the repute of a dreary writer. It is curious how the canon ruled through the Enlightenment.

The one brighter spot is Beaumarchais, born 1732, with his *Barbier*, 1775, *Figaro*, 1784. In spontaneity and charm as well as time he parallels the equally isolated Irishmen Sheridan and Goldsmith in England.

The year 1830 brought the breaking of the bonds with Hugo's *Hernani*. Restraint and the unities were overthrown with a crash. But the "Romantic Revolt" failed to usher in a great drama; though it did result ultimately in the competent theater of Dumas *fils*, Sardou, and Rostand. Dramatic strength was not the prime genius of either Hugo, Dumas *père*, or De Musset. At that, Romanticism came hard to the French, and came late, when it had spent its main force in both England and Germany. The German drama was well over its peak when Hugo sounded the tocsin in Paris. It is true that this German growth was composed of a consciously Classic as well as a Romantic ingredient. But this fact indicates that, whatever its ultimate quality of achievement, it sprang from constructive as well as revolutionary impulses. It is strength of the constructive element that may be questioned in nineteenth-century French drama. It is perhaps for this reason that, before long, marginal countries like Belgium, Norway, Sweden, Italy were equaling or surpassing the drama of France, at least in their influence on the world at large; and this in spite of continuance of French technical skill.

Mediaeval and postmediaeval anticipations, to 1550
  13th-century miracle plays, preserved: Jean Bodel of Arras, *St. Nicolas;* Ruteboeuf, *Théophile.*
  Ca. 1260, Adam de la Halle: *Le Jeu de la Feuillée,* first "comedy."
  14th-century miracle plays of Notre Dame; societies for production of moralities and farces: *Enfants sans souci, Clercs de la Basoche.*
  15th-century mysteries. Acted until 1548.
  15th century, *Pathelin.*

Conscious secular literary drama, beginnings, 1550–1630
  Jodelle, 1532–1573, of the Pléiade: 1552, *Cléopâtre*, tragedy; also *Eugène,* comedy; use of Alexandrines; influence of Seneca and Italians.
  Larivey, 1540–1611, comedy.

Garnier, 1545–1601: *Les Juives;* classical tragedy.

Hardy, 1570–1631. Vigorous drama, without unity, of little literary pretension but wide popular appeal.

Culmination, 1630–1680
  *Corneille, 1606–1684; *1636–1641.
  Rotrou, 1609–1650.
  *Molière, 1622–1673; *1659–1673.
  Pradon, 1632–1698.
  *Racine, 1639–1699; *1667–1677;.*Esther* 1689, *Athalie* 1691.

Continuation, 1680–1800
  La Fosse, 1653–1708.
  Regnard, 1655–1709.
  Campistron, 1656–1737.
  Duché, 1668–1704.
  Crébillon, 1674–1762.
  Marivaux, 1688–1763.
  Voltaire, 1694–1778.

  *Beaumarchais, 1732–1799; *1775–1784.

Nineteenth century
  Scribe, 1791–1861; 1815 seq.
  Hugo, 1802–1885; 1830 seq.
  Dumas *père,* 1803–1870; 1828 seq.
  De Musset, 1810–1857.
  Augier, 1820–1889.
  Dumas *fils,* 1824–1895.
  Sardou, 1831–1908; 1860 seq.
  Becque, 1837–1899.
  Coppée, 1842–1908.
  Rostand, 1868–1918.

GERMANY

Germany failed to participate in the sixteenth–seventeenth-century West European series of national dramas, evidently because her literature was too feeble.

However, the literary growth the inception of which is usually dated from Klopstock's *Messias* in 1748, and which culminated around 1800, carried drama as an essential ingredient. The course of this drama was marked by Lessing's *Barnhelm* 1767, Goethe's *Goetz* 1773, Schiller's *Räuber* 1781, Kleist's *Zerbrochene Krug* 1806, Grillparzer's *Ahnfrau* 1817, as the starting points of the principal careers involved. The climax is probably represented by Schiller's *Wallenstein, Stuart, Orleans, Tell,* 1798–1804. Goethe is much the greater poet and his supreme masterpiece has the form of a play, but in specific dramatic gift Schiller easily surpassed him, as Goethe himself recognized. In about the same mid-moment fall the Shakespeare translations of Schlegel.

Of the three first greater figures, none was exclusively or perhaps primarily a dramatist, and Lessing scarcely even a poet. Here is a definite contrast with the English, Spanish, and French drama. Shakespeare, Lope, Calderón, Corneille, Molière, Racine would probably be unknown today but for their plays. The westerly dramatic growths were essentially self-sufficient; the later German, like the abortive Renaissance Italian one, was only a strand in literature. This difference seems a function of time. The most successful and independent playwriting of Europe was over before 1700, just as it was limited to the western margin of the Continent. Germany began a century too late to attain equality of achievement.

For the same reason, Schiller and his contemporaries achieved no new specific dramatic forms as Shakespeare, Lope, Corneille, or their predecessors had done. His plays are generalized; European rather than typically German in structure. Where the Germans showed anything distinctive, it was in loosening or loss of form, as in *Goetz* and *Faust;* in other words, in invasion of the specifically theatrical by poetic or literary qualities. Schiller's intrinsic ability as a dramatist is shown by the fact that he did not yield seriously to such impulses. His plays are superb acting plays in spite of his rhetorizing poetry, not because of it.

Lessing, born 1729, stands somewhat apart in time. The births cluster thickly from Goethe, 1749, to Kleist, 1777. Then comes an interval of a quarter century with only Grillparzer, 1791; or, if one overlooks a couple of minor figures, to 1811— a full generation. Thereafter come the epigones, from Gutzkow, 1811, to Hauptmann, 1862; with a few lesser stragglers beyond. As usual, it is difficult to set a terminus to the decline.

Geographically the births are rather evenly distributed over German soil, including Austria, except that the Rhine and Bavaria are unrepresented.

So far as I know, the only Jew is the last name on the list that follows.

Born before 1800
  *Lessing, 1729, Lusatia; plays 1755–1779.
  *Goethe, 1749, Frankfurt; 1773 seq.
  Müller, 1750.
  Lenz, 1750.
  Klinger, 1752, Frankfurt; 1776 seq.
  Leisewitz, 1752.
 **Schiller, 1759, Württemberg; 1781–1804.
  Iffland, 1759, Hanover.
  Kotzebue, 1761, Weimar.
  A. W. von Schlegel, 1767, Hanover; transl. 1797–1810.
  Werner, 1768, Königsberg.
  Tieck, 1773, Berlin; translator.
  *H. von Kleist, 1777, Frankfurt on Oder; 1806–1810.
  *Grillparzer, 1791, Vienna; 1817 seq.

Born after 1800
  Grabbe, 1801.
  Bauernfeld, 1802, Austria.
  Gutzkow, 1811, Berlin.
  Hebbel, 1813, Schleswig-Holstein.
  Ludwig, 1813, Eisfeld, Meiningen.
  Freytag, 1816, Silesia.
  Anzengruber, 1839, Austria.
  Lindau, 1839, Magdeburg.
  Wildenbruch, 1845, Beirut.
  Sudermann, 1857, East Prussia.
  Hauptmann, 1862, Silesia.
  Fulda, 1862, Frankfurt.
  Schnitzler, 1862.

MARGINAL LATE EUROPE

The drama shows the same "Hellenistic," pan-European, nineteenth-century spread as most other cultural activities. Here and there a greater figure coincides with a national birth or renaissance and maintains national flavor; but on the whole the impulses at work are international. Ibsen is perhaps the dominant figure. The Low Countries participate with Maeterlinck, Hungary with Molnár. In America O'Neill perhaps represents a belated stir of the same movement. The Slavs have been less prominent in the drama than in several other efforts. France, Spain, England, Germany have already been discussed. Strindberg, Chekhov, D'Annunzio belong, although not primarily playwrights.

Norway: Ibsen, 1828.
Sweden: Strindberg, 1849.
Ireland: Wilde, 1856, Shaw, 1856.
Russia: Chekhov, 1860.
Belgium: Maeterlinck, 1862.
Italy: D'Annunzio, 1863, Pirandello, 1867, Sem Benelli, 1877.
Hungary: Molnár, 1878.

In point of time the following are includable, though they constitute the decline phase of growths whose culmination lay in the first half of the nineteenth century:

France: Dumas *fils,* 1824, Sardou, 1831, Rostand, 1868.
Spain: Echegaray, 1832.
Germany: Sudermann, 1857, Hauptmann, 1862.

§68. Discussion

The history of the drama obtrudes several conclusions.

The first is the definite brevity of nearly all dramatic growths of both performing and literary merit, as distinguished from the mere existence or even popularity of the theater as such, which may go on for centuries. With one exception, to be discussed in a moment, the longest span is three centuries. Even briefer are the periods of high florescence. Not one of these extends over more than a century, and the majority are well under. Wherever there is a really high culmination in Occidental civilization, this is definably limitable within a span of from two to five decades.

As to the reason for this short-livedness, at any rate as compared with literature, it is expectable on the ground that the part is likely to be briefer than the including whole. There is, however, no visible inherent reason why great growths of drama should be shorter, in many instances, than those in sculpture, painting, or music, and never longer.

The one exception is India. Here the plays rated as best were produced strung out through six centuries, though a peak near the middle is conspicuous. All Indian growths are prolix, on a comparative scale. An added factor very likely was the circumstance that the Hindu drama was a court activity rather than a popular one and that it was mainly written in a learned speech, not in a vernacular.

Almost throughout, the growth of drama either begins or ends abruptly. A swift development characterizes Greek tragedy, and the Latin, Chinese, Japanese, English, and German growths. Rapid terminations occurred in both Old and New Attic Comedy and the great Spanish and French dramas.

There are several revivals or recurrences of growth; but nowhere does the recurrence rise to equality with the preceding phase of florescence. Japan is not an exception, because the *No* is of a pattern and aim utterly different from those of the later theater. Rather should Japan be construed as having had two growths, the first directed toward a sort of half drama, the second toward a real one.

All the major dramatic developments except the two Far Eastern ones coincide closely in time and place with major literary ones, as is perhaps expectable from our definition, though it is not a necessary consequence. There is no inherent or abstract reason why, say, lyric poetry should not, in this place or that, have preceded dramatic literature sufficiently to have been finished before the latter was born. In fact, this is just what did happen in China and Japan; although the attendant circumstances were unusual. In both these countries conscious literature was essentially the product of a class, not of the people: of the classic scholars in China, of the aristocracy in Japan. It was only after this upper-stratum literature and the cultural creativeness of its class had withered that popular efforts could come to the surface of the civilization.

The old scheme did not provide for a drama. This accordingly had to spring from the people; and it remained only half-countenanced, and not at all participated in, by the ruling and cultivated class. The considerable gap thus is the result of the fact that these Far Eastern nationalities had really two successive literatures, the first limited in range, the second nonclassical and only semicultivated. From the decline of T'ang poetry to the Mongol drama there were about four hundred years; from the Kamakura historical romances to Chikamatsu, the same lapse. The *No* plays, it is true, came earlier; but they were only semidramas, owing probably to the fact that the class by and for whom they were written and produced was unable to break away from the old literary tradition.

China and Japan also answer the problem of whether a great literature can exist without a drama; though the answer is not unequivocal. The reply is affirmative so far as their classical and recognizedly greatest literature is concerned. On the other hand, the subsequent emergence of a successful drama in these countries might be construed to mean that though dramaless patterns of great national literature may be evolved, the impulses toward a drama in sufficiently high civilizations are strong enough to find ultimate though belated expression. Italy points partly in this direction. Its literature culminated early: evidently before any country in Europe was ready for a drama—perhaps because the populace was still too illiterate for a drama of literary quality. At any rate, the Italian dramatic attempt came during the decline of the literature and remained essentially abortive; but it was repeated two centuries later, with the first renewal of literary stirrings on new lines; though not very much more successfully.

That a literature wholly devoid of drama can flourish is evidenced by the Mohammedan Arabic one. And European mediaeval literature almost furnishes a second example: there was the miracle play, but it was of the feeblest value. Incidentally, the miracle reillustrates the finding repeatedly made before, that in no art is the achievement of highest-potential aesthetic value likely to occur as long as the religious element

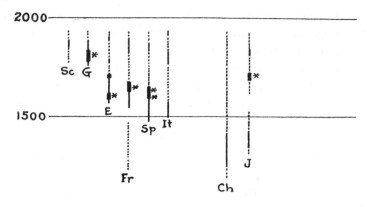

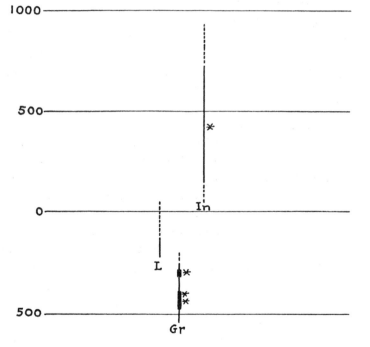

DRAMA

is dominant. How far this conclusion reflects a definable reality or merely flows from the ill-defined concepts with which we are operating, I am not clear about; but it can at least be substantiated empirically.

Most of the greater literatures, however, have included great drama; and all the greatest dramas have formed part of a great configuration of literature. The first finding rests on the literatures of Greece, India, Spain, France, England, and Germany. Those of Rome and Italy, with China and Japan, are to the contrary. The intimate relation is further exemplified by the fact that the dramatists Kalidasa and Shakespeare express the culmination of their countries' literature, and that if the plays of Sophocles, Lope and Calderón, Molière and Racine, and Schiller and Goethe do not represent the absolute summit for Greece, Spain, France, and Germany, they are at least very near to it.

Viewed as a whole, the history has a definite geographical course. This is wholly centrifugal. The first growth is in Greece. This is repeated somewhat to the west, in Latin Italy; and then farther to the east, in India. After a considerable interval, when creative productivity has died out in these several regions, two new growths take place: in eastern Asia and in western Europe. These overlap in time, but the Far Eastern is the earlier. Each is multinational. In the east, China begins, Japan follows. In the west, after a mediaeval religious predrama, Italy starts the first growth, but this never comes into full flower. England, Spain, and France follow, and belatedly, northern Europe. The sequence in summary thus is a literal spread from Attica to the extreme eastern and western margins of the Eurasian continent; a sort of smoldering spark slowly eating its way from point of origin to the edges, with an occasional burst of flame here and there.

By any authoritative standard of historical documentation sufficient for certainty, however, we are dealing not with one transmission but with five separate and more or less "parallel" growths: Greek-Roman, Indian, Chinese, Japanese, modern West European. There is no proof of derivation of any one of these growths from another, unless the Mediterranean elements that entered into the modern European drama at the time of the Renaissance be construed as constituting a derivation. The Hindu theater may have been similarly influenced by the Greek; but the tangible evidence is much slighter.

Equally, however, it would be dogmatic to affirm positively that specific connections of some sort were totally lacking even for any one of the five dramas. The record of history is notoriously almost never complete, and often highly fragmentary. We know of nothing that ties up the Chinese drama with the Hindu. And yet, with second-century manuscripts of Sanskrit dramas actually discovered at Turfan in Chinese Turkestan, who could be sure that something from them had not gone into the making of the plays that began to appear in China in the thirteenth century? The gap in time and religion is less, and in space and language not much greater, than that between Seneca and Trissino. Similarly with Japan's relation to China.

If these potential relations seem slenderly based, it is well to remember how little of the Elizabethan drama can actually be derived from the Italian Renaissance, and how overwhelmingly its distinctive qualities and values are English. Even more striking are the essentially contemporary growths of England, Spain, and France, almost entirely independent of one another—in the usual sense of the word—except for minor influences of the second on the third. And yet, who, looking at the time diagram, and remembering that the three nations are adjacent, would be so rash as to believe that these dramas were mere disconnected, accidental, unrelated coincidences?

It seems evident that, to do full justice to the phenomena, some room must be left to two factors. One is what, in the discussion on Japan, has been called concept diffusion or stimulus transmission, as distinct from the spread of worked-out traits of culture. The other factor is equally hard to detect or define by current methods of historical inquiry, but might be described as common subliminal influences in related cultures: influences, for example, that in themselves, or in their original shared form, might have had nothing to do with the drama, but that ultimately conduced to the formation of similar and seemingly independent dramatic growths, where not inhibited. Such would be similar to the influences operating toward what in another work, some fifteen years ago, I called "secondary parallelism."[2]

Wherever either factor is present, it would appear that the prosecution of historical study merely by the piecing together or weighing of culture-historical items is insufficient for full understanding of what happened. The configurative approach as such is probably less able to produce conclusive proofs. But it will in certain situations arouse suspicions, which, growing into tentative assumptions, working hypotheses, or consciously defined problems, may ultimately enable standard historical method to make well-grounded findings with which otherwise it would not have concerned itself.

---

[2] *Anthropology* (1923), p. 220. This corresponds to Sapir's "drift" in related languages.

Chapter VIII

LITERATURE

Chapter VIII

LITERATURE

§69. General Considerations

As COMPARED with the intellectual and aesthetic activities so far examined, literature is distinctive in two respects. It is capable of becoming more nationalistic; and its medium is on the whole a less specialized and technical one.

A nationalistically directed religion or philosophy is not only conceivable; it has actually happened. Nationalistically colored music, painting, sculpture, drama are also possible: to a minor degree these arts can be used to reinforce national aspirations. But this is definitely more true of literature. It is even generally true. When literature does not at all express politico-national strivings, it is likely to be because, as in China and India, the mass of the population does not participate in either government or literature. An interweaving of literature with competitive nationalistic endeavors therefore seems almost normal rather than unusual.

This relation is further strengthened by the fact that nations are usually set off by languages of their own, which in turn are the organs of literatures.

This brings us to our second point: that the essential medium of every literature is nothing more than the speech which is the common possession of all members of the society. To be sure, there are poetical forms and prosody; but these are slight and simple as techniques in comparison with the technologies of the arts, the instruments of music, the definitions and abstractions of philosophy and science.

It might be expected, accordingly, that as language is perpetually present, literature also would show more continuity of career than the activities previously analyzed. To some degree this is true. The literatures of China and Japan, for instance, and of several Western nations such as France and

England, once they have got started, run along with relatively small fluctuations of level between their best and their worst periods. On the other hand, there are fluctuations even in these. And in many literatures the fluctuations and segmentations are as decisive as in science, philosophy, or the representative arts. On the whole, then, literature will be found to conform to the same constellating habits as other cultural activities.

I take poetry, metrical linguistic expression, as the first criterion of literary achievement. Having a more definite form, it is more purely an art than prose. Moreover, prose shades off into history, philosophy, works of religion and even science, letters, orations, and state documents. Its limits as literature are hard to draw; those of poetry are almost always instantly obvious. Prose may or may not be literature; with poetry the only question is whether it is great, mediocre, or ineffectual literature. This has been the common opinion of men, as is shown by the fact that what peoples conceive as the great or golden ages of their literature are regularly strong in poetry, whether or not they are also strong in prose. Conversely, the "silver ages" show at times no deterioration of prose, but invariably of verse.

A definite, well-worked-out prose style, it is true, is perhaps usually attained later than great poetry, as has long been noted. This, however, seems to mean nothing more than that metrical language is the natural and supreme medium of literature as an art. Unmetrical speech is a more refractory medium, in which only lesser effects are possible, and which is more slowly subjugated to specific aesthetic achievement. The only first-rank literature which has, in the world's opinion, a prose work as its culminating achievement, is Spanish; and possibly Spaniards, left wholly to themselves, would hesitate to accord clear preëminence to *Don Quijote*.

I have followed no very rigorous rule to govern the inclusion or exclusion of writers of prose. Plato cannot be left out of consideration in Greek literature; Aristotle can. Buffon is hard to adjudge; my own opinion is that he was too hybrid between literature and science to be of the first rank in either. Historians I have in general included, though according them less weighting in the determination of climaxes than to poets of equal greatness. Again and again I was tempted to give history treatment as a separate subject, like the narrower activity of philology. But philology is inherently a technical subject, and history is not; at least not as it is represented by the men whom the world calls great historians. Whatever history of today actually is, or is trying to be, the history of all other times has been first of all historiography.

As for the order of treatment by countries, if this were made strictly chronological it would unduly violate geography, and vice versa. I have therefore adopted a compromise arrangement. Occidental literatures being on the whole the latest, I begin with the Far Oriental, among which Chinese is one of the earliest of all; and then proceed in general sequence from east to west. The order thus is Chinese, Japanese; Indian; Ancient Near Eastern; Greek, Latin; Arabic, Persian; and finally the Occidental nations in the succession, so far as possible, of their first important achievements, which is also an approximate geographical arrangement radiating from France as the center to the later peripheries.

§70. Chinese Literature

Chinese literature shows a superficial continuity over more than twenty-five hundred years. Such a continuity is inevitable in a culture which for four-fifths of the time has made high status and successful career dependent on literary training, rigorously tested in examination, and modeled on classic and canonical works in both prose and verse. Some sort of disentanglement of strands is necessary if we are to reach below the apparent uniformity.

First of all, the drama and novel can be set apart as being outside the fixed tradition. They do not count as literature to the Chinese, because they aim to please rather than to adhere to a canon, because they are written in a more or less colloquial or vernacular language instead of the lapidary classical style, and because they address themselves to the ear whereas true Chinese literature has for a long time been not only written but hardly intelligible except as read by the eye. In a comparative view, the novel and drama are therefore no less literature; but they do require segregation in China, and therewith help clarify the configurations involved.

Next, poetry is easily set apart, because it always possesses both meter and rhyme. It is an integral part of true literature, to the Chinese; but it is also a distinguishable strand, which shows clear configurations of its own, and thereby helps to simplify the situation so far as the prose remainder is concerned.

From this remainder, philosophy and history can first of all be taken out, as ingredients which in most civilizations have a recognizable and delimitable identity. We have already considered Chinese philosophy as such, and have distinguished two periods of genuine productivity in twenty-five centuries of commentating. Chinese civilization could not enforce originality of thought; but it could insist on learned preoccupation with wisdom, and reward it. The result has been a unique continuity of stylistically regulated comment on philosophical theme.

History is the subject of two of the five classics, and Chinese civilization is perhaps the most consistently historical-minded of any. Here again is continuity of preoccupation, and the maintenance of a certain rather high level of performance; but above this level two major rises stand out.

What remains is belletristic prose, letters and memorials, exegesis and criticism, informational works and compendia; all alike, however, written in classical language and style by scholars only. Much of this mass would be considered on the fringe of literature, or beyond it, in other civilizations. Our problem is to recognize, so far as is imperfectly possible, the portions which are intrinsically aesthetic, which would be read for pleasure rather than knowledge. Encyclopaedias and textual criticism, for instance, can be omitted without serious remonstrance from a consideration of literature as art. Other classes of writings are more nearly on the border, and their elimination may not be too summary. It must, in any event, be on an international basis; the Western standard would exclude too much, the Chinese too little, for true comparability. When we have proceeded as far as seems reasonable, the residuum is still not very clear-cut, but at least some configurational tendencies are revealed.

The usual periodization of Chinese literature is by dynasties. This is about as summary and ill of fit to the intrinsic literary constellations as the grouping by political periods—or by centuries—is in most other civilizations. Sometimes a growth neatly agrees with the duration of a dynasty; more often it does not. The only other classification I know of is that presented by Erkes as if it were generally accepted, into four periods: before 600; 600 to 100 B.C.; 100 B.C. to 1200 A.D., with a subdivision into pre-Sung and Sung at 900; and after 1200. Each of these terminal dates has undoubtedly a significance as a turning point of some sort, as will be seen. But whether they mark the most crucial turns seems doubtful, in view of the separateness of development of the several strains of the literature.

Poetry.—There are three or four periods of definite poetic originality. The first is that of the composition of the "odes" of antiquity, of which a fragment is preserved in the *Shi-king*. Five of these are said to be pre-1100; the other three hundred from earlier Chou times down to 700, 650, or 600. We may choose the middle date as the probable terminus, because Confucius, about 500, would have excluded from the *Shi-king* anything not bearing some antiquity. Many of the odes are war poems or love songs. At least many were sung as folk songs, and only later endowed with ethical or learned meanings. They are genuinely and simply poetical. The form is also simple; lines of from two to eight but prevailingly four syllables, rhymed, and in stanzas.

Until after 350 B.C. there is no record of further poetry. This is the period of Confucius, Lao-tse, and half of the other great philosophers. The three-century blank is therefore notable. Around 300 a thoroughly new style appears with Ch'ü Yüan's *Falling into Trouble* and the *Elegies of Ch'u*. This is a learned, obscure, allegorical, and subjective poetry, still rhymed, but of irregular line length. Order, however, is one of the deep-rooted objectives of Chinese civilization, and in the next century, under the leadership of Mei Sheng and Sze-ma Hsiang-ju, there was a settling on the seven- and especially the five-syllable line which thereafter remained standard. This growth ended around 100 B.C., and the remainder of Han times, three full centuries, were poetically barren.

With the Han breakup, verse raised its head again with the Seven Poets of the Kien-an era; followed, through the troublous times of the Three Kingdoms, of Tsin, and Liang, by the Seven Worthies of the Bamboo Grove, by T'ao Ts'ien, Pao Chao, the Liang emperors, and others to Sui times. Productivity was continuous to the beginning of T'ang, 618. Poetry was now again essentially personal, instead of heroic, cloudy, and tumultuous.

The T'ang period has always been to the Chinese their golden age of poetry, and they classify it into four stages: Early, High or Glorious (713–762), Middle, and Late. The greatest names, Li Po and Tu Fu, fall, as expectable, in the High T'ang phase. This is no doubt a typical climax growth. On the other hand, if so, what is the relation of the three T'ang centuries to the four that preceded, which possibly show a climax of their own with T'ao Ts'ien around 400?—and which are separated no doubt by a drop in level, but not by any gap?

The answer seems to be that we have indeed a continuous growth from 200 to 900, but near the middle there was a rejuvenation due to the discovery of a new form and therefore resulting in a second and greater peak. T'ang and subsequent Chinese "new style"[1] poetry is described as being characterized by a strict tone pattern in addition to line length and rhyme. The level or flat tone is contrasted with the three nonlevel ones—rising, falling, and arrested or wavering—in certain definite arrangements, which vary for successive couplets, but with each line in a couplet the inverse of its mate. There is also a definite caesura, in both five- and seven-syllable lines, and

---

[1] Old style, nontonal verse continued to be written alongside the new.

the rhyme is between even-numbered lines, except that, in the four-line "stop short" poem, lines 1, 2, 4 rhyme—as in the Arabic-Persian *ruba'i*. Level-tone rhymes are preferred; non-rhyming end syllables must be in the opposite tone class, that is, normally inflected. Altogether, the formal demands are intricate in comparison with those for anything previously written; but the essentially new element is the tone alternation.

Now while all "new style" T'ang and subsequent verse is tonally patterned, it seems hardly likely that this feature was evolved and universally adopted precisely in 618 when a new dynasty came to the throne. There must have been a developmental stage. This evidently filled the sixth century. It is Shen Yo, 441–513, to whom the discovery of the presence of tones is generally attributed, as has been noted in the chapter on Philology. This would place the first recognition of this feature of the language around 480, and 520 would perhaps be a fair date to assume for adoption of the discovery as part of the equipment of all literati. Then in turn we should have left a century for the working out of the application of tones to verse form—a period of experiment and settling on specific arrangements; with the T'ang poets able to start on their course of cumulative achievement with their formal patterns all essentially in hand. I have not found this analysis in any European book on Chinese literature known to me, but it is probable that something of the kind took place around the sixth century.

There is this of theoretic interest in the situation: A poetic growth that began around 200, culminated in 400, and would presumably have died by about 600, through exhaustion of its pattern possibilities, was, by the invention of a new pattern soon after 500, enabled to change into a new growth by 600, which in turn culminated around 750 and ended in 900. The new pattern being literally such—a wholly formal one,—the process at work is clearer than ordinarily, when a "pattern" includes substance and form interwoven.

Hence the seven centuries of Chinese poetry from 200 to 900 can be viewed in two ways: as a single long growth with two peaks, at 400 and 750, and a drop most marked from 500 to

600 though never reaching a cessation; or as two overlapping growths, one from 200 to perhaps 600, the other from 500 or 550 to 900. In either interpretation the significant factor is the development of a totally new pattern element beginning soon after 500.

Incidentally, the Chinese use of tone as a poetical mechanism appears to be a unique event in human civilization, though tonal languages are now known to be by no means confined to the Sinitic speech family. Even more extraordinary—if the full evidence confirms my inferences—would be the circumstances that poetry learned of the existence of the tones, of which it made such fundamental use, from analytic philology; and that philology discovered them because of stimulation by the nontonal philology of India which Buddhism brought in for religious purposes.[2]

Poetry has been written in China on the T'ang model ever since T'ang times; but never equally well. Something of a renaissance seems to have taken place in Sung times, especially through Su Shih in the eleventh century; and again in the eighteenth with Yüan Mei. But the Chinese seem unanimous that the T'ang glory was never again equaled; which, since the form remained unchanged, was almost inevitable.[3]

---

[2] It is of course possible that this was not the course of events, and that it was precisely poetic groping—a feeling impulse—which led to the analytic formulation of philology. Only Sinologists—or better yet, Chinese scholars—are competent to decide this possibility. But if it is true, the accounts now given in Western books are very inadequate.—And still another possibility, theoretically at least, is that the Chinese language has been tonal only since shortly before the fifth century; though this seems highly unlikely in view of Karlgren's statement (*Sound and Symbol in Chinese*, 1923, p. 30) that sixth-century Chinese not only had an even, rising, falling, and abrupt tone, but pronounced each of these on two levels of pitch.

[3] Japanese poetry is of necessity very different from Chinese because the language passes as nontonal. Also, with polysyllabic words lacking stressed syllables, it could not well have employed rhyme, at least not of the Chinese type. Nevertheless, these features are common: 7- and 5-syllable lines, and extreme total brevity in the most common forms: 19 or 31 syllables in Japanese; 20, 28, or up to 84, in Chinese. The Japanese alternation between 7- and 5-syllable lines is evidently a mechanism to avoid monotony, which Chinese achieves by alternating tone patterns in consecutive lines. Chinese verse of the third pre-Christian century, which did not yet recognize tone, or did not yet possess it in the language, attempted something similar to the Japanese method by varying the length of its lines, though with less regularity. What was soon given up again

Philosophy.—With its ethical and human rather than meta-physical or logical bent, philosophy has always stood nearer to literature in China than in most other countries. The incorporation of philosophical with poetical, historical, and magical works into the classical canon which served as the educational vehicle for the governing class strengthened the bond further. From 550 or 500 to 230 or 200, and again from 1050 to 1200, philosophic thought possessing originality was produced in China; as has been discussed more fully in the previous section on the subject. At other times, there was constant comment and criticism, but without new basic ideas.

History.—By an ancient tradition, the *Shu-king* was edited by Confucius. Its dates and no doubt most its events are authentic as far back as about 800 B.C.; beyond that, increasingly less so. Confucius himself contributed a historical work, the *Ch'un-ch'iu,* and since then the stream of historiography has never been interrupted, in fact has always had official sanction and support. The first great historian, however, in fact the greatest of his country and one of the very greatest in the world, was Ssŭ-ma Ch'ien, of about 100 B.C. He was at once critical, perspicacious, synthetic, and interpretive; learned, sage, and vast. In the first century A.C., the Pan family, father, son, and daughter, produced another monumental work. From here it is necessary to pass on to Ssŭ-ma Kuang, 1019–1086, before another historian of the highest rank is encountered. He is considered as rivaling and almost equaling Ssŭ-ma Ch'ien, and as having no subsequent peer. In short, Chinese historiography reached its pinnacles under the Han and Sung.

---

in Chinese, however, became standard in Japanese; probably because of the less variety of resources available in the latter language. It may be added that in both cultures the normal subject of a poem is a mood. It seems impossible to prove the derivation of the Japanese 31-syllable *tanka* from any particular anterior form, because there is no Chinese model with which the *tanka* shows sufficient specific agreement. But the generic resemblances are so striking as to suggest influence, of the type of stimulus diffusion or concept transmission. That is, the Japanese probably borrowed from China certain underlying ideas or attitudes concerning poetry, and then worked them out in conformity with the genius of their own language and current tastes. That the imitation was indirect and characterized by originality rather than slavishness is clear from the fact that for many centuries no Chinese loan words were allowed in classical Japanese poems.

Belletristic prose.—This ill-definable category subsumes the residuum of Chinese literature, the novel and drama excepted. I exclude, however, works of exegesis and comment, and of religious, scientific, or encyclopaedic nature. What is left is the essay, the letter, the introduction, the work of reflection—the primarily literary output of a series of scholars. The perceptible clusterings (see the list below) are in the first century B.C., under Han; around 250–400, under Tsin; 800–900, toward the end of T'ang, when poetry had passed its peak; in Middle Sung, 1050–1100; around 1350, when Mongols were giving way to Ming; toward the end of Ming, 1500–1600; and perhaps in the eighteenth century, under Manchu peace and prosperity. This is not an impressive series of constellations; but the genre is not very definite. Partly it chinks in gaps in the development of other categories.

Chuang Tse, about 300 B.C., had one of the most brilliant and vivid prose styles in Chinese history, and would deserve to be included here if he were not preëmpted by philosophy.

Plays.—The drama has been separately discussed. Its florescence falls between 1200 and 1400 or perhaps 1450. All later plays are considered inferior by both Chinese and Europeans.

Fiction.—Like the drama, the novel emerged into recognition under the Mongol period; but it kept on developing. Three main types are evident. These deal with the marvelous, either in collections of short tales or in larger romances; history; or love and manners. The most famous of the second class, in fact the most famous of all Chinese novels, the story of the *Three Kingdoms,* follows history rather closely; most of the personages are historically authentic. This novel is said to have grown for centuries. Like many others, it was added to or rewritten. For many a work no author is known, or the descriptions of authorship and period are traditional. The historical novels tend mainly to be earlier, and took their essentially final forms about Mongol times. Those of love or manners begin in Ming, and do not reach their best until 1500–1700.

The literature as a whole.—If now we try to see the strands jointly, as indicated in the accompanying diagram, a much less segmented picture results. Chou times yielded the classics, poetic and historic, plus the greatest philosophy. Han produced vigorous poetry, the greatest historian, a good beginning of polite prose; but no one growth lasted through Han. The four following centuries of political division resumed the prose and started poetry toward its final development. T'ang culminated the poetry for all time, but was preëminent in nothing else, except to some degree in literary prose as its poetry declined. Sung produced the second-best philosophy and history, and rather good prose and verse, but was not supreme in any one department. Yüan triumphed in plays; Yüan, Ming, and

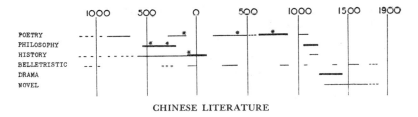

CHINESE LITERATURE

Manchu, in the novel. The one period when no branch of literature was flourishing with particular success was the tenth century, between T'ang and Sung.

The following seems clear. The basic literary formulations of attitude and style were made under Chou. Han, 200 B.C.– 200 A.D., was a varied period of culminations and lapses and new starts, with rapid change and little consecutiveness. The relations are both toward the past and the future. There seems no cogent reason for selecting 100 B.C. as a major turning point. The four after-Han centuries, the three of T'ang, and three of Sung form a larger unit; within which the first period is formative, the second climactic with specialization on poetry (as in art), the third preservative and afterglow. With the melting away of Sung, beginning about 1200, a new era is entered, which continues through Mongol, Ming, and Manchu. The old forms are still standard though they have lost their vigor, and new productivity is through unclassical, semivernacular media. Even this slackens after 1700.

CHINESE LITERATURE

POETRY

To ca. 650 B.C.
Shi-king.

300–100 B.C.

*Ch'ü Yüan, 332–295, *Li Sao* or *Falling into Trouble,* 376 lines,
irregular meters; and followers in the same genre, leading to
the *Elegies of Ch'u;* Ch'ü Yüan's nephew Sung Yü; King
Tsz'e; Kiah I, 199–165; Chuang-ki; Huai-nan-tze the philosopher, d. 122. Also Tung-fang So, 2d cent., and Liu Hsiang, b.
80 B.C.

In regular meters; Liu Heng, fourth Han emperor, d. 157; *Mei
Sheng, d. 140, exponent of 5-syllable line; Ssŭ-ma Siang-ju, d.
126 or 117; Princess Si-kiün, fl. ca. 110; Emperor Liu Ch'ê or
Wu Ti, ruled 140–87.

200 A.D.–618 A.D.

The Seven Poets or Scholars of the Kien-an era (196–221): Hsü
Kan, K'ung Jung (or Ying), Wang Ts'an (177–217), Yin Yang,
Lin Cheng, Ch'en Lin, Yüan Yü.
Ts'ao Ts'ao and his son Ts'ao Chih.
The Seven Worthies of the Bamboo Grove, 3d cent.: Liu Ling,
Hsi (Ki) K'ang. Hsiang Hsiu, Yüan Hsien, Yüan Chi, Wang
Jung, Shan T'ao.
Yang Fang.
Wang Hsi Chi, 321–379: *In the Orchard Pavilion.* Also callig-
rapher.
*T'ao Ts'ien or T'ao Yüan-ming, 365–427.
Pao Chao, d. 466.
Hsiao Yen, first Liang emperor, r. 502–549.
530, Wen Hsüan anthology collected by his son Hsiao T'ung.
Fu I, 554–639.
Hsieh Tao-heng and Wang Chi, ca. 600.
Yang Ti, Sui emperor, r. 605 seq.

Early T'ang, 618–713

Shang Kuan; Wang Po, 648–676; Yang K'iung; Lu Chao-lin;
Lo Pin-wang; Ch'en Tsze-ang (or -ngan), 656–698; Sung Chih-
wei, d. 710.

High (713–762) and Middle (763–846) T'ang

Meng Hao-jan, 689–740.
Wang Wei, 699–759.
Chang Ch'ien, graduated 727.
Ts'ui Hao, graduated ca. 730.

**Li (T'ai) Po, 701–762.

*Tu Fu, 712–770.

Wang Chien.

Han Yü, 768–824, greater essayist than poet.

Po Kü-i, or Po Lo-t'ien, 772–846.

Late T'ang, 847–906

Li Ho, Li She, Chang Chi, Hsü An-chen, 9th cent.

Tu Ch'in-niang, woman, 9th cent.

Tu Mu, 803–852.

Li Shung-yin or Li I-shan, 813–858.

Sse-k'ung Tu, 834–908, "last of the T'angs."

Grube mentions also Ts'en Ts'an, Wei Ying-wu, Chao Han, and Wang Chang-ling without dates.

Sung

Ch'en T'uan, d. 989.

Liu P'u, 965–1026.

Yang I, 974–1030, founder of Hsi K'un school.

Shao Yung, 1011–1077.

Su Tung-p'o or Su Shih, 1036–1101.

Hung Chüeh-fan, ca. 1100.

The Si Ling school of Southern Sung times included Hsü Ling-hui, Hsü Ling-yüan, Wung Ling-shu, Chao Ling-hsiu.

Later

Of recent poets, Yüan Mei, 1715–1797, is perhaps most often mentioned.

PHILOSOPHY

(See the list in Chapter Two.)

HISTORY

Shu-king

Yen-tze-ch'un-ts'iu, about 500 B.C., by Yen Ying.

Ch'un-ts'iu (annals of Lu), ca. 480, "by" Confucius.

Tso Chuan, commentary and elaboration of this, by a pupil Tso, ca. 450–400.

Kuoh-Yü, also attributed to Tso: State Episodes or Conversations.

Ku-liang and Kung-yang also wrote commentaries on the *Ch'un-ts'iu* in the 5th cent.

Chuh-shu-ki-nien, annals of Wei to 299 B.C. Discovered 279 A.D.

Lü-shih-ch'un-ts'iu, by Lü Pu-wei, d. 235.

Chau-kuoh-tz'eh, Plans of the Warring Kingdoms, ca. 200 B.C.

Wu-yüeh-ch'un-ts'iu, annals of Wu and Yüeh; romantic history; 2d cent. B.C.

**Ssŭ-ma Ch'ien, ca. 145–ca. 85 (after 91): *Shi-ki.*
Liu Hsiang, 80–9 B.C.
Pan Piao, 3–54 A.D., and son Pan Ku and daughter Pan Chao.

Fan Yeh, d. 445.   Yen Shih-ku, 579–645.
Li Po-yao, 565–648.   Wei Cheng, 581–643.

Liu Hsü, 897–946.
Ou-yang Hsiu, 1007–1072, and Sung Ch'i, 998–1061.
*Ssŭ-ma Kuang, 1019–1086: *T'ung Chien,* Mirror of History.
Cheng Ch'iao, 1108–1166.
*Chu Hsi, the philosopher, 1130–1200. His revision of Ssŭ-ma
  Kuang is standard.

LITERARY PROSE

(Huai-nan Tze, d. 122 B.C. Taoist.)
Li Ling, fl. 99 B.C.
Lu Wen-shu, fl. ca. 67 B.C.
Yang Hsiung, 53 B.C.–18 A.D.
Wang Ch'ung, 27–97.
Wang Hi-chi, 321–379.
T'ao Ts'ien or T'ao Yüan-ming, 365–427.
*Han Yü, 768–824.
*Liu Tsung-yüan, 773–819.
Tu Mu, 803–852.
Li Hua, 9th cent.
Ou-yang Hsiu, 1007–1072.
*Su Shih or Su Tung-p'o, 1036–1101.
Su Cheh, 1039–1112.

Sung Lien, 1310–1381.
Liu Ki, 1311–1375.
Fang Hsiao-ju, 1357–1402.
Wang Shou-jen, 1472–1528.
Wang Shi-cheng, 1526–1598.
Lan Ting-yüan, 1680–1733.
Yüan Mei, 1715–1797.

DRAMA

(See separate treatment previously given.)

NOVEL

***San-kuo-chi Yen-i,* the Expanded Story of the Three Kingdoms,
  attributed to Lo Kuan-chung of the Mongol period. This, the
  most famous of Chinese novels, may be described as romantic
  history rather than a historical romance. It was probably
  built up gradually from earlier and briefer or partial versions.

*Shui Hu Chuan, the River Margin Story (renamed "All Men Are Brothers" in a recent American translation), by Shih Nai-an, of the 13th cent. A freer fictional treatment of a historical basis of revolt against misgovernment and brigandage.

Yüh Kiao Li, of the 15th cent. The successful love of a young scholar for two charming and learned cousins.

P'ing Shan Lêng Yen, another love story of the learned; also of Ming times, but written in a nearly classical style.

Lieh Kuo Chuan, or Tung-Chou Lieh-kuo-chi, historical novel about the warring Chou states. Written later than the San-kuo-chi, but similar in style and compass. Probably Ming.

**Hsi Yu Ki, the Western Journey Record, by Wu Ch'êng-ên, 1500/05–1580. (Renamed "Monkey" in Waley's recent Englishing.) Fantastic, magical, full of the paraphernalia of Buddhist (and Taoist) mythology, ironic, humorous, episodic, and vivid. Has been confused with an identically named geographical treatise or travel romance by a Taoist patriarch contemporary of Jenghiz Khan.

*Kin P'ing Mei, really the names of the three heroines, but meaning also Golden Vase Plums. A novel of character and manners, full of eroticism; "forbidden" in China. Attributed to Wang Shih-cheng, 1526–1593. Colloquial, easy style.

Hao K'in Chuan, a love novel. Ming.

King Hua Yüan, fantastic, including a visit to the Country of Gentlemen. Ming.

Feng-shen Yen-i, Divinity metamorphoses.

Poh-she K'i-chuan, the Marvelous Story of the White Serpent.

Kin-ku K'i-kuan, Ancient and Modern Marvelous Tales. Forty tales by various authors, collected in late Ming times. Colloquial style.

Erh Tou Mei, Twice-Flowering Plums. A novel of two heroes, each of whom marries two heroines. The style is simple. 16th–17th cents.

*Liao-chai Chih-i, the Refuge-Study's Strange Stories. By P'u Sung-ling, written in 1679, published in 1740. A collection in almost classical, terse, excellent style, but extremely popular in appeal.

**Hung Lou Mêng, the Red Chamber Dream, by Ts'ao Süeh-k'in or Ts'ao Chan, probably of the latter 17th cent. Forty chapters are said to have been added by Kao O in 1792. A long novel of love and domestic manners and the fortunes of a great house. The style is semicolloquial.

Yeh-sao Pao-yen, by Hsia Erh-ming; 18th cent.

§71. Japanese Literature

The literature of Japan is strangely narrow, extraordinarily self-contained and sustained, and unusually lacking in organization into sharp pulses or cycles. It is much less visibly dependent on China than are Japanese sculpture and painting. This is so notwithstanding that the Japanese writing system is Chinese, the Japanese language is full of Chinese loan words, and Chinese-Korean Buddhism has been established for thirteen hundred years.

A fundamental rule of Japanese poetry, strictly observed for many centuries, was that Chinese loan words might not be used, however current in speech, religion, or nonliterary writing. Obviously this proscription is indicative of a persistent attitude of national exclusiveness. But its long observance suggests with equal force the Japanese willingness, or desire, to accept limitation, to operate in a restricted field and with restricted techniques.

Japan has never accepted the rhyme which has always distinguished Chinese poetry. When China added tonal pattern to its verse, the Japanese could not follow if they would. What they took over from the Chinese, or share with them, is brevity of the line of verse, and brevity of the stanza; also, aversion to long poems under any circumstances. In Japan the tendency was carried to the extreme. In their normal poetry, the stanza is the poem.

This condensation brought about grave formal involvements. There is no stress accent in Japanese, and except in rather special cases no quantitative difference of syllables. Tone in the usual sense being also lacking, three of the principal human expedients for singling verse out from prose by internal pattern, within the line, were eliminated. As for external form, rhyme and alliteration not being used, there remained only length of line, as expressed by number of syllables. This one remaining avenue was further narrowed by limitation of the poetic line to either five or seven syllables.

There are some early and again late uses of four- and six-syllable lines; but they are rare, and never classically standard.

Narrative and late dramatic poetry tended to run on an alternation of 7, 5; 7, 5; ... syllable lines. But this was evidently felt as a sort of recitative rather than true poetry, and considered popular rather than refined. The classical form of high poetry, the *tanka,* consists of 31 syllables in five lines, distributed thus: 5, 7, 5, 7, 7 syllables. The tanka was composed in the seventh century and is still composed in the twentieth.

There are a few close variants. The long poem, or *naga-uta,* runs in alternation of 5 and 7 syllables. It is never long by Western standards, and comparatively rare: a collection containing a tenth as many naga-utas as tankas is exceptional. The short poem or *kata-uta* is simply 5, 7, 7 in its old form. A pair of these: 5, 7, 7–5, 7, 7, the second answering the first, makes the *sedo-ka.* About 1100, a sort of interlaced tanka, the chain or *renga,* came into use: 5, 7, 5; 7, 7; 5, 7, 5; 7, 7; 5, 7, 5; ... Out of this, apparently, there evolved by excision the 5, 7, 5 *hokku* for purposes of wit, which in the seventeenth century flourished as the *haikai* and again became lyrical. The difference between the kata-uta of 5, 7, 7 and the haikai of 5, 7, 5 is that the older poem had 19 syllables and consisted of the last three lines of the tanka, the later had only 17 taken from the first three lines. But to the Japanese the implications, the type of feeling, seem to be quite different; and there are centuries between the origins of the two forms.

The tanka all through remained the fountainhead and norm, the poem *par excellence.* But even this underwent a characteristic shift. Until about 800, the typical tanka organization was 5, 7; 5, 7; 7. Since then, it has been 5, 7, 5; 7, 7. What can a non-Japanese do in the face of a literature of such discriminations? He is as helpless as a musician who should encounter a national music built wholly on quarter tones in the compass of a tone and a half. What has been set forth here is the external, because it is describable. Apparently the internals of Japanese poems, their meaning, emotion, or virtue, differ by equally small intervals or shadings. The whole art seems nothing but nuance.

Obviously a 31-syllable poem, averaging scarcely a dozen words, cannot be more than a sketch. It must express by suggestion: by hints, indirections, and intangibles. This quality runs through most Japanese literature. It is allied to the fact that most of the literature is aristocratic—composed by aristocrats and concerned with delicacies. There are also plebeian or bourgeois strains in Japanese literature. But on the whole they are late: preponderantly during the Tokugawa regime, since 1600. And they have never crowded out the aristocratic component, even if in recent centuries they have surpassed it in quantity of product. Apparently the distinction between aristocratic and plebeian art is felt very deeply by the Japanese. They are never in doubt to which category a product belongs, nor how far down or up in the scale of superiority.

The tanka seems to have been well established not later than the Taikwa reform or Sinification of 645. The first and in many ways greatest collection of Japanese poems is the *Manyoshiu,* assembled through private interest about 760, in the Nara epoch. Later collections are official, by imperial order. The *Manyoshiu* contains 4,496 poems, of which 4,173 are tankas. Forty-one are *sedoka,* paired or answering line-triplets; 262 are naga-uta "long" poems—an unusually high proportion.

With the removal of the capital to Heian-jo (Kyoto) in 794, inaugurating the Heian period, the writing of Chinese poetry came temporarily into favor among the Japanese nobility; but the native style went on, just as the native *Hiragana* and *Katakana* syllabaries were developed as an addition to Chinese ideography by 850. The ninth century was the time of the *rok-kusen,* the "six geniuses" or divine poets, including the lady Komachi. The change in the organization of the five lines was accomplished in this period. The "pivot word" on which the final couplet hinges away from the first three lines became more definitely established; also the fixity of associated or "pillow words": *dew* must be accompanied by *tears, thread* must be *thin,* etc. As between the seventh- to eighth-century and ninth-century tanka, the former perhaps excels in feeling, in native estimation; the latter in perfection of form. Which should be accorded superiority is difficult for a westerner even to guess. At any rate, the culmination for the whole thirteen-hundred-year development seems to be placed in these first two to three centuries; which is not surprising. It is hard to imagine so slight a form in continuous improvement for a thousand years.

From 905 to 1187 there were six official anthologies, consisting almost wholly of tankas.

Prose began with mythological history and interest in ritual. The *Kojiki,* 712, is in pure Japanese, without Chinese loan words, though of course the writing was purely Chinese. The second work, the *Nihongi,* 720, shows more Chinese influence, in both style and content. Also from the Nara era are the *Fudoki,* collections of tales and antiquarianism relating to districts, of which only one has been preserved intact. The *Norito* or ritual addresses, prolix and bombastic, date from the same time, though the available collection was made in 929.

About 900 prose began to be private and secular, that is, avowed literature, with the *monogatari,* the tale or story, ultimately developing into the novel, and then into the historical narrative. Special genres that came up soon after 900 are the poem-story, a brief tale written around one or more poems; and the diary. By 950, women were writing perhaps most of the prose, and certainly the best. The chefs d'œuvre, Murasaki's *Tale of Genji,* a long novel, and Sei Shonagon's *Pillow Sketches,* a series of subjective impressions, are from 1000 to 1010, and both by women. It has been supposed that the women learned first to excel in prose on native themes because they were less subject to the rigorous study of the Chinese classics. This prose literature is as marked by subtlety, refinement, indirection, and subjectivism as the tanka, even though it does not aim at all at fragile brevity.

Around 1100, the preëminence of the personal novel and diary yielded to what may be called the historical romance, based on chapters of national history but treated as tales, and still called monogatari. The *Heike,* composed apparently somewhat before 1250, is perhaps the finest of these; but most Japanese and westerners alike seem to rate it as less great than Murasaki's *Genji,* which remains the jewel of Japan's prose literature. Except perhaps for the very earliest, the historical romances were written by men.

In the fourteenth and fifteenth centuries the personal-hero tale replaced the historical romance, but without the sophistication of the *Genji* type of four centuries earlier, and accounted more vulgar in style than the romance.

"Popular" poetry, that is, verse outside the stream of the aristocratic tanka, developed on the plan of lines of 7, 5; 7, 5; . . . syllables. At first, around the tenth century, the arrangement of lines was somewhat irregular, and the subject matter related to Shinto occasions. Later, in the thirteenth and fourteenth centuries—the Kamakura period,—this poetry became Buddhistic and reflective. This *imayo* poetry kept to the 7–5 syllable alternation, but limited itself usually to four or six pairs of lines. It also admitted Buddhistic and Chinese loan words.

The renga or dovetailed tanka series are given a special section in the *Kinyoshiu* anthology of 1127, were fabricated in long chains by paid professionals in Kamakura times, and reached their apogee with Sogi, 1421–1503, in the Ashikaga epoch.

To the same Ashikaga era, but culminating a little earlier, belong the lyric *No* dramas. These consist of prose and verse; the latter has the 7–5 imayo form, but is expected to be largely a tissue of citations. Popular tales, *otogi-zoshi,* were also written in 7–5, 7–5 syllable recitative. One of these, the *Joruri,* became a famous prototype, out of which, after accompaniment by the samisen instrument, one of the two forms of regular drama, the puppet play, later developed.

Thus far, we have had a succession of genres, each with its growth and decline but on the whole rated progressively a little less high as the first few centuries were left behind. The Ashikaga era developed several types, but none of them very great; and the sixteenth century is perhaps the lowest of any.

When the civil wars were over, the Tokugawa regime firmly

intrenched, and Japan thoroughly isolated, soon after 1600, a new trend came into literature. Peace, control, middle-class prosperity brought a literature which was reckoned vulgar, but which nonetheless is far from inconsiderable. From 1600 on, also, the configuration is more "normal": The peaks of the several types or genres tend to coincide. Thus Saikaku, 1642–1693, brought the *ukiyo-zoshi* or novel of realistic life to its climax; Basho, 1654–1694, the 17-syllable 3-line haikai or haiku poem; and Chikamatsu, 1653–1724, the Shakespeare of Japan, the drama, both puppet- and human-acted. This flowering fell around the famous Genroku era, 1688–1703, in which

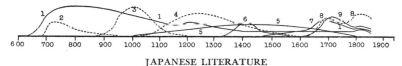

JAPANESE LITERATURE

Solid lines, poetry: 1, *tanka*; 5, *renga*; 6, *No*; 7, *haikai*; 9, drama.
Broken lines, prose: 2, *kojiki*, etc.; 3, feminine court novel, etc.; 4, historic romance; 8, realistic novel.

Tokugawa Japan felt it had reached the zenith of its success and brilliance. It was associated with Osaka as well as Kyoto.

Toward the middle of the eighteenth century, the focal point shifted from Osaka to Yedo, that is, Tokyo. Here, in the first quarter or third of the nineteenth century, there occurred a second, somewhat lesser florescence. This is signalized by the novelists Ikku, 1766–1831, and Bakin, 1767–1848; the playwright Tsuruya Namboku the fourth, 1755–1829; the haikai writer—and painter—Buson, 1716–1784; and by a tanka revival.

Within another generation came the Tokugawa collapse, the Meiji era, and the beginning of sudden westernization.

If now we try to resume the whole course of thirteen hundred years, it is evident that poetry was from its seventh-century beginning set in an exceedingly narrow frame, and within that reached its peak early: in two centuries if not in one. Prose developed more slowly, but culminated after three to four hundred years, around 1000. New genres continued to be developed, but reached, on the whole, lesser and lesser heights; until the later fifteenth and the sixteenth century failed to produce even new types of importance. The first literature not wholly aristocratic and exclusive in manner began to appear in Kamakura times, after 1200. With the Tokugawa epoch, from 1600 on, the slump was emerged from with the development of a series of new vigorous themes and forms, including a true drama, which attained their climax around 1700, plus a secondary echo in the decades following 1800. All the new genres were plebeian, or at least bourgeois semivulgar, by the old aristocratic standards of sophisticated finesse, deliberate limitation and indirection, and cultivated fragility; and, in poetry at least, the classical forms never died out—somewhat as we still write sonnets.

It is perhaps not doing undue violence to the facts to recognize two main configurations in this story. The first would be the history of the literature of a restricted, overcultivated class, from 700 to 1600. In this course, the poetry culminated 700–900, the novel and belles lettres around 1000, heroic semi-history about 1200, the ritual drama about 1400, the order of importance of the successive genres being a descending one, and the last two centuries being relatively barren. The second growth was nonaristocratic, and produced both a drama and a novel of popular appeal but of no great control of form, the peaks falling in the decades after 1700 and 1800.

JAPANESE LITERATURE

Mythological-historical-ritual collections: 700 seq.
  *Kojiki, 712.
  Nihongi, 720.
  Idzumo-fudoki, 733; and other topographies, Nara era, 710–784.
  Norito prayers or speeches, ca. 700, collected 901–923 (929) in
    Yengi-shiki.

Tanka and related poetry: 650 to present
  **Manyoshiu collection, soon after 800, includes poems from 645
    to ca. 760. The longest single piece, by *Hitomaro, ca. 662–710,
    is a 149-line elegy. *Akahito, fl. 724–756, is about equally
    eminent. Also poetesses.
  *Kokinshiu, compiled 905 (922). Mostly near-contemporary, at
    any rate after 760. Included are: Takamura, d. 852; Henjo,

816–890; Yukihira; *Narihira, 826–888; *Komachi, woman; Kuronushi; *Tsurayuki, after 900; Koji, Mitsune.

Gosenshiu, ca. 951, a third anthology.

New official collections ca. 996, 1127 (*Kinyoshiu*), 1152, 1187, 1205 (*Shin-Kokinshiu*).

Izumi Shikita, 988–1074, woman; Tsunenobu, 1017–1097; Toshiyori, his son; Shikishi, woman, d. 1201; Saigyo, monk, 1118–1190; Ietaka, 1158–1237; *Teika (Sadaie), 1162–1241; Jo-Toba, emperor, 1180–1239.

Tokugawa *tanka* revival, births from 1697 to 1828.

Early prose: tales, novels, diaries, reflections, many by women: 900–1350

Taketori monogatari, ca. 900, or soon after 922. Human fairy talc.

Utsubo monogatari, 14 miraculous tales. Longest work before *Genji;* attributed to author of *Taketori.*

Tsurayuki, preface to *Kokinshiu,* ca. 922; and *Tosa Nikki,* diary, 935.

Ise monogatari: 125 incident tales, each with a *tanka.*

Yamato monogatari, ca. 950: 152 tales, type of Ise.

Kagero Nikki, 954–974, diary of a woman.

Ochikubo monogatari, ca. 967–969. Tale of a stepchild.

Hamamatsu Chiunagon, novel, probably before 1000.

**Murasaki no Shikibu, woman: *Genji monogatari,* ca. 1004; diary, 1008–1009.

*Sei Shonagon, woman: *Makura Zoshi,* Pillow Sketches, soon after 1000.

Genji imitations: *Sagoromo,* ca. 1040; *Torikaebaya,* after 1040.

Sarashina Nikki, diary of journeys, by a woman, ca. 1046–1068.

Hojoki, by Chomei (Renin), 1212. A "hermit hut's record."

Izayoi no Ki, diary of travel in 1277, by Abutsu, a woman.

Kenko, ca. 1283–1350: *Tsure-dzure-gusa,* sketches and essays.

Romantic history: 1100–1500

Yeigwa monogatari, probably by a woman, not far from 1100; treats of 930–1088.

O-kagami, Great Mirror, between 1100 and 1150; treats of 851–1036. By Tamenari.

The *Hogen, Heiji,* and *Gempei monogatari* are ascribed to Tokinaga, of early Kamakura period, near close of the 12th cent. They deal respectively with the wars of 1157, 1159, and 1167–1199.

Heike monogatari, between ca. 1225 and 1250. Adaptation of the *Gempei.*

Jinkoshotoki, by Chikafusa, 1293–after 1351; history of Japan with a political philosophy.

Taiheiki, by Kojima (?), d. 1374; history of 1181–1368; its style is the foundation of modern literary prose, with free Chinese admixture.

Renga or chain verses: from before 1100 to 1500
1127, a section in *Kinyoshiu* (see *Tanka*).
In Kamakura period, longer series, by professionals.
1356, first separate anthology.
Nijo Yoshimoto, d. 1388.
*Sogi, 1421–1503.

No, lyric drama: Ashikaga times, 1338–1575
*Peak about 1400 or soon after. (See chapter on Drama.)

Haikai, seventeen-syllable poem: 1500 to present
Haikai no renga, humorous chain, Ashikaga period.
Hokku, same period, 5, 7, 5 syllables, witty; later called *haiku* or *haikai.*
Yamazaki So-kan, 1445–1534.
Moritake, 1472–1549.
Teitoku, 1571–1653.
Nishiyama Soin, 1605–1682: Daurin style.
Teishitsu, 1616–1673.
From here on the *haikai* turned from wit to lyric quality.
Saikaku, 1642–1693.
*Basho, 1643–1694.
Kyorai, 1651–1704.
Ransetsu, 1654–1707.
Raizan, 1654–1716.
Onitsura, 1661–1738.
Kikaku, 1661–1707.
Yokoi Yayu, 1701–1783.
Buson, the painter, 1716–1784.
Issa, 1763–1827.

Realistic novel of life: 1650 seq.
*Saikaku, 1642–1693. Wrote *ukiyo-zoshi* after 1682. Erotic.
*Kiseki, fl. ca. 1715, d. 1736.
*Kioden, 1761–1816, fl. ca. 1780–1790. Romantic novel.

*Ikku, ca. 1766–1831, fl. 1802–1822; developed the *kokkeibon,* humorous novel.
**Bakin, 1767–1848, fl. 1807–1841.
  Shikitei Samba, 1775–1822, fl. 1809–1813. Satirical.
  Tanehiko, 1783–1842.
  Shunsui, d. 1842. Novel of sentiment, *ninjobon.*

Drama, puppet or with actors: 1600 to the present
  *Chikamatsu, 1653–1724, fl. 1703–1713, marks the culmination.
  Secondary peak under Tsuruya Namboku IV, 1755–1829, fl. 1813–1825.
  (See chapter on Drama.)

Kanga-kusha, Scholars of Things Chinese, 1600–1725
  Seikwa, 1560–1619, established Sung philosophy.
  Doshun, 1583–1657.
  Yekken, 1630–1714.
  Hakuseki, 1657–1725.
  Kiuso, 1658–1734.

Waga-kusha, Scholars of Things Japanese, 1675–1825
  Keichiu, 1640–1701.
  Kada, 1669–1736.
  Mabuchi, 1697–1769.
  Motoori, 1730–1801. (On grammar, 1779 [see chapter on Philology]; continued by his son Haruniwa.)
  Hirata, 1776–1843.

§72. Sanskrit Literature

In spite of prolixity, exaggeration, and overornateness, the literature of India ranks high among the great literatures of the world. It is also perhaps the most difficult to assign dates to. I exclude all primarily religious writing: the Vedas, the Brahmanas and Upanishads, the Buddhist canon and works of edification; also philosophy. What remains is mostly in Sanskrit and in Kavya style; that is, a conscious art in a standardized language: Sanskrit means "regulated." Minor portions of this literature are in various Prakrits, that is, "native" or natural dialects of districts or perhaps classes. The whole is in a sense court literature, as it has sometimes been called. More exactly, it is a literature of cultivation, floating on a stream of vernaculars used in daily life.

As in Greece, two great epics precede the more varied and skillful classical literature of the historic period; but they are much less compact and organized than the Greek ones. Valmiki may have about as good a claim to the authorship of the *Rāmāyana* as Homer to that of the *Iliad;* but Vyasa as author of the *Mahābhārata* is clearly mythical. The dates are very uncertain. The *Mahābhārata* especially must have been a long time expanding to its present interpolated and overinterpolated form. Its beginnings are probably the older of the two—it is more national in scope, without a hero; its final form is later. The *Rāmāyana* was, very likely, essentially finished before Christ; the *Mahābhārata* kept on growing for several centuries. The Epic language and style are unornate compared with the Classical. The meter is merely syllabic, with quantitative cadences, as against the long-and-short quantitative meters of Kavya.

The Classic or Kavya or post-Epic literature is attested for the second century after Christ, and its beginnings are probably pre-Christian. There is thus an overlap between the Epic and post-Epic manners—again as in Greece. A proto-Classic phase of Kavya, to the fourth century, may be set off, not only on the basis of this overlap, but because of lesser finish.

The great Kavya literature is that between 350 and 750, with its peak in Kalidasa around 400 or 450; that is, near the beginning. The products are dramatic, lyric, epic, and in prose. But the dramas are more literary and less vigorous on the stage than those in most other languages; and "epic" now means any longer narrative or descriptive poem, not a continuation of the simple, prolix, grandiose manner of the two national epics. A comparison of the Alexandrian brief or episodic epic with Homer roughly illustrates the difference.

The term Gupta is applicable to the best period with the same reservations as in art. The Gupta dynasty held sway only from about 320 to 490. Under it, the styles of poetry, drama, sculpture, and perhaps painting reached their finished perfection; but they continued at a high level two or three centuries longer. The development seems to have been mainly north-central Indian, between the Vindhyas and the Himalayas; there is little to show participation of the Northwest, of Bengal, or of the South.

On the contrary, a post-Classic phase of some four centuries, from about 750 to 1150 or 1200, is mainly peripheral: Kashmir and Bengal predominate. Compared with the past, there is a falling off in quality, though it is gradual, and in the final century 1050–1150 a definite secondary peak is formed by Somadeva, Bilhana, Kalhana, and Jayadeva. The whole Classical Sanskrit cycle is slow-moving: a minimum of a continuous thousand years must be allowed it. This is as in all other activities of timeless India.

After about 1200, Sanskrit literature continued to be produced, but was feebler. Its place was taken by vernacular literatures, especially in Hindi, which attained their culmination in Tulsi Das's reworking in Eastern Hindi of the *Rāmāyana,* under Akbar in 1574. Productions in other dialects point to a general swell of neo-Indian or vernacular literature in the century or so before and after that date. This swell would have its partial parallel in Mughal-Marattha painting. Neo-Indic verse is, like Classical Sanskrit, rigidly quantitative. In addition, it is end-rhymed, and requires double-syllable or feminine rhymes as minimum. Its form is therefore unusually rigorous; and it is obviously much more than a folk product, in spite of the participation of famous weaver and tailor poets in its beginnings. Vernacular prose literature is late, taking shape only around 1800, and hardly standardized as yet.

All in all, Neo-Indic literature is to a considerable degree a product achieved in a new speech medium in continuation of old Indic patterns. There is less mythology and more syncretic theism; but mythology remains. The chief new element of substance is *bhakti,* the love of god; of form, rhyme; both seemingly non-Indian in origin. But the *bhakti* feeling has shown some tendency to clothe its expression in the old Indian eroticism.

Of the Dravidian literatures, Tamil is the most important. There is a recent tendency to date some of its outstanding productions back to the second or third Christian centuries. This seems astonishingly early. Other Tamil works of renown are attributed to the period between the eighth or ninth and the thirteenth centuries; which roughly equates with the time of South Indian important participation in philosophy.

SANSKRIT LITERATURE

I. EPIC PERIOD

Rāmāyaṇa. Books 2–6 probably composed by Valmiki between 400 and 200 B.C.; books 1 and 7 probably added between 150 and 100 B.C.; the whole being famous, in its present size and form, before the *Mahābhārata* attained its permanent shape. There is no Buddhistic or Greek influencing; nor on the other hand is any knowledge of the *Rāmāyaṇa* evident in the early Buddhist Tripitaka canon.

Mahābhārata. Some of the material is older than any in the *Rāmāyaṇa,* but even after it had taken shape in epic form, accretions occurred until the fourth century A.C., after which the work essentially kept its present form and huge compass. It is now something between an epic and a *purāṇa,* and contains references to Buddhism, the Greeks, and stone buildings. Some of the included moral tales presumably date back to sixth-century unwritten literature of asceticism on which Buddhism also drew. The assumed epic kernel can hardly be earlier than 400–300 B.C., else allusions to it would almost certainly have occurred in the home country of Buddhism during its first two centuries. There is no telling how much later than 400–300 B.C. the original narrative was composed, except that time must be left for the enormous accretions to have been made by about 350 A.D.

II. PROTOCLASSIC PERIOD, 1–350 A.D.

? Non-Buddhistic predecessors of Aśvaghoṣa.

Aśvaghoṣa, 2d cent. Buddhistic dramas and epics in court-art style.

Mātṛceta, and Āryaśūra, not much later. Buddhist poets.

The *Kāmasūtra* or *Kāmaśāstra* or textbook of eroticism, whose preserved text by Vātsyāyana is of uncertain date, probably existed in an earlier form before Aśvaghoṣa.

Tantrākhyāyika, oldest form of *Pancatantra,* 3d or 4th cent.

*Bhāsa, about a century before Kālidāsa, viz. between ca. 275 and 350. Dramas.

III. CLASSIC OR GUPTA PERIOD, 350–750

**Kālidāsa, probably of Ujjain, ca. 350–420 or ca. 390–460. Dramas, epics, lyrics.

Hāla or Sātavāhana, about the time of Kālidāsa; 700 lyric stanzas in Māhārāṣṭrī Prakrit.

*Amaru, probably near the time of Kālidāsa; or, not later than 800; most famous love lyricist.

*Śūdraka, period wholly uncertain. Drama *Mṛcchakaṭika*, or *Little Clay Cart.*

Guṇādhya, probably not before 5th cent. Established the tale in literary Sanskrit. His *Bṛhatkathā* in Paiśācī Prakrit is lost but is the source of later works by Kṣemendra, Somadeva, and Budhasvāmin.

Viśākhadatta, early 5th cent., or 8th to 9th. Play *Mudrārākṣasa.*

Bhaṭṭi, between 495 and 641, and Bhāravi, were famous for their epics by 650.

*Bhartṛhari, also widely known by 650. Most famous Sanskrit sentential poet. Also composer of erotic lyrics. Buddhistic elements.

Varāhamihira, d. 587. Poet and astronomer.

*Daṇḍin, probably about 600. Prose romance; also theory of literature.

*Subandhu, not later than the beginning of the 7th cent. His *Vāsavadattā* is sometimes accounted the greatest prose romance, but is overornate.

*Harṣadeva the king, ruled 606–647. Plays.

Mayura, of Harṣa's group. Stanzas in praise of the sun.

Bāṇa, also associated with Harṣa. Prose romance, in the style of Subandhu; also historical romance.

Māgha, of Srimala in Gujerat, between 650 and 700. Epic *Śiśupālavadha.*

*Bhavabhūti of Berar, at Kanauj ca. 730–740, or at Ujjain ca. 700. Dramas ranked second to Kālidāsa's.

Vākpatirāja, pupil of last, also at court of Kanauj. Historic epic panegyric in Prakrit poetry and ultra-artificial style.

IV. POSTCLASSIC PERIOD, 750–1200

In central or western India

Rājaśekhara, at Kanauj, ca. 900. Drama. Occasional rhyme, under influence of popular poetry.

Padmagupta, at Dhara in Malava, ca. 1005. Epic *Navasāhasānkacarita.*

In Kashmir

Ratnākara, during the reigns 826–883. Epic *Haravijaya,* mythological.

Śivasvāmin, before 900, Buddhist. Epic *Kapphiṇābhyudaya.*

Kṣemendra, fl. 1037–1066. Polygraph: epic, drama, abbreviations of *Mahābhārata* and *Rāmāyaṇa.*

*Somadeva, fl. 1063–1081. *Kathāsaritsāgara,* collection of tales in verse.

*Bilhaṇa, ca. 1070–1090. Lyric, historic epic, drama. Style simple. Went to western Chalukya kingdom.

Mankha, ca. 1135–1145. Mythological epic *Śrikaṇṭhacarita.*

*Kalhaṇa, ca. 1148, greatest historian of India. Poetic chronicle of Kashmir.

In Bengal, at the court of Lakshmanasena, 1119 seq.

*Jayadeva. *Gītagovinda.* Sequence of Krishna lyrics, or lyric dance-drama. True end rhyme.

Govardhana. Erotic lyric.

NEO-INDIC LITERATURE, 1150 ON

Bardic chronicles of the Rajputs, beginning in the 12th cent., with lost predecessors several centuries older.

*Chand Bardai, d. 1193, wrote the most famous of these, the *Prithi Raj Raso.*

Jnanesvar, free paraphrase of *Bhagavadgita,* in Marathi.

*Namdev, 1270–1350 (or, fl. 1400–1430), hymns in Marathi.

Janabai, his female slave; the same.

Ramananda, 1400–1470, religious leader, of *Rama bhakti* doctrine; gave up Sanskrit for vernacular.

Vidyapati Thakur, fl. ca. 1400 or 1450. *Krishna bhakti,* in Maithili dialect of Bihari.

Mira Bai, princess, fl. ca. 1470 (or 1420). Religious lyrics, in Braj Bhasha dialect of Western Hindi.

Narsingh Mehta, fl. 1450–1480. Krishna lyrics in Gujarati.

*Kabir, 1440–1518. Mohammedan weaver, turned syncretistic deistic poet.

Nanak, 1469–1538, founder of Sikh religion.

Malik Muhammad Jayasi, influenced by Kabir. *Padumavati,* a romantic historic poem, explained as allegory.

Sur Das, 1483–1563. 75,000 religious verses in Braj Bhasha.

Tan Sen of Gwalior, fl. 1560–1610, poet and musician of Akbar. Convert to Islam.

**Tulsi Das, 1532–1624, ca. 1574 began *Ram Charit Manas,* a reworking of the *Ramayana,* in Eastern Hindi.

Kesav Das, 1555–1617, of Bundelkhand. First important writer on poetics.

Arjun in 1604 compiled the *Sikh Adi Granth* or psalter.

*Tukaram, ca. 1608–1649. Marathi religious songs.

Bihari Lal, ca. 1603–1663, of Gwalior, wrote in Braj Bhasha on poetics.

Dev Kavi, ca. 1673–1745. Erotic-religious poetry in Braj Bhasha.

Lallu Ji Lal, fl. ca. 1804, creator of "High Hindi" literary prose.

§73. Literature of the Ancient Near East

Egypt spoke Hamitic; early lower Mesopotamia, Sumerian; later Mesopotamia, Syria, and Palestine, Semitic. In none of these ancient countries or tongues was a strictly formal poetry achieved, in the sense of verse with regulated number of syllables, accents, lengths, or rhyme. There was what we can still feel as meter of a sort, probably roughly accentual, but loose and irregular. The chief characteristic of poetry was the balanced parallel, repetitive or contrasting. But while this is undoubtedly a poetic device, it is a mechanism which is expressed through content rather than through form as such.

On the other hand, effective prose was developed early in the Near East: in Egypt by 2000 B.C., and for the genuinely literary purpose of giving enjoyment. In Semitic Mesopotamia the growth of literary prose as distinct from poetical utterance is less clear. But little Palestine by the ninth century was writing narrative the religious objective of which was often transcended by delight in the story and effective skill in handling it.

These facts sufficiently controvert the opinions sometimes held that literature of necessity begins with poetry, and that poetry begins with national lays which consolidate into epics.

EGYPT

To our vision, Egyptian literature begins abruptly with the Middle Kingdom Twelfth Dynasty, 2000–1788. Some of the content relates to the Old Kingdom, and may date from that age of great pyramids. But there is nothing to show that the form is old. The Pyramid Texts are confused, vehement, incoherent; even if we allow for their purpose as magical, they give no evidence of any smooth, controlled use of language. Quite likely, writing was still too restricted in the Old Kingdom for a pure literature to develop. At any rate, if there was a formative period, it may be guessed to have fallen not in the great Fourth and Fifth Dynasties but long after, in the unsettlement before 2000; and with the Twelfth, literature emerges ready-made.

It will be recalled that the first burst of preserved science from Egypt also comes to us from the Twelfth Dynasty and the following Hyksos period. Art and architecture were not superior then to those of the Pyramid Age: again we must infer that in the earlier times writing served mainly governmental, fiscal, magical, and religious purposes, but after 2000 came into wider civil use.

After the Hyksos were expelled, Egypt developed for the first time into an empire with foreign possessions. This attainment was achieved by the Eighteenth Dynasty, and an art florescence, around 1400, followed closely on the politico-military peak of about 1450. But there was no corresponding renaissance of literature. We have Eighteenth Dynasty papyri, but they appear mostly to be copies of Twelfth Dynasty compositions. Since preservation probabilities would all be in favor of the Eighteenth, which was four hundred years later, it seems clear that we are dealing with an actual letdown of productivity, and that literature and art did not move abreast.

On the contrary, later in the New Empire, under the Nineteenth Dynasty, when the realm was still holding together with outward magnificence although approaching decline, and beginning about 1300 under Rameses II, there was a new growth of literature. The reason for this development is plain: the literature is now written in New Egyptian. The previous history is also cleared up. Dynasty XII evidently used its speech to evolve a style, built up a satisfying literature, and exhausted the possibilities of this. Meanwhile the spoken language changed, until, when Dynasty XVIII emerged after the liberation from the Hyksos, the written language had become some-

what artificial. After all, the time interval was as great as that
from Shakespeare to ourselves. Just preceding the dissolution
of Dynasty XVIII came the reforms of Ikhnaton. Among these
was the renovation of speech and writing. They were to be
true and natural henceforth. Evidently this refers not so much
to stylistic purification as to a bringing of written and spoken
language into accord. One was to write as one spoke, not as
one's ancestors had written five hundred years before. This
reform prevailed and lasted, at any rate in civil writing; and
the result before long was a growth of literature in what is
called the New Egyptian form of the language. This growth
manifested its best productions in the thirteenth century, but
continued into the tenth under Dynasty XXII. By that time
speech and the literary language had drifted apart again; composition was once more in an artificial medium. That is probably the reason why the seventh-to-sixth-century renaissance
under Dynasty XXVI produced nothing of literary moment
that has come down to us, in spite of its considerable achievements in sculpture and general prosperity.

In summary, the history of Egyptian literature can be only
partly understood in terms of political and economic success.
Architecture and sculpture did go up and down almost like an
index of these nonaesthetic factors. Literature was dependent
on them only negatively: without a strong dynasty and attendant prosperity, literature failed to flourish. Positively, however,
it was dependent on the art of writing, and the degree of accord
of this with actual speech of the day. After all, even China, with
an ideographic writing and a closed system of classical style,
after two thousand years came to a separately compartmented
"popular" literature; and Egypt wrote at least in part phonetically.

Most distinctive of Egyptian literature, both in the Old and
the New Language, is its simple, sober, effective narrative
prose, a thousand years before the Judahist and Elohist story-
writers of the Old Testament.

Perhaps equally significant is the fact that much of the literature is secular. Even where mythological material is dealt

with, it is for literary effect. The *Tale of Two Brothers* seems to be a worn-down myth, but is told purely for its interest as a human story.

The poetry is more easily recognized than defined. It is parallelistic, and repetitive through piling on of figures and half figures of speech. About the only evidence of regular form is when strophes are used; the initial lines are then alike throughout the poem. The question of meter is obscure. The most that is asserted is that the line had from two to four accents. Alliteration and punlike plays on words appear occasionally, but without regularity.

These qualities seem to hold with little difference in the two periods of florescence. It was the language that changed rather than the style. As between the two periods, it is difficult for a non-Egyptologist to assign precedence of quality; but the earlier does not appear in any way inferior, and is represented by at least as many specimens.

EGYPTIAN LITERATURE

In Old Egyptian, 2000–1300

* The Peasant's Complaints. Refers to the kings just before 2000; preserved in four Middle Kingdom papyri; no New Empire copies.

*Precepts of Ptah-hotep (of 2670 or 2875). Middle Kingdom papyrus.

Precepts of King Merikare, and of Duauf. Both refer to the period between the Old and the Middle Kingdom; the papyri are respectively from Dynasties XVIII and XIX.

Precepts of Amenemhet I (1995–1965). Four papyri of Dynasty XIX.

Prophecy of Nefer-rehu. Composed early in Dynasty XII, probably under Amenemhet I, preserved in copy of Dynasty XVIII and variant of XIX.

*The Tale of Sinuhe. Time of story, 2000–1950; three Middle Kingdom papyri.

*Quarrel of One Weary of Life with His Soul. Includes poetry. Middle Kingdom papyrus.

*Tale of the Shipwrecked One. Middle Kingdom papyrus.

Founding of the Temple of Heliopolis by Usertesen I (1965–1934). Preserved in copy of Dynasty XVIII.

Complaint of Kha-kheper-re-seneb. Under Usertesen II, ca. 1900. Preserved from Dynasty XVIII.

Odes to Usertesen III. Papyrus of Dynasty XII.

Admonitions of an Egyptian Sage. Refers to ca. 2500. Poetry. New Empire papyrus.

Fragment: The Herdsman and the Goddess. Middle Kingdom papyrus.

*The Saving of Mankind by Re. Two New Empire inscription copies. Popular style.

Banquet Song. Refers to King Antef, end of Middle Kingdom. Preserved from Dynasty XVIII, also an enlargement from Dynasty XIX.

*Cheops and the Magician. In popular, nonclassic style. Papyrus Westcar, probably Hyksos.

War of King Kamose against the Hyksos. Probably 17th cent.; language has a vulgar cast.

In New Egyptian, 1300–900

*The Bewitched Prince. Papyrus prob. of Rameses II, 1300–1234.

The Capture of Joppa (under Thutmose III, 1478–1447). Papyrus probably of Rameses II.

Victory of Rameses II at Kadesh; also, the City of Rameses II.

*The Quarrel of Two Officials. Two papyri, also ostraca, of the time of Rameses II.

Love Songs, various fragments, in dialogue. Mostly of the time of Rameses II.

King Apophis and Sekenen-re. Papyrus of Merenptah II, ca. 1230. Refers to Hyksos period.

*The Tale of Two Brothers. Papyrus of ca. 1220. Least literary, most popular in style, of all preserved Egyptian products.

*Voyage of Un-Amun to Byblos. Ca. 1100.

*Dispute of the Body and the Head. Probably of Dynasty XXII, 945 seq.

Maxims of the Scribe Ani. Dynasty XXII.

MESOPOTAMIAN LITERATURE

I omit the Sumerian-Semitic literature of Mesopotamia. It is intrinsically important, but is fragmentary; and it is difficult to date its times of composition. Most of the preserved tablets are actually late; some of their content, or its substance, may be immemorially older—perhaps as much older as our Bible antedates us. Technical questions are involved—much as in the dating of Maya sculpture—in which I am incompetent.

PALESTINIAN LITERATURE

Ancient Hebrew literature is on the fringe of our consideration, as being prevailingly religious. Embedded in the Old Testament, however, are secular and semisecular passages which subsequently were given a religious significance. The earliest perhaps is Deborah's song, of about 1100, and various other poetical or gnomic fragments, such as the blessings of Jacob and Moses. Most warped from its original meaning is the erotic Song of Songs. The Proverbs are only half religious, and Job, from near the end of the Biblical procession, is a strange compound of philosophy, religion, and fervid poetry. The themes have changed from the early tribal days, but the parallelistic, balanced, repetitive, image-laden style is the same.

In prose, the earlier narratives of the Pentateuch are believed to have begun to be composed in their preserved form from about 850 on, and passages in Judges and Samuel cannot be much younger. Deuteronomy, of about 600, is full of feeling, but the passion is religious. Still later prose tends to be formal or legalistic. It served conscious, specific purposes, like the first chapter of Genesis, and it suppressed the spontaneous impulses of literature. After 600 the Jews had too little left but their religion for secular poetry or stylistic prose to flourish.

As to form, ancient Hebrew literature shows little that is not manifest also in Egyptian five hundred to a thousand years earlier. The difference is in interests and themes.

Some six or seven centuries after the Old Testament record closed, another Semitic people, the Arabs, burst forth with a literature, which in its beginning was wholly poetical and nonreligious. Some of the Babylonian-Assyrian and Hebrew qualities are still present: the repetition, the parallel balancing, the rich imagery. But other traits are new: rhyme and quantity; and they provide a strict form which the older Semitic—and Hamitic—poetry always lacked. The seven-century gap was filled in the Nearer East by Greek civilization. Its verse was quantitative, and from it the Arabs might have derived the idea of their syllable measuring, as a stimulus at least; though this view is not orthodox. But the origin of rhyming? Evidently much went on below the surface of history among the Semitic nations while they lay just below or beyond the covering range of Hellenistic civilization. More on these matters when we consider Arabic literature.

§74. Greek Literature

Greek literature is distinctive in several ways. First of all, Greek is the only major ancient language which does not begin with, or is not dominated by, a body of religious text. Greek enters into the history of world religion essentially with the Septuagint and the New Testament, when its literature was well over. Or, if one chooses to reckon Stoicism as equivalent to a religion, the picture is not seriously changed; since this morality was the end product of Greek philosophy and contemporary in its development with the last phase of the literature. Literature, in fact, is by long odds the first product of Greek culture. It was Homer and Hesiod, as the Greeks themselves recognized, who gave them their gods: that is, an intellectually organized religion, as distinct from an agglomeration of unrelated local cults. The result was a mythology which overlay the cults, provided at least a pleasing ideology while these retained their sanctity, and thus rendered the cults unobjectionable as the civilization outgrew them in sophistication. This growth of a surrogate religion out of aesthetic impulses proved happy in several results. It left to the pious room enough for real piety, which is always humble, but gave them no opportunity to nourish it into a system tending to dominate the civilization. Philosophy was not faced with the alternative of vindicating an established religion or rebelling against it, but grew up in practically undisturbed freedom, so that, when belief in the mythology and cults waned, philosophy had a coherent ideology all ready not only for the intelligentsia but for the intelligent layman. Finally, all the arts—architecture, sculpture, painting, as well as literature—drew and continued to draw their themes and their stimulus largely from the literarized mythology.

In short, the Homeric epics are not only the chronologically first product of Greek civilization; they are its fountainhead: to a remarkable degree, the determinant of all that followed.

Next, we have the phenomenon of a strange interweaving of subject, literary form, musical style, dialect, and locality, invariably marked in the beginnings of each type of literature and tending to persist as a partial convention to the end. The epics were in continuous hexameters, accompanied by the simple four-stringed lyre. They were also the product of proto-historic Ionia, and were composed in Aeolic heavily overlaid by Ionic—a hybrid dialect which perhaps was never spoken, but which remained the language of the epic.

The first strophic poetry was a variant of the hexameter: the elegiac distich. This was accompanied by the flute, was devised in historic Ionia—from 650 on—and, wherever written, continued to use Ionian speech.

About contemporary was the satiric iambic trimeter, also Ionian in origin and dialect.

Melic or choral poetry, what we should call lyric, with a variety of prosodic and strophic forms, arose most vigorously in Aeolic Lesbos, within sight of the Asian mainland. Terpander is the traditional originator: and he also "invented" the "Dorian" mode of music and the seven-stringed cithara, the instrument of lyric verse. After Arion, Alcaeus, and Sappho, Lesbos lost its supremacy, and the melic dialect tended to shift to Doric, which however was related to Aeolic, at any rate as against Ionic; or to Epic with admixture of Doric and Aeolic words and forms. Lyrics of the same type were part of the drama; in fact, if tradition is right, they were its root, dialogue and action growing out of performance of choral song. Hence the strange phenomenon of Aristophanes, in the prolonged bitterness of the Peloponnesian War, writing choruses in the Doric of Sparta for Athenian audiences. Sicily, Italy, the Peloponneseus, northern mainland Greece, all participated in lyric poetry; no Athenian, except within the drama; and several Ionians—Stesichorus, Simonides, Bacchylides, Anacreon. But of these only the last was an Ionian from an Asiatic island—the others were from Sicilian Himera and Cycladic Ceos—and only he, of those within the canon, prevailingly used his native Ionic; just as, or possibly because, he specialized in songs of wine.

The next developments were dramatic; and both tragedy and comedy were almost exclusively Athenian in origin and achievement, and Attic in language, except for the sung choruses. A partial exception must indeed be made for an early Doric gnomic comedy and prose mime which flourished for a time in Doric Syracuse.

By 300 the *koine* or Common form of Greek had grown out of Attic as the standard and universal Hellenic language which was to prevail through Hellenistic and Roman times. In practice, Doric, Ionic, Attic sank to the level of rural or provincial dialects in the modern sense. Prose was written in the *koine;* but Alexandrian poetry largely kept to the dialects, which were now literary conventions as much as hexameters, distichs, alcaics, and choliambics. Thus Syracusan Theocritus wrote his idyls in his "native" Doric, but his epics and encomia in Ionic; and the mimes of Herodas of Cos—a dramatic form that was to supplant the New Comedy—are in conventional literary Ionic. All this is much as if we were today to write tragedies only in the Elizabethan vocabulary—as in effect we partly do when the tragedies are in verse,—or ballads and bucolics in the Scotch vernacular. Until after 400, however—that is, during the period when almost all Greek poetical forms were being devised,—the dialects were living speeches.

Finally, while it is a frequent phenomenon for prose to develop late in literature, its lag in Greece is decidely great. The origin of hexametric form and manner lies wholly beyond chronology. The Homeric epics are usually assigned to the ninth century, Hesiod to the eighth. The seventh saw the development of the principal strophic and lyric forms. Not until the sixth century does the earliest prose appear, in philosophy, genealogy, geography, and history. The first writer on any topic of whose prose more than fragments are preserved is Herodotus; and his time is that of the very peak of drama, the last major poetical pattern devised by the Greeks: the conventional floruit of Sophocles is 456, of Herodotus 444, of Euripides 440. About the same decade come the first sophists and orators, Protagoras and Gorgias, Antiphon and Andocides. With them, at last, pure literary prose may be said to have been established: writing done for its own sake, as a means of aesthetic expression rather than to convey a nonliterary content. But they are four hundred years later than Homer, two hundred later than Callinus, Terpander, and Archilochus.

Even at that, the Hellenic writers of prose whose names have become household words and ornaments of library façades are philosophers, historians, or patriot-politicians, like Plato, Thucydides, Demosthenes. There is no Greek counterpart to Cicero, Boccaccio, Montaigne, Rabelais, Cervantes, Addison, Swift, or Voltaire. What we would call true *prosateurs* are all from Roman mid-Imperial times, in the second Christian century: Plutarch, Pausanias, Longinus, Lucian; and they smack of the antiquarian. The original prose sophistry and oratory were short-lived—already past in the Alexandrian period.

Quite extraordinary is the virtual absence of any Greek prose novel, romance, or tale as an independent genre until long after the great period. This is the more remarkable in that the gift of telling a fascinating story charmingly was highly developed, as Herodotus and Plato witness; and the unmannered Greek prose would have lent itself admirably to this end. The type simply was not developed. Perhaps the Homeric-Epic pattern was too strong: the hexametric-heroic manner came too easily after centuries of usage. Xenophon made one attempt in his *Cyropaedia;* but it is a novel only as forced into a modern category, and is better described—like Xenophon's own career—as an attempt to hybridize history and philosophy. The other Greek novels, *Apollonius of Tyana, Aethiopia, Daphnis, Leucippe,* are very late, from the pagan breakup in the third, fourth, and fifth Christian centuries. And except for the episodic tale of Psyche—where the Greek was back in his own realm of avowed myth—these novels are strangely inept in invention and characterization. Apparently the Hellenic pattern did not allow place for what we should call realistic fiction. It learned early to deal with phantasy wholly removed from daily life, the legendary and mythical; and later with realities as they actually happened or were believed to have happened; but it did not achieve setting imagination to operate freely on the materials of circumabient reality while preserving the appearance of this. At least not in prose. There is more salt and pungent savor in the mythologically charged verse of Theocritus than in all the Greek prose romances. This seems very significant. The Romans, direct pupils, were able to save some of the same quality; but the Renaissance certainly saw in the idyl only an escape from reality and transmuted it into one of the most artificial forms in all literature. The characteristic quality of Theocritus is that he attained vivid reality through a thoroughly poetic medium. When the Greeks either abandoned this medium or the simple narration of what they believed to be fact, they seem to have been strangely helpless. In their best days, they felt no impulse to abandon them.

Hellenic prose began as Ionic, became Attic, and ended as Common Greek. The Epic, Aeolic, and Doric dialects figured in literature as media of verse, to which they added, by association, both variety and poetic charge. Written prose remained distinctively supple and simple, an instrument for dealing with fact and thought—even the orators reason unduly, by non-Greek standards. There is nothing of the lapidary compression of Chinese, the massive architectonics of Latin, the composition-piling and embellishment of Sanskrit, the metaphor-dealing of Arabic; nor of the baldness of mediaeval prose. It was not until the Renaissance in Italy, the seventeenth century in France, and the eighteenth in England that comparable instruments of directness, effectiveness, and smoothness were forged in Europe; Germany has hardly yet achieved one, except in the conscious imitation of untutored folk speech as a literary device.

So much for some of the outstanding qualities of Hellenic literature: its nonbondage to religion from the beginning; the intimate connection with mythology—an aesthetic surrogate of religion; its local and dialectic diversity, associated in turn with primacy of metric form and even musical accompaniment over type of subject; and its late and unornate prose. Now for its historic configuration.

Three main periods of Greek literature may be distinguished. The first is Greek but protohistoric. It is dominated by Homer, and looks back to Troy and the gods as its central theme. The second is the historic literature from 700 or 650 to 150, and includes all first-rate poetry done in Greek other than the epics; though these continued to be written. The third period, after 150 B.C., includes no important poetry and none of the very best prose, and is humane senescence.

Epic period.—The protohistoric or formative period laid a real foundation by evolving a rich subject matter of legend and mythology on which Greek literature continued to draw for theme or allusion to the very end, plus a single stately meter of quantity; and in achieving a vocabulary and style. It confined itself to narrative, with occasional diversions into gnomic or homespun didacticism: Hesiod has his parallels in parts of the Edda. Subjective expression was scarcely attempted.

Homer was to the Greeks their greatest poet; and he has remained such to most moderns. He is almost certainly more read today than any other Greek poet. No Hellene seems to have resisted his primacy. At any rate, there never was an avowed attempt to throw off his authority and influence. Why then do we set him apart into another cycle or phase?

The reason is that there is little extraneous parallel for a great growth beginning in a culmination; nor is such an event easily conceivable; at least not without strain on historic sense. The usual estimate of his date—or, if one will, of the composition or compilation of the main body of the *Iliad*—is around 850; with the *Odyssey* perhaps a half century after; Hesiod, hardly later than 750. Some of the lost cyclic epics known to the historic Greeks may have been contemporary with Homer. The majority appear to have been post-Homeric, and they continued to be produced, according to Greek tradition, into the historic period. As they begin to be associated with named and more or less dated authors, their rating—by antiquity itself—decreases. Evidently the first growth of hexametric epic poetry had reached its realizable limits; it could and did go on, but its patterns had been filled.

All this is typical growth decline. The first half or rise of the epic curve is unknown. Undoubtedly it existed, but it has been lost in the obscurity of unhistoric and illiterate time. The traditional date of Homer is also the period in which the Greeks first learned to write. His precursors would thus expectably remain unremembered. There must have been such: the hexameter alone, an instrument at once defined and plastic, would take time to work out to its ultimate shape, perhaps from among several formative meters. If our *Iliad* dates from 850 or even 800, the epic growth can reasonably be assumed to have begun around 1000. This would allow three or four centuries for the active life history of the growth.

The locale of epic production presents problems which Homeric scholars have long discussed. Tradition unites with the prevailing evidence of dialect in making Homer and most of his colleagues Ionian. What was not from Ionia was from Aeolis—the Asia Minor coast north of Ionia. Here lay Smyrna, one of the seven cities claiming Homer's birth, and Aeolic-speaking until 700 or after. And from here too would the Aeolic admixture or substratum of the conventional Epic dialect come. And yet, why the tradition which rigorously excluded Ionians and Ionia from mention in the cyclic poems, and left Aeolis a non-Achaean, hostile Asiatic land? The legend took shape, it is usually inferred, before any Greeks settled in Asia. But if so, it is unexplained why it should be those very Greeks that later left the homelands to settle in Asia and Lesbos and Chios, who developed the legend into the poems, and at the same time omitted reference to themselves.

Classic period.—The second period began with the transcending of the Epic frame and form about 650, but still in Aeolis-Ionia: Callinus with the distich, Terpander with songs, Archilochus with iambic invective. We are not yet quite in the full light of datable and verifiable history, but at least entering the realm of history. The moment is about that in which Classic Greek music, architecture, sculpture, and painting (on vases) had their beginnings; and within two generations more, philosophy and science also. There were now the first stirrings toward democracy and tyranny and reconstitution of political institutions. A great series of patterns were born simultaneously around 650. In most of the activities, the seventh-century beginnings were rude, stiff, archaic, and of mainly historic interest even to the Greeks themselves only two or three hundred years later. Poetry, however, with centuries of epic behind it,

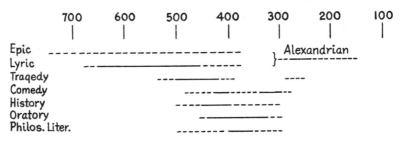

HISTORIC GREEK LITERATURE, BY GENRES

developed swiftly and effectively, and three or four of the canonical nine lyric poets had arisen by 600: Alcman, Alcaeus, Stesichorus, perhaps Sappho. The duration of lyric poetry was also the briefest among the arts. The canon closes with Bacchylides, before 450; and the series of lyrists virtually ends with Timotheus around 400.

The epic continued to be written. The Homeric "hymns," still largely narrative, are anonymous and difficult to date, but are generally ascribed to the centuries following the seventh, perhaps until the Christian era. The last of the cyclic poems, the *Telegonia,* is ascribed to Eugammon, 566. There is a series of non-Trojan epics from the fifth century: a *Heracleia, Thebais, Perseis,* by known authors. Their birthplaces are of interest: Halicarnassus (now speaking Ionian instead of Doric), Colophon, Samos. Evidently we have here a conservative attempt: Ionia persisting in the ninth- and eighth-century manner while Boeotia was producing Pindar and Attica Sophocles and

Aristophanes. The larger significance, as of the third-century Alexandrian *Argonautica,* is in the evidence of how fundamental the Homeric poetry was to all Greek literature. The epic manner never did die out, though it became atypical and less important: somewhat like tragedy in verse in modern English literature.

In the main, however, as lyric poetry approached the end of its course, dramatic poetry took its place. The last two great writers of odes, Pindar and Bacchylides, are about contemporary with Aeschylus and Sophocles; there remain a century and a half of playwrights: Euripides, Aristophanes, Diphilus, Philemon, Menander. The last bring us down to 300 or beyond.

It is probable that so far as a culminating point is definable for the second or historic Greek period as a whole, it is to be sought in the drama; both because tragedy *per se* represents a larger, more sustained effort than any lyric; and because the drama falls most nearly midway in the period. As a precise zenith for 700/650–200/150, Sophocles, around 450, is indicated; or, those who resist the ranking of the heroic above the tender can select Euripides without postponing the climax by more than a decade or two. Aristophanes too has indubitable claims, both as a poet and for his plastic humanity; but his addiction to the contemporary and local, as well as to abuse, are drawbacks to his being selected as the pinnacle. It must be borne in mind that the Greek drama was acted wholly in poetry throughout its career. Even the worldly Menander, who dealt in type and not in nobility of character, and the subsequent writers of mimes, used verse form. And as for Aeschylus, and even Aristophanes in his choral parts, they seem to us too threnodic to be satisfyingly dramatic. The ancients themselves, as their taste in stage performances grew more sophisticated, felt the same way. Menander, who is without choruses, replaced Aristophanes on the stage and in Roman imitation; and in the second Christian century, when the three great tragedians were still occasionally acted—it was only the three,—the choruses were omitted. The entire course of Greek drama may be described as one of origin in choral lyric and progression toward stage play—this end finally realized when poetic subject and feeling were wholly escaped from, although outward poetic form was retained in continuity of pattern.

Alexandrian poetry, from 300 to 150, is the last phase of the great Greek period. Its new styles were few, and in the nature of cameo-like reductions: the brief epic, the bucolic idyl, the mime in place of comedy, the conscious epigram; also the collection of gems in anthologies. But tragedy, the full epic, choral melics continued to be written. There was no break with the past; rather a dignified, cultivated, catholic, elegant preservation of its shrinking essence. The editing and commentating were done in the same spirit. The most complete appreciation of Homer and Sappho and Sophocles was implied in their Alexandrian imitations, but there was no serious attempt to surpass or improve them. Their basic manners and themes were accepted unreservedly; the minor modifications introduced were merely in the direction of a degree of modernization.

Theocritus, Callimachus, and Apollonius, around 280 to 240, mark such climax as the Alexandrian phase of poetry had. It is over by 150, perhaps by 200: the dating is conjectural.

Hellenic prose of the great period, as already remarked, was practically never pure literature, but was history, philosophy, science, pleading, or politicizing in more or less full literary dress. Given as a premise that it came relatively late because frankly imaginative literature had become thoroughly associated with verse form since Homeric times, the pinnacles of prose coincide well enough with those of poetry. The great historians are Herodotus about 450–440, Thucydides around 420, with Xenophon, 394, as a lesser epigone. Then there is a long interval to Polybius, after 170, a poor stylist and therefore second-rank in literature, though a great historian. He falls within the closing limits of Bion and Moschus for poetry. Among philosophers, there will be little question that the palm for writing goes to Plato, 427–347; among orators, to Demosthenes, 384–322. The Alexandrian canon of ten orators runs, in its fortieth-year floruits, from 440 to 320.

It is evident that great prose literature was over by the beginning of the Alexandrian epoch. Or, more realistically, prose literature before 300 was not well differentiated from history, philosophy, and speechmaking. Thereafter there was differentiation: Archimedes is reckoned a scientist, not a scientist and writer. Theoretically, there might have been a school of prose writers as such after 300, if a five hundred years' pattern had not prescribed fixed metrical form for imaginative themes. It was only after the configuration of the great period had lost all vigor, and had been dead for more than two centuries, that there began to be in the Greek language what moderns would unhesitatingly class as pure prose literature.

With 650–150 allowed for the great period, it is evident that the Persian Wars began when it was already a third over, and they are therefore unlikely to have been the cause, except as a secondary reinforcement, of the climax in the second third; *a fortiori,* if we reckon 700–200. It is much more probable, rather, that the complex forces which produced the general cultural upswing around 650, plus the economic prosperity that no doubt underlay or accompanied the upswing, had their share in producing success in the Persian conflict.

Interval.—As in science and philosophy, there was a lapse of 250 years after the Alexandrian era of literature closed. Writing went on, but by the geographer Strabo, by the Jew Josephus about things Judaic, by the Apostles and St. Paul about the new non-Hellenic religion. There is a true continuity of literary production along the lines of the old models, but it is outside the Greek language: in Latin. It is astonishing how almost perfectly Latin literature fits into and fills the void between the great second and poor third period of Greek. Alexandria ends around 200–150. Latin literature begins to create itself, in avowed imitation, about 240 B.C., pauses awhile, and then starts on its full career in 70 B.C., to end around 120 A.D. The Greek third period opens around 100 A.D. The correspondence is not absolute, but close enough to be significant and not an empty coincidence; because it is the Greek patterns of 650–150 which Latin literature was carrying on. In science and philosophy the Roman accomplishment was much slighter than in literature, but such as it was it also fell in the corresponding interval, between Hipparchus and Ptolemy, and between the Stoics and Plotinus.

Third period.—As already said, the third pulse of Greek literature was feeble and retrospective. It is sometimes spoken of as Graeco-Roman; Hellenic Imperial also describes it. It was the literature of the Greek-speaking and -writing half of the Roman Empire and it reached success especially during the second Christian century, the age of Trajan, Hadrian, and the Antonines, when the Empire was at its calmest and seemingly stablest and most prosperous.

The silver age of Latin literature closed chiefly with prose production, and in Tacitus perhaps reached a level comparable to that of Cicero. The Greek revival began where the Latin left off—with prose. We have Plutarch, Herodes Atticus, Pausanius, Marcus Aurelius, Lucian; somewhat later, or of unprecisable date, Diogenes Laertius and Longinus. It is evident from the names how thoroughly this product looks backward into the past. The style, too, is Greek in being still relatively simple, easy, often chatty: the compression and sonority of Tacitus, the whiplash sting of Juvenal, were not taken over into Greek. Second-century Greek verse is very feeble: Oppian's "didactic epic" on fishing is characteristic. This work is essentially an imitation of Alexandrian imitations: Aratus's *Phaenomena,* for instance; for a model to which in turn we have to go back as far as Hesiod's *Works and Days.*

The second century is still practically uninfluenced by Christianity. The third and most of the fourth are taken up, on the one hand, by those of the Church Fathers who wrote in Greek; on the other, by the last stand, or desperate counteroffensive, of paganism as expressed most successfully by Neo-Platonism and Plotinus.

Toward 400, and continuing for a century or so, in the very period when Constantinople had outstripped Rome and the Empire was still barely hanging together, or when a little later the West-East, Latin-Greek severance was accomplished, the powerful root system of the dying Hellenic growth sent up some perceptible and curious shoots. Some of these, as might be expected, were repetitive and revivalistic; others, innovating. A school of writers of epics, mostly episodic, but using the old hexameter and the old Trojan or mythological themes, flourished chiefly in Egypt. Strangely, this revival began just about as Christianity was displacing Greek páganism as the religion of the Empire. The "novels" of Longus, Heliodorus, and Tatius are an endeavor to develop a form not represented before. They also evade the Christianity that surrounded their composition. Of course there was an abundant Christian productivity, too; only it was not literary, and the argument had by now become intersectarian instead of apologetic.

This break of the setting sun from behind the clouds has its equivalent in the Latin West: Ausonius and Claudianus are the counterparts of Nonnus and Musaeus in time and in spirit. Egypt and Gaul were trying to preserve spiritual Hellas and Italy from triumphant Christianity.

Byzantine renaissance.—Because it was thoroughly Christian and coeval with the West European Middle Ages, we are wont to dissociate the thousand-year Byzantine Empire from Antiquity. So far, however, as language is concerned, and the innumerable intangibles that adhere to language, Constantinople of course was Greek throughout its millennium. In the ninth and tenth centuries, from about 850 to 1025, came a revival of power, of prestige, of art, and of writing. This Byzantine literature is known at first hand to only a few dozen scholars. Its reconditeness makes it difficult to treat in a work like the present one. It ought not, however, to be passed over without mention. Its configurational significance is indubitable: as a mark of the vitality persistence of great growths, if for nothing more; even though it seems wholly without transmitted effect on our contemporary lives.

Geography.—Some further remarks on the geographical distribution of Greek poets and writers seem worth while.

In the Epic period, birthplaces tend to confirm the evidence of dialect: Aeolis participates with Ionia. With "Homer" assumed as an Ionian, the second figure, Hesiod, is from Aeolian

Cyme, though reared in North Hellas. The Epic Period poets whose works have not been preserved are from Ionian Miletus, Samos, and Cyprus, from Aeolic Lesbos, from Doric Rhodes. Those who continued the manner during the early half of the Classic period are again mainly Ionians, from Colophon, Samos, and Halicarnassus—the last an Ionianized Doric town; one is ascribed to Doric Cyrene in Lybia. Hellas proper and Magna Graecia are unrepresented. Clearly, the beginnings of poetry were not only peripheral, but sub-Asiatic.

In the Classic period, down to 300, after which birthplace counted for less than living in Alexandria, the situation was roughly as follows. Ionia, with Aeolian Lesbos participating strongly for the first century, produced the overwhelming mass of lyric poetry; Attica, practically all tragedy, comedy, and oratory; history was divided between the two. The rest of the Greek world added very little: Stesichorus from Ionian Himera in Sicily, the Boeotian Pindar, are the chief exceptions. The ancients already noted that Sparta, Argos, Corinth, Thebes were as good as unrepresented by poets, except for Pindar. It must be added that in epic and lyric poetry Athens produced no more than they: local specialization of manner was evidently very strong until the Macedonian supremacy. Sparta made up for the sterility attributed to it by welcoming lyric poets developed elsewhere: Terpander of Lesbos, Tyrtaeus of Athens, Thaletas of Crete, Alcman of Sardes. Another view regards some of these as native Lacedaemonians; but whether it was as mother or as hostess, Sparta functioned only before 600.

Sicily produced more than Italy. Besides Himera with Stesichorus, there was the early comedy of Syracuse, with native-born Sophron and Xenarchus and with Epicharmus drawn in from Cos. Theocritus in the early Alexandrian epoch suggests a continuity of literary productivity at Syracuse. This southeast corner of Sicily and the southwest corner of Asia Minor—Cos, Rhodes, and Halicarnassus—with perhaps Lybian Cyrene, the birthplace of Callimachus as well as of legendary Eugammon, seem to have been the chief centers of Dorian poetry. However, the earlier Alexandrian phase has a strong participation of poets from cities that were Doric by tradition: Tarentum, Epidauros, Crete, Rhodes, Cos.

In pre-Alexandrian time, Ibycus of Rhegium, on the strait facing Sicily, is the only Italian representative; since Thurii, where Herodotus closed his career and whence came Alexis of the New Comedy, was a fresh Athenian colony.

The cities of the Thracian coast, so prominent in philosophy, were almost silent. The one exception, the sophist Protagoras of Abdera, belongs to philosophy as much as to literature.

The New Comedy was a joint product of Athenians—the just-mentioned Alexis and his nephew Menander—and men from the Asia Minor mainland: Antiphanes; Diphilus of Sinope on the north coast; Philemon of Soli on the south. From Soli there also sprang, within the next generation or two, Chrysippus, one of the founders of Stoicism, and Aratus the poet of the *Phaenomena*.

Besides Sappho of Lesbos, the earliest and greatest, a few women poets appear in Greek literature: Corinna of Tanagra or Thebes, Praxilla of Sicyon, Telesilla of Argos, Erinna of Telos near Rhodes, mostly undated. These are all Aeolic-Doric cities. No Ionian-Attic poetess seems to be known.

GREEK LITERATURE

FIRST, EPIC, OR PROTOHISTORIC PERIOD, ± 1000–700/650

Homer, ca. 850–800. Birthplace claimed by six Ionian cities and by Aeolic Smyrna.

Hesiod, not later than 750. Father from Asiatic Cyme; lived at Boeotian Ascra, died in Locris.

The legendary cyclic poets: Arctinus of Miletus, Creophylus of Samos, Lesches of Lesbos, Stasinus of Cyprus, Eumelos of Corinth, ca. 750–700, some perhaps later.

SECOND, GREAT, OR CLASSIC PERIOD, 650–150

(Few birth and death dates are available. The dates given are those of the individual's acme or floruit, which is sometimes when he won a particular success, more often his estimated fortieth year. The places named, unless there is specific contrary statement, are supposed to be birthplaces; how often they are not, I have no means of knowing.)

Epic continuation

Peisander of Camirus in Rhodes, ca. 650: *Heracleia.*

Eugammon of Cyrene, 566: *Telegonia.*

Panyasis of Halicarnassus, 490: *Heracleia.*

Antimachus of Colophon, 404: *Thebais.*

Choerilus of Samos, 404: *Perseis* (viz., the Persian Wars).

Erinna of Telos near Rhodes, prob. 4th cent.: *The Spindle,* brief epic.

Homeric "hymns," from 7th century on.

Lyric: Elegiac distichal, mostly in Ionian

Callinus of Ephesus, ca. 680? 650?

Tyrtaeus of Sparta from Athens? 680? Also Doric marching songs in anapaests.

Mimnermus of Colophon, 630. Erotic.

Solon of Athens, 599.

Phocylides of Miletus, 540. Another of the seven sages.

Demodocus of Leros, 540.

Xenophanes of Colophon, 540, the philosopher.

Theognis of Megara, 520.

Lyric: Melic or choral; primarily in Aeolic or Doric

Terpander of Lesbos, ca. 676. Also "invented" the Dorian mode of music.

†Alcman of Sardes? 650. Many meters. At Sparta.

Thaletas of Crete. Flute dancing songs. Also at Sparta.

Arion of Lesbos, 625. Invented dithryamb and satyr chorus. To Corinth.

†Alcaeus of Lesbos, 612. Alcaic and Sapphic strophes, logaoedic rhythms.

†Stesichorus (Teisias) of Sicilian Himera. Epic themes.

†Sappho of Lesbos, 600 or 570?

†Ibycus of Italian Rhegium, 544.

†Anacreon of Teos, 540.

Corinna of Tanagra or Thebes, 520. Boeotian dialect.

Lasus of Hermione, 520.

†Simonides of Ceos, 516.

†Pindar of Cynoscephalae near Thebes, 480 (522–442).

†Bacchylides of Ceos, in Sicily, nephew of Simonides, 468.

Timotheus of Miletus, to Athens, 400 (447–357).

Philoxenus of Cythera, to Athens, 435–380.

Lyric: Iambic trimeter

Archilochus of Paros, ca. 650, younger contemporary of Callinus. "Inventor" of the form.

_____

† In Alexandrian canon of nine.

Semonides of Samos or Amorgos, 625.

Hipponax of Ephesus, to Clazomenae, 540. Inventor of choliambic (*skazon*).

Tragedy, at Athens, by Athenians

Thespis, 534.

Choerilus, 500.

Pratinus, Dorian from Phlius to Athens, 500.

Phrynichus, 494; first victory, 511.

Aeschylus, 484 seq., *485 (525–456).

Sophocles, 468 seq., *456 (496–405).

Euripides, 455 seq., *440 (480–406).

Ion of Chios, 451.

Agathon, 416 (447–400).

Theodectes of Phaselis, to Athens, 352.

Doric comedy at Syracuse, probably nonchoral

Epicharmus of Cos, to Sicilian Megara and Syracuse, 480. Gnomic comedy.

Sophron of Syracuse, 440. Mimes in rhythmic prose.

Xenarchus of Sicily, 395. Mimes.

Old Comedy at Athens, with chorus; by Athenians

Chionides, 460 (from ca. 480 on).

Magnes, 460.

Ecphantides, 460.

Crates, 450.

Cratinus, 448/4.

Hermippus, 445.

Pherecrates, 430.

Phrynichus, 429.

Eupolis, 421, 415.

Hegemon of Thasos, to Athens, 415.

Aristophanes, 427 seq. *415 (450–385 or 444–380).

Plato, 405.

Ameipsias, 404.

Strattis, 400.

Eubulus, 380.

Anaxandrides of Camirus, to Athens, 370.

Middle and New Comedy at Athens, without chorus

Antiphanes, from Asia Minor, 368 (404–330).

Alexis of Thurii, Athenian colony, 354.

Diphilus of Sinope, 337.

Philemon of Soli, 320.

Menander of Athens, nephew of Alexis, 302 (342–291).

Prose: History

Bion, Proconnesus, ca. 560.

Xanthus, Lydia, ca. 560.

Cadmus, Miletus, ca. 550. Genealogy.

Acusilaus, Boeotia, ca. 550. Genealogy.

Theagenes, Rhegium, ca. 530.

*Hecataeus, Miletus, ca. 520. Geography and history.

Dionysius, Miletus, ca. 520.

Charon, Lampsacus, ca. 510.

Eugaeon, Samos, ca. 510.

Herodorus, Heraclea, 500.

**Herodotus, Halicarnassus, to Athens and Thurii, 444 (484–ca. 425).

Hellanicus, Lesbos, 430.

Antiochus, Syracuse, 423.

Damastes, Sigeum, 420.

Glaucus, Rhegium, 420.

**Thucydides, Athens, 420.

Ctesias, Cnidus, 400.

Philistus, Syracuse, 395.

*Xenophon, Athens, 394 (434–354).

Theopompus, Chios, 340.

Ephorus, Cyme, 340.

Timaeus, Sicilian Tauromenium, 305.

Douris, Samos, 300.

Prose: Oratory. Athenians

(All except the last are in the Alexandrian canon.)

Antiphon, 440.

Andocides, 400.

Lysias, 400. Of Sicyonian descent; at Athens.

*Isocrates, 396 (436–338).

Isaeus, 370. Of Chalcis, to Athens.

Lycurgus, 360 (396?–323).

Aeschines, 349 (389–314).

**Demosthenes, 343 (383–322).

*Hypereides, 340.

Deinarchus, 320. Of Corinth, to Athens.

Demetrius of Phalerum, 305 (345–283).

Prose: Various

Thales of Miletus, 585; and subsequent philosophers.

Pherecydes of Syros, ca. 550. Theologian.

Hippocrates of Cos, 430. Medicine.

Sophists: Bryson of Heraclea, 460; Stesimbrotus of Thasos, 450;

Gorgias of Leontini, 445; Protagoras of Abdera, 442; Hippias of Elis, 430; Prodicus of Ceos, 420.

Rhetoricians, about 470–390: Corax of Syracuse, 466; Tisias of Syracuse, to Thurii; Thrasymachus of Chalcedon, to Athens, 420; Theodorus of Byzantium, to Athens; Alcidamas of Elea, 415; Polycrates of Athens, 395.

**Plato of Athens, 427–347.

Xenophon of Athens, 394. "Novel" *Cyropaedia.*

Theophrastus of Lesbos, at Athens, 332. "Botanist."

Alexandrian Period prose

Hegesias of Magnesia, 290. Asianist rhetorician.

*Polybius of Megalopolis, the historian, to Rome 167 (ca. 210/214–128/122, or ca. 198–117).

Antigonus of Euboean Carystus, to Pergamum. Animal wonder-book.

And philosophers, scientists, critics.

Alexandrian poetry

Philetus of Cos, 290. Elegiac.

Asclepiades of Samos, 290. Melic and epigrammatic.

Isyllus of Epidauros, 280. Choral melic.

Lycophron of Chalcis, 280, and six fellow members of Pleiad. Tragedy and epic.

Leonidas of Tarentum, 276. Epigram.

**Theocritus of Syracuse, 275. Bucolic.

*Callimachus of Cyrene, 270. Brief epic and elegiac.

Herodas of Cos, 260. Mimes in choliambic.

Aratus of Soli, 260. *Phaenomena,* didactic epic.

*Apollonius, from Alexandria to Rhodes. Epic *Argonautica.*

Bion of Smyrna, 250? Bucolic.

Euphorion of Chalcis, at Antioch, 234. Epic.

Rhianus of Crete, 222 (or 250?). Epic *Messenians.*

Nicander of Colophon, ca. 180. Epic.

Moschus of Syracuse, 150? Bucolic.

Meleager of Gadara, Palestine. Epigram; also anthology.

INTERVAL, 150 B.C.–100 A.D.

(The real literature of this period of the civilization is in Latin.)

Poseidonius of Apamea in Syria, 135–51. Polymath.

Philodemus of Gadara, 55 B.C. Epigram.

Diodorus Siculus, 40 B.C. History.

Strabo of Amasia on Pontus, 20 B.C. Geography.

Dionysius of Halicarnassus, to Rome 8 B.C. History, critical essays.

Crinagoras of Mitylene, 50 A.D. Epigram.
Josephus, 77 A.D. Jewish history and apology.
Dio Chrysostomus of Prusa, 80 A.D.

THIRD OR IMPERIAL PERIOD, 100–500 A.D.

Earlier phase, second century, mainly prose
  *Plutarch of Chaeronea, 90. Biography.
  Appian of Alexandria, to Rome, 130. History.
  Arrian of Nicomedia, 135 (95–175). History.
  Herodes Atticus, 140.
  Pausanias of Lydia, 150. Antiquary.
  Marcus Aurelius, emperor, 161 (121–180). Meditations, "To Himself."
  *Lucian of Samosata, Syria, 165.
  Aristeides, pupil of Herodes, 169.
  (Pseudo-)Longinus, date uncertain. "On the Sublime."
  Oppian of Cilicia, 180. Didactic epic on fishing.
  Cassius Dio of Nicaea, 180. History.

Theological-philosophical interval, third and fourth centuries
  (The principal names have been given under Philosophy.)

Later phase, mainly fifth century, poetry and novel
  Novels
    (Philostratus, 3d cent. Apollonius of Tyana.)
    Longus, prob. of Lesbos, between 2d and 5th cent.: *Daphnis and Chloe.*
    Heliodorus of Phoenicia, ca. 390. Tales of Aethiopia.
    Achilles Tatius, 4th or 5th cent. *Leucippe and Cleitophon.*

  Epics in hexameters
    Quintus of Smyrna, 380? Sequel to *Iliad.*
    Soterichus of Egypt, before Nonnus. *Bassarica.*
    Nonnus of Panopolis, Egypt, ca. 400? *Dionysos.*
    Tryphiodorus of Egypt, follower of Nonnus. *Sack of Ilium.*
    Coluthus of Egypt, follower of Nonnus. *Rape of Helen.*
    Musaeus, ca. 500? *Hero and Leander.*

§75. Latin Literature

The Romans produced a considerably greater growth in their
literature than in any other fine art or intellectual activity. A
possible exception might be seen in architecture; but even here
it was in quantity production and engineering developments

that they surpassed the Greeks; whereas in writing it would be fair to say that they rivaled them qualitatively.

The full reasons for this anomaly are not clear, but at least two factors seem to have contributed. In sculpture and painting as well as in science and philosophy, productivity must be expressed through a special and more or less technical medium—the brush, the chisel, abstraction, or logic. These special media or techniques had found no consequential place in the pattern system which grew up in the formative period of Italic and Roman culture. As Rome came to be a world power and civilized, the activities expressed through these techniques became increasingly appreciated and genuinely valued; but it was apparently too late for a productive place to be developed for them in the pattern system or genius of Roman culture. It was easier to let Greeks or Hellenized Orientals perform the activities for Romans, or to imitate or reproduce them. Literature, however, has as its medium only language which is omnipresent, and the Romans evidently felt no handicap in attempting to convert their spoken speech into a literary instrument. Even before Hannibal, in the stern and aesthetically barren days of republican piety and virtue, they commenced this conscious endeavor. Within two hundred years they had succeeded to an amazing degree. In concentration and surcharge, in magnificent sonority and architectonic sentence building, Ciceronian and Vergilian Latin achieved effects beyond those of the Greek instrument, which remained relatively simple at all periods.

As we look backward from the lapse of millennia, the poverty of new content in Latin writing seems appalling. But the Romans took it for granted that both ideas and larger forms had in the main been achieved by the Greeks. They did not even blush for their borrowings and imitations. They felt their sole object to be the transmutation of the Hellenic content and forms into their own medium and the adaption of them to the living Roman background. The case of the Greeks was different. They had long possessed a rich background of mythology and heroic saga for which the Italic peoples had no counterpart.

Here was a content ready-made; and though it grew richer still as literature and art worked it over and over, there was already an enormous mass of it for Homer to draw upon when he gave it the first poetic shaping. All this—both wealth of material and its first formulation in definite metric form—lay available a century to two after Homer when the Greeks began to enter upon the systematic development of their literature. They thus set off with a flying start, and were able to concentrate on problems of form and style as such: the language could become an increasingly effective art medium and yet remain relatively spontaneous and simple. With the Romans, on the contrary, the essence of the task of creating a literature lay precisely in the achievement of the language instrument. Their wine being Greek, they wrought at the bottle, and achieved a vessel of no less merit and greater artifice.

That this process was no hastily imitative one is shown by the fact that the first Latin poet was a Greek, Andronicus, and that though he chose as his subject a translation of the *Odyssey* he rendered this not into hexameters but into the old popular Italic Saturnian meter, probably with change from accentual to length measure. The first Latin-born poet, Naevius, continued with the Saturnian; and it was not until after a full tryout, a generation later, that Ennius introduced the Greek hexameter, gradually modeling the language to a fit with it. The hexameter remained identical; it was the syllabic lengths of the Latin literary language that were determined or altered—fixed, it is usually called. So in the end a complete parallelism was achieved; but the method was gradual and unforced.

A second factor which probably contributed to the preëminence of Roman letters over Roman arts and science was the apparently wide spread of Latin speech through the Italian peninsula with the growth of Roman power and implantation of citizenship. It would seem that even before the first clash with Carthage, Latin was the language of civilization throughout Italy. Not that it had become the mother tongue of the majority; but it was probably the familiar second speech of nearly everyone of influence and relative culture. Only so can we explain the fact that almost no great Roman writers, early or late, were born in Rome; and the still more significant circumstance that of the first seven important individuals in Roman poetical literature, born in the century 290–190, one was a Tarentine Greek, three South Italians, one an Umbrian, one a Gaul of Milan, the seventh an African, possibly born in Carthage itself. Latin literature thus is not the product of a city, but of many nationalities, Italic and non-Italic, which voluntarily accepted Latin speech as rapidly as Roman power grew. The case is the reverse of the Greek, where non-Hellene barbarians began to participate only after the Greek decline was well under way.

In short, by about 250 B.C., the Latin western half of the future Empire, the area of the Dark and Middle Ages and of Catholic Christianity, was already in the making. Rome was no longer a city-state, but the central nervous system of a swiftly growing civilization which it coördinated politically. It was the dominant language of this emergent civilization which set itself the task of forging a literature on the model of that which the Greeks to its east had just finished producing. By the time of Hannibal, this Latin tongue of Rome must have been in such wide use throughout Italy as to dwarf the other languages of the peninsula into provincialistic survivals.

The nascent Latin literature promptly attacked the larger poetical structures. Andronicus produced a tragedy besides his translation of the *Odyssey*. Naevius added comedies and a Roman subject for the epic; Ennius, the satire, the one form of poetry of which the Romans claimed the invention. Only lyric poetry, the ode, the distichal elegy, the epigram came later by nearly a hundred and fifty years. The language apparently had to be filed finer before these more delicate mechanisms could be attempted. Prose lagged behind, as might be expected; but surprisingly little. Cato is just fifty years later than Andronicus, and the almost exact contemporary of Ennius, the first great poet; and Cato wrote orations and history as well as a treatise on agriculture.

After something over a hundred years of growth, there was a

half century of apparent standstill. The period from 120 to 70 is relatively barren: rather conspicuously so.

When the forward movement was resumed, around 70 B.C., the period of great achievement began. Lyric poetry came in with a rush. But the serious drama, tragedy and comedy, was about to die. Before long it did die, except for literary plays not intended to be acted, or occasionally put on the stage in the spirit of the past. The drama had been crowded off the stage by farces and mimes, which in turn were to be replaced largely by pantomimes.

The duration of the great period cannot be fixed with the same precision as its beginnings: of a group of contemporaries, some die young, others live to a ripe age, especially in a group of as variable a life span as writers. Of the great, Livy and Ovid survived until the first years of Tiberius, dying in A.D. 17 and 18. All the others were gone before the Christian era: Horace, the last, died in 8 B.C. If we assume that Livy and Ovid had done most or the best of their work by 10 A.D., we have a total of 80 years for the culmination. If this were cut to 75, 70, or even 65 years, say 65–1 B.C., no large injustice would be done to any career of eminence. The birth dates of the great all fall exactly into the life of Cicero: 106–43. Thus, Cicero 106, Caesar 102, Lucretius ca. 98, Catullus 87, Sallust 86, Vergil 70, Horace 65, Livy 59, Tibullus ca. 55, Propertius ca. 50, Ovid 43.

Obviously this is an "Augustan" constellation only by considerable stretch of the facts. Half the list were dead before Augustus gave peace to the realm in 31 B.C. All the rest, except Livy and Ovid, were gone when Horace died at almost the precise mid-point of Augustus's principate. If this literary culmination must be defined in terms of political periods, it would be much more exact to say that it embraced the last generation of the Civil Wars and the first of the Empire. Actually it is doubtful whether causally either set of political developments had anything to do with the peak. Certainly Augustus did not, because in the forty-five years of his rule not a major figure of Latin literature was born, with the sole exception of Seneca.

The traditional recognition of a Golden and a Silver Age

in Latin literature rests precisely on this dearth of distinguished births under Augustus. But the literature did experience another pulse, perceptibly separated from the first. The births for this began under Tiberius, but constellated most thickly in the still uneasier years of Caligula, Claudius, and Nero, ending by the time of the latter's death. The fruition accordingly fell largely under the Flavian Caesars and Trajan, though it definitely began under Nero. The principal birth dates are: (Seneca ca. –4), Silius Italicus 25, Persius 34, Quintilian ca. 35, Lucan 39, Statius ca. 40, Martial ca. 45, Tacitus ca. 54, Juvenal ca. 58, Pliny the Younger ca. 61, Suetonius ca. 75. To these must be added Petronius, born most likely under Tiberius. This is as definite a clustering as for the Golden Age. The literature, however, has changed. Rhetoric is much more in evidence. In spite of this, prose holds up better than verse: Tacitus is often reckoned the greatest writer of Roman history, and Petronius opened up a new and fresh vein of the picaresque novel. The poetry tends to be either dull or vehement.[4] The best of it cannot match Lucretius, Catullus, Vergil, Horace, Tibullus, or Ovid in either passion or control.

With Trajan, this second pulse was over. The long peace of Hadrian and the Antonines, 117–180, brought nothing notable; nor did the more troubled period that followed. Apuleius is the outstanding literary figure, and even in him the interest in magic begins to adumbrate the preoccupation with philosophy, morals, and religion which dominated Latin writing from the time of Marcus Aurelius to Augustine.

After about 180, there was dearth rather than decline. Christian theology superseded literature. Toward 400 a new stirring is perceptible. It centers about St. Augustine, whose personality was vivid enough to maintain itself irrespective of his theology; but there were also attempts once more in history, in Christian, and even in pagan verse. None achieved greatness, it is true, but at least Ausonius was not a negligible poet.

---

[4] However, this charge holds truest for the earlier men, like Seneca, Silius, and Persius, less for Lucan, Martial, or Juvenal, who were born near the center of the cluster close to Tacitus. Evidently the rhetoricians' influence was largely mastered as the Silver Age swing came into its culmination.

This last phase was almost wholly non-Italian: Africa, Spain, Gaul contributed—even Asia, where the language of culture had been Greek for twenty generations. A century later, Boethius, a Roman patrician, spoke the last utterance of Latin literature which had begun with a Tarentine Greek slave 750 years before.

Summary.—The stages of Latin literature can be recapitulated thus:

240–120, Formative Phase.
120–70, Interval.
70 B.C.–10 A.D., "Golden Age"—a full half pre-Augustan.
10–50, Interval.
50–120, "Silver Age," Nero to Trajan.
120–180, Decline.
180–350, Interval, barren except for theology.
350–460, Afterglow.

This makes a total of 700 years, covering four pulses and three recessions. It is a solidly grounded and genuinely patterned literature that can show so tenacious a life. No other Roman aesthetic or intellectual activity evinced equal duration. However, pure literature for which a quality of greatness can be claimed ended about 120 A.D., reducing the important span to about half. If the formative stage and subsequent lull be also excluded, the duration of best production sinks to less than two centuries, from 70 B.C. to 120 A.D.; and this with a definite sag in the middle.

The causes of the successive rises and falls are not clear. They are certainly not immediately political, as the beginnings of the great phases during the Civil Wars and under Nero show, not to mention that Augustus left his heirs only a void and the great and prosperous peace of Hadrian and the Antonines was marked by a heavy decline. It is evident that the culmination coincides well, in time, with other Roman culminations, such as they were; that the recessions preceding and following it were brief; but that once the second and secondary peak was passed, the recession was long, deep, and followed by only a slight final rise.

Geographically, Latin literature was the product not of a city nor of one Italic subnationality, but of the whole of Italy and then of the western civilized world. Within two generations of the very beginning, Italian Gauls were participating. The great men of the Golden Age were from lower Lombardy—Mantua, Verona, Padua—or from central-southern Italy, in Umbrian, Sabine, Paelignian, Volscian, Samnite territory. Magna Graecia and Campania were represented chiefly in the formative period; Etruria, practically at no time. With the Silver Age, Spaniards became prominent, then Gauls; with the definite decline, North Africans predominated. The final pulse, around 400, is a strange agglomeration of Africans, Asiatics, and western provincials.

LATIN LITERATURE

Formative period, 240–120

Andronicus, ca. 284–204, b. in Greek Tarentum. Translated the *Odyssey* into Saturnian meter; at least 9 tragedies, 2 comedies; first tragedy performed 240.

Naevius, 270–201 or 264–194, b. in Latinized Campania. Ca. 235–205, about 6 tragedies, 35 comedies (*fabulae palliatae*). Epic, *Bellum Punicum*, Saturnian, from Aeneas to his own time.

*Plautus, ca. 254–184, b. Sarsina, Umbria. Comedies, 20 preserved.

*Ennius, 239–169, b. Rudiae, Messapian town in Calabria. Epic: *Annales* (Aeneas, etc.), in hexameters. About 20 or more tragedies. Other poetry, including "satire."

Cato Censorius, 234–149, b. Sabine Tusculum. Prose history (*Origines*), orations, agricultural treatise.

Pacuvius, 220–ca. 131, b. Brundisium, sister's son of Ennius. Next to Accius, best of Roman tragedians.

Caecilius, ca. 219–ca. 168, fl. 180, Insubrian Gaul b. in Milan. 42 comedies.

*Terence, ca. 195/85–159, North African (Afer), probably b. Carthage. 6 comedies preserved.

Lanuvinus, denunciatory rival of Terence.

Togata type of comedy (Roman personages) displaced *palliata* soon after Terence; representatives, Titinius fl. 170?, Afranius, fl. ca. 110 or ca. 90, Quinctius Atta (d. 77).

*Lucilius, ca. 180–ca. 103, b. Suessa Aurunca, Campania. Satires: first important representative of the form.

Hemina, fl. 140 or earlier, first annalist historian except Cato writing in Latin.

Calpurnius Piso, fl. ca. 140, consul in 133. History.

Coelius Antipater, fl. ca. 140. Perhaps the best historian of his time.

Sempronius Asellio, contemporary. Antiannalist historian, influenced by Polybios.

*Accius, ca. 170–ca. 90, b. Pisaurum, Umbria. Titles of 45 tragedies known, 13 of these from the Trojan cycle.

Developmental interval, without greater productions, 120–70

Licinius Crassus, 140–91. Orations.

Displacement of *togata* by *Atellana* type of farce comedy in literary form by Novius and Pomponius, fl. ca. 90.

Sisenna, ca. 110–67; and Licinius Macer, his contemporary. Historians.

Varro, 116–27, b. Sabine Reate. Scholar, polyhistor, on agriculture, etc.; also Menippean satires, mixed prose and verse.

Hortensius, 114–50. Orator.

Great period, 70 B.C.–10 A.D.

**Cicero, 106–43, b. Volscian Arpinum. Orations, philosophy, letters. Peak of Latin prose.

Caesar, 102/100–44. Apologetic history.

Cornelius Nepos, ca. 99–ca. 27, b. northern Italy, probably at Ticinum. Biography.

**Lucretius, 99/97–55/53. Philosophy in epic meter.

*Catullus, ca. 87/84–54, b. Verona. Lyrics.

*Sallust, 86–ca. 34, b. Sabine Amiternum. History.

Valerius Cato. Lyricist and grammarian.

Furius Bibaculus, of Cremona. Satiric epigrams.

Licinius Calvus, 87/82–47. Poet and orator.

Varius Rufus. *Thyestes,* reckoned along with Ovid's *Medea* the best later tragedy.

**Vergil, 70–19, b. Andes near Mantua. Epic, idyls.

Gallus, 70/69–27/26, b. Forum Julii (Fréjus on the Riviera). Erotic lyrics in elegiac distich.

**Horace, 65–8, b. Venusia, in Samnite territory on the Apulian-Lucanian border. Lyrics, satires.

*Livy, 59 B.C.–17/18 A.D., b. Padua. History.

*Tibullus, ca. 55–19 B.C. Personal erotic lyrics, elegiac in form.

*Propertius, 50/49–16/15 B.C., b. Umbrian Assisi. Rival and peer of Tibullus.

*Ovid, 43 B.C.–18 A.D., b. Paelignian Sulmo. *Amores, Heroides, Ars Amandi, Metamorphoses, Fasti.*

Pompeius Trogus, fl. 10 A.D. His *Philippica* (preserved in the reduction by Justin, prob. of the time of Antoninus Pius) is the only world history in Latin literature, omits speeches, and is not pro-Roman in feeling.

Second interval, 10 A.D.–50 A.D.

Germanicus, adoptive son of Tiberius, 15 B.C.–19 A.D. Calendrical poem *Phainomena.*

Manilius, fl. 14 A.D. Astrological poem *Astronomica.*

Velleius Paterculus, fl. ca. 30 A.D. in Campania. History.

Phaedrus, fl. ca. 30 or 40 A.D. Macedonian slave. Fables.

Scaurus. Tragedy *Atreus.*

Pomponius Secundus, fl. ca. 50. Tragedy, probably acted.

*Seneca, 4/3 B.C. (1 A.D.?)–65 A.D., b. Corduba, Spain. Stoic philosophy; tragedies, performance doubtful.

The medical work of Celsus, the geographical of the Spaniard Pomponius Mela, the topical prose writings of Valerius Maximus, the history of Alexander by Curtius Rufus, also fall here.

Second florescence, or "Silver Age," 50–120 A.D.

Columella, under Nero. On agriculture.

Silius Italicus, 25–101. *Punica* in 12,000 hexameters.

Calpurnius Siculus, fl. 55/60. Idyls.

*Petronius Arbiter, d. 65. *Trimalchio;* fragment of novelistic satire with admixture of verse.

Persius, 34–62, b. Etruscan Volaterrae. Abstract satires.

*Lucan, 39–65, b. Corduba, Spain, nephew of Seneca. *Pharsalia,* epic without gods.

Valerius Flaccus, fl. ca. 70/80. Epic *Argonautica.*

Quintilian, ca. 35–ca. 95, b. Calagurris, Spain. Rhetoric.

Statius, ca. 40–ca. 96, b. Naples. Epics *Thebais, Achilleis; Silvae.*

*Martial, ca. 40–ca. 104, b. Bilbilis in Spain. Epigrams, etc.

*Tacitus, 54/55–ca. 120, prob. of south Gallic origin. History.

*Juvenal, 55/60–127/30, b. Volscian Aquinum. Satires.

Pliny the Younger, 61–ca. 113, b. Comum in Cisalpine Gaul. Letters.

Suetonius, 70/75–150/60. Historian, published partly after 120.

Decline, 120–180

Fronto, 90/100–168/75, b. Cirta, Numidia. Rhetorician.

Aulus Gellius, fl. ca. 160. *Noctes Atticae.*

Apuleius, b. 125/30 in Madaura, Africa, fl. ca. 165. *Metamorphosis (Golden Ass).*

The *Pervigilium Veneris,* with its anticipations of postclassic sentiment and form, is considered probably anterior rather than posterior to 200.

Christian writers, third century
> Minucius Felix, fl. ca. 160 or ca. 200.
> Tertullian, ca. 150/60–230; St. Cyprian, ca. 200–258; Africans.
> Commodianus, fl. 249, first Christian poet.
> Lactantius, fl. ca. 300.

Aftermath, centering around 400
> Ausonius, ca. 310–ca. 393/5, of Bordeaux. Poet.
> Ammianus, ca. 330–400, b. Antioch. Historian.
> St. Jerome, 331–420, b. Stridon on Pannonian-Dalmatian border. Chronicle; basis of Vulgate.
> St. Ambrose, ca. 340–397, b. prob. in Gaul.
> Prudentius, 348–ca. 410, b. in or near Saragossa. Christian lyrics.
> *St. Augustine, 354–430, b. Tagaste, Numidia. *Confessions, City of God.*
> Claudianus, fl. ca. 400, b. in Asia or at Alexandria. Last pagan poet; short epics.
> Sidonius Apollinaris, ca. 430–480. Poet.
> Boethius, ca. 480–524. Roman.

§ 76. Arabic Literature

One of the significant features of Arabic literature is that it was well developed before Mohammed. This means that many of its essential patterns had set while the Arabs were still a series of half-civilized tribes, before they united to conquer the world under the Prophet. Among the traits which are known to have been established a century before the Hegira because specimens have been preserved—though the style may go back of 500 for all we know—are: rhyme; the simpler meters; a two-line strophe, with the second of each pair of lines rhyming throughout the poem; and a subjective, lyric approach. The early themes were love, especially on separation; hate or derision of individuals, lineages, or tribes; panegyrics of oneself, one's people, or one's patron; praise of camels, with descriptions of scenery; and laments for the dead—these last often by women. If there was an element of religion in the pre-Islamic poetry, examples have been lost; the strain was at best secondary. Narrative verse as such was lacking: poetry dealt with the feelings spinning around an event or fact, not with the flow of events. Prose literature was also absent, or semimeasured and rhymed,

This early poetry, long remembered but less often written, flourished not only among the Bedouin but also in the cities of Medina, Mecca, and Ta'if, and at the courts of the semi-independent Arab states of Al Hira and Damascus. It is also important that, so far back as is known to us, this poetry is all in one standard or common Arabic language, which evidently prevailed as far as Arabs lived (except in Yemen), without dialectic variation, though everyday speech was locally dialetic. This standardized language argues that a conscious poetic art was probably of some age.[5]

It has already been mentioned that this early sixth-century Arabic verse, which recognized not only rhyme but quantitative meter, may possibly have been influenced beneath the surface—heterodox and preposterous as the idea seems at first—by the quantitative Greek poetry that was being produced in neighboring Egypt during the fifth century. After all, Latin poetry took its quantitative meters from Greek; Persian, from Arabic.[6] As for routes of connection, the Arabs of Palmyra under Odenathus and Zenobia were in intimate contact with the Empire as early as the third century. Later, the Ghassanids or Jafnites of the region from Damascus to Palmyra were allies of the Empire since Justinian, were Monophysite Christians, and fought the Moslems until 635. They ruled from a camp, which means that they remained Arabs in mode of life. Finally, there was the sixth-century conquest of Yemen by Christian Abyssinia, carried almost to Mecca in 570.

---

[5] The Kinda tribe of the Hadramaut is said to have conquered northern Arabia as far as Hira from ca. 500 to 529.

[6] However, a difference in tactical principle of metrics must be noted. Greek meters tend to be fixed with respect to aggregate length units, variable in number of syllables; Arabic, the reverse. Thus the Greek and Latin hexameter consists of 24 morae or minimal length units, alterable only to 23 by substitution of a short for a long final syllable in the line. But the choice allowed between dactyls and spondees in the first four feet results in lines varying from 13 to 17 syllables. In Arabic, on the contrary, while the number of syllables is fixed for a given meter, and the length of most syllables in it is also fixed, there may be particular syllables which can be either long or short. Thus the "tall" or *madid* meter has three feet and eleven syllables; but 17 to 19 morae; thus: ᴗ‿--|ᴗ‿ᴗ-|--ᴗ-. The "long" or *tawil* meter has four feet, fourteen syllables, 20 to 23 morae; thus: ᴗ-‿|ᴗ-‿-|ᴗ-‿|ᴗ-ᴗ-.—Rhyme was being used in Greek Christian hymns by about 500.

Incidentally, we have in this well-standardized, sixth-century, pan-Arabic poetry a setting for Mohammedanism, a soil in which Islam could develop and flourish. The common language is alone enough to indicate that there existed a genuine sense of nationality which needed only a favorable circumstance to divert its energies from clannish feuds to political union and external expansion. And the definiteness of the poetical forms suggests an accumulation of cultural energy ready to be poured into additional channels. In short, already by 500 A.D. there was a rise of culture potential among the Arabs, of which the great burst of the seventh century is only a more intense, and especially a more patently successful, development. It is quite plain that the conventional accounts which make Arab-Islamic civilization begin with—which is, in effect, arise out of—the personality of Mohammed, or which commence with a picture of life in Mecca and Medina in his boyhood, with streaks of Jewish and Christian half-civilization permeating the milieu, are inadequate to an understanding of a phenomenon so vast and enduring in its consequences. The well-knit and cherished art of sixth-century poetry gives an insight into what was brewing in Arabia before the pot boiled over with Mohammed.

Indeed, in literature the pre-Hegiran frame was never very greatly enlarged, except by the addition of prose. The standard form remained the *qasida,* a poem of purpose, usually laudation, which was, however, often reached only after passages dealing with love, camels, battles, the appearance of nature, or other themes. Religion became a subject after the establishment of the Bagdad caliphate, when Persians and other nationalities had begun to help in the reworking and enriching of Mohammedan thought. Drama and epic the Arabs never really attempted. They did put into metrical narrative parts of the legendary history of Persia, Indian tales, and the like; but mainly these have not been preserved, and were therefore evidently not too highly prized. In prose, the Arabs achieved the faculty of telling a story. In poetry, they lacked both native materials preserved so as to lend themselves to epic treatment, and the desire or willingness to free themselves from the habit of subjective attack and of varied restatement of the values or feelings attaching to an episodic fact. The result was that while Firdausi and his Persian-writing successors learned their art from Arabic poets, it was left to them to develop successful epic and romantic narratives in verse.

The whole germinating of mediaeval Persian poetry—the only important literature produced by the Iranian peoples—must be attributed to the influence of Arabic poetry. The specific forms and subjects taken over are too numerous to allow of any other conclusion. Yet Arab-Mohammedan thought and culture were enormously enriched in the same period—except in Arabia itself—by Persian contributions. There was thus a strange interchange: the Arabs giving their religion and their poetical forms outright to the Persians, while receiving from them content and experience in business, administration, knowledge, luxury, and sophistication generally.

The principal other literature affected has been Turkish, and this derived from Persian rather than Arabic, especially in its beginnings.

The Arabic language attained to a very well worked out prose style, which became ornate for some purposes though it could remain simple; but few important prose genres seem to have been developed. The reason perhaps is that in science and philosophy the Islamic world on the whole assimilated and reworked more than it created. In history, it recorded laboriously, but without much synthesis or interpretation. Geography was perhaps the real forte of Moslems. But we are here at the periphery of literature; and how much of the admiration of modern scholars for Al Maqdisi and Al Biruni is for their open-mindedness, power of intelligent observation, and valuable facts preserved, or for their literary qualities?

The one distinctive prose genre developed in Arabic literature is the *maqama,* a tale of the adventures and ruses, mostly verbal, of a vagabond, scamp, or other plastic character—a partial prototype of the Spanish picaresque novel. Apparently the episodic nature of a string of incidents made this form congenial to Arabic literature. Yet even the *maqama* is only partly in prose.

Within the Islamic frame, Arabic soon became the language of philosophy, science, and knowledge like Latin in the West or Sanskrit in India. By the time Persian or Turkish could have asserted claims to be the medium, intellectual activities had much subsided. The result is, as we have seen, that most "Arabic" philosophy and science were produced by men non-Arab in blood, Iran contributing most heavily, Mesopotomia next, Syria and Egypt less, and Arabia least, with Spain undergoing a development separate in time as well as in geography. In history and theology, national participations leaned the same way. But in pure literature, as might be expected, being born to Arabic as one's mother tongue was an enormous advantage. Only, it must be remembered that Arabic before long became the vernacular of Mesopotamia and Syria, and then of Egypt; so that one might be, as now, a true Arab in speech without any Arabian blood in one's veins. As a matter of fact, already in the century after Mohammed non-Arabian poets competed successfully with Arabian ones; and after the Ommayad-Abbasid overturn of 750, and establishment of the Caliphate at Bagdad, born Arabians figured very little in literature. At most did some claim to be of Arabian lineage.

The organization of the history of Arabic literature, and the determination of its climax, are far from simple matters. The usual period classification is into pre-Mohammedan; time of Mohammed; expansion; Ommayad dynasty; Abbasid caliphate at Bagdad, or Golden Age, 750 to 1000 or 1055; Post-Classic or Silver Age, to 1258; and subsequent. But this arrangement is too political to be more than one of convenience. For an analytic understanding of the course of the growth, two primary segregations seem necessary: of Spain, with Morocco and Sicily, from the whole eastern world of Islam; and of poetry from prose literature.

The separating off of Spain we have already found advisable in philosophy and science, and for the same reason as in literature: the Iberian development is clearly later. Two full centuries elapsed after the conquest of the peninsula before Arabic literature began to raise its head there. By that time, the eastern growth had either definitely passed its peak or was approaching the very last stage of its great period, according as one may view its temporal organization. Moreover, Spain contributed new forms: the strophe, including complex rhyme patterns, as contrasted with the typical Arabic couplet with its second-line rhyme throughout the poem; and the use of vernacular. Both these Ibero-Arabic traits appear also in the adjacent Romanic languages of the same period, and the common features in the two growths may therefore be construed as causally connected, although it would require technical competence in two difficult fields to decide in which direction, if either, the causal influences ran.

Arabic prose must also be viewed separately from poetry. The poetry was in full flow a century before Mohammed, and the last great secular poet, Muttanabi, died in 965. Genuinely literary prose, on the other hand, got going only toward 1000, with the invention of its most distinctive form, the *maqama,* and a sudden concentration on the long-known device of *saj'* or rhyming prose.

A further subdivision seems advisable into belletristic prose which was an end in itself and prose which served some specific end such as history, science, philosophy, theology, or law. Speakers of Arabic seem to have been less given than most other peoples to making this distinction, and European historians of their literature have perforce largely followed the nondiscrimination. We have already seen how undifferentiated most Arabic science was: optics, medicine, mathematics, astrology, philosophy were often pursued by the same individual. This fact is surely characteristic of the civilization. But for a comparative treatment a segregation is inevitable. We cannot exclude Aristotle, Archimedes, and Aquinas from literature, but treat Avicenna and Averroës as equivalents of poets merely because these last were Mohammedans and thought in Arabic.

I have therefore separated not only poetry from prose, but

belletristic prose from that in which the substance is more important than the form. This may be contrary to the attitude of Islamic-Arabic civilization, but for present purposes it cannot be helped. I have further segregated the historians from the rest of their group, because in most civilizations they tend to be included among writers as such. The philosophers, scientists, and philologists, having been previously treated in the sections on their fields, need not be relisted here; and theologians we are omitting everywhere.

We have then in effect four strands to review: poetry; literary prose; history; and western Islamic literature.

The poetical growth seems to organize best into four stages: pre-Islamic, with lost beginnings, but known to us from about 500 or 530 on; a first or greater Islamic phase, from about 630 to 830; a second and probably lesser, again of around two centuries, say from 830 to 1030; and one of lower level, from 1030 into the thirteenth century.

As between the second and third stages, it is no doubt somewhat presumptuous for one himself unacquainted with the literature to venture a rating. The histories in European languages are not very committal. They cite Muttanabi as "the last great Arabic poet, if not the greatest." They do admit, however, a gap of more than a century before him; which suggests that he was a belated straggler, or the preëminent figure in a rear guard. Also, in the preceding period we have half a dozen great names, all between 680/700 and 800, whereas Muttanabi stands alone. Incidentally, this clustering shows the inadequacy of the conventional division into an Ommayad and an Abbasid period: 750 splits our natural constellation in the middle.

Indeed, it might be questioned whether the first and greater Islamic period should be reckoned superior to the pre-Islamic. There were quarrels on this point in the early philological schools; perhaps merely because of pedantic antiquarian worship of the past. Nevertheless, the essential forms of Arabic poetry, and much of its content and style, were worked out before Mohammed; and this leaves it an open judgment, on the basis of comparative precedent, whether the quality climax is more probably to be sought in this determinative period or in the unfolding of the subsequent Islamic one.

In any event, it seems reasonably certain that the poetical peak falls before rather than after 800.

For literary prose, on the other hand, a real style was hardly worked out before Al-Jahiz in the ninth century, and the culmination lay in or around the eleventh.

For history, the golden age coincides with the silver age of poetry, 830–1030, with Al-Tabari, 839–923, marking the peak. After 1030 there is an obvious falling off, with a secondary rise from about 1175 to 1275. The great period of historiography coincides rather closely with the great periods of science and philosophy.

In western Islam, literary development is not only later than in eastern, but later than is usually stated. Abd al-Rahman, 912–961, under whom political unity, good government, and economic prosperity evidently reached their height in Spain, was also a patron of letters, learning, and books. Under him, Ibero-Arabic literature, poetical and prose, was born; but the peak was not reached for another century, and new forms continued to be evolved for two centuries. It was in literature as in philosophy and science: the century of Ommayad breakup, and that of Almoravid and Almohad Berber rule, each yielded more and greater cultural products than the reign of Abd al-Rahman and his son. It took two centuries to achieve fusion of ethnic elements and a successful political fabric in Mohammedan Spain; these then bore fruit chiefly in two subsequent centuries.

ARABIC LITERATURE

POETRY IN EASTERN ISLAM

Pre-Islamic phase, 500–630
Bedouins:
  *Imru'ulqays, fl. 530.
  Ash-Shanfara.
  Ta'abbata Sharra.
  *Antara.
  Tumadir, woman, b. ca. 580.
  Zuhayr, saw Mohammed.

*Labid, d. after 652, silent after conversion.
Abu Mikhjan, d. 637+.
Abu Dhu'aib, of Hudhail tribe.

At court of Hira; in Arabian cities; and Jews or Christians:
Aus ibn Hadjar, stepfather of Zuhayr.
*An-Nabigha, 6th cent., at Hira.
Tarafa, next generation.
Al-A'sha.
Qais ibn al Khatim, of Medina.
Umaiya, of Ta'if.
Musafir, of Mecca.
Samaual, Jew, in Arabia.
Adi ibn Zaid, Christian of Hira.

Associated with Mohammed:
Hassan ibn Thabit, mediocre.
Ka'b, son of Zuhayr, one Islamic ode.

Great Islamic phase, 630–830
Qais ibn Dharikh. In Arabia.
(About 700: poetry first regularly written down.)
*Omar ibn Abi Rabia, d. ca. 720, of Mecca. Developed love lyric out of *qasida* introduction.
Al Akhwas, d. 728. In Arabia.
Kuthayir, d. 723. Southern Arab.
Laila al Akhyaliya, d. 707, woman.
*Al-Akhtal, d. 710. Ummayad court poet; Christian.
*Jarir, d. 728. Court poet of viceroy of Iraq.
*Farazdaq, ca. 641–ca. 728. Of Basra.
(The last three were contemporary rivals.)
Walid II, d. 743: wine songs.
Muti ibn Ayas; Palmyra to Kufa to Bagdad; modernist.
*Bashshar, d. 763 or 784, half Persian, at Bagdad, founded "new style," with novel similes.
As-Saiyid al Himyari, 723–789. Greatest provincial poet of his time. Shi'ite.
(Khalil ibn Ahmad, d. 791; formulator of rules of extant prosody.)
Rabi'a, d. 801, of Basra; woman; poems of love of God.
*Abu Nuwas, ca. 750–810, half Persian, court poet at Bagdad.
Abu'l-'Atahiya, d. 826, of Arab blood, developed religious poetry.
Abu Tammam, d. 845, Syrian, followed old style.

Decline, 830–1030
Al-Bokhtori, 820–897, Syria..

Ibn al-Mu'tazz, d. 908, one-day caliph at Bagdad. Poems of revelry and boy-love.

*Al-Mutanabbi, d. 965. At Aleppo. The last great Arab poet. Free of direct Persian influence, but immoderate and hypertrophied in expression.

Abu Firas, 932–967, nephew of ruler of Aleppo.

Abu'l Fatkh, d. 1010; from near Kabul; poet of Mahmud of Ghazna.

Ar-Radi, 970–1015.

Abu'l-'Ala al-Ma'arri, 973–1057, of Aleppo.

After 1030

Ibn al-Habbariya, d. 1100; metric version of *Kalila and Dimna*.

At-Tughra'i, d. 1121, Seljuk vizier; "L-ode of the non-Arabs."

Ibn Sana'almulk, 1150–1211. In Egypt. Introduced Spanish-Arabic strophic *muwashsha* in the east.

Ibn 'Arabi, of Murcia, 1165–1240, mystic. Estabished the *muwashsha* in the east.

*Omar ibn al-Farid, 1181–1235, b. Cairo. Greatest mystic poet in Arabic.

Baba ad-Din Zuhayr, d. 1258, Egyptian.

Al-Busiri, 1212–ca. 1296, Egyptian Berber. "Ode of the Mantle" (of Mohammed).

LITERARY OR BELLETRISTIC PROSE IN EASTERN ISLAM

Ninth century

Al-Jahiz, d. 869, aged. "Book of Animals." Founder of Arab prose style.

Abu Bakr ibn abi'd Dunya, 823–894. Similar vein.

Around 1000

Ibn Nubata, 946–983/4. At Aleppo. First literary sermons wholly in rhymed prose (*saj'*).

Ibrahim ibn Hilal, from Harran, d. 994. Florid secretarial style, rhymed.

At-Tanuchi, 939–997, b. Basra. "Sun Follows Rain."

Abu Bakr al-Khwarismi, 935–1002, Persian. Fictive letters, rhymed.

*Al-Hamadhani, 969–1007/8. From Hamadhan to Nishapur and Herat. Inventor of *maqama*.

Abu Hayyan at-Tawhidi, d. after 1009.

1100–1200

*Al-Hariri of Basra, 1054–1122. *Maqama*.

Az-Zamakhshari of Khwarizm, 1075–1143. Moral apothegms: also grammar.

Usama ibn Munqidh, 1095–1188. Syrian. Autobiography.
Fakhr ad-Din ar-Razi, 1149–1209. Humanist.

HISTORY AND OTHER PROSE IN EASTERN ISLAM

History: 730–830

Al-Kelbi, d. 763. Arab genealogies.
Ibn Ishaq, d. 766. Biography of Mohammed.
Al-Waqidi, d. 823. B. Medina. Expansion of Islam.
Akhmed al-Azruq, d. 834. History and antiquities of Mecca.
Al-Mada'ini, d. ca. 840. Arabian. Historic monographs.

History: 830–1030

Al-Baladhuri, d. 892. Persian. General history, geographic arrangement.
Al-Ya'qubi, d. after 891, or fl. 891. Shi'ite.
*Al-Tabari, 839–923. B. Tabaristan, Persia. Universal history.
Ali al-Mas'udi, b. Bagdad, d. 956.
Miskawayh, d. 1030.
Al-'Utbi, d. 1036. Converted history into laudatory biography.
Ath-Tha'alibi, 961–1038. History of Persia.

History: 1175–1275

Imad ad-Din, 1125–1201. From Isfahan.
Ibn al-Athir, 1160–1234. Arab. Universal history of Islam.
Ibn Khallikan, 1211–1282. Syrian, of Bactrian descent. Biographies.

History: 1375–1450

Ibn Khaldun, 1332–1406. B. Tunis, d. Cairo. Philosophy of history.
Al-Maqrizi, 1346–1442.
Ibn 'Arabshah, 1392–1450. B. Damascus. History of Timur.

Other prose

(See the chapters on Philosophy; Science; Philology.)

ISLAMIC SPAIN, MOROCCO, SICILY

Poetry

(Mohammed ibn Hani, b. Seville, d. 973, Fatimid court poet in Egypt.)
Soon after 1000, development of the strophic *muwashshah.*
*Ibn Zaydun, 1003–1071, of Cordova.
Al-Mu'tamid, 1040–1095, of Seville.
Ibn Hamdis, ca. 1055–1132, Sicilian, to Seville, Morocco.
Ibn Quzman, d. 1160, chief representative of *zajal,* new strophic form in nonliterary vernacular.
(Ibn 'Arabi, 1165–1240, of Murcia, to east.)

Prose

Ibn 'Aba Rabbihi, 860–940, literary thesaurus based on Ibn Qutayba.

Al-Qali, d. 967. Armenian, 942 to Cordova, founder of Spanish school of philology.

Ibn al-Qutiya, b. Cordova, d. 977. History of Spain.

Ibn Hazm, of Cordova, 994–1064.

Ibn Zaidun, 1003–1070. B. Cordova. Rhetorical letters.

Philosophers: Ibn Baja, d. 1138; Ibn Tufayl, d. 1185; Ibn Rushd, d. 1198.

Idrisi, Sicilian, b. 1099; 1154, geography.

Ibn Zafar, Sicilian, d. 1169, belletristic historical novelettes.

Ibn Jubaya, 1145–1217, of Valencia, travel journal.

Ali Ibn Sa'id, b. Granada, d. 1274/86. History.

Ibn Battuta, 1304–1378. B. Tangicr. Travels.

§ 77. Persian Literature

It is peculiar that with their long history the Iranian peoples produced a formal literature only late in their career, after their overthrow by the Arabs, after almost complete Mohammedanization, and while they were under Turkish rule or ravaged by Mongol invasion. The period of this literature is 900 to 1500. It thus began 1500 years after the Iranians entered documented history by participating in the overthrow of Nineveh and establishing the Median empire. Zoroaster, according to Parsee tradition, lived about the same time; some modern scholars incline to consider him from one to several centuries earlier. Since him, the Iranians have had a formulated national religion; which, under the Medes and Achaemenians, perhaps under the Parthians, and certainly under the Sassanids, was the cult of a powerful state as well as the belief and practice of a great nationality. Yet all this success in the spiritual as well as material field produced no notable literature. Evidently the time was too early, and the Asiatic peoples from whom the Iranians drew much of their cultural heritage were too little developed in the production of poetry as poetry; whereas Hellenization, after 300 B.C., was apparently vigorously resisted by the Persians.

There is poetry of a sort in the Avesta: Zoroaster's own *gathas* or songs and some of the *jashts* or hymn-prayers. These are in a syllabic meter, like the older Indic productions; but the form is rude, and the content too directly religious to count as literature. The Middle Persian or Pehlevi stage of the language, in Sassanian times, 226 to 641, is represented only by prose remnants, mainly religious, sober and simple in style. There were also historical and quasi-historical works, some verging on the epic or romance in theme; and there may have been verse which has been lost.

In 636–641 the Arabs toppled this old politico-religious structure. The Iranian lands became part of the Caliphate. Mohammedanism quickly became the dominant belief. Even though the Persians came to embrace the Shi'ite heresy, and clung to it successfully as a sort of protest, they were in Islam; and within a few centuries adherents of the old national religion were a vanishing minority. Arabic was the language not only of government and worship, but of learning, philosophy, and science. With it, Arabic orthography was established.[7] Arabic poetry, which has a pre-Prophet history in spite of the general civilizational backwardness of Arabia, became the model on which Persian poetry was gradually built up. From Arabic were taken the Persian quantitative meters; rhyme, including the habit of having one rhyme run through a whole poem on alternate lines; strophic forms; and types of poems, such as the *qasida* or panegyric. With this borrowed apparatus the Persians set to work, at first in direct imitation of the Arabs. Traditionally, the first longer poem in Persian was recited to the future caliph Ma'mun at Merv in 809. The first great Persian poet, Rudaki, flourished 914–943; Firdausi, toward 1000, when Arabic poetical literature was definitely past its prime. But Persian literature still had nearly five centuries to run.

---

[7] Pehlevi was written with Aramaic letters, but in the main these were used not alphabetically, but as unit ideograms; much as if—for illustration—we wrote "domus" but pronounced the assemblage of the five Latin letters "house." This habit gives an unexpected insight into the cultural retardation, or at least dependence, of the powerful Sassanian monarchy, and perhaps helps to explain why it failed to achieve a formal literature.

Firdausi illustrates the relations of the two literatures. The epic is not an Arabic genre. Firdausi's *Shah-nama* deals with the history of Zoroastrian Iran and its national heroes. But not only its rhyme, its very meter is Arabic, the *mutakarib* of four short and seven long syllables. It is clear that the Islamized Iranians remained no mere imitators of the Arabs. They freed themselves from their model more, probably, than Roman literature became independent of Greek. On the other hand, it does look as if, without the foreign and imposed fertilization, their literature might never have gestated.

Of course the process was not one-sided between the two nationalities, and in business, administration, secretariat, organization, luxuries, and other sophistications the Arabs learned much from the longer-civilized Persians. With it all, the language of the newer culture remained dominant as that of learning. Like Latin in the West, it was the international medium. Persian literature grew up something like a vernacular literature in Catholic Europe.

Whether it outstripped the Arabic is difficult to prove, but might be alleged. Certainly it has evoked more translations in Europe; or at least the translations have met with more response. Western poets, from Goethe down, have been stimulated by Persian poets. There is no Arab writer who has had an influence, or a popular repute in Europe, equal to Firdausi or Omar Khayyam or Jelaleddin or Hafiz. Perhaps the Arab range is too narrow; or perhaps something elusive adhering to Indo-European speech, or possibly even to Indo-European cultural ancestry, has helped the Persian literature to Western favor.

The internal configuration of the Persian growth is difficult to define, except in grand outline: beginnings about 800, earliest full-stature poetry by 900, the great classics from 1000 to 1400, another century with but little falling off, since 1500 stale repetition. This makes a near-thousand-year growth, of which five centuries are original and productive, and several of these can lay about equal claim to greatness. The swing of the rhythm is as slow as in India. The approximate culmination dates of the great seven are: Firdausi, 980; then, after a century and a half, Anwari, 1150, Nizami, 1180, Saadi, 1230, Rumì, 1250, all four within a century; then, a hundred years later, Hafiz, 1360, usually reckoned the greatest if Firdausi is not so rated; then, after another century, Jami, 1450. The irregularity is that the two greatest individuals fall well outside the thickest cluster.

Firdausi's is perhaps the best-known name, and he comes at the beginning of the long "peak." But an epic lends itself better to transmutation into other languages than lyrics; less of the essential flavor is lost; and how much discount should be made for this factor? Perhaps we have here one of the literatures like the Italian, which begin with their greatest genius but nevertheless last well.

Persian literature of the great period is poetry. Prose was less ambitious and less successful, except incidentally as by Saadi in the thirteenth century. Arabic, being the language of learning as distinct from enjoyment, evidently retarded the development of Persian prose for its own sake.

To what degree men born between 900 and 1400 in the northeastern border areas, from Merv and Khiva to Bokhara and Samarkand, which are now mainly Turkish-speaking, were respectively Turkish or Iranian in descent, it seems difficult to ascertain. The culture and the language of culture in this region were undoubtedly Persian. However, Mohammedanized Turks did much of the ruling in Iran from the tenth century on, and many followers must have come with them. Ethnically and in vernacular speech, many populations were probably composite.

Ottoman Turkish literature, a sort of imitation of Persian, might have its culmination set perhaps in the latter half of the sixteenth century.

Persian Literature

From 800 to 950, traditional originators of panegyrics, quatrains, mystical poetry: Abbas at Merv; Bayezid of Bistam; Hanzala of Badaghis; Mahmudi Warrak of Herat; Abu Shukur of Balkh.
*Rudaki, of Khurasan, d. ca. 954. Court panegyrics. "The Adam of poets."

Al Bal'ami, first connected prose in Persian: translation of Tabari's *History*. Under Samanid (874–999) dynasty.

Dakiki, first 1,000 verses of *Shah-nama*. Under Samanids.

Unsuri of Balkh, d. ca. 1050, poet laureate of Mahmud of Ghazna.

Farrukhi and Asjadi, Unsuri's associates and pupils. Farrukhi was the best of the three.

**Firdausi, 935/6–1020, b. Tus, Khorasan. National epic, the *Shah-nama*, written 964–999, revised 1010; 60,000 couplets. Also the romance *Yusuf and Zulaykha* in rhymed couplets. Firdausi almost alone is uninfluenced by mystic Sufiism.

Asadi the Elder, d. ca. 1038, introduced from Arabic the *munazara* or disputation poem (*tenzone*).

Minuchihri of Damghan, d. soon after 1041. *Diwan* of panegyrics.

Abu Said, 968–1049. First Sufi or mystic poet; revived the *ruba'i* or quatrain.

Sana'i, whose career began under Mahmud, first employed the rhymed couplet (*masnawi*) for mystic expression.

Al Jurjani. Historical romance *Wis and Ramin*, ca. 1048.

Asadi the Younger, nephew of Firdausi, d. before 1100. Epic *Kershasp-nama*.

Nasiri Khusrau, 1004–1088. Mystic; *Safar-nama*, "diary" in prose; also poems.

Ansari of Herat, later contemporary of Nasiri Khusrau, mystic, quatrains.

Al Ghazzali, the philosopher and theologian, 1058–1111, of Tus, wrote mostly in Arabic, but a summary in Persian.

Ibn Sina, Avicenna, the philosopher and physician, 980–1037, from near Bokhara, may have written many of the quatrains attributed to Omar.

*Omar (Umar al) Khayyam, 1038/48–1123/4, the astronomer, b. Nishapur. Mystic-philosophical quatrains.

Nasru 'llah ibnu 'l Hamid, fl. in reign 1118–1152, transl. *Bidpai* (*Pilpai*) fables from Arabic.

Suzani (Sozeni), d. 1173/4, satirist.

Mehisti, a woman, fl. ca. 1157? Erotic lyrics.

**Anwari (Enweri), fl. under Sanjar 1117–1157, d. ca. 1189–1191 at Balkh. Best Persian panegyrics (*qasida*).

Aṣiru 'l Din Akhsikati, contemporary of Anwari, almost equaled him.

Khakani, d. 1199, almost as famous as Anwari for panegyrics; also couplets.

Amir Mu'izzi, d. 1147, court poet of Sanjar.

**Nizami, 1140/41–1202/3, b. Tefrish or Kum. Romances *Khusrau* *and Shirin, Layla and Majnun,* etc.; also *Iskandar-nama* in Firdausi's epic meter.

*Attar, 1119–1230 (*sic*) or fl. 1119–1130? Sufi couplets. Faridu 'l Din, predecessor of Sa'di, who influenced him.

**Sa'di (Saadi), 1184–1283/91 (*sic*), b. Shiraz. Most popular of the moralist-mystic poets. *Bustan* (Orchard) and *Gulistan* (Rose Garden) in prose mixed with verse.

**Jalalu'l (Jelaled) Din Rumi, 1207–1273, b. Balkh, settled in Iconium (Rum). Most serious and perhaps greatest mystic poet. Founder of Mawlawi order of dancing dervishes.

Nasiru 'l Din of Tus, d. 1274. Hulagu's astronomer. Wrote *Nasiri's Ethics,* in prose.

Ata Malik, b. Nishapur, d. 1283. History of Jenghiz.

Iraki, d. ca. 1288; prose and verse *Flashes,* dealing with "mystic" love.

Rashid, d. 1318. Compendium of histories.

Wassaf. Euphuistic continuation of last.

Mahmud of Shabistar, d. 1320. Sufi couplets.

*Amir Khusrau of Delhi, born and lived in India, d. 1325. Quintet of romances almost equal to Nizami's.

Hamdullah, *Zafar-nama,* rhymed history continuing Firdausi; also *Select History* (to 1330).

Khwaju, 1281–1352, of Kirman. Another quintet in imitation of Nizami.

Ubaydi Zakani, of Shiraz, d. 1370/71. Satire.

Salman of Sawa, d. 1376/7. Panegyrics and romantic couplets.

**Hafiz, b. Shiraz ca. 1320, d. there 1389/90. Most popular and perhaps greatest Persian poet. Panegyrics, quatrains, and lyrics of love and wine, with ambiguous mystic secondary meaning.

Abu Ishak (Bushak), of Shiraz, d. 1427. Parodist, writing of food.

Kasimi Anwar, d. ca. 1434. *Diwan* of Sufi couplets.

Katibi of Nishapur, d. 1434/6, panegyrist. After him, romances and mystic poetry tend to fuse.

*Abdur-Rahman Jami, 1414–1492, of Jam in Khurasan. Lyric, romantic, and mystic verse. The last great Persian poet.

Hatifi, his nephew, of Jam, d. 1521. Epic *Timur-nama,* and romances.

Fighani, contemporary, d. 1516 or 1519.

Hilali of Astarabad, d. 1532.

Persian poets in India under Akbar: Urfi of Shiraz, d. 1590/91; Fayzi, d. 1595; Zuhuri of Tihras, d. 1616. These are rated higher than their contemporaries in Persia. Cf. also Khusrau of Delhi, d. 1325.

§ 78. Occidental Literatures

With mediaeval and modern Europe we come to a group of literatures that are similar to one another and historically inter-related because they are the products of a series of nations largely sharing a common civilization. Yet they are separate because each nation possessed its distinctive language and therefore a distinct medium for its literature. Such a relation holds also as between Greek and Latin, and between Arabic and Persian literatures; but in the Occident it is a whole array of nations that march abreast. Essentially the literatures of Europe are the literatures of the vernaculars which gradually established themselves alongside Latin, and finally in place of it, as the media of religion, learning, law, and record.

The lead in the achievement of literary forms and contents was taken by France, both southern and northern; and what-ever the fluctuations in any one nation, Europe as a whole has produced a fairly steady stream of productivity for nearly eight centuries thereafter. Italy was relatively late in participating, England still later, Germany early but then long inactive; the smaller or peripheral peoples contributed little until after the Middle Ages.

There is one exception to this intricate but coherent growth: the Norse literature of the close of the Viking period. This is earlier than the main growth; it alone is wholly uninfluenced by Classic Mediterranean traditions; and it is the only Occi-dental literature produced by a non-Christianized people. Also, in origin and course it is geographically peripheral, in the strictest sense. It stands so apart from everything else in the Occident that it should probably be regarded as a coördinate historical growth rather than as a subordinate part. I have left its discussion under the caption of "Scandinavian Literatures," in § 87 (p. 590), for the practical reason that conformity to the general scheme of treatment by nationalities is the simpler pro-cedure; but I do not believe that this grouping is historically defensible in terms of basic cultural affiliation.

The general order of examination that follows is chronological, on the basis mainly, however, of the time of beginning rather than of culmination of each literature.

§79. French Literature

From before 1100 on, French literature manifests a continuity of performance unequaled in Europe. There are admitted ups and downs of quality, but nothing like the nullity of quality for considerable periods in Italy, Spain, England, Germany, and smaller countries. Once the French began to write, they never fell below a certain level. It is as if, after they had first glimpsed higher civilization, they reached and held it easily, without the struggles, triumphs, and failures of other nationalities. Their literature therefore resolves itself less satisfactorily into periods of distinctly different level than any other European one. There are peaks, but they are hardly grandiose; and the intervening stretches, while often somewhat arid, are never so sterile as to warrant apology or misprizal.

The French is also the earliest Occidental literature. It shares this priority, it is true, with its sister Provençal. But, contrary to a widespread impression, it is not in the least later. The conventional golden age of Provençal, 1150–1280, is also exactly the golden age of mediaeval North French writing. The real difference is that Provençal poetry died about 1350, or was superseded by Italian, but French went on. This is no doubt connected with the fact that Provençal literature centered almost wholly in the lyric, while French developed also poetical narrative, the *fabliau*, drama, and prose.

This High Mediaeval literature commenced simultaneously with the early burst of French philosophy at Paris and with Romanesque architecture and sculpture. It ended about simultaneously with the best phase of Gothic sculpture and architecture, and with the thirteenth-century monarchical consolidation of France.

By about 1300 a literary falling off is perceptible, and it continues for more than two centuries. The decline is presumably connected with the growth of the bourgeoisie, which required time to absorb traditions of higher culture. One great poet falls in this lapse: Villon, 1431–ca. 1465. He stands isolated and unexplained by context. He might well be construed as an antibourgeois revolt.

Around 1520 or soon after, there begins a half century of relatively high performance. Between 1490 and 1535 were born Rabelais, Marot, Calvin, Ronsard, Montaigne. Yet France had not found her direction. There were conflicting Renaissance, Reformation, humanistic influences. No unified pattern system was worked out. The outstanding quality of the period was its diversity. In this it was abnormal, if not unique. Other nationalities also groped, more or less at the same period; but mainly with failures.

There followed a sixty-year period of lesser lights, born 1535 to 1595. Of these Malherbe is the outstanding name; and he can mean little, intrinsically, to any but a Frenchman. His role was the initiation of the restrictive attitudes through which the following great "Baroque" period was to express itself in France: restriction of theme, manner, diction.

The great Classic age, somewhat inaccurately known as that of Louis Quatorze, extended from 1630 to 1700; the births, which will hereafter be followed because they constellate more regularly, run from 1595 to 1655. Corneille was at his peak 1636–1641, Molière 1664–1668, Racine 1667–1677. After 1680 we have, as the best, Racine's religious plays, Fénelon, part of Boileau. Nearly half of the highest product is therefore pre-Louis XIV: nearly half of his reign is beyond the zenith. He capitalized on a period of strength: as its product, not its cause.

In some respects this growth has a "silver" rather than a "golden age" character. There is no outstanding, dominant figure. It submits willingly to rules. It retracts its vocabulary instead of trying to enrich it. It is a period of founding of academies: of the Française in 1635, of painting, sculpture, sciences, architecture, and music from 1648 to 1672.

After 1700 there is a lull. Among the births for a generation, 1655–1685, the outstanding one is the Spanish imitator Le Sage.

The next thirty years, 1685–1715, still in the reign of Louis XIV, see the birth of the leaders of the Enlightenment: Montesquieu, Voltaire, Buffon, Rousseau, Diderot. This is a positive growth. But it is marginal to literature, to philosophy, and to science. There is no very great poet, philosopher, or scientist in the group. Ability of a high order there is, but no new forms of literature, unless it be limpid, effective prose, such as Chinese literati might write on subjects of generic intellectual interest.

Even this development, high in its intelligence but lacking in the emotional vitals of literature, is followed by another lull of births, of nearly half a century, 1715–1760. Beaumarchais is the most prominent figure.

So far as it relates to pure literature as something felt rather than cultivated, the whole French eighteenth century, births 1655–1760, can easily be seen as an interval between two greater periods, in spite of the genius of Voltaire and Rousseau. They influenced European thought rather than the art of literature.

The next century is one of positive growth, and in directions which may be characterized as expansive in contrast to the restrictive ones of the seventeenth century. In short, we have the Romantic-Realistic development. The births begin soon after 1760, culminate around 1800 with Hugo, and go on to 1850; 1800–1900 encompasses the productivity of the movement.

Three subperiods can be recognized. A preliminary one includes Chénier, De Staël, Chateaubriand, born 1762–1768. Then there is a gap to Béranger 1780, Stendhal 1783, Lamartine 1790; after whom follows the climax: De Vigny, Balzac, Hugo, Dumas, Mérimée, Sand, De Musset, Gautier, 1797–1811. As in contemporary England, poets and novelists come interdigitated. Another gap lasts ten years, after which Flaubert and Baudelaire, 1821, initiate the descent, to be followed by Renan, Daudet, Zola, Verlaine, France, De Maupassant, 1823–1850.

If one prefers, the middle subperiod could be made to run to 1825 instead of 1820 in births, with the tipping of several more distinguished names into the culminating phase. But the objective gap in births between 1811 and 1820 seems a reliably significant index of subdivision.

Romanticism, so-called, of course came earlier in England and Germany, in a sense even in Italy, than in France. It did not triumph in Paris until 1830, when its greatest achievements were finished in the other countries. The French had a much tighter tradition of so-called Classicism to unlearn: a tradition of poetry that aimed at the virtues of elegant prose.

After 1900, or births later than 1850, it can hardly be pretended that there is anything but a lower level.

This analysis yields five positive periods of French literature:

1. 1070–1300, High Mediaeval.
2. 1520–1580, Renaissance-Reformation Experimental.
3. 1630–1680 (1700), Classic-Baroque.
4. 1720–1770, Enlightenment.
5. 1800–1900, Romantic-Realistic.

The total is 500 years in the 850 from 1070 to 1920. This seems too high, by precedent elsewhere. Moreover, we have 230 years of High Mediaeval productivity and 220 of Late Mediaeval relaxation, or a total of 450 accounted for by the first crest and trough. The 400 years that remain are too little for four florescences and four relatively sterile periods—at least if experience in other areas and fields is to be a guide to probability. A reduction by consolidation seems in order.

Such a consolidation can be effected most naturally, it seems, by union of positive periods 2, 3, and 4—Renaissance, Louis XIV, and Enlightenment—into a larger unit of three pulses. From 1520 to 1580 France was exposed to, and also resisted, strong Reformation influences from the Germanic peoples and Renaissance influences from Italy; much as Italy, two and three centuries before, partly accepted but also resisted French "Gothic" influences in architecture, sculpture, and literature. No consistent set of patterns was therefore formed in sixteenth-century France, and it required a lull, the 1580–1630 interval, before the conflicting impulses could die down and a fresh start be made. The direction of this fresh start is already evident in Malherbe; and in the great Classic phase of fifty or sixty years following 1630 a truly national and harmonious expression was achieved. The limitation of this to so short a period as two active lifetimes is to be construed as perhaps at least partly due to the fact that restrictiveness was a fundamental quality of the pattern system.

After a generation of second lull, there follows the Enlightenment phase. In spite of great names like Voltaire, this did not produce a single great poet or dramatist. The literary forms established a century before continued to hold absolute sway, but of course could no longer be filled with content of equal value; especially so because the deliberate narrowness of forms allowed only a narrow range of content, which had been quickly traversed and exploited. The writers of the Enlightenment therefore turned to new subjects which lay outside the unshaken forms and could be handled in prose. Their themes, at least those in which they succeeded best and for which they are remembered, are social-philosophic, not poetic. Voltaire was facile and great enough to go successfully through the motions of poetry; but Rousseau and Montesquieu scarcely even attempted the motions, and Diderot failed in them.

These three phases, together with their intervals, fill a quarter millennium: 1520 to 1770. This period seems more proper. Sixty years is too short a lapse for a constellation qualitatively as great as that which centered in Molière. On the other hand, the forms finally settled on were too narrow to allow of a growth filling two hundred and fifty years. Hence the three pulses, respectively: of attempted finding; of achievement; and of dissolution not by dilation or alteration of form but by escape from poetic preoccupation.

The nineteenth century finally brought rupture of the old forms and an intense endeavor at poetic accomplishment. However, the interval preceding it is also brief. One can therefore conceive of the nineteenth-century growth as a reaction formation against what preceded, and in that sense part of it. Such a view is supported by the lateness of the Romantic impulses in France. In England, Germany, even Italy, the tradition against which their Romanticism revolted was, it is true, in established control. But the victory was hollow, because the restrictive tradition in these countries had never produced important values and was therefore a formal fashion that had been accepted because native expression was in a lull, rather than being a genuinely rooted force as in France.

In any event, whatever the reasons, French literature remains the most continuous in Europe. It produced, in common estimation, no one genius equal to Shakespeare, Goethe, Dante, or Cervantes. On the other hand, most of its low-level intervals lasted only a generation or two, and the longest little over two centuries. Also, each interval contained at least one figure of definite distinction: Villon, Malherbe, Le Sage, Beaumarchais. And three times French influence was widespread and profound in Europe: during and after its High Mediaeval growth; again after its Baroque; and, at least in Spain and peripheral countries, during the Romantic phase.

French Literature

High Mediaeval florescence, ca. 1070–1300

Eleventh-century gestes: *Roland* (prob. Norman); *Pélerinage de Charlemagne* (in 12-syllable lines).

Twelfth-century gestes: *Huon de Bordeaux; Aliscans; Raoul de Cambrai.*

Tristan et Iseult, by Beroul, ca. 1150, Thomas, ca. 1170, both Anglo-Norman.

*Chrétien de Troyes, fl. ca. 1160–1175: *Tristan; Erec; Cligès; Lancelot; Yvain; Perceval (Le Graal).*

Aucassin et Nicolette, between 1150 and 1200.

Roman de Renart, 12th–13th cent.: 8-syllable couplets.

Marie de France, end of 12th cent., in England.

Lambert le Tort, 12th cent.: *Roman d'Alexandre,* in 12-syllable lines.

Villehardouin, 1164–1213.

Thirteenth-century gestes: *Aimeri de Narbonne; Renaud de Montauban.*

Fabliaux.

Roman de la rose, by Guillaume de Lorris, ca. 1236, and Jean de Meung, ca. 1276, in 8-syllable couplets.

Adenés, ca. 1260.

Adam de la Halle: *Le Jeu de la Feuillée,* ca. 1260.

Thirteenth-century miracles.

Joinville, 1224–1319.

Rutebœuf, ca. 1230–ca. 1290.

Dissolving Mediaeval interval, 1300–1520: Births ca. 1270–1490
   Miracles de Notre Dame, 14th cent.
   Griseldis, 14th cent.
   Froissart, 1337–ca. 1405.
   Christine de Pisan, 1363–1431.
   Gerson, 1363–1429.
   Chartier, 1386–1458.
   Juvenal des Ursins, 1388–1473.
   Charles d'Orléans, 1391–1465.
   La Salle, 1398–1461.
   Mysteries, moralities, *soties,* farces, until after 1500.
   Pathelin.
  *Villon, 1431–1465?
   Comines, ca. 1445–1511.

Productive diversity, after 1520: Births 1490–1535
  *Rabelais, 1490–1553.
   Marguerite de Navarre, 1492–1549.
  *Marot, 1496–1544.
  *Calvin, 1509–1564.
   Amyot, 1513–1593.
  *Ronsard, 1524–1585.
   Du Bellay, 1525–1560.
   Baïf, 1531–1589 (Metrical quantity instead of rhyme!).
   Jodelle, 1532–1573.
  *Montaigne, 1533–1592.

Interval: Births 1535–1595
   Brantôme, 1540–1614.
   Larivey, 1540–1611.
   Du Bartas, 1544–1590.
   Garnier, 1534/45–1590/1601.
   D'Aubigné, 1551–1630.
  *Malherbe, 1555–1628.
   Satyre Ménippée, publ. 1594.
   Honoré d'Urfé, 1568–1625.
   Hardy, 1569?–1632.
   Régnier, 1573–1613.
   Montchrétien, 1575–1621.
   Théophile de Viau, 1590–1626.

Seventeenth-century restrictive florescence: Births 1595–1655
   Chapelain, 1595–1674.
   Descartes, 1596–1650.
   Balzac, 1597–1654.
   Voiture, 1598–1648.

*Corneille, 1606–1684; *1636–1641.
Mlle de Scudéry, 1607–1701; *1649.
Rotrou, 1609–1650; *1638–1645.
La Calprenède, 1610–1663; *1642.
Scarron, 1610–1660; *1649.
La Rochefoucauld, 1613–1680.
Retz, 1614–1679.
*La Fontaine, 1621–1695.
*Molière, 1622–1673; *1659–1673.
*Pascal, 1623–1662.
Thomas Corneille, 1625–1709.
Mme de Sévigné, 1626–1696.
*Bossuet, 1627–1704.
Perrault, 1628–1703.
Bourdaloue, 1632–1704.
La Fayette, 1634–1693.
Quinault, 1635–1688.
*Boileau, 1636–1711.
*Racine, 1639–1699; *1667–1677.
La Bruyère, 1645–1696.
Bayle, 1647–1706.
*Fénelon, 1651–1715.

Interval: Births 1655–1685
Regnard, 1655–1709.
Fontenelle, 1657–1757.
Massillon, 1663–1742.
*Le Sage, 1668–1747.
Crébillon, 1674–1762.
Saint-Simon, 1675–1755.

Enlightenment: Births 1685–1715
Marivaux, 1688–1763.
*Montesquieu, 1689–1755.
La Chaussée, 1691–1754.
*Voltaire, 1694–1778.
L'Abbé Prévost, 1697–1763.
*Buffon, 1707–1788.
*Rousseau, 1712–1778. Swiss.
*Diderot, 1713–1784.

Interval: Births 1715–1760
Vauvenargues, 1715–1747.
Sedaine, 1719–1797.
Du Bellay, 1727–1775.
*Beaumarchais, 1732–1799.

Ducis, 1733–1816.
De Saint-Pierre, 1737–1814.
Mirabeau, 1749–1791.

Preliminary to florescence: Births 1760–1780
Saint-Simon, 1760–1825.
Chénier, 1762–1794.
*Mme de Staël, 1766–1817. Swiss descent.
*Chateaubriand, 1768–1848.

Nineteenth-century expansive florescence: Births 1780–1820
*Béranger, 1780–1857.
Lamennais, 1782–1854.
*Stendhal, 1783–1842.
Guizot, 1787–1874.
*Lamartine, 1790–1869.
Scribe, 1791–1861.
Cousin, 1792–1867.
Thierry, 1795–1856.
Mignet, 1796–1884.
Thiers, 1797–1877.
*De Vigny, 1797–1863.
Michelet, 1798–1874.
Comte, 1798–1857.
*Balzac, 1799–1850.
*Hugo, 1802–1885.
*Dumas *père*, 1803–1870.
*Mérimée, 1803–1870.
Quinet, 1803–1875.
*George Sand, 1804–1876.
Sainte-Beuve, 1804–1869.
De Tocqueville, 1805–1859.
*De Musset, 1810–1857.
*Gautier, 1811–1872.

Aftermath of florescence: Births 1820–1850
Augier, 1820–1889.
Leconte de Lisle, 1820–1894.
Fromentin, 1820–1876.
*Flaubert, 1821–1880.
*Baudelaire, 1821–1867.
Feuillet, 1821–1890.
Murger, 1822–1861.
De Goncourt, 1822–1896, 1830–1870.
Banville, 1823–1891.
Renan, 1823–1892.

Dumas *fils,* 1824–1895.
Taine, 1828–1893.
Fustel de Coulanges, 1830–1889.
Meilhac, 1831–1897, and Halévy, 1834–1908.
Sardou, 1831–1908.
Becque, 1837–1899.
Prudhomme, 1839–1908.
Hérédia, 1839–1907. Cuban.
Daudet, 1840–1897.
Zola, 1840–1902.
Coppée, 1842–1908.
Mallarmé, 1842–1898.
Tarde, 1843–1904.
Verlaine, 1844–1896.
*France, 1844–1924.
Brunetière, 1849–1907.
Loti, 1850–1923.
De Maupassant, 1850–1893.

Interval: Births 1850——
Bourget, 1852.
Bergson, 1859.
Prévost, 1862.
Maeterlinck, 1862. Belgian.
Rostand, 1868.
And others may easily be added.

§ 80. Provençal Literature

The influence of the Provençal troubadours on mediaeval European literature is notorious. Their lyrics were the first formalized, skilled poetry of the Occident. Poems in Provençal were written by Catalans and Italians; and were imitated by North French, Germans, Sicilians, Portuguese, and by Castilians writing Galician.

The period of this growth was brief: 1100 to 1280. It is sometimes stretched to 1350, but by courtesy. Guiraut Riquier, 1230/35–1294, "the last of the troubadours," was the last figure of importance, and lesser than a dozen or more predecessors. At the other end, the earliest troubadour whose work has been preserved, William IX of Poitiers, shows enough development of verse artifice to make it sure that he was not the first representative of the growth. What its origins and early developments were, is unknown. Arabic influence is now usually denied. But it is difficult not to think of some Arabic stimulation: the fixed forms, rhyme, the prevailing themes, the place for the poet's naming of himself in the last strophe—coupled with the contiguity of place and time—all suggest at least indirect or subsurface diffusion as underlying a native growth.

Unless the lost developmental period was of considerable length, Provençal literature was not notably earlier than North French. By 1100 the latter was also already definitely on its course. The chief time difference is in the close. The best period in the Midi ended about 1220; the movement proper was essentially over by 1280; French Mediaeval literature must be recognized as in its higher phase until about 1300.

This difference is probably associated with the fact that North French verse had a broad narrative base, and skilled form was achieved slowly, but Provençal literature was overwhelmingly lyrical and structurally complex and its theme mainly a special type of courtly love which was a manner rather than a passion; or if the latter, a strained neurotic one. There was Provençal narrative poetry, and prose; but their bulk is small, and they exerted little influence abroad.

All the *langue d'oc* territory shared in producing Provençal troubadours. Seeing that even Italy contributed them, it would be strange if it were otherwise. However, of the principal dialects: those of Provence, Languedoc, Gascony, Auvergne, and Limousin including part of Poitou, it was the last that furnished the first troubadour and the basis of literary Provencal. This is remarkable, in that it indicates the origin of the poetry to have occurred on the northwestern frontier of the language, in Loire drainage. It suggests a parallel and closely related source for Provençal and French literatures. Survivals of Roman culture in the old Provincia are rather minimized as a cause of the growth, by this recognition; and, it must be admitted, Arabic stimulation also becomes more difficult to understand.

Five phases can be recognized in Provençal poetry.

1. Before 1100. Formative and unknown.
2. 1100–1150. Early.
3. 1150–1220. The culmination.
4. 1220–1280. Late, largely by Italians.
5. 1280–1350+. Aftermath.

How far the Albigeois crusade, in the decade or two following 1209, destroyed troubadour literature, or how far this had already passed its zenith, I leave unanswered. Most of the greater poets began their floruits between 1150 and 1180.

PROVENÇAL TROUBADOUR POETRY

1. Formative phase, before 1100
No documents preserved.

2. Early phase, 1100–1150
  *William IX, Count of Poitiers, 1071–1127.
  Cercamon, fl. 1137–1152.

3. Culmination, 1150–1220
  Raimbaut d'Aurenga, Count of Orange, 1150–1173.
  *Marcabrun, fl. 1150–1195.
  Jaufre Rudel, contemporary.
**Bernard de Ventadour, fl. ca. 1150–1194.
  Beatrice Countess of Die.
  *Peire d'Auvergne, fl. 1158–1180. B. in Clermont-Ferrand.
  *Bertran de Born, ca. 1140 to 1202 or after. B. on border of
    Limousin and Périgord.
  *Arnaut de Mareuil, fl. ca. 1170–1200. B. Périgord.
  *Arnaut Daniel. B. Périgord.
  *Guiraut de Borneilh, ca. 1175–1220.
  *Peire Vidal, fl. 1175–1215.
  The Monk of Montaudon, fl. 1180–1200.
  *Folquet of Marseilles, fl. 1180 seq. B. Marseilles of a Genoese
    father; merchant; bishop of Toulouse 1205; d. 1231.
  Guillem de Cabestanh, fl. 1181–1196.
  Raimbaut de Vaqueiras, fl. 1180–1207. B. in Orange; to Mont-
    ferrat.
  Raimon de Miraval, of Carcassonne.
  *Peire Cardenal, fl. 1210–1230. Of Puy-Notre-Dame in Velay.
*4. Late phase, 1220–1280. Largely Italians composing in Provençal.
  Sordello, fl. 1225–1269. B. near Mantua.
  Lanfranc Cigala, of Genoa.

*Guiraut Riquier, ca. 1230–1294. B. Narbonne. "Last of the (Provençal) Troubadours."
Bonifacio Calvo, of Genoa, fl. ca. 1270.
Bartolomeo Zorzi, of Venice, fl. ca. 1270.

5. *Aftermath, more bourgeois, 1280–1350 or later*

§ 81. German Literature

Among European literatures, that of Germany has an aberrant course. Above all, it lacks any successful Renaissance-Baroque pulse,[8] either in time or in inclination of spirit. This absence cannot be attributed to the Reformation: because there are no effective Renaissance-like symptoms or stirrings previous to 1517. Rather must both the Reformation and the lack of a Renaissance be laid to a common underlying cause, or set of causes, which are difficult to describe specifically but are indicable by the concept that Germany from 1250 on, in trying to remain German, also remained Mediaeval. As the remainder of Europe gradually worked toward clarity, balance, organization, regularity, practical attitudes, the Germans clung increasingly to the disordered, bizarre, fantastic, irrelevant, unpractical. A certain originality cannot be denied them, but its products meant and mean as little to the rest of the world as they were satisfying to the deliberately provincial Germans. Dürer, with all his genius, illustrates the quirks, fumblings, and harshnesses of the period, which so fail to be Renaissance-like in quality; and in fact, as soon as he was gone, contact with the Italian Renaissance withered what there was of German painting.

At any rate, 1250 to 1750 is an arid half millennium of literature in Germany,[9] but a productive one, in either one or two pulses, among other major European nationalities.

A second peculiarity is that the genuine and successful Mediaeval burst is both remarkably brief and remarkably early in

---

[8] Except—as discussed below—for the definite classic or neoclassic counterpoise to the romantic element in the growth culminating in Goethe.

[9] Hans Sachs, intrinsically rather negligible, is made much of in German histories of their literature apparently because he is a satisfying nationalistic symbol of Germany at its peak of nonparticipation in European civilization; perhaps also because he seems to help fill an immense void.

Germany. Its best is confined to the generation 1190 to 1225. By the second quarter of the thirteenth century, "artificiality," that is, decadence, is manifest; in the third, important products are beginning to cease. This means that all the greater poets were almost exact contemporaries. Moreover, they included men who wrote on German themes in essentially German-evolved meters, as well as those who used French plots and forms; also, writers of epics and writers of lyrics. Whether one sees this as a coincidence or a significance depends ultimately on whether one's habits of thought prefer to construe historical happenings as a series of accidents or a series of pattern constellations. In any event, it is surprising how quickly the German culmination followed on the French. The best Provençal period was 1150–1220; the North French peak is marked by Chrétien de Troyes, who flourished 1160–1175. We have observed a similarly precocious florescence of French-derived Gothic sculpture in Germany.

The one post-Mediaeval period of great literature in Germany falls into the four-thirds century 1750–1880, with its culmination around 1800. This coincides very closely with the great German periods in music and philosophy, precedes science by a half century, but has no serious counterpart in sculpture or painting.

This modern German literature is doubly out of step with the European development.

As a romantic development, it is premature, because it developed that quality to a high degree by 1780, whereas England attained it successfully only after 1800 and France after 1830. Obviously, there is no reason why Germany should not precede. Only, the visible currents were into Germany, not out of it. The abortive effort of Macpherson's "Ossian" was more influential in Germany than in England. Goethe admired Byron, and Heine translated him; but the influence was one-way. Until Carlyle's subsequent propaganda, even Goethe seems to have been nonexistent for Englishmen, except for sporadic tributes like Shelley's. As for the French, with the exception of Swiss-descended De Staël, they also largely ignored the German growth, whether by choice or imperviousness. Napoleon indeed had *Werther* burned into his memory; but how much influence of *Faust* does Hugo admit?

In short, the Germans were hungry for whatever romanticism was lying about, assimilated it even though half-baked, and pushed their urge for it to a climax before anyone else. They were then followed, rather than imitated, by the rest of Europe. We have seen their same priority in romantic painting, meager as the results were. And presumably their French-derived poetry and sculpture around 1200 followed an analogous course: the national attitudes worked themselves out with similar quickness.

However, the 1750–1880 growth was not wholly romantic and Storm-and-Stress. There is a definitely classic strain, of which Goethe and many others were conscious, perhaps over-conscious. There can be cited his *Iphigenie,* hexameters, *Helena, Elegien, Xenien;* Schiller's classicistic language; Lessing's *Laokoon.* The aspiration was toward the Greek as such, of which the later eighteenth century first became aware as something distinct from Graeco-Roman civilization or the generic Antique. But, in addition, how much of the tendency was due to a Renaissance impulse, modified from the Italian one of 1500 by being three hundred years belated? Could a nation contiguous to Italy permanently escape the Renaissance as a genuine motivating factor? The French were a century and a half behind the Italians—1650 as against 1500—before they fully assimilated the Renaissance and pseudo-classicism to their own taste in literature. The English took two centuries. There would thus be nothing abnormal in the Germans' being three hundred years late. By that time, perspective on the classic had changed. Also, a new current toward the romantic and Mediaeval was setting even more strongly. The consequence was that the Renaissance influence on German literature, arriving post-Baroque and even post-Rococo by European standards, manifested very little of typical Italian Renaissance traits. The contention is that what really successful influence the Renaissance had in Germany it achieved belatedly in Goethe and his contemporaries rather than in the sixteenth or seventeenth centuries.

In brief, the great German cycle of literature was a full generation ahead of Europe in romanticism, from one to three centuries behind in classicism as first formulated by the Italian Renaissance.

As for chronological definition of the German culmination, there is an old textbook dating which makes it begin with Klopstock's *Messias* in 1748 and end with the death of Goethe in 1832. For the compass it encloses, this frame is rather good; but a publication and a burial are haphazard as the sort of termini which could be applied elsewhere. There will be more comparability if we adhere to our usual procedure of birth dates. Accepting Klopstock as the herald of the new era, we have this era beginning with men born from 1724 on. This takes in every author who definitely has turned away from the direction of the previous arid period; except a handful of semi-precursors who, if not intrepid pioneers, were at least anti-Gottsched and anti-Boileau: Gellert 1715, E. von Kleist 1715, Gleim 1719. There are even earlier antecessors, downright contemporaries of the strawman Gottsched whom they opposed: Bodmer 1798, Breitinger 1701, Haller 1708; but they were Swiss.

The culmination can be set at almost exactly 1800, or at any rate within the decade enclosing it. These were the last and best ten years of Schiller; and while they represent the age from 46 to 56 for Goethe, his genius, though not late in unfolding, was unusually long for a poet in maturing and sustaining itself. Also, the number as well as quality of men whose main work fell respectively before and after 1800 is about equal.

The conventional 1832 also comes reasonably near the point at which a change is first evident. I would date this with Heine's *Harzreise* and *Buch der Lieder*, 1826–1827. We can therefore select his birth in 1797 as the turning point in birth dates.

Heine's repute is in a peculiar status. Outside of Germany his poetry is certainly felt as poetry far more immediately and poignantly than that of any other German save Goethe; much more so than that of Schiller, for instance, whom Germans have agreed upon as their second, and, if they are bourgeois enough, sometimes prefer to Goethe. Yet Schiller, except for his dramas as acted on the stage, leaves nearly every non-German cold, if we disregard those who are partisan to his propaganda for human liberty rather than to his poetry. In his native country, on the other hand, Heine has always been viewed with ambivalence. "One of the greatest of German poets, but unfortunately . . ." runs the formula. The disparity of judgment is not due to translatability, for in that Heine, as a pure lyricist, would suffer most, whereas his most undiluted appreciation has come from aliens. Nor is the case like that of Byron, whom Continental textbooks are wont to rate as third, or even second, to Shakespeare. Byron, after all, dazzled his fellow countrymen as thoroughly as he dazzled Europe, and the chief difference is that his fame wilted faster at home than abroad. Heine, however, stands at least as high today as in his own time, in the world at large, and was distrusted and resented and whittled at in Germany from the beginning. For the same reason anti-Semitism can be discounted as the cause: in Germany, anti-Semitism is far younger than the resistance to Heine.

What almost certainly it is that sticks in the German crop is that Heine is unnationalistic. Not merely politically, which many Germans also were; but he is, two-thirds of the time, at war with Germanness, with those impulses that made for Germany's rejecting the Renaissance and Revolution. What Germans allege is his negativism: his *Zerrissenheit,* which enrages and discourages them as irony of disillusionment. This quality he undoubtedly possesses. And because of it, he can, although a truly great poet, be rightly taken as marking the inception of dissolution of the German pattern. With all his romanticism and all his idealism for freedom, he is essentially destructive; just as is his pity for himself.

What is interesting is that a somewhat later *Zerrissenheit,* that of Nietzsche, Sudermann, and Hauptmann and nearly all their contemporaries, seems on the whole less objectionable to Germans. But it is a quality of breakdown which at least accepts Germanicness as it is. German instinct has therefore been sound in its consistent hostility to Heine, though formulated in untrue rationalization. Up to about 1830, universal pattern and German pattern did not conflict, in fact were blended in unusual harmony in Goethe and many of his lesser contemporaries. But, after that date, Germanicness gradually came to be valued more highly than universality, in Germany. And Heine was as sound in his resistance to this as the Germans were sound in their resistance to him. All that his Judaism probably had to do with the matter was that as a Jew he was more sensitive to the first subtle currents—politically as yet wholly blocked—toward nationalistic self-centering.

That he felt ahead of his time is shown by the fact that for a long generation after him there was no aggressive nationalism in German literature. The later men were obviously of lesser stature; their preoccupation was with smaller horizons; but it was not until men born after 1840–1850 came to maturity that there was a real drive to dissolve the established patterns. As some of the histories put it, German literature since 1885–1890 has been in a state of chaos, revolt, and eccentricity. In our terminology, the old great patterns were by then exhausted, and the process of disintegrating them had got fully under way.

One other great figure is involved in an ambiguity more or less analogous to that of Heine, though quite different in outcome: Richard Wagner, born sixteen years later, in 1813. With all his being first of all a musician; with all his ultramannerisms in writing, and receiving only mentions of courtesy in most histories of literature, he probably remains the German poet of greatest stature subsequent to Heine. After all, he did aim at universals and ultimates; and in spite of turgidity and strain, and blindness to the existence of serenity, he came nearer to attaining universality than anyone else. And yet, nationalism is equally powerful in him. The rude Germanic past is his ideal. Five centuries of growing cultivation of European civilization have flowed past him without leaving a mark. And he has rightly become one of the most powerful symbols of modern German nationalism. But the contradictory impulses are as deep in him as in Heine. Both men, the Jew and the gentile, were torn by their time and place.

As for organization of the great period, then, half a dozen phases can be distinguished.

(Born 1698–1723: Precursors.)

Born 1724–1745: Early phase: Klopstock, Lessing, Wieland, Herder.

Born 1745–1770: Great phase: Goethe, Schiller; and the Sturm-und-Dränger. The difference seems due to this: the great figures rode out the storm, the others never got over it.

Born 1770–1795. The "romanticists." Actually it is questionable whether this group is more romantic than the last, except in being less neoclassic; but their achievement is of smaller quality. Uhland is probably the largest figure.

Born 1795–1820: Heine and Wagner both evidence strain; the serener figures are lesser.

Born 1820–1840: Chiefly novelists and narrative poets, both of secondary rating.

(Born after 1840: Dissolutionists.)

On the broadest view, both the prologue and epilogue must be counted as part of the cycle, which would thus run from 1725 to the present, or more than two centuries. If we limit the growth to 1748–1880, it is in the sense that all the greater productions emanate from the four generations comprised in that span. On either view, it is an ample growth, by European standards, and thereby presumably indicative of high quality. Whether we accept the more compact or the more extensive period, the culmination falls before the middle: at about a third or two-fifths of the total course.

Kant was born in the same year as Klopstock; Fichte, Schleiermacher, Hegel, Schelling, all between 1762 and 1775, or in the fifteen years following Schiller.

The Franco-Prussian War of 1870 should probably be absolved from being a cause of the literary disintegration after 1880. The literature was evidently through, war or no war. The connection is probably one of common functional effect. The great literature grew up under political disorganization and nationalistic impotence. The causes, however they be defined, which finally put an end to that condition, became effective while the literature, which had taken shape under the condition, was declining.

German Literature
CAROLINGIAN, IN OLD HIGH GERMAN, UNTIL 1050

Wessobrunner Gebet, alliterative fragment, end of 8th cent.

Hildebrandslied, alliterative fragment, ca. 800.

Heliand, Biblical, in Old Saxon (Low German) alliterative verse, ca. 830.

Muspilli, fragment, ca. 850.

Evangelienbuch, by Alsatian Otfried, first German rhymed verse, ca. 863 or later.

Ludwigslied, earliest "ballad," 881.

From 900 to 1050 almost all preserved productions are in Latin.

MEDIAEVAL, IN MIDDLE HIGH GERMAN, 1050–1300
(FLORESCENCE: 1190–1230)

Early, 1060–1170, largely religious

Memento Mori, ca. 1060, Alemannian.

Das hohe Lied, ca. 1060, Bavaria.

Ezzolied, 1063, Bamberg.

Annolied, ca. 1080, near Cologne.

Vom Glauben, soon after 1100, Thuringia.

Kaiserchronik, 1130–1150, Regensburg.

Von des Todes Gehugede, and *Priesterleben,* ca. 1160, by Heinrich von Melk, Austria.

Lieder von der Jungfrau, ca. 1170, by Wernher, probably Bavarian.

Popular epic, on national themes, by anonymous Spielleute, 1160–1280

König Rother, Bavarian, ca. 1160.

Herzog Ernst, ca. 1180.

**Der Nibelunge Not,* composed in Austria prob. ca. 1190–1200.

Gudrun, Austrian version of 1210–1215, based on lost North German one.

Heldenbuch, short popular epics, mainly grouped around Dietrich von Bern; ca. 1220–1280.

Court epic, on themes of French origin, 1130–1300

Lamprecht, of Rhineland, *Alexanderlied,* ca. 1130.

Konrad of Regensburg, *Rolandslied,* ca. 1135.

Heinrich von Veldeke, of Maestricht, Netherlands, usually considered the real founder of the court epic with his *Eneit,* 1175–1186.

Eilhart von Oberge, *Tristant,* ca. 1180.

Heinrich der Glichezare, Alsatian, ca. 1180 wrote the first German adaptation of the *Roman de Renart,* based in turn on the Latin poem *Isengrimus,* composed in Ghent ca. 1150.

Herbort von Fritslar, Hessian, *Lied von Troja,* ca. 1195.

*Hartmann von Aue, from the Rhine side of the Black Forest, ca. 1170–1220 or earlier. *Erec* ca. 1191, *Gregorius, Arme Heinrich, Iwein* ca. 1201/06, partly adapted from Chrétien de Troyes.

Ulrich von Zatzikoven, Swiss, *Lanzelet,* ca. 1195. Hartmann influence.

*Wolfram von Eschenbach, from near Ansbach (then Franconian), ca. 1170–1220 (?): *Parzival,* 1205–1210; *Titurel; Willehalm,* from the *Bataille d'Aliscans,* 1210–1215.

Wirnt von Gravenberg, Bavarian, *Wigalois,* ca. 1205. Hartmann influence.

*Gottfried von Strassburg, *Tristan,* ca. 1210–1215.

Heinrich von Türlin, Carinthian, *Die Krone,* ca. 1220. Hartmann influence.

Konrad Fleck, *Flore und Blancheflur,* ca. 1220. Gottfried influence.

Rudolf von Ems, Swiss, fl. ca. 1225–1235, d. 1254. Gottfried influence.

Ulrich von Türheim, continuation of *Tristan,* ca. 1240. Gottfried influence.

Reinbot von Duren, Bavarian, *Heilige Georg,* ca. 1240. Wolfram influence.

Konrad von Würzburg, fl. ca. 1260–1280, d. 1287. Gottfried influence.

Der Pleier, of Salzburg, ca. 1265–1275. Hartmann influence.

Albrecht von Scharfenberg (?), Bavarian, *Der jüngere Titurel,* ca. 1270. Wolfram influence.

Lohengrin, 1276–1290, by a Bavarian. Wolfram influence.

Heinrich von Freiberg, continuation of *Tristan,* ca. 1300.

Lyric, Minnesang, 1160–1300

Herr von Kürenberg, Austrian; Dietmar von Aist, Austrian; Burggraf von Regensburg; Meinloh von Sevelingen; 1160–1180.

Heinrich von Veldeke, as above, fl. ca. 1180.

Friedrich von Hausen, from the Rhine, d. 1180.

Heinrich von Morungen, Thuringian, ca. 1190.

Reinmar von Hagenau, at Vienna, fl. ca. 1190, d. ca. 1210.

*Walther von der Vogelweide, prob. Tyrolean, ca. 1170–1228/30, left Vienna 1198.

Neidhart von Reuental, ca. 1180–1250. "Niedere Minne," "höfische Dorfpoesie."

Ulrich von Singenberg of St. Gallen; Leuthold von Säben; Burkhart von Hohenfels; Ulrich von Winterstetten; Gottfried von Neifen, ca. 1234–1255; (Berthold) Steinmar (von Klingenau); Johannes Hadlaub of Zürich, ca. 1300.

Various: Didactic, gnomic, humorous, satiric, 1200–1300

Herr von Windesbach, Bavarian: *Der Winsbeke,* ca. 1205.

Thomasin von Zirclaere, Italian by birth: *Der welsche Gast,* 1215.

Stricker, from Rhine, lived also in Austria, ca. 1220: *Pfaffe Amis.*

"Freidank": *Bescheidenheit,* ca. 1217–1230.

Reinmar von Zweter, ca. 1200–1260, from the Rhine, in Austria, Spruchdichter.

Wernher der Gartenaere, before 1250: *Meier Helmbrecht,* peasant romance.

Ulrich von Lichtenstein, Styrian: *Frauendienst,* 1255.

Der Marner, Swabian, d. ca. 1270.

Hugo von Trimberg, near Bamberg, end of 13th cent.: *Der Renner.*

LOW-LEVEL PERIOD, (1250) 1300–1750

(Language New High German from about 1350)

Bourgeois Meistersänger from 1300, in Nuremberg, Augsburg, Ulm, etc. Heinrich von Meissen, ca. 1250–1318; Michael Beheim, 1416–ca. 1480; Hans Sachs, 1496–1576.

Earlier Mystics: Eckhart, ca. 1260–1327/9; Suso (Seuse), of Constance, 1295–1366/8 (1300–1365); Tauler, Alsatian, ca. 1300–1361.

Volkslied, 1350–1550.

Prose Volksbücher, generally anonymous: *Reinke de Vos,* Low German, 1498; *Tyl Eulenspiegel,* 1515; *Schildbürger; Haimonskinder; Schöne Melusine; Doktor Faust,* 1587.

Reformation: Luther, 1483–1546.

Satire: Brant, 1457–1521, *Narrenschiff,* 1494; Murner, 1475–1537, *Narrenbeschwörung, Schelmenzunft;* Fischart, ca. 1550–1590, *Geschichtsklitterung,* 1575.

Humanism: Reuchlin, 1455–1522; Hutten, 1488–1523; Melanchthon, 1497–1560.

Later Mystics: Böhme, 1575–1624; Arndt, d. 1621; Scheffler (Angelus Silesius), 1624–1677.

First and Second Silesian Schools: Lauremberg, b. 1590; Opitz, 1597; Logau, 1604; Dach, 1605; Fleming, 1609; Gryphius, 1616; Hoffmannswaldau, 1617; Lohenstein, 1635.

Grimmelshausen, b. ca. 1624, *Simplicissimus,* 1669.

Gottsched, b. 1700.

Swiss "precursors" of Great period: Bodmer, b. 1698; Breitinger, 1701; Haller, 1708.

Germans, also anti-Gottsched: Gellert, b. 1715; E. von Kleist, 1719; Gleim, 1719.

GREAT PERIOD, OR SECOND FLORESCENCE, 1750–1880

From Klopstock: Births 1724–1796

*Klopstock, b. 1724

*Lessing, 1729.

*Wieland, 1733.

Gessner, 1730. Swiss.

Hamann, 1730.

Musaeus, 1735.

Jung-Stilling, 1740.

Claudius, 1740.

Hipfel, 1741.

Lavater, 1741. Swiss.

Richter, J. P., 1743.

Jacobi, 1743.

*Herder, 1744.

Hölty, 1748.

Bürger, 1748.

**Goethe, 1749.

Lenz, 1750.

Müller, 1750.

Voss, 1751.

Klinger, 1752.

Leisewitz, 1752.

Knigge, 1752.

**Schiller, 1759.

Iffland, 1759.

Hebel, 1760.

Kotzebue, 1761.

Richter, 1763.

Schlegel, A. W. von, 1767.

Werner, 1768.

Arndt, 1769.

Hölderlin, 1770.

Zschokke, 1771.

Schlegel, F., 1772.

Novalis, 1772.

Tieck, 1773.

Hoffman, 1776.

Kleist, H. von, 1777.

Fouqué, 1777.

Brentano, 1778.

Arnim, 1781.

Chamisso, 1781. (Champagne.)

Schenckendorf, 1783.

Grimm, J., 1785.

Grimm, W., 1786.

Börne, 1786.

Kerner, 1786.

*Uhland, 1787.

Eichendorff, 1788.

Rückert, 1788.

Körner, 1791.

Grillparzer, 1791.

Müller, 1794.

Platen, 1796.

Immermann, 1796.

From Heine: Births 1797–1840

**Heine, 1797.

Droste-Hülshoff, 1797.

Grabbe, 1801.

Hauff, 1802.

Bauernfeld, 1802.

Lenau, 1802. (Hungary.)

From Heine: Births 1797–1840—(Continued)

Mörike, 1804.
Laube, 1806.
Grün, 1806.
Freiligrath, 1810.
Reuter, 1810. In Low German.
Gutzkow, 1811.
Auerbach, 1812.
Hebbel, 1813.
*Wagner, 1813.
Geibel, 1815.
Freytag, 1816.
Storm, 1817/18.

Jordan, 1819.
Fontane, 1819.
Bodenstedt, 1819.
Keller, 1819. Swiss.
Scheffel, 1826.
Spielhagen, 1829.
Heyse, 1830.
Busch, 1832.
Wolff, 1834.
Lindau, 1839.
Anzengruber, 1839.
Baumbach, 1840.

From Nietzsche: Births after 1840

Nietzsche, 1844.
Liliencron, 1844.
Wildenbruch, 1845.
Sudermann, 1857.
Fulda, 1862.

Schnitzler, 1862.
Hauptmann, 1862.
Frenssen, 1863.
Mann, 1875.

§ 82. Italian Literature

The course of literature in Italy is rather atypical, both as compared with other countries and with painting and sculpture in the peninsula.

First, the beginnings are later than in Spain, France, or Germany. This seems associated with the lack of national narratives put into rude but vigorous verse by unknown poets. The first poetry in Italy is an imitation of South French. Up to within a generation of 1300, all of it is formal and lifeless. On the one hand, native literary impulses were apparently still too weak to achieve patterns of their own. Hence the French patterns were copied. Yet, on the other hand, one has a feeling that the French patterns have been resisted too, as something alien in spirit.

Next, when this deadlock was broken, toward 1300, Italian poetical energy reached its full strength almost instantly. Dante remains the greatest poet of his country, but he has no predecessors of consequence. For the six centuries since, the course of Italian literature is, on the average, a descent. This is an anomaly, especially as the Italian climaxes in painting, sculpture, music, and science were not reached until two to three hundred years later.

Broadly, the great period of Italian literature extends from Dante to Tasso, from just before 1300 to just before 1600. This of course is the era of the Renaissance in a larger sense; but literature does not follow the typical Renaissance configuration, because it is greatest in 1300 instead of in 1500. Also, in the other activities the growth course is continuous, but Italian Renaissance literature breaks into three well-marked pulses.

The first of these contains the Florentines Dante, Petrarch, Boccaccio, born in 1265, 1304, 1313. The last of them died in 1375. This is a well-defined constellation.

Then follows an interval of more than a century without the birth of even a second-magnitude figure: from 1313 to 1432! This astonishing gap is certainly well glossed over in most histories of literature.

When births resume, they cluster thickly for 50 years, in northern Italy generally: Pulci 1432, Boiardo 1434, Sannazaro 1458, Macchiavelli 1469, Bembo 1470, Ariosto 1474, Michelangelo 1475, Trissino 1478, Castiglione 1478, Guicciardini 1483.

Another period of sixty nearly empty years, and we come to Tasso, born 1544. He stands isolated in his day, except for Guarini, born six years earlier.

By the usual ranking, the great four of Italian literature are Dante, Petrarch, Boccaccio, Tasso. Possibly Ariosto might be added as a fifth. But what does this mean? That the great names come at the beginning and the end of a period. Such a configuration would be unparalleled. Precedent is all in favor of not accepting such a period, but of breaking it up into separate growths, as the dates have already suggested.

What we really have seems to be this:

1. High to Later Mediaeval growth, 1275–1375.
2. True or High Renaissance growth, 1450–1540.

Tasso is not enough to constitute a growth: he stands too much alone. He may be set down as a belated and uneasy straggler of the Renaissance growth; perhaps a greater poet than any one individual in this, but lighter than the group. Also, he has had little influence compared with them, abroad or at home. He is an aftermath much like Milton, but without Milton's ruggedness.[10]

The three growths or pulses, or at least the first two, differ in substance as clearly as they are separate in chronology. Dante is still High Mediaeval in his essential ideology—classically so. Voltaire's age was correct in characterizing him as Gothic. He is fervidly Catholic. His work is a vision, not an epic; a static organization of the world, not a flow of narrative. Petrarch, it is true, was the first humanist; but his poetry is again Mediaevally spiritual. Boccaccio's verse is also of Mediaeval cast; his tales, Mediaevally broad in humor.

The second pulse is true or High Renaissance. Where Mediaeval themes are utilized, they are treated playfully, even ironically. A pseudo-Antique is reëvoked: the pastoral or idyl flourishes. A drama is created, though it never quite comes to full life; and epics are attempted. Breeding is given a higher value than spiritual intensities; wit is rated perhaps higher than humor.

Tasso differs from this second group in his elegiac quality, his sensitivity and strain, his lack of playfulness.

The fourteenth-century Florentines were still genuinely religious. The High Renaissance writers had liberated themselves from piety, though they were careful not to break with the forms of Catholicism: the opposite of contemporary northern Europe, where Protestantism stood for breach of the forms but persistence or renewal of piety. Tasso, however, was devout once more, but as a child of the Counterreformation.

From 1575/80 to 1725/30 is another long gap of low-level productivity. The period is one of sag in quality of almost all activities of culture in Italy.

The eighteenth–nineteenth-century revival is not defined

---

[10] If a subjective reaction may be injected, I would add that he is probably an overrated poet, whose aim to achieve the great Italian poem came to be traditionally accepted as achieved. Posterity has been enormously interested in his personality; but, has it not found *Jerusalem Liberated* dull?

sharply; perhaps because it did not reach very high peaks. At any rate, it evoked almost no repercussions outside of Italy, in contrast with the Florentine and High Renaissance growths. On the other hand, there were eighteenth-century Italian efforts to understand, imitate, or translate French, English, and German literature.

Metastasio, born 1698, and Goldoni, 1707, represent a first, light-dramatic attempt.

Alfieri, 1749, brings up heavier artillery, but stands nearly alone in time.

A generation later begins a series of births that do cluster: beginning with Foscolo, 1778, and culminating with Leopardi, 1798, and ending perhaps with Carducci, 1835. There is a gap before Carducci, however, and he might be reckoned the earliest member of a group which continues to D'Annunzio, 1863.

ITALIAN LITERATURE

Phase of French dominance and native stirrings: 1200–1275

Italian poets composing in Provençal, ca. 1200–1250/60: Malaspina, Lanfranco Cigala, Calvo, Sordello, Zorzi.

North French gestes and fabliaux recited in Italy first in French, then in Italianized French, then in Italian with French admixture.

Sicilian school at Palermo, under Frederick II, 1208–1250, Enzo, Pier della Vigna, Lentino: Provençal imitations in Sicilian.

St. Francis of Assisi, 1182–1226: *Cantico del Sole* (but perhaps only the Latin original is his). Also in Umbrian and religious, Jacopone de Todi, and anonymous *Laudes*.

Tuscan, 1250 seq.: Guittone del Viva of Arezzo, 1220/30–1294; Brunetto Latini of Florence, ca. 1220–ca. 1294; encyclopaedic, French-imitated *Tesoretto*.

Guinicelli, of Bologna, ca. 1230–1276: best pre-Dantean poetry.

Great period, High to Late Mediaeval, Florentine, 1275–1375

Guido Cavalcanti, of Florence.

**Dante, 1265–1321, of Florence, 1295, *1300 seq.

Minor figures: Cino da Pistoja, d. 1336; Franceschino degli Albizzi, d. 1348; Sennuccio de Bene, d. 1349; Matteo Frescobaldi.

**Petrarch, 1304–1374, Florentine, born at Arezzo.

**Boccaccio, 1313–1375, of Florence. *Ca. 1350.

Fioretti di San Francesco, ca. 1350.

Sacchetti, 1330–1400?, of Florence: Novelle.
St. Catherine of Siena, 1347–1380.

Interval, 1375–1450
Salutati, 1331–1406, humanist.
Giustiniani, 1388–1446, Venice, satiric verse.

High Renaissance period, 1450–1540
  *Pulci, 1432–1484. Florentine.
  *Boiardo, 1434–1494. B. Scandiano.
  Lorenzo the Magnificent, 1449–1492.
  Poliziano, 1454–1494.
  *Sannazaro, 1458–1530. B. Naples. *Arcadia,* 1502, 1504.
  Macchiavelli, 1469–1527. Florentine.
  Bembo, 1470–1547, at Venice.
**Ariosto, 1474–1533. Born at Reggio Emilia. *1516.
  Michelangelo, 1475–1564. Florentine.
  Trissino, 1478–1550. *Sofonisba,* 1515.
  Castiglione, 1478–1529.
  Bandello, 1480?–1565.
  Guicciardini, 1483–1540. Florentine. History.

Aftermath, mainly of epics, 1540–1580
  Bernardo Tasso, Venetian, 1493–1569; Alamanni, 1495–1556;
    Cinthio, 1504–1573.
  Guarini, 1538–1612, b. Ferrara. *Pastor Fido,* 1580–1590.
**Torquato Tasso, 1544–1595. B. Sorrento, son of Bernardo.
    Aminta 1573, *Gerusalemme Liberata* 1575.

Interval, 1580–1725
  Chiabrera, 1552–1638.
  Tassoni, 1565–1635, of Modena.
  Marini, 1569–1625, of Naples.
  Testi, 1593–1646.
  Maffei, 1675–1759. *Merope,* 1713.
  Martelli, 1655–1721. Imitation of French tragedy in couplets.
  Zeno, 1668–1750, of Venice.

Modern growth, 1725–ca. 1925, in four pulses:

I

Metastasio, 1698–1782, of Rome.
Goldoni, 1707–1793, of Venice.

II

Parini, 1729–1799.
  *Alfieri, 1749–1803. Of Asti. *1775–1786.
  Monti, 1754–1728.

III

Foscolo, 1778–1827. Born on Zante, Greek Venetian.
Niccolini, 1782–1861.
Rosetti, 1783–1854, b. Vasto, Abruzzi.
*Manzoni, 1785–1873, of Milan.
D'Azeglio, 1798–1866, of Milan.
*Leopardi, 1798–1837, b. Recanati, Papal State.
Mazzini, 1805–1872, b. Genoa.
Giusti, 1809–1850. Tuscan.

IV

*Carducci, 1835–1907, b. near Pisa.
Fogazzaro, 1842–1911, b. Vicenza.
Pascoli, 1855–1912, b. San Mauro, Romagna.
D'Annunzio, 1863–1938, b. Pescara.

§ 83. Spanish Literature

The configuration of Spanish literature is unusually marked and simple. There is one great period, from about 1500 to 1660 or 1670, with its climax after rather than before the turn of the century. A much smaller, preliminary growth came in and around the thirteenth century; a third, in the nineteenth, when all Europe was attempting a revival. The fifteenth and eighteenth centuries, with considerable parts of the preceding ones, produced almost nothing of note.

Thus the general picture is that of five periods, each about a century and a half in length. The middle one is occupied by a great peak. Beyond the flanking valleys rise two hills. Both these lesser growths, the mediaeval and the nineteenth-century one, are the Spanish expressions of general European developments. But the major growth does not agree with any other European one, either in substance or in time. It comes nearest to coinciding in culmination with the English, though it begins much earlier. It is also earlier than the French. It is definitely later than the Italian, which, roughly, ended about as the Spanish movement came into full swing.

The great period in Spanish literature is also that of greatness in painting and sculpture, and in conquest and political dominance, except that in the latter the movement got under way before 1500 and culminated before 1600—say a generation earlier than the literature. The mediaeval literature also coincides with a time of national vigor: the first half of the thirteenth century saw Mohammedan power in the peninsula broken and almost expelled. On the contrary, the nineteenth century was politically and nationally a time of continued ineffectualness and often of humiliation for Spain.

In summary:

Mediaeval development: 1150–1350.
Interval: 1350–1500.
Great period: 1500–1670.
Interval: 1670–1830.
Modern development: since 1830.

Mediaeval period.—Early Spanish writing shows some French influence, like every High Mediaeval literature, but is thoroughly national in most of its subjects and its feeling. There are several strains: the popular epic in Castilian; more formal verse, partly in Galician; and prose, largely historical, again in Castilian.

The most famous production is the *Poema del Cid,* of about 1150 or somewhat after. This is probably the best example of a class of narrative poems springing from the people, which continued to be composed until around 1250, but are mostly lost. They were probably stimulated by the *chansons de geste.* The number of syllables is not fixed, the line is long with a caesura, the rhythm trochaic, groups of lines roughly rhymed or assonanted.

The learned poetry is largely religious, partly of love. There are Gonzalo de Berceo, Fernán Gonzáles (with a stanza of four alexandrines), King Alfonso X, and, after 1300, Juan Ruiz.

In prose, Alfonso X, el Sabio, 1220–1284, is reckoned the creator of literary Castilian and the best mediaeval Spanish stylist, in his national and general histories. He is also famous as the framer of the *Siete partidas* code, the promoter of the astronomical tables named after him, and the instigator of translations of the Koran, Talmud, and other non-Christian works. His nephew Juan Manuel wrote prose tales after 1300.

Late Mediaeval recession.—In the main the period between 1330/1350 and 1490/1500 is one of Italian, classical, and Provençal inspiration and forms; translations, imitations, and allegories loom large. Ayala, Pérez de Guzmán, Villena, Santillana, Mena are the principal names. Ayala could perhaps still be reckoned with the preceding period.

The most important work of the time is probably the *Amadís de Gaula,* with origin still uncertain between Portugal and Spain, and with date not fixed except in the vicinity of 1350 or later. It enjoyed much vogue in the latter fourteenth century, and a revival in the early sixteenth.

About 1375–1400, Castilian supplanted Galician as the dialect of literary poetry. The priority of Galician has a parallel in the earlier florescence of Portuguese than of Castilian Spanish literature in their great periods. Portugal is a historic offshoot of Galicia, and their speech was similar, as compared with standard Spanish or Castilian. One important strand of the peninsular literature was therefore west Iberian. This is of interest because of the geographic separation of Galicia and Portugal from southern France, where European poetical forms and themes of modern type first evolved. Catalan, on the contrary, is a half-Provençal language and is spoken in a territory contiguous to southern France, yet was less important in literary history.

Great period.—The beginning is somewhat indefinite, and 1500 an arbitrary date. The later fifteenth century was particularly empty, so there is nothing to prevent our setting back the starting point to 1490, to include Encina's *eglogas* or pastoral mysteries, the first of which was produced in 1492. They are counted as marking the beginning of the Spanish drama, though they are still a long way from real or secular plays. Everything else early comes after 1500: the dialogue-novel *Celestina* about 1501; Torres Naharro's Italian-influenced plays of intrigue, 1517. The first vein to come to maturity was lyric poetry, when Boscán in 1526 introduced the Italian hendecasyllabic line. The births in lyric achievement run from 1490. With Ledesma, born 1552, and Góngora, 1561, the *con-*

ceptismo and *cultismo* manners were introduced, and lyric poetry had transcended its peak. It is the only Spanish literary genre that was heavily influenced by Italy.

Narrative was written in verse and prose, but the latter has been more famous in the world at large. The series is impressive: Montalvo, revision and continuation of *Amadís*, 1508; the anonymous *Lazarillo de Tormes,* the first picaresque novel, 1554; Montemayor, *Diana,* 1558; Alemán, *Guzmán de Alfarache,* 1599–1605; Rojas Villandrando, *Viage entretenido,* 1603; Cervantes, *Don Quijote,* 1605–1615; Espinel, *Obregón,* 1618; Quevedo, *Don Pablos,* 1626. *Don Quijote* is much the best-known and esteemed, in the world at large, of any work of Spanish literature; and its date serves well for the apex of the period.

The drama culminated later. Lope de Vega was born in 1562, Calderón in 1600; the next greatest figures, like Tirso de Molina and Alarcón, fall between them. Only Moreto is later: he was born in 1618. Calderón lived till 1681, but wrote no secular plays after his ordination in 1651. The only greater dramatists to live beyond that date were Rojas Zorrilla, till 1661, and Moreto till 1669. The high period is thus the half century from 1600 to 1650; its mid-point is only one to two decades after *Don Quijote.*

The first quarter of the seventeenth century thus holds the climax of the era as a whole.

The decline was as startingly rapid in other phases as in the drama. We have noted the same phenomenon in painting. Calderón and Velásquez were exact contemporaries; and both left not even lesser successors. By 1660–1670 the great period was suddenly exhausted.

Interval.—How complete this exhaustion was, is shown by the fact that not a single really notable figure appeared for a hundred and fifty years. The Jesuit satirist Isla, flourished 1758, and the poet Meléndez Valdés, 1785, come the nearest to renown. Nor was it foreign influence that swamped Spanish writing: it was not till 1770 that a native play on strict French lines was performed. Rather did Spain stir feebly in the direction of international eighteenth-century enlightenment because at last she felt her own fire darkened.

Modern development.—The rise of a new drama, and its stimulation-dependence on France, have already been described. Campoamor, Arçe, Bécquer in poetry, Fernán Caballero, Trueba, Valera, Alarcón, Pereda, Pérez Galdós in the novel, are the principal precontemporaneous figures.

It is difficult to evaluate modern Spanish literature. The peninsula seems to remain a small world apart, occasionally discovered by seekers of the picturesque and intense; but they describe or use it as background, rather than let themselves be influenced by it. Little Spanish literature has been translated, and less has made a real impression elsewhere. The exceptions of temporary success abroad, like Blasco Ibáñez, are perhaps least representative. Yet, in very recent time, it would be difficult to name a national group of novelists superior to those of Spain.

SPANISH LITERATURE

MEDIAEVAL FLORESCENCE, 1150–1350

Poema del Cid, ca. 1150, or 1150–1200; ms. of 1307.
El Rodrigo, Crónica rimada del Cid, ca. 1250.
Other epic poetry, 1150–1250, mostly lost.
Gonzalo de Berceo, 1220–1246, religious tales in verse.
Poema del Conde Fernán Gonzáles, ca. 1240. In learned stanza of 4 alexandrines.
*Alfonso X, el Sabio, 1220–1284, *Estoria (Crónica) de España.* Stimulated or edited *Grande y general historia; Siete partidas;* translations of Koran, Talmud, Kabbala, *Secreta Secretorum;* creator of literary Castilian prose and its best mediaeval exponent. *Cantigas* in Galician.
Don Juan Manuel, 1282–1348, his nephew. 1328, prose tales: *Conde Lucanor.*
Juan Ruiz of Hita, 1330 seq., *Libro de buen amor,* in Castilian verse.

INTERVAL, 1350–1500

Ayala, 1332–1407. Chronicle *Rimado de Palacio.*
Amadís de Gaula, ca. 1350. Original doubtful between Spanish and Portuguese.
Villena, 1384–1434. Translator of Vergil and Dante.
Santillana, 1398–1458. Allegory, songs.

Juan de Mena, 1411–1456. More allegory and Provençal and Italian verse forms. *El labirinto*, 1444.

(Juan del Encina, 1492, first pastoral mystery.)

GREAT PERIOD, 1500 (1520)–1670

Lyric poetry

Castillejo, 1490/91–1556, b. Ciudad Rodrigo.

Boscán, ca. 1493–1542, of Barcelona. 1526, introduced Italian hendecasyllabics.

Garcilaso de la Vega, 1503–1536. Pastoral eclogues.

Mendoza, 1503–1575.

Luis de León, 1527–1591, b. La Mancha. Religious verse.

Herrera, d. 1597. School in Seville.

Ledesma, 1552–1623. *Conceptos espirituales*, 1600. (Conceptismo.)

Góngora, 1561–1627, b. Córdoba. (Cultismo.)

Argensola, Lupercio, 1559–1613; Bartolomé, 1562–1632. Aragón.

Quevedo, 1580–1645. b. Madrid. Satirist; also prose.

Narrative poetry

Ercilla y Zúñiga, 1533–1594, b. Madrid. *Araucana*, 1569–1590.

There were about 200 other epics or narrations, many dealing with recent or contemporary historical events. In Portugal, Camoëns, ca. 1521–1579, brought the type to its most illustrious development.

Vague de Salas. *Amantes de Teruel.*

Drama

(This has already been given.)

Prose novel or romance

La Celestina, 1499/1502, book drama or dialogue novel.

*Montalvo, revision and continuation of *Amadís de Gaula*, 1508–1510.

Lazarillo de Tormes, first picaresque novel, ca. 1525?, 1554.

*Montemayor, d. 1561. Portuguese. *Diana*, 1558/9.

Alemán, *Guzmán de Alfarache*, 1599–1605.

Rojas Villandrando, *Viage entretenido;* 1603.

**Cervantes, 1547–1614, Alcalá. *Don Quijote*, 1605–1615. Also drama, poetry, novelas.

Espinel. *Obregón*, 1618.

Guevara, 1579–1644. *Diablo cojuelo*, 1641.

History and other prose

Hurtado de Mendoza, 1505–1575, b. Granada. *Guerra de Granada,* wr. 1572, publ. 1627.

Santa Teresa, 1515–1582, of Avila.

Mariana, 1536–1623. *Estoria de España,* 1601.
Garcilaso Inca de la Vega, *Royal Commentaries,* 1609–1617.
Navarrete. *Conservación de Monarquías,* 1621.
Gracián, 1601–1658, of Aragón. Criticism.

Humanism, Scholasticism, philosophy, science
Nebrija, 1444–1532.
Nuñez de Guzmán, 1473/88–1552/3.
Vives, 1492–1540.
Cano, ca. 1509–1560.
Serveto, 1509–1553.
Loyola, 1492–1556.

INTERVAL, 1670–1830

Isla, *Gerundio de Campazas,* 1758, satire.
Meléndez Valdés. 1785, poems.

MODERN, SINCE 1830
Drama
(Already cited.)

Poetry
Campoamor, 1817–1901, b. Asturias.
*Arce, 1834–1903, b. Valladolid.
Bécquer, 1836–1870. German ancestry; infl. by Heine, but knew
no German.

Novel
Fernán Caballero (Cecilia de Arrom), 1796–1877.
Trueba, 1821–1889, Basque.
Valera, 1827–1905, b. Córdoba.
Alarcón, 1833–1891, b. Guadix.
Pereda, b. 1834, Santander.
Pérez Galdós, b. 1845, Canaries.
Unamuno, b. 1864, Bilbao.
Blasco Ibáñez, b. 1869, Valencia.
Baroja, b. 1872, San Sebastián.

§ 84. Portuguese Literature

Portuguese literature is essentially as much a part of Spanish
as Provençal is of French, Scotch of English, Plattdeutsch of
German. It would be strange if it were otherwise within the
peninsula, with Portugal so definitely minor that it is limited
to part of the west coast. In fact the most distinct Iberian

language is not Portuguese but Catalan, which is South French as much as it is Spanish. Portuguese goes with Galician, while "Spanish" is Castilian plus nonliterary dialects. Historically, Portugal is one of four or five former Iberian states, which by the accident of history was kept out of union with the others until discovery, foreign conquest and colonization, and rivalry with Spain had established a separate national tradition. Had union come by 1450, perhaps as late as 1480, it would probably have been permanently successful: perhaps more so than that of Aragon-Catalonia, with its French-Balearic-Italian preoccupations. But when union was established in 1580, it was too late. Especially so in literature: the languages and orthographies had been standardized separately, and most of the specifically Portuguese products were already achieved.

Culturally the two "countries" have a single history, with the smaller and marginal one consistently leading in time. This priority cannot be due to geographical position, except so far as the very aloofness from Europe may have allowed more rapid development on a local basis. In the main perhaps the cause of the precedence is Portugal's smaller size: not too minute for achievement, yet homogeneous, not held back by internal pulls in different directions.

We have already seen that early Spanish court poetry was Galician, virtually Portuguese, until nearly 1400. The original *Amadís de Gaula* is in dispute as between Castilian and Portuguese. One of the early dramatists of importance, Gil Vicente, who flourished about 1502–1536, was a Portuguese, but composed in both languages. So did the dramatist Sá de Miranda, 1496–1558. Encina and Naharro were from Salamanca and Estremadura; *La Celestina* was written in the Salamanca region. In fact, until Rueda, the Spanish theater is essentially an affair of Portugal, Leon, Estremadura. Montemayor of the *Diana,* 1558, was another Portuguese, although he wrote in Castilian.

Camões was born in Lisbon about 1521. *The Lusiads* were published in 1572; he died in 1579, a year before the annexation. In general estimation the greatest poet of his country, his summit may serve as the peak of Portugal's great period. As compared with that of Spain as represented by Cervantes, Portugal is a full generation earlier.

PORTUGUESE LITERATURE

King Diniz, 1261–1325, *Cancioneiro.*
Canção de Figuereido, mid-14th cent.
Amadís de Gaula, prob. mid-14th cent.
Chronicles: Fernão Lopes, d. 1451/4; Zurara, 1410/20–1473/4; Pina, fl. 1482–1495.

1490–1600
*Gil Vicente, 1460/70–1536.
Bernadim Ribeiro, 1482–1552.
Rezende, 1470/90–1554, *Cancioneiro geral* 1516/20.
*Sá de Miranda, 1490/94–1558.
Cristovam Falcão, b. prob. 1510–1520.
Caminha, prob. 1520–1589.
**Camões, ca. 1521/4–1579/80; *1572.
Antonio Ferreira, 1520/28–1569.
Diogo Bernardes, 1530?/1540–1594/1596/1605.
Corte-Rial, d. 1588.
Alvares de Oriente, 1540–1595?

History, same period
Castanheda, d. 1557/9.
*João de Barros, 1496–1570; *1532 seq.
Gois, 1501/2–1574.
Couto, 1542–1616.

After 1600
Pereira de Castro, 1571/2–1632; Mascarenhas, 1596–1656/8; Sousa da Macedo, 1606/12–1682/7; successors of Camões.
Lobo, prob. 1556–1623/7.
Faria e Sousa, 1590–1649.
Melo, 1608–1666.

§ 85. English Literature

English literature shows three configurations. The first, around 1400, is signalized by Chaucer, was brief, and is followed by a full century of low level. The second begins in 1575, or possibly 1525 at the earliest, includes the Elizabethan drama, but continues almost a century beyond Elizabeth, until 1700. The third configuration perhaps begins about 1760, is definite by 1780, centers in what usually is called or miscalled the romantic burst of the decades around 1800, and essentially ends not far from 1875 or soon after.

This is not the conventional organization, which is primarily concerned with content, style, and trend, and only incidentally with quality level. The usual designations of Elizabethan, Restoration, Queen Anne, Eighteenth Century, Romantic, and Victorian need not of course be rejected. These represent real directions or tendencies; but they cut across the time-quality constellations sufficiently to leave these disfigured or concealed. It is a case much like Romanesque, Gothic, Renaissance in sculpture and architecture.

Preliminary growth: Chaucerian, 1360–1415. — Chaucer's eminence has never been questioned. He overtowers everyone within centuries. However, he does not stand alone. A few historic figures group close enough around him to make a group in time: Langland, Gower, Occleve, Lydgate in poetry, Wyclif and Mandeville in prose. This is not much of a constellation, it is true; but it is more than anything that appears earlier or for a century and a half after. What raised Chaucer above his contemporaries seems to have been a combination of personal ability with exposure to Italian influence. At the same time there was no overexposure; so that he remained English. He is recognized as a definitely conscious poet; one less so might have been either uninfluenced or overwhelmed by impact with Italian literature. Generic French civilizational influence of course had been universal in England for three hundred years. It is rather remarkable how little effect the great twelfth- and thirteenth-century growth of French literature had in England, then or later.

So far as I know, there was no other notable pulse or growth of cultural activity in late fourteenth-century England. Since Chaucer's constellation stands alone, and he is far preëminent within it, he approaches somewhat the isolated but culturally effective genius who is the exception in history; though without quite attaining that status.

Wyclif, ca. 1320–1384.
Gower, 1325/30–1408.
Langland, ca. 1330–ca. 1400, *1362.
Mandeville, 1377.
*Chaucer, ca. 1340–1400, *1385 seq.
Occleve, ca. 1370–ca. 1450, *1411.
Lydgate, ca. 1370–ca. 1450, *1415.

The two brief generations from 1360 to 1415/25 amply cover this pulse.

Interval, 1415–1525.—Compared with the Chaucerian pulse, the dearth of quality for more than a century afterward contrasts strikingly. In England there is nothing worth mentioning besides Malory, ca. 1470, Skelton, ca. 1460–1529, and two anonymous folk ballads. Scotland shows somewhat better with Dunbar, 1460–1530, but he looms seemingly large because of the contemporary British void; and the succession of poets whom he capped were Chaucerians belated a century in a marginal province.

Stirrings, 1525–1575.—The first stirrings of the great growth that was to follow are evident around 1525, but for fifty years more there was no poetry or drama of import.

Tyndale and Coverdale's Bible, 1525–1535.
Wyatt 1503–1542, and Surrey 1517–1547.
Book of Common Prayer, 1549.
More, *Utopia,* in English 1551.
Drama: *Gorboduc,* 1561; *Roister Doister,* publ. 1566; *Cambises,*
    1569; *Gurton's Needle,* 1575.

First great growth, 1575–1700.—Between 1575 and 1580 there began a sudden burst of growth. We have Lyly's *Euphues* 1578/9 followed by plays; Spenser's *Shepherd's Calendar* 1579; Sidney's *Arcadia* 1580. By 1590 the movement was in full swing: the *Faerie Queene* had begun to appear, Shakespeare had commenced to write, Marlowe had done half his work.

In drama the climax followed quickly. Shakespeare was at the height of his stride by 1598, and stopped writing in 1613. The best products of his lesser contemporaries were completed within another five years. This story is reviewed separately in the chapter on Drama.

In poetry, it is a long leap from the *Faerie Queene* in 1589 to *Paradise Lost* in 1667, but there is much to fill the gap, including Milton's earlier work of 1632–1638. Elizabethan and Jacobean prose is often still as unknit as it is colorful, and the Restoration is generally considered the time when English prose really took form, but Bacon and the King James Version witness the earlier period's ability to attain high levels.

The end of this great period may be set at 1700, for the following reasons. Dryden, the great figure of his day, died in that year. Two of his best poems were written in 1697 and 1698. In 1698 Jeremy Collier's puritanical blast is supposed to have withered the Restoration drama. However that may be, Congreve, who was easily the leading dramatist of his generation—and the last great one of England except for two brief clusters of Irishmen,—produced his best play in 1697 and his last one in 1700. In short, almost exactly at 1700 both poetry and drama dropped abruptly; and within a few years, it may be added, prose took new directions and manners with Addison and his contemporaries.

The period of 125 years from 1575 to 1700 was of course not uniform in content. Drama was first in culmination, but after a lapse was also last. The problem is where to divide the long span into phases. The midway point of 1638 or 1640 separates nearly all the greatest productions from those not so great. The Elizabethan drama is universally considered to have been internally finished before the playhouses were closed in 1642. The lyrics fall about equally before and after the mid-point. All of Milton's great poetry—that which is still read—except *Paradise Lost* is previous to 1638. This epic, it is true, was composed after the Restoration and was published in 1667, as a seeming anachronism. Milton was then 59: an age at which practically no poets have attained their greatest heights. But between his earlier and his later activity there lay twenty years of politics, secretariat, prose and Latin writing. During this time Milton the poet was completely suspended, where a lesser one would have been permanently diverted or extinguished. The result was that he did in his sixth decade what in an uninterrupted normal career he would have done in his fourth or fifth—presumably by 1650 at latest.

As to the culmination of the whole, one thinks inevitably of Shakespeare's last fifteen active years. So far as drama is concerned, these years were no doubt the center of the moment of glory, even with him left out. But for literature as a whole it is difficult to fix a single point: its different departments did not march abreast, as they mostly did in Rome, France, Spain, Germany. The reason for this anomaly is perhaps connected with the suddenness of the growth: the complete void after Chaucer, the near-insignificance of the 1525–1575 half century of preparation. The configuration is of a different type from, say, Renaissance painting, when Leonardo, Michelangelo, Raphael, Correggio, Titian all fulminated simultaneously for a decade or so. But Renaissance painting was two hundred years building up to its peak, whereas Elizabethan literature shot up to the first part of its summit in twenty-five. It is true that often the productive time of the greatest individual is also the mean time of highest achievement by lesser men. But it must be recognized that this is not always so; that genuine and important configurations do not regularly conform to one strict outline. Seventeenth-century English literature rather resembles Greek sculpture in the relative diffuseness of its peak.[11] It was over a century from Phidias and Polyclitus to Praxiteles and Lysippus; and who would rashly wish to rate one of these as decisively overtopping the others? The really significant feature of both configurations is the length of time over which work of high order was produced. Compared with the continuous elevation of the two ranges, their precise highest points are of less moment than in most cases.[12]

Two other English growths coincide quite closely in absolute chronology with this literary one: music and science; and a third is not far away: philosophy. Music and science also ended

[11] Though from different causes, no doubt, for Greek sculpture had been continuously developing for nearly two centuries before Phidias, and was not segregated into departments corresponding to English drama, poetry, and prose.

[12] The exact culmination of modern German science is also difficult to define, though no doubt again for somewhat different reasons.

about 1700 or 1710 after a career of a century. Philosophy culminated 1680–1710 in England: Hume is somewhat later, 1740–1748, but Scotch. As there has never been any real growth of sculpture in England, and that in painting was secondary and the architectural one was mediaeval, it follows that the seventeenth was on the whole the great century of England for the unfolding of intellectual-aesthetic energy. Internally, the synchronism is less exact, because music and science clearly culminated just before 1700, philosophy just after as well as before, but literature probably soon after 1600. This fact may serve as a safeguard against construing similar configurations as identical ones, or forcing their fit into too rigid a scheme. Nevertheless the near-synchronism is striking and must be historically significant.

It helps, for one thing, to show what is sound and what is exaggerated in the widely held concept of the greatness of Elizabethan England. Take away Spenser, Shakespeare, Bacon, and a daring freebooter like Drake, and what is there left of greatness in Elizabethan England that any but historians really know anything about? At that, the very best of Shakespeare's and Bacon's work was done under James I, not Elizabeth. The famous Armada outcome obviously represents mainly ill-planned Spanish overstraining plus some storms; the Queen herself was an able, unscrupulous, cautious, and vacillating woman. What her reign really contained was the beginnings of a period of high achievement for a century after. Before her, England was little and culturally produced less; after her, much. This fact popular historic instinct has soundly seized upon; but it has also exaggerated the fact into exalting her reign into one of greatness over that of stubborn and weak Stuarts and the Civil Wars; whereas her time only laid the foundation for larger accomplishments actually realized under these same Stuarts.

The Civil Wars evidently shook England deeply—more so than any other internal or external war. Without exception every cultural activity sagged deeply during their continuance, or was entirely suspended. But also without exception the cultural activities resumed afterward, and without impairment, though with some change of direction. Since the other growths all reached their heights after 1660, the falling-off in literature cannot be attributed directly to the Civil Wars as such. This finding fits with the selection of 1638–1640 as the point of division between the earlier greater and later lesser half of the literary growth. Without the Civil Wars, the point might have been delayed to about 1650.

FIRST PHASE, 1575–1638: BIRTHS TO ABOUT 1600

Drama

Lyly, 1553/4–1606.
Kyd, 1558–1594.
Lodge, 1558–1625.
Peele, 1558–1598.
Chapman, 1559–1634.
Greene, 1560–1592.
*Marlowe, 1564–1593.
**Shakespeare, 1564–1616,
     *1598–1613.
Nashe, 1567–1601.
Dekker, 1570–1641.
Middleton, 1570–1627.
*Jonson, 1573–1637, *1598,
     *1605, *1609.

Marston, 1575–1634.
Heywood, 1575–1650.
Tourneur, 1575–1626.
Webster, 1575–1624, *1612–
     1616.
*Fletcher, 1579–1625, *before
     1616.
Beaumont, 1584–1616.
Massinger, 1584–1639.
Rowley, 1585–1642.
Ford, 1586–1639.
Shirley, 1596–1666.

Poetry

*Spenser, 1552–1599, *1579 seq.
Donne, 1573–1631.
Herrick, 1591–1674.

Herbert, 1593–1632.
Carew, ca. 1598–1639.

Prose

Lyly, 1553/4–1606, *1578/9.
Sidney, 1554–1586, *1580.
*Bacon, 1561–1626.

King James Version, *1611.
Burton, 1577–1640, *1621.
Walton, 1593–1683, *1653!

SECOND PHASE, 1638–1700: BIRTHS AFTER 1600

Poetry

Waller, 1607–1687.
**Milton, 1608–1674, *1632–
     1638, *1667.
Suckling, 1609–1642.
Crashaw, 1612–1650.
Butler, 1612–1680, *1663–1678.

Denham, 1615–1669.
Cowley, 1618–1667.
Lovelace, 1618–1658.
*Dryden, 1631–1700, *1667–
     1698.

Drama

Davenant, 1606–1680.	Lee, 1653–1692.
Dryden, 1631–1700, *1674.	Vanbrugh, 1664–1726.
Etheredge, ca. 1634–ca. 1690.	*Congreve, 1670–1729, *1697.
Wycherley, 1640–1716.	Farquhar, 1678–1707, Irish,
Shadwell, 1642–1692.	*1699–1707.
Otway, 1652–1685.	

Prose

Browne, 1605–1682.	Bunyan, 1628–1688, *1677.

It appears from the list that it was mainly the living drama which carried the larger growth on to 1700. The prose production was actually less in the second half, unless the prose plays be included. Except for the drama, 1670/80 could be set as the end of the whole growth. This would take in all of Milton, part of Dryden, and just cover Bunyan, leaving the Congreve prose drama to be thrown in with the following age of prose. This alignment, however, splits the Restoration period in the middle.

Another way of recognizing the situation is that no poets or prose writers were born after Dryden, 1631, but that all the Restoration playwrights were born after him; the Vanbrugh-Congreve-Farquhar constellation, in fact, from thirty to forty years after.

The difficulty is evidently with the Civil Wars, including the Protectorate, which were disruptive enough to suppress almost all nonpolemical cultural activity for twenty years. With the Restoration in 1660 there was an effort to restore pre-1640 activities. This, however, was necessarily abortive except for a few hangovers like Milton. By about 1680 this endeavor had spent itself, and the new attitudes which had come to the surface in 1660 were beginning to be dominant—with their froth blown off. The growth of poetry was over, the stage set for an age of prose literature which began to realize itself about 1700.

If we accept this alternative construction, the difference between the cycle of literature and the cycles in music, science, and philosophy is that literature had passed its culmination in 1640 and it was its tailings-off which were interrupted and dislocated by the Wars. The three other activities, however, were still formative in 1640. The Wars therefore delayed their progress; but after the suspension they resumed growth without impairment. On this view, had England remained internally peaceful, the growth of literature which began in Elizabethan days might have fulfilled itself by 1650–1660, and died quietly a generation later. Actually, there was enough vitality left in the growth in 1640 for it to send up new shoots after 1660.

Interval, 1700–1760.—It may seem strained to call the age of Pope, Addison, Swift, Defoe, and Fielding a trough. But, in the first place, it was a period overwhelmingly of prose. Pope is the one notable exception; and with all his admitted artificer's skill, he dealt mainly with trivialities, platitudes, or his personal spites. No great patterns of poetry can be evolved for such content devoid of broader and deeper feelings. Pope has been admired by some poets for his technical workmanship, and by part of the nonpoetical public precisely because he gives the semblance of poetry without its uneasy substance. In his case the sustained formal skill, probably, is at least in part the inverse product of poverty of emotional content.

The period is an interval in the sense that the patterns of the preceding great growth had been worn through, and those of a new future growth of poetry had not begun to form. Hence the strong French influence: emphasis on precision, *netteté*, urbanity in both senses, the reintroduction of rhyme into narrative verse. This French influence began with the Restoration, as the great previous vigor, then nearly a century old and suspended for two decades, began to grow feeble; it got the upper hand by 1700. The introductions did much to give the English language, especially as a prose vehicle, a degree of regularity which it had not previously been able to attain consistently; and part of the gain was permanently retained. However, primary emphasis on the new virtues was un-English, in view of the past, and was evidently instinctively felt as such, as soon as the acquisition had been made; and the future also relegated them into secondary place. The main point is that the foreign influences were accepted in an interval between the development of native English forms, especially in verse.

English tradition continued with greater strength after 1700 on the inevitably much less patterned level of prose, where the primary emphasis is on content. Hence *Crusoe, Gulliver, Tom Jones*. Probably it is the very lack of specific English form which has allowed the first two of these three works to become international books for children.

Poetry

Prior, 1664–1721.

Young, 1683–1765, *1742.

Gay, 1685–1732.

*Pope, 1688–1744.

Thomson, 1700–1748, Scotch.

Gray, 1716–1771, *1750.

Collins, 1721–1759.

Prose

*Swift, 1667–1745, Irish, *1704, *1726.

Arbuthnot, 1667–1735.

Steele, 1672–1729, Irish.

*Addison, 1672–1719.

Bolingbroke, 1678–1751.

Mary Montagu, 1689–1762.

Chesterfield, 1694–1773.

Johnson, 1709–1784.

Novel

*Defoe, 1660–1731.

Richardson, 1689–1761.

*Fielding, 1707–1754.

*Sterne, 1713–1768.

Smollett, 1721–1771, Scotch.

1760–1780.—The third quarter of the eighteenth century can be reckoned either with the preceding interval or as the first stirrings of the growth that followed. Macpherson's "Ossian," 1760–1763, Walpole's *Otranto,* 1764, Percy's *Reliques,* 1765, show a new direction: romanticism is raising its head, looking toward mediaevalism.

The decade 1770–1780 produced one of the two approaches to a revival of living drama of literary value which England experienced. Goldsmith, 1773, and Sheridan, 1775–1779, were both of them Irish, spontaneous, finished, and writers of genuine comedy. The other flare-up, more than a century later, was also Irish: Wilde, Shaw, Synge.

Poetry

Percy, 1729–1811, *1765.

Macpherson, 1736–1796, Scotch, *1760–1763.

Prose
  Walpole, 1717–1797, *1764.
  Burke, 1729–1797, Irish.
  Gibbon, 1737–1794, *1776 seq.
Drama, Irish
  Goldsmith, 1728–1784, *1773.
  *Sheridan, 1751–1816, *1775–1779.

Modern growth, 1780 to 1880, or to the present.—The climax
of modern English literature is clearly between 1790/95 and
1825. A sort of silver age after 1825 was over by 1870: Tennyson, Browning, Swinburne wrote after that date, but with
definite falling off. The novelists of the same period had done
their work by 1870. As between the earlier and the later phase,
1795 marks the boundary in birth years. Keats and Carlyle
were both born then: the poet died in 1821, the prose writer
first attained his level in 1833.

As for after-1870/80, the one thing that is sure is the decline
as against the century before. Whether we have by now come
to the point of emergence of new patterns which will have a
future, or which still are only disintegrating past ones, can
hardly be more than an opinion. The decline in values is clear;
whether it is also the prelude to a new growth of greater values
will be known when the new values have been produced.

FIRST PHASE: BIRTHS TO 1795

Poetry
  Cowper, 1731–1800, *1785.
  Crabbe, 1754–1832, *1783.
  Blake, 1757–1827, *1789 seq.
  *Burns, 1759–1796, Scotch,
    *1786 seq.
  Rogers, 1763–1855, *1792.
  *Wordsworth, 1770–1850.
  Scott, 1771–1832, Scotch,
    *before 1815.
  *Coleridge, 1772–1834, *before
    1798.

  Southey, 1773–1843.
  Campbell, 1777–1844.
  Moore, 1779–1852, Irish,
    *1807–1817.
  *Byron, 1788–1824.
  Hood, 1790–1845.
  *Shelley, 1792–1822.
  Felicia Hemans, 1793–1835.
  *Keats, 1795–1821.

Prose
  Coleridge, 1772–1834.
  Lamb, 1775–1834.
  Landor, 1775–1864.

  Hazlitt, 1778–1830.
  Hunt, 1784–1859.

Novel

Frances Burney, 1752–1840, *1778–1782.

Ann Radcliffe, 1764–1823, *1794.

Maria Edgeworth, 1767–1849, *1800 seq.

*Scott, 1771–1832, Scotch, *after 1814.

Lewis, 1775–1818, *1795.

*Jane Austen, 1775–1817, *1811–1813.

Mary Shelley, 1797–1851, *1818.

SECOND PHASE: BIRTHS 1795–1840

Poetry

Elizabeth Barrett, 1806–1861.

*Tennyson, 1809–1892.

Fitzgerald, 1809–1883.

*Browning, 1812–1889.

Arnold, 1822–1888.

Patmore, 1823–1896.

Rossetti, 1828–1882; half Italian.

Christina Rossetti, 1830–1894.

Morris, 1834–1896.

Thomson, 1834–1892, Scotch.

*Swinburne, 1837–1909, *1855, *1856.

Prose

Carlyle, 1795–1881, Scotch.

Macaulay, 1800–1859.

Ruskin, 1819–1900.

Pater, 1839–1894.

Novel

Lytton, 1803–1873.

Disraeli, 1804–1881.

Elizabeth Gaskell, 1810–1865.

George Eliot, 1810–1880.

*Thackeray, 1811–1863.

*Dickens, 1812–1870.

Trollope, 1815–1882.

Charlotte Brontë, 1816–1855.

Emily Brontë, 1818–1848.

Kingsley, 1819–1875.

Collins, 1824–1889.

Meredith, 1828–1909.

Butler, 1835–1902.

Hardy, 1840–1928.

BORN AFTER 1840

British

Stevenson, 1850, Scotch.

Kipling, 1865, b. in India.

Irish

Moore, 1851.

Yeats, 1865.

James Stephens, 1882.

Irish dramatists

Wilde, 1856.

Shaw, 1856.

Synge, 1871.

These lists show, for the first phase, a heavy clustering of births in the decade 1770–1780, alike in poetry, prose, and novel, with the density thinning out for fifteen years before and after, in a normal frequency-distribution curve. The second phase is similarly constellated, for both poetry and novel, around the years 1809–1812; but its subsequent thinning out is somewhat slower, being spread out over twenty-five years. The interval between the peaks of the two phases, again as expressed in births, is a generation, 1775 to 1810; the gap in which no great figures were born lasted fourteen years, from 1795 to 1809. As compared with the two phases together, the meagerness of higher quality in the two generations after 1870/80, that is, emanating from men born after 1840, forms a startling contrast. With Ireland subtracted, Great Britain has two figures of prominence to show in sixty recent years: the Indian-born Englishman Kipling and the Scotchman Stevenson; and neither of them, probably, is able to match at least a dozen individuals born in the seventy or eighty years of the preceding era. This in the face of an indefinitely greater quantity of production since 1875.

It is also evident that poetry, novel, and miscellaneous prose tend to rise and decline together in the modern era, while what there is of drama is set apart, in fact comes just before and after the limits of the main bursts of growth. This of course contrasts with the seventeenth-century development, in which drama led, attained the greatest heights, and longest maintained itself.

Curious is the participation of women in the novel: at its peak around 1800, when they surround the solitary figure of the virile Scott. In point of dates of production, indeed, they mostly precede him. In the second phase, too, they come early. The last woman to write an English novel which can lay claim to the quality of full greatness was born in 1818.

Summary.—The periods and their subdivisions recapitulate thus:

 I. 1360–1415. Anticipatory or Chaucerian growth. Post-Mediaeval, pre-Modern. Unaccompanied by growths in other higher cultural activities.
X1. 1415–1525. Barren interval.
 II. 1525–1700. First major growth. "Baroque" in time.
    A. 1525–1575. Preliminaries, but so faint that the period might be reckoned as part of the preceding empty one.
    B. 1575–1700. Main growth, divisible into:

B 1. 1575–1638. Greater phase, corresponding to beginnings in music and science.

B 2. 1638–1700. Lesser phase, corresponding to peak in music and science.

X2. 1700–1760. Interval. Prose literature. "Enlightenment" in time. Corresponds to end of philosophy and beginning of painting.

III. 1760——. Second major growth. "Modern" or "Romantic" in time. Corresponds closely to second growth of science.

A. 1760–1780. Stirrings, still overlain by qualities of preceding prose interval.

B. 1780–1870/80. Main growth, divisible into:

B 1. 1780–1830. Greater pulse; births to 1795.

B 2. 1830–1870/80. Second pulse; births 1795–1840.

C. 1870/80——. Decline.

SCOTLAND

Scotch literature is of course hardly dissociable from English, even when in "vernacular" or dialect. It shows two growths, one centering about 1500, the second more diffusely around 1800.

The first begins with the influence of Chaucer soon after his death. Besides the *Kingis Quair* of James I, reigned 1424–1437, there are mentioned Blind Harry, Clerk, Holland (fl. 1482), Mersar, Roulls, Quentin Schaw (d. ca. 1504), Henryson (still under Chaucer tradition), Kennedy (ca. 1460–ca. 1507), and, most important, Dunbar, 1460–1530. There followed Gavin Douglas and David Lindsay. With the Reformation, this growth ended. It had coincided with the sterile interval in England; and, in spite of the traditional hostility of the two nations, the Scotch movement is obviously the marginal counterpart of the Chaucerian growth, belated by a century.

The Elizabethan-Stuart period is empty in Scotland.

The second growth is largely intertwined with the English current. Scots staying at home were likely to use the vernacular, especially until about 1800. Others went to England and of course wrote standard English. Births begin just before the Union of 1707, and productivity was in flow within two decades of that date. The Pope-Addison current of finished endeavor hardly affected Scotland. The growth there was local in origin, and is to be construed as part of the general heightening of cultural activity for a century after the Union. It showed also in philosophy and science, in a minor way in painting. Somewhat after 1800 this Scotch configuration tended to fade out into a proportional representation of Scots in undifferentiated British activity.

Ramsay, 1686–1758.
Ross, 1699–1784.
Thomson, 1700–1748.
Skinner, 1721–1807.
Smollett, 1721–1771.
Fergusson, 1750–1774.
Burns, 1759–1796.

Joanna Baillie, 1762–1851.
Scott, 1771–1832.
Campbell, 1777–1844.
Carlyle, 1795–1881.
Ballantine, 1808–1877.
Thomson, 1834–1892.
Stevenson, 1850–1894.

IRELAND

Irish participation in English literature begins about 1700, and remained a participation, almost exclusively enacted on English soil, until the late nineteenth century.

In order of birth dates, the principal Irish writers are:

Swift, 1667.
Steele, 1672.
†Farquhar, 1678.
†Goldsmith, 1728.
Burke, 1729.
†Sheridan, 1751.

Th. Moore, 1779.
Geo. Moore, 1851.
†Wilde, 1856.
†Shaw, 1856.
Yeats, 1865.
†Synge, 1871.

There is a gap of half a century between Farquhar and Goldsmith, and three-quarters between the two Moores. The latter gap means a lack of productivity from 1810 to 1880, and must be significant. The earlier date perhaps corresponds to the union with Great Britain in 1800; the later, possibly to the rise of constructive nationalism in Ireland and of Home Rule attitude in Britain.

The daggers above indicate dramatists, who make up half the list. The last real dramatist of greatness who was an Englishman was Congreve; the dramatist who closed the Elizabethan-Restoration procession was the Irishman Farquhar. The only subsequent minor bursts of comedy in English are the brief ones beginning about 1770 and 1890, and these are wholly the product of Irishmen. The parallel is in British music, which has also been almost sterile, or dull, since 1700/10, except for such spontaneity as Balfe and Sullivan contributed.

§ 86. Dutch Literature

The Low Countries are, and have been since their emergence into history, from two-thirds to three-fourths Germanic, from a third to a fourth Romance in population. The Romance language, Walloon, is a well-differentiated dialect of French; its area, a belt bordering France. Literarily, it has long been tributary to the larger nationality, and has developed no serious product of its own. The Germanic speech, Dutch-Flemish, is basically a form of Low German, and perhaps no more different from this than Walloon from standard French. But it is more different from standard German, which is High German. Also, the Dutch-Flemish territory forms a tongue jutting out from the general Germanic area: it is connected with this only on the east. To the south, Walloon and French are spoken; to the northwest lies the sea. More opportunity was thus given for the Germanic Netherlanders to develop independently from Germany than for the Walloons from France.

Dutch and Flemish even today do not differ much more than dialectically. But they are spoken in separate countries: Holland and Belgium. Until after 1500, the Flemish-Walloon Netherlands much outweighed the Holland Netherlands in population, wealth, and cultivation. In fact, the Flemings alone counted for more, culturally, than the Dutch. The balance between the two halves had become more nearly even when friction with sovereign Spain began soon after the mid-sixteenth century. After a decade or so of hesitant participation, the Catholic Flemings-Walloons refused to rebel further, and reëstablished terms with the Spanish monarchy. The Dutch, largely Calvinist, and reliant in their new prosperity and vigor, fought it out and achieved a separate nationality.

From about the time of the beginning of their political revolt, their science, philosophy, painting, and literature began to flourish in pace with their navy, industry, and trade. Evidently a silent change of center of gravity from southwest to north-east had been going on for some time. Ghent and Bruges had been outdistanced first by Antwerp, now by Amsterdam. What had been the humbler provinces made a bid for Netherlandish leadership. The older, Belgian districts refused to follow. After the split, they still produced great painting for two genera-tions: their science and music were already finishing. The Dutch, on the other hand, went on up in everything they at-tempted, to a culmination which was attained toward 1650 and which did not close until 1700. It was probably not resubmis-sion to Philip II or Catholicism which brought the earlier decline to the Belgian provinces: their course seems already pointed downward, relatively at least, when the revolt for in-dependence began. Historically, the Netherlands were a unit from time immemorial until the internal displacement of focus of activity and prosperity broke them apart in the sixteenth century.

One result is that what literature there was before the Revolt was essentially Flemish; after it, Dutch.

High and Late Mediaeval Flemish literature was inevitably modeled on French. Not only did twelfth- and thirteenth-century France influence all Europe; but the Belgian Nether-lands were half Romance. Essentially, the Flemings translated and adapted from French; and, prosperity being greater than cultivation among the burghers, they translated without high distinction. Germany had, on the one hand, a group of aristo-cratic poets; on the other, some remnant, because of its eastern remoteness, of native themes like the Nibelungen saga. The Flemings had neither. They transmitted some material from France to Germany. But the High Mediaeval German great literature had flashed and extinguished before the Flemings, except for Veldeke, had more than started.

Then comes a century and a half with very little: say, 1425 to 1575. The greatest figure in letters is Erasmus, 1466–1536, who wrote in Latin. He was from Dutch Rotterdam—a premonition of a weighting that was to come.

The Dutch burst began about 1575, and was essentially over by 1675. In this century, lyric, didactic-reflective, descriptive, and dramatic poetries were produced. The greatest figure is Vondel, 1587–1679. His fortieth year, 1627, is about midway of the century of productivity, and indicates the region of the culmination: say 1620–1640. This is slightly earlier than the climaxes in philosophy, science, and painting under Spinoza, Huygens, and Rembrandt. The concentration is quite definite, and a century sufficiently long for a small country.

By 1700, foreign imitation was current, presumably because the native growth was spent. Pels's dramas modeled on French rules, about 1695, are a symptom. The eighteenth century has been called the Dutch Augustan age, but it copied Addison and Voltaire.

A smaller peak was attained in the early-middle nineteenth century, from about 1810 to 1870. The births run from 1780 to 1820/30. This was evidently part of the international romantic-realistic revolt current that swept most of Europe. I do not know what to do with Bilderdijck, 1756–1832, usually reckoned the greatest Dutch poet after Vondel. He seems too early for the nineteenth-century movement. If he belongs, he at once initiates and climaxes it. Superficially, his configuration fit is not good. Those acquainted at first hand with Dutch literature may be able to explain his place.

Flemish adaptations of Romance literature, 1200 or after to ca. 1425
  Heinrich von Veldeke, ca. 1200.
  Jakob von Maerlant, 13th cent., translations.
  Willem, ca. 1250. *Reynard,* from the French.
  Jan Boendale, 14th cent. Didactic poems, rhymed chronicles.
  Sprekers or wandering minstrels.
  Dirk Potter, d. 1428. *Der Minnen Loep,* poem based on Boccaccio.

Dutch literature, 1575–1675
  Visscher, 1545–1620. "The Dutch Martial."
  Spieghel, 1549–1612.
  Coster, 1579–1665, b. in Amsterdam. Pioneer in drama.

Bredero, 1585–1618, b. Amsterdam. Drama.

Cats, 1577–1660, b. Zeeland. Didactic; school of Dordrecht.

Hooft, 1581–1647, b. The Hague. Drama.

Camphuyzen, 1586–1627, b. Gorkum. Lyrics.

*Vondel, 1587–1679, b. Cologne, to Antwerp, to Amsterdam; Anabaptist, turned Catholic 1641. Dramatic, lyric, epic, satiric writings.

Huygens, 1596–1687, b. The Hague, father of physicist. Didactic writings.

Heemskerck, 1597–1656, b. The Hague. Pastoral.

Asselijn, 1620–1681, b. Dieppe. Comedy.

Van der Goes (Antonides), 1647–1684. *De Y Strom,* descriptive poem.

Luyken, 1649–1712.

Interim, 1575–1810

Pels, ca. 1695, strict-rule drama.

Van Effen, *Hollandsche Spektator,* 1731–1735.

Feitama, 1694–1758, translated Voltaire's *Henriade.*

Hoogvliet, epic *Abraham,* 1763.

Unplaced

*Bilderdijck, 1756–1832, b. Amsterdam. Lyric, epic, drama. He stands outside of any apparent configuration.

Nineteenth century, 1810–1870

Tollens, 1780–1856.

Bogaers, 1795–1870.

Van Lennep, 1802–1868, "The Dutch Walter Scott."

Beets, 1814–1903.

Dekker ("Multatuli"), 1820–1887.

De Genestet, 1830–1861.

§87. Scandinavian Literatures

Literary productivity of the Scandinavian peoples falls into two far-separated pulses: the Viking, Icelandic, or Eddaic, climaxing around 1000 and continuing until 1300; and the Modern, scarcely beginning before 1700 and centering around 1800. As already stated, the Viking phase, being pagan, pre-French, uninfluenced by Rome, and peripheral to the Continent, is really separate from the great growth of civilization, many-stranded but unified, which we call Occidental.

ICELAND, 900–1300

The preserved Eddaic literature is Norwegian and especially Icelandic.[13] Its materials, mythological and heroic, are common Scandinavian and in part pan-Germanic; but the working out in literary form was west Scandinavian and largely Icelandic. The art was conscious, in part highly mannered. Out of epic materials, episodes were shaped into strophic lyrics; then into prose sagas. Themes and forms are uninfluenced by the literatures of civilization: they spring wholly out of a barbarian and pagan soil. In fact it is remarkable that a culture otherwise so undeveloped should have produced so great, if limited, a literature. The oldest portions of the poetic Edda are dated about 900, possibly a little earlier. The culmination, as marked by the *Voluspo, Thrymskvidha,* and *Lokasenna,* is tenth-century; in 1000 Iceland adopted Christianity; but parts of the Edda are as late as the twelfth century.

The inception of the composition of the Edda is approximately the period of Viking expansion. Beginning about 790, this expansion had its peak from 830 to 900. Around 1000 fell a second phase, of which Canute is typical: conquests by established kings who had accepted Christianity—a powerful instrument of royalty as against tribal disorganization. Roughly, the two activities, fruitful war and literature, correspond in time, with the poetry a little in arrears. On a closer view, the best poetry seems to come mainly in the interval between the conquest-expansion and the achievement of kingdoms; the prose development, after the latter. However, the seat of composition of the best of the preserved literature was Iceland; and Iceland, though a product of Viking expansion, lay pretty well outside the course of raids, conquest, and kingship.

---

[13] The *Thrymskvidha* and *Völundarkvidha* are believed to have been composed, possibly in Norway, ca. 900; the *Grimnismol* and *Skirnismol* not much later; the *Voluspo* ca. 950 in Iceland; the *Rigsthula* "in Scotland or Ireland," or by a Norwegian acquainted with Ireland, for a Danish king ca. 950±; the *Atlakvidha* and *Atlamol* in Greenland in the eleventh century. The *Alvissmol* and *Hyndluljodh* are thought to be twelfth-century, the *Gripisspo* late twelfth-century.

It is a fair question whether Christianity did not have an indirect influence on Eddaic literature. The missionary Ansgar entered Denmark and Sweden about 827. In the tenth century both Denmark and Norway had Christian kings, though most of the population may still have been pagan. The period of the production of much of the best of the poetic Edda is just before the collapse of the old beliefs. The suggestion is that the native culture, now under pressure from outside, was stimulated into a reaction formation, a higher tension and sharper formulation than before. The Edda on this view would be a collision product—a mobilization or manifestation of activity due at least partly to the old culture's finding itself on the defensive in spite of its outward successes. Sweden was remote enough to escape this pressure at the critical moment. Its first king was baptized around 1000, but his successors relapsed, and it was not until well after 1100 that Christianity was established. By then, the drives of the Viking era were over. On the other hand, Germany and England lay nearer civilization, and were Christianized earlier, so that their pagan Germanic poetry failed to reach an equal quality as literature, and in fact was largely lost.

Considerable has been made recently of Irish influence on the development of the Edda in Iceland; but the effect appears a minor one, especially on the poetry.

Alongside the Eddaic poems ran those of the skalds, composed by historic personages, mostly about contemporary or recently dead kings or chiefs. The kings were mostly Norwegians; the earlier bards, from 880–900 on to Eyvind Finnson, who flourished about 961–986, were also Norwegian; after that, Icelandic. The ablest, perhaps, was the Icelander Egill Skallagrimsson, 900–982. Ulfr Uggason, about 985, was the last skald to treat myths. Others followed Haakon and Canute. Harald Hardraade, who reigned in Norway 1047–1066, was himself a skald. After 1100 there was decline; but the professional and panegyric genre continued till about 1300. In 1153 Einar Skulason composed the religious *Geisli,* on St. Olaf the king; the bishop of Orkney, Bjarni Kolbeinsson, 1188–1222, wrote the *Jomsvikingadrapa* on a Viking battle of 986. The

Solarljod of about 1200 belongs in theme to the Mediaeval literature of visions—it is on the Resurrection—but is in the Eddaic manner, evidently influenced by the *Havamal*. Even the monk Eysteinn Asgrimsson's Christian *Lilja* of about 1340 is still in skaldic verse. Some twenty years later Einar Gilsson's *Olafsrima* is written in end rhymes introduced from Europe.

The skaldic poetic form is basically the Eddaic alliterative one, but stricter and more elaborate. Syllables are counted rather than accents, there is internal syllabic rhyme, and more variety of meters. Far-fetched metaphorical allusions abound. All this artifice is achieved at the expense of the natural word order, on which intelligibility so largely rests in the Germanic vernaculars.

A third strain in Icelandic literature, culminating somewhat later, is the prose sagas. These began as biographies on individual Icelanders of the period 950–1030, commenced to be written down about 1170, and gradually became true history. The language is that of speech, simple and unornamented, the narrative straightforward and accurate, the psychological insight, as in the Edda, astonishing. The four greatest *Islendinga-sögur* are the *Egilssaga*, composed about 1200; the *Eyrbyggja*, around 1225; the *Laxdöla*, about 1230–1240; and the *Nyalssaga*, a combination in the second half of the thirteenth century of two sögur which may have been composed about 1200. The first true history is that of Iceland by Ari Thorgilsson, 1067–1148. The outstanding historical work is the *Heimskringla* or *Noregs Konunga-sögur* by the great Icelander Snorri Sturluson, 1178–1241. Snorri and his two nephews were also skalds. By 1300 the saga movement was over. In 1262, after more than three centuries of organized independence, Iceland had become subject to the Norwegian kings.

The Icelandic growth is remarkable in a number of ways. It has strictly its own themes and its own forms, is rooted wholly in the Germanic past, began to take shape in pagan Scandinavia, culminated, so far as myth and legend are concerned, in remote Iceland as it came under the impact of Christianity, and continued, with native themes and native styles, although now Christian, nearly three centuries longer before it succumbed under the weight of Occidental civilization, then closing its High Mediaeval phase. If contact with European-Christian culture helped stimulate this growth, surely the remoteness of marginal Iceland gave it the opportunity to flower in spontaneous originality before the mass of Continental culture assimilated it.

EUROPEANIZED SCANDINAVIA

The long interval.—Once Christianized, the Scandinavian lands soon became merely the frontier outposts of Europe, backward in population, wealth, and development, and necessarily laggard in cultural productions of all kinds. The Late Mediaeval and Renaissance ages find them without literature, art, or thought of moment. The more France and Italy developed, the more was Scandinavia outdistanced, as measured by the patterns and standards achieved. Denmark, the nearest of the northern countries, was no doubt somewhat the most advanced. But it was concerned, on the one hand, with preserving its national integrity against adjacent Germany; and on the other, it had little to take from this spiritually in the long period from 1250 to 1750, when German literature was particularly sterile.[14]

Sweden.—The first of the three nations to emerge into European participation was Sweden, probably the most populous, sheltered from attack, but so situated as to participate easily in European affairs once it chose to become aggressive. The expansion began with Gustavus Adolphus, and for most of a century Sweden essayed the role of a great power, far beyond its resources, until the inevitable collapse soon after 1700. Definite as was its mark in European politics in this period, the country was still too raw to produce culturally by European standards. In literature it was schooling itself in imitations.

However, about 1730 an organized growth of literature got under way; and after a generation, the leading poets began to appear: Bellman, 1740–1795; Kellgren, 1751–1795; Tegnér,

---

[14] Some examples of Danish lag are cited in § 109 (p. 734).

1782–1846. It will be seen that these fall into the eighteenth, the century of Swedenborg and Linnaeus, rather than into the nineteenth. In consequence, the foreign influence which was digested and nationalized was French rather than German, "classical" rather than "romantic": the rhymed Alexandrine became the typical Swedish verse. In fact, the Swedish literary growth could not have leaned on the German: Bellman was born earlier than Goethe, Kellgren than Schiller. When, after 1800, German and romantic influence penetrated, the Swedish growth was already declining.

Soon after 1800, there is a slackening of the number of births of men of importance; but they resume in the quarter century 1840–1865, with a grouping around Strindberg, 1849–1912. This cluster represents a distinguishable pulse, but probably within the limits of the single growth that began around 1730. There is a further difference, in that Swedish writers before 1850 are very little known in the outside world, but the near-contemporaries Strindberg and Lagerlöf are much read. This may be a function of the circumstance that the earlier writers were primarily poets, the later, prose writers; plus the growing internationalization of literature.

At any rate, Swedish literature, however schooled on Italian and then French imitation, is national in that it underwent a full half of its development before the romantic-realistic early nineteenth-century wave flooded most of Europe.

Denmark.—Modern Danish literature, on the contrary, belongs largely to this international movement. It did not emerge from the formative, apprentice stage until after 1750, instead of before; and the majority of its more distinguished writers fall after 1800. The great figure is considered to be Oehlenschlaeger, born 1779, as against the Swede Bellman, 1740; the most widely read abroad is Andersen, 1805.

The dominant recent figure, at least in international recognition, is Brandes; but, being a critic, he almost surely marks the weakening of creative production.

The Danish growth is therefore definitely briefer than the Swedish one. It is essentially comprised between 1760 and 1860.

A curious fact is that the formative stage is dominated by a Norwegian, Holberg, 1684–1754; and that the growth proper began to take shape in the hands of Norwegians living in Copenhagen or at any rate writing Danish. None of these eighteenth-century Norwegians attained top eminence; but as a group they antedate the early Danes. Norway at the time did not yet have a speech vehicle of its own. Again, the pioneer propagandist for romanticism was a Norwegian, Steffens. After him, Hauch, born 1790, is the only Norwegian of consequence. Oehlenschlaeger was of German descent. Brandes was preceded by two other Jews: Hertz—the exact contemporary of Heine—and Goldschmidt. The total picture is much less intensely national than in Sweden.

Norway.—Technically, Norwegian literature is of the mid-nineteenth century only: Ibsen was born in 1828, Björnson in 1832. However, this is largely a matter of denomination in terms of national consciousness. Until after 1800, Norwegians participated in Danish literature, as just set forth. In fact, their role there was that of pioneers: they did not make the greater achievements, but they led the way in each new development.

Ibsen and Björnson, with contemporaries such as Lie, are a notable enough group to constitute a constellation.

International currents.—In the ensuing lists, I have followed the conventional plan of grouping into Enlightenment or Classicism, Romanticism, Realism. In the main, these trends predominated within the dates shown. But the trends are never unmixed; and I employ them only as more or less factitious labels for subdivisions of the several growths. The essential facts, from the point of view taken for the present treatment, are the dates of the individuals and the degree of their quality or greatness.

In the larger prospect, it would be venturesome to suppose that small and culturally recent countries like these Scandinavian ones could ordinarily produce fundamentally original trends in literature. Their basic trends, like almost all their forms, are generic European, first crystallized into definiteness in one or another great nationality of the Continent. Essentially all that any Scandinavian, to date at least, has been able to do is to flavor one of these trends or forms with a special national quality. A man born in 1750 inevitably became more or less of a classicist of enlightenment, in 1800 a romanticist, in 1850 a realist, however much he might as a personality swerve from or struggle against the current. That Sweden leans more to the "classic," Denmark to the "romantic," Norway to the "realistic," does not in the least mean that these are deeply ingrained propensities of the three nationalities, but that each moved onto the cultural stage at a time when the prevailing European current is conventionally assigned that epithet.

MODERN SWEDISH LITERATURE

Formative, 1600–1730
   Messenius, 1579–1636.
   Bärgbo (Rosenhane), fl. 1630; sonnets.
  *Stjernhelm, 1598–1672; hexameter.
   Wivallius, 1605–1669.
   Dahlstjerna, 1661–1709; transl. *Pastor Fido;* *1697.
   (Swedenborg, 1688–1772; revelations 1745 seq.)
*"Classical" or "National," 1730–1800/10: Enlightenment, French
      influence, Alexandrines; births 1700–1760*
  *Dalin, 1708–1763.
   Mörk, 1714–1763; first novelist.
   Hedvig Nordenflycht, 1718–1763.
   Gustavus III, born 1746, reigned 1771–1792.
   Creutz, 1731–1785. Finn.
   Gyllenborg, 1731–1808.
  *Bellman, 1740–1795.
   Oxenstjerna, 1750–1808.
  *Kellgren, 1751–1795. Finn.
   Leopold, 1756–1829.
   Lidner, 1758–1793.
   Thorild, 1759–1808.
"Romantic," 1800/10–1860: German influence; births 1760–1820
   Hoijer, 1767–1812.
   Franzén, 1772–1831. Finn.
  *Tegnér, 1782–1846.
   Geijer, 1783–1847.
   Atterbom, 1790–1855.
   Stagnelius, 1793–1823.

Almquist, 1793–1866.
Sjöberg ("Vitalis"), 1794–1828.
Runeberg, 1804–1877. Finn.

Recent, since 1860; prose dominant; births from 1820
Rydberg, 1828.
Snoilsky, 1841.
*Strindberg, 1849.
Geijerstam, 1858.
Selma Lagerlöf, 1858.
Fröding, 1860.
Karlfeldt, 1864.

MODERN DANISH LITERATURE

Formative, to 1750
Arrebo, 1587–1637. "Father of Danish poetry."
Kingo, 1634–1703; father Scotch. Hymns.
*Holberg, 1684–1754; Norwegian. Shaper of literary prose. Plays.
Falster, 1690–1757.
Brorson, 1694–1764. Hymns.

Norwegians writing Danish, 1750–1800; births, 1725–1765
Tullin, 1728–1765.
Bredal, 1733–1778.
Wessel, 1742–1785.
C. Frimann, 1746–1829.
Storm, 1749–1794.
P. H. Frimann, 1752–1839.
Rein, 1760–1821.
Zetlitz, 1761–1821.

"Enlightenment," 1760–1800; births, 1740–1775
*Ewald, 1743–1781.
P. A. Heiberg, 1758–1841.
Rahbek, 1760–1830.
*Baggesen, 1764–1826.
Malte Bruun, 1775–1826.

"Romantic," 1800–1860; births, 1770–1820
Staffeldt, 1769–1826. German.
Steffens, 1773–1845. Norwegian.
Gyllembourg, mother of J. L. Heiberg, 1773–1856.
**Oehlenschlaeger, 1779–1850. Part German.
Blicher, 1782–1848.
*Grundtvig, 1783–1872.
Bredahl, 1784–1860.
*Ingemann, 1789–1862.

Hauch, 1790–1871/2. Norwegian.
*J. L. Heiberg, 1791–1860, son of P. A. Heiberg and Gyllembourg.
*Winther, 1796–1876.
Hertz, 1797–1870. Jewish.
*Andersen, 1805–1875.
*Paludan-Müller, 1809–1876.
*Kierkegaard, 1813–1855, the philosopher.
Goldschmidt, 1819–1887. Jewish.

"Realism," since 1860; births from 1830
Schandorph, 1836.
*Brandes, 1842. Jewish.
*Drachmann, 1846.
Jacobsen, 1847.
Pontoppidan, 1857.
Wied, 1858.
Larsen, 1860.
Jensen, 1873.

Modern Norwegian Literature

Before 1830
(See Denmark.)

Since 1830

Welhaven, b. 1807.	Elster, 1841.
Wergeland, 1808.	Kielland, 1849.
Munch, 1811.	Garborg, 1851.
Asbjörnsen, 1812.	Heiberg, 1857.
Moe, 1813.	Hamsun, 1859.
*Ibsen, 1828.	Bojer, 1872.
*Björnson, 1832.	Undset, 1882.
Lie, 1833.	

§ 88. Polish Literature

Poland possessed two periods of successful literary productivity in its own language, each rather more definitely marked than those of Bohemia. The other Slavic nationalities attained at most one. The two Polish growths differ from each other radically in that the first falls in the time of the nation's greatness, the second during its dismemberment and political extinction.

Until after 1500, apart from a few religious attempts, what literary efforts were made in Poland were in Latin. When a native literature developed about 1550, it followed Italian, not German models, and took on a Renaissance cast. This "golden age" is conventionally dated from 1541 to 1606. It fell toward the end of Poland's national greatness, which, in terms of reigns, can be dated from 1319 to 1572 or 1586. The real national consolidation occurred under Casimir the Great, 1333–1370; the expansion, on the union with Lithuania in 1386. Sigismund I and II, 1506–1572, are known as the Humanist Kings; one of them married a Sforza. With apparent stability and outward success, the political-economic fabric was already deteriorating in their day; but the cultural upswing was late in developing, presumably because Poland's position was marginal to Catholic Europe; and the literary growth does not begin until the second of the Sigismunds and continues after him.

>   Bielski, b. 1495. Calvinist. First native history of Poland.
>   Rej (Rey) of Naglowice, 1505–1569. Protestant. First Polish poet.
>   *Kochanowski, 1530–1584. "Prince of Polish poets."
>   Szarzynski, d. young in 1581. Introduced the sonnet.
>   Klonowicz (Acernus), 1545–1602. *Flis the Boatman.* Also Latin
>   verse.
>   Górnicki, 1527–1591/1603. Adapted Castiglione's *Cortegiano.*
>   Skarga, 1552–1612. Pulpit rhetorician.
>   Szymonowicz (Simonides), 1554/7–1624/9. Pastorals.
>   *Memoirs of a Polish Janissary,* 1601.
>   Also Latin odes, histories, etc.

The "Macaronic Period," 1606–1764, is described as one of stiltedness and absence of originality. It contained no productions of note.

The conventional end date 1764 was quickly followed by the partitions which put an end to the independence of Poland. Literature, however, began to rise somewhat in this period of national collapse. There are a few respectable names, but no great ones. The births fall between 1735 and 1757.

>   Krasicki, 1735–1801.
>   Niemcewicz, 1754–1841.
>   Woronicz, 1757–1829.

The main phase of the modern period of greatness is the product of men born in a thick cluster between 1790 and 1815. Their activity thus began around 1815, when Polish nationalistic hopes had been definitely undone for a century to follow. Here belong Mickiewicz, Slowacki, Krasiński, Kraszewski, and half a dozen others. Many were exiles.

Rzewuski, 1791–1866.	Zaleski, 1802–1886.
Brodziński, 1791–1835.	Grabowski, 1805–1863.
Fredro, 1793–1876.	Gorczyński, 1805–1876.
Malczewski, 1793–1826.	*Slowacki, 1809–1849.
Korzeniowski, 1797–1863.	*Krasiński, 1812–1859.
**Mickiewicz, 1798–1855.	*Kraszewski, 1812–1887.

The closeness of this concentration is succeeded by a quarter century of lull in births. Then follows a smaller cluster, in which only Sienkiewicz is outstanding.

Asnyk, b. 1838.
*Sienkiewicz, 1846.
Maria Konopnicka, 1846.

It is evident that we have here three phases of a growth of well over a century. Its tripartite chronological organization is unusually well marked: a quarter of a century without births of note separates the introductory from the great phase, and another separates this from the aftermath. It is perhaps not unfair to reckon Sienkiewicz in this last. It is true that he has been more widely read abroad than his predecessors, but as a popular novelist whose works were easily translatable, whereas they were rather poets and definitely Polish in preoccupation. But the reason for the gaps between the phases is wholly obscure to me.

Also it is not at all clear why the growth as a whole should have fallen in the period of Polish national failure between 1764 and the World War. It is too long and too early a growth to be accounted for completely as a phenomenon of the post-1830 international spread to the peripheries of Europe. Chronologically it resembles the Russian growth in literature. The great phase of this is marked by births from 1795 to 1830, as against 1790 to 1815 for the Polish. There is also an eighteenth-century initiating phase in Russia, and a rather high-rank epigonal period, signalized by Chekhov and Gorky, born 1860 and 1868, as counterpart of Sienkiewicz, 1846. In view of the geographical contiguity, the time parallelism is almost surely significant. But of what? Certainly not of political fortunes, since Russia's grew steadily for more than two centuries while Poland's declined and vanished. Nor can the reason be attributed with any assurance to the simple, gradual, eastward spread of West European civilization; since Poland had already participated productively in this in the sixteenth century—somewhat superficially and spottily, no doubt, by more advanced Western standards, nevertheless definitely—while Russia was still proceeding on her leisurely semibarbaric way, far from anything like a classical culmination.

It is true that from about 1700 on, Russia, while conscious of her potential strength, also became aware of her backwardness and set herself humbly to learn in the school of Occidental civilization. What she needed was experience and assurance. Poland, on the contrary, from about that time, felt her growing weakness, but both refused to face it and insisted on acting as if culturally she were abreast of western Europe. It required collapse and disillusion before she reversed her course. She had to unlearn her past which had become false. Just because the two nations were neighbors, the failure of the one became also the success of the other. It may therefore be thought strange, though it is not, that in the field of literature they entered upon their upswings almost together, though from opposite antecedents.

I do not press this explanation, because, like most westerners, I am necessarily on unsure ground in understanding Slavic history and culture. Also, the explanation leaves residual problems: such as the growth of a national school of music in Russia but not in Poland. However, whether the suggestion advanced be sound or unsound, it is scarcely credible that the close concordance in time and contiguity in space of the two literary growths should be a nonsignificant coincidence.

§ 89. Russian Literature

Russian literature consists mainly of an effort to learn and apply Western patterns in the eighteenth century, and successful achievement with them, nationally colored, in the nineteenth.

Mediaeval products are of historic rather than aesthetic value: the *Chronicle of Nestor,* the lives of various saints, the *Testament of Vladimir Monomach,* the voyage of the abbot Daniel, the patriotic poetic prose of the *Battalion of Igor* (if authentic), and the *Zadonschina.* The stimulus, of course, was Byzantine. What is remarkable is that there was Russian composition in Slavonic at all, earlier than the West Slavs seem to have attempted writing in vernacular Polish and Czech. After 1100, Constantinople was weak, but Rome strong.

The almost uninterrupted growth after 1300 of Moscow, from a local principality to a vast empire, long had no literary effects. The expansion for centuries was to the north, east, and south. Kiev did not rebecome Russian until 1667; the western Ukraine, not until the Second Partition of 1793. Between Russia and the West, Poland-Lithuania lay as a barrier for 250 years after the establishment of Tsardom. Occidental influences were slow and gradual. Printing was begun in Moscow in 1552 (1562). The first Russian grammar, by Smotritsky, was published in Polish-Lithuanian Vilna in 1618, in Moscow thirty years later. During the same century, Jesuit influence at Polish Kiev tried to introduce syllabic verse, with Latin and Greek, to Moscow. Two interesting symptoms are the Pan-Slavic writings, at Moscow, in a mixture of Russian, Croatian, and Church Slavonic, by the Roman Catholic Serbian Krijanich, about 1650; and the work of Kotoshikhin, who died in 1667, on Russia for westerners.

Under Peter the Great, 1682–1725, westernization became conscious, official, and compulsory. Literarily, however, the immediate effects were slight. Trediakovsky, 1703–1769, and Kantemir, 1708–1744, could do little better than imitate Chapelain and Boileau. The enlightened prelate Prokopovich, 1681–1736, remained in the Old Russian Byzantine-Kievian tradition.

The first positive landmark is Lomonosov, 1711–1765. The son of an Archangel fisherman, he became not only a poet, but an engineer, chemist, and professor of literature, helped create the literary language of Russia out of the Moscow dialect, published its standard grammar in 1755—thirty years after the establishment of the St. Petersburg Academy,—and fixed its prosody.

However, even a great organizing genius—and organization was above all needed in half-civilized Russia—cannot create a great literature at one stroke; and two generations had to elapse before Lomonosov's work bore worthwhile fruit. One after another writer shows the influence of La Fontaine, Voltaire, Gellert, Sterne, or Tibullus—an impartially conflicting enough array; or is notable chiefly as the first head of the theater or literary academy of St. Petersburg. The most important figure, or influence, was Karamzin, 1765–1826, who in his history, novel, and letters helped to free Russian prose.

Realization was attained with the men born from about 1795 on, under the leadership of Pushkin, 1799–1837, followed a decade and a half later by Lermontov, 1814–1841, around whom cluster in time the great novelists Gogol, Goncharov, Turgenev, and Dostoyevsky. Even Tolstoy, 1828, is not much later; and the poets and dramatists Khomiakov, Alexis Tolstoy, Nekrasov, Ostrovsky, and the founder of criticism Bielinsky, were born in the same thirty-three years, 1795 to 1828. These men obviously constituted the florescence of Russian literature, the period of which can thus be set as from about 1820 to 1890.

The early poets Ryleyev, Griboyedov, Pushkin, Koltsov, Lermontov were a short-lived lot—their average was only thirty-three years, and most of them met a violent death: one assassinated, one executed, the two greatest killed in duels. The five great novelists averaged only fifteen years later in their births, but managed to live more than thirty years longer, or to a mean of sixty-five. It is a commonplace that poets can die young and

still be great, but prose writers mostly season gradually and
therefore need to attain middle age. Here is an instance, then,
of the accentuation of a slight chronological priority of verse
over novel by the varying duration of lifetimes.

The two outsanding figures since the culmination, at least
in Western repute, are Chekhov, 1860–1891, and Gorky, 1868–
1936. Although Chekhov's work overlaps that of Tolstoy, and
he died earlier, he and Gorky are separated from Tolstoy by a
generation, and from Pushkin by two. They must therefore be
regarded as epigones of the great period; especially so because
they in turn have had no peers in the generation that followed
them.

With all its distinctive flavor, Russian literature is, like
Polish, also the child of the nineteenth century: romantic and
vehement, then realistic and disillusioned. In short, it is part
of an international advance or movement. Nevertheless, its
integral value and duration, its long formative period and attainment of florescence before 1830, stamp it as no mere echo
from an outer hall, but as a genuinely national growth. It was
foreign-induced, especially in its conscious aspects, but became Russian in its expression. Its historic configuration was
evidently essentially concluded before the World War and
Revolution.

The parallelism in time to Polish modern literature has
already been discussed.

Russian Literature

Initial stage, formative of the language medium
>   Trediakovsky, 1703–1769.
>   *Lomonosov, 1711–1765. From Archangelsk.
>   Sumarokov, 1718–1777.

Imitative developmental phase, to 1820
>   Novikov, 1744–1818.
>   Radishev, 1749–1802.
>   *Karamzin, 1765–1826, b. near Simbirsk.
>   Krylov, 1768–1844.
>   Zhukovsky, 1783–1852.

Principal period, 1820–1880/90
>   Ryleyev, 1795–1826.

Griboyedov, 1795–1829, b. Moscow.
Delwig, 1798–1831.
*Pushkin, 1799–1837, b. Moscow.
Baratinsky, 1800–1844.
Tiuchev, 1803–1873.
Koltsov, 1809–1842.
Gogol, 1809–1852, b. Poltava.
Bielinsky, 1811–1848. Founder of criticism.
Goncharov, 1812–1891/4, b. Simbirsk.
*Lermontov, 1814–1841, b. Tula.
A. Tolstoy, 1817–1875.
*Turgenev, 1818–1883, b. Orel.
Polonsky, 1820–1898.
Pisemsky, 1820–1881.
*Dostoyevsky, 1821–1881, b. Moscow.
Maikov, 1821–1897.
Nekrasov, 1821–1876/7, b. Podolia; half Pole.
Ostrovsky, 1823–1886.
Saltykov, 1826–1889.
*Tolstoy, 1828–1910, b. Tula.
Chernishevsky, 1828–1889.

Decline, from 1880/90; births all after 1830, mainly after 1850
Lieskov, b. 1831.
Dobroliubov, 1836.
G. Uspensky, 1840.
Pisarev, 1840/41.
Korolenko, 1853.
Garshin, 1855.
*Chekhov, 1860.
Nadso(h)n, 1862. Jewish.
Sologub, 1863.
Merezhkovsky, 1865.
*Gorky, 1868.
Bunin, 1870.
Andreyev, 1871.
Artsybashev, 1878.

§ 90. American English Literature

English literature of quality produced in the United States begins about 1800 and has passed its zenith by 1870. The culmination is quite visibly between 1840 and 1860. Since then a long lifetime has passed, or two full generations, as they are reckoned here. It is thus clear that the recent failure of America to produce any very notable literature is not due to retarded cultural growth of the country: a peak of higher performance already lies well behind us.

Being in the same language, the literatures of England and America should expectably show a time relation; and they do. The whole American growth falls within the compass of the modern English one. On the whole, it corresponds in time to the second main phase of the British modern movement, the Tennysonian rather than the Byronian. In fact, most of the more eminent Americans were born in the decade and a half between 1795 and 1810, when British births were few as compared with the years before and after.

With the exception of Bryant, whose best poem was written at seventeen, most the Americans came into their full powers rather slowly: rarely before thirty, often much later. Emerson, Hawthorne, Whittier, Holmes reached their zenith only in their fifth decade. This may be a result of the lack in the diffuse American cultural setup of any mechanism for facilitating early forcing of talent, comparable to the class schools and groups of England.

The range of the contemporary British and American literatures is quite similar: lyric and narrative poetry, novel and belletristic prose, but no drama of moment. There is probably a somewhat more outright didactic flavor to the American output as a whole. Attempts at new forms are not wholly lacking: Poe with the lyrical short story, Whitman with his broken-down poetry, even Longfellow's Kalevala meter. Incidentally, the first two of these are the ones who have earned the most attention in Europe, both in England and on the Continent—besides of course the perennial boys' vogue of Cooper's Indian novels.

That we are dealing with a genuine national expression, which was felt as such, is clear from the fact that there is not a single born Britisher in the American list, nor any American who transplanted himself to England until Henry James in

1869. This is not true of all American cultural activities. It will be recalled that early American painters went to England, and then there followed a period of British painters in the United States; and the same tendency is observable in science.

The American growth is traditionally associated with New England, especially with the environs of Boston. This is correct for the period of concentration, 1840–1860, births 1800–1820. The two principal exceptions are Poe and Whitman. As these are also the two personalities that from an international point of view are considered the most original—as well as imperfect in execution,—it follows that the best "normal" American literature was almost wholly a New England product, with its focus in Boston.

Rather remarkably, however, the first American pulse was associated with New York City. Irving was born there; Cooper in near-by New Jersey, but reared at Cooperstown in upstate New York; Bryant was from Massachusetts, but spent the last fifty years of his life in the metropolis. Several lesser contemporaries either lived or were born there. Toward the end of the second or culminating phase, New York produced Whitman and Melville. Post-Revolutionary New York grew with extreme rapidity in wealth and population. But if this fact accounted for the burst, it is obscure why within thirty years leadership in literature passed back to the older tradition and culture of New England while this was slipping back in relative importance in general national activity.

Philadelphia and the South can claim but a pair of names each, and these only of second rank at best, even by American standards: Brockden Brown and Bayard Taylor, and Simms and Lanier. Poe cannot be provincially assigned. He was born in Boston of a Baltimorean actor father and English actress mother, schooled in Virginia and England, and spent six years of his manhood in Baltimore and Richmond, six in Philadelphia, six in New York. It is only possible to say that he was not of New England.

The trans-Appalachian land emerges with Mark Twain, born 1835 in Missouri, and Howells 1837 in Ohio. If the whole growth had not been by then well on the decline, the West would undoubtedly have shown a more prominent absolute participation.

Rise: 1800–1840; births 1770–1800
    Brockden Brown, 1771, Philadelphia; *1798–1804.
    Daniel Webster, 1782, New Hampshire; *1820–1843.
    *Irving, 1783, New York City; *1809–1820.
    *Cooper, 1789, New Jersey, 1790 to Cooperstown, N. Y.; *1821–1828 (–1841).
    Halleck, 1790, Connecticut; to New York City.
    *Bryant, 1794, Massachusetts, to New York City 1825; *1811.
    Drake, 1795, New York City.

Culmination: 1840–1860; births ca. 1800–1825
    Prescott, 1796, Massachusetts; *1843.
    *Emerson, 1803, Massachusetts; *1841–1844.
    Simms, 1806, South Carolina.
    *Longfellow, 1807, Maine; *1839–1858.
    *Whittier, 1807, Massachusetts; *1854.
    *Holmes, 1809, Massachusetts; *1858.
    *Poe, 1809 (see text: 1831–1837 in the South, 1838–1844 in Philadelphia, 1837–1838, 1844–1849 in New York City); *1838–1849.
    Margaret Fuller (Ossoli), 1810, Massachusetts.
    Harriet Beecher Stowe, 1812, Connecticut; *1851.
    Motley, 1814, Massachusetts; *1856–1860.
    Dana, 1815, Massachusetts; *1840.
    Thoreau, 1817, Massachusetts; *1854.
    Lowell, 1819, Massachusetts.
    Melville, 1819, New York City; *1851.
    *Whitman, 1819, Long Island near New York City; *1855.
    Mitchell (Ik Marvel), 1822, Connecticut; *1850–1851.
    Parkman, 1823, Massachusetts; *1849–1869.

Decline: 1860——; births 1825–1850
    Bayard Taylor, 1825, Pennsylvania; *1870.
    Emily Dickinson, 1830, Amherst, Massachusetts.
    Clemens (Mark Twain), 1835, Missouri; *1876–1884.
    Aldrich, 1836, New Hampshire.
    Howells, 1837, Ohio.
    Harte, 1839, Albany, N. Y.
    Sill, 1841, Connecticut.
    James, 1843, New York City. Grandfather from Ireland, father from Syracuse, N. Y.
    Lanier, 1849, Georgia.

§ 91. European Literature as a Whole

Since western Europe has a single civilization underlying its manifold national manifestations, its literature should also be examined as a whole.

In such a broader perspective we must first of all set apart the Norse-Viking myth and saga literature as a growth separate from all the others. It culminates around 1000, and is essentially over before the other European literatures really stir. It is also geographically marginal: in fact, its peak was reached off the European continent, in Iceland halfway across the Atlantic. It is also the only European literature emanating from a non-Christian people,[15] and the only one uninfluenced by ancient Mediterranean tradition. Its themes are wholly indigenous, and so are its forms: it ignores syllabic measure and rhyme, and considers stresses and initial alliteration. It is "Occidental" merely in geography, and in some subject stimuli which it has imparted to a few Christian literatures. It is nearly as separate a growth from European literature as Sanskrit or Chinese are, and less related than Helleno-Latin or perhaps even Arabic.

Occidental literatures proper begin about 1050 or 1100 with two parallel but related developments, in *langue d'oc* and *langue d'oïl,* in central-southern and northern France. Both probably culminated within a decade or two of 1170, or about contemporaneously; but the southern French growth confined its endeavors to a narrower range, achieved formal mastery and artifice more quickly, and died earlier.

The example of these two French literatures spread to Italy and Spain on the south, to the Netherlands and Germany on the northeast. The Germans were the most rapid followers; the Italians, the latest and greatest. The German zenith was passed by 1225. The Italian growth did not begin to move suc-

---

[15] This does not necessarily contradict the suggestion made above that this pagan poetry conceivably reached its climax as a result of pressure impinging on its native ideology from the encroaching Christian world.

cessfully until 1275, and culminated, for Italy and for all mediaeval Europe, with Dante in the decades immediately after
1300. The Netherlandish and Spanish growths were much
more diffuse, only partly renationalized, and produced neither
a concentrated nor a great configuration. When the Italian
growth ended, about 1375, mediaeval literature was essentially
over.

Now comes an interlude, around 1400, when no continental
European country was producing superior literature. The one
exception was England with its Chaucerian burst, the French
and Italian borrowings of which show it to have been a belated
mediaeval bloom from across the Channel. Between 1375 and
1450 Chaucer was the sole important European poet or writer.
This late mediaeval slump has its counterpart in philosophy,
architecture, and sculpture.

Around 1450, a second phase of European literatures was
initiated—in Italy, which had closed the preceding phase. This
was part of the Renaissance movement, and its influences persisted until 1680/1700. In spite of its priority and dominance,
the literature of Italy of this period did not equal its mediaeval
one: it produced no Dante, nor even a Petrarch. The duration
was 130 years with Tasso—a somewhat belated aftermath—
included; only 90 without him.

Portugal, Spain, Poland, England, Holland followed Italy
in that order: 1490, 1500, 1530, 1575, 1575. France began to
follow about 1520, experimented, stopped around 1600, evidently because the Italian manner proved uncongenial, and
resumed, in more native form and with much greater success,
about 1630. Germany did not respond at all with creative
productivity. All the nations undergoing Italian influence
achieved styles of their own which increasingly diverged from
the Italian models. Hence the culminations were late: between
1600 and 1660 in Spain, England, Holland, and France. The
peaks before 1600 were, singularly enough, attained in remote
Portugal and Poland. The reason must be that these were
smaller nations with quantitatively lesser growths, whose
course was run sooner. That the greater climaxes fell after

1600 is significant in that the initiating Italian growth began by 1450, and was over, except for Tasso, by 1540. The reason for the retardation is almost certainly that each receiving literature had to rework its Italian stimuli into consonance with national tastes and its own language.

Around 1670–1700 the induced literature of the four greater nations—Spain, France, England, Holland—ended abruptly and almost simultaneously. We have seen the same sort of sudden termination occurring in the same countries—and in all Europe—at the same period, in painting, music, and science, to be followed by a lull. The "Renaissance-Baroque" terminated in 1680 or 1700.

This fact is curious: Mediaeval literature was initiated in France and reached its highest European culmination in Italy, the last country to participate in the mediaeval poetical growth.[16] In the Renaissance phase, this same Italy was the initiator and influencer, but attained lesser heights than in the Middle Ages; whereas Portugal, Spain, France, Netherlands, and England, which now depended on Italy, all reached higher peaks of literature than before. It seems as if, within the multinational arena of Europe, the pioneer nation that first evolved a new set of poetical patterns was thereby prevented from carrying them to their highest expression.

The second pan-European lull is the first half of the eighteenth century, the beginning of the time of "Enlightenment," of lucid, effective, easy, and polished prose, and of no poetry of consequence anywhere on the Continent.

Around 1750 begins the third Occidental growth of literature. This is both Romantic and Enlightened at first, Realistic—and turgidly emotional—later. It begins actually somewhat before 1750 in peripheral and long-quiescent Italy and Sweden; sets in with fuller force just at 1750 in Germany which has been unproductive for a half millennium; passes on successively to England and France; and spreads to a series of countries uninvolved before: Denmark, Russia, the United States, Norway; with revivals of some sort also in Spain, Holland, Poland. By

---

[16] Except belated England across the Channel,

1860 the zenith has been passed everywhere except in Norway. By 1900 there is no Western nation whose literature has not admittedly declined from its state in 1800, 1830, or 1870. And of course the generation since 1900 has shown only increasing disintegration of patterns.[17]

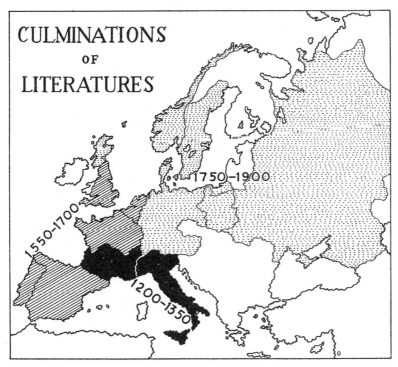

OCCIDENTAL LITERATURES: CULMINATION PERIODS

Which are the literatures that attained the highest levels in their own total histories in the first half of the nineteenth century—between 1780 and 1880, to be more exact? The list is illuminating: Germany; the three Scandinavian nations; two Slavic ones, Poland and Russia; and English-speaking America across the sea. All are peripheral to the previous centerings of Occidental development.

---

[17] The disintegration appears to have proceeded most slowly in Spain and Italy, where the Romantic pulse had beat most weakly.

The little map on the preceding page shows clearly the centrifugal wandering of national climaxings in the three grand periods of Occidental literature.

The greatest Mediaeval figure, by common consent, is Dante; the greatest of Renaissance-Early Modern times, Shakespeare, with Cervantes and Molière as competitors; of the Later Modern period, Goethe. The crown goes first to Romance Italy; next is more or less in balance between Romance Spain and France and Germanic England; and finally rests in German territory.

The period summary is:

1900–	Interval.
1750–1900	3. Later Modern ("Romantic-Realistic").
1700–1750	Interval: "Enlightenment," continuing into next pulse.
1450–1700	2. Early Modern ("Renaissance-Baroque").
1375–1450	Interval: Late Mediaeval widening of interests, continuing into next pulse.
1075–1375	1. High Mediaeval (in England to 1415).
–1075	Formative, unproductive.

The durations of the three active pulses successively decrease: 300, 250, 150 years, in round numbers.

§ 92. Historical Summary

By including the products of the Middle and New periods in Egypt, we can carry the analyzable history of literature back about four thousand years in the aggregate.

For the first of these four millennia, the story is mainly that of Egypt, but too imperfectly dated to be segregable with surety. The surviving products also are, or seem to us, deficient in passion, and relatively formless. It is remarkable that they are mainly in prose. Early Semitic literature of Mesopotamia, and the somewhat later one of Palestine, also appear lacking in close patterns, except for the poetic balanced parallel which is of substance as much as of form. Both these literatures, so far as we know them, seem less extricated from religious functioning than the Egyptian.

Probably next to emerge was the poetry of the Greeks, soon after Egyptian literature atrophied into repetition. It may or may not have had some roots in the Aegean-Minoan civilization that preceded it on the same soil. This older language is unknown; whether it carried a literature is wholly problematical. Early Greek poetry, the Epic or Homeric, constitutes a separate pulse in the entire Greek growth. It remained a living, influential factor in Hellenic culture to the end; but Epic productivity faded as general Greek literature arose. It did determine very sharply a formal pattern out of which all other Greek forms developed. The Homeric poetry grew in isolation: there were no worthwhile architecture, sculpture, painting, science, or philosophy at the time. On the other hand, Classic Greek literature was almost exactly contemporary with florescences in these fields. Also, it diversified into lyric, dramatic, historic, and other prose activities. Its duration of production was five centuries; its florescence lasted for three. After two hundred and fifty years of comparative aridity, there was a much feebler revival, mainly in prose; and after another lapse, a second, in which poetry—especially the epic!—tried to resuscitate itself.

Latin literature, of course, is historically only an adaptation of Greek literature to another language vehicle, although it is a remarkably successful adaptation. Its main growth was fairly brief, although broken into three definite pulses. These fit in time exactly, except for part of the formative stage, into the arid quarter-millennium Greek interval, thus further evidencing the singleness of root of the growths in the two languages.

In the East, Chinese literature can be traced back to nearly as early a date as Greek—technically perhaps farther, if we are ready to give serious weight to some poems and passages attributed to pre-Chou times. The salient characteristic of the history of Chinese literature is that it both is nearly continuous for more than two thousand years and yet shows well-marked pulses. One genre replaces the other, but at least one is almost always flourishing, so that total gaps are few and relatively brief. The most evident intervals center somewhere about 550 B.C., 50 A.D., 950 A.D. Lyric and reflective poetry flourished twice in the pre-Christian periods; and again—in two styles, though these flowed into each other in time—for the long span from 150 to 900, with a recognized culmination at 750. Epic or narrative poetry is lacking; the drama and novel came late, from 1200 to 1700, and were composed in vernaculars not admitted into the accepted literature.

Japanese literature shows a similar succession of genres: poetry, novel, historic romance, drama, overlapping into a continuum much as in China. A genre sometimes continues a long time, but it usually develops and culminates quickly. The difference between these two Far Eastern literatures and the Greek is quite marked. The Greek peaks, with the exception of the Epic one, were all concentrated within three hundred years, and essentially simultaneous; the Japanese kept evolving new climaxes in new types for a thousand years, and the Chinese, for more than two thousand. Moreover, two climaxes in the Far East almost never coincided in time. The Indian, Near Eastern, and Occidental literatures on the whole developed more nearly on the Greek pattern. While the distinction is not absolute, it is marked enough to seem significant. Its best explanation seems to be the long-continued relative isolation of the Far Eastern cultures, at any rate so far as competitive impingements and shocks are concerned.

The relation of Japanese to Chinese literature is curious and far from simple; owing probably to the fact that what influence there was flowed one way only, but met with varying resistances and transformations in Japanese institutions and speech. The order in which the several genres developed is therefore by no means the same in the two countries. In fact, in two forms of prose narrative, the historical romance or romantically treated history and the novel of manners or psychology, the Japanese climaxes are the earlier. For the former, it is possible that the Japanese product was preceded by Chinese output which remained below the surface of literary history and survives only in forms made over later. However, even in that case the later forms were no doubt superior in China; so that the climax remains earlier in Japan. For the novel of manners the Japanese precedence is indubitable by five hundred years. The Japanese simply forced each of their growths quickly, the Chinese worked on them slowly. T'ang poetry was six continuous centuries reaching its climax, after two poetic florescences in previous ages. Japanese Nara poetry culminated within four hundred years after writing was first introduced.

In both classical poetry and drama the Japanese peaks follow very soon on the Chinese. There was no direct imitation—the patterns that were assumed in the two countries are too diverse for this to have happened.[18] Yet a stimulus influence seems indicated, as has been discussed under Japanese Drama.

The long Japanese development began earlier than anything in western Europe; the first climax was reached by 800.

Sanskrit literature is like Greek in showing a homogenous, concurrent growth; though a very much slower one, as in other fields of civilization. Also like the Greek is its beginning with its national or popular epics in a preliminary pulse, separate from the rest of the development. Among both peoples the final poetical forms were not achieved by the epics. In India, syllabic quantity was still lacking in the epic. In Greece, the epic had quantity, but in only one meter as against many later on. Lyric, drama, narrative poetry, and prose culminated close together in India as in Greece. Sanskrit literature, however, trailed off for seven or eight centuries after its peak, Hellenic for at most three. Sanskrit, over most of the period of its active literature, was a learned language. Vernacular Indian literature, in Hindi and other spoken dialects, began to flourish, or at least to be recognized as literature, about the time genuine productivity in Sanskrit came to an end. The two growths are therefore really one, in somewhat different media—like the Chinese drama and novel in the nonclassical style following after classical literature. This continuity is substantiated by the fact that while the Indian vernacular languages added rhyme, they kept the syllable-length meters of Sanskrit. The vernacu-

---

[18] Chinese T'ang verse rhymed and tonal, the Japanese language nontonal and ill-adapted for rhyme. Yet there are the common features of rigorous syllabic count, overwhelmingly of 5 or 7 syllables, great tonal brevity—as discussed in §70 (pp. 458–460).

lar poetry originated and grew in northern India in times of foreign conquest and domination and culminated under the early Mongol-Turk Mohammedan rulers.

Next in order of time of beginning we have Arabic literature. This is characterized by a paucity of genres, a combination of narrowness of range with high development of medium, and a lack of sharp historic climax. The peak could be or has been set almost anywhere within five centuries; which means that there can hardly be a very definite one. The known beginning is around 500 A.D., just when Greek poetry had attempted its last renaissance in adjacent Egypt and Syria. Moreover, the earliest Arabic meters known are already quantitative, as in Greece. Are we to think of a connection? It seems a far cry between Nonnus and Musaeus looking back to Homer, and the Bedouin Imru'ulqays with his vehement *qasidas*. But can we disregard the contiguity of geography, period, and metrical device as wholly nonsignificant coincidences?[19]

Western Arabic literature in Spain and Morocco was brief and not of prime importance. Essentially its course was run during the definite decline of Eastern Arabic; of which it may be regarded as a local variant. Its new features centered around strophic forms analogous to those arising in the Christian West about the same time.

The most remarkable feature of Persian literature is its entire dependence on Arabic. It took over its themes, genres, metrical principles from conquerors speaking a fundamentally different language and imposing an undesired religion. It commenced just as Arabic literature was definitely declining; and, like it, flourished for several hundred years without any clear peak. Evidently the Iranians had been unable in more than a millennium of intimate contacts with the peoples on their west, and of frequent rule over them, to achieve an important literature of their own; whereas the Islamic conquest within three centuries precipitated them into one, perhaps as a nationalistic compensation. They did give their poetry a somewhat wider range than the Arabic by adding epic and narrative verse. Per-

---

[19] See §76 (p. 519), esp. footnote 6.

sian literature got going something like two centuries before any Christian vernacular literature of moment.

The native Germanic literatures have their own subjects and their own forms: accentual stress and alliteration as the expression of verse. They must therefore be regarded as an independent growth. Most of this literature has perished. Except for some Old English and Old German remnants, enough to show the basic alikeness of all the pre-Christian Germanic verse, it is represented by the Viking-Icelandic Edda around 1000. This flowering is of narrative themes utilized lyrically or semidramatically with a conscious inner and outer technique. The time of this peripheral peak is that of the falling off of Arabic and rise of Persian poetry, and just before any of the Christian cultures of Europe had evolved anything comparable in literary skill and intensity. The growth was evidently choked by the import of Christianity which remade the civilization. Whether or not the literary growth would in continued isolation have produced much more seems doubtful, in view of the possibility that the Norse cultural florescence as a whole may itself be a stimulation phenomenon due to the pressure of this same Christian-Occidental culture.

The unique characteristic of the non-Norse literatures of the West is their multilingual character, in spite of their constituting a single international growth as evidenced by overwhelming resemblances in metrical form, genre, and themes. This similarity is really remarkable in view of the fact that a literature is necessarily expressed in a nontransferable language medium. It is therefore significant that the relation of the several national strands in Occidental literature is parallel to that of the same strands in other aesthetic and intellectual departments of culture, into which language does not enter seriously as a barrier. The only similar happenings elsewhere in the history of literature are the transfers from Greek to Latin and from Arabic to Persian. And there the later growths arose as the earlier declined. These, accordingly, are instances of transfer, but the West European one an instance of continued interaction.

At the same time, the historic configuration of the several national growths in the West is by no means uniform. France begins, Italy climaxes the Mediaeval phase, Germany definitely participates in it, England scarcely and late. Italy opens the Renaissance pulse, Spain and England carry it farther, France joins late, Germany not at all, so far as products of value are concerned. The sole common-European phenomenon is two fallings-off of poetical productivity in the early fifteenth and early eighteenth centuries. From these, no European people escapes; nor from the decline now in progress. The whole picture is amazingly intricate and yet amazingly ordered as a total configuration. We have noted this before, in other domains; but it is striking to see it repeated in a field of culture so dependent on the ethnically diversifying medium of language as is poetry.

The three main pulses of Western literature—the Mediaeval, Renaissance, and Modern—differ among themselves in configuration. The Mediaeval was the longest and the slowest to develop. The peak comes near the end. The Renaissance phase was somewhat briefer and culminated near the middle of its duration. The Modern phase was considerably the shortest, climaxed early, then diffused and diluted.

Prospect

I have reserved to the last a pair of questions relating to the present which tend to involve attempts to forecast the future. We have determined a decline as occurring in the literature of every country in Occidental civilization since 1860. Inasmuch as this same civilization is destroying or radically transforming every other culture, and thus either terminating or rechanneling its native growth, the dearth in the Occident means that there is a dearth of great literature in the whole world.

First of all, has this happened before? There are no very clear-cut instances, but there are approximations.

1. Around 1000 B.C., by actual records, Egypt had definitely declined; Mesopotamia was probably in a sag; Greece and

China had not yet begun to produce "literature," though we know little about this period in their history.

2. The second century after Christ shows Latin literature over, Greek in a very pallid revival, Sanskrit active in a formative way preparatory to its great growth, Chinese actually starting its greatest development about the middle of the century. There is nothing of the first order in the period, but scarcely a universal absence of quality.

3. The mid-eighteenth century just escapes being an interval. There are only four literatures at all active. Of these the Chinese and Indian are on the ebb, the Japanese is just closing its great phase of novel and drama, the Occident has been quiescent for half a century. However, just as we must set the end of the Japanese pulse at 1750, we must allow the same date for the opening of the great burst of German literature and therewith of the Romantic-Modern phase of Occidental. We have here, then, an abutment rather than a lapse.

In contrast, the present shows the peak definitely passed everywhere by 1860, in many literatures well before; a fair level of quality maintained among some marginal and minor European literatures until 1900; and nothing of first or even second magnitude anywhere since. Moreover, the evidences of disintegration of patterns, even of pride in their destruction, are multiform and obvious.

The second question then arises: Is the contemporary lack of higher literary quality a transient phenomenon, or a symptom of the general breakdown of the one civilization which has become universally dominant by stifling all competitors?

I do not wish to prophesy, and give no categorical verdict. In another twenty-five years the answer may be plainer. Since about 1830 there have been no births of very great writers. By allowing the inclusion of some that approximate greatness, we may stretch the date to about 1860. The majority of writers born since 1930 will come into their essential powers by 1960. If the literature being produced then is still at the present level, and continues to show no signs of successful integration of forms, there will have been an interval of seventy-five to a

hundred years of no significant births or significant productions respectively. In that event we may more justifiably face
the possibility of a long hard winter ahead.

On the other hand, the actual interval so far elapsed is,
according as one reckons less or more pessimistically, from
thirty-five to seventy-five years. And such a pause Europe has
experienced twice—around 1420 and 1720—and resumed with
a new swing thereafter. These precedents are no evidence that
the contemporary depression will end after the same number
of years. They do suggest that possibility; it may or may not
be realized.

It is true that 1420 had just produced Chaucer, if we count
England as already part of Europe, and 1720 had Voltaire, and
that the present shows no equivalent phenomenon. It is also
true that modern painting, sculpture, music, philosophy are
evincing disintegration symptoms quite parallel to those of
literature—only science and wealth-production probably are
still holding up their heads. In 1420 the Renaissance was in
full growth in Italy, except only in literature; and in 1720
philosophy and music, at least, were flourishing in northern
Europe.

On the other side, contemporary civilization still has science;
and until this becomes sterile and our wealth shrinks—in other
words, while we still have active ingredients in our culture,—it
would be rash to predict the impending death of this. Historical precedent should be well-nigh unanimous before it is accepted as a basis for prediction; and it rarely is overwhelming.

The alternatives seem still more or less in balance. Even another quarter century may not bring decision. But at least by
then the outcome—say for the hundred years ahead—may be
probable.

In the last analysis, questions such as these must be examined
with reference to all strands that make up a culture. When all
of them have withered and shrunk, we can legitimately speak
of the end of a civilization, of a type of culture. The date 600
A.D. in Europe marked such a death. If we are approaching
such another death, as conceivably we are, it is still far too

early to affirm it. The vats of our own and other civilizations have at times run turbid before now without a final descent to the dregs.

Finally, if we view the whole of human culture as distinct from its Occidental form, to which we belong, nothing at all can be predicted with any show of reason. It is true that the civilizations of Islam, India, China, Japan seem definitely ended in their historic forms. But who can tell whether after an interval wholly new cultures, rooting both in these old ones and in the Occidental one, may not spring up as independent growths, on old soil? We do have the precedent of Italy partaking in Classic Mediterranean civilization, and a millennium and a half later participating actively in Occidental culture and leading it. Also there is Mesopotamia, a full millennium after its native culture was superseded, harboring the flowering of Islam. There simply is no precedent for the contemporary situation of one culture growth crushing all others out of existence; and hence no basis for any prediction.

Chapter IX

MUSIC

Chapter IX

MUSIC

§93. European Music

USIC has the advantage for this study of being a pure art. Architecture is involved in the practical needs which nearly all edifices serve, and in mechanical problems. Literature fades out into prose speech and inevitably roots in language and nationality. Music, however, might logically be international as easily as national; and there is, too, no *a priori* reason why it should not be timeless. On the contrary, it is produced in phases, and these are about as sharply localized in space as other cultural activities.

It is necessary to limit inquiry to the music of Modern Europe. The ancient data are too scant. As for both ancient Greek and all non-European musics, perhaps no Occidental of today could really distinguish better and worse, or at least good and best. Even Mediaeval music is almost too remote for judgment of aesthetic quality; and it will be touched on only as an antecedent of Modern. The period actually to be covered is thus only of about five hundred years' duration.

Also, reference will be wholly to the composition of music, not to its execution; and to written music, exclusive of folk song—a limitation obviously necessary for precision of data.

§94. Netherlandish Music

European music is generally traced back to North French sources in the twelfth and thirteenth centuries. We know more of the musical teaching or theory of those days than of the music itself. But the two were probably closely associated, and it can be inferred that composition and execution flourished in Paris, northern France, and adjacent regions from England to the lower Rhine.

About 1350 or soon afterward, this growth was replaced by one in the southwestern Netherlands, corresponding more or less to the modern Belgium. By some this is called the First Netherlands, by others the Gallo-Belgic school. It seems to have been more Netherlandish than French, but evidently was a precursor of the main Netherlands movement which began about 1450 with Okeghem.

The principal names in these early developments are:

Mediaeval French school, ca. 1100–1350
Leoninus, before Perotinus.
Perotinus, 12th cent. in Paris.
De Garlandia, French, fl. ca. 1210–1232.
Petrus de Cruce, born at Amiens, 13th cent.
Franco of Paris, 13th cent., after De Cruce.
Franco of Cologne, perhaps a younger contemporary.
De Vitry, 13th–14th cent.
De Machault, ca. 1284–1369+, b. near Rethel, Champagne.
De Muris, born in Normandy; at Paris; fl. 1321 seq.
Tunstede, Englishman, d. 1369.

First Netherlands or "Gallo-Belgic" school, ca. 1350 (1400)–1450
Dufay, born at Chimay in Hainault, fl. 1380?, d. 1432.
Binchois, b. Bins in Hainault, ca. 1400.
Dunstable, Englishman, 1390–1453/8, contemporary of Dufay and Binchois.
Faugues, 15th cent., Netherlander.
Busnois, Netherlander, fl. 1467, d. 1481.
Regis, Belgian, contemporary of last.

Within the principal Netherlandish movement, ca. 1450–1600, four stages are recognized, headed successively by Okeghem, 1460;[1] Josquin Deprès, 1480; Willaert, 1520; Lasso, 1550. Opinion seems to differ upon which of the last three marks the culmination. Lasso died in 1594—the same year as Palestrina;—most of his associates, soon after. There is thus justification for the assignment of 1600 or a decade or so afterward as the date of expiration of the school.

It appears that Walloons and Flemings contributed about

---

[1] I assume that a composer begins to attain his full capacity, on the average, at the age of thirty, and rarely maintains it beyond fifty or sixty. Where only one date is given, accordingly, it is the nearest third decade after his birth.

equally to this movement, for which the name Belgian is therefore not inappropriate; but that Holland had no active part in
it. Individual Dutchmen who participated were drawn into the
Belgian current, as in painting, sculpture, and architecture.

That this growth was for its time the dominant one in
Europe is shown by its influence on English, German, and
Italian music. That it had freed itself from its French origin
and become truly national is evident from the fact that it sent
musicians to France. Deprès was choirmaster to Louis XII,
Mouton to Francis I. The English school beginning with the
middle of the sixteenth century was under Netherlandish influence; so was the German, from the early part of the same
century, and again that following Sweelinck after 1600. Dufay,
died 1432, already went to Rome. Willaert "founded the
Venetian school" in 1527, and Van Rore was his successor at
St. Mark's. Some prefer to look upon the Venetian school as
Belgian rather than Italian. Even the Roman school was influenced: Palestrina was a pupil of Goudimel.

Phase 1
    *Okeghem, 1415/30?–1512/27; b. Termonde.
    Hobrecht, ca. 1430–ca. 1506; b. Utrecht.
    Tinctor (Baerwere) ca. 1446–1511; b. Poperinghe.
    Brumel, Netherlander, pupil of Okeghem.
    Compère, Netherlander, d. 1518 at St. Quentin.

Phase 2
    *Josquin Deprès or des Près, ca. 1450–1521?; b. Hainault (or
        Cambrai?).
    Agricola, 1446?–1506?, Belgian, pupil of Okeghem.
    Mouton, d. 1522; b. near Metz? Pupil of Deprès, teacher of
        Willaert.

Phase 3
    *Willaert, ca. 1480–1562, b. Bruges. Pupil of Mouton. 1527 to
        Venice.
    *Goudimel, ca. 1500–1572, b. near Avignon, 1535 to Rome, teacher
        of Palestrina and Nanini.
    Gombert, fl. 1530–1543; b. Bruges.
    Arcadelt, Netherlander, 1536 to Rome, fl. 1536–1557.
    Van Rore, 1516–1565, b. Malines, pupil and successor of Willaert
        in Venice.

Phase 4
  *Lasso or De Lattre, 1520–1594; b. Mons, Hainault; 1532 to Italy,
    1548–1557 at Antwerp, d. Munich.
  De Monte, 1521–1603; b. Mons (or Malines).
  Pevernage, 1543–1591; b. Courtray, d. Antwerp.
  Waelrant, 1517–1595; b. Tongerloo in Brabant, d. Antwerp;
    pupil of Willaert.
  Claude LeJeune or Claudin, French, fl. 1585–1610.
  Sweelinck, ca. 1560–1621; b. Deventer, Holland, d. Amsterdam.
    Teacher of Germans.

The phases of the Netherlandish development are sometimes
differently given. Riemann's *Lexicon,* for instance, recognizes
three: 1400–1450 (Dufay, etc.—the "Gallo-Belgic" school
above); 1450–1525 (Okeghem, Deprès, phases 1 and 2 above);
1525–1600 (Willaert, Goudimel, Lasso, with Palestrina, etc.).
The interrelations of the subschools are complicated, to much
the same degree as the minor schools of Italian Renaissance
painting.

What is much clearer is the general configuration of development. In this, the first stage is a genuinely Mediaeval and
genuinely French one, which ended about 1350. Performers,
composers, and theoretical writers were predominantly North
French; the growth centered in Paris. It was under way in the
twelfth century, and culminated in or soon after the end of the
thirteenth—the great era of Mediaeval France. About 1350 or
1400 the center of gravity of musical production shifted, with
the prevalence of counterpoint over discant, to the Belgian
Netherlands. Some Frenchmen continued to participate, as
did occasional Burgundians and Hollanders; but their relation
to the Netherlanders was like that of the occasional Germans
and Englishmen to the French themselves in the mediaeval
centuries. The most significant Frenchman was Goudimel,
from Avignon in the south, and his primary significance lies
in stimulating the Roman school of Palestrina. Until about
1525 the Netherlanders chiefly influenced their nearer neighbors; after 1525, Italy as well; and when the Low Countries
development ended about 1600, the Italians had surpassed
their teachers.

Herewith other members of the Netherlands movement:

Barbireau, d. 1491, in Antwerp.

Divitis, La Riche, fl. ca. 1515, French.

Larue, fl. 1492–1510 in Burgundy and Courtray, pupil of Okeghem.

Ghiselin, 15th–16th cent., Netherlander.

Orto, De Horto, Dujardin, 15th–16th cent., prob. Belgian.

Pipelare, 15th–16th cent., Belgian.

Fevin, contemporary and rival of Deprès, prob. Netherlander.

Bauldewijn, in Antwerp 1513–1518, d. 1529.

Bassiron, 16th cent., Netherlander.

Jannequin, 16th cent., French or Belgian.

Carpentras, 1475–1532. French, b. Vaucluse. At Rome and
Avignon.

Ducis, b. ca. 1480 at Bruges, pupil of Deprès.

Gombert, b. Bruges, pupil of Deprès, fl. 1530–1543.

Richafort, Belgian, in Bruges 1543–1547, pupil of Deprès.

Clement non Papa, 1475/1500?–1558. Netherlander, in Netherlands.

Verdelot, Belgian, 1530–1540 in Florence, d. before 1567.

Danckerts, Dankers, b. Tholen, Zeeland, fl. 1540–1560.

De Hollandia, 1520–1568+.

§95. Italian Music

The history of music in Italy lends itself to organization with
some difficulty. It begins abruptly, apparently under foreign
influence; but then flows for four hundred years, with pulsations indeed, but no interruptions; and the pulsations not only
tend to overlap one another, but are of more nearly equal
strength than is usual. Sometimes there is a change of musical
direction within a temporal continuity; sometimes a temporal
near-break in an essential continuity. Although the initial stimulus to the growth as a whole is alien, Italian music soon takes
the lead in originating new aims and mechanisms, affects or
dominates other countries, and, even after leadership has
passed from it, remains productive, self-sufficient, and impervious to foreign influences for a century. But a single outstanding peak is not convincingly discernible. The history is rather
that of a series of wave crests.

Nevertheless, configuration is not wholly wanting. It merely is not simple. Such as it is, it seems to run about as follows.

The first record of the history of Italian music begins at the moment of the peak of the High Renaissance in painting and sculpture. In 1516 Willaert visited Rome and Ferrara; in 1527 he settled with permanent appointment in Venice, and taught Gabrieli. About 1535 Goudimel came to Rome and became the teacher of Animuccia, Palestrina, and Nanini, according to the usual account, although this has also been denied. In any event, during the second quarter of the century the Venetian and Roman contrapuntal schools took their origin under avowed Netherlands stimulation. Such development of native music as the Belgians may have found in Italy, the ordinary histories of music are silent about. Within a generation the Italians had made the northern choral counterpoint their own and brought it to its climax under Palestrina. The birth dates of the members of these first Venetian and Roman schools fall within 1500–1560; the peak comes perhaps a decade later than the latter year; soon after 1600 the movement wanes.

The Roman development drew to itself two Spaniards, Morales and Vittoria. While sometimes spoken of as a "Spanish school," they were active in Rome. Spain never possessed a national school such as existed elsewhere.

In 1594, the year of Palestrina's death, Peri produced in Florence the first opera, so called, *Dafne*. However thin musically this work was, it set a new form. Not only was there a dramatic skeleton, but polyphonic counterpoint was replaced by melody, or recitative, with accompaniment. The early Florentine operatists, Peri, Caccini, Monteverde, Cavalli, were born between 1550 and 1600; so that this innovating impulse overlaps the Venetian-Roman contrapuntal movement.

More or less contemporary is a second Roman school, that of Allegri, Frescobaldi, Carissimi, who were born between 1580 and 1605; in other words, so as to overlap with the Florentines. They preëminently composed church music; and Allegri, the oldest of them, was a pupil of the elder Nanini. However, the direction of their work was away from counterpoint toward harmony. The books are therefore not wholly in error when they make the group part of the "Roman school," and have this continue until Carissimi's death in 1673/4. The significant thing about the group is the new turn in its methods.

Thus far we have a development continuous in time, its exponents born within a century and producing their work within a century and a quarter. And yet this period witnessed first the culmination of a style—contrapuntal—which had been nearly three centuries developing in alien lands, and then the laying of the foundations of a new style—harmonic—which in turn was to reach its culmination beyond the Alps. So at least the histories of music tell the story. But it is an anomalous one.

There follows a rather barren period of forty or fifty years, in which the only musicians of note to be born were Cesti, 1620; Legrenzi, 1625; Lully, 1633, who are difficult to affiliate.

About 1650 there begins a new accumulation of births which lasts until 1700; but the music produced is segregated into three groups: the school of Naples, by Neapolitans and Sicilians, under the leadership of Scarlatti; the later Venetian school, by Venetians like Lotti and Caldara; and the early Sonatists, such as Corelli, Torelli, Veracini, Tartini, from North Italy generally. The Neapolitan school was evidently the most vigorous, and certainly the most active in opera.

Evidently dependent on it was the later eighteenth-century opera and *opera buffa,* sometimes called decadent. Its composers were partly from the Two Sicilies, like Jommelli, Piccini, Paisiello, Cimarosa, Zingarelli, partly from central and northern Italy, like Pergolesi, Salieri, Righini. Their birth dates range from 1710 to 1756, with a tendency to shift northward with time. Boccherini, born 1743, fits with these in time, but is an instrumentalist. Cherubini, born 1760, belongs to opera until the age of forty-five, but his fame rests rather on religious compositions.

The next pulse of Italian music, in the nineteenth century, was also operatic. It rose higher than eighteenth-century opera, but is distinguished from this more by its increased vigor than by a marked time interval. Spontini, Rossini, Donizetti,

Bellini, Verdi were born between 1774 and 1813. Paer, 1771, may be included because of his date; in quality he perhaps belongs rather to the eighteenth-century group. These names certainly constitute a culmination. It is, however, remarkable that this culmination was not achieved until opera, though invented in Italy, was more than two hundred years old, and had reached several previous crests. Also notable is the fact that the achievements of the group were essentially limited to opera, which therefore eventuates as the end product of Italian music. Finally, it is significant that this culmination, though appearing after the climax of the German one, remained substantially unaffected by it. Music had changed from Piccini to Rossini; but except for some Haydn and Mozart in Rossini himself, there is little non-Italian influence in this group of operatists. Again Italian music proved itself self-sufficient.

Verdi's adhesion to this group will perhaps be questioned. He was born a little later and was slower realizing himself. The floruit of the others falls between 1807 and 1835; his commences only in 1851.[2] Also, he lived, and composed, so much longer that he seems almost a modern contemporary in comparison with the others. Nevertheless, the melodic fertility of Verdi's earlier works classes him with Rossini and Donizetti; and the time separation is not excessive.

Verdi's later works, especially *Otello* and *Falstaff*, in which he abandoned *bel canto* for dramatic sincerity and instrumentation, place him with Boito, Puccini, Mascagni, and Wolf-Ferrari, with most of whom these late Verdian productions were actually contemporary. These operas of Verdi's old age are sometimes pronounced his greatest. But this is an opinion probably based on the bias of the time, which is away from organized melody as such. The dullness from which *Otello* and *Falstaff* are not free is a greater fault in a work of art than can be compensated by earnestness. As a matter of fact the later nineteenth-century composers, however able, represent a partial breakdown of purely Italian tradition. They are, if not

[2] (*Ernani* 1844), *Rigoletto* 1851, *Trovatore* 1853, *Traviata* 1853, *Aida* 1871, *Otello* 1887, *Falstaff* 1893.

under German, at least under European musical influence; a thing which had not happened to Italians since 1550. They and the later Verdi can therefore hardly be construed other than as marking the declining phase of an old, continuous national tradition.

PERIOD I: 1530–1650
CONTRAPUNTAL

Venetian school
  (Willaert, 1480–1562, Belgian, from 1527.)
  (Van Rore, 1516–1565, Belgian, successor of Willaert.)
  A. Gabrieli, 1510–1586, b. Venice.
  Zarlino, 1516/19–1590, b. near Venice.
  Merulo, 1533–1604, b. Correggio.
  Donati, d. 1603 in Venice.
  G. Gabrieli, 1540/57–1612, b. Venice.
  Orazio Vecchi, ca. 1550–1605, b. Modena.
  Porta, d. 1601, b. Cremona.
  Asola, d. 1609, b. Verona.
  Croce, ca. 1560–1609, b. near Venice.

Roman school 1, contrapuntal
  (Goudimel, 1500–1572, b. Avignon, in Rome 1535 seq.?)
  Ferrabosco, fl. 1542.
  Festa, d. 1545.
  Animuccia, ca. 1500–1570/71.
  Morales, b. 1510 in Seville.
  Palestrina, 1514/15–94, b. Palestrina.
  G. M. Nanini, 1540–1607, b. Vallerano.
  Vittoria, 1540/60–1608, b. Avila, Spain.
  Marenzio, 1550/60–99, b. near Brescia. To Poland.
  Anerio, b. 1560.
  G. B. Nanini, ca. 1560–1624.

Various or transitional
  Viadana, 1564–1645, b. near Mantua.
  Banchieri, 1567–1634, b. Bologna.

TENDING TO HARMONY

Florentine school of opera (recitative and melody with accompaniment)
  Peri, 1561–ca. 1630, b. Florence, 1594 *Dafne*.
  Caccini, ca. 1550–ca. 1615, b. Rome, collaborator with Peri.
  Monteverde, 1568–1643, b. Cremona; 1607 *Arianna*, 1608 *Orfeo*.
  Cavalli, 1599/1600–1676, b. Crema.

Roman school 2, tending to harmony
    Allegri, 1580?–1652, b. Rome, pupil of G. M. Nanini.
    Frescobaldi, 1580/84/87–1640, b. Ferrara.
    Carissimi, (1580) 1604–1673, b. Marino.

Various or transitional
    Cesti, ca. 1620–1669, b. Florence.
    Legrenzi, 1625–1690, b. near Bergamo.
    Lully, 1633–1687, b. Florence. To France.

PERIOD II: 1680–1800

School of Naples
    Stradella, ca. 1645–1681, b. Naples.
    A. Scarlatti, 1649–1725, b. Trapani, Sicily.
    D. Scarlatti, son of preceding, 1683–1757, b. Naples.
    Durante, 1684–1755, b. near Naples.
    Porpora, 1686–1767, b. Naples.
    Leo, 1694–1746, b. near Brindisi.
    Logroscino, ca. 1700–1763, b. Naples.

Later Venetian school
    Lotti, 1660/67–1740, b. Venice (or Hanover).
    Caldara, 1678–1763, b. Venice.
    Marcello, 1686–1739, b. Venice.
    Galuppi, 1703/6–1785, b. Venice.

Sonatists, violinists
    Corelli, 1653–1713, b. near Imola.
    Torelli, ca. 1660–1708, b. Verona.
    Vivaldi, d. 1743, b. Venice.
    Somis, 1676–1763, b. Piedmont.
    Geminiani, 1680–1762, b. Lucca; in England.
    Veracini, 1685–1750, b. Florence.
    Tartini, 1692–1770, b. Pisano, Istria.
    Locatelli, 1693–1764, b. Bergamo.

Eighteenth-century opera and opera buffa
    Pergolesi, 1710–1736, b. near Ancona.
    Jommelli, 1714–1774, b. near Naples.
    Piccini, 1728–1800, b. Bari.
    Sacchini, 1734–1786, b. Puzzuoli.
    Paisiello, 1741–1816, b. Taranto.
    Salieri, 1750–1825, b. Legnano, d. Vienna.
    Cimarosa, 1749–1801, b. Aversa.
    Zingarelli, 1752–1837, b. Naples.
    Righini, 1756–1812, b. Bologna; in Germany.

Various
   Boccherini, 1740/43–1805, b. Lucca.
   Cherubini, 1760–1842, b. Florence.

PERIOD III: 1800 SEQ.

Earlier opera of bel canto
   (Paer, 1771–1839, b. Parma.)
   Spontini, 1774–1851, b. Majolati, Ancona, fl. 1807.
   Rossini, 1792–1868, b. Pesara, Romagna, fl. 1816–1832.
   Donizetti, 1797–1848, b. Bergamo, fl. 1835.
   Bellini, 1801–1835, b. Catania, fl. 1831.
   Verdi, 1813–1901, b. near Busseto, Parma, fl. 1851–1871.

Later opera
   (Verdi of 1887, 1893.)
   Boito, b. 1842, Padua.
   Leoncavallo, 1858, Naples.
   Puccini, 1858, Lucca.
   Mascagni, 1863, Livorno.
   Wolf-Ferrari, 1876, Venice.

§96. German Music

German music began as early as Italian, but was much slower in reaching a first climax, and this was not specially well defined. Then a slump of a half century or more ensued, to be followed by a long and great culmination. The first formative influences were from the Netherlands. These were added to by Italian ones from the time of Palestrina on.

For the earlier period, the following currents are recognized: a polyphonic movement from about 1500 to after 1600, with stimuli first from the Belgians and then from the Venetians; Protestant church music of chorales beginning with Luther, but by 1600 coming to include also Catholic passions; two schools of organists, ca. 1620–1720, a north German one originating under the influence of Sweelinck and a central and southern one under that of Frescobaldi; and toward the end, the beginnings of the *Singspiel* or native opera. So far as it was not religious, music was predominantly bourgeois, and it produced no master of the first rank. The climax, in the first half of the seventeenth century, during the Thirty Years' War, is

constituted by Schütz, 1585–1672, the "father of German ora-
torio" and composer of the first German opera—another
Daphne,—performed at Dresden in 1627.

After Schütz there is a pretty barren three-quarters of a century until Bach, with organ music and *Singspiel* and other
activities continuing, but so little of permanent merit being
produced that some of the historians are exercised over filling
the gap between the two masters.

The great period begins abruptly with Bach, 1685–1750,
whose *Wohltemperierte Klavier* in 1725[3] established the scale
system of all subsequent music until today. It therefore marks
an epoch intrinsic to the art, just as Bach's greatness marks
the beginning of a major historic configuration. There follow
Händel, Gluck, Haydn, Mozart, Beethoven, Weber, and Schubert, undoubtedly the greatest constellation of musicians of
whom there is record. The end of the period can be fixed
within a few years. Weber, Beethoven, Schubert died in 1826,
1827, and 1828. On the other hand, Weber and Schubert are
reckoned among the romantics as well as among the masters;
and by some the beginning of the romantic movement is dated
from Weber's *Freischütz* in 1821. Of Beethoven's nine symphonies, eight had been composed by 1812.[4] On the basis of
greatness of achievement, which primarily concerns us here,
1828 is therefore the close of the climax. With reference to
style, 1812 to 1821 marks the transition from full "classicism"
to definite "romanticism." As the movement begins in 1725,
or, if one will, about 1715 with Bach's thirtieth year, the duration of the great period is almost exactly a century.

Bach and Händel were Thuringian and Saxon like Schütz;
Haydn, Mozart, Schubert, south Germans; Beethoven, from
the lower Rhine. The shifts follow chronology. The last one is
substantiated by Spohr, Mendelssohn, Flotow, Brahms among
the successors—all north Germans; while Schumann and Wagner continue to keep Saxony represented.

---

[3] Written in 1722 and 1724.
[4] The overlap is slight: *Erlkönig* 1815; *Freischütz* 1821; Beethoven's Ninth
Symphony 1822/3.

Minor figures of course were not lacking: Hasse, Graun, and Naumann, who composed in the Italian style; Hiller, Dittersdorf, and others in the *Singspiel* tradition; Stamitz, Albrechtsberger, Himmel, Hummel, and younger Bachs and Haydns.

Soon after 1812 began the romantic or "expressionist" movement, represented among the masters of the great period by Weber, Schubert, and Spohr. In general, music produced by men born after 1790 is romantic, or at least not "classic." About 1815, too, begins the German *Lied,* as a conscious art form— initiated by Schubert, specialized in by Franz and Silcher, and practiced by many others. The most significant birth dates for the phase are Meyerbeer 1791,[5] Moscheles 1794, Mendelssohn 1809, Schumann 1810, Liszt 1811,[6] Flotow 1812, Wagner 1813, Raff 1822. Though largely an epigone of the classics in spirit, Brahms, 1833–1897, belongs here in time.

In many quarters this postclassic period has not been felt as one of decline. It is, however, one of expressed rather than controlled emotion—like the Pergamum sculptures. It also contains no individual figure—with the possible exception of the propagandist and controversialized Wagner—who in general estimation equals the great masters of the preceding classical phase. The period must accordingly be construed as the descending phase of a larger cycle that began with Bach. This interpretation is confirmed by the character of German music after about 1890, of which Strauss, born 1864, is representative: loosened in form, uncoördinate, an art of disintegration.

Two matters of national affiliation remain to be considered about German music: the participation of foreigners, and that of Jews.

Occasional foreigners practiced and composed music in Germany before Bach: Senfl, Reinken, Buxtehude, Biber, were respectively Swiss, Dutch, Danish, and Bohemian. After Bach, the Czechs and Hungarians were increasingly drawn into German music. Kauer, Stamitz, Benda, Hummel, Moscheles, Liszt,

---

[5] Meyerbeer and Wagner, like some other essentially operatic composers, reached their full capacity later in life than most musicians.

[6] Liszt was born in Hungary, but is generally reckoned among the Germans.

Goldmark were active on German soil and participated in German developments. Not only was Germany a musical center, with Vienna long its metropolis, but it was preponderant in general culture, with Czech nationalistic aspirations not developing until well into the nineteenth century. Then too, it is in part a matter of Germans in Bohemia-Moravia or Hungary, or Czech or Magyar districts adjoining the German-Austrian border. Klein-Thaya, Deutsch-Brod, Pressburg, Oedenburg, where Kauer, Stamitz, Hummel, and Liszt were born, are in one or the other of these categories. In short, these men were born in bilingual and binational territory. All such are placed in parentheses in the summary list that follows; and the Czechs are reviewed again under their own heading.

As for the Jews, the series begins with Meyerbeer, 1791–1864. There follow Moscheles, Mendelssohn, Offenbach, Goldmark; to whom may be added the Bessarabian Rubinstein, born 1829. Meyerbeer and Offenbach flourished in Paris, with Halévy, 1799–1862. There seems no record of any Jewish composer—or, for that matter, performer—of note previous to these in the whole history of European music. The innate Jewish musical temperament or special aptitude is obviously a myth, else it would have broken through into manifestation before 1820. What apparently happened was that about 1800, or shortly before, especially in Germany, a certain proportion of Jews ceased feeling themselves as Jews and entered European culture. The Rothschilds, Heine, Disraeli are examples in other lines of activity. Once having made the step, those who entered music threw into the new pursuit the characteristic Jewish energy and mobility. The "naturally musical" Jew is a phenomenon of only a little more than the last century.

For the German second or major cycle as a whole, there is this problem. We have allowed a century for the high development, another for the decline. Before Bach is an arid three-quarter century. There is thus no "rise," no growth period. Also, a century is unduly long for a culmination, by other precedent. It is therefore a fair question whether the great or classic era should not be subdivided into a first and a culminating period, characterized respectively by Bach and Händel and by Mozart and Beethoven. About 1780–1828 would seem adequate for the latter. On this view Bach would presumptively be a lesser artist than Mozart and Beethoven, but of fundamental importance as the establisher of a scheme or canon for all successors.[7] Händel certainly cannot be considered of a class with Mozart and Beethoven, except in the belated opinion of some in England—which has had almost no worthwhile music of its own in more than two centuries, and where Händel is still often reckoned as English.

This classification has the further merit that it puts Beethoven in the latter half of the culmination, and Beethoven is certainly the personage singled out by most books on music as representing the peak of "absolute" music, if they express themselves at all.

PERIOD I: 1480–1710

Polyphonists, first under Flemish, then Italian influence
    Isaak, ca. 1450?–ca. 1518.
    Hofhaimer, 1459–1537, b. Rüdstadt, Salzburg.
    Finck, ?–?, trained and lived in Poland.
    Rhaw, 1488–1548; b. Eisfeld, Franconia.
    (Senfl., ca. 1490–1550/60; b. Basel-Augst; pupil of Isaak.)
    Stoltzer, ca. 1490–1526; b. Silesia.
    Dietrich, 1490/95–1548; b. Augsburg.
    Paminger, 1494–1567, b. Aschau, Austria.
    Gallus, ca. 1550–1591; b. Krain, d. Prague.
    Gumpeltzheimer, b. 1559, in Trossberg, Bavaria.
    Hasler, 1564–1612/18; b. Nürnberg; pupil of Gabrieli in Venice.
    Aichinger, ca. 1565–ca. 1613; b. Augsburg?
    Praetorius, 1571/2–1621; b. Kreuzberg, Thuringia; pupil of Sweelinck.

Protestant and Catholic church music
    Luther, 1483–1546.
    Walther, 1490/96–1555/70; b. Thuringia.

---

[7] In the most recent decades attempts have been begun toward breaking down this canon—quarter tones, wholly random consonances, etc. This endeavor to disintegrate the basic law or frame of the art is a typical end-of-cycle phenomenon, and emphasizes the importance of Bach's formulation of 1725. He established, and all successors unhesitatingly accepted, the limits of the system within which music was to move. Its products have shown it to have been a great system—even though potentialities inside it may by now be about exhausted.

Eccard, ca. 1545/53–1611; b. Mühlhausen, Thuringia; pupil of Lasso.

Calvisius, 1556–1615; b. Thuringia.

Franck, ca. 1580–1639; b. Zittau.

Schein, 1586–1630; b. Grünhain, Saxony.

Lossius, 1508–1582; b. Bacha, Hessen.

Vulpius, 1560–1616; b. Wasungen.

*Schütz, 1585–1672, Köstritz, Saxony; pupil of Gabrieli till 1612; 1627, *Daphne,* first German opera.

(Biber, 1638–1698; b. Wartenberg, Bohemia; violinist, instrumental music).

J. C. Bach, 1643–1703; b. Arnstadt.

J. M. Bach, 1648–1673; b. Eisenach; brother of preceding.

Organist school, north German, Sweelinck influence

Scheidt, 1587–1654, b. Halle.

Scheidemann, d. 1654; at Hamburg.

(Reinken, 1623–1722; b. Deventer, Holland.)

(Buxtehude, 1637–1707; b. Helsingör, Denmark.)

Kuhnau, 1667–1722, b. Geising, Saxony.

Central and south German, Frescobaldi influence

Kerll, 1628–1693; b. near Ingolstadt; pupil of Carissimi and Frescobaldi.

Froberger, ca. 1610?–1667; b. Halle; pupil of Frescobaldi.

Pachelbel, 1653–1706; b. Nürnberg.

G. Muffat, d. 1704; in Passau.

PERIOD II: FROM 1710

"Classic masters"

*Bach, 1685–1750, Eisenach. *1725.

*Händel, 1685–1759, Halle. *1741. To England.

*Gluck, 1714–1787, Weidenwang, Oberpfalz. *1762–1774.

*Haydn, 1732–1809, Rohrau, Lower Austria. *1798, 1801.

*Mozart, 1756–1791, Salzburg. *1781–1791.

*Beethoven, 1770–1827, Bonn. *1800–1812.

*Weber, 1786–1826. *1821–1823; b. Eutin, Oldenburg.

*Schubert, 1797–1828. *1815–1828; b. Lichtenthal near Vienna.

Contemporaries

Keiser, 1673–1739; b. near Weissenfels. Singspiel.

Hiller, 1728–1804; b. near Görlitz. Singspiel.

Dittersdorf, 1739–1799; b. Vienna. Singspiel.

(Kauer, 1751–1831; b. Klein-Thaya, Moravia. Singspiel.)

Schenck, 1761–1836; b. Wiener-Neustadt. Singspiel.

Hasse, 1699–1783; b. near Hamburg. Italian opera.

Graun, 1701–1759; b. Wahrenbrück, Saxony. Opera, church music.

Naumann, 1741–1801; b. near Dresden. Operas, oratorios, symphonies.

K. P. E. Bach, 1714–1788; b. Weimar.
(Stamitz, 1719–1761; b. Deutsch-Brod, Bohemia.)
(Benda, 1721/2–1795; b. Jungbunzlau, Bohemia.)
J. C. Bach, 1735–1782; b. Leipzig.
Albrechtsberger, 1736–1809; b. Klosterneuburg near Vienna.
M. Haydn, 1737–1806, brother of J. Haydn. Church music.
Neefe, 1748–1798; b. Chemnitz.
Himmel, 1765–1814; b. Treuenbrietzen, Brandenburg.
Wölfl, 1772–1812; b. Salzburg.
(Hummel, 1778–1837; b. Pressburg).
Spohr, 1784–1859; b. Brunswick.

Successors and romanticists
Silcher, 1789–1860; b. Schnaith, Württemberg.
Meyerbeer, 1791–1864; b. Berlin, d. Paris.
(Moscheles, 1794–1870; b. Prague.)
Franz, 1815–1892; b. Halle.
Mendelssohn, 1809–1847; b. Hamburg.
Schumann. 1810–1856; b. Zwickau, Saxony.
(Liszt, 1811–1886; b. Raiding near Oedenburg, Hungary.)
Flotow, 1812–1883; b. Teutendorf, Mecklenburg.
Wagner, 1813–1883; b. Leipzig.
Offenbach, 1819–1880; b. Cologne.
(Raff, 1822–1882; b. Lachen, Zurich.)
J. Strauss, 1825–1899; b. Vienna.
(Goldmark, 1832–1915; b. Keszthely, Hungary.)
Brahms, 1833–1897; b. Hamburg.
Humperdinck, b. 1854, near Bonn.
R. Strauss, b. 1864, Munich.

§97. French Music

France, whose mediaeval, thirteenth-century development was the great-grandfather of all those we are considering here, has little real history of music for nearly half a millennium thereafter, and achieves an active growth only during the last century. At that, this growth is not autonomous, but Italian- and German-derived.

It is really remarkable how empty of names of great or original ability the French record is for century after century. From 1350 to 1650 there is not one, except for Goudimel—who stands so nearly alone that the histories generally merge him in the Netherlands movement. In 1645 Mazarin imported Italian opera—then a half century old—ready-made to Paris. From 1672 to 1687 Lully, an Italian, was the leading musician— operatic—of France. About 1680 he originated the overture. In 1659 Cambert had composed the first all-French opera, *La Pastorale*.[8] This was an event of a certain significance, but Lully displaced Cambert in establishing French opera. A half century later, Rameau, 1683–1764, was the leading French composer of his time—again operatic. He stands as a nearly isolated figure, until, when he was in his old age, Philidor and Monsigny took up the task.

In 1752, Italian *opera buffa* was introduced in Paris. Gluck and Piccini were imported, and in 1776 the contention of the factions grouped around their names was fashionable news. Later, Cherubini, Spontini, Rossini were all drawn to Paris and spent most of their maturity there. Grétry, 1741–1813, a Belgian, and Isouard, born in Malta in 1775, are generally reckoned as among the founders of the later French grand and comic opera.[9] Still later, Meyerbeer, Offenbach, Flotow, and even Wagner were drawn from Germany—the first two to become French musicians.

The persistence of Parisian opera as an institution was evidently founded on a predilection, and finally bore fruit in a continuous crop of native composers. From Rameau to Philidor and Monsigny was nearly a half century; from them to Dalayrac, a quarter; thereafter, not a decade lacked the birth of one or more successful operatic composers in France: Méhul, Berton, Catel, Boieldieu, Auber, Hérold, Halévy, Berlioz, Thomas, Gounod, Delibes, Bizet, Massenet, Godard, Charpentier—nearly half of them natives of Paris itself. This list represents, if not a growth of first magnitude, a notable one, shaping

---

[8] Thirty-two years later than Schütz's *Daphne* at Dresden.

[9] Comic, with some spoken words; grand, wholly sung.

a real style. French opera has consistently followed a specific tradition; it is essentially dramatic, with emphasis on plot, enunciation, ballet, and scenic effect; the orchestra as well as the voices are kept in their place. It is in line with this fact that French instrumental music was later in developing, and, in comparison with opera, has tended to remain struggling.

Instrumental music begins with Chambonnières, Le Bègue, Couperin, Rameau, Leclair in the period 1630–1750. This is a far from notable showing, as compared with Germany or England, let alone Italy. Though Rameau, with his *Traité de l'harmonie*, 1722, contributed to the basic theory of the music of the next two centuries, his work was scarcely as fundamental in practice as Bach's synchronous *Wohltemperierte Klavier*, 1725. Not till the nineteenth century did Baillot, Rode, Berlioz, David, the half-Pole Chopin, the Belgian Franck and the French Walloon Lalo, and then Saint-Saëns, Massenet, Godard, D'Indy, Charpentier, Debussy, Dukas develop a successful school of French instrumental music, which lasted into the twentieth, but seems by now to have run its course. It began about fifty years later than the operatic movement, and lasted nearly fifty longer. This precedence of opera is a uniquely French phenomenon in the history of music.

Berlioz is perhaps the greatest name in this list; at any rate, he was the first to have aimed at musical fullness and profundity, with the result that for a time his European reputation exceeded that at home. From the beginning to the end of the century of duration, style and content changed, of course; but not more than German music in the century from Bach to Schubert.

It is of interest that in the foregoing enumeration of nineteenth-century instrumentalists, which is in sequence of births, the first seven Frenchmen were all born in the provinces or abroad, but five of the second seven in Paris.

Mediaeval French school, 1100–1350
As above, under Netherlands: Leoninus, Perotinus, De Garlandia, Petrus de Cruce, Franco of Paris, De Machault, De Muris (also Franco of Cologne and Tunstede of England).

Frenchmen participating in the Netherlands contrapuntal development, 1350–1600
  Mouton, d. 1522, b. near Metz?
  Goudimel, ca. 1500–1572, b. near Avignon.
  Lejeune (Claudin), fl. 1585–1610.

French instrumental and operatic composers, 1630–1750
  Chambonnières, ca. 1600–1670. (I)[10]
  Cambert, ca. 1628–1677; b. Paris. (O)
  Le Bègue, 1630–1702, b. Laon. (I)
  (Lully, 1633–1687; b. Florence.) (O)
  Couperin, 1668–1733; b. Paris, of family from Brie. (I)
  Rameau, 1683–1764; b. Dijon; 1722, *Traité de l'harmonie*, 1726,
    Nouveau Système. (I, O)
  Leclair, 1697–1764; b. Lyon. (I)

Foreigners participating in opera in France
  Piccini, Gluck, Cherubini, Spontini, Rossini, Bellini; besides
  Lully and those mentioned under the next caption.

French operatic and instrumental composers, 1750 seq. (including
    foreigners active in Paris)
  Philidor, 1726–1795; b. Dreux; fl. 1759–1788. (O)
  Monsigny, 1729–1817; b. near St.-Omer; fl. 1759–1777. (O)
  (Grétry, 1741–1813; b. Liège; Belgian.) (O)
  Dalayrac, 1753–1809; b. Muret, Haute-Garonne. (O)
  Méhul, 1763–1817; b. Givet, Ardennes. (O)
  Berton, 1767–1804; b. Paris. (O)
  Baillot, 1771–1842; b. Passy. (I)
  Catel, 1773–1830; b. L'Aigle, Orne. (O)
  Rode, 1774–1830; b. Bordeaux. (I)
  (Isouard, 1775–1818; b. Malta.) (O)
  Boieldieu, 1775–1834; b. Rouen. (O)
  Auber, 1782/4–1871; b. Caen. (O)
  Hérold, 1791–1833; b. Paris. (O)
  (Meyerbeer, 1791–1864; b. Berlin.) (O)
  Halévy, 1799–1862; b. Paris. (O)
  Berlioz, 1803–1869; b. near Grenoble. (I, O)
  David, 1810–1876; b. Cadenet, Vaucluse. (I)
  Chopin, 1810–1849; b. near Warsaw; half French. (I)
  Thomas, 1811–1896; b. Metz. (O)
  (Flotow, 1812–1883; b. Mecklenburg.) (O)
  Gounod, 1818–1893; b. Paris. (O)
  (Offenbach, 1819–1880; b. Cologne.) (O)
  (Franck, 1822–1890; b. Liège; Belgian.) (I)
  Lalo, 1823–1892; b. Lille. (I)

---

[10] I denotes instrumental composers; O, operatic.

Saint-Saëns, 1835–1921; b. Paris. (I)
Delibes, 1836–1891; b. St.-Germain du Val. (O)
Bizet, 1838–1875; b. Paris. (O)
Massenet, 1842–1912; b. near St.-Etienne. (O, I)
Godard, 1849–1895; b. Paris. (O, I)
D'Indy, 1851–1931; b. Paris. (I)
Charpentier, 1860——; b. Dieuze, Lorraine. (O, I)
Debussy, 1862–1918; b. St.-Germain, Paris. (I, O)
Dukas, 1865–1935; b. Paris. (I)

To summarize: In the twelfth and thirteenth centuries, France—North France—seems to have been the musical leader of Europe. This burst is undoubtedly part of the great French culmination which climaxed the florescence of truly mediaeval architecture, literature, learning, and feudal institutions. By 1350 this early growth of music was over; and for three centuries, while productivity and innovation grew up in the Netherlands and passed to Italy, France contributed less to European musical development than Germany and England. The period of Louis XIV and XV saw some awakening, but on a minor scale, and with native music on the defensive against Italian. Paris was a music center: but mainly for foreigners; and the opera held primacy. Only in the later eighteenth and the nineteenth century did native French opera, and then instrumental music, begin to attain considerable achievement. Even then it remained largely self-sufficient, without much influence on Europe, not superior to that of declining Germany and rising Russia. Its culmination can fairly be set as starting about 1830, when romanticism finally reached France, and when the series of supreme German masters had just been concluded.

If French postmediaeval music is in a sense secondary, it is, however, not imitative. If it is not highly characterized by a definite style, this is probably for the one reason that it is not the very greatest art. The Italian and German influences that have gone into it are thoroughly remodeled, the German ones so well as virtually to defy specific identification. In this sense modern French music, when it finally achieved itself, was genuinely native, even if not strongly national in character. It is as if the French, while welcoming foreign music, had kept themselves from being swamped by admiration for it until they were able to produce it adequately themselves, when the danger of imitating something un-French had been passed. This is a national attitude which they have evinced also in other domains of culture, and which they largely share with the English, but not with the Germans. These accept freely and sometimes avidly, like inferiors; but keep assimilating foreign material and styles until finally they produce now and then something that is both nationally German and so great as to transcend nationality in its importance.

At bottom, this probably means that the French feel themselves as civilized, the Germans as experimenters; and that on the whole they have been such, relatively to each other. All Latins have in general manifested reluctance to accept anything Germanic; and when they have done so it has first been thoroughly reworked or refined to suit their national taste. It has been better, as Latins see it, to continue with a shopworn or second-rate style produced in civilization than to accept a potentially greater or more significant one emanating from barbarism. Their true fidelity is thus to an ideal of civilization as such, irrespective of the price of belatedness or nonaccomplishment which they now and then pay in this or that domain. The Germans, by contrast, have never really absorbed the idea of civilization as something finished and maintainable. When they cease groping or imitating, they grapple with universals, attempting to transcend the limits of what may strictly be called civilized. Hence their Kant, Goethe, Beethoven.

If these remarks seem to be contradicted by the Italian acceptance of Netherlandish music, it may be recalled that the Belgian Netherlands were and are half French in language and nationality.

§98. English Music

English musical history, in the postmediaeval period, is as brief as French, but early where this is late. English music had died before French was born. Italian and German each lasted as long as English and French added together.

There are some indications of English musical activity in the genuine Middle Ages. "Sumer is icumen in" is attributed to the early thirteenth century. Simon Tunstede is mentioned as a fourteenth-century contributor; Dunstable as important in the early fifteenth. In the absence of fuller knowledge, these scattering evidences may be interpreted as English reflections of French and Belgian activities.

The total period of spontaneous native English musical development in the Modern period is comprised within a span of less than two hundred years, from about 1520 or 1530 to 1710. This is broken by a semihiatus from 1620 or 1625 to 1660. The prehiatus growth is said to have had two phases, the first under Netherlandish influence, the second under Venetian. The passage from one to the other took place about 1560 or soon after. The principal relevant names and dates are listed below. There was a burst of madrigal development from about 1580 to 1620, culminating in the *Triumphs of Oriana* collection of 1601. This madrigal growth runs an almost exact duplicate of the time curve of Elizabethan drama. The greatest figure in the joint phases perhaps was Orlando Gibbons, 1583–1625.

After the death of Gibbons the books speak of a decline, and the dates of such composers as there are confirm the statement. Conventional historic interpretation no doubt assigns the rise of Puritanism and the Civil War as causes.

However that may be, music became active again soon after 1660. There have been few actively living Englishmen since 1700 who followed music with the zest of Pepys. In 1673 the first English opera, Lock's *Psyche,* was put on—14 years after the corresponding French attempt, 46 after the German, 79 after the Florentine. Italian opera was not tried in England until 1706, nor launched until 1720. The course of the process thus was the reverse of that in France. Humfrey, Wise, Blow were other composers of the Restoration period. The leading figure was Purcell, 1658–1695, unanimously accepted as the acme of English musicians, and generally accorded high rank by international standards. With the possible exception of Scarlatti, he was the greatest musician of his day in Europe. By the time of

Purcell's premature death, the movement was nearly over. Blow lived until 1708, and two slightly later men, Clark and Aldrich, died in 1707 and 1710. With the latter date, the school was finished. Händel and other Germans and Italians were imported; and what native music was produced, was spiritless. The Purcell movement had been undoubtedly English in character, and if brief and not of the greatest, was vigorous.

The little Purcell cycle, it will be noted, about coincides in time with English bursts of science, philosophy, and drama.

Why English music in the two centuries since has never risen above mediocrity, it is difficult to explain. That great nations can go long without higher musical achievement has already been established for France, and is a fact to be accepted. That English music after Purcell is of a lower order is not always avowed by English books, which make up for the qualitative deficiency by quantity of obscure names. The fact of lack of higher creativeness, if it needs establishment beyond common notoriety, is confirmed by the way the English cling to Händel after two hundred years as if he were God-sent, and sometimes even treat him as English; and by the fact that most of what they have produced, and best like to discuss so far as the Continent is concerned, is religious music; which, a century after Beethoven, seems rather belated.

Mediaeval
  "Sumer is icumen in," 1226 or 1230.
  Tunstede, 14th cent.
  Dunstable, d. 1458, contemporary of Dufay and Binchois.

First Period, first phase, Flemish influence
  Taverner, fl. ca. 1530.
  Redford, 1491–1547.
  Johnson.
  Tye, ca. 1500–1572.
  Merbecke, 1523–1585.

First Period, second phase, Venetian influence
  White, d. 1575/80.
  Tallys, 1510/29–1585.
  Edwardes, 1520/23–1566.
  Farrant, ca. 1530–1580.

Byrd, 1538/43–1623; b. London.
Wilbye, 1560–1612.
Dowland, 1562–1626; b. Westminster.
Morley, 1563–1604.
Bull, 1563–1628; b. Somersetshire.
Benet, 1565–1605.
*Gibbons, 1583–1625; b. Cambridge.

Interim
Lawes, 1595–1662.
Child, 1606–1697; b. Bristol.

Second Period, "Restoration"
Lock, 1620–1677.
Humfrey, 1647–1674; b. London.
Aldrich, 1647–1710; b. London.
Wise, ca. 1648–1687.
Blow, 1648–1708; b. Nottinghamshire.
*Purcell, 1658–1695; b. Westminster.
Clark, d. 1707.

§99. Marginal Developments

Beginning about 1830, a series of east and north European countries manifest musical developments. The dates conventionally given for the rise of these "schools" are: Poland, 1835; Russia, 1836; Hungary, 1840; Scandinavia, 1840; Finland, 1850; Bohemia, 1860. These are obviously marginal growths, the commencement of which follows close upon the great culmination in Germany. This does not mean that they carry on the manner of Beethoven, but that they presumptively stand in a relation of marginal dependence, as the geographer or anthropologist would say, both in time and space, to that growth in Germany the culmination of which is typified by Beethoven.

Poland.—The Polish growth is irregular, and dominated by Chopin, whose father was a Frenchman and most of whose adult life was spent in Paris. Like Copernicus, Chopin appears cometlike out of cultural space; he is scarcely part of national growth. Nevertheless he does form part of a system, in one sense: the constellation of musical geniuses who began to appear, in countries without an independent musical history, after 1830, when the climax of European music came to a close in Germany. Schubert, in fact, could be construed as a predecessor within Germany.

Apart from Chopin, there scarcely is a distinctive Polish school.

Dobrzynski, 1807–1867; b. Romanow, Volhynia.
Chopin, 1810–1849; b. near Warsaw, of French father; in Paris 1832 seq.
L. P. Scharwenka, b. 1847, F. X. Scharwenka, 1850, Samter, Posen.
Moszkowsky, b. 1854, Breslau.

Hungary.—A Hungarian "school," in the sense of a conscious art tradition beyond folk productions, is not recognized by many of the books. Liszt was born in 1811, which makes the beginning of his maturity coincide with several of the eastern and northern starts; but he was born on the western border of Hungary, in a German-speaking district; and the affiliations of his adult life were German. What is popularly known as Hungarian music is Gypsy ornamentation of European music.

It rather seems as if both Poland and Hungary had been too close to the German center, too immediately marginal, to make it easy for them to develop musical independence successfully. As fast as their nationality produced, its products tended to be absorbed into the cultures of the center. Russia, more remote in both distance and culture, had the better chance of undisturbed native growth.

Bohemia.—From their position and old close relations with Germany, the Czechs should expectably have had the first musical growth among the Slavic peoples; whereas it comes last. Actually they did precede; but their products were long absorbed into the German development. The Czech national school is usually dated from Smetana about 1866.

Isaak, ca. 1450?–ca. 1518; probably German, possibly Bohemian.
Biber, 1638–1698; b. Wartenberg; to Austria, Bavaria.
Stamitz, 1719–1761; b. Nemečky-Brod; to Mannheim.
Benda, 1721/2–1795; b. Jungbunzlau; to Germany.
Kauer, 1751–1831; b. Klein-Thaya; to Vienna.
Dussek, 1761–1812; b. Czaslav; to Paris.

Gyrowetz, 1763–1850; b. Budweis; to Vienna.
Moscheles, 1794–1870; b. Prague; to Vienna, Paris, Leipzig.
Chwatal, 1808–1879; b. Rumburg; to Germany.
Smetana, 1824–1884; b. Litomyšl.
Dvořak, 1841–1904; b. Mühlhausen.
Fibich, 1850–1900; b. Seborschitz.

It would be interesting to know the precise nationality of all the earlier of these Bohemians and Moravians; that is, if they were born into Slavic- or German-speaking families. But the inquiry would probably be difficult.

Russia.—Russian music, although a limb on the European tree, is distinctively national. It is dated from Glinka's *Life for the Tsar,* 1836. There is a clustering of births in the decade 1834–1844, with Borodin, Cui, Balakirev, Mussorgsky, Tchaikovsky, Rimsky-Korsakov; another, 1865–1872, with Glazunov, Scriabin, Rachmaninov. These clusterings are symptoms of a normal or healthy cyclical growth. The birthplaces point the same way. Bortniansky, the first on the list that follows, is from the Ukraine, and the only one from there. The majority of the others are from the western frontier of Great Russia: Novgorod, Pskov, Vilna, Smolensk; Tchaikovsky from eastern Great Russia, in Kama drainage; only Borodin and Glazunov were born in Leningrad, and Scriabin in Moscow. Rubinstein, a Bessarabian Jew, does not fit into the development qualitatively, though he does fit fairly in time: his music is West European rather than Russian.

The Russian growth, the culmination of which begins about 1870, is marked by vigor while contemporary German, Italian, and French productions show symptoms of decadence. As a style it is formative until well beyond 1900, whereas other European styles are then tending toward dissolution.

Bortniansky, 1751/2–1825; b. Glukhov; pupil of Galuppi; 1799 seq. in Russia.
Glinka, 1803/4–1857; b. near Smolensk, d. Berlin.
Dargomyzhski, 1813–1869, b. province of Tula.
Rubinstein, 1829–1894; b. Bessarabia. Jew.
Borodin, 1834–1887; b. Leningrad.
Cui, b. 1835, Vilna.

Balakirev, 1836/7–1910; b. Novgorod.
Mussorgsky, 1835/9–1881; b. Karev, Pskov.
Tchaikovsky, 1840–1893; b. Votinsk, Perm.
Rimsky-Korsakov, 1844–1908; b. Tikhvin, Novgorod.
Lyadov, 1855–1914.
Taneyev, 1856–1915.
Arensky, 1861–1906.
Glazunov, b. 1865, Leningrad.
Scriabin, b. 1872, Moscow.
Rachmaninov, b. 1873, Novgorod.
Stravinsky, b. 1882.

Scandinavia.—In the Scandinavian movement, the time progression is from Denmark to Norway to Sweden and Finland, that is, geographically outward from the center. The music remains European with minor peculiarities, rather than natively founded.

Gade, 1817–1890; b. Copenhagen.
Grieg, 1843–1897; b. Bergen.
Sjögren, b. 1853, Stockholm.
Sinding, b. 1856, Kongsberg, Norway.
Sibelius, b. 1865, Finland.

Spain.—Spain enters the procession of marginals with a "school" beginning about 1890, as yet too recent to judge for our purposes. Sixteenth-century musical Spaniards—Morales and Vittoria—were absorbed into Italy. The country has therefore never had a musical history in the sense of participating with coherent contributions of consequence to the growth of European music.

Belgium, Holland, and Switzerland.—These three minor countries have been musically tributary to their larger neighbors—Belgium to France, Holland and Switzerland (Raff) to Germany, in accordance with basic speech affiliation. Of the three, Belgium, whose music flourished with such distinction before 1600, is the only one to have produced considerably since 1750; although at first drained almost wholly into French channels. Benoit's nationalistic Flemish school seems to have remained a wish rather than a reality. But the historians Fétis and Coussemaker are significant, in view of Belgium's past.

Gossec, 1733–1829; b. Vergnies; to Paris, 1751.
Grétry, 1741–1813; b. Liège; to Paris, 1768.
Gresnick, 1752–1799; b. Liège; to London 1785, Paris 1793.
Campenhout, 1780–1848; b. Brussels.
Fétis, 1784–1871; b. Mons; historian.
Franck, 1822–1890; b. Liège.
(Lalo, 1823–1892; b. Lille; Walloon French.)
Benoit, 1834–1901; b. Harlebecke.
(Coussemaker, 1835–1876; b. Bailleul, Dept. Nord; French Walloon; historian.)

The whole course of European development in the last hundred years is a sort of Hellenization and the period a Hellenistic one: 1830 corresponds to 323. What before was a localized and nationalized art spreads out internationally. Slavs, Scandinavians, Spaniards, Jews appear alongside Germans, as Bithynians, Cilicians, Syrians, and Jews once participated beside Hellenes in philosophy, science, and the arts. So far as there still is originality and leadership in new production, it seems to have passed in large part to Russia, only recently admitted, or half admitted, within the pale of civilization.

It is also a fair question whether modern French music, which as a nonoperatic school scarcely dates from before 1830, must not be construed in the same light as the Slavic and Scandinavian movements. After all, France is geographically no farther from Germany—or, if one will, from Germany-Italy—than these eastern countries. In relation to the average level of whole culture, or degree of civilizedness, it would of course be nonsense to think of France as dependent. But this fact would not prevent dependence in a particular field of culture, especially a highly separate domain like music.

§100. Review and Conclusions

West European music since the early Middle Ages is a fundamental unit. Its development from singing in unison to discant and from that to contrapuntal polyphony; the change from consonances in octaves to fifths and fourths, then sixths and thirds, and finally more complex relations; the gradual development of a sense of harmony, with reassertion of a dominant melody first harmonically accompanied and then also itself harmonically constructed; the growth of a sense of tonality and modulatory variety; the escape from the nearly rhythmless chant of the Church, until rhythm was again an integral element of music; the development of instruments until purely instrumental music was attained and the timbre of orchestration became a factor—all these matters of growth of content and form of the music itself are set forth in many histories. With all the multiple threads of the narrative, there runs through it a complete continuity. There is not a single break in the story, not one full-fledged sudden birth of an element out of nothing. The present examination does not quarrel with the standard historic account, but accepts it. It differs in attempting to shift examination from the continuity relations as main theme, to the organization of the surface of this continuity into configurations of time, space, and nationality.

Limitation to the higher manifestations is unavoidable, because only these possess a historic record, in general. Folk music of course also varies according to time and place; but it is anonymous, not written down; a new phase obliterates the older one. Folk music also is unconscious, historically speaking; like speech, it is unaware of its own grammar or theory; it is scarcely taught or studied or formulated. It is obviously the foundation of the art music we have been considering; but it seems impossible to consider in the same way. It is also well to remember that folk music, being universally persistent, goes on when self-conscious art music lapses or sinks to a level of sterility. The greater continuity is thus in its domain; so that professional historians of music lose more by inability to deal adequately with folk music than we who deal primarily not with connections but with the organization of such continuity as is visible.

European music as an art is an international thing. Characteristically, it emerged in the Middle Ages out of the Church. Rather typically too, its first recorded formulation was mainly North French, in the period when France was most fully expressing the High Mediaeval culture. Like so many other

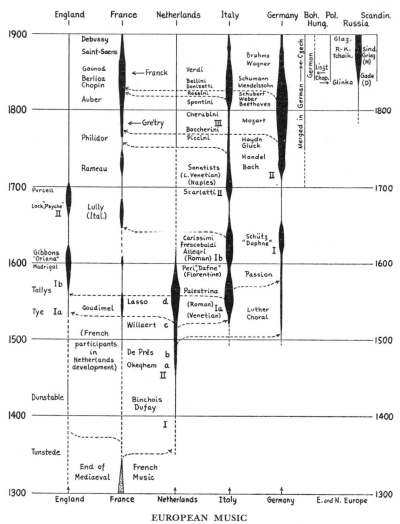

EUROPEAN MUSIC

French activities, this music waned in the fourteenth and fifteenth centuries. Unlike literature and philosophy, it did not experience a notable rebirth in the French nationalistic florescence of the seventeenth century.

The southwestern or Belgian Netherlands—equally Romance and Germanic—took up music where the French left it, and carried it to the high development of its complex, almost artificial, contrapuntal stage. Holland, and later Germany, followed humbly in their train; France participated sporadically and apparently diminishingly. This Low Countries development of music is obviously part of the same growth that produced the flourishing industry, commerce, science, painting, and town architecture of the Netherlands in about the same period.

Just before or at its culmination in the Netherlands, contrapuntal music was taken up by the Italians in two centers, Venice and Rome, and then developed to its peak under Palestrina. Just what led to this transfer, and what preceded it, is not clear. There must have been a considerable antecedent development of music among Italians, else they could not have achieved European leadership so quickly as they did. This antecedent, though obscure, was probably a more important factor than the known relations of Italy and the Netherlands in commerce and painting.

The Italians promptly moved on to new styles and forms: the beginnings of harmony and the opera; whereas when counterpoint composition had been carried to its limits, the Belgians knew nothing further to do, and ceased being a factor in music. The reason for this difference seems to be that the Netherlanders, having begun one and a half to two centuries earlier, had their music rooted in Late Mediaevalism, whereas the Italians, coming into theirs at the very peak of the Renaissance, carried on with the impetus of this into the Baroque and Modern periods. At that, from Palestrina to Verdi is a full three centuries—a long period for one people to maintain an art at a distinguished level. As usual, Italy runs atypical to Europe.

English music maintained itself as an honorable appanage to French, Belgian, and Italian from the Middle Ages on, achieving a minor climax just after 1600 and a somewhat greater one just before 1700. The former coincided with the "Elizabethan" period; the "Restoration" one, approximately with peaks in science and philosophy.

The German development may be compared to a large mass slowly acquiring momentum. From about 1500 on, there are

German composers in considerable numbers. Music must have been rather widely cultivated and appreciated. Italian influences were absorbed as receptively as Netherlandish ones. Opera was introduced earlier than into France. But for a full two hundred years no notable composition or composer appeared; nor any national style of European significance. Toward the end of the two centuries there was, if anything, a sag. Then Bach appears over the horizon, not as an isolated comet but as the first of the greatest constellation in musical history, stretching over a century to Beethoven. As large a growth as this does not die at once; and the century since has produced many important German composers; but it has been a century of decline nevertheless. What is unexplained is the sudden rise of level after 1700. Bach, for all his predecessors, mounts almost as abruptly at the beginning of his period as Palestrina at the onset of Italian music. Beethoven was a contemporary of Goethe and Kant; which speaks for itself.

France reëntered the lists half-heartedly under Louis XIV—primarily leaning on Italians, but with a degree of reserve. Certain forms of music, especially opera and dance, were persistently cultivated in specifically French form; others, except for Italian opera, were long ignored. Instrumental music finally came into its own about 1830, at the very moment when the great climax of European music had been achieved through the Germans and epigone national growths were begining to spring up in many parts of Europe; when, in fact, German music was turning from being European to being Germanic.

All these new developments, however, in the Slavic and Scandinavian countries, in Belgium, in a measure in France, finally even in Spain and Italy, have this in common: they are more or less consciously nationalistic efforts to participate in a growth which, though given its shape largely by Germans, had become international. They are therefore secondary products of the breakup of a greater thing. The one exception is the music of Russia, which, no doubt on account of the very late and incomplete entry of Russia into European civilization, was able to grow up in relative independence and to work out, to some degree, novel creative impulses instead of carrying farther, like the rest of Europe, tendencies which had already found their most balanced expression.

If now we turn from sequential to abstract considerations, we find that there are nations, like Spain and Holland, which have never possessed an art music of international European significance, although they passed through definitely high florescences in other domains of culture. England is an example of a people that once achieved a rather notable musical productivity and then lost it. France, and to a degree Belgium, lost and after centuries measurably regained it. Rather early investment of musical production with a specific national quality—after Palestrina—seems to have helped prevent the Italians from rising to the sheer peaks, or from profiting from non-Italian music after this was greater, until too late. The Germans, on the other hand, went humbly to school with their foreign betters for two centuries. Perhaps for this very reason they were able, when once they started, to reach broader and deeper achievements; at any rate, relatively supernational ones.

There are also instances of a conscious cultivation of foreign music by a court or aristocracy: Netherlandish by the Italians, Italian by the French, German and Italian by the English. But the consequences were wholly different. The Italians profited immediately, the French slowly and gradually, the English not at all, so far as stimulation of native productivity goes. Evidently the pupil is a more important factor in the outcome than the teacher.

A somewhat reversed process is also visible, in which the musical genius of a smaller or more backward people is drained off into the achievements of a more outstanding one, permanently or for a period: Dutch into Belgian; later, Belgian into French; Czech and Hungarian into German.

That the final climax arose in Germany and not in Italy appears to be largely a function of its date. During the seventeenth century, cultural primacy in the whole of civilization was passing across the Alps. By 1725 the process was completed. A culmination in any field thereafter had to be northern.

Chapter X

THE GROWTH OF NATIONS

THE GROWTH OF NATIONS

T HIS CHAPTER could well be designated Part Two if all that has gone before were gathered into a Part One. So far, the treatment has been topical, by activities. Here it is by areally and ethnically defined cultures and subcultures, each seen as a sum of its various activities. The data are the same, but harrowed across the furrows. The chapter therefore contains little new material, except for references to politics, and a few to architecture. It is the focus of consideration that is different: historic culture-wholes instead of abstracted activities like science or sculpture.

§101. Egypt

Egypt's culture is of special interest because its historic record goes back farthest into the past. Probably Mesopotamia is equally ancient, but her story is much less continuous. Moreover, she harbored several distinct peoples who overlapped and succeeded one another. In ancient Egypt there was, so far as we know, only one people with one speech from first to last.

More interesting still is the fact that Egyptian civilization uniquely rose and fell four times within the same essential pattern frame before it exhausted itself.[1] At that, a long formative period of a millennium is not counted in because its history is inferential.[2]

---

[1] Petrie, *The Revolutions of Civilizations,* 1911, on the basis of sculpture and carving, sets up an additional florescence probably culminating with the third king of the First Dynasty—around 5400 by his reckoning, about 3250 by standard chronology.

[2] Historic Dynasty I of united Egypt is believed to have been established not far from 3315. The calendar was set up on June 15, 4241, in southern Lower Egypt, not far from Heliopolis or Memphis, according to astronomical and historical calculations. An appreciable amount of record keeping and other cultural progress must of necessity have preceded the invention of so serviceable a calendar. It seems theoretically unlikely that an accurate calendar should

Why this special Egyptian faculty of reflorescence? Impingements and competitions were relatively few. The number of existing civilizations was small, and the greater ones, like Mesopotamia and India, were at considerable distances. Between were situated peoples of less advanced culture. Egypt lay isolated by desert and sea. Agriculture was enforced in the fertile land; beyond it, occupation of the soil could be only of the sparsest. The basic economy is therefore essentially unchanged even today. A fairly high idea-system, once having been worked out, was thus reached rather feebly by outside idea-systems. When it met misfortune, from internal causes, it tended in time to right itself from internal stability rather than by outside help or borrowing. When finally it failed to resurrect, it withdrew within itself, defensively, and gradually wasted away before fresher Greek, Roman, Christian, and Arabic influences, leaving relatively little trace of effect on these other cultures.

The histories recognize as eras of Egyptian success: the Old Kingdom or Pyramid Age, Dynasties III, IV, V, especially the two latter; the Middle Kingdom, Dynasties XI, XII, particularly the last; the New Kingdom or Empire, Dynasties XVIII, XIX, with the former the more illustrious; and the Renascence of Dynasty XXVI. These were periods of prosperity and wealth, a strong central government, satisfactory foreign relations and often conquest. Seven or eight flourishing dynasties out of the thirty-one counted to the Ptolemies may seem to make the history of Egypt a long desolation broken by occasional oases of prosperity. However, not all the other dynasties were downright unsuccessful; and the poor ones were generally also the shorter. If we classify them into three grades, we have:

Prosperous, III–V, 2895–2540;[3] XII, 2000–1785; XVIII–XIX, 1580–1200; XXVI, 663–525.

---

precede writing and the rest of the higher civilization by a thousand years; but Meyer and Breasted concur in accepting 4241—the first date in history. With the lately prevalent retraction of the date of beginning of Dynasty I to about 3000 (see footnote 4, below), the difficulty of accepting 4241 is of course increased.

[3] The chronology is Meyer's, from which most others vary inconsiderably. The principal aberrant chronology is Flinders Petrie's. Going backward, this runs

Middling, I–II, 3315–2895; XI, 2160–2000; XX, 1200–1085.
Unsuccessful, VI–X, 2540–2160; XIII–XVII, 1785–1580; XXI–
 XXV, 1085–663.

Adding up, we have seven definitely prosperous dynasties,
with 1,088 years; four satisfactory, with 695; fifteen disturbed
or unsuccessful, with 1,007. This makes 1,783 years in reasonably successful dynasties, out of a total of 2,790 years, or 64 per
cent—nearly two-thirds. Also, the average duration of prosperous dynasties is 162 years, of poor ones only 67.

The peaks may clearly be set in Dynasties IV (or V), XII,
and XVIII, with XXVI a partly successful attempt to bring
back the old power and glory. In approximate dates, we might
say 2650, 1900, 1450, 600.

The books regularly describe the architecture, sculpture,
and painting as rising and falling in accord with the politico-
economic fortunes to a most surprising degree. It would seem
that when there was no strongly established government to
collect revenues, no one—neither courts nor officials nor
temples—had a surplus, building undertakings were few and
small, materials inferior, and the quality of workmanship in
royal sculpture as well as private tomb decoration became low.
All this is plausible enough; but the relation as depicted between economics and aesthetics seems almost too direct. Historical determinism is not often so simple. The situation makes
of the Egyptian artist nothing but an artisan, and a wage-
dependent one at that. This may have been true in some degree, but can hardly have held absolutely.

It is therefore somewhat reassuring to find that in science
and literature the case is presented differently. There is noth-

---

almost abreast of Meyer's to the inception of Dynasty XVIII: 1587 against 1580.
By the beginning of Dynasty XII, it has, however, got more than 1300 years
ahead: 3400–3300 against 2000. Dynasty I is put at 5500–5400 instead of 3315.
It is only fair to add that Meyer does not insist on precisely 3315, but does
regard 3400–3200 as sure.

[4] A belief is gaining ground that 3315 may have to be reduced to about 3000,
most of the "saving" coming out of the obscure 380 years now allotted to
Dynasties VI to X. This correction, if confirmed, would diminish the total of
1,007 low-level years to 700 or 800, and correspondingly reduce the percentage
of low-level periods from 36 to about 28.

ing known earlier than Middle Kingdom, nor anything of note later than Dynasty XXII. In both these activities we are dependent on papyrus preservation. This might militate against Old Kingdom chances, but ought to favor post-1200 material. Moreover, there seem to be both literary and scientific productions from the Hyksos period of alien dominance. The record of literature thus falls between 2150 and 750, with the best discovered products between 2000 and 1200. In science, the most notable manuscripts date from between 1900 and 1500. It does look as if profane activities dependent on writing by hand had taken a notable development around 2000, with Dynasty XII. Perhaps this was part of a trend toward secularization of thought and activity in general and of writing in particular.

The Ikhnaton reform deserves a comment. In a military sense, the New Empire attained its crest under Thutmose III from 1480 to 1450, according to Meyer, but the aesthetic peak was not reached until about 1400 under Amenhotep III, 1405–1370. His successor was the reformer Ikhnaton, 1370–1352, crowned Amenhotep IV. Religion, both doctrinal and ritual, art, painting, writing, and literature were to be changed in the direction of "truth." Ikhnaton is best known as a monotheist, but this was probably an incident of his struggle with the clergy and of his attempt to remodel the Egyptian culture pattern generally. There must have been a leftist or anticlerical intelligentsia from whom he drew his inspiration and direction. Naturally, most of the innovations seem mild enough from our point of view: one mannerism is replaced by a similar one. There is nothing to show that Egypt had been absorbing much culture from outside, beyond what came in piecemeal and had been readily accommodated in the existing idea-system. The reformist impulse must therefore have been preponderantly of internal origin. The sequence: politico-military peak, peak in art, reform movement, indicates a case of pattern saturation. The patterns of the culture, having been developed to their limits of potentiality, had to be expanded or altered unless repetition and retrogression were to set in. This appears to be what the "reform movement" was. The attempt failed, and with it passed the opportunity for the culture to attain to anything beyond. Thereafter it was condemned to iteration, more or less successful according to circumstances. As a matter of fact, as soon as conservatism had become definitely reëstablished, and a new dynasty, the XIXth, had emerged, this dynasty produced a long-lived ruler, Rameses II, a sort of Grand Monarque, who successfully imitated the more genuine triumphs of warfare and art achieved by the dynasty preceding his own. And six hundred years later, even after a transient conquest by Assyria, the XXVIth dynasty effected a renascence which outwardly followed the age-old lines as closely as possible.

It would be interesting but probably unprofitable to speculate what would have happened in Egyptian culture if the attempt at modification symbolized by Ikhnaton had succeeded. Another question is whether it could have succeeded. The answer to this involves a basic principle: whether a civilization, starting with a definite set of patterns and having reached the apparent limit of these, can through its own efforts reconstitute them and thus achieve a new growth; or whether such a new growth is only possible after a long period of pattern breakdown has elapsed, or through the introduction of foreign culture evolved in a different context. In short, can successful cultural movement in any one direction persist indefinitely, or is a sort of rejuvenation through cultural cross-fertilization necessary sooner or later? I pose the problem as intellectually significant, without being able to offer an answer.[5] There has as yet been too little sustained inquiry into the dynamics and processes of pattern sets or culture wholes. The mass of available data is vast, but conceptual organization of it is only in the beginnings. History is not subject to experiment, and its own endless experimentation is without control.

We can, however, be somewhat more confident about another inference: that the Ikhnaton movement determines the culmination of all Egyptian civilization as having been reached

[5] It is not Spengler's problem, because he begins with the answer that cultures—pattern sets—must die.

in the generation just preceding, say around 1400. If we have interpreted the movement rightly, it could have originated only when the patterns were saturatedly mature, not while they were still in development. On this view, the Pyramid Age, thirteen centuries earlier, and the Middle Kingdom, five centuries before, were preliminary efforts toward what was finally realized in the latter half of Dynasty XVIII, around 1400 B.C.

On the whole, of course, the civilizational process moved slowly in Egypt; but we must guard against conceiving it as unduly slow, for a country unusually sheltered from forcible contacts. It is nearly two thousand years from the beginning of authenticated history to the Hyksos; and nearly three thousand to the first conquest by an organized, civilized power, the later Assyrians. In view of this protection by nature, the intervals of 380 years between the successful periods of the Old and Middle Kingdoms, 205 between Middle and New, and 422 between New Kingdom and the feeble Renascence, are essentially moderate, as compared with some low-level periods in the history of European cultures, which are only parts of a larger whole: France and Germany after their mediaeval florescences, for instance. The slowness in Egypt was rather in the maturing. From the calendar of 4241, or from Dynasty I in 3315 if one wishes to be conservative, to the presumed peak around 1400 is a long span.

§102. China

Before about 1200 B.C., Chinese history is largely inferential and reconstructed. After about 800 B.C., it seems essentially authentic, however trickling the stream of cultural information may at times become.

Two pulses of Sinitic culture growth must be recognized: a protohistoric and a historic. The first outlined and the second developed the same patterns. As in India, the time of the earlier pulse was well pre-Christian; of the second, wholly subsequent to Christ's birth. The second came into its zenith while Europe was still in its Dark Ages, and substantially ended about as the Italian Renaissance dawned.

The earlier or protohistoric Chinese growth is characterized above all by its philosophy, which began developing around 600 or soon after, had ended by 200, and has ever since been accepted by the culture as fundamental. Of other florescences we really know very little—as in India. There was poetry, of which some preserved examples are perhaps centuries older than Confucius; but it is difficult to speak of a peak in folk-song remnants of varying age. About 300 a consciously sophisticated poetry began to be produced for some two centuries. This is difficult for the foreigner to evaluate; perhaps for the modern native also. A very great historian, Szŭ-ma Ch'ien, appears around 100 B.C. Inasmuch as there is continuity of deliberate history writing back not only to Confucius but for some centuries before him, and as excellent history continued to be produced to 100 A.D., we can regard Szŭ-ma Ch'ien as the zenith of a growth. Of what was produced in pre-Han China in painting, sculpture, and architecture we know almost nothing. It is likely that there was little, because archaeology has discovered nothing notable, whereas it does know technological and decorative products of a high order, especially in bronze. Apart from these, however, early Chinese culture seems to have developed chiefly on a basis of verbalizing patterns: philosophy and ethics, subjective poetry, history.

After an interval of several centuries, about the time of the breakup of the Hans, there began, one after another, a series of developments which constitute the historic growth as compared with the protohistoric. Literature began around 150, sculpture 200, philology 250, painting by 400 if not earlier, science around 400. These are all pre-T'ang beginnings. The culminations for poetry, sculpture, and painting are usually set around 700–750, midway in the T'ang dynasty; scientific productivity ended then; the philological development was completed soon after 600.

All these intellectual-aesthetic growths with T'ang culmination were more or less Buddhist-influenced, in part even "derived" from Buddhism. As a propagandizing religion, however, Buddhism spent its force in T'ang times. Thereafter, Chinese civilization remained Buddhistically colored, but never again in danger of becoming Buddhism-dominated. Enough of the Buddhist influence was sublimated off into aesthetic, intellectual, and social expressions for the remainder to suffice only for an ingredient in a religious blend or composite.

The ninth and tenth centuries were, on the whole, a pause in culture growth.

Then developments recommence, to form a second, differently constituted phase of the historic growth. We have: literature, 1000–1050; painting, which had never wholly declined, reached new peaks around 1100, 1200, and perhaps 1350; philosophy, 1050–1200, with culmination just before its close; history, 1050–1200; drama, soon after 1200 to perhaps 1400; and, in science, a brief burst of algebra from 1240 to 1320.

In this "Sung" phase, Buddhism is no longer a driving force. As a cult and faith, it has shrunk to a place in a larger whole; its general cultural effects have been long since assimilated.

After 1400, decline. Only the novel written in nonclassical language made progress.

Of the two phases of the historic growth, the first with its mid-T'ang culmination is usually reckoned the greater. The second tended either to develop new specialties, like the theater and algebra, or to subtilize toward preciosity, as in painting. The Sung "Neo-Confucian" philosophy has had only limited repute and less influence outside of China. To a westerner it seems efficiently compact but lacking in variety of fundamental ideas, and surprising in some of its retentions, like that of the philosophically immature and gratuitous *yin-yang* dichotomy.

The distinctness of the two phases of the historic growth ought certainly to be recognized; but they are so close in time, and in many of their patterns, that they probably belong within one growth.

Correlation between national solidarity and cultural achievement is obviously only partial in China. The later Chou period was certainly one of high accomplishments: the characteristic Chinese ideology was then given its form. But the time was one of warring states and political chaos. Ts'in brought unity and expansion, and Han carried these further; but culturally there was consolidation rather than progress. After the Hans, for 400 years the Empire was broken into rival dynasties and northern China was most of the time under the rule of barbarian invaders; yet the great historic culture cycle had its definite beginning then, so that it was able to culminate immediately afterward under the T'angs. Late T'ang and early Sung marked a temporary recession of culture; which became productive again, in several activities, under the decaying fortunes of the later or Southern Sung and under the early foreign Mongols. Subsequently Ming and Manchu witnessed revivals of political strength and economic prosperity, with encouragement of higher culture, but without any important measure of cultural creativeness of patterns. It is clear that any formulation of culture history in terms of Han, T'ang, Sung, and Ming as "prosperous," and Ts'in (Three Kingdoms) and Tsin (Six Dynasties), Mongol, Manchu as either tyrannous or riven and disastrous, is simplistic.

As a matter of fact, very few dynasties anywhere are genuinely successful for four, three, or even two continuous centuries, and it is wise to guard against evaluating as real units in this regard the dynasties by which Chinese history is usually reckoned. As for strong rule internally, and ability to act offensively on the frontier, few Chinese dynasties show more than one or two genuinely able and successful rulers. Ts'in, the first house to unite China, collapsed immediately after its founder's death. Han is really two dynasties, separated by a usurper. Wu Ti, 140–86, is the outstanding monarch. Sui, like Ts'in, was unifying, able, but brief. T'ang got off to a good start under T'ai Tsung; but within a century the reign of Hüan Tsung, 712–756, ended in revolt, flight, and destructive civil war. The Mings produced two able early rulers, Hung Wu and Yung Lo, 1368–1424; the Manchus, K'ang Hsi and Chien Lung, 1661–1722 and 1736–1796. Almost always, the strong rulers come early in the succession. The dynasties being so far from politically uniform units, it is natural that they have even less relation to cultural growths.

The developmental relation between the two Chinese growths seems to be somewhat as follows.

In the Chou cycle a classical literary ideology was worked out. This provided for metaphysics, ethics, politics, magic and cult, history, poetry—all verbalizable activities. Science had no place in the pattern, except as a technology of inferior prestige; nor did tangible art, except again as technology; it therefore remained on a decorative level. Music was the only aesthetic function which received genuine sanction from the culture; partly because the associated song was verbal and therefore conformable to the ideological pattern, partly because of its tie with cult and its supposed ethical effect.

The Ts'in book-burning edict was a transient reaction, a sort of Spartacus revolt from above, against this system. Under the Han, the Chou ideology was promptly restored, and perpetuated by the institution of examinations in scholarship. That the scholarship became increasingly written and textual did not alter its essential nature, though it became thereby less easily permeable by outside influences. Metaphysical inquiry was felt as a disturbing factor, and it was therefore gradually outlawed as unclassical; Taoism, the strongest ingredient of metaphysics, was depressed into survival affiliation with a popular cult of religious magic. This antimetaphysical attitude was already present in Confucius; it achieved realization with his canonization. Obviously, Han sought and accomplished little except a sort of codification. In the field of history its advance was perhaps due to the increasing specialization and professionalization of scholarship.

However, Buddhism had gained entrance during Han; and, as a world religion always does, it carried many values and much ideology which was unrelated to it in origin but which had become interknit with it. From the end of Han to mid-T'ang was the period when Buddhism as a force was most active in China and came nearest to challenging the established order of culture; with Taoism as a minor but adaptive and imitative competitor. It is due to Buddhistic influence that Chinese sculpture, painting, and architecture developed in the four post-Han centuries. This is generally admitted. The same is probably true for philology, and at least in part for science. Here then was a series of activities, not intrinsically in conflict with the old scholarly system but unprovided for in it, which were pushed up into the national culture pattern from below, through popular acceptance of a great alien religion and therewith of its extrinsic attachments. The one old Chinese manifestation which reflowered in T'ang was poetry, now viewed for the first time as a self-sufficient aesthetic objective. Incidentally, it also had the new element of tonal arrangement.

Such was the first phase of the second or historic Chinese growth. After a lull in the passage from T'ang to Sung, the second phase emerged to prevail through Southern Sung and Yüan. This phase took two directions. On the one hand, the old scholarly tradition reasserted itself. History revived; the ancient philosophy was given reëxpression; and painting, long associated with calligraphy, flowered in the hands of "superior" or "cultivated" persons—that is, tended to become sophisticate, specialized, and precious. On the other hand, new popular activities, now no longer carried by the flood of Buddhism but, like it, essentially bourgeois or plebeian in appeal, won themselves a place in the culture as a whole, though scarcely achieving recognition from the scholarly class. Such were the drama, and then the novel; and mathematics. The latter is distinctly specified as popular in origin and appeal; and the literati very soon managed to misunderstand and then to forget it.

By 1400 or soon after, these new impulses from below, except the novel, had exhausted themselves; and so had the Neo-Confucian and supercultivation efforts of the scholars.

Will four centuries of import of Occidental culture material lead before long to a new Chinese growth, as Indian Buddhism once did?

§103. Japan

Japanese culture and nationality are marked by less rise and fall than is usual. Isolation is the evident cause. There are no actual neighbors. Korea is the nearest country, and is itself marginal to China, through which culture influences from the rest of the world had mainly to filter, until about 1400, in order to reach the island empire. In historic times, there has never been a successful invasion. Kublai's armadas of 1274 and 1281 did not penetrate beyond the coast of landing. Japanese participation in mainland affairs, until the eve of the twentieth century, was not much greater. From perhaps 364 to 562, Japan maintained a feudatory Korean province. Just a century later, she locked horns disastrously with a T'ang army in defense of one of the Korean kingdoms. From 1592 to 1598, Hideyoshi kept armies in Korea. They defeated the natives, ravaged the peninsula, fully held their own against the Chinese, accomplished little, and were withdrawn on Hideyoshi's death.

Overseas relations accordingly were in the main peaceful, and the Japanese received of foreign culture only what they accepted voluntarily, or believed they wished to accept. Military energies were spent internally, in civil or feudal family wars. When these became unusually frequent or chronic, the adverse effect on cultural productivity was similar to prolonged internal dissension or unsuccessful foreign wars in other nations. Such periods were the *Gempei* or Taira-Minamoto conflict of 1159–1199, the struggle of the Northern and Southern Courts of 1337–1392, the *Sengoku* or Epoch of Wars from 1490 to 1600. Not one of these contained a prime efflorescence in any department of culture.[6] On the contrary, periods either of quiescence or of strong centralized rule, like Nara–Early Heian, Kamakura, and Tokugawa, hold the great civilizational achievements.

A further appearance of continuity is given by the unbroken dynasty which has nominally ruled the land since prehistoric times. Not that this mattered much in itself, since the feeling of the Japanese for at least twelve centuries has been that government should be indirect, through and not by the sovereign. But the sense for continuity is symptomatic. In the same way the primitive national set of cults and shrines,

---

[6] Except that a full half of the era of great Ashikaga painting falls after 1490; though the peak, as calculated in § 51 (p. 341), probably came before 1490.

the Shinto, has persisted unbroken, though of course not un-altered, since pre-Buddhist times.

The relation of cultural dependence on China is illustrated both by priority and by contribution.

The antecedence of China will be taken for granted: but the variability of the interval according to item is of interest. As the little tabulation shows, the Japanese lagged from one or two centuries to more than a thousand years behind. Of course, in addition, they never accepted certain features of Chinese culture at all, and retained or developed others of their own.

	China	Japan
Bronze	—1500 or earlier	^{k}—4th cent.?
Writing	Established by —1200	^{k}405
Iron	Common in —7th cent.	^{k}—4th cent. or later
Coins minted	—4th cent.	677
Abolition of "feudalism"	Ca. —220	1868
Last burial of live retainers	—209?	Ca. 123?
Buddhism officially recognized	"65"	^{k}552
True block printing	7th cent.	8th cent. (extant spec. 770)
Printing with movable type	1049	^{k}1592–1595
Southern-Sung-style painting	*1210	*1460
Neo-Confucianism	*1180	*1720
Algebra	*1303	*1675
Drama	*1280–1370	*1400, *1703
Novel	13th–17th cents.	*1807 (1682 seq.)†

Minus sign (—), B.C.; asterisk (*), culmination; raised "k" (^{k}), via Korea, or probably so.

† An earlier novel of court life flourished around 1000.

On the side of contributions to the world's civilization, the disparity is as one-sided as in time. China invented silk, paper, book printing, gunpowder at least for use in fireworks, rhyme in poetry, playing cards, paper money, porcelain, and admin-istration by examination-tested civil service. As against these, there is not one cultural contribution of consequence which can be credited to Japan and which was later taken up in other parts of the world. Items like folding fans and a revolving theatrical stage about represent the level of Japanese original invention.

Of course this is no evidence of any intrinsic inferiority of the Japanese. It is the result of their being shut off from the whole world except China and Korea during most of their history; whereas China, remote though accessible to other centers, began to receive foreign culture early and continued to receive it, and could make return. That the Japanese possess sufficient originality is shown by the way they grafted onto their own tradition and made over almost every institution and art which they took from China. On their periphery, origination perforce became almost equivalent with remodeling. The generalization which one is tempted to venture to draw from their case is that an isolated people will change its culture but is unlikely to produce much that will pass on to others even when the barriers are removed. Egypt supports the idea.

Considering now more particularly the swells in the continuity of Japanese civilization, I would recognize four such: Nara–Early Heian, 700–900; Kamakura, 1200–1300; Middle Ashikaga, perhaps 1400–1500; and Middle Tokugawa, 1650–1800.

When the Nara period opened in 710, writing had been introduced in Japan three centuries before, Buddhism a century and a half, Korean artists nearly as long, Japanese students had begun to visit China a century before. Time had therefore passed for the assimilation and nationalization of what had come in from the great civilization overseas; even for the dropping of what was impractical in the Taikwa or Daika reform or administrative overimitation of 645. National consciousness was just crystallizing in the compilation of the *Kojiki* and *Nihongi* legends and records. The eighth century produced probably the greatest religious sculpture; the ninth, the flower of Japanese poetry and the early great painting. The poetry was wholly nonreligious; the painting, like the sculpture, was fervently Buddhist.

Three centuries of Fujiwara regency or ascendancy followed, with extreme cultivation of taste but without any very great productions except in prose literature around 1000. This prose is insufficient to constitute a national swell: first, because it is only prose; second, probably, because the best authors were women; and third, because the most successful genre was the novel, a relatively unformalized type. Toward the end of the long period fall the fierce Taira-Minamoto wars.

The second swell is the Kamakura period, 1192–1333; let us say the thirteenth century. Now, for the first time since civilization had been installed, the warrior dominated the court aristocrat, and austerity and frugality were exalted by him. This is the century of the second great sculpture of Japan, still religious but less fervidly and exclusively so than before; of the superb paintings of episodes of national history; and of vigorous prose narratives of romantic history.

The first part of the Ashikaga shogunate, 1337–1392, was filled with the conflict of the Northern and Southern courts. The second part, say 1400–1490, was the period of the *No* plays, of the *renga* or chain poetry, and of the painting which the Japanese consider their greatest. If one rates Motonobu, 1476–1559, equal to Sesshu, 1420–1506, the florescence should be prolonged somewhat beyond 1500. All the arts that culminated in this time are definitely specialized. Ashikaga was a period of luxury, public extravagance, overbreeding; also the one in which the virtues of loyalty and devotion were weakest, according to native historians.

The Ashikaga or Muromachi regime lasted until 1573, after European influences had entered; but its last chapter falls into the long Sengoku unrest, 1490–1600; and it produced nothing but a declining painting. Toward the end of the conflicts, three strong men emerged: Nobunaga, Hideyoshi, and Ieyasu, born in 1534, 1536, and 1542. Through them peace was restored, and Ieyasu initiated the Tokugawa shogunate, 1603–1868, under which government was centralized, Christianity was suppressed, isolation enforced, but Japan participated in the growth of wealth and population of most of the rest of the world.

It took the stable Tokugawa conditions about fifty years to bear their cultural fruit; and their last fifty or more evince decline. This leaves a century and a half, say 1650–1800, for the florescence. In this there fall the only science which Japan ever developed, a remarkable algebra carrying further the forgotten one of China, with culmination around 1675–1700; a true, nonreligious drama, wholly new to the country, with its peak in the decade or so after 1700; the *hàikai* type of poetry around 1675; and the realistic novel, from about the same date on. This last, in fact, is generally recognized as having culminated in Bakin, 1767–1848, or after 1800. Painting subsequent to about 1700 followed lines similar to the novel, in representing *ukiyo* or "life"; but it rated lower than in pre-Tokugawa days. Other symptoms are: a systematic preoccupation with Neo-Confucianism, especially in the earlier Tokugawa time—the Japanese never accomplished much in philosophy, but this was at least an endeavor to deal with it; an attempt to understand Shinto and national institutions in an anti-Chinese spirit, somewhat later; and an analysis of grammar, beginning in 1771.

If it were not for the great group of painters toward 1500, the Ashikaga florescence could be omitted. Its chain verses and *No* semiplays could be ignored without much concern. In that case we should have three swells: 700–900, 1200–1300, 1650–1800, plus or minus, separated by intervals of about three centuries: a much simpler configuration. I do not know what attitude to take toward this possibility. As I have said before, I am left without the help of evaluation of a subjective reaction toward Sesshu, Motonobu, and their contemporaries.

Somewhat of the obverse holds for the *ukiyo-e* or low-life art of the eighteenth and early nineteenth centuries, as typified by by Hokusai. The nonsubtle vigor of this made it the first Japanese art to become appreciated by westerners. Then, as they learned from the Japanese, and came to feel themselves into native attitudes, there was a reaction; and possibly an underappreciation. We of the West are so new to these things that the pendulum may swing back. In general, a nation's own judgment of its best qualities may be safely trusted. But the Japanese have been so long under the spell of aristocratic refinement that it may have become a fetish which warps them unduly against whatever smacks of the bourgeois-plebeian; and they may not yet have overcome this bias sufficiently to be safe guides. They have only just entered cosmopolitan civilization, and we do not know what their own verdict on Tokugawa bourgeois art will be a century hence. The Chinese may be equal newcomers in evaluations from the Western standpoint, but at least they possess the perspective of nearly a thousand years since the great fabric of their own culture was woven into its pattern. Therefore I affirm nothing on these respective merits of Sesshu and Hokusai, of Ashikaga and Tokugawa, but present the alternatives.

It is evident that from one point of view the whole history of Japan has been the dissipation of culture outward from the nucleus of the entourage of the sacred emperor. Writing was adopted by or for the court when it became of use to the court. Buddhism became the religion of the country when the court decreed. Painters and sculptors were imported from foreign courts to work on court-decreed temples. Literature was the recreation of princes, nobles, and court ladies, who alone could read. Philosophy and science, which are hard work, were of course not developed by these people. The Fujiwara period mainly carried all these inclinations farther out on a limb of the tree, and of course added little.

The first break came around 1200 with the triumph of the Kamakura-Hojo regime—the warrior class. They seized power, but maintained it by separating themselves from the court. They still ranked lower—not above the sixth grade of officials.

Under Ashikaga-Muromachi, military power weakened but military status improved; until, by 1600, order was reëstablished by the three great military leaders. Hideyoshi, the second of these, was a commoner, the son of a farmer.

In the Tokugawa peace, industry, trade, and cities grew, and with them, for the first time apparently, a class of wealthy commoners, educated plebeians, a true bourgeoisie. Incidentally, it is one of the problems of history why this phenomenon should have occurred so closely parallel in time in western Europe and in self-excluded Japan. For this bourgeoisie there were developed the new novel and drama, new verse forms, the new painting, and color blocks; also the belated mathematics, which was popular, not classical, in its appeal.

The Meiji era of 1868, with Constitution, elected Diet, universal conscription instead of service by a military class, obviously carries the centrifugal democratization or plebeianization another step along. It is not a question here of who really governs, but of formal participation in the nation's cultural functioning.

We can observe something similar in China, but on a much milder scale; because China on the one hand has long since stripped off her formal aristocracy, and on the other, except temporarily under the Sungs, did not overvalue preciosity and refinement. The corresponding Chinese phenomena therefore have manifested themselves chiefly in an ignoring of new and popular forms like novel and drama, and in some measure science, by the orthodox tradition of the literati.

The other difference is that China, after a pre-Christian period of gestation, gradually developed her cultural patterns in one great configuration, the peak of which is long since past; whereas Japan progressed by a series of pulsations, of which it is difficult to say whether the earlier or the later come nearer to the ideal goal of fruition.

§104. India

India, in the last three millennia, shows two periods of florescence. The first, some five centuries before Christ, groups around the name of Buddha, and is protohistoric or traditional. The second is historic, in a long swell from 100 to 1200 A.D., with the greatest average altitude around perhaps 400–600.

These are the phenomena with which it is possible to deal historically; but they do not exhaust the story. First of all, there is the Indus Valley or Mohenjo-daro civilization of around 3000 B.C., or at least not later than the third millennium. We cannot yet say whether its recently discovered remains represent a peak or a level, nor whether they characterize only the northwest frontier or a larger part of India.

Then there is the civilization of the South of India, including perhaps the East of the peninsula also. It has lately become fashionable to postulate a florescence of this Dravidian culture around the beginning of the Christian era, or even earlier. This helps to solve certain ethnographic or culture-historical problems, such as the change from Aryan Vedic frontier culture to historic Aryan-Dravidian pan-Indian Hinduism. But, so far as I can control the literature, both the nature and content of this early South Indian civilization, and its time and geographic range, remain hypothetical if not speculative. At least, if there exists substantial evidence, this appears not to have been presented as at all extricated from technical argument and supposition.

At any rate, it is important to remember that the culture history of India which we can deal with here is, presumably, only part of a longer history.

To the protohistoric florescence are attributed the following names and achievements:

Kapila, traditional founder of Samkhya philosophy, ca. 600 B.C.
Buddha, d. 543 or 483/77.
Mahāvīra, contemporary, founder of Jainism.
Suśruta, of the time of Buddha, head of school of medicine at Benares.
Ātreya, rival head at Taxila.
Śulvasūtra mathematics, date of the older portions guessed variably from the 8th century to the 4th.
Pānini the grammarian, date sometimes estimated as early as the 8th or 7th century, more likely of the 5th or 4th.

This looks as if it might be in large part a legendary golden age, a creation of the imagination of an unhistorical-minded people, made at a time when they did not yet possess the faculty of writing or at least exercised it but slightly. On the contrary, it would be hard to imagine Buddhism alone, not to mention historically authentic Indian culture in general, casually growing out of nothing, without some constellational antecedents. The Vedas are distinctly too meager to prefigure later India; and the crystallization of the great mass of cultural ideas subsequently added to the Vedic ideology, whether by absorption or by evolution, ought to have led to a configuration. The rather definite localization of the tradition is also confirmatory: on the lower-middle Ganges around old Magadha, and secondarily on the northwest frontier.

We can grant, accordingly, that all the dates of this earlier Indian peak may be unauthentic, that names and accomplishments many centuries earlier or later may have been projected into it, and that yet an essential historic truth is likely to underlie the systematized traditions. One might even suspect that the period of high cultural productivity had been long and that the error of tradition lay in part in having overconcentrated it.

There follows an interval of five or six centuries with less clustering. Into this there fall:

> The essential creation of the two national epics, as distinct from their subsequent interpolation and expansion; period perhaps 400 B.C.–200 A.D.
>
> Sculpture at Sarnath, Sanchi, Mathura, Amaravati, Peshawar, 300 B.C.–400 A.D.
>
> Philology, say 500–100, with the culmination under Pāṇini most conservatively put around 350 B.C., unless he belongs to the protohistoric growth.

Some of these may be the aftermath of the assumed florescence that preceded.

The productive constellation of India which is historically documented, even though many of its dates remain only estimates, begins perhaps a century after the Christian era, is mainly over by 900, and wholly so by 1200. Its principal components are the following.

	Total period	Climax
Philosophy I	100–500	150–450
Sculpture	– 300–800	400–500
Drama	?100–750	350–450
Literature	200–1200	350–750 (*ca. 400)
Science	400–1150	500–625
Painting	450–750	550–650
Philology	600–650	
Philosophy II	600–1000	800–850

It is evident that, with the exception of the two philosophical phases, the climaxes all begin between 350 and 550 and end between 450 and 750, or with one exception by 650. This yields 350–650, or, more reductively, about 400–600, as the period of greatest average florescence. The one departure is philosophy, of which the gross duration of 900 years, from 100 to 1000, seems to be interrupted by a sixth-century near-suspension and by an interval of about 350 years between its climaxes. In short, two philosophical peaks mark the beginning and end of a cluster of peaks in other activities.

If it were not for the preëminence accorded in native opinion to Sankara, ca. 800—perhaps because he summed up orthodox Vedanta thought—the second philosophic phase could be relegated as an aftermath, the total span of climaxes would be shortened by a century, and we should not be faced by the discrepancy of a temporary slump in philosophy at the very moment when most of the other activities were at or near their peaks.

Nationalism has remained relatively undeveloped in vast, amorphous, caste-segmented India. It is customary to associate some of the florescences with the Gupta dynasty of 320–490, ruling from the seat of ancient Magadha; and the peak phase of sculpture is named from this line of rulers. Kalidasa also belongs to this period. But science and painting are at their best later, and philosophy before and after. As a political structure the Gupta dominion was both superficial and transient: certainly evanescent and local when one compares it with the millennium-long pan-Indian cultural growth. One would almost incline to look for a political-cultural correlation rather in India south of the Vindhyas, where fairly stable kingdoms, Dravidian as well as Aryan, flourished from the sixth century.

After the Guptas, there seems to have existed but one major or international native kingdom in northern India, that established in the first half of the seventh century by Harsha and barely outlasting him. For the rest, whenever consolidated rule was achieved, it was by Afghans, Turks, Mongol epigones, or Britishers—Mohammedans or Christians. This Indian helplessness, it is well to remember, antedates the close of the cultural growth by a full five hundred years.

At that, India has been exposed to conquest by foreigners almost constantly though intermittently since Darius, without ever reciprocating. Her colonial empires in Indo-China and Indonesia were autonomous, among willing semiprimitives, and conquests of culture rather than of the sword, so far as we can judge.

The first great native empire within India of which we have record, that of the Maurya, immediately after the invasion of Alexander and possibly stimulated thereby, coincides with little that is definite in cultural peaks.

The correlation of national achievement and intellectual-aesthetic achievement seems, in short, to be low in India; which is what might be suspected from the unusually abstruse cast of Indian civilization.

Since 1200, little of a very high cultural order has been accomplished in India. There are Mogul-Rajput painting and vernacular poetry, the latter especially in Hindi, both culminating around 1600. But neither of these growths can pretend to genuine first rank of value by world-wide standards: they rate rather with the near-contemporary Chinese novel and drama, in quality as well as in their epigonal character.[7]

The relation between the Buddhist and the Brahmanic or Hinduistic components of Indian civilization has been much discussed, but is by no means clear. We do know that the Vedas are earlier than anything Buddhistic, and that they have been sacrosanct in the Brahmanical cults to the present day in spite of the enormous non-Vedic elements which have accreted to Indian civilization. Buddhism, on the contrary, not only began later than the Vedas, but essentially rejected them; and, after long flourishing alongside Brahmanical cults, died out on most of the mainland of India by about 1000 A.D., and on the eastern periphery, in Bengal, some two centuries later. Buddhism meanwhile had spread over all eastern Asia; whereas Brahman-

---

[7] Jayadeva's *Gītagovinda*, before 1200, has already something of the new patterns of the future: rhyme and simplicity, for instance.

ism scarcely got any foreign foothold except in the coastal portions of Farther India and Indonesia, where it competed with Buddhism. Within India, accordingly, Buddhism is a sort of episode encapsulated in the more permanent continuous history of Brahmanism; outside, Brahmanism was the episode, and Buddhism one of the enduring world religions.

Now what were the respective parts of these two strands in the culture history and florescences of India? This is an important matter which has never been satisfactorily defined. Most of the sculpture and nearly all the preserved painting of India are Buddhist. But some of the best is Brahmanical. The formal systems of philosophy are perforce Brahman, because orthodox. But the earlier development of logic seems Buddhist. And how far the Samkhya system is a philosophy extricated in acceptable Hinduistic form out of the nonacceptable Buddhist religion, or, on the contrary, how far the religion grew out of the partly developed philosophy, as legend has it, is not clear. In general, it seems as if the Buddhistic ingredient had been more oriented toward the world at large, and was therefore not only more influential outside of India, but more receptive internally to stimuli from without and thus quicker to originate new features. Brahmanism was more self-centered and resistive, but also more intent on the sharply defined working-out of an interrelated set of highly specialized patterns. It therefore consistently rejected Buddhism as such, but gradually accepted as much of Buddhist content and influence as it could work over into its own specifically Hindu system of ideals. On this view, there was little in the nature of a conflict, like that of Christianity with Mohammedanism, between Buddhism and Brahmanism. Rather were they expressions of polar attitudes within one civilization: one assimilative, expansive, and leveling, the other contractive, refining, and accentuating. Had the Buddhist attitude wholly prevailed, most of the finest qualities of Indian culture would have been dissipated; if Brahman, they might early have atrophied into sterility. Both attitudes were necessary to the full fruition of the civilization. Such at least is one way of conceiving the relation.

It is clear that Buddhism, even more as an attitude than as a cult, appealed to the masses and the lowly. That occasional kings embraced it within India is no wonder. We do not know how far they felt themselves hampered by firmly rooted privileges; and alliances of king and demos are frequent in history. As in China and Japan, the civilization tried hard to hold fast to what it had achieved, whether through literati, aristocrats, or priests and allied castes; but there was also a countercurrent of the popular-nonclassical, the plebeian-bourgeois, the Buddhistic-Bhakti, respectively. Not all conflicts of this sort are fought out along consciously economic lines of holding or seizing power. Some are not fought at all, but result in constant slow readjustments through many centuries.

Returning once more to the great historic growth of India, we must note its length: a thousand years as against about half that for the Greek and Islamic-Arabic growths. Occidental civilization has until now had some seven centuries of florescences, and may well persist for a total of ten, or more; but it has come in pulsations and with replacements of nation by nation; so that the case is not parallel. In short, growth and decline have been slow in India. Evidently the basic cultural patterns have been deeply characterized, and persistent both for that reason and because of the size of the populational mass.

As for absolute time relations: The period 100 to 1200 is almost exactly that of the interval between the last Ancient Mediterranean and the first Occidental florescences. Moreover, if we accept 400 to 600 as the Indian peak, it coincides rather closely with the depth of the trough between these two western civilizations. The best of the Indian growth was over before the Islamic one began; the two ended together because of the greater brevity of the latter. As for the Far East, India and China have their historic growths of cultural productivity almost contemporary, but with the Indian slightly in advance both in inception and in average peak. The two regions are alike also in possessing an earlier, somewhat shadowy, but indubitable growth of importance centering not far, either way, from 500 B.C.

§105. The Ancient Mediterranean
(Hellenic, Roman, Byzantine)

The Classic or Antique or Greek-Roman culture was essentially European—though corner European—as compared with the Afro-Asiatic cultures of Egypt, Syria, and Mesopotamia which preceded it; and it was very largely carried by Indo-Europeans instead of by Hamites, Sumerians, and Semites. The only non-Indo-Europeans who seriously participated in it—and they are, more strictly, not known to be Indo-European rather than provenly non-Indo-European—were the Minoans of the Greek prologue and the Etruscans who provided an analogous preface for Rome.

Outside of Europe, the coasts of Anatolia have long held a Greek fringe. With Alexander, a flood of Greek culture was poured over all the Near East. It maintained itself a thousand years in Syria and Egypt, at least as a heavy and influential veneer, and longer in Anatolia. In Mesopotamia and Iran its influence was more superficial and its permanence much more transient. These inner lands, like Arabia, remained basically Asiatic in civilization. Somewhat later, the Romans laid a similar coating of culture and partly of speech on coastal North Africa. This too, like the Hellenization of Asia and Egypt, dissolved before Islam if not earlier.

With these Macedonian and Roman extensions, the civilization changed spatially from a marginal southeast European one—originally dependent on nearer Asia and Egypt—to a pan-Mediterranean one; and such it was, without residue, at its greatest extension. It penetrated farthest inland on its northwest, into Europe, where the Danube, Rhine, and Clyde became its frontier. These European gains were made after the temporary spread into and beyond Mesopotamia had in large part been lost.

As the culture aged and contracted, it shrank back upon itself spatially, until it ended where it began: on the Aegean. Today Greek speech—one of the two languages in which this culture was expressed when it became international—has very nearly the same focal geographical distribution as it had twenty-five hundred years ago.

With the other great European civilization, the Occidental, the Mediterranean had these relations of time and space: It was earlier to the degree that all its genuine productivity was over before the specific patterns of Occidental culture began to form. There was, it is true, a temporal overlap: the Occident was producing before the atrophied Byzantine end of Mediterranean civilization was quite extinguished. But the significance is in chronology rather than in cultural values.

Geographically, Italy, Spain, France, England, parts of Germany, Austria, Hungary were covered by both civilizations. But to the older culture these were peripheral provinces, last conquered and assimilated and first given up—except, in a measure, Italy. To the later civilization they were the lands both of its crystallization and its climaxing, and for long it did not extend beyond them except in much weakened form. Italy is the one country which is integral to both.

It will be evident that the Greek and Roman civilizations are here treated as closely related parts of one great culture growth, the Roman being the western manifestation and the more transient one—much more transient, within the civilization itself, though important for the nourishment it long afforded the young Occidental culture which succeeded it.

The full sequence of culturally productive phases is:

Minoan, pre-Greek
Mycenaean, proto-Greek
Homeric
Hellenic and Hellenistic
Roman
Imperial Hellenic or mature Graeco-Roman
Early Byzantine
Byzantine Renaissance.

Aegean phase: Minoan and Mycenaean.—The prologue to Mediterranean civilization was performed on the Aegean coasts and islands, especially in Crete. Here grew up, under influences generally accounted more Egyptian than Asiatic, a semi-independent Minoan culture which passed out of the Neolithic stage around 3000, and had become largely autonomous soon after 2000. In the periods which first Evans and then custom have designated as Middle Minoan III, Late Minoan I, and Late Minoan II, the Cretan culture reached its apogee. The time may be 1700 to 1400. There was a vivid, lively, nonmonumental plastic and pictorial art—vases, frescos, and inlaying are all known—possessed of certain curiously anticipatory Greek qualities. We know something of buildings, dress, games, cults, conveniences of life; hardly enough, however, to trace cyclic growth. Many of these activities already seem more Greek than Egyptian or Asiatic. There was writing; it is undeciphered, and the language therefore unknown; it is supposed to have been non-Greek. About 1400–1350—the date is uncertain,—sudden ruin by violence overtook this Minoan civilization at Cnossos and elsewhere in Crete. The following Late Minoan III phase is a feeble attempt to resume and carry on.

Meanwhile, other phases of this culture had established themselves around the shores of the Aegean, their relations of influence, time, and locality complex and not always clear from the solely archaeological evidences. Among these was a mainland facies, the Mycenaean, which is believed to have been also Aegean—that is, non-Greek—in origin, but maintained by Greeks, for the most part, by the time the Cretan Minoans collapsed. Late Mycenaean therefore carried on, approximately, where Late Minoan II ended; and it continued to flourish until perhaps 1200 or after. Then came the Iron Age, invasions by ruder branches of Greeks, and a general degradation of higher culture for several centuries.

Homeric phase.—Around 850—some would have it by 900 or even earlier—and continuing to 750 or after, the Homeric and Hesiodic poems originated or took substantial shape. The culture they describe is half Mycenaean, half Hellenic; the language, myth, and meter are wholly Greek. In fact their poetical form is the foundation of all Greek poetical form.

Here, then, we have one definitive Hellenic pattern well established. The trouble with our understanding it is that it stands alone. There is as yet no Hellenic architecture, sculpture, painting, philosophy, science. The time gap to the earliest of these is not very great, and it is threaded if not bridged by the continuance of production of epic poetry well into the historic Greek period. Still, there appears to be a gap. All that we can say in the present consideration of the Homeric phase is that it is a definitely Greek beginning—a swallow of spring.

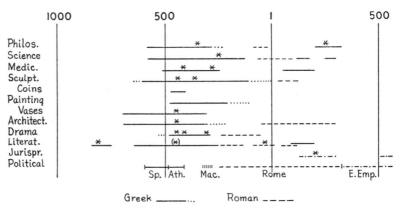

SEGREGATION OF THE HELLENIC-ROMAN CULTURE GROWTH

Hellenic-Hellenistic phase.—The main or great phase is shown in the accompanying diagram. It may be said to have lasted from 700 to 1 B.C. If we cut off the very earliest vase painting of promise, and the last scattering examples of noble sculpture, the duration can be reduced to but little over five centuries: 650 to 125.

The flowering of this civilization has become one of the familiarities of history. From it the notions are perhaps derived that sculpture normally precedes painting, that philosophy is earlier than science, and that literature is associated with military success. Each idea contains some truth. Greek sculpture did attain mastery before picture painting, but was preceded by vase painting of an extraordinary spiritedness and charm. Philosophy and science started abreast, or rather as one, but philosophy exhausted itself a century or two sooner. The association of successful war with literature holds only for drama, in time, and has been made unduly vivid and mnemonic by legend or epigram with regard to the participations of Aeschylus, Sophocles, and Euripides in the victory of Salamis.

Actually, what is specially characteristic of the great Hellenic configuration is the near-synchronism of its various developments. They rose swiftly, they culminated high, they lapped each other closely when they were not wholly contemporary. It is the typical but ultranormal picture of a great civilization on its great surge, and it has indelibly impressed human imagination since.

It was obviously a culture too great for its area and population. Hence, perhaps, the unquenchable internecine rivalries. A lack of room for expansion without larger political leadership, and inability to change the political pattern after the patterns of other activities, which had grown up in association with this, were full-fledged, are perhaps the reason why the Greeks succumbed to Macedon and then to Rome, rather than the presence of a mysterious blind spot among their many acuities of vision and ability.

Macedon was truly the precursor of Rome. It may have been, as late as the Persian Wars, as non-Hellenic as Lydia. We do not even know whether its speech was an aberrant Greek dialect or a member of some very different branch of Indo-European. By Philip's time Macedon had Hellenized. We know very little of the process, but it must have been rapid, because relations with the Greeks had become very different in the intervening century and a half. Hellenized Macedon was promptly able to master not only Greece but nearer Asia as well. The only culture which it had, for carrying into Asia and Egypt, was the Greek one; and the Hellenization of the Near East was the most important result of Alexander's conquest. Already at his death, what was left in Asia that was Macedonian? A few myriads of veterans and some generals to seize old kingdoms. Within a few generations, their descendants were Greek so far as they were not Oriental—the Attaluses,

Seleucids, Antigonids, Ptolemies. One cannot think of Cleo-
patra as a Macedonian, unless Macedonian has first been
equated to Greek.

The Philip-Alexander episode was but a forerunning parallel to longer and more solid Roman domination. The chief
difference is that while the Macedonians spread Greek civilization, the Romans fixed it enduringly over most of the same
area.

Specific Roman phase.—The diagram shows how neatly
Roman higher culture began to flourish when Greek left off.
Its culminating period is essentially that of the century before
Christ and the century after; only the drama is essentially of
the second pre-Christian century. Law, it is true, runs from
the second century after Christ through the third; but, though
the language remains Latin, many of the great jurists were
easterners, and their period is that of the next phase.[8]

Graeco-Roman or Imperial phase.—Shortly before 100 A.D.,
Roman imperial rule passed out of its frenetic throes and became firmly established with a sense of responsibility. A century of profound peace followed this resurrection of the old
Roman spirit. Then the legions and the barbarians began to
batter the order, until the West finally crumbled away; but in
the East the Empire maintained its solidarity till long after
500, and several times reaffirmed it.

In the second century, Greek literature enjoyed its silver
age—with an attempt at resilvering in the fifth. In the same
second century it put its scientific structure into final shape,
though now without originating enterprise, under Ptolemy.
Diophantos, toward the end of the third, proves that at least
in mathematics new approaches were still possible. About the
same time, Plotinus and the Neo-Platonists gave Greek philosophy its final new ingredient—after nearly five hundred

---

[8] Salvius Julianus, fl. 117–138. Gaius, fl. 138–180. Papinian, possibly a Syrian,
d. 212. *Ulpian, of Tyre, d. 228. Paulus, d. after 228. Modestinus, born in a
Greek-speaking province, d. after 244. Gregorius, at Beyrut, end of third century.
Hermogenian, in the eastern half of the Empire, before 324. The second to sixth
are "the five fundamental jurists." The culmination of the growth obviously fell
around 200 A.D.

years of quiescent lapse. Roman jurisprudence as an articulate system of thought dates from the same second to third century, as just said. With this one exception, however, all the Graeco-Roman renascences were expressed in the Greek language and in the eastern half of the Empire. The Latin contribution died out soon after 100.

During the latter half of the Graeco-Roman phase Christianity got the upper hand and lent a new coloring to all that followed.

Byzantine phases.—During the fifth century, while the West was slipping under barbarian control, the Eastern Roman Empire enjoyed relative peace internally. During the sixth, under Justinian, it began to reassert itself. Italy, the islands, Africa, part of southern Spain—most of the Mediterranean parts of the old West—were reconquered from German invaders. The idea and claim of the Empire were still strong, its powers far from feeble. To Justinian's reign there belong also the great structure of St. Sophia and the famous organization of law in his *Institutes* and *Code;* and to his period, the mosaics at Ravenna and some revival of sculpture.

By about 600, this florescence was over; and Greek civilization—Byzantine, now, in historic terminology—went on the defensive until 850. The western reconquests had begun to be lost. Persia made a final thrust which carried it for the first time to the Mediterranean shore; and hardly was this repelled when the Arab storm broke, and permanently wrested away Syria and Egypt. The Greeks managed to hold Asia Minor, but early lost control of the sea and were twice besieged in Constantinople by Arab fleets. On the northern frontier, the Avars passed on into Hungary and were succeeded by the Bulgars, who in 679 crossed the Danube and established themselves permanently on Imperial soil as rivals of Constantinople. Both intellectually and aesthetically there was recession from the sixth century. Most of the eighth century and a part of the ninth were filled by a sterile puritan dissension, the Iconoclast controversy, which involved state, church, and population alike.

When finally the controversy was settled, the Greek World entered on a final sort of flowering; without greatness, it is true, but with a successful functioning. Both art and literature underwent revivals, beginning around 850 and lasting until about 1000 and 1050 respectively. The former contributed ivory carvings of a certain exquisiteness. Until the tenth century, ancient Greek remained more or less intelligible. What might be called encyclopaedias were produced. Bulgaria and then Russia were Christianized under the influence of Constantinople. A line of fairly competent Basils and Constantines, the Macedonian dynasty, held the throne stably and expanded the frontiers until 1025. The Frankish power in the West and the Caliphate in the East had passed their zenith and in their disintegration were no longer a menace; Turks and Mongols had not yet appeared; the Hungarians raided mainly to the north of Roman domain. The Bulgars, it is true, strained at seizing the Empire; but they were the smaller people, far less mature in civilization; and in the end the effort brought about their own political annihilation. Constantinople was much the largest, wealthiest, and most refined city of Europe, perhaps in the Near East also.

We have traveled a long way from fifth-century Athens, into Mediaeval Christianity and a bureaucratic Empire of the "Romans"; but the soil, the speech, the fundamental tradition, are still mainly Hellenic. The civilization, like the empire, had shrunk back to the Balkan and Anatolian peninsulas. Still centering around the Aegean, its distribution differed from that of fifteen hundred years before chiefly in extending farther inland from the coasts. Even in South Italy there was still a foothold.

During the eleventh century, dissolution finally set in. Literature and art receded. The Macedonian house ended in feeble empresses. Soon after them, nearly all of Asia Minor was lost to the Seljuk Turks, and Bari to the Normans. Venice strangled the commerce. Then the Crusades marched through, and the fourth one seized the impregnable city. After sixty years, the Greeks regained it, only to find their remnant of empire become a small island in an engulfing sea of Turkish territory. That anything survived at all for the four centuries preceding 1453 would be a mystery, were it not that it was the residuum of one of the great civilizations of the world, at once battered and seasoned, and therefore wrecked but slowly, by the passage of more than two thousand years.

§106. Islam

Arabic Islamic civilization, that is, the civilization carried by Mohammedans using the Arabic language as their medium of culture—that most of them were not Arabians by blood does not matter in the present connection,—is peculiar in several regards.

First, it began, definitely and almost completely, with a new religion. The only phenomenon which is in conflict with this statement is the existence of a pan-Arabic lyric poetry for at least a century before Mohammed.

Second, this religion was a hybrid and contained no essential element of novelty—other than relation to personality, speech, and place—except its extreme simplification.

Third, superficially due to association with an accidental feature of this religion, but in reality probably owing to more complex and less obvious causes, this civilization did not attempt visible aesthetic representation. Sculpture, painting, and drama, in the ordinary sense, are therefore lacking.

Fourth, the civilization was predominantly a verbalizing one, in its higher accomplishments. Its principal achievements are religious, literary, philological, philosophical, scientific, and architectural. Of these, only architecture and, in part, science are nonverbal. There is an old proverb: that God gave the Greeks skill with the head, the Chinese with the hands, but us Arabs with the tongue.

If one were to venture on a single keynote as characteristic of the culture (though such of course are always overcharacteristic), it might be skill in simplicity of organization; with variation in repetitiveness rather than richness of fundamental complexity. In some measure this quality seems to hold of every Arabic-Islamic activity and attainment.

The periods of productivity are:

Lyric poetry, 530 (or earlier) to 1030; florescence to 830, but no sharp crest.

Religion, 622 to, say, the destruction of the Califate by the Mongols in 1258.

Political, 632, to ca. 825, when the Califate began to disintegrate.

Philology, 650 to 1000, with peak at 800.

Science, 750 to 1125, best period 820 to 1050, climax about 1020 with Avicenna, Alhazen, and Al-Biruni.

Philosophy, (800 or) 850 to 1120, climax 1020 with Avicenna.

Prose literature, 830 to 1130, with prolongation.

Some of the foregoing can be lengthened somewhat by including western or Spanish-Moroccan Islam, the florescences of which fall later, as follows:

Politics, 912–976.

Philology, 950–975.

Science, 950–1250, climax at 1130, with Geber and Avenzoar.

Literature, 1000–1200.

Philosophy, 1050–1200, climate at 1175 with Averroës.

It seems somewhat arguable whether Western Arabic civilization is better linked with Eastern on the ground of speech and belief, or with Spanish Christian on the ground of proximity and intimate interinfluence. This doubt has been discussed in the chapters on Philosophy and Literature. On the whole, the fit with the Eastern Arabic configurations seems the better, as might be anticipated. However, the best construal seems to be as a semiautonomous, peripherally belated, minor growth derived from the Eastern or principal Arabic one with some Christian Occidental stimulations.

The maximum duration of the larger Islamic florescence is about seven centuries, from 530 (?) to 1250 at utmost. It is only literature which can be said to have been productive as long as this; and that only as an aggregate, successful poetry and prose having had shorter individual lives. Seven centuries are less than the period of Egyptian, Indian, Chinese, Greek, or Occidental civilization, and argue for a certain meagerness of the Arabic one. As a matter of fact, Islamic history fills such space as it does occupy in our usual Europocentric history, chiefly for two reasons: the politico-military impingements of Moslems on Christian nations; and the fact that the culture partly bridges the gap between Greek and Occidental philosophy and science, which we tend or try to regard as a continuum or single permanent growth.

For Oriental Arabic civilization by itself, five centuries about comprise the essential growth span.

The last culminations of East Arabic growths were over by 1050, which confirms this date as the approximate turning point of the balance, both of national strength and of cultural development, between Islamic and Occidental Christian civilizations. The success of the First Crusade less than a half century later is corroboration.

Also, there were no revivals or renascences. Persian and Turkish developments establish the vitality of the Mohammedan religion as such, but prove little so far as culture is concerned, because both were national growths, the former in some respects a conscious secession.

In the discussion of Science, it has already been mentioned that Mesopotamia-Iran-Turkestan produced a surplus of productive talent over Arabia-Syria-Egypt-North Africa. The same seems to hold for philosophy. In literature (and philology) this geographic relation does not hold, not only because the start had to come from Arabs, but because Arabic literature stimulated the Persians to develop their own literature as a separate product.

IRAN

The Iranian peoples play a peculiar role in culture history, a role which might be designated as both partial and secondary.

First, they achieved nationalism and its effective political expression twenty-five hundred years ago, when the Medes helped destroy Nineveh. Fifty years later the Persians established a greater empire than had yet existed, and governed it fairly successfully and humanely. Overthrown by Alexander, Iranian nationalism resurrected itself in less than a hundred and fifty years under Parthian leadership, which absorbed the eastern Macedonian successions, matched itself with Rome, and held Mesopotamia against it. As the Parthian power crumbled, the Sassanian succeeded it, again to hold its own— including Mesopotamia—against both Rome and Byzantium, and to succumb only to the Arabs. In summary, in a stretch of twelve centuries the Iranians were independent more than ten, and during most of that millennium controlled either Mesopotamia to their west or Bactria-Turkestan to their north, or both.

Also, they had a religion which was not only national in origin, but formulated in doctrine and ideology. This religion was active. It appears to have influenced primitive Christianity or its subsoil—Paradise and Satan concepts,—and again in its Nestorian form; not to mention later Bogomils, Albigenses, and the like. It sent the Mithraic sect over the extent of the Roman Empire. It hybridized Manichaeism—a double heresy— out of Christianity, and was a component in Gnosticism and Mandaeanism.

However, neither national success nor religious activity were able to produce a first-rank productive growth even in any one department of Old Persian culture. Achaemenian as well as Sassanian architecture, plastic art, literature, science, and philosophy are either lacking or are imitations of neighboring ones. Whereas the Arabs used their simple religion of borrowed materials as an instrument for forging a civilization, the Iranians seem to have become involved in their richer and more original religion to a degree which perhaps was obsessive, and which at any rate appears to have blocked their efforts on non-religious and nonpolitical lines.

It is after their conquest by the Arabs, and after their acceptance of Islam, that the Iranians began to make new cultural achievements: in Arabic philosophy and science and mysticism, in Arabic literature even, and then in a national literature of their own, in Persian, clearly built at first on Arabic models, but going beyond these to achieve successful epics. The great period of this literature is about 950 to 1450.

In painting too—forbidden to orthodox Moslems—a Persian school sprang up, though in European Renaissance times, well after the literature was ended.

TURKISH PEOPLES

Any treatment of culture history is incomplete which omits the Turks. This group of virile peoples long transmitted culture material between China and the West, gave the Mongols most of what civilization they acquired, formed the backbone of the Mogul conquest of India, for nearly a thousand years have been the prop of Asiatic Islam, and still hold Constantinople. Their greatest construct was the Ottoman or Osmanli state, which, originating soon after 1300, climaxed under Suleiman the Magnificent, 1520–1566, continued to grow until 1670, and began its decline with the defeat before Vienna in 1683. The Turks have not, so far, achieved high productivity in any activity other than conquest; but they have participated in many civilizations, even though perhaps as much to tear down as to build up. If they are passed over here, it is because understanding of them involves knowledge of many countries, cultures, and languages—in short, a scholarship more intensive at innumerable points than I control.

§107. The Occident: Nuclear Nations

This is a polyphonic civilization: multinational and multilingual. Latin was its language of learning and religion; but only for part of the course of the civilization. It was Christian; but there were important bodies of Christians in other major cultures. It centered in western Europe; but it cannot accurately be designated European because at first it failed to include much of Europe—Byzantium and Spain—and later came to extend beyond it. Hence the advantage of the term Occidental: it is free from inexact amplications of speech, religion, and geography.

Each important nationality obviously deserves consideration of its own development. At the end, a section on the West as a whole reviews the larger civilization of which the separate national cultures are only strands.

FRANCE

The higher cultural luster of France was shed in three periods: Mediaeval, Louis XIV, Napoleonic.

The first of these was the longest. It extended, roughly, from 1100 to 1300, or, more exactly, from 1075 to 1325. The times of achievement are: in philosophy, 1075–1160; architecture, 1050–1300, with the highest product probably between 1175 and 1250; sculpture, 1140–1325; literature, 1075–1300, with the peak around 1170. Politically, three successful kings nearly fill more than the thirteenth century: Philip Augustus, St. Louis, Philip the Fair, 1180–1314. Under them the monarchy was strengthened, the towns grew, the royal domain was increased. By a reckoning in of French leadership in the earlier Crusades, the period of politico-military success can be pushed back of 1100; by inclusion of Norman conquests in Naples-Sicily and England, beyond 1050.

Southern France, contrary to what is often implied, did not enjoy a civilization essentially Mediterranean, apart, and earlier than that of northern France. Important surviving Norman architecture dates back about as far—to 1050—as South French. The same time relation holds for literature. North and South French poetry appear in the same half century, 1050–1100. The main difference seems to have been that southern activity was narrower and ended earlier. The troubadour poetry was essentially finished by 1225, the southern Romanesque architecture largely so by 1175. The North went on with its building, carving, writing until 1300/25, and then passed these activities on to a bourgeois florescence in the Netherlands, obviously by the route French-Walloon-Fleming.

It must also be borne in mind that Troubadour and Romanesque were not limited narrowly to Provence and Toulouse. Poitou, Limoges, Auvergne, Burgundy spoke the *langue d'oc,* and the center of Mediaeval South French lyric and architecture lay rather in Loire drainage than on the Mediterranean. In short, the first stirrings of French civilization were incipiently Occidental rather than lingeringly Roman in geographical nexus as well as content.

Mediaeval French philosophy was somewhat out of step with other activities, as regards time. Its florescence centered around 1120, and the important growth was over by 1160. The mid-thirteenth century, when Italian, German, British philosophy, and that of mediaeval Europe generally, culminated, was one to which the French contribution was secondary, although the University of Paris was still the great gathering point.

After 1300/25 French decline is manifest in all departments. In music, literature, architecture, sculpture, before long in painting, the Netherlands—Flemish at least as much as Walloon—go up absolutely as France moves back actually or relatively. For a century or more, the best musical, sculptural, and pictorial talent in France was imported from Belgium.

The first half of this long low-level interval is the time of the Hundred Years' War. It seems dubious whether the English invasion and conquests can legitimately be accepted as cause. Most lines of intellectual-aesthetic activity were in retrogression before the war began. The two sets of phenomena are almost surely related, but as joint effects or in reciprocal function.

The one outstanding exception of a great talent partially realized in this period is Villon, born 1431.

Around 1500, France was perceptibly on the upgrade once more, first in sculpture, then in painting, literature, science. Momentum gathered slowly, however, as also politically, and with no effectiveness toward concerted development until after 1600. The post-Mediaeval interval was thus of three full centuries' duration. As Netherlandish influence began to be outgrown, the full force of the Italian Renaissance burst on unorganized France soon after 1500; with the minor but militant Reformation disrupting it further.

By 1620/30, the preceding century of slow recovery bore

fruit in a rather sudden integration and culmination of which the nation was sharply conscious. Within a decade philosophy, science, painting, literature, and drama broke into organized flower. Almost simultaneously Spain was humbled and France became the leading and aggressive power of Europe. Around 1680, or, if one will, 1690, the cultural burst was essentially exhausted, and traveling chiefly on name and momentum. The growth was thus an unusually brief as well as compact one. Attention has several times been directed, in preceding chapters, to the fact that more than half the development fell in the time of Richelieu and Mazarin, or Louis XIII and the minority of Louis XIV. Conversely, most of the Grand Monarch's long, unguided rule of fifty-four years was a period of slowing of cultural creativeness; as it was also one of wars more exhausting than remunerative, and leading from dominance to stalemate.

The eighteenth century, in gross, was one of French slackening. There were no wars of success, and India and Canada were lost. Enlightenment, however valuable a development, produced no literature of the greatest—perhaps prevented it. Painting from Watteau to Ingres was competent or clever rather than of the first order. Conditions were as in Europe generally: 1700 to 1750 was a breathing spell.

The third swell was longer than the seventeenth-century one, and more concentrated than the Mediaeval. Nationalistically and politically the crest comes, of course, under Napoleon—say at 1810,—whose cradle of destiny was rocked by the Revolution, 1789. Science and music had begun definite growths around 1750; literature and drama commenced only about 1800. The peaks are hard to define, because the French tendency to produce high ability rather than towering genius leaves the focuses somewhat diffuse, except when the growths are quite brief as in the seventeenth century. In literature the crest probably lay in the quarter century before 1850, in painting around that date, in music probably and in sculpture almost certainly after it. French science from 1750 to 1860–1870 shows a strangely even level. If it possesses no high point, its median at least falls earlier than the peak of any of the arts.

All in all, then, the third French growth began on some fronts by 1750, in others not till 1800, with culminations all the way from perhaps 1800 to 1880, and no recoveries since declines set in.

Of the three growths, it would be difficult to judge which attained the highest level. They differ in concentration and integration rather than in degree of attainment. There is no other European nation which has three separate growth pulses so neatly separate and so nearly equal in importance.

ITALY

Italian configurations are sharply differentiated from French, and from most European ones. Three can be recognized—the usual Mediaeval, Renaissance, and Modern; but the first is partial, the last feeble, and both grade into the Renaissance in one or more activities. No serious violence is done to truthful conception, accordingly, if Italian civilization is viewed as centered in the Renaissance, with a slight prelude and aftermath.

For the three concrete arts, this is very much so. Italian painting begins at 1250, is established at a high level with Giotto in 1300, begins to culminate at 1500, but continues until Tiepolo and Canaletto—to beyond 1750. The development is unbroken for five centuries, with the mid and high point in the Renaissance, but the beginning and end of the configuration respectively Mediaeval and Modern in spirit as well as time. For sculpture, the corresponding stretch is from 1400 to 1800, Ghiberti to Canova. Three centuries of low-grade sculpture precede, but they are a formative period, not a separate growth with its own curve. Architecture begins to be significant soon after 1000, and again develops continuously. I do not venture to define the culmination and end, but they would hardly fall before 1500 and 1600 respectively. There are no other instances in Occidental culture history of unbroken national growths of such duration.

In other domains there are breaks, or limitations of florescence to periods. Italian music does not get going till the High Renaissance, but then culminates quickly under Palestrina and goes on to Verdi three centuries later. There is a sag toward the end of the seventeenth century, but scarcely a break. Literature comes in three well-marked pulses, characterized say by Dante, by Sannazaro or Tasso, and by Alfieri—distinctly Mediaeval, Renaissance, and Modern in time, form, and content. Yet the Italian is the latest Mediaeval literature in Europe, except for the English, and the earliest in the Renaissance. The two pulses are only 75 years apart, as against 300 in France. Petrarch and Boccaccio are certainly only semi-Mediaeval, in spite of their pre-Renaissance century: they foreshadowed and influenced the future instead of summing up the Middle Ages. Thus, though there is a gap between pulses, and the first pulse is reckoned the greater, there is almost a leaning forward on the Renaissance. Only in philosophy was Italy truly Mediaeval— and wholly mediaeval: Aquinas had no followers of eminence in his own country.

Very marked too, except in philosophy, is the resistance which Italy manifested to Mediaevalism, whether of international, French, or Byzantine cast. In architecture, national growth was earliest: so-called Romanesque and Gothic in Italy is specific Italian architecture with minor transalpine acceptances. Sculpture was imitative and poor until 1400, when it freed itself and became Italian and great. Painting, where the influence resisted and absorbed was largely Byzantine, got its liberation by 1300. Poetry was imitation of French, or outright done in French, until 1275; but by 1300 came Dante, intensely, even locally, Italian, and the greatest single personage in Mediaeval literature.

At bottom this resistance was probably a resistance to what was felt as barbarism; the gulf was one of culture manners. As soon as the foreign forms could be reworked, they became material for the building up of Italian Renaissance civilization. From probably as early as 1000, Italians labored at the edifice of this civilization; blindly and helplessly at first, but with a certain stubborn integrity which kept them from being swamped by the French influence which overran the rest of western Europe.

Why in philosophy alone Italy integrated with Mediaeval Europe and produced its crown in Aquinas, is not clear, unless it is the simple fact that scholasticism was Church-dominated, and the Church was felt as a primarily Italian institution.

The Risorgimento of 1750–1850 was a feeble thing intrinsically, compared with the Renaissance. Moreover, it was a parallel phenomenon to the contemporary growths in France, England, Germany, and was lesser than they; whereas the Renaissance had no strict contemporaries but did have a hand in the making of the Late Renaissance–Baroque growths of Spain, France, and England. In science and literature the 1750–1850 Italian pulse was obviously not much more than second-rate. In music it was much stronger, and in sculpture produced in Canova the leading European figure of his time. But in both these fields Italian nineteenth-century activity was part of a configuration the culmination of which lay in the sixteenth. There had been a dip, but there was also continuity.

All in all, then, while the configuration of the culture history of France is best viewed as a series of three parallel mountain chains with intervening valleys or plateaus, that of Italy is rather a single great system with subsidiary ranges of foothills—often respectable enough in themselves—flanking this on both sides. More or less from 1000 to 1100 on, and clearly from 1300, everything can be seen oriented toward the early sixteenth-century peak; and to 1850, perhaps until this day, the configuration also seems oriented from this same peak.

As for politico-nationalistic development in its usual forms, Italian culture does not fit at all. The moment when the Renaissance comes into full flower is precisely when France and Spain begin to contend for mastery of the peninsula. The cultural Risorgimento is mainly over when the political one commences to be effective. Legnano, 1176, seems to be the last battle of consequence won by Italians from non-Italians. The whole great cultural movement falls into the victoryless centuries since.

In fact, it is difficult to define achievement in the politico-military sphere in Italy. Is it exemplified by the small, party-torn communes of Dante's day? The somewhat larger tyrannies of the Sforzas and Medicis? The foreign-propped kingdom of Victor Emmanuel? The large, national, strongly organized, aggressive state which so often accompanies bloomings in the cultural sphere, and sometimes underlies them—as in ancient Italy—is simply absent. In this point Italy is historically anomalous.

South Italy went its own course, independent of the rest of the peninsula. It had no hand at all in the building of the Renaissance. Not until the Renaissance had passed its zenith, after 1550, did Naples and Sicily become an area of cultural productivity. Southern Italy accordingly flourished in the Baroque era, under Spanish and Bourbon rule. Eustachius, Tasso, Marini, Bernini, Salvator Rosa, Vico evidence this growth. In music, the time of preëminence averaged somewhat later, mainly in the eighteenth century, with Bellini an early nineteenth-century straggler. Since Bellini, there do not appear to have been many South Italians of the first magnitude. On the whole, then, the Two Sicilies enjoyed a local and late prosperity during about two centuries when the Central and North Italian culture configuration was on the downgrade.[9]

Science: Eustachius, birth date unknown, d. 1574; Della Porta, b. 1543/5. Literature: Sannazaro (of Spanish family), 1458; Tasso (of a Venetian father), 1544; Marini, 1569. Painting: Caravaggio, 1569; Ribera (b. in Spain), 1588; Salvator Rosa, 1615; and others born between 1576 and 1657. Sculpture and architecture: Bernini, 1598. Philosophy: Bruno, 1548; Vico, 1668; Croce, 1866 (from Aquila, Abruzzi). Music: Stradella, ca. 1645; Scarlatti, A., 1649, D., 1683; Logroscino, ca. 1700; Jommelli, 1714; Piccini. 1728; Paisiello, 1741; Cimarosa, 1749; Zingarelli, 1752; (and Bellini, 1801; Leoncavallo, 1858).

One more consideration remains to be examined: the relation of mediaeval-modern Italy to ancient Italy—Rome, as we generally call it. The soil of the two is the same; the speech not radically changed; the lapse of time—two and a half millennia— no greater than we unquestioningly construe as within one

---

[9] St. Thomas Aquinas belongs to High Scholasticism, which was the philosophy of the Church and was strikingly international.

frame in China or India or Egypt. It is fair to ask whether it would not be more valid to consider all growths on Italian soil, from Romulus to Mussolini, as a unit, instead of dividing them between an earlier Mediterranean and a later Occidental set.

We should in that case have two six-century periods of creative productivity, say −300 to 300 and 1250 to 1850, with about a millennium between. This is undoubtedly one justified way of looking at the phenomena.

But historians are probably right in their habit of not considering this the alignment of most fundamental significance; for several reasons: 1, The area of Italy is small. 2, The sterile interval of time is long: a thousand years—longer than we get within one civilization anywhere else. 3, Ancient Italic—Roman—higher civilization was a marginal, rather late extension from an older East Mediterranean center, and crumbled sooner than the center. Mediaeval-modern Italian culture, on the contrary, is the smaller fraction of a West European growth which was mainly transalpine, and to which it was accordingly also more or less marginal. Culture-historically therefore, Italy was temporarily a part of two larger growths distinct in area, in period, and in content; though in certain domains it dominated each for a time.

It is curious that the Italian role in these two episodes was almost opposite. The Romans entered Mediterranean civilization when this had passed its apogee in aesthetic-intellectual achievement and had shown its incapacity for greater political attainment. This these ancient Italians supplied equally on the military, administrative, and juridical sides; and meanwhile absorbed an aesthetic-intellectual veneer strong enough to lead to real creativeness at least in literature. In Occidental civilization the situation was reversed. Italy now made the weakest politico-military contribution, and the heaviest aesthetic one.

But it is significant that even where Italy now contributed preponderantly, she did not lead the Occident in time, as might be expected in view of her having been the western country first and longest exposed to participation in Ancient Mediterranean culture. The lead was taken by France, politically as early as Charlemagne, and in sculpture, new architectural forms, poetry, and philosophy somewhat later, but still earlier than Italy; and even after 1500, music, anatomy, astronomy were still being imported into the peninsula from the Netherlands and other North European countries.

The Italian resistance of which we have spoken above, or, perhaps better, the unwillingness to accept European culture until it could be made over into something Italian—a reluctance which by the very delay of digestion enabled the Renaissance to grow greater,—is probably due to the geographic continuity of culture in Italy; which in turn implied many continuities flowing largely below the level of recorded history. After all, for Gaul, Belgica, Germany, and Iberia, Italy had been the civilizational mother. It is perhaps not unexpectable that, when a new type of civilization began to grow, the nations of younger generation should participate more readily, Italy more hesitantly, but that in time her greater depth of cultural experience should enable her to remodel the vigorous but crude transalpine efforts into what we call the Renaissance. That in the end the Renaissance in turn yielded to the Modern phase of Occidental civilization, and that this was again transalpine, is no wonder: not only were the transalpine peoples greatly in the majority; they had gradually learned war and coherent political control, as well as cultivated themselves by absorptions from the Italian Renaissance.

SPAIN

Spain resembles Italy in that its greater growths are concentrated in one time pulse. The concentration is in fact more extreme: neither mediaeval nor modern Spain has produced a single personality reckoned as of the first cultural magnitude. There is no Iberian counterpart to Aquinas, Giotto, or Dante, nor even to Canova or Alfieri;[10] nor, to enter the political field, to Mazzini or Mussolini. There is, to be sure, a Spanish mediaeval pulse, and a modern, post-1830 one; but they are both barely recognizable and of little European importance.

---

[10] Goya, yes; but he is notorious for his nonconstellation.

The main Spanish growth falls between 1470 and 1690. It came fastest in the political field, where Lepanto, 1571, probably marks the culmination. In painting, sculpture, poetry, and drama the developments were slower, the peaks fall between 1600 and 1650, and the terminations come within a decade of 1680. A musical beginning was drained off into Italian channels; and in philosophy and science Spain never produced much. The explorers and conquistadors of course fall into the sixteenth century; so does Loyola. This means that expansive nationalistic forces were most effective in the three-quarter century 1500–1575, aesthetic ones 1575–1650, intellectual ones not notable.

The greater brevity of the Spanish growth probably correlates with its being of less weight culturally, on the whole, than the Italian one. It certainly influenced Europe but little. Spanish aesthetic activities were Italian-influenced at first, with a gradual liberation during the sixteenth century, and independence in the seventeenth.

Do Spanish Christian growths show any relation to Arabic Mohammedan in the peninsula? As already discussed under Islamic civilization, the Spanish-Moroccan Islamic florescences on the whole fit the Eastern Islamic ones better: they are pretty consistently somewhat belated and lesser counterparts of these. However, they are not markedly out of fit with the Mediaeval Christian Spanish ones; they abut on them in time; and an argument might be put up about the balance of their relation to each other.

It must be borne in mind that Mohammedan power in Spain was broken at Navas de Tolosa in 1212, and that by 1264 all the peninsula except Granada was under Christian dominion. This means that two and a half centuries elapsed before there was any further impulse toward Christian Spanish expansion. In this period Christian and Mohammedan must have lived rather intimately side by side in the southern half of the peninsula.

Portugal behaves as a lesser and slightly premature Spain. Its main growth curve moves parallel and in advance. Portuguese exploration was a few decades earlier than Spanish; the first Iberian dramatic efforts were half Portuguese; Camoëns preceded Cervantes by a generation; in 1580 Portugal was absorbed into Spain. The time precedence probably reflects only the quicker mobilizability of the smaller unit.

ENGLAND

England presents the usual three peaks: High Mediaeval, Early Modern, Late Modern. The first, however, is partial only; and the second and third separated by but a brief interval.

Because of the position of the island of Great Britain off the French coast, one would expect English cultural dependence on France. This holds, in fact, for the Middle Ages; but very little since.

Mediaeval England reached high attainments in philosophy and architecture and in nothing else. The philosophy was, in a sense, French-induced, like that of all Europe; but not directly dependent. It began a half century after the great French Early Mediaeval growth ended, and coincided with that in international Europe. With Alexander of Hales, Grosseteste, Bacon, Duns Scotus, and William of Occam, England probably contributed more intellects of the first rank to High Mediaeval philosophy than any other single country.

In architecture, England, under French stimulus, followed hard on France in time. The first or Romanesque phase is usually made to begin with 1066 or even 1050. To this are due Exeter, Norwich, and Durham, and parts of Rochester and Canterbury. The great phase is the Early English or Lancet Gothic, 1189–1307, with Wells, York, Canterbury, Lincoln, Salisbury, Westminster, Litchfield cathedrals. At least some of the architects were French, but the style is individualistically English. The Decorated and Perpendicular Gothic, to 1485, are generally considered as constituting a decline.

English sculpture never amounted to much. The best of it dates from about the second quarter of the thirteenth century.

The literary burst constituted by Chaucer and several lesser lights just before 1400 is probably to be construed as a belated

High Mediaeval phenomenon. It was belated because it involved transmutation of Continental models into the medium of an unformed and inexperienced language. Philosophy which operated in Latin, and architecture in stone, could be transplanted without such delay. However, Chaucer came late enough to undergo Italian as well as French influences, which diminished his Mediaevalism and kept him more palatable to modern tastes.

In general, the fourteenth and fifteenth centuries and most of the sixteenth produced little realized genius in England. The second or Early Modern growth begins rather abruptly about 1575 and lasts until 1725. The specific durations are: literature and drama, 1575–1700/10; music, 1580–1700/10; science, 1600–1700; philosophy, 1640–1730, peak 1680–1710. Each of these except the last suffers an interruption from about 1630 to 1660, in which fall the Puritan tension, the Civil War, the Protectorate. Each activity, however, resumes with the Restoration, music, science, and philosophy in fact reaching their peaks only just before 1700. This break is a rather unusual historic phenomenon. It ought either to have failed to suspend the intellectual-aesthetic growths,[11] or to have distorted or wrecked them. It can be inferred that the intellectual-aesthetic and the politico-religious movements of seventeenth-century England lay on separate planes which cut each other without much entanglement; though at least Milton operated on both. At any rate, the religious quarreling and the fighting, while vigorous enough to interrupt the cultural activities, only suspended them. Perhaps the whole episode was dissonant enough with basic English orientation for the country to put it aside, as soon as it could, like an unpleasant dream.

At the risk of repetitiousness it may be remarked again that this period of England's greatness was seventeenth-century— Baroque, in Continental terminology—to an infinitely greater degree than it was Elizabethan. The growth began in the second half of Elizabeth's reign; but in the long view James I and Charles I and II are the characterizing monarchs.

[11] Like the Fronde and the Revolution-Empire in France.

The interval that succeeded was brief. In philosophy, in fact, inclusion of the Scotch growth, 1740–1790, would bridge it entirely. But music and drama did not revive, painting arose, science and literature followed new bents after 1750; so there can be little doubt that we are dealing with a genuine rest period before a new pattern formation.

The third or nineteenth-century cultural florescence of England shows the following dates of activities: Science, 1750 to the present, peak probably 1800–1875; painting, 1750 to 1850; literature, 1780 (or, if one will, 1760) to 1880, peak from 1790 to 1825; philosophy, of secondary magnitude, 1820 to 1870. Roughly coincident are leadership in the so-called Industrial Revolution, an unparalleled accumulation of capital, the progressive erection of an overseas empire uninterrupted except for defection of the American colonies, the continuing maintenance of primacy on the sea, and a series of technological inventions of paramount industrial importance. To all these achievements seventeenth-century England had no parallels, or only slight premonitory anticipations; on the intellectual-aesthetic side, on the contrary, she both developed more activities and perhaps reached greater heights in them.

Nationalistically, England does not show the periods of alternate strength and weakness of most European countries, no doubt because as an island she was exempt from the unceasing competitions and shocks of the Continent. She has not even had a monarch surnamed the Great since Alfred the Saxon and Canute the Dane. If any one sovereign has been set on a pedestal by English sentiment, it is Elizabeth: not only a woman, but one who refused initiative. Edward I, 1272–1307, was probably the most successful ruler in the Middle Ages.

Scotland, as the more remote and barren extremity of Britain, should have lagged culturally behind England, and through most of history has done so. As the poorer and smaller nation, she has produced less—so much less, for many centuries, that the stream is intermittent, and most earlier Scotchmen are without place in a configuration unless it is an English one: Napier, for instance.

With the Union of 1707 this condition changes, and Scotch births of genius show a definite constellation. There are Hume, the Scotch school of metaphysicians, Adam Smith and James Mill; Hutton, Black, Hunter, Rutherford, Lyell in science; Raeburn and Wilkie the painters; Smollett, Burns, Scott, Carlyle, and others in literature—evidently a larger number of able men per million inhabitants than England of the same period produced. Instead of submerging Scotland, the Union gave her assurance, opportunity, and a wider clientele. Before, she had been a much smaller brother to England—weaker, poorer, proud, resistive, and yet by force of circumstances largely imitative.

For men of eminence born after about 1800, the Scotch-English ratio seems more in accord with population, and Scotch productivity more absorbed into the generic British configurations.

GERMANY

German culture growths come in four periods, besides the feeble "Carolingian renaissance," which was still undifferentiated French-Netherlandish-German.

1. Around 1000 there occurred an early development of architecture[12] and sculpture. The former was mainly Rhenish, the latter Saxon. Politically, the period was closing Othonian and after. That is, the growth overlapped the first post-Frankish national German dynasty, the tenth-century Saxon, under which the last independent ethnic group to be integrated politically into German nationality took the leadership. Under the Saxons, also, the Magyars were definitively turned back, and the eastward reëxpansion into Slavic territory got under way. Absolutely, the cultural achievements of the growth were slight; but, for the period, they were definite and vigorous. Slightly later, Denmark, Poland, Hungary, Russia underwent a similar political integration and no doubt the laying of a cultural foundation also; though, being farther on the peripheries, they could scarcely yet make a positive contribution to nascent Occidental civilization.

---

[12] Cathedrals of Trier, 1016 seq., Speyer, 1030, Mainz, 1036.

It is significant that this early German growth preceded the French Mediaeval one by a century or more.

2. Around 1200 there was a second accumulation of growths, which may be labeled Hohenstaufen. It is difficult to see what this famous dynasty achieved politically other than failure, but it certainly has symbolized greatness to Germans. The cultural accomplishments were in literature, on both native and French themes, with the peak at 1190–1225; in "Gothic" sculpture and architecture, culminating in the former around 1230–1260, in the latter perhaps prolonged somewhat later; and, more or less contemporary, in philosophy under Albertus. As in the first constellation, the cultural peaks lagged a little behind the political. In this period, French influencing is definite, but not at all overpowering.

3. About 1500–1560 Germany experienced a sort of equivalent or counterpart of the Renaissance, not influenced from Italy, and much lighter and briefer. This growth included Luther; Dürer and his contemporaries; and a scientific constellation respectable without Copernicus and eminent if he is included. The painting and science were under way by 1450. The development of printing around 1450 can therefore be confidently counted as part of the development. Other technical inventions fall into the same period: watches, iron casting, and various metallurgical advances. Politically there was nothing beyond chronic German disorganization; literature was very arid; architecture and sculpture, mediocre.

In the interval that followed, Kepler and Leibnitz stand out in isolation. All the arts, being in a slump, underwent Italian or French imitation.

4. The great German period centers around 1800. It is indicated by Kant, Beethoven, Goethe, and a host of their contemporaries. In music, which had the longest course, the growth extends back to nearly 1700 with Bach. Science was definitely later, beginning only about 1800, and being presumably still in flux today. The same holds for philology. The concrete or tangible arts—architecture, sculpture, and painting—underwent no corresponding developments. The configuration as a

whole thus has an abstract character: philosophy, music, literature. Perhaps therefore it is significant that science definitely
followed philosophy in time.

This configuration was predominantly middle-class. Courts
participated little, the aristocracy as such hardly at all. Vienna,
Weimar, and later Munich are only partial exceptions.

Political correspondences are hard to find. Frederick the
Great's victories about coincided with the beginning of burst
of the growth. But contemporary with the culmination were
the successive defeats by Napoleon and his manhandling of
Germany politically. After his fall, there was ineffective political reactionarism. By 1870, when unity was achieved and
national aggressiveness developed, literature and philosophy
were ended, music declining, only science still flourishing.

It is clear that German culture growths, like Italian, cannot
be brought into concordance with politico-national developments, whereas French and Spanish can be.

This is also evident: Germany is the only European country,
except for the marginal Scandinavian and Slavic nations,
whose indubitably greatest period is that after 1750. Italy,
Spain, France, the Low Countries, England—the western
peoples—all had one great period before 1750. Germany is later
than they: evidently because she lies eastward of them. The
Germans were slow to come to full civilization, in short.

On the other hand, their strange anticipations must not be
overlooked: the Othonian sculpture and architecture, the poets
Wolfram and Walther a century before Dante, the first science
in Europe, printing, the Reformation. Germans simply have
not moved in accordance with the generic European pattern.
Early and thoroughly original in spots, they have nevertheless
done much imitating, have often proceeded confusedly, and
have been retarded in growing to full civilizational maturity.

THE NETHERLANDS

Belgium and Holland form a cultural unit, in full perspective.
I therefore use the term Netherlands for them jointly, in its
older sense.

They formed the heart of the Frankish domain, and of its royal fisc. With the gradual dissolution of the Frankish realm into French-speaking France and the mainly German-speaking "Empire," the Netherlands found themselves on the border, linguistically and politically divided, prosperous, and without powerful local rulers. The towns, and with them industry, grew to importance early, as in North Italy and to some extent up the Rhine. The cultural development, as compared with both France and Germany, therefore soon took on a relatively bourgeois character, which has never been lost. In the burgher atmosphere, aesthetic development was slower than at national or provincial courts; but, once rooted, it tended to persist with less fluctuation. The result is that in one activity after another the Netherlands became active a century or two after France, following French Mediaeval models, but with modifications and extensions which reflect not only their burgher environment but also the passage of several generations of pan-European development. Thus thirteenth-century France built cathedrals, but fourteenth-century Netherlands built belfries and town halls.

This belatedness throws the first Netherlandish cultural productivities mainly out of the High Middle into the Late Middle Ages. This in turn means that the Netherlands growth coincides roughly in time with the Italian Renaissance, though largely stemming separately. The contemporaneity, in turn, together perhaps with the fact that up to about 1500 the development in both countries was urban rather than courtly, led to active interrelations. Among such are the import of Willaert in 1527 to "found" Italian music; of Vesalius in 1540 to become the first great figure in Italian science; the Italian appreciation of the Van Eycks, and the desire to learn their technique of oil painting. In all three activities the Italians soon surpassed their Netherlandish preceptors because their Renaissance expressed a greater cultural force.

Then came the backwash, most evident in painting but perceptible also in sculpture and literature. The sixteenth century is one of Italian domination in Netherlandish painting. Only with the seventeenth, approximately, do the Belgians under Rubens achieve partial, and Rembrandt and the Dutch complete, liberation and national expression. But by this late period the Netherlands growth finds itself paralleling the "Baroque" or Early Modern growths of France, England, and Spain—in literature, philosophy, science as well as the concrete arts.

By this time also a shift of internal center of gravity had taken place. Until the sixteenth century, the focus of population, wealth, and productivity had lain in the southwestern half of the Netherlands—Ghent, Bruges, Antwerp, Brussels, Malines, Louvain—half Flemish and half Romanic Walloon in speech. In the northwest, Hollandish Utrecht lagged behind these cities as a cultural center, and Amsterdam, Leyden, Rotterdam, Middelburg scarcely counted. But in the sixteenth century, while Walloon-Flemish "Belgium" remained prosperous, Dutch "Holland" began to draw more abreast. Also, it was more infected by the Reformation. When, around 1570, the Netherlands as a whole grew restive under Spanish dominion, it was the northeastern Dutch provinces that provided most of the initiative, and certainly most of the persistence, in opposition to Spain. The difference is usually laid to their Protestantism. But how far was their Protestantism itself the result of economic-political restiveness and separatist impulses, due in turn to cramped growth?

At any rate, within a few years the seven Dutch provinces committed themselves to the precarious but successful adventure of revolt, the Belgian ones to return and compromise; with the result that higher cultural productivity in Belgium soon declined, except in painting, whereas in Holland it opened up, and marched abreast of that of France and England in philosophy, science, painting, and, in a measure, literature.[13] Concurrent were naval and military successes, exploration and colonization, the East India Company, an enormous accumulation of wealth, a raising of the standard of living and educa-

---

[13] Grotius, 1583–1645, belongs to this constellation. Erasmus of Rotterdam, 1466–1536, is definitely prior, and not part of a national configuration.

tion—everything that makes for a "golden age." But all this was a definitely Dutch development, not a joint-Netherlandish one.

The Dutch growth came to an end suddenly, by 1700. One is inclined to think that the pace had been too rapid for a small country. But it is well to remember that all the West European Baroque growths, in Spain, France, England, ended between 1680 and 1710. Size of nationality therefore probably had little to do with the termination. But it very likely did determine that France and England resumed growth before the eighteenth century was over, and that Holland did not.

The nineteenth century brought the usual new growths. In both Belgium and Holland they were minor—in science, literature, painting, and sculpture—and not highly nationalized. In nearly every growth Belgium preceded Holland by an interval of a decade to a generation; which is expectable in that the seat of stimulation was largely France.

In summary, the Netherlands show essentially a single cultural growth, which became productive as the High Mediaeval patterns began to be transcended around 1300–1325; continued as a joint Flemish-Walloon product, but without any sharp culmination, until 1550–1575; and then passed into a specifically Dutch national flowering, with a marked culmination around 1650, and a close by 1700. The time span, 1300–1700, is that of the Italian growth which we call the Renaissance, but is nonconformable with the nearer French, German, and British periods of growth.

SWITZERLAND

As Belgium is, and the larger Low Countries were, binational, Switzerland is trinational. In both areas, Germanic people have long constituted a majority, but the Romanic element has been an integral factor, with the result of a non-German nationality. In both, there has been a strong local centering of interests. Both regions, finally, are among the most densely populated of Europe, and appear to have been so for a long time.

Swiss history begins about 1231 with stirrings toward separatism or independence in the original three forest cantons, takes form with their documented league in 1291 and the victory of 1315 over the Austrians at Morgarten. Then, one after another, Luzern, Zurich, Zug, Glarus, Bern joined and brought an urban element into the confederacy. The Austrians were defeated again in 1386 and 1388, and for nearly a century the Swiss league grew piecemeal and slowly. Then Charles the Bold became involved with the stubborn peasantry and townsmen, and in 1476 and 1477 the Swiss crushed the Burgundians at Grandson, Murten, and Nancy, and found themselves an international power. The first French-speaking canton, Fribourg, became associated soon after. The Empire was defeated in 1499, Milan manhandled, the French beaten at Milan and Novara in 1512 and 1513. Then, in 1515, came the first defeat, by French and Venetians at Marignano; a moral victory for the Swiss, it is true, but also a warning that they could not permanently compete with the great powers of Europe; and they deliberately withdrew from international politics. Geneva was helped to freedom, associated, and finally leagued between 1526 and 1584, and Neuchâtel received in 1529; but there was no further expansion.

This is a neat instance of a nationalistic growth and florescence. A cultural counterpart is less definite, but is present.

Paracelsus, semiscientist, born in Basel, 1493–1541.
Zwingli, religious reformer, born at Toggenburg, 1484–1531.
Vadianus, humanist, of St. Gallen, 1484–1551.
Tschudi, national historian, of Glarus, 1505–1572.
Gesner, biologist, in Zurich, 1516–1565.
Swiss painters of second rank in the contemporary German schools (ca. 1490–1590).

The seeming incoherence of product is probably due in part to the fewness of men of superior ability in a limited population, in part to nondistinctiveness of cultural patterns in an emergent nationality. As might be expected from the period, the constellation is German-speaking. An international touch is, however, given by the Dutchman Erasmus and the German Holbein, who lived at Basel; and by the North Frenchman Calvin, who labored at Geneva.

The nationalistic peak preceded the cultural one by some forty years: 1476–1516 as against about 1520–1560.

Since 1516, the Swiss have been deliberately self-contained and neutral in European affairs. Attempted maintenance of a status quo of course carries dangers; and politically Switzerland stood very nearly still for three centuries. Perhaps that was why, after some years of internal unsettlement during the French Revolution, the national fabric crumbled in 1798 at the touch of France; and in 1803 the Swiss came under Napoleonic moderation for twelve years. Then the old aims of independence, self-sufficiency, and nonparticipation reasserted themselves, and with their long training the Swiss became leaders in experimenting with democracy. Even a brief civil war—along lines of religious denomination in 1847!—did not interfere with their successful functioning.

The second and greater cultural florescence of Switzerland lasted a full century and a half, from soon after 1700 to nearly 1900. It is therefore just about cut in half by the political collapse under Napoleon. The sometimes assumed normal correlation with politico-military success is therefore not so much lacking in this Swiss instance as negative.

> Bernouilli, Jacob, b. 1654, and John, 1667, mathematics.[14]
> Bodmer, 1698, Breitinger, 1701, Von Haller, 1708, literature and criticism; the last-named also a biologist.
> *Euler, 1707, mathematics.
> *Rousseau, 1713.
> Bonnet, 1720, geology.
> Gessner, 1730, idyls.
> De Saussure, 1740, geology.
> Lavater, 1741, physiognomy, literature.
> Füssli (Fuseli in Eng.), 1741, Angelica Kauffmann, 1741, painting.
> Pestalozzi, 1746, education.
> *De Candolle, Augustin, 1778, botany; Alphonse, son, 1806.
> Agassiz, 1807, geology, biology.
> Raff, 1822, music.
> *Boecklin, 1827, painting.
> Forel, 1848, biology.

---

[14] Several other Bernouillis became eminent in science, like Daniel, the physicist, born in 1700 at Groningen. The family was Flemish, moved to Basel via Frankfort.

This list shows several things. The births run from 1700 to 1850, approximately, if the Bernouilli family be omitted as immigrant. The range of activity was wide. If there are few men eminent in any one field, this is no doubt due to the smallness of numbers that could be drawn from. An innovating spirit is prominent throughout. Rousseau is obvious in this connection. Euler was one of the founders of the modern movement of science; in fact, along with Linnaeus, the earliest post-Newtonian scientist of prime rank. De Saussure and De Candolle did fundamental work on which modern observational science is still building. Pestalozzi was an influence second only to Rousseau in education, and more specific; Lavater at least attempted something original. The Bodmer group are precursors of the German literature after 1750.

The growth has some coloring of Enlightenment; but this movement, as a generic European one, was over, and Romanticism predominant, when the Swiss growth was still going on. Nature and ethics continued to engage much of its attention.

Productions by the French- and German-speaking elements in this growth are about proportionate to the populational composition.

What we have, then, for Switzerland, is a slow nationalistic growth for two to three centuries in late mediaeval times, ending in a brief climax around 1500 and followed by a somewhat sputtering little cultural burst in succeeding decades; then quiescence; and, beginning in the earlier eighteenth century, a much larger and purely intellectual-aesthetic movement of at least a century and a half, punctuated near its middle by a transient political collapse.

§108. The Occident: America

In continents as new to Western civilization as the Americas, historic precedent would hardly lead to expectation of great cultural achievements; especially as the New World nationalities have been independent only a little more than a century to a century and a half.

United States.—English-speaking America began to be settled about a hundred years later than Latin America, and was overrun and occupied much more slowly. On the other hand, it was rather loosely administered from home, in spite of charters and governors, and its inhabitants came to make their way by their independent efforts, not through the government or by exploitation of a resident native population. Thus, favorable conditions of self-sufficiency existed, even though the area settled and the wealth produced long remained small. However, it took time for money, towns, and industry to become established, and until there was a certain accumulation of these, America could not hope to compete civilizationally with urbanized, courtly, and affluent Europe within the frame of the same culture.

Intellectually or aesthetically gifted and ambitious Americans of the later Colonial period tended to seek their futures in England. Such were the painters Copley and West, born 1737 and 1738, and Stuart, born 1755, though Stuart returned; and the physicist Thompson (Count Rumford), born 1753. More or less contemporary with these were the men of practical or political turn who remained in the country and became its traditional founders and fathers: Franklin, born 1706, Washington 1732, Jefferson 1743, Hamilton 1757, and their associates. They are difficult to evaluate, especially for an American, on account of the fetishistic halo which has come to surround their names. It is as easy to underrate them sophisticatedly and countersuggestibly as to overestimate them naïvely and patriotically.

Whether according to their opportunities these men went to England or remained in America, their birth dates brought them to the prime of their efficiency in the term of the Revolution and the formative years of the new nationality. We are therefore evidently dealing with an ability configuration of normal type.

After this, the picture changes. There is only one large, generally recognized figure in public life—Lincoln, born 1809. There are several growths in intellectual-aesthetic fields; and while none is of first magnitude, some are distinct. Also, they remain American, in spite of occasional flights of sensitive individuals to Europe.

The most clean-cut growth is that in literature, with a total range from about 1800 to 1900, or perhaps better 1810–1890, and a culmination at 1840–1860. The births run 1780–1850, climax 1800–1825. The growth is shorter than the nineteenth-century one in England.

Painting comes somewhat later. The birth dates range from 1825 (Inness) to 1856, with Whistler, 1834, marking the undoubted culmination. The relative weakness of the growth is shown by Whistler's leaving America. Sculpture is feebler and later still. Saint-Gaudens, born in Dublin in 1848—his father, however, a Frenchman,—perhaps comes as near to being a peak as could be named. Architecture and music scarcely come into consideration by world standards.

In philosophy, William James, born in 1842, is perhaps a symptom.

In science, the situation is obscure. The appearance is that of a development beginning to come into its growth at present; but it is risky to evaluate the contemporary in linkage with the past; wholly unwarranted, when its only connection is with the future. Good scientific work has been done in America during the nineteenth century; but it has been respectable rather than great, and it does not seem to constellate well.

This leaves us, then, small but definite developments in literature and painting culminating respectively around the middle of the nineteenth century and soon after, and over by about 1900. In view of the growth of the United States in wealth and population, neither its eighteenth- nor its nineteenth-century culmination seems adequate. Rather are they indicated as preliminary attempts or pulses of a greater movement ahead; unless Occidental civilization as a whole should prove already to have passed its zenith leaving America an unsuccessful because belated starter. After all, peace, population, and wealth alone do not produce great achievement; as second-century Rome shows.

Latin America.—For three hundred years, Latin America—primarily its native population but incidentally its white also—was closely ruled by and for the Iberian peninsula. In all this time it made no cultural contribution, but remained a colonial dependency. The only man of genius whom I am aware of its having produced is the dramatist Alarcón, who was born in Mexico in 1580, of course of Spanish parents, and who flourished in Spain.

Liberation produced the usual crop of national heroes, with Bolívar and San Martín the most eminent; but apparently no other distinguished ability. Spanish America had possessed families of wealth and a certain refinement all through the Colonial centuries. These have since produced a stream of polished prose and poetry, of greater finish probably than that produced in English America; but evidently also not of genuine originality of content, since the products have made little impress in the mother country and are practically unknown in the rest of the world. In philosophy, science, and organized music it would hardly be expected that Latin Americans would, as yet, do more than the Spaniards and Portuguese from whom their culture stems.

The northernmost Ibero-American nation, bordering the United States, has, possibly by reaction to that fact, been led into a program of social philosophy somewhat aberrant from that of its sisters. Coincident is the development of a Mexican school of painting, headed by Orozco and Rivera, born 1883 and 1886. How much of the acclaim of this school is due to actual aesthetic achievement and how much to its socio-economic bias, it is as yet too early to say. However, the group fits equally into the general recent phenomenon of spread to the peripheries and into the conscious effort of Mexico to overturn its past.

§109. The Occident: Peripheral Europe

Scandinavia and the Slavic countries, being marginal to western and central Europe, evince certain common features in their cultural history.

Christianization

Apparently the two significant events in their earlier history were the acceptance of a block of new cultural ideas and habits along with Christianity, and their emergence from a tribal status as signalized by the establishment of national kingdoms. Actually the two tended to go together, Christianity and royalty becoming allies against the old order.

In each case Christianity was either established by a monarch of power, or its introduction was promptly followed by the accession of a king who ruled with firmness and success, became a national symbol, and often earned the epithet "Great."

However much political power might thereafter again decentralize, it remained in consciousness as an ideal, and after centuries was regularly reattained.

The amount of new cultural material introduced along with Christianity is hard to estimate. The tenth-century Church was scarcely the agency to stimulate enough aesthetic and intellectual activity to result in products of intrinsic permanent cultural value. On the other hand, it did bring a new horizon of ideology, a considerable heritage and some knowledge of the past, and a valuation of certain crafts and skills, as in building and the decoration of objects of religious use. A foundation was therefore laid which was all-important for future higher attainments. Moreover, the beginnings of town life, of the minting of coins, of a social and political officialdom, sometimes date from the same period.

Integration

The table given overleaf shows the close correspondence in time of the corresponding events among several Scandinavian, Slavic, and Finno-Ugric peoples. Where there are differences, they follow distance from the centers of civilization. Bulgaria precedes Russia; Denmark precedes Norway and Sweden. That the influences from Constantinople should bear fruit simultaneously with those from Rome and the Franks is presumably a coincidence, but at least it simplifies the picture.

Peoples	Christianization	Political founder, historical or legendary	Ruler at early peak
Franks	496	Clovis, 481–511	Charlemagne, 768–814
Saxons	780		Otto I, 936–973
Danes	(826), 975	Gorm, –935, Harold Bluetooth, 935–	Knud, 1014–1035
Norwegians	1015–1030	Harald Haarfager, 863–930	(Magnus, 1035–1047)
Swedes	1150	(Olaf, 933–1024)	
Finns	1157–1293		
Bulgars	*864/5	Asparukh, 679, Krum, 802	Boris, 853–888
Russians	*988	Rurik, ca. 862	Vladimir, 972–1015
Moravians	**863	Moimir, 824	Svatopulk, 870–894
Czechs	845	Boleslav I, II, 929–967	First king, 1157
Magyars	1000	Arpád, before 900	Stephen, 1000–1038
Poles	963 seq.	Piast, ca. 850, Mieszko, 963	Boleslav, 992–1025
Lithuanians	1386	Mindvog, 1247, Gedymin, 1316–1341	Jagiello, 1377–1434

* Greek orthodox; ** Greek at first, then Roman; all unstarred, Roman.

The precedent, in one sense, for all these constructs was of course either Byzantium or the Frankish kingdom with its culmination in the empire of Charlemagne; back of which, in turn, lay the ideal of the Christianized world-empire of Rome. It is tempting to see in the tenth-century Saxon Imperial dynasty—now specifically German as it emerged from the Roman-Frankish composite—the slightly earlier German counterpart of the Scandinavian and Slavic political fabrics. At any rate, the Saxons were the last Germans to be Christianized and incorporated in the Frankish empire.

A few variants from the generic pattern may be commented upon, as follows:

Viking integration.—The Scandinavian peoples were obviously on the way to some sort of national florescence before Christianity and kingship knocked at their doors. This is shown by the successful expansions of the Viking-raid period. The movement falls into four phases:

Preliminary raids, mostly in Scotland and Ireland, 790–830.
Most active raiding and conquests, 830–900.
Lull, 900–980.
Conquests by kings, 980–1066.

The Varangian penetration and organization of Russia are the Swedish counterpart of Danish and Norwegian attacks on the West.

The Eddaic poetry is the one important literary growth on European soil which did not have knowledge of Ancient Mediterranean models and grew up without serious absorptions of Christian or Southern form or content.

In Scandinavia, then, and there alone in peripheral Europe, a perceptible native cultural growth was in progress when Christianity and political constitution arrived. Whether, left undisturbed, this growth would have progressed farther, it is impossible to say. At any rate it appears not to have affected the tempo of the spread of Christian Occidental civilization from its center outward.

The several Slavic integrations.—The West Slavs received their first Occidental civilization from the Germans. The time-

space relation seems regular for the Poles. They lost some territory to the Germans, but on the whole checked the German
eastward reëxpansion, thanks to their nationalization and
Christianization, as the pagan and tribal Slavs and Balts along
the Baltic could not.

The Czecho-Slovaks occupy a tongue jutting into German
territory. They therefore tended to become more Germanized
than the Poles, and their early national florescences are less
marked. That of ninth-century Moravia seems premature—an
interlude between Charlemagne and the Hungarians. Bohemian growth was retarded: the nation grew up under German
tutelage, accepted or imposed. There was no king until 1086,
no attempt at expansion until Ottokar II, 1253–1278, toward
the end of the Przemysls. Both Moravia and Bohemia became
an integral part of the Holy Roman Empire, as did Slovene
Styria and Carniola; whereas Poland virtually freed itself from
the Empire under Boleslav, 992–1025, who assumed the title
of king.

The South Slavs had in part moved into the limits of the
Byzantine Empire, in part had come under Avar and then
Magyar or Holy Roman Imperial domination. Perhaps this is
why they showed little tendency toward either national or cultural independence until considerably later, when a Serbian
growth was checked by the spread of the Turks in Europe.

The one exception among the South Slavs is formed by the
Bulgars—a Slavic people overrun and organized by a non-Indo-
European horde—probably Finno-Ugric from the Volga, but
possibly Turkic. The Bulgar state reached its real climax under
Boris, 853–888. Simeon, miscalled the Great, 893–927, wasted
his people's strength in futile efforts to overthrow Byzantium,
while losing his important trans-Danubian provinces.

As for the East Slavs or Russians, it evidently required foreign leadership, furnished by Scandinavians, to unite their
tribes into some sort of state with capital at Kiev. It seems that
the coöperation and fusion of the two nationalities was more
or less willingly accepted by the numerically preponderant
Slavs; as it must have been in Bulgaria also.

Disintegration

In every case, Christianity stuck but the early monarchies soon broke up. In Denmark an attempt at revival was made by the Valdemars and Knud around 1200, but it failed in 1227. Sweden, which had missed the first phase, finally settled down to Christianity about 1150 and a measure of political stabilization around 1250–1300. The Bulgars, who had already succumbed to the tenacious Greek Empire about when the peripheral nations were establishing their first kingdoms, made a gallant but unsuccessful attempt to re-form a state. Poland and Russia were in obvious disintegration when the Mongol storm broke over them.

Slavic Reintegration and Cultural Growth

Productive cultural florescence was slow in being attained, both because of distance from the higher centers and because politico-national reconsolidation was often very late.

In Poland.—The clearest instance of a civilizational flowering in the marginal lands earlier than Late Modern times is furnished by Poland. Here political integration recommenced under Ladislas the Dwarf, 1319, was developed by Casimir the Great, 1333–1370, and bore fruit in an enormous political expansion on the voluntary union with rising but rude Lithuania under Jagiello in 1386. Culturally, the Lithuanians soon subordinated themselves, the political union of the two peoples gradually became more intimate, and Poland-Lithuania retained its possessions, including all of White and most of Little Russia, until well into the seventeenth century; though under the last two of the Jagellons, the "Humanist" Sigismunds, 1506–1572, and the earlier of the following elective kings, royal power, and therefore political coördination, were weakening. The University of Cracow, founded in 1364 under Casimir, with Prague the first north of the Alps and east of the Rhine, served to indicate intent and direction. A national literature began to raise its head soon after 1500, and flowered about 1550–1600. Copernicus, 1543, falls into this constellation.

There were conscious borrowings from the Italian Renaissance in this growth; and in the main it was non-German in origin.

The Czechs.—Bohemia underwent something similar, but its course was blurred by immersion in the greater German unit. Ottokar II, 1253–1278, the next to the last Przemysl, is also reckoned the greatest. The real prosperity of Bohemia-Moravia, and its political importance, however, began with the accession of a foreign line, the Luxemburgers, 1311–1437, who generally became Holy Roman Emperors. Bohemia was the largest compact political entity in the Empire; and in turn the Luxemburg line gave Bohemia consciousness and importance through providing Imperial sovereigns. It is in this phase that the founding of the University of Prague falls.

Czech literature, founded in the days of Hus, reached a "golden age"—seemingly much overestimated by subsequent patriotism—in the later sixteenth century, about contemporary with Polish.

The real expression of Bohemian nationality was in the religious field, as symbolized by Hus, burned in 1415, and the successful popular Hussite wars of resistance, ending, in part, in a compromise of semi-independence within the Church. But, as usual, overinterest in religion tended to drain cultural energy away from other activities; especially as the religious conflict soon involved sectarian differences. Bohemia was both too small and too backward, on the whole, to evolve a new religion for Europe. With the definitive Protestant Reformation breaking in Germany a century after Hus, Bohemia again became the breeding ground of sects, and finally drew Germany into the Thirty Years' War; from which she came out ruined, crushed, and compelled to orthodoxy.

Russia.—The Russians emerged from the Mongol storm, and the Lithuanian conquests in the following century, with their western divisions, the White and Little Russians, under Polish sovereignty, and the Great Russians, now centered farther east than the former Varangian realm, divided into a series of principalities and republics under Mongol overlordship. Constantinople had become too feeble to exert serious influence. Even the Turks turned their main attention westward after they entered Europe. The Great Russians were thus cut off pretty completely from Europe. Their first concerns were to achieve unity and to free themselves from the Mongol yoke, real or nominal. The instrument of the former was the principality of Moscow, which in the fourteenth century began to absorb its neighbors, by 1462 had grown north, east, and south to rule over ten degrees of latitude. In 1480 the Mongol-Tatar over-lordship of the Golden Horde was broken. Ivan the Great, 1462–1505, also added Novgorod, Perm, and domains to the Arctic Ocean. Ivan the Terrible, 1533–1584, Tsar in 1547, con-quered southward and eastward. With him, all Great Russians may be considered as united under one rule. Also in his reign, with Yermak in 1582, falls the beginning of the marvelously rapid expansion over Siberia. In 1589 Moscow received its own Patriarch.

Here, then, was a great unified power, but severed from all higher centers of culture, and correspondingly rude. General European influences percolated slowly. Printing, for instance, reached Cracow in 1474 within two or three decades from Gutenberg, but Moscow only after a century, in 1552.

However, westward expansion soon commenced. Access to the Baltic was gained in 1617, and, though lost, was restored by Peter the Great. The Ukraine was partly wrested from Po-land in 1667, and other territory followed. Finally, around 1700, Peter the Great turned Russia on a deliberate course of cultural Westernization.

Productivity of moment by international standards, how-ever, did not begin to be achieved until 1800 and after. There came in succession the Russian growths in literature, science, and music, with culminations beginning around 1820, 1820, and 1860. These dates put them largely into the time of Pan-European or cosmopolitan nationalistic culture growths. But in spite of Pushkin's and Lermontov's Byronism, these growths were more than local reverberations—no mere "we too" efforts. The ground had been consciously cultivated for them for a century, and the Russian people had found successful nationalistic expression for three hundred years previously, though still too unformed, until the nineteenth century. to participate intellectually or aesthetically with Europe.

The course of development of the three greater Slavic peoples after the eleventh century thus was markedly different. The Czecho-Moravians, half-surrounded by Germans and under their cultural impact, remained almost a German appanage within the Holy Roman Empire. Their sense of nationality remained only half developed and long found its chief expression in religion. Psychologically as well as culturally they are perceptibly more similar to the Germans than are the Poles.

The Poles were farther removed, and never swamped by Germany. They reintegrated from their thirteenth-century slump, and achieved a definite nationalistic as well as cultural florescence in the fifteenth and sixteenth centuries; after which they sagged again, until a nineteenth-century revival, which was cultural only.

The Russians were long wholly beyond direct German and Latin influences, and when regrowth began after 1300, Byzantium, in which their higher heritage rooted, was itself almost extinguished as a stimulus. They had thus first to found and achieve an effective nationality, and then to extend it westward to meet the Occident, before higher culture could blossom among them. This Westernization hardly began, even on a sporadic scale, much before 1600, became conscious around 1700, and attained positive productivity of quality only after 1800.

Scandinavian Reintegration and Cultural Growth

The post-Viking Scandinavians were culturally in some ways more remote than Russia, which lay open to Byzantium and Asia. After the kingship, Papal recognition reached them, and finally the Reformation and pale reflections of the Renaissance. Always there was a belatedness of arrival—at first of about five centuries as compared, say, with the Franks, but with the span gradually decreasing. Protestantism alone was quickly adopted from Germany. Slow as the irradiations from the south and west were, they were persistent enough to check for long any serious growth of genuinely native productiveness. The result was a rustic, behindhand sort of culture. It was not till nearly 1600, with Tycho Brahe, that the first Scandinavian appears who contributed importantly to general European higher civilization. Soon after, Sweden began a brief career of nationalistic military expansion. It was the eighteenth century before either Denmark or Sweden attained a literature of any consequence even from the national point of view; and the nineteenth before there were authors read outside of Scandinavia. Since its Christianization, in short, Scandinavia has been humbly going to school, and not until the most recent centuries has she ventured to speak up in class.

As between the three countries, Sweden was long the most in arrears, as might be expected from her position. However, her greater isolation perhaps was the circumstance which enabled her earliest to work out a typical national florescence; which, bursting on Europe politically in the seventeenth century, culminated in spiritual fields at home in the next. Denmark had evidently been too immediately adjacent to overwhelmingly greater Germany, and too much influenced by her, or by France in conscious counterbalance, to develop for herself the same sort of a national destiny. In some degree, the culture history of Denmark is fairly conceivable as that of a semi-independent province of Germany. Norway, finally, stands rather clearly in the same relation to Denmark, the relation being facilitated by the close relationship of language. In spite of all recent separatist emphases, which extend even to the manufacture of a national Norwegian speech—or two, to be exact,—the summary culture history of Denmark and Norway is therefore most intelligible as a unit.

Denmark and Norway.—After Canute (or Knud), Denmark and Norway and England fell apart. After more than a century, the Danes resumed an expansion, into Schleswig and eastward along the coasts of Mecklenburg, Pomerania, and Esthonia. This was under Valdemar I, Knud VI, and Valdemar II, who reigned from 1157 to 1241, contemporary with the German

Hohenstaufens. But the effort collapsed under Valdemar II, in 1227. Culturally there were Bishop Absolon or Axel, died 1201, and Saxo Grammaticus, died 1204, and Svend Aageson, who compiled history under his patronage. About the same period, Iceland enjoyed a cultural florescence, which Sarton has enlarged upon.[15]

Norwegian consolidation occurred somewhat later; under Haakon and Magnus, 1217–1284, when the crown became powerful, the laws were codified, Iceland and Greenland were annexed, and Scotland invaded.

The following are characteristic of the Danish lag in subsequent centuries.

Heidelberg, first German university, 1386.
Rostock, first in northern Germany, 1418.
Copenhagen, 1478/9.[16]
Printing in Germany, about 1450.
In Denmark, 1490.
Luther's translation of the Bible, 1522–1534.
Danish, 1550.
Science, culmination in Germany, ca. 1550. Tycho Brahe, ca. 1600.

Denmark in the period of its best literature, say 1770–1860, as marked by Ohlenschläger, born 1779, and Andersen, 1805, also produced Thorwaldsen, born 1770, in sculpture; Oersted, 1777, in science; Rask, 1787, in linguistics; Kierkegaard, 1813, in philosophy; Gade, 1817, in music. This is clearly a constellation, and though the array seems scattered it is not unduly so for a small country.

Norwegian participation in modern European cultural productivity is perceptibly later, and mainly post-1850. Thus, in mathematics, Abel, born 1802; literature, Ibsen 1828, Björnson 1832; music, Grieg 1843, Sinding 1856.

The Norwegian contributions possess more originality and force. This seems a function of greater remoteness and there-

---

[15] *Introduction to the History of Science,* Vol. 2.
[16] Sweden preceded with Upsala, 1477; and Scotland with St. Andrews, 1411, Glasgow, 1450 (and Aberdeen, 1494). Norway appears to have had no university until Christiania-Oslo, 1811.

fore independence. Norway still savors of the soil, whereas Denmark lies closer to the heart of Europe. The relation in this point is much like that of Russia and Poland.

Sweden.—Here, as in Norway, geography dictated a lag as compared with Denmark. Christianity was first preached by the same Ansgar in the ninth century, but paganism re-arose in the eleventh, and it was only the reign of Erik IX, 1150–1160, that brought an archbishop and a church to long-sacred heathen Upsala. This was when the burst of Early Scholastic philosophy was ending in France.

The first monarchs to exercise reasonably firm authority were Birger, Valdemar, Magnus Ladulaas, and Birger, 1250–1319. The only expansion was across the Baltic to Finland, which was crusaded, Christianized, and conquered somewhat earlier, from 1157 to 1293.

A growth began with Gustavus Vasa in 1523, who made Sweden independent of Denmark and strengthened and enriched the crown by introducing the Reformation. Under a line of strong if often erratic successors, of whom Gustavus Adolphus is the most famous, a career of nationalistic expansion took place.

Esthonia, acquired 1561.
Karelia, Ingria, 1617.
Livonia, 1629.
Gothland and Oesel, 1645.
Herjedalen, 1645.
Pomerania, Bremen, 1648.
Southwest Swedish provinces, 1658.

For more than half a century, Sweden was one of the quasi-great powers of Europe, like Switzerland around 1500. Then Charles XII precipitated overstrain, with collapse at Poltava in 1709, and the conquests crumbled away.

Bremen, lost 1719.
Part of Pomerania, 1720.
Karelia, Ingria, Esthonia, Livonia, Oesel, 1721.
Finland, 1808.
Rest of Pomerania, 1815.

This is a symmetrical curve of growth and decline.

The cultural development began a century later than the military one. In literature, the classical writers were born from 1729 to 1759, corresponding to productivity from about 1760 to 1810. In science, Celsius, Linnaeus, Bergman, Scheele, were born from 1701 to 1742; Berzelius in 1779. To the same period belong Swedenborg, 1688, and Celsius the historian, 1716. This is as definite a cultural constellation for the later eighteenth century as the politico-military one in the seventeenth.

Why Sweden, after lagging behind Denmark for a thousand years, should finally have anticipated her culturally, is not clear. It may be because she had had a successful nationalistic growth; and this in turn may be the result of greater sheltering in remoteness plus greater population.

§110. The Jews

The Jews, beginning as a small localized nationality, became to most intents a self-segregated, sectarian, but widely scattered caste in later antiquity, and have remained such through the Islamic and Occidental civilizations. Three thousand years of separateness merit them consideration here; and their abnormal history serves as a reminder that at least a quasi nationality is attainable without territory or even distinctive speech.

Originally a group of tribes, the Hebrews took gradual possession of Palestine toward 1200 B.C., and around 1000 attempted to consolidate themselves into a monarchy. After an initial reverse, they succeeded, and for perhaps eighty years, under David and Solomon, they managed a successful minor or local kingdom comparable to, say, Tyre or Damascus. This happened in a period of Egyptian and Mesopotamian nonintervention in Syria. At Solomon's death about 937, the kingdom broke into northern and southern portions, which were subjected to intermittent Egyptian, Assyrian, and Neo-Babylonian overlordship until their respective extinctions in 722 and 586.

To the Hebrews themselves, their little temporal glory seemed very great; and as hope of its reattainment receded, they substituted the concept of the unlimited and universal supremacy of their national deity. Such is the modern reading of the Old Testament in culture-historical terms. This volume was composed from about 850 to 150, with a few older inclusions, and is at once a nationalistic philosophy, history, and literature. In a work which still has so much religious connotation for us, and with parts so diverse, it is difficult to make qualitative evaluations as between the straightforward, affective narratives of Genesis, Judges, and Samuel, the thundering denunciations of the prophets, the fervor of Deuteronomy, the resignation of the Psalms, or the glowing metaphors of Job. On the side of literary expression, the passages written before 600 will perhaps have the most enduring and unusual appeal; but the Hebrew religious philosophy was not clearly evolved until about that date. It would therefore be difficult to date a culmination for the Old Testament. It is, after all, part of the Bible of the religion of our Occidental civilization, and it is still almost impossible for each of us to be wholly without bias for or against this religion. The verdict, some day, of a group of sufficiently informed Chinese scholars in history and art might be worth much more than ours.

It is important to bear in mind that in the ability to compose clear and effective narrative prose, in the forms of their lyrical or rhapsodical poetry, as well as in a monotheistic concept of a certain grandeur, the Old Testament Hebrews had been anticipated by several centuries by Egyptian Hamites and in part by Mesopotamian Semites.

In 168 B.C., just about as the very last portions of the Old Testament were being added, there was a successful national revolt under the Maccabees; which, however, on the one hand soon dissipated into a series of minor Oriental autocracies, and on the other produced nothing culturally, beyond a refanaticizing of nationalistic orthodoxy. The one cultural product of the ancient Hebrews, the Old Testament, falls precisely between Solomon and the Maccabees.

In the full Graeco-Roman civilization—the Hellenes before Alexander barely knew of the existence of Hebrews—the Jews

took relatively little part, other than in unconsciously preparing the soil of Christianity. Around the beginning of the
Christian era there were St. Paul, Philo the Helleno-Judaic
philosopher, and Josephus the historian of Judaea. All three
were engaged in pouring the essence of the wine of Judaism
into the newer and greater bottle of a cosmopolitan age; and all
three expressed themselves in Greek.

The Talmud or traditional Hebrew law was gradually built
up between 450 B.C. (legendary date) or 150 B.C. (historical)
and 500 A.D., mainly in Palestine and Mesopotamia. It is thus
wholly subsequent to national independence, and in part post-
Diaspora. It consists of the law and the commentaries, which
are separated in time by about 200 A.D. In spite of some eminent
leaders like Hillel (about the time of the birth of Christ) and
Rabbi Jehuda (toward 200 A.D.), the Talmud is a gradual
growth, scarcely measurable by the standard applied in the
present work.

For six or seven hundred years after the Diaspora, we hear
of Jews in various Christian, pagan, or Muslim lands without
their making notable contributions to Jewish or Gentile culture. Then comes their florescence under Islam, in whose
science and philosophy they participated, without furnishing
any of the very greatest names, it is true, but with a proportion-
ately greater representation, it is probable, than their numbers
in the population. In eastern Islam, half a dozen eminent
scholars were Jewish, from about 800 to a little beyond 900.
More of them were scientists than philosophers. In western
or Spanish-Moroccan Islam, there were about the same number, all but the two earliest between 1100 and 1200, and with
the philosophers Avicebron, Ibn Ezra, Maimonides outweigh-
ing the scientists. The two bursts are, culturally, primarily
Arabic—miniature samples of the stream of Arabic thought of
the period with a greater or less Jewish coloring. In philology,
the Jews accepted the Arabic techniques worked out by 800
and applied them to Hebrew during the century 950–1050.

In Occidental civilization, the Jews begin to participate
creatively very late. The first familiarly great name is that of

Spinoza, born 1632. In Dutch culture history he stands in a closely clustered constellation, with Huygens, Vondel, Rembrandt; among Jews, he is very isolated.

The next appearance of Jews is again in philosophy, but in Germany and a century later. Mendelssohn, Jacobi, Maimon, born between 1729 and 1754, were younger and minor contemporaries of Kant, 1724. Once the Kantian philosophy began to be established, in the period of Fichte and Hegel, Jews receded from the scene; and even among the epigones they re-emerge only with the quasi philosopher Marx, born 1818.

Into Occidental science the Jews ventured very late. The German Jacobi, born in 1804, and the British Sylvester, 1814, both mathematicians, are apparently the first. Up to 1900, or perhaps a decade or so before, I can recall no first-magnitude Jewish reputation. The noticeably great Jewish contributions to mathematico-physical science, and biological as well, have been made essentially since 1890. One is likely to forget the recency of the phenomenon because of its brilliance.

In music, we have previously seen that the list of Jewish composers opens with Meyerbeer, born 1791. Moscheles, Halévy, Mendelssohn, Offenbach, Rubinstein, Goldmark bring the birth dates in that order down to 1832, and include France and Russia with Germany. Then there is a comparative lull until the immediately contemporary period.

In literature, the outstanding figure remains Heine, born 1797. In Germany, he had as predecessors Börne, 1786, chiefly remembered for Heine's attacks on him; and the philosopher-authors Hamann and Jacobi, 1730 and 1743. Heine is not followed by any German Jewish writer of notability until the Viennese Schnitzler, born in 1862, six years after Heine's death.

In other languages we have, in English, Disraeli, 1804;[17] in Danish, a little group: Hertz, 1797, Goldschmidt, 1819, Brandes, 1842; in Russian, Nadsohn, 1862; in French, the philosopher Bergson, 1859.

That there are no great historic names of Jews in painting,[18]

---

[17] Disraeli counts in politics also, along with the Genoese-French Gambetta.
[18] Joseph Israels, born in Holland, 1824, is scarcely a vigorous exception.

sculpture, and architecture is sometimes explained by a supposed inherited manual deficiency, which of course is biologically unproved. It is, however, remarkable that in the verbalizing activity of dramatic writing no Jew seems ever to have
attained genuinely high rank, in spite of the success of Jews in
acting since Rachel (1821, Swiss) and Bernhardt (1845, half
Jewish, Dutch), and more lately in the producing of plays.
Evidently the factors involved are highly complex and vary in
strength rapidly.

Witness the history of chess, in which championships, challenge matches, and open tournaments furnish a continuous
record of superiority since a full century ago. The earlier masters, such as Philidor, Anderssen, and Morphy, were gentiles.
There follows an unbroken series of Jewish champions: Zuck-
ertort, Steinitz, Lasker; plus a crowd only a shade weaker.
Excellence in chess seemed a distinctively Jewish trait. Then
suddenly Cuban, Russian, Dutch gentiles succeed one another
in the championship. There is nothing long-range in the situation to indicate any deep-seated correlation. Evidently Jews,
on account of their smaller numbers and caste coherence, perhaps sometimes also on account of previous caste training in
allied activities, tend to mobilize more quickly than gentiles
in fields which they enter newly, and temporarily win brilliant
successes. Then after a time the balance is restored. There is
no reason to suppose that in physics, medicine, psychoanalysis,
cinematography, or communism the apparent recent swamping
by Jews is anything but a similarly transient phenomenon.

If now we bring together the Jewish participation in Occidental civilization, we find a thousand years in which they
made no cultural contribution, then Spinoza, and then another
century in which they did not participate. About 1760 they
commence to enter German philosophy, for which the Talmud
had given training. The chief historic contribution in the
modern West is from Jews born between 1790 and 1830 mainly
in Germany, but also in Denmark, France, England, and Slavic
countries. This group achieved excellence but not dominance
in literature and music, modest success in science and philoso-

phy, nothing in drama, painting, or sculpture. Then comes a definite tapering off for nearly a generation; and then once more, with births from about 1855 on, a successful Jewish drive mainly into new fields, such as certain areas of science and theatrical production. The essential characteristics of the movement are its recency, its fluctuations in time, and its variability in activity entered upon.

It is evident that the causes which have made for the exceedingly spotty Jewish participation in three great civilizations must have been highly variable. It is easy to see why no Jew contributed directly to European Mediaeval philosophy. which began with orthodox Christian assumptions; but in Arabic philosophy there was a place for them. There is no doubt that European eighteenth-century Enlightenment was bound to end in opening many gates to Jews. It is equally clear that they moved through these at quite different times, and as determined by variant factors—some of their own making, such as readiness to discard Orthodoxy for Enlightenment, and others due to gentile attitudes. The one constant element in Jewish culture history in two thousand years has been the religious caste sense. Everything else has been too intermittent to suggest that it springs from any permanent, consistent, and developable pattern.

§111. The West as a Whole

Occidental culture is to a much greater degree a multiple-national one than any other great civilization. We have reviewed the configurational history of its principal ingredients. It remains to consider the totality in sequence.

The Dark Age of Germanic preponderance: 500–800.—The pit of the Dark Ages is the point up to which Mediterranean civilization was disintegrating or atrophying faster than the forming Occidental civilization could effectively develop its new patterns. Just when the deficit piled up highest in distinction from the assets of the past and the future, it is difficult to say with precision, and varied locally; but an average for western Europe would presumably fall between 600 and 700. About the year 500, Germanic tribes were ruling Italy, Spain, France, the Netherlands, Austria, Germany, Scandinavia, and part of Britain. On the whole, however, they were still receiving much more from Mediterranean civilization than they were visibly contributing. By 800 the balance had shifted. The formal patterns were still largely ancient: the Empire, the Church, Latin writing, many technologies and names of things. But the content of institution and custom was dominantly Occidental. Christianization had been completed, except among marginal Scandinavians and Slavs.

Politically, in 800, one German nation, the Frankish one, had emerged and absorbed the others. Its center lay between Paris and Cologne: on old Roman soil, but near the Roman frontier. Spain had been lost to the Arabs, southern Italy in part to the surviving old Empire, so that the vicinity of the Netherlands constituted a fair geographical as well as gravitational center for the new Europe, as the Frankish kingdom-empire really was. Eastern Germany had been abandoned and occupied by the Slavs, who were still thoroughly uncivilized. The only Germanic peoples not under Frankish rule and influence were the Scandinavians, who were just beginning to find that raiding or conquering the fairly settled lands was more profitable than fighting one another in the poverty-stricken north; and the Anglo-Saxons, who had slumped down in the isolation of Britain. In Hungary the Avar power was just collapsing and the Magyars had not yet come in, and the Franks had little trouble in dominating a belt of Slavic peoples from the nearer Baltic to the head of the Adriatic. The Byzantine Empire, with half its realm lost to the Arabs and with the Bulgars bored into its northern flank, was in no position to be an active competitor, either inland or in southern Italy.

At the same time, the unity of rule in western or Latin Christendom, around 800, was keeping down the sense of nationality which was gradually to grow so large in the culture of Europe. Nationalism was still essentially tribal where it was unsubdued. Within the Frankish empire, nationality had sunk rather to the role of local custom, such as was taken for granted, but as something that underlay the great and symbolically worthwhile things—Christianity and the Church, the power of rule and kingship, writing and law, and everything else that was seemingly fixed or wide-scale.

Most histories seem to find it difficult to make clear the significance of Charlemagne other than as a personality, a somewhat rude but firm and capable ruler of many lands. Others dwell on the Carolingian cultural renaissance. This latter was a very feeble phenomenon in comparison with most of the configurations considered in the present work. That centralized order and internal peace should bring with them a degree of promotion of wealth, trade, the condition of the arts, and learning, is to be expected. But when we look about for specific products of the Carolingian renaissance, for something done in a characterized manner, there is very little, either in thought or art. There is more style, more sense and control of form, in the Edda of the heathen Norsemen than in anything accomplished by tongue or hand in Carolingian Christendom.

On the contrary, the realm of Charlemagne was the product of a three hundred years' growth, which began with half a dozen Germanic kingdoms and as many more tribal nationalities, some Arian, some Athanasian, some pagan; and ended with a unified empire and unified Roman Christianity. Beginning in 486, Clovis more than doubled the Frankish dominion by taking over the Seine basin to the Loire, and then extending his rule to Toulouse. He also turned Athanasian, that is, Roman Catholic. From that time there is a steady growth of Frankish power, at the expense of the Burgundian and Visigothic kingdoms, and of the Alemannian, Thuringian, Frisian, Bavarian tribal confederacies. Meanwhile the Vandal, Ostrogoth, and Visigoth kingdoms fell before the resuscitated Byzantines or the Arabs. The latter were definitely turned back behind the Pyrenees by the Franks after the victory of Tours in 732. When Charlemagne came to the throne in 768, he had only to overthrow the Lombards, reconquer the Bavarians, and subdue the Saxons, and every Germanic or German-ruled people of the mainland was brought under the single Frankish sovereignty. In short, he completed a long process of unification and of attainment of the degree of order which springs from unity.

In brief, the Franks gradually achieved a state at once multiple and centralized enough to deserve the name of empire. They did not achieve a civilized culture; they ruled like Romans, or like other Germans since 300, over other peoples; but, for a time, they ruled successfully. Why their state broke up is not clear. There were two factors that certainly contributed: one, the lack of a developed higher culture to reënforce with its content and associations the ideal of the empire; the other, the lack of place for nationality in the Frankish political scheme. With an impressive culture to offer, Charlemagne might have induced his polyglot peoples to identify themselves with this. Without it, his empire was subject to disruptive forces even stronger than the personal ambitions of his heirs.

National crystallization: 800–1050.—When the Carolingian breakup came—wholly from within,—the French emerged as a clean-cut people. Their state was long politically feeble, and it failed to include all Frenchmen; but it was as much of a national unit as was possible at the time. Frankish speech and specific German habits and institutions were shed. The French thus were set to lead the way toward the development of Occidental culture, which proved to be organized on an increasingly nationalistic basis.

The Germans achieved nationality of a sort. They substituted a Pan-German ideal for that of Frankish German overlordship. But at the same time they refused to let go of the multinational empire which the Franks had achieved as a fact rather than with a conscious purpose. The total German nation, as expressed by their collective princes and the leader chosen by these from among themselves, was to rule; and over French, Italians, and Slavs as well as over Germans. It was easy for Frenchmen to renounce a corresponding ambition: after all, the dynasty which had achieved it was an alien one. Two-thirds of France in French hands was better than being part of a Germanic empire.

For a time it looked as if most of the Germans might also segregate themselves as a national unit, plus backward Slavic tributaries. A Lotharingian empire was actually set up between the French and the German block, stretching from the mouths of the Rhine to those of the Po and the Tiber, and composed of both Romance and Teutonic peoples. This scheme failed, and the strip fell back into the German empire—France was still too weak to absorb it. But the Lotharingian strip was never firmly controlled; and sooner or later, at varying times but ultimately, the Netherlands, Burgundy, Switzerland, and Italy became *de facto* and then admittedly independent of the empire. Two of these, the Netherlands and Switzerland, were preponderantly Germanic in population. It is only the stretch of the Rhine between them that has remained politically German; and even that has been subject, in the end, to French encroachment.

Culturally the Lotharingian corridor seems to have represented a certain reality, in spite of its monstrosity from the twentieth-century point of view which assumes political and national identity as unarguably right and desirable. The strip was probably in most of its parts culturally more advanced than the pure French and pure German blocks on its left and right. It continued, on the whole, prosperous, and at least its two ends, the Netherlandish and the North Italian, accumulated unusual density of population and wealth and advanced into relative urbanization. In the fifteenth century especially, in fact largely from, say, 1325 to 1625, not only Italy but Switzerland, the Netherlands, even northern Burgundy, achieved definite florescences of one sort or another, while France and Germany lagged, on the whole. The Lotharingian lands resisted the Middle Ages to some degree, one feels. They took relatively little part in the formulation of the High Mediaeval pattern.[19] With the breakdown of this pattern in the Late Middle Ages, beginning soon after 1300, they came into their own.

---

[19] They tended toward the urban or cantonal, and away from the feudal, for instance. And the one outstanding contribution of Italy to Scholasticism, Aquinas, came from Naples, not Lombardy or Tuscany. Perhaps this is only an accident; but it deserves consideration.

We cannot yet quite leave the Franks. Their accomplishment of a state more firmly organized than anything the West had yet seen since the days when the Roman Empire still held together, had a series of repercussions. The less civilized peoples on the east and north made the same attempt and several times succeeded.

The first effort was by the Germans, under the Othonians, in the mid-tenth century.[20] Otto the Great—crowned 962—perhaps came nearer to being a successful emperor than any other German. The home domain of the dynasty was Saxony—the last German territory conquered by the Franks, and a frontier. There was also a transient cultural development: small but perceptible, and localized in and about Saxony.

A little later, clustered around the year 1000, the marginal Scandinavians, Poles, Magyars, and Russians all achieved successful kingship and Christianity, as shown in the table under "Peripheral Europe" (p. 726, §109). They were too little civilized as yet to do more: there is no counterpart of accomplishment in art, letters, or thought.

High Mediaevalism: 1050–1325.—The first European cultural products of superior intrinsic value appear in the eleventh century: poetry, cathedrals, sculpture, philosophy. By 1050 the High Mediaeval pattern was beginning to form; by 1150 it was taking definite shape; around 1250 it came into culmination. By 1325 it was dissolving. Around 1050 the last Byzantine resuscitation ended, and Arabic culture was turning downgrade, or had turned downgrade, in one after another activity, except in its one European territory, Spain. This inverse correspondence may be pure coincidence. But possibly the European-Mediterranean area is enough of a historic unit for something like "cultural potential" to flow reciprocally between its major divisions; what one gains being at the expense of the other. This would be like pattern productivity flowing from Greek East to Latin West and back to Greek within the Ancient Mediterranean civilization. Both Arabic

---

[20] Possibly the Anglo-Saxon reunion under Alfred the Great, 871–901, should be counted as prior. It was, however, the success of consolidating a remnant, rather than an expansive movement like the others.

and Occidental culture are rooted in the older Mediterranean one. Their philosophies, for instance, up to 1300, were re-workings of Greek thought; their architectures, transformations of Roman prototypes. Viewed configurationally, the idea of such an inverse or complementary relation does not seem preposterous; though it must be admitted that the mechanism at work remains hazy.

At any rate, when the balance began to tip around 1050, Europe, with its patterns in growth, was in a position to nourish these with Ancient Mediterranean, Byzantine, and Arabic absorptions; whereas these last two civilizations, their patterns having passed the stage of growth, could only take over Occidental culture material by accretion, inorganically as it were, and not digest it into new-patterned products. Spanish Arabic culture remained for a time in the condition of West European. At least, both were late because both were distant from their stem in the East Mediterranean.

By 1100, the dip of the balance was clear. The First Crusade had taken place—a successful expansive effort of the Occident against Islam and by implication Byzantium.

The area in which the Mediaeval patterns took their shape was usually France, both northern and southern, and almost synchronously, though the southern florescence ended earlier. That 'the cultural center of southern France was the Loire drainage rather than the Mediterranean coast, makes the movement a genuinely French one, and removes it from the sphere of Roman persistences or renascences in the old Provincia Romana.

The preëminence of France in the formation of High Mediaeval culture is clear. French building, French sculpture, French verse forms, sentiments, and themes were copied or adapted in varying degree through civilized Europe. There is no nationality uninfluenced by France; but no single pattern of importance which France took from another European nationality. Sometimes the adoptions were marvelously rapid, as of architectural features in England, literary ones in Germany, so that it has been questioned whether this or that pattern trait may not have been of native origin rather than transferred out of France. But what flow is traceable, is always one-way; and at least French priority and probable stimulus-influence are almost always discernible, no matter how original the non-French native treatment.

In philosophy the situation is particularly neat. In a Latin Europe that acknowledged the spiritual supremacy of the Church to which thought bowed, philosophy had almost to be Pan-European; at least was extremely likely to be so. And High Mediaeval philosophy in its culmination was actually international. The greatest single figure was a South Italian; the largest number of thinkers of high rank was probably contributed by Britain; Germany and Catalan Spain participated vigorously. France alone added no first-magnitude philosophers in the thirteenth century—because the whole Scholastic movement had originated and flowered there in the early twelfth. Early Scholasticism is almost wholly a French product. France set the pattern; the rest of Europe collectively filled it a century later.

The dominance of France was cultural, not political. Even though she enjoyed a prosperous thirteenth century, with relatively successful kings, she was in no sense preponderant in strength of arms. She did influence and stimulate every West European country; but whether these produced works of high quality in this or that cultural activity depended on factors within their own situation. Thus, as has been shown, Germany had a literature of a certain greatness touched off by France, and some good sculpture. In England neither art attained to anything much worth while; but architecture kept close step with that of France. The Netherlands absorbed French influences generally, but began to achieve notably for themselves only after the French productivity was in decay. Contrariwise, Italy, especially in the focal north, either resisted the foreign impingements or imitated frankly and badly.

In the thirteenth century, accordingly, Europe under the leadership of France realized an international set of distinctive and productive patterns. There was a fairly successful balance between kingship and feudalism; the towns, while still small, had their place in the scheme, and there was a definite bourgeoisie. The Church was strong and united, and its Franciscans and Dominicans had identified themselves with intellectual activity. A totally new and ambitious order of architecture, mainly ecclesiastical, had been evolved, and with it a flourishing sculpture. Literature had developed in several vernaculars, with definite metrical forms and an abundance of new themes. Philosophy had achieved high technical competence and genuine systematization within the framework allowed by the Church. Science, technology, painting, the drama stayed rudimentary; but enough had been accomplished to assure that if the growth of Europe had been cut off by a cataclysm in 1300 or 1325, a relatively high and distinctive Occidental civilization would have remained inscribed on the pages of history.

Late Middle Ages and Renaissance: 1325–1575.—However, this High Mediaeval set of patterns was only a forerunner of greater ones. In the generation following 1300, the patterns began to dissolve. This is specially patent in philosophy, which turned upon itself in skeptical negativism. Architecture became mannered or extreme, sculpture lost its vigor and plasticity. The Church underwent a political schism, and was widely assailed as a corrupt and frivolous perversion of a God-given instrument. The strong or successful monarchs of France, Spain, Germany, England were succeeded by less fortunate or weaker ones. In the fourteenth or fifteenth century each of these countries in turn was torn by long internal wars.

On the other hand, population and wealth increased in these two centuries, in spite of the devastating plague of the mid-fourteenth. The horizon widened: Farther Asia came into the ken of Europe, and then America. Technology made enormous advances. Firearms, paper, printing, seaworthy ships, cast iron were developed in this period, along with a host of more special inventions and introductions: spectacles, playing cards, coaches, watches, spinning wheels, insurance, double-entry bookkeeping. These all preceded any organized development of science. In 1500 or 1550 the cultural inventory of western Europe was far richer than in 1300, especially on the material and economic side.

It was different with patterns of aesthetic and intellectual culture, and sociopolitical ones. A new set, at least of the former, had developed by 1500; but in new centers. France had yielded leadership; Spain and England had not yet achieved it. The hearth of higher cultural productivity lay farther east than before: in the Netherlands, Germany, and Poland, especially in northern Italy. The radiant area now was central instead of west European—the old Lotharingia, mainly, but with a definite accentuation at its southern end. The seat of high cultural potential had shifted out from the former center in France.

Around 1300, northern Italy, which until then had rather kept out of Mediaevalism, and had either refused or slavishly accepted French models, found itself. Dante and Giotto are the symptoms. The specific Renaissance, in the sense of a certain degree of control in the visual arts, may perhaps be more properly datable from about a century later. But in larger view the Renaissance is all one growth, with great culminations in sculpture, painting, and architecture in the first decades after 1500, and a little later in science and music; the literary configuration is more diffuse, but ends about 1580. Here was an entirely new set of attitudes and patterns: secular in spite of acceptance of the Church, nonfeudal, non-Gothic, urban; never stiff, never overloaded with detail, poised rather than committed; and therefore seeming infinitely more modern than true Mediaeval culture.

While most outstandingly Italian, this growth was not confined to Italy. The Netherlanders underwent a similar urban bourgeois development, and soon surpassed the French whom they began by imitating. In sculpture, painting, music, and science they accomplished notable things. In the last three of these activities they contributed to the Italian growths. The relations in painting have been discussed above. Netherlandish artists executed much of the fifteenth-century sculpture and painting of France, Spain, and especially Burgundy. Toward 1500, Switzerland found itself an international power and began to take part in cultural productivity. Germany's mathematicians and astronomers set off the procession of Western scientists in the fifteenth century, and a minor peak in science was reached there around the mid-sixteenth. The majority of the inventions and technological innovations just cited were made either in Germany or Italy. In painting, too, the Germans reached a culmination with Dürer and Holbein. Their achievements, it is true, were spotty: in sculpture, architecture, literature, music, and politically, they remained mediocre or worse. Whether the Reformation is to be counted a cultural asset or liability is an arguable matter. Bohemia produced Hus a century earlier. Poland was politically prosperous through the whole period, and in the sixteenth century produced not only Copernicus but a worthwhile literature. It is evident that the frontier peoples of east-central Europe were participating in the developments that were most active along the Rhine-Tiber line and culminating in North Italy.

Apart from Italy and the Netherlands, it is true that these achievements scarcely aggregated enough to constitute a great phase of a great civilization. But they become significant by contrast: in the same period of 1325 to 1550, France, Spain, and England produced nothing equal to them.

The Netherlands were too small and too bourgeois to influence Europe very profoundly except in particular crafts. Around 1500, however, the Italian Renaissance began to spread its influence strongly: first to Spain and the Netherlands, then to France, later to Germany and England, ultimately even to Scandinavia. However republican its beginnings, the Italian Renaissance had always emphasized grace, and had adapted itself to courtly life in the Italian tyrannies. The Papacy in fact was the first large court to discover and foster the Renaissance. There was thus nothing to hinder the spread of Italian patterns to any people sufficiently advanced to appreciate refinement and charm; or, for that matter, simplicity of objective and structure. The fonts of roman and italic type promptly added

by the Italians to the German invention of printing are highly
characteristic in this connection. Their significance lies less in
their return to ancient classic forms than in their simple, elegant directness, which made their acceptance inevitable by all
nations that had not somehow got stuck fast in Mediaevalism.
Similarly with architecture. There can be little doubt that the
Romanesque-Gothic order is a more ambitious, original, and
intense one than the Renaissance order: in short, capable of
more grandeur. But it is intricate, overloaded, inconvenient
to live in. A Renaissance palace is fundamentally a modern
building; the climax of Mediaeval architecture was a cathedral
or abbey. It was because of essentially "modern" though buried
attitudes that the Italians so tenaciously resisted transalpine
Mediaeval influences, and, when these had lost their force,
were the first people able to offer Europe a set of thoroughly
non-Mediaeval forms.

Earlier modern culture in western Europe: 1575–1700.—
The crux of the story of the spread of the Italian Renaissance
to Spain, Portugal, France, the Netherlands, Britain, is, however, the way in which each of these national cultures reworked
what it got from Italy until it could express the acquisition in
its own patterns. This gradual reworking occupied most of the
sixteenth century; in France it was not completed until the
early seventeenth.

The outcome was a post-Renaissance or Baroque century or
more in which five West European nationalities attained definite cultural florescences stimulated ultimately by Italy but
always intensely national in form: Portugal, Spain, France, the
Netherlands, England. The approximate periods were:

Portugal, 1550–1600 (political, 1475–1550).
Spain, 1575–1650/60 (political, 1500–1575).
France, 1620/30–1680/90.
The Netherlands, 1600–1700 (mainly Dutch; Belgian also in
   painting).
England, 1575–1700.

These florescences always included several of the arts; and,
except in the two Iberian countries, bursts of science and phi-

losophy. The science carried on that of Galileo; but the philosophy was new, Italy having never found a successor to Aquinas. In this field, France was the initiator, and England carried on well beyond 1700, owing largely to late Scottish reinforcement.

Outside of these West European countries, the Renaissance influence was a veneer, and often an unfortunate one. The Germans, Scandinavians, and Slavs profited little and late; so late, often, that they took over more Boileau than Guarini. Germany, in fact, receded culturally from after about 1550–1575, as compared with the two centuries before. The desolating Thirty Years' War may be construed as an overt symptom of the general disintegration and regression that were under way, rather than as their cause. In fact, it occurred in the very middle of the slump.

The Enlightenment interval: 1700–1750.—Around 1700, the Early Modern west-European growths were finished, and something of a lull ensued in nearly all fields of higher culture in all Europe. This interval lasted about a half century, and is the era roughly of Enlightenment, Rococo, and the example of Versailles. The interval is not absolutely universal: English-Scotch philosophy lasted through it, and German music began its career soon after 1700. No one cultural activity, however, reached its peak, and no one nation was definitely in culmination, between 1700 and 1750. It was a time of balance of power, relative tranquillity, intellectual enlightenment and diffusion rather than enterprise, lack of aesthetic ardor: a period of diminished tension, in short. As in the Late Middle Ages, population, wealth, and total amount of culture grew, but patterns were being relaxed rather than channeled. Voltaire is typical: neither a true poet nor a real philosopher, but enormously intelligent and always on the side of intelligence, and influencing a larger public than any seventeenth-century writer.

Later Modern culture, north-European and peripheral: since 1750.—Around 1750 begins the period of modern science, of industrial development, of romanticism, and of unsettlement and revolution. This third positive phase of European culture history commenced almost simultaneously in Italy,

Switzerland, Sweden, France, England, and Germany, but by 1900 had become Pan-European; or, perhaps better, Pan-Occidental, in view of American participation. The route followed by the several countries was quite diverse, yet brought them to strangely similar results in the main; and the total European picture is consistent rather than blurred.

On the whole, it is the North European countries that dominate in new and high contributions during this phase: France, England, Germany, with Scandinavia, Russia, and America beginning to participate. Spain remains inactive, and the role of Italy is ambiguous and far from outstanding: she was wanting to be modern, but still rooted in the Renaissance.

France got going early with her science, but her music, literature, drama, painting, sculpture are definitely nineteenth-century. What quality of the "romantic" there is in them had been developed previously in England or Germany. Between the beginnings of the intellectual and the aesthetic growths of modern France, roughly, fall the Revolutionary-Napoleonic achievements, which exerted a profound influence on all Europe. It is true that large-scale democratic institutions had been evolved in England and carried farther in North America, but these had had almost no direct influence among the Continental nations.

The English growth was unusually smooth. An overseas world empire was built up with little effort and little conscious plan. In industrial development, the English preceded the Continent. Their modern phase of science got under way as early as the French and has lasted about as well as the German. About the same time, they finally developed a school of painting. Their literature reculminated in the early nineteenth century.

On the whole, primacy of rank though not of visible influence in this period must probably be awarded to the Germans. In philosophy, in music, and again in literature they reached greater heights of attainment than any other modern Occidental people. Their science was later in getting started than British, French, Swiss, or Italian science, but has almost certainly outstripped them, and for say two generations has come near to being dominant. The same may be said for German scholarship in philology and history. There has also been since about 1750 a continuous growth of German nationalism; but long without corresponding development of institutional patterns. Nor have German manners become urbane in the eyes of the rest of Europe, which has therefore tended to resist German influence even when it acknowledged German superiority, to a greater degree than it resisted Italian influence in the Renaissance. France has continued to be recognized as more civilized than Germany even in fields in which she was obviously second in performance.

There is nothing anomalous in this German disparity of political and intellectual-aesthetic success. It held also for Renaissance Italy. And twelfth- and thirteenth-century France, though relatively unified, was very far from being nationalistically dominant in western Europe; certainly much less so than culturally.

Switzerland seems to have profited by being both French and German in speech, and began early its modern growth—in fact, helped fertilize those of both its greater neighbors. Sweden too was early.

The remaining nationalities in Occidental civilization have all played a similar part. They entered as national contributors in an international scene, some of them around 1800, others not till 1830 or 1860. In fact, with the re-creation of nationalities as a result of the World War, the process was intensified. On the one hand, there were vast peoples like the Russians and North Americans who on account of their geography and a separate history had for some time been participating in the bases of Occidental civilization, but could hardly mature any of its fruits till 1800 or after. On the other hand, there was a long series of medium-sized and small nationalities, who either, like Spain and the two Netherlands, had had a great cultural past but had sunk from it; or, like Poland and in a measure Bohemia and Hungary, had enjoyed a florescence that was transient or partial or fictitious; or, like the South Slavs,

Finns, Irish, Norwegians, and Latin Americans, had long been submerged as inferiors; or finally, like Denmark, had remained free but impotent. All these, since 1800, have enjoyed some sort of cultural surge, coming from outside and tending toward assimilation to an international standard, but at the same time animated by a fervid national zeal. The Olympic Games and League of Nations express formally and by articles something of this attitude that had begun to find aesthetic-intellectual expression a century before. In some of these instances, mainly of the larger nationalities, traditions or patterns of a certain originality of national twist or flavor were developed, and successful schools can be spoken of: Russian music and literature, for instance, or the Spanish novel, possibly also recent Mexican painting. More often, however, the stream of cultural influence was socially limited, the total population of the country small, the number of individuals genuinely affected remained few, and those able to attain the productivity of genius were but a handful. Consequently, one country, on the scattering of probability, managed to produce perhaps an eminent scientist and an eminent painter, another a distinguished novelist, a third a composer and a political leader of note. It is when the marginal countries are added together that a nearly normal configuration is seen to emerge for their totality in the recent period.

Another factor in this nationalistic internationalization is that by about 1850 most of the aesthetic themes of the modern phase of Western civilization were tending to be exhausted. There was accordingly a desire for new content and forms. Whatever a new or newly raised nationality could offer that had a novel color or aspect was thus eagerly "discovered" and temporarily accepted, though genuine absorptions have tended to be rather slight.

The following semitabulation attempts to review compactly the principal stages of Occidental civilization as a whole. Of course all dates are to be construed as averages expressed in round numbers.

Periodic Summary of the Course of Occidental Civilization

500–800. Gradual consolidation of the Germanic kingdoms and tribes into one international Christian empire under Frankish rule. Low point of cultural recession, due to more rapid loss of Mediterranean patterns than building up of new Occidental ones, reached about 600–700: "Dark Age."

800–1050. Cultural energy directed chiefly to establishment of politico-socio-religious order on the basis of incipiently nationalistic Christian kingdoms, first in France and Germany, then in Scandinavia, Poland, Hungary, Russia. Intellectual and aesthetic productivity quantitatively increased and ordered during the "Carolingian Renaissance" and subsequent kingdom florescences, but nominal in quality and rudimentary in formation of patterns.

1050–1325. High Mediaeval florescence, first phase of constructive Occidental civilization, with well organized and highly distinctive and interintegrated patterns of society, religion, philosophy, architecture, sculpture, and literature, culminating around 1250; under French leadership, but internationally European. From the beginning of this phase, Occidental civilization established competitive superiority over Islamic and Byzantine cultures.

1325–1575. Late Middle Ages and "Renaissance." Quantitative growth of Occidental civilization with dissolution of the High Mediaeval patterns. Loosening of politico-religious organization in western Europe; achievement of new cultural patterns, from about 1400 on, in middle Europe, from the Netherlands through Germany, including the West Slavs, to North Italy, most intensively in the latter, where the Renaissance was in full maturation 1500–1575, with influencing of the rest of Europe. Most of the fine arts were involved, and the foundations of science; but technological developments were earlier and much greater than scientific ones.

1575–1700. Florescence in western Europe, through nearly concurrent but separate Iberian, French, Dutch, and English national patterns containing reworked Renaissance forms. Philosophy and drama developed in addition to previous activities; first phase of Occidental science in culmination. "Baroque."

1700–1750 (1775). Lull in creation of new patterns, with social and geographical diffusion of knowledge and taste. "Enlightenment" and "Rococo."

Since 1750. Third phase of formation of Occidental culture patterns, with "romantic," democratic, and industrial coloring, the aesthetic impulses attempting to tie up with Mediaeval achieve-

ments in an effort to break the Renaissance-Baroque forms, and
science entering a new, experimental phase, with enormous technological extensions. Primarily north European, Italy contributing
secondarily and Spain scarcely at all; with gradually increasing
participation of Scandinavian, Slavic, and American peoples; in
other words, extension toward expanding peripheries.

NOTE. It is also justifiable, and more in accord with the current
usage of history, to split the 1325–1575 period into Late Middle
Ages and Renaissance at about 1450 or 1500, and then to unite the
Renaissance with the "Baroque" of 1575–1700. This arrangement
is less consistent with unity of geography and time, since in Italy,
and in a measure in the Netherlands, the Renaissance was definitely
launched by 1400, whereas in German-Slavic central Europe the
Late Middle Ages continued a century longer—in fact in some
respects until 1750. The advantage of the arrangement is that it
leaves Late Mediaevalism as a stage of dissolution of High Mediaevalism, and unites into another phase the creative productions of
the Renaissance and Baroque, 1450/1500–1700.

Chapter XI

REVIEW AND CONCLUSIONS

Chapter XI

REVIEW
AND CONCLUSIONS

§112. Universals in History

IN REVIEWING the ground covered, I wish to say at the outset that I see no evidence of any true law in the phenomena dealt with; nothing cyclical, regularly repetitive, or necessary. There is nothing to show either that every culture must develop patterns within which a florescence of quality is possible, or that, having once so flowered, it must wither without chance of revival. After all, cultures merge into one another, and so cannot have the individual entity of higher organisms. Nor is there reason to believe that historians are wrong in having consistently refused to believe, or at least in doubting, the presence of strict universals in the record of human and social events. Experience attests that universals are to be found in abstracted properties or processes, not in specific phenomena. And in the light of such physical and biological constants or regular properties as have yet been discovered, the facts of history and culture appear not even phenomena so much as epiphenomena.

What I have done is to present a mass of data in a manner that is essentially descriptive; and descriptive—or, if one will, narrational—in a manner not fundamentally diverse from that of historians and most anthropologists; though with different emphasis in at least two respects. One of these respects is that persons have throughout been viewed as indices, not as agents or even as if they were agents. The result is that culture configurations tend to stand out as stripped skeletons rather than softened, mixed, and blurred. Here the training of the ethnologist concerned with primitive cultures no doubt shows.

The second way in which this work differs from straitly historical ones is that in the endeavor to be broadly comparative it has had to be in some degree "sociological" in its approach. That is, it has violated historical context. I trust, however, that the ruptures of context have been no greater than need be; in other words, that they were not made lightheartedly and blindly; and that the pieces have been in some measure associated in the chapter immediately preceding this one, in which the national cultures dealt with have been reëxamined as wholes. After all, if comparative study is to be undertaken seriously at all, it must be through analysis. Studies of particular periods and areas, or of special activities within them, or of their specific interconnections, or of the forms taken by historyless cultures, must of course always underlie all historic or anthropological work. But, just as obviously, no multiplication of such efforts will *per se* lead to more than implicit comparative understanding. If there are to be explicit comparative findings, comparison must be undertaken as such; and if the chief conclusion proves to be the difficulty of comparing precisely and reliably, that will be at least a wholesome if disappointing result. I confess to some lowering of expectations in the course of my work.

§113. Cultural Patterns and Growths

What the material arranged in the foregoing pages does seem to show that is positive, is the strength and significance of cultural patterns or plans,—as I must continue to call them for lack of a better term. That culture patterns have a conceptual validity in some way reflecting phenomenal reality, appears to be shown by the fact that those to which we assign products of high value appear definitely limited, even concentrated, in time and space, with a usually continuous rise and fall of value. In fact, one conceivable way of defining higher values would be as those qualities of human productions which normally appear in historic configurations thus limited and shaped. Such a definition has this virtue: it deals with something which is accepted as necessarily transcending the individual, without reference either to individual personality or to any a-prioristic standard or measure. At the same time, personality is not denied: it remains unimpaired, but as a vehicle or instrument instead of as an agent.

What it is that binds high-value culture patterns to such transience—lower-grade ones can apparently go on with much less change and much longer—is far from clear. It may be something in the constitution of the human mind. But direct psychological explanations have never got anyone very far in reducing the phenomena of history to order, and I shall not fall back on them. This much is clear: the patterns which we adjudge as of higher quality are selective from among a number of potentialities. They cannot remain undifferentiated and attain quality. As they begin to select, early in their formation, they commit themselves to certain specializations, and exclude others. If this arouses conflict with other parts of the culture in which the pattern is forming, the selection and exclusion may be abandoned, the pattern as something well differentiated be renounced, and nothing of much cultural value eventuate. If, however, this does not happen, but the other patterns of the culture reinforce the growing one, or at least do not conflict with it, the pattern in question tends to develop cumulatively, in the direction in which it first differentiated, by a sort of momentum. Finally, either a conflict with the rest of its culture arises and puts an end to the pattern, or it explores and traverses the new opportunities lying in its selective path, until less and less of these remain, and at last none. The pattern can be said to have fulfilled itself when its opportunities or possibilities have been exhausted. Or more exactly, the value culmination comes at the moment when the full range of possibilities within the pattern is sensed; the decline, when there remain only minor areas of terrain to be occupied. After this, development may quietly subside, the results achieved being retained as institutions, but with repetitive instead of growth activity; and quality atrophies. Or again, energy still being vigorous in the field of culture in question, the limitations imposed on itself by the growing or culminating pattern are felt as restraints, and there is an effort to disrupt them. Such efforts may end in incoherent conflicts which sooner or later level out in undifferentiation.

An example of strain tending toward pattern rupture is late Greek sculpture. After the pattern had been achieved and its main possibilities exhausted in the Great phase, there came a period of representations of vehement emotion or of complete calm, of insipid idealism, standardized symbolism, and realism, all approximately contemporary. There were no such contradictory currents in the time of Phidias or even of Praxiteles. Similarly, Mediaeval philosophy, within fifty years after Aquinas, was diverging into the negativistic skepticism of Occam and into mysticism. Gothic architecture, about the same time, entered a more extreme phase, as compared with its thirteenth-century culmination; and still later tended to become flamboyant. Modern philosophy reached its zenith with Kant: Hegel and his contemporaries mopped up or elaborated within the confines he had staked out; Schopenhauer manifested prejudices and dogmatism; the next generation or two developed Comte, Marx, Nietzsche. All European fine arts since about 1880, and more strongly since 1900, have displayed increasing symptoms of what may be called pattern dissolution: jagged rhythms and dissonance in music, free verse in poetry, plotless novels, cubism, abstractionism, and surrealism in sculpture and painting.

These remarks on contemporary conditions are not introduced as judgments according to an absolute standard of aesthetics, but as more or less objective descriptions of phenomena. When concord governs music, harmony may be simple or subtle, but there are rules. Dissonances, however, can be innumerable, and when they are freely permitted there can no longer be a harmonic pattern, or it survives only as a background against which dissonant effects are exploded. Free verse is avowedly a revolutionary disintegration of meter and rhyme. Once we paint hands on trees and cogwheels in men, we can just as well put spectacles on mountains or make any other combination. True, a Perugino saint on a cloud is just as contrary to nature; but he represents a traditional belief, in other words a genuine and living pattern elsewhere in the culture, and not an arbitrary or personal collocation. The difference is between responsibility and irresponsibility toward some form.

Nor ought the contemporary arts to be censured. Harmony or rhyme or symmetry can be used until they have become mechanical and dull. The choice then is between going on with them perfunctorily, or revolting against them. Of the two, revolt is not necessarily the worse course. Certainly in the last half-dozen decades far more energy and imagination have been developed by the pattern wreckers than by the pattern preservers still trying to travel in the channels of a century ago. And therefore extravagances like the horizon line carried in front of a tree, a piano struck with full forearm length, lines of verse beginning with small letters or full of stammers, can be accepted as neither wicked nor insane. In part they represent the zeal of the revolutionist who needs first to wreck everything, whether significant or not, before he can reconstruct; in part, responses to a condition in which, accepted patterns having gone stale, any upsetting novelty is rewarded for being startling, and the shrewd exploit the situation. The fundamental fact is that while twentieth-century Occidentals can still write in the manner of Goethe and compose in the manner of Beethoven, they evidently cannot do so with the same quality, else presumably some of them would be doing it. That is, the pattern possibilities of the Goethe and Beethoven configurations are obviously exhausted. Such being the case, does it matter much whether the successors revolt and wreck or peacefully atrophy into senility? Revolution may at least be followed by new growth; and whether this is to be greater or less, no one can foretell.

Examples of the contrary process, of patterns dying away into feebler and feebler repetitions, are also numerous. For instance, Greek and Latin and Sanskrit literatures; post-T'ang and post-Kamakura sculpture in China and Japan; Greek and Arabic science.

§114. Pulses and Lulls in Growth

Sometimes a lull occurs in a pattern growth, after which development is resumed, always with some reshaping of the pattern. Of these I have spoken as pulses in a growth. The second pulse may be the greater; the earlier then becomes construed as prodromal or introductory. Or it may be inferior: I have then characterized it as an aftermath or revival. There may be a lull or pause both before and after the culminating period. Latin literature shows this type of configuration. There is first an initiatory pulse, still under direct Greek influence but with deployment of notable dramatic skill. The time is around 200 B.C., say from 240 to 120. A low-level interval follows for fifty years. Then, 70 B.C. to 10 A.D., comes the great pulse, with Vergil marking the apogee, during the years of dissolution of the Republic and first half of Augustus. The latter end of his rule and some decades after, 10 to 50 A.D., are again relatively barren—a fact glossed over in most accounts as if it were shameful, or stressed lightly as if nonsignificant. Then from about Nero to Trajan, say 50 to 120, literature of quality is once more produced. We have here the conventional "Early," "Golden," and "Silver" ages of development, which have obtained some usage as a formula of descriptive nomenclature; though they have also been applied where there were no distinct pulses separated by lulls, and with other varying connotations. There is no doubt that Latin literature was a single growth. But, equally clearly, it grew in three main pulses, somewhat different in content and form, interests and techniques, and definitely separated by time gaps during which the quality level of products was lower.

Other lulls occur in European science after Newton, say roughly the first half of the eighteenth century; in Attic drama between Aristophanes and the New Comedy; apparently between Homeric and post-Homeric poetry; and in Indian philosophy around the sixth century after Christ. Italian music too shows several sags suggestive of the same phenomenon.

Grading by degrees into such lulls are longer or more incisive intervals, which, however, are still internal to a single culture growth. These longer intervals, and the pulses or subgrowths separated by them, are of several kinds. The simplest type is that presented by ancient Egypt, which started to develop its basic patterns in relative isolation, or with rather slow infiltrations from outside, but had its growth checked, apparently by internal factors, three times.[1] After each pause, growth was resumed. New elements were added, or there were alterations; but basically, according to all accounts, the direction remained the same: the old patterns were either revived or slightly extended with success. This Egyptian case, to be sure, is unique in the stark rigidity of its configuration, if the facts are as outlined; but it will serve to illustrate an extreme type of interrupted growth.

Incidentally, within a century of the probable zenith of the entire Egyptian configuration around 1400, there occurred typical symptoms of revolt and attempted rupture of the successfully established patterns. These "Ikhnaton reforms," which have been more fully discussed in §101, failed; which means that the culture preferred being locked up repetitively in its patterns to breaking them down and starting afresh. It seems likely by analogy that, in the contrary event, a successful reformation would not have stopped where Ikhnaton's coterie intended, but would have gone on to fairly thorough dissolution; whether with ultimate reconstruction of an allied but new set of national patterns, or not, is more speculative.

In Mesopotamia there were not only more exposures to the outside world, but several peoples, with the result that the configurations are not so simply recurrent. They are in fact irregular and intricate enough for the historic data—at least as controlled by a nonspecialist like myself—to be insufficient for a clear recognition of the course of the total configuration or even of its several national parts.

For Europe, on the other hand, the record is so much fuller

---

[1] Four times, if the activities culminating in the establishment of the First Dynasty be counted a florescence.

that, although the total Occidental configuration is compos-
itely intricate, most of the several nationalities show clear
enough profiles, including several with interruptions. France
is a case in point. She was undoubtedly most instrumental of
all European countries in shaping the characteristic High Mediaeval patterns. In the twelfth century she was definitely in
the lead in this work, and in the thirteenth she enjoyed a clear
culmination in which most of western Europe shared to a
greater or less degree. Then came recession, with both dissolution and some atrophy. About 1500, French cultural energy
was mounting again, but no distinctive patterns had yet been
worked out. This however had been done, during the preceding two centuries, in central Europe, especially in Italy. The
result was that during the sixteenth century nascent French
patterns tended to be swamped by more developed Italian
Renaissance ones, and it was not until the seventeenth that
characteristically French patterns were evolved in philosophy,
science, literature, painting, warfare, politics, and manners.
That these were patterns of considerable intrinsic value is
shown by the fact that they influenced not only backward countries like Germany, but Spain, Holland, and England, which
had undergone florescences with Renaissance absorptions
about synchronously with the French one. Unquestionably,
the seventeenth-century French culmination was truly nationalistic. But it obviously was not a simple redevelopment of
where France had left off in 1325. Besides the specific Renaissance, there were all sorts of other influences that had been
produced somewhere in Europe in the interval: Protestantism,
for instance, which France had to digest as it did the Renaissance; or, in science, what the Germans, Poles, Netherlanders,
Italians, and British had successively developed, without which
the Descartes group could hardly have made its contribution.

Then, after an eighteenth-century lull in which France
maintained moral ascendancy in Europe but was dissipating
or popularizing or repeating culturally, came her third florescence. In this, the international strands are intricately woven.
As for new political patterns, France definitely initiated them

for the Continent, but followed Anglo-Saxon precedents. In science, she got going earlier than some of her neighbors, but simultaneously with several others. In literature and music, her characteristic nineteenth-century patterns did not become established until about 1820–1830, well after those of Germany and, in part, England. In painting and sculpture, she mainly led the way for Europe. The result is that by 1875 France maintained many direct continuities of flavor and mannerism with 1675, but was probably more internationally European than French in her culture patterns, with, however, a considerable French ingredient in the international element. Her situation may be compared with that of Athens in the Hellenistic world around say 275.

It will be clear that the three French pulses developed and expressed quite distinct patterns, and that the pauses between them, besides differing from each other, were filled to a considerable extent by manifest or latent influences from elsewhere in Europe. The total picture is therefore at the opposite end of the scale from that of ancient Egypt; mainly because France is only part of the larger totality of Occidental culture.

This larger Occidental entity, viewed as a whole, has not only, of course, greater continuity than any of its parts, but has had a high degree of developmental continuity for at least nine hundred years past. Something of a slowing of productivity can be discerned toward 1400, and again after 1700; but occasional activities continue into or begin within these intervals, so that there are only near-lulls, never complete pauses in quality production.[2]

§115. Types of Growth Configurations

It is evident from these instances that the pauses, lulls, regressions, or barren intervals are only the minor part of a set of problems the center of which lies in the question of the in-

---

[2] If the first slowing down is put in the decades before 1400, Petrarch and Boccaccio, and Chaucer in England, persist into it; if after 1400, it contains commencement of specific Renaissance painting and sculpture. Similarly with Bach in 1725.

trinsic relation to each other of the productive periods of a
nation or civilization; and the further question arises, how far
some of these productive periods might not be reckoned as
separate cultural growths rather than as pulses or phases of
one growth. It is plain that we are dealing with an intergrading
series of phenomena, without either measure or touchstone,
and can only hope to arrange them in order from the more
clear-cut to the more difficult or dubious instances.

Simple cases are those like unilingual, uninational, relatively
isolated Egypt.

Simple also are the prelude growths, like the Carolingian
renaissance if there was one; the tiny Othonian florescence;
the Chaucerian constellation. These are premature stirrings
the patterns of which may be real but which remain abortive,
presumably because the culture as a whole is insufficiently
developed.

Equally intelligible are the aftermaths and attempted revivals. For instance, the Twenty-sixth Dynasty "renaissance"
in Egypt; probably the whole Neo-Babylonian Empire; Latin
and Greek pagan poetry of the fifth century after Christ; the
tenth-century Byzantine renaissance; the Ming revival.

Sometimes there is both prologue and epilogue. Spain, for
instance, had essentially one great growth, like Italy, though
the Spanish one was somewhat briefer and came a little later.
She had, however, also a minor, not very sharply configured,
thirteenth-century growth, much less than that of France; and
something similar and partial in the nineteenth century.

Less obvious, but still not seriously doubtful so far as pattern
is concerned, are instances in which an aftermath has a semblance of equality or superiority because a mainly quantitative accumulation of cultural content has occurred in the
interval. The Ptolemaic-Galenic science of the early second
post-Christian century is typical. It came two hundred and
fifty years after Greek science had stopped progressing. The
later pulse contained few ideas and almost no ways of thinking
which it had not taken over from the previous one. It did have
at its command two and a half centuries of added observations,

of repetitive industry, and of accumulated knowledge, which enabled it to make a more comprehensive and final summary, which in turn passed usefully and authoritatively down to later times and other civilizations.

Of similar type I would reckon the semiflorescences of the prosperous century or more of the Manchu dynasty in China, after the absorptions from Jesuits and other Europeans. Also, much of the arts of Europe in the later nineteenth century, when Poland could build on French productivity and Finland on German. On the whole, I would incline to set down Sung philosophy as related in type. So far as I can judge, it is mainly a true Neo-Confucianism—a superficial reworking of the old patterns, or a putting of them into more modern dress. Neo-Platonism would be suspect of the same quality, except that it selects the minor mystic ingredient of Hellenic philosophy for reworking into a definitely religious philosophy. But its urge represents an accretion that had come into late Greek civilization from non-Greek sources; and to this extent Neo-Platonism also belongs to the category. On the whole, this class of growths approaches the epilogue or revival type, with a factitious appearance of being new—owing, however, to content assimilation rather than pattern development.

A somewhat special type of configuration has a prodromal growth which, however, is determinative, to an appreciable degree, of the larger growth that follows. Later Chou China, and post-Vedic protohistoric North India of the days of Kapila and Buddha, have been construed in the preceding pages as of this class. The Epic growths of Greece and India bear a similar relation to their later literatures. What we have in the first two of these instances is an early development of a philosophy, or philosophy-religion, sufficient to constitute a basic idea-system for a great culture, before other cultural activities had been developed sufficiently to attain to any considerable quality. Later, these other activities grew, owing to internal factors or to stimulation and impact from outside, and the entire culture matured, but with its thought patterns already provided. Thus Chinese painting and sculpture seem pretty clearly due to Buddhistic influences; also some at least of the science; and the "new style" T'ang poetry owes its most distinctive trait, the tonal pattern, to a recognition which I have conjectured to be due to Indian language study. How far Hindu science, sculpture, and painting were induced by Mediterranean models is an obscure problem; but for the first two, at least, some Greek absorptions are indubitable, and there may have been much basic stimulus-diffusion, quickly disguised by native reworking.

The Hindu and Greek literary growths are parallel to the foregoing two, to some extent. The two epics of both peoples produced at least one definite and adequate, though limited, poetic form, and a mass of themes. The later literatures added further forms and drew very heavily on the Epic themes, however much they reworked or elaborated them. In a sense, therefore, the Epics also provided an idea-system which could be adhered to throughout the more complex growths which followed. Incidentally, foreign influence may have entered into one of these later growths. It has been debated, though inconclusively, whether the Sanskrit drama is derived from the Greek. The probability seems fair that this is another instance of stimulus importation, with the specific resemblances, which alone can prove historic derivation, either remaining lacking or having been quickly lost.

In some measure Arabic civilization might be considered as also partaking of this type of an early basic idea-system culminating only when filled out considerably later. Its organization begins with the thought-system formulated by Mohammed. Before this event, Arab culture contained nothing whatever of notable quality except some lyric poetry. With Islam established, absorptions of culture material began on a large scale, and philosophy, science, literature, and architecture were developed. These, however, were largely the product of Persians, Syrians, Egyptians, and the like, who were held together by a common adopted speech and religion plus a common tradition which they themselves had in large part evolved on the basis of this speech and religion; also, they operated chiefly on material inherited from a previous civilization. The Arabs themselves faded from the productive cultural scene rather quickly. This submersion of the originators or stimulators is not, except for its accentuation, a unique event: Greek and Roman civilization also became international; and in some degree the phenomenon occurred elsewhere, and will be discussed below. What is distinctive is the degree to which the Mohammedan religious system furnished almost the whole occasion for the far fuller and richer civilization which later evolved around it. In this respect, namely, that a set of formulations about human belief and conduct preceded the development of the larger culture, and was retained through it, Arabic civilization resembles Indian and Chinese.

§116. The Question of Growth Curves

The question arises, how far culture-growth florescences tend to follow a symmetrical normal curve in their configurations. It is clear that they do not always take such a path. There certainly are some for which a diagrammed profile would be skew. But still it is conceivable that for most of them the rise and fall would be substantially symmetrical. Or again, one might imagine that when cultural energy was released into productive patterns, the release would tend to come with a rush, but would taper off more gradually. On the other hand, it is possible to think of a pattern as being achieved slowly by a long series of men; but, once realized in its fullness, and its prelimited possibilities exhausted, dissolution would begin. The problem is: which of these possible courses does occur most often in human experience, as we review the historic facts?

The difficulty in answering is primarily the difficulty of measuring. As for the peak of the profile, there usually is general agreement, which I have accepted as an approximation to measurement. As we get away from the peak, however, forward or backward, differentiation of quality tends to be made with less decisiveness. As between fourth and fifth rank, the world's opinion is likely to be expressed with hesitance.

Moreover, another factor enters. As quality diminishes—forward or backward in time from a culmination,—historical interest and inquiry tend to shift from quality of product to alteration of pattern, and even to introduction of new content as having bearing on form. For an investigation like the present one, there are thus fewer judgments available on the low ends of growths than on the peaks. An example or two will illustrate.

The drama as a literary form differentiates fairly distinctly and easily and there is general agreement that the Modern, Ancient Mediterranean, Indian, Chinese, and Japanese civilizations evolved dramas sufficiently similar to be comparable, and possessing definite aesthetic value. There is a large fringe, extending all the way from dances, processions, ceremonies, and mysteries, to mystery and morality plays. These we can rule out as being both avowedly religious in purpose or subject and crude in aesthetic execution. The Japanese *No* plays can be included, in spite of their religious themes, because they make use of consciously literary language.

Now in general the emergence of true, aesthetic, secular drama can be fairly well defined historically; also the point at which permanent quality, recognized as of value in other cultures, enters. Soon after culmination, however, the drama usually becomes fairly repetitive at a constant low level of quality; but it continues on this level. It has become a fairly fixed or institutionalized activity, well rooted in its culture and affording unquestionable satisfactions; an activity which does not aim at, nor can longer achieve, high values, though it may be practiced with genuine competence. Now where shall we assign the end, as must be done if we are to judge as to skewness or symmetry?

English drama supplies an example. The first literary gropings begin about 1560. Around 1580 a true popular drama, in verse, commenced. This rapidly developed quality, with Marlowe and then Shakespeare joining in. The culmination, Shakespearean and other, can be quite precisely set at 1601–1616. Then there was rapid decline, until the playhouses were for a time closed in 1642.

So far, we have fairly symmetrical development: twenty years for the rise if we exclude the prepattern false starts, or forty if we admit them; twenty-six for the fall. But the Civil War was an external cataclysm from the point of view of the drama. Is it justified to end the profile there? After 1660, the drama re-arose, with a mixture of rhymed heroic play, Elizabethan revivals and imitations, and Restoration prose comedy. The last underwent an indubitable culmination by 1700, but then died quickly. Whether this 1660–1700 growth should be considered a postponed terminal phase or epilogue of the greater Elizabethan growth has been discussed in the chapter on Drama; with a preponderantly affirmative answer. But if it is an epilogue, we have a definitely skew configuration: 20 or at most 40 years before the peak, 85 to 95 after.

Nor is this all, for English drama was not dead as an institution in 1700; only the higher qualities had gone out of it. In fact, there were flashes of resurrection: by Sheridan and Goldsmith around 1775, by Wilde and Shaw around 1900, in prose comedy. These can be disposed of as minor revivals in a pattern essentially exhausted long before; but even that makes something of the pattern live on for two centuries beyond the termination previously determined.

It is one thing to view the growth of English drama as a thing apart and to recognize a configuration which, with certain qualifications and special features, seems definite enough to be convincing to oneself and perhaps to others. It is another thing to take this configuration schematically and numerically and set it alongside others thus treated: the special traits which qualify and individuate the configuration get lost, and the mere numbers of years for rise, peak, and fall may be more misrepresentative than true.

Each case compared increases the difficulties. For instance, Spanish and French drama, the florescences of which are nearly contemporary with English, have also remained living activities; but their developmental periods are longer, hesitantly gradual, and groping, so that a beginning date would be harder to fix, and judgments perhaps farther apart.

Returning to the field of culture as a whole, we may say with assurance that clearly some patterns productive of high values have been developed with astonishing rapidity; and that there have been others in which such productivity fell off and ceased with equal rapidity, the withering apparently not having been enforced by any external factor. There are still others in which either the growth or the exhaustion was relatively slow and gradual. Just so, some culminations are brief, others sustained. All these traits presumably can combine, so that we have occurrences of long and short, peaklike and plateaulike, fore-skew, aft-skew, and symmetrical configurations.

It will be worth while to cite in review some examples of each type.

Peak early in configuration
   German philosophy
   Chinese sculpture
   Cham sculpture
   Mughal-Rajput painting (Persian-derived)
   Chinese painting?
   English drama
   Latin drama
   Japanese poetry (*tanka*)
   Greek literature (with Homer included in the configuration)
   Italian literature as a whole

Configuration approximately symmetrical
   Italian sculpture
   Italian painting
   Indian sculpture, probably
   Sanskrit literature
   German music

Peak late in configuration
   Greek philosophy
   Arabic philosophy
   Spanish Arabic philosophy
   Sung philosophy
   Mediaeval philosophy
   Greek science
   Earlier phase of English science
   Chinese algebra
   English music

Mesopotamian sculpture
Cambodian sculpture, probably
Japanese sculpture
Nineteenth-century French sculpture
Greek vase painting
Japanese painting
Renaissance Italian literature
Spanish drama

This is not a very impressive array. It represents a minority of the growths examined in the course of this book. The others I cannot conscientiously assign to one or another class. What this fact chiefly suggests is that even estimates in lieu of measurements are difficult to make with assurance. About a third of the listed cases of aft-skewness are in philosophy, where the culmination would normally consist of the system which substantially fulfilled the potentialities of the pattern, after which there would be little left to do. In the arts, the number of instances of early and late peak is about the same. Symmetrical configurations come out fewer than either. This suggests that there may be no single normal type. If there were, and this were symmetrical, its class should be the most numerous. If a one-way asymmetrical profile were normal, the opposite asymmetry would presumably be less frequent than approximate symmetry.

I can only conclude that either there is no normal form of time-quality curve in florescences, or that the difficulties of quality estimation at a distance from the peak render curve representation too uncertain for determination at present.

§117. Interrelation of Cultural Activities

Another question that arises is whether the several activities which have been examined possess any fixed relation to one another of time or order of appearance, or any tendency in that direction. Associated with this, or underlying it, really, is another question: namely, whether all activities regularly appear in each civilization, so that one can infer a "must."

To this last query, the answer can only be a categorical No. At any rate, the denial holds for productions of significant intrinsic value; as for fumbling efforts, one might argue at length how they were to be construed. The obvious example of Islam as lacking in representative art suffices to settle the matter negatively, whether one accept as cause a puritanical whim of the person Mohammed or look for broader and more impersonal factors.

It may be worth while to list some conspicuous absences of successful development of activities in the greater civilizations.

ABSENCES

Philosophy: Egypt, Mesopotamia, Rome, Japan; also the Renaissance period in Europe.

Science: Rome and mediaeval Europe; also, except for algebra, Japan and largely China.

Sculpture: Arabic civilization.

Painting: probably Mesopotamia; Rome; Arabic Islam.

Architecture, other than in wood: Japan.

Drama: Arabic civilization; also Egypt and Mesopotamia.

Political integration during period of culture florescence: Greece; Germany and Italy.

To be sure, there is the fact that the Persians, always somewhat recalcitrant, and heretical in their Mohammedanism, and the Mohammedan Indians, did finally develop a school of painting. This flourished well after Islamic civilization as a whole had declined, and after Persian culture had pretty well detached itself from Arabic in speech vehicle and had developed an independent literature. This means that by the sixteenth century we are dealing with a substantially separate daughter culture in Persia. Not every culture carried by peoples professing Islam is necessarily to be construed as part of the one integral growth.

If activities which are usually developed may be wholly or almost altogether lacking from some cultures, there can hardly be any necessary interdependence between the activities. This in turn renders it less likely that there can be any very constant relation of order of appearance among activities, or at any rate a significant order. However, as sculpture has been asserted by Petrie to be regularly early in its culture appearances, at any rate preceding painting, and since there is a widely prevalent feeling of a nexus between philosophy and science, it will be worth while to review the facts on both points.

SCULPTURE AND PAINTING

The following are the instances which I am able to assemble of a sufficiently defined occurrence relation of florescences in sculpture and painting.

Egypt. Sculpture fully developed in Dynasties IV and V, painting peak perhaps in Dynasty XVIII; but preservation conditions may be involved.

Mesopotamia. Sculpture at peak very late, in Assyrian Empire. Painting unknown, perhaps absent.

India. Sculpture known since 275 B.C., culmination probably 400–500 A.D. Painting at peak about 450–750.

China. Sculpture at peak 600–750, then decline; painting, culmination about 750, but again around 1100 and 1200.

Japan. Sculpture, peaks in 8th and 13th centuries; inferior thereafter. Painting, culmination in 15th to 16th centuries.

Greece. Best sculpture between times of Pericles and Alexander, painting not at its zenith till the latter. Vase painting, on the contrary, passed its zenith and died earlier than sculpture.

Mediaeval Europe. Sculpture; no painting except book miniatures, stained glass, crude murals, etc.

Italy. Sculpture and painting synchronous, as shown by the participation of Michelangelo in both culminations. With rude beginnings counted in, sculpture can be traced back farther, to about 1100 as against 1250; but this may be a matter of preservations. The first great painter, Giotto, precedes the first great sculptor, Ghiberti, by a century. At the end, Canova is sixty years later than Tiepolo and Canaletto.

Spain. Martínez Montañés was born about 1564, Cano in 1601, Mena in 1628; all the greater painters between 1547 and 1599, except Murillo, 1618.

Earlier Netherlands. Sluter, died 1406; the Van Eycks, 1426 and 1440. Painting kept a high level longer.

Later Netherlands. The Rubens and Rembrandt culminations have no counterpart in sculpture.

England. There is no sculpture to compare with the Reynolds-to-Turner growth.

France. Modern painting culminates with men born about 1790 to 1830; sculpture, probably with Rodin, born 1840.

In these thirteen instances—several others are unclear or doubtful—sculpture develops earlier than painting five times, simultaneously twice, later twice, and four times one or the other is lacking. This is not a decisive showing for any uniformity or constant relation. Nor is the situation better when we consider the duration instead of the absolute time incidence of the two arts. In the nine comparable instances, painting lasts longer three times; as long, once; less long, once; and the relation is not construable with certainty four times.

Also, the three instances of definitely greater duration of good painting—the Netherlands, China, Japan—possess special features. The Netherlands never produced any great sculpture. Their painting was of high order in the fifteenth century, went on through the sixteenth, and rose to a new culmination in the seventeenth. The two activities are therefore not fully comparable. In China and Japan, a verbally directed type of civilization achieved very little in representative art until Buddhism introduced both painting and sculpture. Through calligraphy, painting acquired a tie-up with upper-class verbal culture; while sculpture remained in the status of artisanship. When Buddhism in China settled down to being the property essentially of the lower orders of society, sculpture tended to suffer the same fate, whereas painting continued to be practiced by Mandarins. The case is not quite the same in Japan, because Buddhism acquired a more national status. But sculpture did remain associated with Buddhism, and the best it could finally attain, in the thirteenth century, was a secular treatment of certain aspects of religion; after which it deteriorated. Painting, however, about the same time, had entered the profane field, and achieved its fullest development thereafter, in the fifteenth and sixteenth centuries. It is obviously nothing in the nature of the two arts that caused their different histories in the Far East; it was the circumstances of their introduction and the particular condition of Chinese-Japanese civilization when they were introduced.

This however must be admitted, and it is the probable basis of Petrie's intuitive judgment: no nation has ever acquired sculpture late in its growth. Many have developed it early. Successful painting, on the contrary, is often lacking in early stages, as in Europe when we consider Occidental civilization as a whole: there is no adequate counterpart in two-dimensional art to Mediaeval sculpture. Also, painting can arise late: as in England not until 1750.

The basis of this difference lies in the arts themselves. Sculpture represents objects in nature simply and directly. It has to acquire manual and sometimes technological skill, but otherwise its task is only to see, choose, and control the forms it is reproducing. The subtlest and completest sculpture cannot do more. Painting, on the other hand, which has to represent three-dimensional nature in two dimensions, begins by selecting objects and aspects which lend themselves readily to this treatment, such as profiles; but can proceed, and sometimes has proceeded, to handle other and more resistant aspects, or, ideally, all aspects of the visible world. The result is a whole series of new problems to be successively mastered: color, modeling, foreshortening, perspective, cast shadows, light values, luminosity, atmosphere. To attack these problems seriatim takes time; to handle most of them simultaneously with adequacy is a complex task, which usually means that each has had to be solved in a separate stage of tradition. Great sculptures in a rich and sophisticated and in a simple civilization will therefore differ in theme, emotion, and the forms selected, far more than in their physically definable objectives and skills. Great styles of painting will differ in both.

All this does not mean that high-quality painting must develop later or more slowly or last longer than high-quality sculpture, for there is no need for either to develop at all. It does mean that sculpture, being a relatively simple art, may grow up quickly, and may develop effectively in a relatively primitive culture; whereas, with its more numerous and diverse potentialities, painting can develop longer and still keep growing. One can understand primitive Chams and Khmers producing vigorous sculpture after two or three centuries of Hindu tutelage; it is difficult to imagine them producing Gainsboroughs and Turners. One can perhaps go even a step farther and see that a mature culture like that of eighteenth-century England, which happened to be lacking in any creative native tradition of representative art, would be more likely to adopt a sophisticated Claude and Watteau manner of painting, and build it farther with fair success, than to adopt a simple, direct, and drastic manner of sculpture. On the contrary, a sophisticated and mature style of sculpture is already too nearly exhausted to be developed profitably by newcomers. The nearest partial exception in history is the Roman success with realistic portrait sculpture—the Greeks, in their search for varied types, having left the field of completely individuated representation relatively uncultivated. Possibly it is significant that the English latecomer painters also specialized most successfully in portraiture.

In short, such difference as exists in the two arts lies in their respective relations to the physical world. This makes possible a quick development of one, a prolonged growth of the other; it enforces neither. What determines which art, if either, is taken up by a given civilization; when; and whether with qualitative success, depends on culture-historical factors which are of the most varied and inconstant character. Thus, of two religions, Buddhism essentially introduced and enormously fostered both arts in Eastern Asia, Islam long helped to inhibit them in Western Asia.

PHILOSOPHY AND SCIENCE

The relation of philosophy and science also is worth examining. Both, as intellectual activities, are of course abstracting: philosophy dealing primarily with problems of human existence and the psyche, science with the world outside man—in terms of a somewhat crude and overlapping dichotomy. Both also are concerned with relations, and build up systems of relations. In fact, until there is something of a system, we ordinarily have only prolegomena to or materials for philosophy and science, rather than activities fully deserving those names. That there should be a relation between the two activities is ⁻perhaps due to the fact that it is difficult to conceive of human existence and its problems quite separately from the world that men live in. At any rate, there are familiar historic associations: Thales as the traditional first name in Greek philosophy and science; Aristotle, two hundred and fifty years later, preëminent in both; Descartes as the originator of modern European philosophy as well as of analytical geometry; and innumerable thinkers in the Arabic-speaking civilization.

Again, however, there are dissociations: Greek and modern science going on productively after the exhaustion of the philosophies which for a time ran concurrently with them; the Middle Ages with a highly refined philosophy but without any productive science; China beginning its civilization with diversified philosophizing but scarcely any science.

There are also instances which can be ambiguously construed. For India, the record is obscure: her science may largely be import disguised by native reworking, or it may be an original creation. In Occidental civilization, if we consider the period since the Renaissance, there is a continuous growth of science from about 1450 on, while philosophy is encapsulated within it in the much narrower limits of 1630 to, say, 1880. But if we take Occidental civilization as a whole, philosophy begins three to four centuries the earlier, lapses while science is starting, then flashes up again transiently while science continues.

The data on time concurrence, already summarized in a tabulation (pp. 208–209), will now be reviewed with reference to the intrinsic historical relations.

Egypt and Mesopotamia. There were some scientific achievements, but hardly organized into a system except, toward the end, in astronomy. Philosophy scarcely if at all emerged from religion, magical and mythologic.

Greece. Science and philosophy began as one, slowly differentiated, but maintained connection as late as Aristotle. Science remained productive a century and a half longer. It also experienced an organizing or summating phase two hundred and fifty years after creative thinking ended. To this there was no philosophic counterpart. Still later, there was a contemporary aftermath in both activities: Neo-Platonism and Diophantine algebra.

India. Traditionally, the foundations were laid in both philosophy and science around the sixth pre-Christian century. The philosophy is certainly native in origin; the science may or may not be; except in philology, where the Indians were originators and surprisingly early ones. The final achievements seem to have taken place in philosophy in an abnormally long stretch occupying most of the first thousand post-Christian years, and in science in a briefer span roughly coincident with a sag or pause in the middle of this long philosophic growth. Again, this final philosophy seems wholly spontaneous and native; the late science contains Greek materials.

The Occident. The Western nations also possessed no organized intellectual heritage, except a trickle of the diluted Latin version of Greek productivity. This, after centuries, they proceeded to build over into Mediaeval philosophy, but without any creative counterpart in science. The growing civilization was vigorous, however, and such a one-sided reworking did not satisfy it. It therefore turned away from systematization to a phase of acquisitiveness of cultural content; from which before long a growth of science emerged, which resolutely began where the Greeks left off. After the foundations of a new astronomy, physics, biology, and in part mathematics had been laid, a new philosophy also emerged, equally emancipated from the Greeks in the sense of possessing new problems. It is, however, significant that Copernicus, Galileo, Vesalius, Harvey, and Napier preceded Descartes. It is also significant that after him and his French contemporaries, there was, except for Leibnitz, no great philosopher who was also a great scientist. The philosophical growth, although initiated later, culminated within two centuries, and is as obviously past as the scientific one is in full activity. Occidental science has already lasted as long as Greek and longer than any other. Its sag in the early eighteenth century proved to be a pause in which it reconstituted itself to deal with new problems by somewhat new methods—notably, increased experimentation.

China. The situation is as in India, and its beginning is synchronous: fundamental philosophic attitudes are outlined in Chou times. Scientific achievements are much less, and later, apparently for the most part in Han. Another small scientific growth centered about five centuries later. The pre-T'ang mathematics of this later growth seems native, the T'ang astronomy Indian. In the Sung period there was a philosophic reformation; and following this, a brief but remarkable algebra, which quite likely contains Indian absorptions but is developed on strictly native lines. After another sag, there was some Chinese scientific activity, not well constellated, due to Jesuit instruction. In general, as in India, science limps behind philosophy, and is partly foreign-derived.

Japan. There is no independent systematic Japanese philosophy, and only one scientific growth: a carrying further, after European contacts, of the Chinese late-Sung algebra.

Islam. Greek philosophy and science were taken over together and developed concurrently, often but not always by the same men, in Islam. The duration of the two activities is about the same, first in the East and then in Spain; with some afterglow of science lingering on a while longer. The Arabs and most of the peoples who came into Islam had developed their previous cultures in emotional rather than in rational patterns. They therefore took over Greek intellectual activity bodily, science and philosophy together; and on the whole carried them on competently and encyclopaedically rather than creatively. The greatest Islamic productivity centered in lands like Mesopotamia and Iran, which had experienced only a thin and transient veneer of Greek civilization, rather than in Syria and Egypt, where the dominant civilization had once been Greek for many centuries.

Summarizing, we can say that in spite of whatever sense of problems or empirical acquisitions there may have been before, there was no successfully organized intellectual endeavor in human culture until about the sixth century before Christ, but that then it arose in China, India, and Greece. The three growths were of two types. In China and India philosophies were worked out with little reference to nature.[3] They were able to become the basic idea-systems of the cultures, and were integrated with, or even productive of, religions. In Greece, the pattern of the growth was from the first directed as much to the concrete as to the relational, to nature as to man. Hence science flourished alongside philosophy, but there was little integration or even contact with religion. The higher levels of the culture became religionless. This gave Christianity its opportunity—precisely because it started unencumbered with intellectual preoccupations.

From this point on, the three growths split and diverge. The two Asiatic civilizations reformulated their philosophies as they became more mature and expert; the Indian one, with increased competence. In both, science tagged behind, in achievements and usually also in time, and probably always dependent on stimulations from outside, which entered in a thin and intermittent stream. There is something genuinely pathetic in the Sung algebra—a high intellectual endeavor narrowly limited by possessing no antecedents in its own culture other than a method of arithmetical manipulation, and foreign sources so trickling that we can no longer trace them. Even more extreme is the case of Tokugawa Japan, which, apparently made to realize by European contacts that there were such things as scientific possibilities, knew no other outlet than to take up the Sung algebra which the Chinese had dropped three centuries before, and to specialize this further.

In the Near East and Europe, after possibilities in the specific Greek patterns were exhausted, Mohammedanism was added to Christianity. Originating in a culturally more remote area, it crystallized without even an attitude toward intellectual en-

---

[3] The amazingly early and perfect philology of India does not contravene this statement. Not only is philology verbal, but grammar is the discovery of unconscious logic.

deavor, whereas Christianity already with St. Paul was using some weapons of Greek intellect against the Greek system. Also, Islam captured peoples long inured to a considerable measure of civilization: Egyptians, Syrians, Mesopotamians, Iranians; whereas Christianity soon settled down to becoming the basic idea system of barbarians or peoples of recent barbaric antecedents, except for the Greeks. Such seem to be the chief reasons for the earlier development of philosophy and science in Islam than in the Occident: ideational indifference of the cultural frame, with some experience in abstraction on the part of the included cultures; plus geographical proximity to the Greek area. The consequence was that the Islamic peoples were able to appropriate the Greek products of a millennium before, rapidly and almost whole; with the result that they remained essential imitators, or reproducers with some enrichments. At any rate, they produced little in the way of fundamentally new thought-patterns. The West, on the contrary, in its isolation was thrown more on itself and developed more slowly. All it had to start from was a theology that was well trained logistically in support of a nonrational dogma— the sort of theology that Mohammedanism acquired chiefly after, or as a result of, its philosophy. The West's first effort therefore had to be within this dogmatic frame. The resulting Scholastic philosophy is a compromise formation: astonishing in its acuity and skill, but of little value to human culture as a whole except as a virtuoso performance. Its own civilization *de facto* dropped the Scholastic system as soon as it was completed, and after some groping found the path of natural science. This path theology could prescribe less rigorously, especially as the total culture was growing too large and rich to be confined in a strait pattern of dogma. By the time the Occidental pattern of religion was cracking, before and during the Reformation, Occidental science was respectively being born and winning its first great successes.[4] When Europe settled down again to

---

[4] The Jesuit Order represents the attempt of the Church, now on the defensive, to renew the tactics of its early days from Paul to Augustine, namely, to use ideational weapons forged outside, in its own behalf. It was the new science that the Jesuits largely relied on, and with profound effect in the Far East.

religious peace—a peace of division and exhaustion,—her science was well established, and a new nontheological philosophy could arise. The starting point, the *Discourse on Method,* is only eleven years from the Treaty of Westphalia, but is preceded by the great scientific discoveries of the century before. One interesting by-product, or partial by-product, of this situation is that modern Western philosophy centers in time around the early eighteenth-century pause or slowing of science—the inverse of post-Christian sixth-century India. Descartes, Spinoza, Locke preceded the scientific lull, Leibnitz and Hume flourished within its borders, Kant and Hegel followed within some thirty and sixty years.

All of which, I admit, eventuates in what is, after all, a historical summary: historical in the sense of being variably individuated, rather than shaped by fixed principles. What there is of the latter, is a few approximations: that science and philosophy, being ideational, are likely to have relations in their historic occurrence, but need not have them; that a philosophy which is also a religion, or is capable of developing one, can become and remain the fundamental idea-pattern of a civilization, in which case scientific growths are likely to lag or be left to foreign introduction; whereas a nonreligious philosophy is likely to be accompanied by a growth of science; but also to be unable to withstand the vigorous activities of a growing organized religion, or to be delimited by an established organized one. This, after all, might be inferred from the implicit definitions of the concepts: religion as something impelled basically by emotional interests, but, if it is to be more than a series of incoherent local or national cults and myths, needing organization in formulable ideational terms, which in turn bring it into relations, hostile or amicable, with philosophical activity; science, related to philosophy in its goal of inquiring and its method of generalizing or abstracting, but, primarily concerned with understanding nature instead of human conduct, therefore more remote from religion, and consequently less likely either to conflict with it or to receive stimulus and support when religion and philosophy become allied.

As a sociological finding, this seems reasonable enough, but too airy to serve as a foundation for further investigation. While I have followed a factual route, it ends about where deductive reasoning would have led us more quickly: from ill-defined (though perhaps important) concepts of cultural activities to ill-definable concepts of their relations.

More significant seems the historical fact that coherent and developable systems of philosophy grew up seemingly independently, and so far as we can see *de novo*, three times in history; but an important system of science only once, and that in close linkage with one of the three philosophies. All subsequent growths of the two activities, however much they developed what was new and of their own, also derive in some measure from these four starts, by stimulus, absorption, or direct taking-over. The tracing of the threads between them is a fascinating pursuit; but it is pure history.

What remains remarkable, on the face of the record, is that these three primary growths—for the Greek one is double,— coming as it were out of nothing, should be simultaneous. One aspect of this fact has been examined in the chapter on Philosophy. It was there shown that the total distribution of periods of productivity throughout history is such that simultaneous occurrences appear with almost exactly the frequency expectable under the laws of chance, and that there is therefore no need to assume any generic factor which at certain times or stages impels humanity toward such activity. It is, however, not precluded that there might be a specific historical causality connecting these first three recorded philosophies; such as, for example, the introduction or sufficiently widespread use of writing.[5] At any rate, such efforts at philosophizing as there might have been previously, would be likely to be lost: it is through writing that preservation to us was made possible. The much earlier use of writing in Egypt, Mesopotamia, and the Indus Valley would be no necessary bar to such a view,

---

[5] Early Indian philosophy and Buddhism are said to have been orally transmitted, but writing must have come into use almost immediately afterward. In China, writing is archaeologically attested for at least seven centuries before Lao-tse and Confucius; in Greece, not much more than two or three before Thales.

because it would be gratuitous to assume the inverse proposition, that writing *per se* will produce philosophy. All I am contending for is the possibility of specific connections between the beginnings of Chinese, Indian, and Greek philosophies; not indeed in their content, but as functions of other cultural activities which were carried and transmitted by contact. In other words, it is an ordinary historical problem which is being suggested—one that is orthodox except for the fact that it falls so near the beginning of the written record that it may remain insoluble.

This is a problem of a different nature from the question raised in the chapter on Philosophy. That question concerned the possibility of there being immanences inherent in the totality of human culture, of which the three simultaneous sixth-century philosophies might be an example. The answer was that, the total space-time distribution of philosophies being in accord with chance, there was no need to assume an immanence in this instance. The problem now suggested is historical in that it is specific: did the development or diffusion of something else than philosophy, such as the growth of the use of writing, help to bring about the philosophical growths as a function of itself, and therefore contemporaneously?

§118. Special Problems of Growth Interrelation

The problem of whether different activities are necessarily interrelated, and how they tend to be actually interrelated, has just been answered to this effect: that no activity need be present in a culture with a force sufficient to reach high values, even if others do rise to that level; nor is there an important relation of time or order of appearance between the several activities. There remain, however, several more special questions. Such are: the likelihood of high achievement in a single art or activity; the frequency of nationalistic achievement without corresponding aesthetic or intellectual development; and the possibility of considerable cultural achievement without coördinate national development.

By nationalistic development I mean coherent internal organization, especially on the political side, although economic success may also be involved; and, normally, external military success as expressed by victory or conquest. Naturally the two criteria tend to be associated.

That nationalistic organization and expansion can occur without notable achievement in the fields of art and thought is evident from numerous examples which have been touched upon here and there in the foregoing pages. In fact, it follows almost from the definition of cultural achievement as dealt with in this work: the achievement must attain a certain level of intrinsic or world-wide value before it is entered upon the record with which we have concerned ourselves. Consequently, any barbarian people which consolidates and expands by force of arms is a case in point.

The Mongols, with their brief but vast empire, come to mind at once, especially as their work was accomplished by a remarkably small population, numbering only a few millions today, and presumably fewer in the thirteenth century.

The Turks are another such people. Their effects were less concentrated and spectacular than those of the Mongols, but more enduring. They bulwarked and preserved Islam for centuries, and they did leave more behind them than the Mongols in the way of constructive products. Nevertheless, their contributions were effected mainly through Arabic and Persian civilization and to a large extent through the medium of these languages. What the Turks evolved of their own, other than in statecraft and conquest, such as in Turkish literature, appears to be a rather feeble imitation of Arabic and Persian.

The Lithuanians are still another such. In the fourteenth century they built up a formidable and successful power in eastern Europe. But they were too backward to do anything civilizational with this. By the time they had learned enough, they had channeled their energies into the Polish cultural medium. Historically their principal role may be said to have been to make possible the higher development of Polish nationality and civilization.

Before them, around the year 1000, a whole series of peoples, marginal to what then was civilized Europe, underwent a similar development; Russia, Hungary, Poland, Denmark succeeded, almost contemporaneously, in establishing a fairly firm rule, in maintaining or expanding their borders, and in developing a persistent national consciousness. All were too little civilized for higher cultural attainments, and their civilizational accomplishments came later.

Still another illustration is supplied by Macedon, which realized for the Greeks the old Greek dream of the conquest of Asia, but in the very act of so doing was absorbed in the Greek civilization.

In most of these examples we can trace a connection between the nationalistic florescence and previous exposure to higher culture. It does not seem to matter much whether this exposure was amicable or hostile: it occurred in equal strength. Macedon came into conflict with the remnant of the Athenian dominion and then with other Greek cities. The Russians before their rise had attacked Constantinople, and the Hungarians had been checked by the Germans. The Poles had been in the situation of barely sustaining themselves against Othonian Germany, and the Danes likewise. So far as the Turks are concerned, the surface record is clearer for dynasty than for nationalities. But it is evident that both before and after 1000 many of the men of genius in Islamic philosophy, science, and literature, both in their Arabic and their Persian phases, were natives of what we now call Turkestan. Whether these districts were then ethnically still Iranian, or whether they were already predominantly occupied by a Turkish population with an Iranian veneer of higher civilization, I cannot say. If the former was the case, there certainly were Turks only a little beyond the city-bearing oases, and these ruder pure Turks must have been receiving some effects of exposure to Iranian culture before they proceeded successfully to invade and annex. This at least is certain: that before Turks entered and dominated lands such as Anatolia and Balkan and Danubian Europe they had had from two to five centuries of intimate contact with

Islamic civilization as its military and then political masters in Iran and Mesopotamia.

As for the Mongols, I do not know the antecedent situation, and doubt that anyone does except conjecturally. However, on the basis of the illustrations just cited it seems not unlikely that the same process was at work on them also. The people who trained them may have been the semicivilized Uigur Turks whom they subsequently conquered and utilized. At any rate, there appears to be as much warrant for looking for cultural causes for the Mongol burst as for attributing it somewhat crassly to changes of climate. At least, the two factors may have been operative in the same direction, in case evidence does establish the climatic one. Necessity alone is a simple and dangerous explanation to invoke in history. No matter how great the need, a people must be militarily equal or superior to its neighbors before it can conquer them; and whether the superiority be in equipment, organization, or morale, these in turn are unquestionably more directly dependent upon cultural factors than upon environmental ones. To explain the always complex events of history by direct appeal to raw psychological factors resulting from environmental ones is inevitably naïve.

We have another illustration in the relation of the Germans to the Roman Empire. They made their first eruption a hundred years before Christ. For centuries thereafter they were a trouble and a menace. But it was not until about 250 A.D. that they broke through and began establishing themselves on Roman soil. What were they doing during the intervening three centuries and a half but inevitably learning from the Romans, who consistently defeated them? It may be that the Romans had weakened in the interval; but this can hardly be the sole cause. As a matter of fact, when the Goths and other nations began breaking the barrier in the third century, it is clear that they were quite different people in their skills and their degree of organization from the Cimbri and Teutons and the followers of Ariovistus and Arminius.

Our second question concerns a definite cultural achievement without accompanying nationalistic achievement. The whole trend of the facts reviewed is contrary to this; but there are instances enough to prove it possible. Outstanding is the pre-Islamic poetry of Arabia—the more striking because it appears to have been a growth that stood isolated in its day.

Then there is the florescence of Polish literature in the early nineteenth century, falling precisely into the period of national humiliation and subjugation. This is the more remarkable because it reached its full development at the very moment when the hopes of a restoration of Polish independence had finally collapsed with Napoleon. The instance is also strengthened by not standing wholly isolated: Chopin's music is contemporary.

In China we have noted that the beginnings of the second and greater cultural constellation which culminated under the national prosperity of the T'angs seemed to go back to about 200 A.D., when the country passed from the relatively successful, and at any rate symbolically nationalistic rule of the Hans, to division and partial rule by barbarians from the outside. It is true, however, that here the full development of the patterns was not attained until T'ang reunification and success.

On the other hand, it is certainly true that high achievements by suppressed nationalities are rather rare. If such a nationality contributes, it is usually through the medium of the culture of the ruling people; like the Irish, who have participated in English literature and music.

As for the third question, which, apart from considerations of relation to nationality, asks whether a people can do great things in one activity while remaining mediocre or backward in all others, it is rather evident from all we know about civilization, as well as from the evidence laboriously adduced in these pages, that such an event is unlikely; but it does occur. The just-cited instance of pre-Islamic Arabic poetry is sufficient indication that exceptions can occur. This is really an unusually clear-cut example because of the complete lack of achievement by the Arabs in all other domains until after 622. It is difficult to find another occurrence that approaches this one in decisiveness.

In short, we may conclude that, on the whole, ethnic or national energy and higher cultural energy tend to be related; but that the relationship is not complete. Often enough, cultural development precedes the ethnic one, at least in its beginnings; and the reverse is even more frequent; in part because our definition of cultural achievement involves a certain threshold, and that of national achievement implies at most an indefinite one. That there should be a prevalent relation seems to follow from the fact that, after all, even the more elementary forms of national success presuppose at least some cultural development. Patriotism needs symbols around which it can rally. Ardor and patriotism require a certain skill in armament and in organizational order and control before they can become effective; and these latter are of course patterned cultural achievements, technological and social.

Finally, the quantitative factors of population and wealth no doubt tend, other things equal, always to play a part. They can, however, only be mentioned here. How important on the average they may or may not be, it is difficult to state. As I have said before, I should have liked nothing better than to be able to consider population and wealth in the course of this work. But it is a curious fact that as soon as we pass beyond the last century or two in the Occident, quantitative estimates on these two supposedly measurable factors become much more vague and conflicting in human history than opinions on qualitative achievement.

§119. Relation of Culture Content and Climax

The relation of cultural quality to quantitative content of culture is an important problem which remains rather obscure. *A priori,* one would expect this relation to be rather strong. A culture with a content several times as great as another—let us say with a total inventory of items several times larger—has more material to operate on, and ought therefore to be able to produce more combinations of items and richer or more intensive patterns. An art of painting which employs color as well as line ought, other things being equal, to achieve a greater variety of effects than one limited to line; and among this greater variety, or because of it, there ought to be some pattern effects which the world at large would rate qualitatively superior to the best produced in the simpler art. If to color and line we add also, let us say, perspective and values, the range is further widened, and the potentiality of still greater and more satisfying patterns is correspondingly enhanced. I am of course not saying that this must happen. It is entirely possible for a culture not to seize upon its finest pattern potentialities; to be lacking in the ability to select and concentrate, and, instead, to dissipate its energies in random or conflicting endeavors at expression. Still, if the factors bearing on this matter are at all equal, and in the long run they are likely to average more or less equal, one could expect qualitatively greater patterns to eventuate most often in cultures of the richest and most varied content. On the whole, it will probably be admitted that this is what has occurred. At any rate, there is no art of a primitive culture which can fairly be rated as equal to the qualitatively finest arts produced in so-called high civilization.

However, like most things in history, the matter is not simple. In a great civilization, which is necessarily slow-growing, it is entirely possible that a certain pattern formulation occurs fairly early during the development. The basic patterns may in fact be worked out into a consistent and expressive system in this relatively early phase of growth. The culture as a whole may, however, continue to grow by either absorbing or developing new content; and before long this content may become more than the patterns already formed can accommodate, because they had their development while the content was considerably less. In this event, it seems likely that the patterns will stretch to a certain point and then begin to disrupt or dissolve. Inasmuch as what we feel as cultural quality is apparently more directly a function of pattern than of content, the phase of stretch or disruption is likely to be construable as one of decline. At any rate, a period of apparent disintegration follows, during which the patterns are no longer dominant but are being reconstituted. As soon as this has been successfully achieved, and the new patterns are able to absorb and mold the increased body of constituents, a new phase of florescence is entered upon in which higher results are attained. The whole process just summarized may conceivably be repeated more than once.

I construe as a striking example of this type of configuration Europe as a whole in the interval between the High Middle Ages and the High Renaissance, say about the fourteenth and fifteenth centuries. There is no question of the growth of knowledge, inventions, varieties of ways of living, wealth, and population in Europe during this period. On the other hand, there is also little question that there was less coherent systematization, many more conflicting outlooks on life, and few products of a really high sort in the arts or science or philosophy. When, around 1500, under the leadership mainly of Italy but with some contribution from Germany and the Netherlands, Europe set out to reformulate its standards and to recreate its world, which it succeeded in doing between 1600 and 1700. it evolved a set of patterns which were considerably deeper and richer than those of the Middle Ages, considerably more numerous also, and almost as much unified into a coherent system.

I have previously indicated that a similar process is probably observable in China. Here an early set of patterns was formulated and brought to a very high pitch, although covering a rather narrow range, in the last Chou centuries. Then followed a period of formal disruption of these patterns, of little productivity of the highest type, and of introduction of a great mass of new cultural material from the West, mainly as the accompaniment of the introduction of Buddhism, but probably accompanied also by internal originations stimulated by the introductions. This period lasted perhaps four centuries. Upon these four centuries followed another four in which we see new patterns beginning to emerge, of limited scope and somewhat scatteringly, but on the whole increasingly; until, after 600, during the first two T'ang centuries, we have a new culmination which includes products of a high order in more activities than the Chou florescence. I realize that this is not the conventional presentation of Chinese culture history. But then, this history has scarcely been scrutinized with an eye to its configurations, except in native terms of prosperous and unprosperous dynasties, and in the classification of these the ethical element figures largely.

Something similar seems also to have occurred in India, where there was a preliminary or premature formulation of patterns in the sixth or fifth century B.C., and a later one, of considerable duration, centering perhaps around the fifth century A.C. I bring this up with reserve, however, and advance it only as a suggestion, because the earlier period is legendary and the chronology of the later one vague at many points.

When it is a matter of civilizations of less compass—a smaller population or territory, a briefer total duration of growth and decline, or fewer attainments,—the prodromal stage may of course be entirely lacking. A set of culture patterns is worked out in conformity with the culture content, a florescence is attained, and therewith the growth is ended.

It is also possible that patterns are swamped by content, the preliminary dissolution occurs, but reconstitution does not take place because the culture is overwhelmed by the impact of greater ones. It may come into direct conflict with another culture, civilizationally or nationalistically, and be defeated or superseded; or, owing to the influence of a larger culture, the influx of content may continue in sufficient quantity to prevent the reconstitution of patterns. In such cases, what in isolation would have been temporary pattern loss preliminary to new pattern growth may become the permanent death of higher pattern formation. There have probably been a number of such cases in history which we can more easily imagine than demonstrate. Pagan Norse culture is probably an example; at any rate, a partial one.

One other observation ought to be added. I have spoken in the foregoing paragraphs of culture patterns and culture content as if they were easily contrastable phenomena: the form and the substance of culture, so to speak. I am fully aware that this distinction is beset with difficulties: cultural form and content are both merely aspects of the same phenomena as they occur in nature. With analysis a point is soon reached where distinction becomes ambiguous. We can abstract an art style or an intellectual process, in the more favorable cases, and deal with it as pattern or form. We can also extract from the body of a culture individual items like the wearing or not wearing of shoes, or the lighting of candles as a religious offering, and treat these as if they were pure content or substance. Nevertheless, it is obvious that culture form can exist only with reference to culture content. A style can exist only in the presence of certain techniques. A way of thinking can be applied only upon a body of factual knowledge. And, on the other side, there is always a tendency for the items of culture content, as they come in contact with one another, to form associations or complexes which in turn inevitably have form. We simply have no rigid criterion by which we can say that this cultural phenomenon is form and that is content. The two are necessarily in relation and must be considered as no more than useful abstractions of phenomena. At times we can fruitfully separate these aspects and give consideration chiefly to the one or the other; but this does not mean that they are separate realities. They occur interwoven.

§120. Religion

Religion has not been included among those activities the florescent configurations or climaxes of which are examined here. I definitely considered including it, but could find no satisfactorily feasible procedure. Though religion contains both intellectual and aesthetic elements, its essence is of a different nature. So far as a given religion varies temporally, it is in the intensity of emotion with which it is felt, and in its organizational expression and status. Its growths and declines in these respects would be hard to estimate. Moreover, they would be something different from the growths and declines in intellectual and aesthetic products. They might be compared, but only partially.

A concrete example will illustrate the situation. Are we to consider as the high point and culmination of Christianity the period of its origin or some later period? Certainly there was no later time in which ardor of adherence and purity of conviction were greater, if as great. On the other hand, doctrine was still undifferentiated and vague, its formal expression unprecise or personalized, and wider cultural significance was as yet almost nil. In brief, we have in primitive Christianity the generalized outlines of a pattern for the future to fill in, rather than an expressed pattern.

In western Europe, it might well be argued that Christianity had reached a culmination around the twelfth and thirteenth centuries. Certainly after that time it underwent external shocks and internal dissensions, and both its hold and its influence gradually weakened. There is also little doubt that the Christianity of thirteenth-century Europe was a more evolved product, one that ramified at many more points into the lives of men of the time, than it was at earlier periods, say in the Carolingian epoch. But I doubt whether preponderant consent would be found for the assertion that the thirteenth century marked the culmination of Christianity. There is practically unanimous agreement that Shakespeare was a greater dramatist than Marlowe, and Marlowe a greater one than Peele; and more or less similarly for most of the other judgments on which the treatment of the present book rests. I do not believe that a corresponding consensus could be found in regard to Christianity or any other religion as a culture pattern.

As a matter of fact, when we analyze Christianity in thirteenth-century western Europe, such culmination as it had will probably be found expressible chiefly in two respects. First, it was probably best integrated and strongest as an institution. Second, it had then, on the whole, the most and finest intellectual and aesthetic expressions.

As for the first point, that of institutional efflorescence, it is true that institutions are also patterns, that apparently they also culminate, and that their configurational history as such could very probably be studied by the same approach which I am following in this work. Kingship, for instance, or almost any political or social institution, is theoretically amenable to the same treatment. I simply have not considered the history of institutions in the ordinary sense of the word, because a limit must be drawn somewhere.

The influence of Christianity on the sciences and arts, I have considered: but among these activities the High Mediaeval philosophy was not only the product, in a full half of its representatives, of Franciscans and Dominicans, but it moved wholly, as a system of thought, within the framework provided by the Church. The great tangible arts of the same period, architecture and sculpture, were almost wholly ecclesiastical in their preoccupation. Much of the literature of the time, it is true, was secular, but at least the greatest single poet of the Middle Ages, Dante, also operated strictly within the confines of Christian concept and sentiment. Much of what the Christian Church produced culturally in the Middle Ages has therefore already been covered in the course of this book. The remainder, its institutional realization, is obviously also of importance, but happens to fall outside the limits of space and range which I have felt it necessary to observe.

The example just discussed, however, touches on a matter which is germane to the scope of the present work: namely, the relation of religion to aesthetic and intellectual culminations, the part which religion plays in helping the arts and sciences to reach their highest peaks—or, on the other hand, how far it may be a hindrance. On this matter there is a point of view to be presented which cannot pretend to being susceptible of proof, nor indeed can its generality be easily tested. But on the other hand there are a number of instances in which the thesis seems to apply.

The suggestion which is therefore advanced is that often, perhaps more often than not, a religion which is actuated by powerful drives or possesses established strength is likely to annex and subordinate the arts and sciences and use them primarily for its own purposes. Lacking the freedom of autonomy, these activities accordingly remain on a relatively low level.

Their attempts at distinctly intellectual or aesthetic expression are constantly limited or checked in favor of religious expression. In spite of this, however, these nonreligious activities may grow until they more or less liberate themselves; or the strength of the essentially religious impulses may wane, and rational understanding and self-contained art may profit by this weakening of suzerainty over them. If this happens, the arts turn more and more in their preoccupations, their content, and the feelings rendered, from the religious or ecclesiastical to the profane and secular.

This course of events has been several times mentioned in preceding pages: for the Occidental arts, for instance, and for the Greek and Japanese; and some evidences seem to be apparent in India and China. In fact, where religion and the arts are at all closely associated it is tempting to set up the general proposition that the configuration of the arts can be expressed, in one of its aspects, in terms of this association. Art emerges timidly as a handmaid in the service of religion. After a more or less long apprenticeship she achieves competences and develops faculties of her own, but has not yet cast off the relation of dependence. It is at the moment when essential independence is attained and art freely pursues her own objectives, although perhaps still paying superficial homage to her former mistress, that an art is likely to come into culmination. A few generations more of secularity, and it tends to become too profane. Room is made for the shallow and the frivolous, for the purely formal and precious, and decline has set in. In the Italian Renaissance this process is clearly evident. Raphael, Leonardo, Michelangelo represent at once the climax and the moment of liberation. So, correspondingly, does Phidias. Early Western music was, in its supposedly finest exemplification, Church music. The seventeenth century began to bring, and the eighteenth achieved, emancipation; and by about 1800 the peak had been reached.

In Eastern Asia there is no doubt that the pictive arts were enormously indebted to Buddhism in India and almost wholly dependent upon it in China and Japan for their origins. At the same time, the finest achievements of the arts in these countries seem, on the whole, to have occurred in later periods when the first fervor of strictly religious enthusiasm had subsided, and the arts, while still formally Buddhistic, were operating on a more secular plane.

Something similar may easily happen in the field of the intellect. The Mediaeval Church helped produce the Scholastic philosophy which moved within the bounds set it by the Church. When this frame had been filled, the philosophy began to disintegrate. By this time also the first symptoms of disintegration were manifest within the Church. After three centuries of quiescence, philosophy began to be active again; but now outside the Church and with only partial reference to religion. Science, which the Church could not use for its purposes as it used philosophy and the arts, never came up at all during the High Middle Ages. After the hold of the Church relaxed, empirical Western science came into being.

We know little about the strength of religion in Greece before 600 as compared with the centuries after; but we can at least guess that it may have been stronger because of the lack of systematized intellectual activity to compete with it. Certainly, from 600 on, as science and philosophy increasingly flourished, the hold of religion in the Greek world grew progressively less. After science and philosophy had run their active course, religion once more became important; until we have in Neo-Platonism an attempt to revive philosophy upon a religious motivation.

I do not wish to set up this thesis as a universal. Obviously there are sooner or later likely to be cultures in which religion remains dominant and in which the arts and sciences, either because of this fact or because the frame of the cultural whole makes little provision for them, remain relatively ineffectual. I am only suggesting that the process tends to be operative when there are strong tendencies toward religious expression and strong tendencies toward aesthetic or intellectual expression within the same culture, or potential within its larger system. At any rate, I cannot think of a single people which

first evolved a high science, philosophy, or art, and thereafter
a religious pattern which was important intrinsically and
institutionally; at any rate; not within the bounds of duration
of what we customarily consider one civilization. If there is a
relation or association, within any one civilization as it affects
one population, it seems normally to be religion which first
reaches its chief climax, and then the aesthetic and intellectual
activities as they free themselves from religion. Pre-Islamic
poetry and perhaps pre-Deuteronomic Hebrew poetry are the
seemingly contrary examples which come most readily to mind.

§121. Durations of Growths

From what has been said concerning lack of regularity of form
and relations of florescent growths, it is expectable that there
would also be no standard durations. Indeed, there is no regularity in these. They range all the way from a single productive
lifetime, say thirty or forty years, to a thousand years. The
briefest ones usually represent a localized pulse in larger
growths, like French seventeenth-century philosophy and science. The longest-seeming ones occur in Asia, in civilizations
intimately known to very few westerners, and therefore difficult to analyze or to evaluate comparatively with regard to
their historic parts. The extreme instance, on the whole, is
supplied by India. Here we have a great culture notorious for
being exceptionally indifferent to and uncritical of its own
history, but fond of exaggeration. In the face of the eternal
verities with which the Hindu is preoccupied, time perspective
is bound to be a rather trivial consideration. It may therefore
prove, when we control Indian culture history better, that
some of its growths will prove less unusually long than they are
now estimated. Nevertheless, the indications at hand are that
all growths in India have been comparatively slow, and that
anything established tends to relatively fixed repetition there.
India is culturally a continent, not well segregated into parts
nor organized in relation of parts. It moves as a huge, somewhat inert mass. In spite of some possible reduction of the

time values here assumed, it is therefore probable that the actual durations of Indian growths will prove to average longer, both on the up- and the down-swing, than elsewhere. This seems to be an inherent quality of the set or orientation of Indian culture. In very virtue of that, however, the fact argues against any absolute norm for the length of growths.

This much can probably be affirmed inductively from the data reviewed: that qualitatively great growths tend to be of considerable duration. A greater pattern takes longer to fill and to exhaust, at any rate within the same or similar cultures. This indeed may seem deductively expectable. However, here are some examples.

Science. Greek, main pulse, five centuries; Occidental to date, five; against Eastern Islamic, Western Islamic, and Indian of the historic period, somewhere between one and a half and four; second Chinese, three; third Chinese, less than one; Japanese, two centuries, approximately.

Music. Italian, nearly four centuries (several pulses, but difficult to segregate); German, about two; British, little more than one; modern French, perhaps one and a half; Russian, less than one.

Sculpture. Greek about five centuries, with aftermaths; Italian, Renaissance-centered, four to seven; French (earlier and later), Spanish, and Netherlandish, one to two each.

Painting. Italian, five centuries; Netherlandish, three from Van Eyck to Hobbema; German Renaissance, about one; Spanish, not more than two, important, one; French, seventeenth century, less than one, modern, about one; British, one.

Literature. Greek, without epics or silver age, five continuous centuries; Latin, total with intermissions, less than four; golden age, less than one. Italian with three pulses, France with two postmediaeval ones, England with two, Germany with one, Spain with one: no one growth or pulse exceeding two centuries, most not far from one.

These are some qualifications or limiting circumstances that must be kept in mind in comparisons:

Parts cannot legitimately be matched against the whole: the drama against a whole literature, mathematics against science, would be inadmissible.

Nonculminating growths, or those that seem to be such, like Arabic and Persian literature, are not satisfactorily comparable to those with obvious rise, peak, and decline.

In India and China we really have entities more comparable to Europe than to any one European nationality. When matched against Occidental civilization as a whole, Chinese culture does not show longer growths in particular activities, and the excessiveness of Indian becomes less extreme.

I admit a certain degree of outward inequality in my delimiting of certain growths. From 1100 to 1800 doubtless seems a maximal length for the growth of Italian sculpture, when for instance French modern philosophy is allowed only the thirty years from 1630 to 1660. However, the endeavor is to define, literally, sculpture as a growth in Italy; of this, the typical Renaissance pattern is only part; the growth is continuous; and, just because it was prolonged and reached high, it seems valid to include in it all sculptural activity continuous with it in space and time. Descartian philosophy, on the contrary, begins without gropings, says its say, and as abruptly ends; its continuation is elsewhere, in Holland, Britain, Germany. While Renaissance Italy also helped stimulate other nations— France and Spain—into activity, its sculpture went on with high competence, in fact the best in Europe; just as it had fumbled some centuries over its beginnings. The two growths in question differ in type; the nature of their configurations seems to demand that one be construed narrowly and the other largely.

If we consider the lengths of time for which *whole* cultures are actively creative in some department—with reference to quality values, not to production of new culture material as such,—my impression is that they do not differ very notably, except in some measure in proportion to the values which they achieve.

China, not quite two thousand years, say from −600 to 1300. Japan should perhaps be added, but is difficult to judge, for reasons already discussed.

India, somewhat less, −600 to about 1000.

Mediterranean, or Greek plus Roman, from −900 or −800 if we include Homer, to perhaps 400. This allows the inclusion of Neo-Platonism, Diophantine algebra; also of St. Augustine, if one will. The total is twelve or thirteen centuries. This could be lengthened about seven centuries by admitting pre-Greek Minoan culture, and two more with Byzantine architecture and law under Justinian. The Byzantine tenth-century renaissance belongs to the growth historically, but produced insufficient quality.

Arab-Islamic, seven hundred years, 500 to 1200; with inclusion of Persian, perhaps two centuries more. This will be generally conceded to be the narrowest in quality of the five here listed.

Occidental, since 1050 or 1100, eight or nine centuries to the present; the future, of course, indeterminate.

It will be seen that, in spite of the apparently slow rate of growth of separate Indian activities, Indian civilization as a whole was not unusually slow in working out its total of productive patterns.

National culture-wholes of course are normally longer in growing than their constituent parts. This is almost inevitable. Some one activity gets going before the rest, another lingers when they have died. More significant is the fact that sometimes the whole flourishes but little longer than its parts: the duration of these, and their absolute time incidence, are so similar that their aggregate but little exceeds any one. Greek culture is a striking example. Not only its higher values but even the formation of its specific patterns were accomplished between 650 and 100; and several of its activities, like sculpture and literature and science, run for almost that period. In fact, the chief reason for counting the Greek epic outside the main growth as prodromal is that it alone, if the conventional chronology is right, falls essentially outside the span of all other successful Greek activities.

Not only are great growths long, generally, but they show a tendency to recurrence. These recurrences are the prodromal and aftermath phenomena which have been discussed. The total period within which an area is productive in the higher fields of culture may therefore be remarkably long. Thus, the main growth of Greek literature is enclosed between 650 and

150. But if we count in the epics and the "silver age," the span
reaches from about 900 before Christ to 200 after, or eleven
centuries instead of five. Similarly, we have in Imperial times
the recrudescences of Ptolemaic astronomy and Neo-Platonic
philosophical mysticism. These revivals are all Greek, not only
in speech and mainly in extended or transferred geography,
but also in their basic orientations; though their patterns all
have a specific new twist. They are epilogues, genuinely, in that
they primarily relate to what went before. As for the configuration of the Greek culture-whole, they cannot be omitted. Their
significance lies precisely in their evidencing that when the
great Greek effort was over, a century before Christ, life had
not yet wholly gone out of the culture. After a rest period, or
relief by Rome, it resumed; and while the second crop may
have been pitiful in comparison with the former, it showed that
the culture was still far from dead.

It is therefore equally legitimate to construe Greek literature, philosophy, and science to have lasted more than a thousand years over all, or to have realized their essential patterns
in a short half millennium. The latter view is legitimate when
interest centers on specific pattern achievements of value; the
former, when concern is with the whole nexus of patterns
which make up an idea-system or culture-whole growth; a
"civilization," in everyday language. There need be no confusion if the breaks or gaps in growth are recorded as clearly as
the growth pulses.

Another problem is whether the rate of progress within
growths has gradually accelerated in history. The data indicate
rather conclusively that the rate has not gained in speed. So
far as high-quality growths are concerned, they seeem to take
about as long now as they did one or two thousand years ago,
speaking in terms of estimated averages of fairly variable periods. The widely spread contrary notion that there is acceleration rests on reference to the sum total of production of new
cultural content in the world, irrespective of value patterns.
For this, the notion may be correct. An acquisition once made,
like the plow, ironworking, writing, printing, tends both to be

retained and to spread to other cultures. However, the matter of losses and displacements in the totality of human culture has never been adequately investigated. Also, we are still under the influence of the eighteenth- and nineteenth-century assumption of human progress—a pulling down to earth of the millennium and transfer of divine agency to ourselves. This assumption, backed by projection of the special course of Occidental civilization in the last five centuries into a universality, may account for much of the idea. At any rate, whatever its foundation, this concept of accelerating progress deals with something different from what we are discussing here. For the rate of development of growths productive of high intellectual and aesthetic values, there is little warrant for believing in any material change in history. Such growths are variable, but there is nothing positive to show that they are growing faster now than they did in the past. Greater speed of modern communications is often thought to speed up the processes of history. But the two need not have any relation. Even if they do, the brute mass of contemporary culture, being larger, may take longer to affect or move. And further, the populations which carry recent culture are larger than those of the past.

These are some examples suggesting that growths do not rise and fall faster than in the past:

The productive periods of Chinese, Greek, Arabic, Mediaeval, and Modern philosophy do not exceed three to four centuries; and, for the main phases, do not fall much lower than that duration. The one notable exception is post-Christian India; and in this there may be two pulses, and the entire chronology is somewhat conjectural.

There is no growth in science that has lasted as long as the contemporary Occidental one, seeing that it is still in full activity after five centuries.

Italian sculpture and painting both endured successfully as long at high level as ancient Greek, although they are only parts of a multinational Occidental growth.

Literatures vary in range and content, but the drama as I have defined it is a limited form suitable for comparisons. The total range of Greek drama is comprised within two centuries. The glory of Greek tragedy falls within less than a century; of comedy, in two pulses each less than that. Latin, Chinese, Japanese, French, Spanish, English dramas are all growths of similar duration, so far as acting drama of literary value is concerned and as distinct from mere performances in a theater. Only the Sanskrit drama is much slower in its course—again an example of the slow-moving rate of nearly everything Indian.

These findings refer to the past twenty-five hundred years. Before then, in Egypt and Mesopotamia, the case may have been different. We have noted Egypt as anomalous in its seemingly repetitive pulses. But isolation rather than antiquity may be the cause of the phenomenon. In Mesopotamia, the record is broken, and the cumulative culture total is much clearer than the course of the several growths. The two that are most clearly delimited, middle Sumerian and late Assyrian sculpture, certainly seem to have had rapid and brief careers.

§122. Retarded and Insular Growths

There is no need to assume that each area or every nationality will produce its peculiar flowering of intellectuo-aesthetic culture. That some do, is owing to the accidents of where and on whom civilization alights; that others do not, is to be taken for granted. And as there is no definable threshold of higher civilization, there will be peoples that have worked out cultures of lesser values, or have long gone without florescences and then attained them late. In the latter class are all the populations of Europe, if viewed with an eye to total culture history: none of them participated with distinction until less than three thousand years ago. Even since there has been a European or Occidental form of civilization, the marginal peoples of the far north and east of Europe contributed almost none of its accepted higher values until barely two centuries ago.

There is, however, one historic instance of a population that verged on florescence productivity for more than a thousand years, then seemed to be defeated, and thereafter achieved what it had never accomplished before: the Iranians. Or perhaps it would be better to say that they early achieved empire—Achaemenian, Sassanian—and a distinctive religion—Zoroastrianism —and a fairly high level of general culture, but very little in the arts or in the field of intellect; and at a later period, some centuries after Mohammed, with their empire gone and their religion shattered, they attained to a great poetry, respectable painting, and important participation in the international science and philosophy of Islam. Their case has been discussed somewhat more fully in its proper place. It serves here to dispel any possible impression that, because high florescences in different cultural activities tend to come associated in time among a people, they must do so. When the Persians emerged from tribal culture, it was to find themselves precipitated into a world of competitive empires in which the victors progressively dominated more widely. On this level, plus that of an approximately contemporary organization of their tribal religion, they fixed the patterns of their civilization. Before long, this civilization came into competition with Hellenic civilization under Macedonian organization, and succumbed; only to regather itself under Parthian leadership, and consolidate under Sassanian, as a mass resistive to most Hellenic-Roman patterns and attempting to maintain the integrity of its own narrower ones. Only after a second collapse at the hands of the Arabs, a people geographically closer and more nearly related culturally, did the Iranians relinquish their fixation on their old cultural patterns, or most of them, and, opening their culture to new values, develop activities to which they had been relatively impervious before.

In one sense this unusual growth parallels that of the Hebrews. Both peoples achieved certain values only after they had essentially renounced their ambitions of nationalistic empire. The Hebrews then experienced a religious growth. With the Iranians, on the contrary, the religion was associated with empire, and fell with it, and the subsequent growths were intellectual and aesthetic. A historic parallel almost never proves to be a complete parallel if all relevant facts are considered.

Insular cultures present a problem of their own. There have been three higher ones: Britain, Japan, the East Indies. The history of the last-named is not very fully known, and its recorded attainments are notable only in sculpture and architecture, through preservation of work in stone. So far as can be judged, the Indonesian civilizations, whether actually on the islands or on the Indo-Chinese mainland, remained rather fully colonial, that is, culturally dependent on India, and lagging a few centuries behind.

Japan was never colonized from China; nor, for that matter, except for certain crafts in the early period, from Korea. At the same time, until the Portuguese arrived in the sixteenth century, all external influences of higher civilization which reached Japan at all reached her from China or through a Chinese or Korean medium. The result was a curious combination of dependence and independence. Nearly every activity successfully prosecuted to a higher level in Japan has a Chinese antecedent; and yet it rarely is wholly imitative, and sometimes surpasses its prototype in quality of pattern. Evidently the cultural inflow was at all times limited and never overwhelming. The Japanese exercised a control that at times seems to have been almost deliberate and skillfully took in only as much as they could assimilate. At any rate, the periods of greater and less absorptions from China-Korea are not very strikingly differentiated. In times of little direct import there was likely to occur a working-out of materials previously introduced: like algebra and philosophy in the Tokugawa period of non-intercourse.

I suspect that the unusual nature of these relations is the main factor in the unusually level character of the configuration of Japanese higher culture. The culminations in different activities tend to succeed one another rather than to cluster. There is nothing like the T'ang peak or the Ming-Manchu trough in Chinese art and literature.

England appears to show a little of an analogous steadiness of level. She too was backward in becoming civilized. In the High Middle Ages, she participated with western Europe in philosophy and architecture, hardly at all in literature or sculpture. Her mediaeval peak having been only partial, the several centuries of slump which France and Germany underwent are less evident: England seems continuingly backward from 1350 to 1550, rather than caught in the disorganization of a recession. On the other hand, the average level of total cultural productivity has probably been maintained more steadily since 1575 in England than in any continental country of Europe, except possibly France. These peculiarities must not be stretched too far. But they seem real to a certain degree, and so far similar to the peculiarities of Japanese development.

§123. Growth at the Peripheries

Alongside the measurability of growths in time, there is often also observable a measurability in space: that is, gradual extension from a center outward or from a periphery toward the center. The increasing spread outward of culture is a familiar enough phenomenon to the anthropologist and culture historian. The diffusion of a culture, or for that matter of a single culture element, is ordinarily supposed to take place in this way. The event has been observed sufficiently often; anthropologists have even ventured to use it as an approximate formula for reconstructing the course of events where this has not been recorded. The age-and-area principle explicitly embodies this concept. It has been employed in anthropology in a manner quite parallel with its use in biology and palaeontology. Whether anthropologists discovered it for themselves as a working method, or took the idea over from biologists, is not wholly clear. At any rate they employ it to reach corresponding results. Like every reconstructive principle, it must of course be used with both caution and tact; that is, it may never be relied upon excessively, and it is also necessary to abandon results reached by it as soon as they begin to conflict with conclusions inferable from other evidence.

The process of spreading outward from a focus is illustrated over and over again in the foregoing pages. It would no doubt have been exemplified even more often if the geographical evidence available had been more specific or detailed. Instances of movement in the opposite direction, from a condition in which the geographical margin of a culture is at first more active than the central regions, to a stage in which the center finally overtakes them, are, as might be expected, definitely less frequent; but they do occur.

The spread inward seems to be of two types. The first occurs when a culture, still in the formative stage as far as higher developments are concerned, is exposed on one or more of its frontiers to contacts with other cultures which stimulate or fertilize it. In this event the contact frontier is likely to show the first development and the central area to participate in the growth somewhat later. Of this type is the precedence of Ionia in Greek philosophy, sculpture, painting, literature, and probably music, to judge by the geographical names of the modes. Ionia lay in Asia and was therefore more directly open to all eastern influences than was the mainland of Greece.

However, the factors at work are rarely unique, and even this seemingly simple instance has a complicating aspect. Ionia was immediately followed in most of these activities by the western marginal Greek world, the cities of southern Italy and Sicily. No historian, so far as I know, has ventured an explanation of stimulation of these western outposts by Carthaginian or Etruscan influences. We must therefore fall back on another explanation. The most plausible one that occurs to me is that the peripheral and younger settlements were, on the whole, in a state of greater ferment and activity, and therefore readier for new undertakings, cultural as well as practical, than the relatively conservative populations which had remained on the long-settled Greek mainland.

Roughly, all higher cultural activity in the Greek world during most of the sixth century was Ionian. Toward the end of the century the western settlements began to participate; but the Greek mainland not until the fifth. During the remainder of the fifth century and the fourth, all three areas were productive, although the central one was probably most so. It was not so much a matter of one area superseding the other as of relative succession in entering upon activity.

Up to 330 the process was thus one of inward extension. This corresponds with the fact that there had been no material spread of Greek civilization beyond the confines of Greek territory. Influences into the barbarian world can be traced; but no solid taking over of Greek culture.

Around 330, with the Macedonian conquest of the Near East, the picture changed. The Greek cities witnessed this expansion with reluctance, because its prerequisite was the relative diminution of their own power. Nevertheless, adjacent Macedon had been pretty effectually Hellenized during the preceding two centuries, and from the point of view of the conquered Asiatics, as well as in effects upon the Asiatic culture, Alexander's conquests were a Greek conquest, of which the Macedonian king and Macedonian phalanx were merely the instrument. In other words, Macedon did for the expansion of Greek civilization what the Greeks themselves had been unable to do on account of their peculiar political underdevelopment. The result was that leadership in the arts and sciences was transferred from Athens to Alexandria, and that Antioch and Pergamum became more important culturally than Sparta or Corinth. Toward the end of the specifically Greek culture growth, accordingly, the direction of extension was reversed: the centripetal spread became centrifugal.

The second type of centripetal change is illustrated somewhat later, if we consider that in higher civilizational respects Roman culture was only a proliferation of Greek. The warrant for this view has been set forth in a previous chapter. Essentially, Rome at first followed the precedent of Macedon: consolidating and then extending its power, but becoming Hellenized in the process, in fact being already so, in the higher levels of civilization, before it began its career as a world power. Now the aesthetic-intellectual achievements of the Romans fell preponderantly in the century before and the century after the birth of Christ. Not only were these Roman achievements definitely modeled after the Greek ones; this two-century period in which they were at their highest was also the period in which Greek productivity was at its lowest for a millennium.

After about 100 or 120 A.D., the situation was reversed. The Greek-speaking world underwent a partial renaissance in science, philosophy, and literature, but quality of productivity fell off in the Latin-speaking half of the Empire. Soon after, the political fabric of the Empire began to show internal strains, and then followed pressure from the barbarians outside. It was in the east, and mainly by easterners, that the Empire was politically reconsolidated; and it was the east which, in spite of suffering some ravaging incursions, held its frontier against the barbarians, whereas the west was more and more overrun and gradually detached from the Empire by Germans. By this time, too, the arts and learning had sunk to a definitely low level in the west, but were being tolerably maintained in the east. Significant is the fact that, by the fifth century, Italians who knew Greek had become rare, whereas Latin was still the official language of the law and of the armies in the east.

In short, Italy and the western provinces, which had entered Graeco-Roman civilization late, were also the first to drop out of it. By 500 the shrunken domain of this civilization was confined to the eastern Mediterranean; and this equally whether one thinks of the political Empire or of the state of the arts and learning.

The process of shrinkage, in fact, went on for nearly a thousand years more, with several oscillations. Until the rise of Mohammedanism the Eastern Empire successfully maintained itself and even underwent a temporary expansion. It then lost half its territory to Islam, politically, culturally, and linguistically; and four centuries later half of the remainder to the Turks; although again there was a temporary expansion of frontier and culture intensification in the interval.

In the larger view, then, what we have here is a single growth beginning on a unilingual basis, becoming multilingual with prevalent bilingualism, and then contracting again in its decline to unilingualism, with corresponding changes in geographical extension. The whole Roman development is in one sense only an episode in this larger life cycle. It was Latin participation which brought the political resultant to its peak; but it was also the Latin portion of the totality which first sloughed off again. In brief, this Graeco-Roman or Mediterranean or Classical civilization expanded its area during a time in which the quality of its cultural products was, on the whole, declining; that is, there was a lag of the territorial and political growth behind the intellectual and aesthetic growth. There can be little doubt that the general parallelism of growth and decline, or of expansion and contraction, in the two sets of activities, must be related, even though our understanding of the connecting mechanism remains vague.

This second is apparently the more normal type of centripetal change: it is an accompaniment of the waning of cultural energy, of the atrophy of cultural patterns. Normally, it would seem, geographical expansion is a symptom of the growth, and contraction, of the decline, of a culture. The instances of the first centripetal type, like Greece in the sixth century, seem definitely in the minority.

Nevertheless the potential influence of the frontier or march must not be underestimated. Even where it faces a lower instead of a higher culture it may call for an increase in energy, which in turn leads before long to a higher degree of productivity. Germany has twice manifested this phenomenon of the frontier culturally in advance: in the minor Othonian florescence; and again, five centuries later, in assuming the lead in the development of European science. The latter instance is the more remarkable because, in the mediaeval centuries between, Germany had been subjected to a definite process of civilizing from France.

In one sense even the Italian Renaissance can be construed as partaking somewhat of the nature of a frontier development. In spite of more survivals from Ancient Mediterranean times in Italy than elsewhere in the west, the origins of Occidental culture are to be found not there but in France. The first effective centralization under Charlemagne took place in France and the Netherlands: and to this empire Italy was only marginal; in fact, was only partly included in it. It was also in the heart of Charlemagne's domains, especially in France, that the full development of the specific Mediaeval phase of Occidental civilization later took place; and Italy entered this development hesitantly and late. It was after the High Mediaeval patterns began to disintegrate that the Italians successfully developed their own, on soil which until then had been peripheral to Occidental culture.

It is true that this post-Mediaeval Italian growth was intensive enough to become the most important one in Europe; and from about 1500 on, cultural influence radiated from Italy to the remainder of Europe for a time. The civilizational center might be said to have moved to Italy. This, however, was only a transient occurrence, and within little more than a century the focus or hearth had begun to move back to the northwest, to France, Holland, England, and finally Germany. From the point of view of Occidental civilization as a whole, there can be no doubt that Italy lay, for the greater part of the duration of this civilization, on the geographical margin; and the period of Italian cultural dominance was, in accord with this fact, a relatively brief one; as indeed it had been in earlier Mediterranean civilization.

§124. The Question of Cultural Death

The problem arises, in what sense a culture can, or cannot, die. The issue is one of definition.

That a given society, in a given area, can ever become cultureless, seems an impossibility. We have no record of culture-less human societies, and we do possess archaeological records showing the existence of cultures—rudimentary to be sure, but cultures—for at least several tens of thousands of years. Cultures can evidently deteriorate, in the sense that their total content as well as their highest values may shrink; but there is nothing to show that the process can go on to the point of extinction. In fact, it would be very difficult to imagine circumstances or a process by which a society might lose all culture.

The whole population older than infants in arms would have to be simultaneously exterminated, and the infants would then have to rear themselves unaided.

On the other hand, specific cultures, that is, particular, geographically limited forms of culture, can and do die. They die not only by complete extinction of the populations which carry them, like the aboriginal Tasmanians, but by absorption of societies into larger societies which carry different cultures; and even by displacement of one culture by another, without any annihilation, absorption, or fundamental damage to the underlying society or population. Primitive cultures are dying in this way every year before the "impact of civilization." Popular imagination sees them dying in the death of their last survivor. This happens occasionally; yet more often part or all of the population remains, of mixed blood or still preponderantly native in blood, but with the old culture exchanged, overwhelmingly or wholly, for a new one, or a humble part of a new one. In spite of "The Last of the Mohicans," there is a Mohegan population today; but Mohegan culture has been substantially extinct for a century or more.

The case is really parallel to that in language. We cannot imagine a human society divesting itself wholly of speech. We do know that populations often exchange their former language for another, for a variety of reasons. There is record of many languages that have become wholly extinct, and there must have been even more that perished without progeny and without leaving a record of their existence.

The real question is why particular cultures die. Usually, the cause no doubt is the impingement of other cultures which are in some way "superior" or more viable. In what the superiority consists we do not really know. The specific causes which are alleged in particular instances may or may not be the real ones. Essentially, the culture which survives in competition is the more viable and therefore the one we consider superior; though under different circumstances the qualities which make it superior may differ widely. It may be armaments or organization or training in physical courage or numbers or wealth or cohesion or fanaticism or mechanical inventions or habits of adaptability or education or the lack of it, which seem to be the decisive factors in this or that case.

One problem remains, though it is probably insoluble at present. Can any given particular culture, as an interrelated body of culture traits—that is, as a body of content plus a nexus, —die of itself, from internal causes alone? As "dying" cannot mean complete evaporation of all culture, it must mean a replacement of most of the material and patterns with new material and patterns developed within the culture, until, after a sufficient length of time, the transformation is so great that it is descriptively more useful to speak of the end product as a new culture, or one different from the original one. The reason we cannot give an answer to this question is that nature, so far as we know, has not performed the experiment. Other cultures always do impinge, and the result is that sooner or later we have extinction by replacement, or cultural hybridization. No culture in history has been left in isolation long enough for us to tell whether it would ultimately have remained essentially unchanged, or developed into something basically different, or atrophied indefinitely. Perhaps the native Australians have remained in substantial isolation long enough; but we know nothing of their original culture; and cannot even tell whether it has grown or retrograded.

A concrete case may illustrate. Ancient Egyptian culture is a stock example of a dead culture. The opinion is certainly substantially correct, in that relatively few elements or items of the old Egyptian civilization are elements or items of existing cultures, and none of the basic groupings or patterns, and no part of its total nexus, still lives, in or out of Egypt. We know that after flourishing, largely autonomously, for more than two thousand years, it began to decline by 1000 B.C., more so after 500 B.C., and by 500 A.D. was extinct, essentially as much so as it is now. The outlines of what happened are clear. Control of Egypt was seized by Libyans and Nubians, then the land was overrun by Asiatic conquest, thereafter by Macedonian conquest and Hellenization, then came Romanization in the Empire, and finally Christian ideology and practice. Whatever sporadic remnants of the culture survived 500 A.D. were simply absorbed soon after into Islamic culture. As is well known, even the language was replaced by Arabic.

Two questions suggest themselves. Was the gradual displacement of Egyptian culture by Asiatic, Greek, Roman, Christian, and Islamic culture due to some intrinsic superiority of these in competition? Or had the Egyptian culture "lost its vitality" and become "senile"—that is, were there internal or inherent causes which finally rendered it weaker than the neighboring cultures? In other words, did other cultures outgrow Egyptian culture until they smothered it, or did it of itself age and become feeble until it was extinguished?

I do not see how an answer can be given other than as a personal opinion. It would be easy to argue at length for either view, or that both processes were operative; but very difficult to adduce conclusive evidence. The senility interpretation will seem to some to savor of mysticism, of analogy to vitalism in biology. However, the biological situation is really quite similar. We know that all higher organisms age and die. We know a good deal descriptively about aging, and some of the ways in which freshly mature individuals differ in their physiological processes from senile ones. We do not, however, know why after a certain period these processes increasingly alter one way, and irreversibly so. With all the progress of biology, death remains something we only partly understand, something endowed with an infallibility we cannot explain, though we accept it as a fact and can describe many of its symptoms.

To be sure, that individual organisms must die is no proof that particular cultures must die. We can only say that it leaves room for that possibility to be true; and that, as long as we accept natural death in the organic world without really understanding it, we are not forced to deny cultural death because we cannot explain its processes.

The contrary view, that cultures do not die, age, or necessarily weaken of themselves but are superseded by others, tends to rule out retrogression and to imply constant progress. As soon as a given culture ceases to advance or hold its own, others near it are ready to extend themselves to its carrying society and to replace the existing culture, if lack of communication or isolation do not prevent. It seems difficult to adhere to this view without tacitly subscribing to the assumption that cultures inherently tend to progress. This assumption widely dominates the thought of our time, but is, of course, an untested and emotional one. It is certainly not supported by any more critically tested evidence than there is for the opinion that cultures naturally age and die.

A third view is also possible: that cultures do not necessarily either age or progress, but that they do undergo variations in vigor, originality, and values produced. A culture exposed to the competition of a number of other cultures may be partly made over or largely replaced by one of these, as soon as it has fallen below its own optimum. A greater or more sheltered culture may pass through several internal crises without experiencing serious threat of modification or extinction from outside. But sooner or later, merely on the probabilities of chance, it will lie exposed to competition in one of its weak phases, and one of its neighbors will happen to be in a strong, expansive phase, and then replacement will begin to occur; and after two or three repetitions, extinction ensues.

This interpretation does not assume that either death or progress is inherent; it does assume that fluctuations of cultural vigor are normal. This assumption suffices for the type of analytical study made in the present volume. I have gone one step farther and added the working hypothesis that the reason for the fluctuation is that any notable cultural achievement presupposes adherence to a certain set of patterns; that these patterns, to be effective, must exclude other possibilities, and are therefore limited; that with successful development they accordingly become exhausted; and that there must be a breakdown or abandonment and reformulation of patterns before the culture can go on to new high achievement. That there is some tendency for the several patterns of one culture to form, to culminate, and to dissolve or atrophy simultaneously, is, I think, obvious. How far this tendency is or is not actually realized, has been one of the principal objectives of the investigation.

How little we really know of these matters will be evident from the second point I wish to illustrate concretely by Egyptian civilization; though this will be entirely hypothetical. About 1400 B.C., this culture was at its last great peak, perhaps at its all-time peak. Let us assume that in that year Egypt had by some miracle been entirely cut off from the rest of the world, and had remained until now without communications, impacts, or competition. What then would have been the course of events? I am, of course, not referring to particular happenings in regard to particular cultural features, but to the ensuing configurations of Egyptian culture as a whole and the values attained. That all this could not have happened, that nature would be extremely unlikely to perform such an experiment for us, does not matter. If there were any general understandings which we derive from history, they ought give us some indications, to which we could hold with a certain confidence, of the probable outline of events.

What we are actually justified in concluding is very little. We know that during the century following 1400 there was an attempt to recast several of the patterns of Egyptian culture—the reform of Ikhnaton—and that, except for some conformation of the written to the spoken language, the attempt essentially failed. Egypt reaffirmed her adherence to her old patterns. With this commitment she tended to become repetitive, and in consequence, we may infer, she was, within a few centuries, at a disadvantage in competition with other cultures and nationalities, until, before she knew it, she was essentially swamped by them, beyond recovery. Now in our hypothetical case the fourteenth-century recasting of patterns would no doubt have been attempted and have failed much as in actuality, and perhaps have been followed by the vigorous but shallow reëxpression of the Ramessids. But thereafter? Would culture simply have become more and more stereotyped and empty *ad infinitum,* with new elements or subpatterns admitted only as they conformed to the traditional great patterns, thus helping to reinforce these? Would such new culture material, perhaps not always strictly conformable to the patterns but also not in overt conflict with them, gradually have been evolved, until at last its sheer mass would break down the old patterns and lead to a new ideology? Or is there something in human nature which makes men increasingly restive under the unmitigated ban of past generations, until revolt breaks through to overthrow and reconstitute the whole culture? And, if so, what reconstruction can there be along genuinely new pattern lines if the culture has been wholly isolated and inbred? Will there be anything more than a recombination of old material into nominally rather than intrinsically new patterns? If, on the other hand, reconstruction did not take place, would the ancient patterns have been accentuated to the point of bizarrerie, just short of breakdown through physical impossibility? Or would the fact of repetition as an end in itself have led to automatizing, slovening, abbreviation, and indefinitely progressive deterioration of cultural functioning and achievement, perhaps so far that barbarism or primitiveness would be reattained in a sort of second childhood? Or again, if the patterns had been ruptured from inside, would this have paved the way for a second and third reconstitution, until we might today rediscover an Egypt far more different from than similar to that of 3400–1400, though historically continuous with it? To be specific, might a genuine science of geometry have developed out of the old Egyptian land-measuring in the more than three millennia since 1400, in our hypothetical insulated Egypt? Or was this possible only to a culture which, starting in other directions, was able to combine Egyptian material with non-Egyptian patterns?

Easy as it is to have answers of opinion to such questions, it is plain that, in honesty, anything more than opinion can hardly be claimed. To be sure, where there can be no experiment, wide predictability cannot be looked for. But if we knew any-thing very fundamental about the nature of culture and how it works, we might hope to be able to attach at least partial probabilities to some of the answers to these questions, seeing that we start not only from a defined point, but from a point at the end of a fairly well-known line of development two thousand and more years long. The one thing that seems clear from this hypothetical example is that even the questions could hardly have been asked very intelligibly except in terms of patterns; and demonstrated answers, or partially demonstrated ones, would almost certainly involve understanding of the relation of culture material to patterns and of patterns to the culture whole.

Whether cultures can properly be construed as undergoing something like inherent aging and death, or whether they succumb only to the accidents of competition; whether they depend for their notable growths on refructification or cross-fertilization from other cultures, or can rejuvenate themselves indefinitely until they have become quite different entities, are problems which I thus leave unanswered. With all we know of history, we understand too little to give conclusive judgments. What I have dealt with primarily in this work is the life histories of some of the better-marked patterns in the larger civilizations, and secondarily their interrelations within culture wholes.

§125. Spengler

Certain resemblances of the approach here followed to that of Spengler will be obvious, so that it seems necessary to define our respective positions.

Spengler's contribution to history seems to be his recognition of the importance of the fundamental patterns of cultures. As against these qualitatively distinct patterns, the quantitative aspect of culture content and still more the personalized events of history are to him relatively insignificant. This attitude implies that what is being sought is an understanding of history with emphasis upon culture as such, extricated from the web of biographic personalities and their individual acts in which the raw phenomena lie before us. With this attitude my own concurs: not as alone legitimate, but as valid and fruitful. Where we differ is that Spengler has attempted the difficult task of expressing the essential patterns themselves, which necessitates an intuitionally subjective approach; while I have set myself the more specific problem of defining the time-space configurations of part of the patterns as they find expression in their florescences. As a quasi-objective mechanism for this defining, I have used the roster of genius as generally accepted in dated history: individuals are dealt with, but not as an end: they are no longer personalities, but measures of culture growth. Spengler uses individuals as material only sporadically, and chiefly as exemplary illustrations. But our point of view with regard to them as historic material is the same: essentially, persons are indicators of cultural phenomena.

Spengler also assumes that the important patterns of any one culture are bound by some nexus into a grand master pattern; and that, this nexus being inherent, great cultures can never blend or assimilate. Each is distinct and, having expressed or exhausted itself, must die, to be superseded by others. They may take over nonsignificant material content from former cultures, but they work this over into their own forms according to their own master plan, which begins unconsciously. Cultures are therefore as distinct as personalities, or even as organisms of different genus.

This view I do not share; but also do not believe that it may be unqualifiedly discarded. I speak with hesitancy because I do not see that we can yet discriminate satisfactorily and consistently between culture material or content and culture forms or patterns. The two are certainly different things, but often not easily kept apart. Culture material is surely borrowed on an enormous scale. With it some patterns are also usually taken over from alien cultures. Spengler presumably would hold that these remain organically unincorporated or that the absorbed patterns are made over in conformity with the pattern system of the absorbing culture. That the latter is true to some degree is clear. It is recognized by all anthropologists. The Japanese reworking of Chinese forms, the Renaissance reworking of Classical and Mediaeval ones, are cases in point. But is there really an inherent master pattern or plan existing as something individuate and unalterable? Or is the seeming master plan the result largely of the more or less fortuitous aggregation of component material and forms from many sources, gradually working itself into a secondary integration, which in fortunate cases may gradually attain a high degree of internal concordance? The general trend of anthropologists, and apparently of historians, is to assume the latter; at least, to assume that accident plays a part. And I see no reason for disregarding their cumulative experience. On the other hand, specific items, which normally are cultural material, are easiest to deal with reliably in history and in comparison, and are most often dealt with; and it is easy to become so preoccupied with them as to forget the deeper patterns, or to tend to argue from experience with items to disbelief in patterns. At any rate, the working-out of a coördinating system of high-value patterns into an integrated culture, however it may come about, is one of the great and rare events in the life history of mankind. The distinctiveness of these larger growths Spengler feels with deep intensity.

The conviction of an inherent and indestructible nexus between all the patterns of a culture is cardinal with Spengler, and leads to his organic parallel, which so irritatingly rasps most of his professional audience.

The fact that the paralleling of culture phenomena and organic phenomena constitutes an analogy is not necessarily and *per se* a fatal defect; it is only a limitation. A whale is not a fish, but it functions like one at so many points that its aquatic adaptation is certainly an important part of the phenomena it presents. The question at issue in all such cases is to learn how far the analogy extends and where it ends. To discard the analogous phenomena or refuse to see any significance in them is as one-sided as mystically to see significance only in the parallels. There is nothing in Spengler that I can find which would suggest that he considers culture growth an organic process in the modern biological sense of the word organic. On the contrary, his whole endeavor is to understand specific culture phenomena in terms of larger culture totalities. These larger wholes are, naturally enough, not so sharply definable as their constituent parts; much as the abstract concept of a mammal cannot be presented with the same precision as the concept of a whale or a mouse. In dealing with these larger entities, and with their major parts or stages, Spengler therefore falls back on analogical or figurative language. It is the metaphors like "spring" or "ripening" or "senility" of cultures that have aroused particular opposition. It is, however, pedantic to take these figures of speech literally. Precisely denotive terms would no doubt be better; but if he had been able to find them, Spengler would presumably have used them. And, it might be added, let those who can supply better ones suggest them, if they wish to do something constructive. In the history of art styles no one objects, in the absence of anything better, to terms like "archaic" and "flamboyant," the significance of which is also connotive rather than denotive.

Whether particular cultures really pass through fixed parallel stages and then inevitably die is another problem, and an important one. Spengler takes the fact for granted. I have tried to proceed by more inductive examination, and have come to much less positive conclusions.

The two Spenglerian principles with which this study is, then, in essential accord are, first, the existence of certain fundamental patterns characteristic of each major culture, and second, that these occur in limited growths. The opinions at which I halt are three. The first is that the basic patterns of each culture can necessarily be reduced to a single master or key pattern which controls the culture. The second is that the cultures necessarily develop through essentially parallel stages; and the third, that they die of themselves. All three of these "necessarily's" I hold to be legitimate problems, but wholly unproved, and difficult to investigate because it is difficult to evaluate the objective comparability of the facts.

On the matter of procedure, it is difficult to analyze Spengler because he is so little a scientist or historian that he does not really present evidence. He is an intuitive dogmatist perfervid about a completed system. Facts which do not fit into the system, he simply does not see, ordinarily, and so does not have to meet. Those which do fit are only exemplifications, and so do not have to be arranged in any order. It is always the system, the cardinal idea, which counts, so this is restated and restated in a variable context. It is really an attitude which he is illustrating over and over. As for inductively built-up proof, there is none. When he has a telling bit of evidence, it is merely mentioned; it is not analyzed, but used as a springboard for another restatement of the system and its a-prioristic value perceptions. It is hard to judge how much or little his case rests on, because evidence is never presented coherently.

The nearest he comes to an orderly array of data in historical terms is in the three folded-in tables at the end of his Introduction. These are designated as a conspectus of results, but are scarcely referred to again; they are evidently regarded as illustrative. They aim to show developmental "contemporaneity" or equivalence, and contain dates. They are the only passage in Spengler which is at all orderly or methodical in the customary sense of the words. They are therefore worth analyzing a bit.

The three tables present epochs or stages of Geist, Kultur, and Politik. The content shows Geist to mean thought, and Kultur, art. Each contains four columns, each of which is devoted to the developments in one culture. The Occidental and Ancient (Antike) cultures appear in all three tables; the Arabic (perhaps more often called Magian in the text) in tables 1 and 2; Egyptian in 2 and 3; Indian in 1; Chinese in 3 only. Table 1 is arranged to show four successive stages, called Spring, Summer, Fall, Winter. Tables 2 and 3 follow a different plan: Vorzeit (prodromal), Culture (Early and Late), and Civilization. Not a word is wasted on the difference of organization; nor on the fact that the two plans do not agree temporally. I tabulate their dates for the Classical, Arabic, and Occidental cultures.

"Spring" and "Early Culture" are made to begin at the same dates for each culture, and "Winter" and "Civilization" also begin simultaneously. "Civilization" is carried on much farther, however. And "Summer" is silently divided up between

"Early" and "Late Culture" in tables 2 and 3. Not only do dates fail to agree, but stages appear and disappear without a word of comment.

There is a similar indeterminateness with regard to geographical and national limits. The prodromal stage of Arabic-Magian culture is characterized as Persian-Seleucid. The earlier stages include primitive Christianity at least to St.

FROM THE SPENGLER TABULATION

1. THOUGHT

	Classical	Arabian	Occidental
Spring	1100–700	1–400	900–1400
Summer	700–500?	400–700	1400–1700
Fall	500?–300	700–1000!	1700–1800
Winter	300–200[b]	800 seq.	1800–1900+

2, 3. ART, POLITICS

		Classical	Arabian	Occidental
	Prodromal	1600–1100	500–1	500–900
[Spring]	Culture, E.	1100–650	1–500	900–1500
[Summer] [Fall]	Culture, L.	650–350	500–800	1500–1800
[Winter]	Civiliz. 1	350–100[b]	800–1050	1800–2000
	Civiliz. 2, 3	100[b]–200[a]	1050–(1600)	2000 seq.

[b] Before Christ; [a] after Christ.

Augustine, then Mohammed and Islamic thinkers and movements, but also Byzantine elements (Iconoclasts, St. Sophia, mosaics, in tables 1 and 2). In the text, Roman architecture is made Syrian and therefore Magian, the Pantheon is the first mosque, Diocletian the first Khalif.[6] But elsewhere,[7] Roman architecture falls into the final stage of Civilization of Ancient culture, and so is the *panem et circenses* homeless mob housed in metropolitan tenements.[8]

I concede that the limits of cultures can be drawn differently from the limits which I have observed. An argument could

---

[6] I, 272–276, 1923 ed.
[7] Table 2.
[8] I, 46.

easily be maintained, for instance, that Byzantine culture should be reckoned rather as part of a Syrian-Christian-Magian-Islamic one, emerging around the turn of the era, characterized by successive Magian, Syncretistic, Christian, and Mohammedan stages, and really dominating most of the Roman Empire even in the west. I believe that more evidence is on the side of the view that Roman civilization was but an interlude, and Byzantine a final phase, in a larger Hellenic-Roman or Mediterranean civilization. It is, however, a question of preponderance and therefore of construal of evidence, and Spengler's view may prove to be the deeper and juster. But even then, Roman data cannot be assigned both to Magian and to Classical civilization; at least not without stated criteria for the discrimination. Cultures are complex and may participate in more than one major movement. Such a situation calls for analytic distinction and assignment of parts or trends. I would not go so far as to say that Spengler uses the identical evidence in contrary arguments. But he does fail wholly to state the basis on which he allots historically associated material to diverse culture growths. He seems as constitutionally incapable of analysis as of methodical order. Besides apperceiving intuitively, he can only synthesize. This seems the basis of the "mysticism" with which he is so often charged.

It may be worth while to examine another specific case. According to Spengler,[9] the Renaissance is a purely Florentine phenomenon, and at that merely the ideal of one social class; it mastered only certain arts of picture and word, penetrated to costume and gesture, but did not alter the Denkweise or Lebensgefühl of western Europe. The Renaissance is a local countermovement against the Faustian Gothic current of European culture, of whose Weltanschauung the Baroque is a continuation even in Italy. The Renaissance is definable only negatively, in terms of the Gothic which is its foundation. It is not a renewal of Antiquity, only an Occidental Faustian dream of a supposedly antique existence which, however, was more Magian-Syrian than Classic. So far his interpretation.

---

[9] I, 302–310, 1923 ed.

That the Renaissance was not a rebirth, except superficially, is a commonplace. That it represents an Italian reworking of High Mediaeval (Gothic) form more acceptable to Italians, and that Florence took the lead in this movement, is the view which I have developed in preceding pages. That the Renaissance remained uninfluential in Europe is a paradox intelligible only in terms of Spengler's preconceived definition of the Renaissance as a brief, local reaction. This definition in turn flows from his monistic urge to conceive every major culture as a harmonious whole, expressing one set of attitudes at every point and without remainder. In Spengler's own language, my interpretation of the Renaissance as the culmination of the Italian growth within the multinational Occidental growth to which it contributed importantly, while yet remaining a truly national expression, would be a "polyphonic" or "contrapuntal" interpretation in distinction from his compulsively simple one. With all his demand for recognition of "das Werdende," Spengler sees "becoming" occurring only within a set of predetermined, unalterable frames of fundamental culture patterns. It is in these unalterabilities that his restless drives evidently find repose.[10]

There is a certain strange parallel between the ways of thinking of Spengler and of the Graebner-Schmidt Kulturkreis school, in spite of his emphasis on organic, determinative relations within cultures and the Kulturkreis method of operating with culture material as something randomly cast and carried about and forming innumerable associations that are mainly fortuitous. Both do recognize the phenomenal variability of human culture, and have therefore shrunk from a monogenetic explanation. But both have recourse to some seven or eight entities in terms of which culture is explainable with no important residuum. These entities as the Kulturkreis doctrine operates with them—totem culture, two-class culture, etc.—are,

---

[10] Another dogmatic evaluation is of Chinese culture as running its course between 1300 B.C. and 200 A.D. (table 3). I do not characterize this interpretation as wrong or absurd; I can understand it; I have divided Chinese culture history into two phases at about the same point of 100–200 A.D. But one cannot summarily dismiss T'ang and Sung art, poetry, philosophy, and science as nonexistent or as mere Byzantine repetitions of no inner cultural weight.

historically, wholly hypothetical, and only secondarily buttressed by selected evidence from ethnography, archaeology, and history. In one sense Spengler's entities are, or appear to be, accepted historical entities, like Egyptian or Occidental civilization; but actually these terms seem rather to cover, in his mind, certain concepts of essential qualities inwardly related each into a system which can be better apperceived than expounded. These are his unalterables just referred to; and to them he allocates what is significant in culture; the rest can be ignored. The quality common to the two systems is the essentially complete resolution of the totality of human culture into a number of ultimate and definitely limited entities of assumed but really unexamined historic reality and separateness.

There is a certain injustice in dissecting Spengler as I have done in the preceding pages. He is not trying to work empirically and he is not writing history. He is interpreting history as part of a philosophy which he feels passionately. The very titles of his chapter subdivisions show this: The Meaning of Numbers, The Idea of Fate and the Principle of Causality, Macrocosmos, Soul Image and Life Sentiment. When Italian Renaissance art and Chou Chinese political thought are touched on under captions like these, it is evident that they are not being treated systematically as a historian would treat them, but as exemplifications of a larger scheme. Spengler is really telling us how he believes all history should be dealt with, rather than dealing with it specifically and in order. He need therefore not have been considered at all here: technically, he could have been ignored as a philosopher, as he disdains historians. Inwardly, his interpretations and my approach do bear kinship; which is the reason I have tried to trace the degree and distance of relationship.

A much less weighty but more systematic effort to establish repetitive regularity in culture history is the essay—perhaps originally a lecture—by Flinders Petrie, *The Revolutions of Civilization,* first published in 1911. In 15,000 words and 55 pictures he outlines the beginnings, culminations, and decay of sculpture, painting, literature, mechanics, science, and wealth in five successive western growths of civilization—Egyptian, Mycenaean, Classical, Arab, European; finds these activities each reaching its "liberation" in the same order, though with lengthening interval; compares these civilizations with eastern ones, which fall into the same scheme of an average duration of 1,300 to 1,500 years, but precede the western by two to five and a half centuries; determines that culture adheres to race rather than land; and pays his respects to causes of change, including climate and migration. Apart from the Petrie chronology for Egypt, Mesopotamia, and Crete, now accepted by no one else, we get such judgments as European sculpture attaining its peak around 1240, the Renaissance being "but the resort of copying an earlier period"; and of European literature—characterized by plain prose—achieving its liberation from Archaism under Bacon and Jonson in 1600. Evidence, though systematically marshaled, is obviously treated as cavalierly here as by Spengler. At the same time, the booklet is not without insights, which render it perhaps as stimulating as irritating; which is the reason for its mention here. Of the fluctuation in quality-achievement of patterns, Petrie has a very clear if often dogmatic perception. He also realizes that there is a problem in this culture-quality growth and in its time limitations—though his answers are hasty.[11]

§126. Exceptional Isolated Genius

The procedure followed throughout this work has rested on the assumption that geniuses tend to cluster in time and space, as well as in their relation to particular pattern growths. All in all, it will probably be conceded that the mass of material presented tends overwhelmingly to substantiate this assumption, which indeed many would be ready to accept as so plain from common knowledge as hardly to need verification by cited evidence. There are, however, exceptions; and if there

---

[11] The works of Toynbee and Sorokin have pertinence here, in that they also are synthetic interpretations of broad masses of historical data. They did not come to my notice until the present study had been written. Brief comment on them will be found in the Bibliography.

were enough of these exceptions, the assumed principle would become correspondingly dubious. It thus seems only fair that the exceptions should be considered collectively, instead of being admitted, or explained away, scatteringly. In this section, accordingly, I have gathered the principal instances of admitted genius that do not occur in a constellation nor in relation to a pattern growth.

Philosophy.—Erigena, 815/25–ca. 880, stands alone. His predecessor Alcuin, 735–804, the theologian-humanist of the Carolingian renaissance, was hardly a philosopher. Leibnitz, 1646–1716, stands definitely isolated in Germany. He has no predecessors, and, except for his expositor Wolff, born 1679, no successor of consequence until Kant, born 1724. In Occidental philosophy as a whole Leibnitz is not particularly isolated: witness Pascal, born 1623, Geulincx 1625, Locke 1632, Spinoza 1632, Malebranche 1638, Berkeley 1685.

Science.—Diophantos is isolated in the nature of his mathematics rather than in time and place; witness Pappos, his near-contemporary.

The Pole Copernicus, 1473–1543, the Dane Tycho Brahe, 1545/6–1601, the Germans Kepler, 1571–1630, and Leibnitz, 1646–1716, are the outstanding examples. They were all northeast Europeans, as the cultural Occident was constituted then; but the time span which includes them is too long for a constellation, even for the three astronomers alone. Copernicus, who is said to have been half German by descent and was born in the once-German city of Thorn, would fit into a contemporary minor German constellation;[12] but the others will fit nothing. Tycho had a contemporary in the mathematician Finck, 1561, but then there was nothing Danish until Steno, 1638, and Roemer, 1644. I cannot rid myself of a half persuasion that the three astronomers, at least, form some kind of configuration;[13] but if so, it is of a laxer order than the other con-

---

[12] But he is also said to have had a Czech grandfather, and to have been taught by the Polish astronomer Brudzewski, 1445–1497.

[13] My colleague R. H. Lowie contributes the pertinent suggestion that common use of Latin made the scientists from Copernicus to Leibnitz "virtually men of one country."

figurations dealt with in this work, with regard to limitation in time, geography, and nationality.

The French mathematician Vieta, 1540–1603, is not a good fit; nor the Swiss Bürgi, 1552–1632.

Painting.—Goya, 1746–1828, is the most flagrant case of isolation; François Clouet, ca. 1500–1572, a milder one.

Sculpture.—Thorwaldsen, born in 1770 in Denmark, comes nearest to being an exception. He is a full generation too early for inclusion in the crop of talents produced in peripheral Europe during the internationalistic phase of the nineteenth century. However, the tendency is to regard him as no more than of second or third rank—a sort of Mengs famous in his day because the day was otherwise nearly empty. He is certainly a lesser figure than his contemporary Canova, who, while also isolated in stature and time, is nevertheless connected with the greater past of Italian sculpture by a groundswell of continuous pattern tradition.

Literature.—Villon, born 1431, is probably the outstanding exception to the rule. His vein is narrow and his output small, but its quality has never been denied, and he stands wholly alone.

Tasso is a troublesome fit, as discussed under "Italian Literature." He was born in 1544, sixty years too late for the Renaissance group. Guarini, 1538, suffices neither as a bridge to the past, nor for a quite satisfactory constellation around Tasso.

The Norwegian Dane Holberg, born 1684, is too early for a configuration.

Bilderdijck, 1756–1832, rated the second greatest Dutch writer, is outside any constellation.

Of another order are the writers who fill certain periods of several European literatures: notably the sixteenth century in France, with Rabelais and Montaigne, again the eighteenth with Voltaire and Rousseau, the eighteenth in England, and perhaps lesser groups elsewhere. Here we are dealing not with individuals outside of constellations, but with constellations which, contrary to conventional histories of literature, I rate as relatively low-level. Perhaps my judgment is somewhat forced because I am interested in variations of level. On the contrary, literary historians are generally interested in continuity; or start from it as an unavowed postulate. The chief justification of my view is the fact that the periods in question produced only prose which can be regarded as of enduring value; and that, in spite of the quality of the form of this prose, its content is overwhelmingly not aesthetic in nature, but rational. Voltaire and Pope, I would admit as mere virtuoso poets.[14] In other words, I am more rigorous in separating out what might be called pure literature. The histories in their horror of hiatus create a continuum by treating two orders of writing as if they were one. Some prose is certainly literature in every sense; but not all prose, not even all well-written prose, is fully such.

It is also observable that the periods thus in question, at least those most decisively questionable, fall after the invention of printing, with its inevitable tendency to increase readers' consumption and the mass production of writing. On a close enough view of China we should probably perceive a similar situation there, since printing became established by Sung times.

Apparent but unreal exceptions to the rule are eminent men born in the Scandinavian, Slavic, Hungarian, and Spanish peripheries of Europe in the nineteenth century, when West European active civilization doubled its area by extending to these areas. The nationalities involved, except Russia, are relatively small either in territory or in population. The total number of geniuses produced in all activities by each country would therefore expectably be few, and the number in any one activity would be only one or two, sometimes none. Hence Chopin and Curie in Poland, Smetana in Bohemia, Sibelius in Finland, Abel and Bohr nearly a century apart in Denmark, Bolyai in Hungary, Unamuno and Picasso in Spain, and so on. These men do not stem from truly national growths, but rather from a cosmopolitan growth with a series of minor national

---

[14] Rabelais, on the contrary, is a pattern-destroyer, or the attempting shaper of a pattern directly contrary to the one which French literature was evolving.

facies. As soon as they are reckoned together, therefore, as they deserve to be, they constellate into sizable groups of scientists, writers, musicians, and even painters. Or, if we disregard the nature of their activities, there is usually a fair-sized cluster in each nationality. That this interpretation is warranted is confirmed by the fact that Russia, more or less equal in population to the other culturally marginal countries considered as a unit, shows a nineteenth-century constellation of its own, of about equal size and importance, in science, literature, and music. This series of exceptions, then, is only seeming.

I may have overlooked some names, especially near-second-rank ones, that occur in my own previous pages. But in the main the foregoing bill of exceptions is perhaps reasonably complete. It is, I think, not a heavy list as compared with the immense number that fit into either a major constellation or a pulse or phase constellation. As social and historical phenomena in general run, the data dealt with may be fairly said to yield an unusually good fit to the configurational principle assumed at the outset. Whatever the cause, genius and the higher cultural values do appear in nature with a definite tendency to segregation in space and time.

As to the reason for this tendency, I advance none, other than to suggest that all human beings are the products of their culture to a much greater degree than we ordinarily imagine, and that cultures appear to grow in patterns and to fulfill or exhaust these. Why cultures so often behave in this way, especially in their intellectual, aesthetic, and nationalistic aspects, is not clear; but it seems to be one of their most distinctive properties.

§127. Conclusions

For convenience, the principal conclusions arrived at in the foregoing pages are summarized.

It is clear that aesthetic and intellectual endeavors resulting in higher values preponderantly realize themselves in temporary bursts, or growths, in all the higher civilizations examined. The same sort of bursts or growths tend to characterize nationalistic development, as expressed in successful political organization and expansion. Whether the phenomenon holds also for wealth and population, is a separate question, which I have not gone into because the data are of a different order and seem much more difficult to acquire over continuous long ranges of history. It seems possible that the behavior of wealth and population may prove different, because these phenomena are naturally expressible quantitatively, whereas the index for those considered is essentially qualitative through the medium of genius. At any rate, genius is one way in which the degree of aesthetic and intellectual achievement can be expressed. The world has, however, never been ready to admit any strong correlation between genius and wealth accumulation; and the peculiarly quantitative consideration of population size is obviously also a distinct matter.

It is entirely conceivable that there may be a connection between growth of population and wealth and the achievement growths which have been analyzed. It would certainly be somewhat difficult to imagine highly cultural achievements reaching their culmination among a population whose size and wealth were consistently declining. No serious long-range and comparative studies appear, however, to have been undertaken on this problem, and it seems wise to defer opinion until they shall have been made.

The tracing of the degree or quality of value growths has been made on the assumption that genius is a fair representative of cultural value. It is the clustering of recognized genius in time and space and common speech which is the basis of the value-growth appraisals which have been outlined in this book.

This implies a definition of genius supplementary to the customary or popular one that a genius is an individual who is eminently superior in his mental endowment. A social definition of genius may also be offered. Geniuses are the indicators of the realization of coherent pattern growths of cultural value.

A corollary is that most of the potential geniuses born are never realized, so far as history or human values are concerned. The supply of genius, physiologically or psychologically speaking, ought to remain essentially constant in any one race within any period which is not unduly long. However, inasmuch as even the peoples possessing higher civilization have produced cultural products of value only intermittently, during relatively small fractions of their time span, it follows that more individuals born with the endowment of genius have been inhibited by the cultural situations into which they were born than have been developed by other cultural situations.

The reason for the transience of high-value patterns is not altogether clear. It is evident that such patterns must be selective and somehow differentiated or specialized. This in turn necessitates that any such pattern fairly early takes a particular direction. The pattern is then gradually pushed to its limits in that direction. These limits may be the limitations of the physical world. But they need not be such. The very selection which at the outset is necessary if a distinctive pattern is to be produced, is almost certain later on to become a limitation. It is then often or normally too late to go back and widen the scope of the pattern without undoing the entire growth which it has achieved. It seems to be historically almost as difficult to reconstitute a pattern fundamentally, or to widen greatly the scope of a growth, as at an earlier stage it is difficult to get a distinctive pattern growth or pattern value started. Not infrequently, when a pattern has attained realization or reached saturation, its limitations appear to be felt and efforts are made to alter or enlarge it. If these efforts take the form of a pause in activity, there may be a reconstitution of energy and direction, with the result that, after a lull, growth is resumed along somewhat new and broader lines. The early eighteenth-century pause in the growth of European science is an illustration of this type of phenomenon.

More often, perhaps, there is no such abatement or recession once a peak of pattern realization has been attained. Endeavors become evident toward strain and rupture of the pattern. The impulses toward change and growth persist, but take the form of extravagance, flamboyance, or alteration for the sake of novelty. At other times these endeavors are repressed, with the result that, change, or at any rate important change, being no longer tolerated, there is no recourse for activity other than in essential repetition, which necessarily brings with it deterioration of quality. This is the condition familiar as Byzantinism. Such Byzantinism need not be permanent, nor need it involve the whole of a civilization. If it remains sufficiently brief, it may behave somewhat like one of the temporary lulls and be followed by a period of renewed activities with more or less reconstituted patterns. If the interval is not too long, and the reconstituted growth reaches higher values than the original one, the type is that of a lull followed by the second phase of a greater growth. If, on the other hand, the interval is longer, and especially if the second-growth pulse fails to reach as high an achievement as the first, the later effort is of the type of an attenuated renaissance episode in a Byzantine decline.

Particular attention has been paid both to these lulls and to the pulses or phases which they separate. Latin literature, with its three or four pulses separated by definite time intervals, is a case in point. So is Egyptian art in a very much longer time span.

In well-unified and well-defined civilizations the configuration of growth and decline may be clean-cut even though marked by several crests. In a multinational civilization like that of Europe, each nation shows its own crests, and at the same time the several culminations replace each other, like instruments in an orchestra, so that there is a larger polyphonic configuration for the supernational civilization as a whole.

There are a number of configurations with several crests, of which the middle one is clearly the highest. In them, the first and last growth pulses partake of the nature of prologue and epilogue; or, prodromal and aftermath efforts may be better designations. The total culture history of Spain, and again that of ancient Greece, seem to fall into this form.

The growth curves are sometimes symmetrical like a normal variability curve; sometimes skew, the crest appearing either before or after the middle of the duration. Skew curves are, if anything, more frequent for single activities. The curves for total cultures show somewhat more of a tendency toward symmetry, presumably because they are a composite of curves for several activities. There is enough variability to make it uncertain whether growth is typically expressible by a symmetrical normal curve.

The duration is also extremely variable, ranging from as little as thirty or forty years to as much as five hundred or a thousand. On the whole, it can be said that growths tend to be longer in proportion as they produce what posterity has recognized as great values. There are, however, large differences in duration, apart from this consideration. Thus the Sanskrit drama took several times as long to develop and decline as the Elizabethan, even with the Restoration drama counted in as part of the latter. There do seem to be significant national differences. Irrespective of kind of activity, all datable growths in India are slow.

There is no clear evidence of a tendency toward acceleration of growth as we pass from ancient to modern times. Of course, in this connection, comparison would be illegitimate between a culture like that of France, which is only one strand of the larger European culture, and, say, that of India or China, which, culturally speaking, are continental rather than national. Occidental culture as a whole has already developed about as long as ancient and Asiatic ones.

I do not set a norm of duration for the growths of larger civilizations, though the usual estimates of a thousand to fifteen hundred years are probably approximately right as an average. It seems doubtful whether any absolute figure can have much meaning: it would be only the doubtfully significant statistical average of a small number of instances. That is, it is uncertain whether duration values *per se* are significant of anything inherent. It seems reasonable that conditions of area, population, and kind of culture developed, which are almost necessarily variable, would be of sufficient influence to prevent any standard duration. The similarity between instances is probably less in tempo than in configuration; and this suggests that the real constants lie in the growth processes involved.

There is an evident tendency for growths in distinct activities to be associated in time, but no clear indication that a successful growth in one activity must be accompanied by growths in other activities. In other words, successful activity growths in one culture may be few or solitary; and many civilizations have failed to attain high achievement in one or another activity. That, on the contrary, growths tend to occur associated may be attributed to the fact that distinctive success in one activity presupposes a high degree of cultural energy, and once this is aroused it is unlikely to remain restricted to a single activity. But again, there is no reason to believe that once such cultural energy is aroused it must necessarily spread to all possible fields of cultural activity, since it is notorious that civilizations differ in their interests and emphases. The most marked example toward close clustering in time of the culminations in diverse activities is furnished by Greek civilization. Here the unusually small population involved may have been the cause; not only the number in any one city-state, but the total number of Greeks, was small. Our familiarity with Greek history has, then, served to set up this case as a type. Actually, it is almost unique in its degree of simultaneity of activity developments.

There is no marked evidence of an inherent order of succession in which the several cultural activities develop. So far as there is a tendency for sculpture to precede painting, the cause lies not in anything cultural, but in the fact that sculpture is the physically simpler art. The tendency toward sequence, if there is one, lies in the laws of nature rather than in some law of culture. Science possesses certain inherent relations with philosophy, and philosophy again with religion, and religion again with art. But these relations have been worked out quite diversely in their cultural manifestations. Science, philosophy, and religion impinge on one another psychologically, but their expressions in cultural growth do have manifold, and may have minimal, relations.

Religion, however, in general precedes aesthetic and intellectual developments of note, and a history of the arts is frequently one of gradual emancipation from religion as they attain their culminations. This relation appears to inhere in the definition of the concepts. We hardly recognize philosophy and science as such until they have reached a certain level of development and organization. Below this threshold, which we do not avow but nevertheless recognize, we tend to treat these activities as nonexistent. Somewhat similarly for the arts, though there the threshold is a certain degree of quality attainment. Religion, on the other hand, is more or less omnipresent. At any rate, we tend to deal with it as if there were no corresponding threshold. The result is that when we begin our consideration of florescences in art, science, or philosophy, it is against a background of preëxisting religion, which has inevitably had relation with the formative or prethreshold stages of the other activities. Nevertheless, the criterion of emancipation of these activities from religious influence has a certain empirical value of defining their degree of development.

To the question whether there may be national florescences without accompanying cultural ones, or vice versa, the answer must be yes, although such happenings are rare in history. It is evident that ethnic or national energy and cultural energy are related but are not the same thing. Ethnic energy may be conceived of as potential cultural energy, or as cultural energy expressed in simple and immediate forms, with more emphasis on specifically social than on specifically cultural ends.

Of some importance is the relation of cultural content, which is fairly readily expressible quantitatively through descriptive enumeration, and cultural forms or patterns, which we apperceive qualitatively and which seem quantitatively expressible only by the indirect method of estimating the rating of genius. The difficulty of dealing with the relation lies in the fact that culture content and culture form occur only in association with each other, and are therefore imperfectly distinguishable. Here is a fundamental problem of anthropology which still awaits most of its solution. It will probably be conceded that more growth of value can be attained on a larger body of content or material. Content tends to grow cumulatively, whereas forms are more or less predetermined by their origins. The result is that a certain set of forms may be realized or fulfilled while the content of the culture is still growing. In that event, the consequence is a partial dissolution with reconstitution on an ampler scale; after which the patterns may proceed in a new growth or pulse. Fourteenth- and fifteenth-century transalpine Europe is an example of such an interval between pattern growths, while culture content was rapidly expanding.

The more insular cultures, like those of Japan and England, seem to possess a somewhat retarded growth, which, however, is steadier and less intermittent than that of corresponding mainland cultures exposed to more numerous and sharper competitive contacts.

Geographically, a radiating spread of culture growth can usually be traced from a first hearth or focus over the larger area finally occupied. This is in accord with what anthropologists have again and again noted in regard to specific diffusions. They have, it is true, mostly dealt with items of culture content; but the same process of spread seems to apply more or less to culture patterns and values. The spread is perhaps most often from the center outward; but the original focus may be situated on a geographical margin and the spread therefore be fanwise rather than radiating. If so, the focus is likely to lie on a frontier exposed to foreign stimulation. It is also possible for much of the periphery to develop first, and the remaining spread then to be centripetal.

Another type of centripetal change sometimes occurs during the decline of a large civilization: it then shrinks upon itself; as Mediterranean or Classic civilization, after having spread from the Hellenic area to include the Roman West, retracted later within its original Greek limits, the West relapsing into barbarism.

Cultural death has here been construed only as the death of particular cultures or forms of culture; that is, as the replacement of particular patterns, which may be of higher value, by other patterns. The question whether a whole culture can die of itself through internal causes or inherent aging is not answered.

A final review listing of such genius as has occurred in isolation shows such occurrence to be definitely rare, and justly to be designated as exceptional. The methodological assumption on which this volume rests seems therewith to be vindicated, at any rate approximately. A derivative corollary is that we human beings are, at least so far as our accomplishments go, the products of our cultures much more than we ordinarily recognize.

As for findings that are universal, or such as might express a general sociology of human history, this investigation has attained only to approximations, though some of these may stimulate further inquiry. My own feeling is that the growth-configuration approach results rather in a multiplicity of specific historic findings. These are occasionally new, more frequently a shifted emphasis or realigned interpretation. And the endless events of history are lifted out of their level of near-uniformity into organized relief, by an attitude which consciously recognizes pattern-growth configurations in their space-time relations as well as in their value relations.

BIBLIOGRAPHY

BIBLIOGRAPHY

THE FORMAL bibliography which follows includes only part of the books consulted. Much of the raw material used was taken from encyclopaedias. A compiled work often possesses the advantage of giving compactly the factual data needed, without undue ramification or originality of judgment. An elementary textbook of, say, a literature is likely to present only the greater names with which the present undertaking is concerned: it is in itself a precipitate of many opinions.

Of encyclopaedias, I have used, in English, the Britannica and several American ones, according as they were available or convenient at one time or another; in French, Larousse; in German, both Meyer and Brockhaus.

BIOGRAPHICAL, GENERAL

HOEFER, ed. Nouvelle Biographie générale. 46 vols. 1862–1877.

Lippincott's Pronouncing Dictionary of Biography. Philadelphia, 1930.

MICHAUD, L. G. Biographie universelle, ancienne et moderne. 52 vols. 1811–1828.

PETRIE, W. M. FLINDERS. The Revolutions of Civilization. 1911 (1922).
> Discussed in Chapter Eleven, §125, pp. 833–834.

SOROKIN, P. A. Social and Cultural Dynamics. Vols. 1–3, 1937. (Fluctuation of forms of art, Vol. 1; of systems of truth, ethics, and law, Vol. 2; of social relationships, war, and revolution, Vol. 3.)
> This work, like my present one, deals analytically with variations in the intensity of cultural activity. It differs in being based on a scheme: the classification of cultures into Sensate, Ideational, Idealistic, and Mixed. Its underlying data are more elaborate, Dr. Sorokin having had the benefit of a corps of research assistants. I did not use the book: when it began to appear in 1937, my writing was nearly completed.

SPENGLER, O. Der Untergang des Abendlandes.
> I have used the two-volume German edition of 1923. Discussed in Chapter Eleven, §125, pp. 825 ff.

TOYNBEE, A. J. A Study of History. 6 vols. 1935–1939.
> An interpretation of the cultural aspects of human history in an endeavor to find constants; hence more or less sociological, with leaning on concepts such as challenge-and-response, withdrawal-and-return, and genesis, growth, breakdown, and disintegration of civilizations. The plan embraces thirteen sections, of which five are treated in the six volumes published by 1939. The value of the work lies in its many amazingly penetrating and

Toynbee, A. J.—(*Continued*)
original historical insights, not in its sociological frame or mechanisms.
The civilizations recognized are: *Abortive:* Old Irish, Viking Scandinavian,
Far Eastern Christian (Nestorian, etc.), Syrian (?); *Arrested:* Polynesian,
Eskimo, Nomadic, Ottoman, Spartan; *Unrelated:* Egyptian, Sumerian, Old
Chinese ("Sinic"), Minoan, Andean, Mayan; *Sub-affiliated:* Old Indian,
Hittite, Hellenic (including Roman), Syrian (?); *Related:* Arabic, Iranic
Islamic, Hindu, Buddhistic Chinese, Japanese, Near Eastern Christian,
Russian, Western; *Supra-affiliated* (virtual continuations): Babylonian-
Assyrian, Mexican, Late Maya or Yucatec. I read the work only after con-
clusion of my own.

Philosophy, Science, Philology

Aster, E. von. Geschichte der Philosophie. 2d ed., 1935.
Contains "Zeittafel," pp. 446–459.

Buckley, H. A Short History of Physics. 1927.

Cajori, F. A History of Physics. 1899.

Cantor, M. Vorlesungen über Geschichte der Mathematik. 4 vols.
1880 seq.; 2d ed., 1894 seq.

Dampier-Whetham, W. C. D. A History of Science, and Its Relations with Philosophy and Religion. 1929 (and 1930, 1931, 1932).

Darmstaedter, L. Handbuch zur Geschichte der Naturwissen-
schaften und der Technik. 1908.

Deter, C. J. Abriss der Geschichte der Philosophie. 13th ed., 1913.

Feldhaus, F. M. Lexikon der Erfindungen und Entdeckungen. 1904.

———. Die Technik der Antike und des Mittelalters. 1931.

Grousset, R. Histoire de la philosophie orientale. 1923.

Heath, T. (L.). Aristarchus of Samos, the Ancient Copernicus: A
History of Greek Astronomy to Aristarchus. 1913.

———. A History of Greek Mathematics. 1921.

———. A Manual of Greek Mathematics. 1931.

Holmyard, E. J. Makers of Chemistry. 1931.

Keith, A. B. The Samkhya System. (1918), 1924.

Kugler, F. X. Sternkunde und Sterndienst in Babel. 3 vols. 1907–
1924.

Maspero, H. La Chine antique. 1927.

Masson-Oursel, P. Esquisse d'une histoire de la philosophie indienne. 1923.

———. La Philosophie comparée. 1923, 1931. (Eng. trans., 1926.)

Messer, A. Geschichte der Philosophie im Altertum und Mittel-
alter. 1912.

Mikami, Y. The Development of Mathematics in China and Japan.
1912. Abh. z. Gesch. d. math. Wiss., No. 30.

Mumford, L. The Culture of Cities. 1938.

———. Technics and Civilization. 1934.
The tabular list of inventions seems to be the best in English.

NEUGEBAUER, O. Vorlesungen über Geschichte der Antiken Mathematischen Wissenschaften. Vol. 1: Vorgriechische Mathematik. 1934.

NEUGEBAUER, O., *et al.*, eds. Quellen und Studien zur Geschichte der Mathematik. 1929 seq. (Vol. 3, 1936.)

OLMSTEAD, A. T. Babylonian Astronomy: Historical Sketch. Amer. Jour. Semitic Lang. and Lit., Vol. 55, pp. 113–129. 1938.

REY, A. La Science orientale avant les Grecs. 1930.

ROUTLEDGE, R. A Popular History of Science. 1881.

SARTON, G. The History of Science and the New Humanism. 1937.
———. Introduction to the History of Science. (Vol. 1, from Homer to Omar Khayyám, 1927; Vol. 2, from Rabbi Ben Ezra to Roger Bacon, 1931.)
  This work of reference is of fundamental importance, and I have drawn upon it heavily for philosophy as well as science.

SEDGWICK, W. T., and H. W. TYLER. A Short History of Science. 1917. (1939 ed. revised by Tyler and Bigelow.)

SMITH, D. E. History of Mathematics. 2 vols. 1923–1925.

SMITH, D. E., and L. C. KARPINSKI. The Hindu-Arabic Numerals. 1911.

SMITH, D. E., and Y. MIKAMI. A History of Japanese Mathematics. 1914.

SMITH, PRESERVED. A History of Modern Culture. 2 vols. 1930–1934.

STURM, A. Geschichte der Mathematik. 1906.

SUZUKI, D. T. A Brief History of Early Chinese Philosophy. 1914.

TANNERY, P. Pour l'histoire de la science hellène de Thales à Empédocle. 1887, 1930.

THOMSEN, V. Geschichte der Sprachwissenschaft. 1927. (Danish in 1902.)

WHITEHEAD, A. N. Science and the Modern World. 1925.

WIELEITNER, H. K. Geschichte der Mathematik. 1922–1923. (Vol. 1, to 1700; Vol. 2, 1700 to 1850.)

SCULPTURE AND PAINTING: OCCIDENTAL AND CLASSICAL

BEAZLEY, J. D., and B. ASHMOLE. Greek Sculpture and Painting. 1932.

CAROTTI, G. A History of Art. 3 vols. 1908–1929.

CHASE, G. H., and C. R. POST. A History of Sculpture. 1924.

FAURE, E. History of Art. 5 vols. 1924, 1937.
  Has chronological table.

FLETCHER, B. A History of Architecture on the Comparative Method. 1901. (6th ed., 1921, rewritten by B. F. Fletcher.)

HALL, H. R. Aegean Archaeology. 1915.

HAMANN, R. Geschichte der Kunst. 1933.

HAUSENSTEIN, W. Die Bildnerei der Etrusker. 1922.

HERRMANN, P. Denkmäler der Malerei des Altertums. 21 nos., 1906–1931.

LANGLOTZ, E. Griechische Vasen [in Würzburg]. 3 vols. 1932.

———. Griechische Vasenbilder. 1922.

MARTHA, J. L'Art étrusque. 1889.

MONKHOUSE, C. Heaton's History of Painting. 1893.

PEYRE, R. (R.). Histoire générale des beaux-arts. N.d.

———. Répertoire chronologique de l'histoire universelle des beaux-arts. 1899.

PFUHL, E. Malerei und Zeichnung der Griechen. 3 vols. 1923.

———. Masterpieces of Greek Drawing and Painting. 1926.

REINACH, S. Apollo: An Illustrated Manual of the History of Art. 1907, 1924, 1935. (1904 ed., The Story of Art throughout the Ages.)

VAN DYKE, J. C. A Text-Book of the History of Painting. 1915.

SCULPTURE AND PAINTING: ORIENTAL

ARDENNE DE TIZAC, J.-H. D'. L'Art chinois classique. 1926.

ASHTON, L. (A. L. B.). An Introduction to the Study of Chinese Sculpture. 1924.

———, ed. Chinese Art. 1935.

AYMONIER, E. Le Cambodge. 3 vols. 1904.

BINYON, L. Painting in the Far East. 1908 (1913).

BUSHELL, S. W. Chinese Art. 2 vols. 1905, 1914.

CAPART, J. L'Art égyptien. 1909.

———. Leçons sur l'art égyptien. 1920.

———. Propos sur l'art égyptien. 1931.

CHAVANNES, E. Mission archéologique dans la Chine septentrionale. 1909.

———. La Sculpture sur pierre en Chine. 1893.

CODRINGTON, K. DE B. Ancient India from the Earliest Times to the Guptas. 1926.

CŒDÈS, G. Bronzes khmèrs. 1923.

COMMAILLE, J. Guide aux ruines d'Angkor. 1912.

COOMARASWAMY, A. K. History of Indian and Indonesian Art. 1927.

———. Introduction to Indian Art. 1923.

———. Portfolio of Indian Art [in the Boston Museum]. 1923.

———. Rajput Painting. 2 vols. 1916.

———. Selected Examples of Indian Art. 1910.

COX, WARREN E. [The Romance of] Chinese Art. N.d. (Reprinted from Encyclopaedia Britannica, copyright 1929–1936.)

DIEZ, E. Die Kunst Indiens. N.d.

FENOLLOSA, E. F. Epochs of Chinese and Japanese Art. 2 vols. 1921.

FERGUSON, J. C. Chinese Painting. 1927.
———. Outlines of Chinese Art. 1918.
FINOT, L. Le Temple d'Angkor-Vat. Mém. Arch. de l'Ecole Française d'Extrême-Orient, Vol. 2, 5 parts, 1929–1932.
FOUCHER, A.-C.-A. L'Art grécobouddhique du Gandhara. (1905–) 1922. Publ. de l'Ecole Française d'Extrême-Orient, Vols. 5–6.
———. The Beginnings of Buddhist Art. 1917.
FRENCH, J. C. The Art of the Pal Empire of Bengal. 1928.
GRIFFITHS, J. The Paintings of Ajanta. 1896.
GROUSSET, R. Les Civilisations de l'Orient. 4 vols. 1929–1930. (1, L'Orient; 2, L'Inde; 3, La Chine; 4, Le Japon.) (The Civilizations of the East, 4 vols., 1931–1934.)
GRÜNWEDEL, A. Buddhistische Kunst in Indien. 1900.
HARCOURT-SMITH, S. Babylonian Art. 1928.
HAVELL, E. B. The Ancient and Mediaeval Architecture of India. 1915.
———. A Handbook of Indian Art. 1920 (1927).
———. The Ideals of Indian Art. 1911.
———. Indian Sculpture and Painting. 1908 (1928).
KROM, N. J. L'Art javanais dans les musées de Hollande et de Java. 1926. Ars Asiatica, VIII.
———. Inleiding tot de Hindoe-Javaansche Kunst. 3 vols. 1923.
KROM, N. J., and T. VAN ERP. Beschrijving van Barabudur. 2 vols. and atlas. 1920–1931.
KÜMMEL, O. Die Kunst Chinas, Japans, und Koreas. 1929.
LAUFER, B. Archaic Chinese Bronzes of the Shang, Chou and Han Periods. 1922.
———. The Beginnings of Porcelain in China. 1917. Field Museum, Anthr. Ser., Vol. 15, No. 2.
———. Chinese Clay Figures. 1914. Field Museum, Anthr. Ser., Vol. 13, No. 2.
———. Chinese Pottery of the Han Dynasty. 1909.
———. Jade. 1912. Field Museum, Anthr. Ser., Vol. 10.
LE MAY, R. A Concise History of Buddhist Art in Siam. 1938.
MARCHAL, H. Guide archéologique aux temples d'Angkor. 1928.
MASPERO, G. Art in Egypt. 1912.
MINAMOTO, H. An Illustrated History of Japanese Art. 1935.
MORI, O. Ying-Ch'êng-Tzŭ. 1934. Archaeologia Orientalis, Vol. 4.
Han tomb with frescos, in Manchuria.
MÜNSTERBERG, O. Chinesische Kunstgeschichte. 2 vols. 1910–1912.
———. Japanische Kunstgeschichte. 1904.
PARISH-WATSON, M. Chinese Pottery of Han, T'ang and Sung Dynasties. 1917.

PARMENTIER, H. Les Sculptures chames au Musée de Tourane. 1922. Ars Asiatica, Vol. IV.

PETRIE, W. M. FLINDERS. The Arts and Crafts of Ancient Egypt. 1909.

POPE, A. U. An Introduction to Persian Art. 1930.

ROSS, E. DENISON. The Art of Egypt through the Ages. 1931.

SALMONY, A. Sculpture in Siam. 1925.

SARRE, F. Die Kunst des Alten Persien. 1923.

SCHÄFER, H., and W. ANDRAE. Die Kunst des Alten Orients. 1925.

SIREN, O. La Sculpture chinoise du Vᵉ au XIVᵉ siècle. 5 vols. 1926.

———. A History of Early Chinese Art. 4 vols. 1929–1930.

———. A History of Early Chinese Painting. 1933.

SMITH, VINCENT A. A History of Fine Art in India and Ceylon. 2d ed., 1930.

STEIN, M. A. Ancient Khotan. 2 vols. 1907.

———. Innermost Asia. 4 vols. 1928.

———. Serindia. 5 vols. 1921.

STERN, PH. Le Bayon d'Angkor et l'évolution de l'art khmer. 1927. Ann. Mus. Guimet, Bibl. de Vulgarisation, Vol. 47.

TAJIMA, S. Masterpieces Selected from the Fine Arts of the Far East. 12 vols. 1909 seq. (Original text, Vols. 9–12, by S. Omura.)

———. Masterpieces of Sesshû. 1910.

TAKI, S. Japanese Fine Art. 1931.

VERNEUIL, M.-P. Les Temples de la période classique indo-javanaise. 1927.

WALEY, ARTHUR. An Introduction to the Study of Chinese Painting. 1923.

WASHBURN, O. M. The Art of Ancient Egypt. 1938. Univ. California.

WEIGALL, A. Ancient Egyptian Works of Art. 1924.

WITH, K. Java. 1922.

WOOLLEY, C. L. The Development of Sumerian Art. 1935.

———. Excavations at Ur, 1929–1930. Museum Journal, Vol. 21, pp. 81–105. 1930.

WORRINGER, W. Egyptian Art. 1928.

LITERATURE AND DRAMA: OCCIDENTAL AND CLASSICAL

BECKER, P. A. Geschichte der spanischen Litteratur. 1914.

BOOR, H. DE. Schwedische Litteratur. 1924.

BRONSON, W. C. A History of American Literature. 1900.

BRÜCKNER, A. Geschichte der polnischen Litteratur. 1901.

———. Geschichte der russischen Litteratur. 1905.

CHAYTOR, H. J. The Troubadours. 1912.

DOTTIN, P. La Littérature anglaise. 1931.

FIGUEIREDO, F. DE SOUSA. História da literatura portuguesa. 1918.

FOWLER, H. N. A History of Roman Literature. 1923.

GUDEMAN, A. Geschichte der lateinischen Literatur. 2 vols. 1923.

JÖRGENSEN, (J.) J. Geschichte der dänischen Literatur. 1908.

LAIGNEL, M. TH. La Littérature italienne. 1926.

LEGER, L. Histoire de la littérature russe. N.d.

LOISEAU, A. Histoire de la littérature portugaise. 1887.

MURRAY, G. A History of Ancient Greek Literature. 1915.

SAFARIK, P. J. Geschichte der slawischen Sprache und Literatur nach allen Mundarten. 1869.

SAINTSBURY, G. Primer of French Literature. 1888.

LITERATURE AND DRAMA: ORIENTAL
(Asiatic, Egyptian, Islamic)

ARLINGTON, L. C. The Chinese Drama. 1930.

ASTON, W. G. A History of Japanese Literature. (1899), 1933.

——. Shinto. 1905.

BAZIN, M. Théâtre chinois. 1838.

BEZOLD, C. Babylonisch-assyrische Literatur. 1886.

BREWITT-TAYLOR, C. H., trans. San Kuo, or Romance of the Three Kingdoms. 2 vols. 1925.

BROCKELMANN, C. Geschichte der arabischen Litteratur. 1901.

CHI-CHEN WANG, trans. Dream of the Red Chamber by Tsao Hsueh-chin. 1929.

DOLE, N. H., and B. M. WALKER. The Persian Poets. 1901.

FRAZER, R. W. A Literary History of India. 1907.

GIBB, H. A. R. Arabic Literature. 1926.

GILES, H. A. A History of Chinese Literature. (1901), 1930.

GRUBE, W. Geschichte der chinesischen Litteratur. 1902.

HART, H. H. The West Chamber. 1936.

HORN, P. Geschichte der persischen Litteratur. 1901.

HSIUNG, S. I., trans. Lady Precious Stream. 1934. (=*Wang Pao-chuan.*)

HUART, C. I. A History of Arabic Literature. 1903 (1915).

KAO TONG-KIA (Mao-Tseu, ed.). Le Pi-pa-ki, ou l'histoire du luth; trans. Bazin, 1841.

KEAY, F. E. A History of Hindī Literature. 1920.

KEITH, A. B. Classical Sanskrit Literature. 1923.

——. A History of Sanskrit Literature. 1928.

——. The Sanskrit Drama in Its Origin, Development, Theory and Practice. 1924.

LEVY, R. Persian Literature. 1923.

LOMBARD, F. A. An Outline History of the Japanese Drama. 1928.

MACDONNELL, A. A. A History of Sanskrit Literature. 1900.

(MIALL, B., trans. from German translation of F. Kuhn.) *Chin P'ing Mei.* 1939.

NICHOLSON, R. A. A Literary History of the Arabs. (1907), 1930.
OU ITAÏ. Le Roman chinois. 1935. (Preface by F. Strowski.)
WALEY, A. The Book of Songs. 1937.
WINTERNITZ, M. Geschichte der indischen Literatur. 3 vols. 1907–1922.
WYLIE, A. Notes on Chinese Literature. 1867 (1901).

MUSIC

BALTZELL, W. J. Dictionary of Musicians. 1914.
————. History of Music. 1905.
GROVE, G. A Dictionary of Music and Musicians. 4 vols. 1879. (Later editions 5 vols. and suppl., then 6 vols.)
MASON, D. G. The Art of Music. 12 vols. 1915–1917. (Vols. 1–3, narrative history; Vol. 12, dictionary-index of musicians.)
PARRY, C. H. H. The Evolution of the Art of Music. (1883), 1930.
————. Summary of the History and Development of Mediaeval and Modern European Music. 1904.
RIEMANN, H. Musik-Lexicon. 1884. (And later enlargements; 9th ed., 1919, ed. by A. Einstein.)
UNTERSTEINER, A. A Short History of Music. 1902.
WOLF, J. Geschichte der Musik. 3 vols. 1929.

NATIONS: OCCIDENTAL AND CLASSICAL

BAIN, R. N. Slavonic Europe. 1908.
BOUSQUET, G. Histoire du peuple bulgare. 1909.
BRETHOLZ, B. Geschichte Böhmens und Mährens. 4 vols. 1921–1925.
BRÜCKNER, A. Bilder aus Russlands Vergangenheit. 1887.
————. Geschichte Russlands bis zum Ende des 18. Jahrhunderts. 2 vols. 1896–1913.
CAVAIGNAC, E. Population et capital dans le monde méditerranéen antique. 1923.
DÄNDLIKER, K. Schweizerische Geschichte. 1904.
GOTHEIN, E. Die Culturenentwicklung Süd-Italiens in Einzel-Darstellungen. 1886.
JIREČEK, C. J. Geschichte der Bulgaren. 1876.
JOYCE, P. W. Concise History of Ireland. 1903, (1918).
KLYUCHEVSKY, V. O. History of Russia. (C. J. Hogarth, trans.) 1913.
LOT, F. Les Invasions barbares et le peuplement de l'Europe. 2 vols. 1937.
NADLER, J. Von Art und Kunst der Deutschen Schweiz. 1922.
OLRIK, A. Nordisches Geistesleben in heidnischer und frühchristlicher Zeit. 1908.
————. Viking Civilization. 1930.

Otte, E. C. Scandinavian History. 1874.

Paul, J. Nordische Geschichte. 1925.

Rachel, H. Geschichte der Völker und Kulturen. 1922.

Rambaud, A.-N. Histoire de la civilisation française. 2 vols. 1887, (1909, 1921).

——. Histoire de la Russie. 1878. (6th ed., 1913.)

Runciman, S. Byzantine Civilization. 1933.

——. A History of the First Bulgarian Empire. 1930.

Saillens, E. French History. 1932.

Tarn, W. W. Hellenistic Civilization. 1930.

Vasiliev, A. A. History of the Byzantine Empire. 2 vols. 1928.

Wilcken, U. Griechische Geschichte. 1924.

Nations: Oriental
(Asiatic, Egyptian, Islamic)

André, P.-J. L'Islam et les races. 2 vols. 1922.

Aymonier, E. Le Cambodge. 3 vols. 1904.

Beal, S. Buddhist Records of the Western World. (Trans. of Hiuen Tsiang.) N.d.

Bose, P. N. The Hindu Colony of Cambodia. 1927.

Brinkley, F. A History of the Japanese People. 1915.

Chamberlain, B. H. Things Japanese. 1905.

Chatterji, B. R. Indian Cultural Influence in Cambodia. 1928.

Clement, E. W. A Short History of Japan. 1926, 1936.

Close, Upton. Behind the Face of Japan. 1942.
  Cited in footnote, p. 225, in § 30.

Cœdes, G. Le Royaume çrivijaya. Bull. de l'École Française d'Extrême-Orient, T. 18, N° 6, 1918.

Couling, S. The Encyclopaedia Sinica. 1917.

Creel, H. G. The Birth of China. 1937.

——. Studies in Early Chinese Culture. 1937.

Czaplicka, M. A. The Turks of Central Asia. 1918.

Ferrand, G. L'Empire sumatranais de Crivijaya. 1922.

Franke, O. Geschichte des Chinesischen Reiches. 3 vols. 1930–1937.

Giles, H. A. The Civilization of China. 1911.

Gowen, H. H., and J. F. Hall. An Outline History of China. 1927.

Harvey, G. E. History of Burma. 1925.

Havell, E. B. A Short History of India. 1924.

Hirth, F. The Ancient History of China. 1911.

——. China and the Roman Orient. 1885.

Huart, C.-I. Ancient Persia and Iranian Civilization. 1927.

——. Histoire des Arabes. 2 vols. 1912–1913.

HUNTER, W. W. A Brief History of the Indian Peoples. 1907 (24th ed.)

IBN BATTUTA. Travels in Asia and Africa, 1325–1354. (Trans. by H. A. R. Gibb, 1929.)

JACKSON, A. V. W., ed. History of India. 9 vols. 1906–1907. (Vol. 1, R. C. Dutt, to the sixth century; Vol. 2, V. A. Smith, to the Mohammedan conquest.)

———. Persia, Past and Present. 1906.

KROM, N. J. Hindoe-javaansche Geschiedenis. 1926.

KUNO, Y. S. Japanese Expansion on the Asiatic Continent. Vol. 1, 1937; Vol. 2, 1940.

LAMMENS, H. Islam: Beliefs and Institutions. N.d., (1929).

———. L'Arabie occidentale avant l'Hégire. (1914), 1928. (Le Berçeau de l'Islam.)

LATOURETTE, K. S. The Chinese: Their History and Culture. 1934.

LEE, J. S. The Periodic Recurrence of Internecine Wars in China. China Journal, Vol. 14, pp. 111–115, 159–163. 1931.

LEE, M. PING-HUA. The Economic History of China. 1921.

LIN, YU-T'ANG. My Country and My People. 1935.

LONGFORD, J. H. The Story of Old Japan. 1910.

MASPERO, G. Le Royaume de Champa. 1928.

MASSON-OURSEL, P., et al. L'Inde antique et la civilisation indienne. 1933. (Ancient India and Indian Civilization, 1934.)

MEYER, E. Geschichte des Altertums. 5 vols. 1884 seq. 5th ed., 1925 seq.

MURDOCH, J. A History of Japan. 3 vols. 1903, 1910.

PARKER, E. H. China and Religion. 1905.

RAPSON, E. J. Ancient India. 1914.

SANSOM, G. B. Japan: A Short Cultural History. 1931.

SMITH, V. A. The Oxford History of India. 1923 (2d ed.).

STEIN, M. A. Ancient Khotan. 2 vols. 1907.

TAKEKOSHI, Y. The Economic Aspects of the History of the Civilization of Japan. 3 vols. 1930.

WILHELM, R. A Short History of Chinese Civilization. 1929.

WOOLLEY, C. L. The Sumerians. 1928.

———. Ur of the Chaldees. 1929.

INDEX

THIS INDEX omits proper names occurring in formal lists and the text discussions accompanying such lists in the same section. For instance, Cervantes and *Don Quijote* would naturally be found first of all, and more quickly, in the chapter on Literature (VIII), and within that in the section on Spanish Literature (§83); so would Alcalá, the birthplace of Cervantes. These mentions accordingly do not appear in the Index. But all other references to Cervantes, *Don Quijote,* or Alcalá, anywhere in §§1–82 and §§84–127, have been indexed. This procedure has reduced the Index by a full half of its bulk without impairment, it is believed, of its serviceability—in fact, with its utility being perhaps the readier.

INDEX